FROM GOSPELS *to* GLORY

FROM GOSPELS *to* GLORY:
EXPLORING THE NEW TESTAMENT

KENNETH G. HANNA

CrossBooks™
A Division of LifeWay
1663 Liberty Drive
Bloomington, IN 47403
www.crossbooks.com
Phone: 1-866-879-0502

© 2014 Kenneth G. Hanna. All rights reserved.

No part of this book may be reproduced, stored in a retrieval system, or transmitted by any means without the written permission of the author.

First published by CrossBooks 01/17/2014

ISBN: 978-1-4627-3448-1 (sc)
ISBN: 978-1-4627-3450-4 (hc)
ISBN: 978-1-4627-3449-8 (e)

Library of Congress Control Number: 2014900961

Printed in the United States of America.

This book is printed on acid-free paper.

Scripture quotations taken from the New American Standard Bible®, Copyright © 1960, 1962, 1963, 1968, 1971, 1972, 1973, 1975, 1977, 1995 by The Lockman Foundation. Used by permission. (www.Lockman.org)

Because of the dynamic nature of the Internet, any web addresses or links contained in this book may have changed since publication and may no longer be valid. The views expressed in this work are solely those of the author and do not necessarily reflect the views of the publisher, and the publisher hereby disclaims any responsibility for them.

PREFACE

From Gospels to Glory: Exploring the New Testament aims to provide a map and guide service for students seeking to explore the New Testament. To achieve this the author has sought to give the reader a balanced treatment of important introductory features, deal fairly with critical issues, summarize the essential message, and provide a working outline for each book of the New Testament.

The author has benefited greatly from reading other writers and seeks to introduce the reader to the wealth of literature available for New Testament studies. Documented quotations link the reader to other sources and provide an easy to use reference guide for the reader to explore an idea or issue more deeply.

Maps are essential to an explorer. A thematic chart gives the reader a "satellite view" of each book. The central theme, key words, major divisions, and structural elements are made evident at a glance. This alerts the reader on what to look for as they read and enables them to understand the biblical author's flow of thought.

Each book of the New Testament was written to a select audience and for a specific purpose. The introductory material supplies the reader with essential background information that illuminates the message of the book. Every book has something unique to contribute to the New Testament and this is highlighted in the distinctive features section. The essential message of each book is summarized and followed with a working outline to assist the reader in understanding that message.

Source information (footnote) follows immediately after each quote. There are frequent references to additional resources that are not quoted but provide helpful information. This is to aid the explorer wanting to dig more deeply into a given topic. All resources mentioned in the book are fully identified in the bibliography.

Maps are copyrighted by Carta, Jerusalem and used by permission under a licensing agreement. Scripture quotations are taken from the *New American Standard Bible* (NASB): 1995 update. LaHabra, CA: The Lockman Foundation, unless otherwise indicated. Scripture quotations are placed in italics for easy identification.

ACKNOWLEDGMENTS

"Never has one man owed so much to so many."

The author owes much to more people than can possibly be identified in this brief tribute, but these merit special mention. (With apologies to Winston Churchill for altering his famous quote).

First and foremost, I am indebted to Mary, my wife and mainstay. She has been a lifelong partner in ministry, a faithful friend, and a constant source of support. She has joyfully endured the hours of preparation, proofread the manuscript, and used the information in her own study.

Children are a special gift from God and we have been doubly blessed. Our son, Gordon, is now with the Lord and experiencing the fullness of God's grace that he treasured. Our daughter, Libby, and her husband Chris are models of faithfulness in servant leadership. They have also brightened our life with three loving grandchildren who have blessed us with four delightful great grandchildren.

The author has been privileged to study under a host of outstanding teachers, most notably J. Dwight Pentecost, Howard Hendricks, John Walvoord, and Charles Ryrie. I trust that their love for the Bible and their ability to expound it clearly are reflected in this book.

Colleagues have contributed much by their example and through their fellowship, especially the faculty of Dallas Theological Seminary. Roy Zuck edited this manuscript while in the final days of his battle with cancer. Larry Waters shared his insights and we have collaborated on many course projects. Will Johnston has been a friend and an indispensible technical advisor. The author has been privileged to be part of the administration and faculty at four schools. Each has played a role in fostering the research and making this work possible. Bill Eichhorst and Cary Perdue have been supportive friends since student days.

Students are a delight. Their warm response in class has lifted the author's spirit time and again. Their diligence and enthusiasm for the study of the New Testament has sharpened the author's thinking and made the preparation of this book a labor of love.

To these and the "host of un-named encouragers" my heartfelt thanks.

TABLE OF CONTENTS

Exploring the New Testament	1
Matthew	7
Mark	37
Luke	61
John	91
Acts	121
Romans	159
1 Corinthians	183
2 Corinthians	207
Galatians	227
Ephesians	251
Philippians	275
Colossians	291
1 Thessalonians	307
2 Thessalonians	323
Pastoral Epistles	331
1 Timothy	341
2 Timothy	353
Titus	361
Philemon	369
Hebrews	379
James	401
1 Peter	415
2 Peter	431
1 John	443
2 and 3 John	459
Jude	465
Revelation	477

Exploring the New Testament

The Bible is a story. It contains 66 books but it has only one story to tell, God's story. What begins in the book of Genesis climaxes in the book of Revelation. The story begins with the creation of "the heavens and the earth" in Genesis and concludes with "the new heavens and the new earth" in Revelation. All of the books in between form part of the seamless garment we call "Scripture."

The Old Testament introduces the story; the New Testament explains the story. The Old Testament is foundational; the New Testament is fulfillment. The New Testament is enfolded in the Old Testament; the Old Testament in unfolded in the New. One cannot fully understand or appreciate the New Testament without being familiar with the Old Testament. Conversely, one is left with an unfinished story without the New Testament. The designations "Old" and "New" are unfortunate since they are really only two parts of one story. Both are essential to God's story. Together they tell a complete and compelling story.

Studying the Bible is like examining a forest. We need to see the entire forest but must not overlook or ignore the distinctive trees that make it a forest. The Bible is one continuous story but each book is a separate, stand-alone chapter in that story. The Bible is understood best when we approach it like we would view a forest, as a complete area that is created and defined by the trees it contains. Thus we study each book of the New Testament as a separate chapter but one that is part of and contributes to the story that we call the Bible. Background matters! The message of each book is set in a historical context. Each book has an author, a target audience, and was written for a specific purpose. Our understanding of the New Testament will grow when we discover the unique contribution of each book to the New Testament.

When we begin our exploration of the New Testament, God's voice has not been heard for centuries. It has been 700 years since Isaiah promised that a voice would one day be heard in the Judean wilderness crying out, *Clear the way for the LORD in the wilderness* (Isaiah 40:3). It has been 400 years since Malachi, the last prophetic voice of the Old Testament, declared, *Behold, I am going to send My messenger, and he will clear the way before Me. And the LORD, whom you seek, will suddenly come to His temple* (Malachi 3:1). With the Gospels of the New Testament that voice is heard. John the Baptist appears in the Judean wilderness and announces the arrival of the promised Messiah (Matthew 3:3; Mark 1:3; Luke 3:4-6; John 1:23). The One whose saving presence has been sought since sin and death entered the Garden of Eden (Genesis 3:15-16) has now appeared in the person of Jesus of Nazareth, who is the Christ, the Son of God.

The New Testament contains twenty-seven books. Each contributes to the unfinished story begun in Genesis. The New Testament is the "watershed" of history, the "continental divide" of time. Time is measured and history is distinguished by B.C., "Before Christ," and A.D., "Anno Domini" (the year of our Lord). Time is no more when the New Testament closes with the book of Revelation.

The New Testament opens with the four Gospels, Matthew, Mark, Luke, and John. They offer four distinct but complimentary portraits of Jesus. Matthew portrays Jesus as the promised King of Israel. A king must have a genealogy and so Matthew traces Jesus' roots through David and all the way back to Abraham (Matthew 1:1-17). Mark portrays Jesus as the Servant of God. A servant needs no genealogy so Mark provides none. Luke portrays Jesus as the perfect man who should have a genealogy and thus Luke traces Jesus' roots all the way back to Adam (Luke 3:23-38). John portrays Jesus as the Son of God. God has no genealogy and John gives none. Each Gospel must be studied in its entirety but not in isolation from the others. Together they present a full and harmonious record of the life and legacy of Jesus Christ.

All four Gospels accentuate the last week of the life of Jesus. The cross and the resurrection are essential to the saving purpose of God that is introduced in the Old Testament. The cross was part of God's plan from eternity past (Acts 2:22-24; 1 Peter 1:18-21). However, the cross is not the end, rather, it marks a new beginning. All four Gospels close with a declaration that the saving message of Jesus Christ is destined to go global. The book of Acts was authored by Luke as the second volume of the ongoing witness of Jesus (Acts 1:1-11).

Most of the original disciples (apostles) of Jesus died a martyr's death but the good news continued to spread. Persecution scattered the early Christians (Acts 8:1) but accelerated the witness from Jewish enclaves to Gentile and pagan communities. James, the younger brother of Jesus, became a believer and wrote "James," the first of the New Testament books to be written. The author of Hebrews remains anonymous but his readers were among those dispersed believers.

Acts is the lone book of "history" in the New Testament. Acts is a book of transitions. It begins with the advent of the Holy Spirit and the birth of the church in Jerusalem. At Pentecost the newly formed church is entirely Jewish, by the close of Acts it is largely Gentile but includes all ethnicities. Acts records the spread of the Christian gospel throughout the Mediterranean region and closes with the apostle Paul in a Roman prison. Acts is an "unfinished symphony" because the good news of Jesus Christ was still spreading throughout the Roman Empire. Paul and his coworkers planted churches in every major Mediterranean city. The New Testament contains 13 letters (epistles) written by Paul to those churches and to his coworkers. But Paul is not the only apostle, church planter, and author of the New Testament.

The three synoptic Gospels, Matthew, Mark, and Luke, along with Peter's two letters and that of Jude, round out the early writings of the New Testament. Early church fathers placed Matthew as the first Gospel written, followed by Mark and Luke. Recent scholars place Mark first but all three were likely written in a short time period (AD 55-65) and completed before the destruction of Jerusalem and the dispersing of the Jewish people in AD 70. John, the youngest of the original disciples was the last voice to be heard in the New Testament. John's three letters were probably written from AD 85 to 95 and the book of Revelation around AD 95. With the book of Revelation the last chapter of God's story in the Bible has been written. Its ultimate fulfillment awaits the return of Jesus Christ (Revelation 19-22). The New Testament closes with the cry of John echoed by Jesus' followers through the centuries, *Amen, Come Lord Jesus* (Revelation 22:20).

Luke's keen interest in history and his commitment to accurate reporting shapes our knowledge of chronology of New Testament events. Luke corelates events in his Gospel and in Acts with the career of Roman administrators making it possible to establish strategic dates. This author is indebted to Harold Hoehner (*Chronological Aspects of the Life of Christ*) and other scholars for their research and findings. A suggested chronology for New Testament events appears on the following page.

Suggested Timeline for Major New Testament Events

Jesus and His Disciples	B.C.	Roman Officials
		Herod the Great- King over
Birth of Jesus	5/4	all Palestine- 37-4 BC
	A.D.	Herod Phillip- Tetrarch of Iturea and Trachonitus- 4 BC - AD 34
Baptism of Jesus	29	Herod Antipas- Tetrarch of
Jesus' public ministry	29	Galilee, Perea- 4 BC - AD 39
Martyrdom of John	32	Pontius Pilate- Procurator of Judea- 27-36
Jesus' death, resurrection	33	
Pentecost	33	
Stephen's martyrdom	35	Herod Agrippa I- King over
Saul's conversion		all Palestine- 37-44
James' martyrdom	44	
Paul's first mission	48-49	
Jerusalem Council, Acts 15	50	
Paul's second mission	50-52	Felix- Procurator- 52-59
Paul's third mission	53-57	
Paul in prison at Caesarea	57-59	Festus- Procurator- 59-61
Paul in prison at Rome	60-63	
Peter's martyrdom in Rome	64-65	Nero- Emperor- 54-68
Paul's martyrdom in Rome	67-68	
	70	Jerusalem destroyed

Selective Bibliography for New Testament Studies

Bible Atlases

Beitzel, Barry J. *The New Moody Atlas of the Bible.* Chicago: Moody Press, 2009

Brisco, Thomas V. *Holman Bible Atlas.* Nashville: Broadman & Holman, 1998.

Dowley, Tim. *The Kregel Bible Atlas.* Grand Rapids: Kregel Publications, 2003.

Pfeiffer, Charles F. *Baker's Bible Atlas.* Grand Rapids: Baker Book House, 2005.

Rasmussen, Carl G. *Zondervan Atlas of the Bible.* Rev. ed. Grand Rapids: Zondervan Publishing House, 2010.

Wright, Paul H. *Rose Then and Now Bible Map Atlas with Biblical Background and Culture.* Torrance, CA: Rose Publishing, 2012.

New Testament Introductions

Carson, D. A., Douglas J. Moo, and Leon Morris. *An Introduction to the New Testament.* Grand Rapids: Zondervan Publishing House, 1991.

DeSilva, David A. *An Introduction to the New Testament.* Downers Grove, IL: InterVarsity Press, 2004.

Guthrie, Donald. *New Testament Introduction.* Downers Grove, IL: InterVarsity Press, 1990.

Hiebert, D. Edmond. An *Introduction to the New Testament.* 3 Vols. Chicago: Moody Press, 1975. Reprinted in 1 vol. Waynesboro, GA: Gabriel Publishing, 2003

Kostenberger, Andreas J., L. Scott Kellum, and Charles L. Quarels. *The Cradle, the Cross, and the Crown: Introducing the New Testament.* Nashville: B & H Academic, 2009.

New Testament Backgrounds

Barnett, Paul. *Jesus & the Rise of Early Christianity: A History of the New Testament Times.* Downers Grove, IL: InterVarsirty Press, 1999.

Bock, Darrell. *Studying the Historical Jesus: A Guide to Sources and Methods.* Grand Rapids: Baker Academic, 2002.

Ferguson, Everett. *Backgrounds of Early Christianity.* 3rd ed. Grand Rapids: Wm. B. Eerdmans Publishing Co., 2003.

Hoehner, Harold W. *Chronological Aspects of the Life of Christ.* Grand Rapids: Zondervan Publsihing House, 1982.

Bible Dictionaries and Handbooks

Butler, Trent C. *Holman Illustrated Bible Dictionary.* Nashville: Holman Bible Publishers, 2003.

Douglas, J. D. and Merrill C. Tenney, eds. *New International Bible Dictionary.* Grand Rapids: Zondervan Publishing House, 1987.

Evans, Craig A., and Stanley E. Porter, eds. *Dictionary of New Testament Background.* Downers Grove, IL: InterVarsity Press, 2000.

Green, Joel B. and Scot McKnight, eds. *Dictionary of Jesus and the Gospels.* Downers Grove, IL: InterVarsity Press, 1992.

Halley, Henry H. *Halley's Bible Handbook.* Grand Rapids: Zondervan Publishing House, 2007.

Hawthorne, Gerald F., and Ralph A. Martin, eds. *Dictionary of Paul and His Letters.* Downers Grove, IL: InterVarsity Press, 1993.

Martin, Ralph P., and Peter H. Davids, rds. *Dictionary of the Later New Testament & Its Developments.* Downers Grove, IL: InterVarsity Press, 1997.

Youngblood, Ronald F., ed. *Nelson's New Illustrated Bible Dictionary.* Nashville: Thomas Nelson Publishers, 1995.

Matthew: Jesus is the Messianic King

Key verse: 16:16, "You are the Christ, the Son of the living God."

Key Words	Jesus is the Messiah:		Preparation of Jesus the Messiah
Kingdom, King, Christ, Followed, Fulfilled, Prophet(s), Law	His Presentation 1:1-4:11	1:1	

From that time Jesus began... (4:17)

Discourses	His Proclamation 4:12-7:29		Proclamation of Jesus the Messiah
Sermon on the Mount 5-7		4:17	
Instructing, sending disciples 10	His Power 8-10		
Parables of the kingdom 13			
Kingdom life and relationships 18	His Progressive Opposition 11:1-16:12		
Olivet Discourse 24-25			

From that time Jesus began... (16:21)

Prophetic Fulfillment	His Preparation 16:13-20:34	16:21	Passion of Jesus the Messiah
1:22-23			
2:15	His Presentation and Official Rejection 21-25		
2:17-18			
2:22-23			
4:13-16	His Passion 26-27		
8:16-17			
12:14-21			
13:13-15			
13:13-15	His Proof 28		
21:1-5		28:20	
27:5-10			

Matthew—AD 45-55, Purpose: to assure Jewish Christians and as an apologetic for non-believers

7

MATTHEW

The record of the genealogy of Jesus the Messiah, the son of David, the son of Abraham (Matthew 1:1).

Now Jesus stood before the governor, and the governor questioned Him, saying, "Are You the King of the Jews?" And Jesus said to him, "It is as you say" (Matthew 27:11).

And Jesus came up and spoke to them, saying, "All authority has been given to Me in heaven and on earth. Go therefore and make disciples of all the nations, baptizing them in the name of the Father and the Son and the Holy Spirit, teaching them to observe all that I commanded you; and lo, I am with you always, even to the end of the age"
(Matthew 28:18-20).

The Gospel of Matthew stands first in the New Testament for compelling reasons. It is the indispensable link between the Old Testament and the New. It is essential in demonstrating that Jesus is the Messiah promised in the Old Testament. Matthew continues the history of Israel and documents the nation's rejection of Jesus as her Messiah. Among the four Gospels, Matthew alone mentions the church and gives the most comprehensive teaching regarding the course of the present age in the parables of the kingdom (chap. 13). All four Gospels are inspired records of the life of Jesus Christ, but Matthew enjoys "pride of place" in the early collection of New Testament writings and in the circulation of the apostles' writings.

Author
The Gospel of Matthew is anonymous but it was consistently and universally credited to the apostle Matthew by the early church fathers. The superscription *kata Matththaios,* "according to Mathew," appears in all the earliest manuscripts and the association with Matthew was well established by AD 125. As Guthrie claims, "There is no positive evidence that the book ever circulated without this title" (*New Testament Introduction*, 43). External and internal evidence alike support the authorship of this Gospel by the apostle and former tax collector, Matthew.

External evidence. Direct references and allusions to Matthew appear often and early in the writings of the church fathers. Matthew was the most frequently quoted of the four Gospels and the most widely used and circulated in the early church. The *Didache* (AD 110) quotes Matthew more than any other Gospel. Ignatius' *Epistle to the Smyrneans* (AD 110) and letters by Polycarp indicate familiarity with the Gospel of Matthew. In his *Ecclesiastical History* Eusebius cites Papias, Clement of Alexandria, and Origen as identifying Matthew as author of the Gospel.

"Numerous quotations and allusions to the gospel of Matthew in the patristic writers firmly establish that it was known early and unhesitatingly accepted as authentic and authoritative. The first gospel is an anonymous document, yet the early church had a specific and unvarying tradition as to its authorship" (Hiebert, *An Introduction to the New Testament*, 1:47).

According to Leon Morris, "The external evidence is unanimous that the author was Matthew, one of the twelve apostles" (*The Gospel According to Matthew*, 12).

Internal evidence. Several lines of evidence point to Matthew as the author. All three synoptic Gospels use the same phraseology in describing Jesus' call of the tax collector but Mark and Luke identify him as "Levi" whereas he is called "Matthew" in this Gospel (Matthew 9:9). It is possible that Matthew preferred to be known by his new name as a follower of Christ. Luke notes that *Levi gave a big reception for Him [Jesus] in his house* (Luke 5:29) and Mark records that the dinner occurred *in his house* (Mark 2:15), but Matthew simply states that the dinner was *in the house* (Matthew 9:10). The payment of the temple tax (17:24-27) occurs only in Matthew. Matthew uses three words for money that occur nowhere else in Scripture. The language of the book points to someone proficient in Hebrew, Greek, and Aramaic, and Matthew would likely qualify. The apologetic nature of the narrative and the orderly arrangement of material are often cited as appropriate to a tax collector.

Audience and Occasion

The location and circumstance of the original audience has been debated and remains unresolved. The close connection with Abraham and David (1:1-17), the frequent reference to fulfillment of Old Testament prophecies, and the dominance of the messianic King and kingdom theme indicate that the book was written from a Jewish perspective and for a Jewish audience. The references to Jerusalem and the Sanhedrin argue for a location in or near Palestine and a date before AD 70. Jerusalem was totally destroyed by the Romans in AD 70, and the Sanhedrin ceased to function after that date.

With the martyrdom of Stephen in Acts 8 many Jewish Christians were driven out of Jerusalem and settled in surrounding territories of Judea and Samaria. This dispersion of the Christians from Jerusalem and their isolation from the apostles (Acts 8:1) created a need for reliable teaching concerning Jesus Christ and the events that occurred in Jerusalem. A date between AD 45 and 55 is reasonable if the priority of Matthew as the earliest Gospel is maintained. A date of AD 65 for Matthew is more likely if one holds to the priority of Mark. Though decidedly Jewish, Matthew shows Gentiles in a favorable light. Climaxing the book with the great commission (28:18-20) is appropriate for an expanding Christian witness. Several authorities suggest Antioch of Syria as a point of origin since it was home to a thriving church and became the center of missionary activity by AD 45. Fortunately the interpretation of Matthew does not depend on the location of the audience.

Purpose for Writing

Matthew was written to a Jewish audience to prove that Jesus is the messianic King as promised in the Old Testament, to explain God's kingdom program for the present age in light of Israel's rejection of the King, and to assure them that Jesus is alive and will return in triumph as King to establish His kingdom. Matthew is written as an apologetic and his evidence is presented in a rational and systematic fashion. He cites the fulfillment of Old Testament prophecies in the life of Christ as proof of his thesis that Jesus is the messianic King who has come to claim the throne of David and is the descendant of Abraham through whom all nations will be blessed.

The apologetic nature of Matthew suggests that he may also have had a second and wider audience in mind. Jewish believers driven out of Jerusalem were engaged in active witness wherever they went (Acts 8:4). They needed a clear presentation of the gospel of Jesus Christ that was appropriate to both Jewish and Gentile audiences and that related to both Israel and the newly formed church.

Structure

Biographical/chronological markers. The statement "from that time Jesus began" occurs twice in Matthew and may be used to define Jesus' ministry. It occurs first in 4:17 when Jesus begins His public ministry after receiving word that John the Baptist has been arrested. *From that time Jesus began to preach and say, "Repent, for the kingdom of heaven is at hand."* The arrest of the Messiah's forerunner signals the start of Israel's resistance to the Messiah. Jesus moves His base of operations from Nazareth to Capernaum in a region identified as "Galilee of the Gentiles" which Matthew cites as a fulfillment of Isaiah's prophecy (Matthew 4:14-16 with Isaiah 9:1-2). Jesus' public ministry is initiated here and reaches a crucial turning point when the phrase is used a second time in 16:21. The opposition of the Jewish religious leaders has solidified and now the movement toward the cross intensifies. *From that time Jesus began to show His disciples that He must go to Jerusalem, and suffer many things from the elders and chief priests and scribes, and be killed, and be raised up on the third day.* Using these two statements as structural keys, the Gospel of Matthew may be divided into three sections. Turner offers this resulting outline but does not support this as the best arrangement (*The Gospel of Matthew*, 11).

    I. The Preparation of Jesus the Messiah   (1:1-4:16)
    II. The Proclamation of Jesus the Messiah   (4:17-16:20)
    III. The Passion of Jesus the Messiah   (16:21-28:20)

Discourse/narrative pattern. Matthew records five major discourses by Jesus and a narrative section follows each one. Many scholars seem to prefer this structure as the outline of Matthew's life of Christ. Matthew marks the end of each discourse with the phrase *when Jesus had finished these words* (7:28; 11:1; 13:53; 19:1, and 26:1). This statement delineates the following five discourses,

    I. Sermon on the Mount   (chaps. 5-7)
    II. Instructions of the twelve disciples   (10:5-11:1)
    III. Parables of the kingdom   (chap. 13)
    IV. Life and relationships in the kingdom   (18:1-19:1)
    V. The Olivet Discourse   (chaps. 24-25)

Logical/thematic approach. Matthew is preeminently the gospel of the King and the Kingdom. When this theme is traced throughout the book, a structure appears that is logical and cohesive. The opening verse establishes the messianic theme of Matthew, *the record of the genealogy of Jesus the Messiah, the son of David, the son of Abraham* (1:1). Jesus is identified as the Messiah and His lineage is traced to David and to Abraham, thus making Him the rightful claimant to the throne of Israel (2 Samuel 7:16; Isaiah 9:6-7). Jesus is also the One through whom God will fulfill His promise to establish Israel and bless "all the families of the earth"

11

(Genesis 12:1-3). Dispensational and older commentaries usually favor the thematic approach and identify the structure as follows:

I.	Presentation of the King	1:1-4:11
II.	Proclamation of the King	4:12-7:29
III.	Power of the King	8:1-10:42
IV.	Progressive Opposition to the King	11:1-16:12
V.	Preparation in Light of His Rejection	16:13-20:34
VI.	Presentation and Official Rejection of the King	21:1-25:46
VII.	Passion of the King	26:1-27:66
VIII.	Proof of the King's Right to Rule the Kingdom	28:1-20

Literary devices. The Gospel of Matthew contains a wealth of literary devices in addition to the structural features noted above. Matthew frequently uses numerical groupings. In the opening he arranges the genealogical record in three groups of 14 each. There is a connection between David's name and the number fourteen. The three Hebrew consonants for David (DWD) each have a numerical value, and added together total 14. D = 4 + W = 6 + D = 4 = 14. In the Sermon on the Mount there are two roads (7:13-14), two trees (7:15-20), two claims (7:21-23), and two houses (7:24-27). Seven petitions are in the Lord's Prayer (6:9-13) and Jesus gave seven parables (chap. 13). Matthew records the miracles performed by Jesus in three cycles of three miracles each and intersperses these miracle cycles with discipleship narrative:

1a. Three miracles of healing: leper, centurion's servant, and a woman (8:1-17).
1b. Two would-be disciples fail the test of discipleship (8:18-22).

2a. Three miracles of power: sea, demons, and paralytic (8:23-9:8).
2b. Two discipleship events, call of Matthew, inquiry of John's disciples (9:9-17).

3a. Three miracles of restoration: life, sight, and hearing/speech (9:18-34).
3b. Disciples challenged: a plentiful harvest awaits laborers (9:35-38).

Distinctive Features

Kingdom teaching. Matthew uses the term *basileia*, "kingdom," fifty-four times. He refers to the kingdom more frequently than any other Gospel writer and is the only one to use the designation "kingdom of heaven." He refers to the kingdom of heaven thirty-two times and to the kingdom of God five times. "Kingdom" includes three elements, a ruler, a people (subjects) who are ruled, and a sphere, realm or territory of rule. The kingdom theme is paramount in Matthew, but how is the author using "kingdom?" What "kingdom" is Jesus offering in Matthew? Matthew's concept of the kingdom is the major interpretive issue in this Gospel and will be considered later.

Discourses. All three synoptic Gospels record some of Jesus' teaching ministry, but Matthew does so with the greatest detail. He provides the fullest record of Jesus' Sermon on the Mount and His Olivet Discourse. Both discourses are unequaled in length, clarity, and significance. Luke's record of Jesus' discourses may refer to the same occasions but they have much less detail. Each of Jesus' five discourses ends with the phrase *when Jesus had finished these words* and is followed by a shift in the geographical scene and in the narrative.

1st	The Sermon on the Mount	5:1-7:29
2nd	Instructing and sending the twelve disciples	10:1-11:1
3rd	Parables of the kingdom	13:1-53
4th	Life and relationships in the kingdom	18:1-19:1
5th	The Olivet Discourse	24:1-26:2

Prophetic fulfillment. Matthew refers to the Old Testament 129 times including 53 citations and 76 allusions. Reference is made to 25 of the 39 Old Testament books (Scroggie, *A Guide to the Gospels*, 270-71). Matthew uses the fulfillment formula in eleven strategic passages.

1st	Virgin Birth	Isaiah 7:14	1:22-23
2nd	Move to Egypt	Hosea 11:1	2:15
3rd	Slaughter of the Children	Jeremiah 31:15	2:17-18
4th	Called a Nazarene	Isaiah 40:3	2:22-23
5th	Ministry in Galilee	Isaiah 9:1-2	4:13-16
6th	Healing Ministry	Isaiah 53:4	8:16-17
7th	Servant Ministry	Isaiah 42:1-4	12:14-21
8th	Rejection of the King	Isaiah 6:9-10	13:13-15
9th	Parables of the King	Psalm 78:2	13:13-15
10th	Triumphal Entry	Zechariah 9:9	21:1-5
11th	Buying the Potter's Field	Zechariah 11:12-13	27:5-10

Parables. Much of Jesus' teaching was given in parables and the Gospels record approximately 70 of them. Matthew records 40 of Jesus' parables including 13 that appear exclusively in this Gospel. His reporting of the parables of the kingdom in chapter 13 is the most extensive disclosure of the kingdom during the present age.

Church. Matthew is the only Gospel writer who mentions the church and he does so three times. Jesus' announcement that He will build His church, that it is yet future, and that the gates of Hades will not overpower it (16:18) introduces the new revelation regarding the church that is developed in Acts and the Pauline epistles. Matthew also records Jesus' teaching regarding corporate fellowship and discipline in the church (18:15-20).

Synoptic Problem

The major debate regarding Matthew remains unresolved though intensely researched and debated. The issue is called the "synoptic problem," that is, did Matthew write his Gospel before and independently of Mark and Luke, or did he rely on Mark for much of his material? The early church considered Matthew the first Gospel written, and viewed it as independent of the others. Farnell claims, "From early church times through the Reformation in 1517 and until the rise of Deism, Rationalism, and Enlightenment philosophies in the 1800's, the Independence View of the synoptic origins dominated orthodox Christianity" ("The Case for the Independence View of Gospel Origins," in *Three Views of the Origin of the Synoptic Gospels*, 235). However, the close similarity of the three synoptic Gospels and particularly of Matthew to Mark has prompted most recent scholars to claim Markan priority, that is, that Matthew was written after Mark and drew heavily from Mark's Gospel. This has further developed into the two-source view, that Matthew used Mark and also another unidentified source *Q* (from the German, *Quelle,* which means "source"). When Luke and his proposed Q source are added to the discussion, the view is called the "four-source view," or "two/four source view."

Markan priority (two/four source view) has become the major opinion. "Most scholars conclude that the phenomena of the Gospels are inexplicable without some literary interrelationship. ... While some still hold to Matthean priority, the scholarly consensus today favors Markan priority, with Matthew and Luke composing their Gospels in dependence on Mark and another hypothetical source known as *Q,* which purportedly contained a collection of the sayings of Jesus" (Turner, *The Gospel of Matthew*, 9). Glasscock supports the priority of Matthew but notes that Markan priority has become so entrenched that, "if one is to be a true scholar in the contemporary arena of biblical learning, to question the synoptics' chronological order of writing and to assume their dependence upon each other as well as dependence on noncanonical sources is considered necessary" (*Matthew*, 13).

This study does not undertake to resolve the current debate but adopts the traditional independence view of synoptic Gospel origins. Several lines of evidence support this view. (1) Matthew was an apostle and an eyewitness of the events he records. (2) The unanimous conviction of the early church fathers was that Matthew wrote this Gospel and that he was the first to do so. (3) Oral and written records regarding Jesus' life were numerous and well known according to Luke 1:1-4. (4) There are no known copies or fragments of the proposed *Q* source. (5) Inspiration by the Holy Spirit combined with the previous reasons may account for some similarities and does not require a dictation view of inspiration. A growing number of authors are sympathetic to and lean toward the traditional independence view. After reviewing problems facing the two/four document theory Morris notes, "Such problems have caused some scholars to rethink the process, and in recent years there has been a revival of the hypothesis of J. J. Griesbach. This view dispenses with Q and takes Matthew to be the first Gospel to have been written, followed by Luke and then Mark. On this view Mark was produced by reworking some of the material in the other two Gospels" (*The Gospel According to Matthew*, 16).

Aramaic or Greek Original?

A second but lesser problem is whether the Gospel of Matthew was originally written in Aramaic and then translated into the current Greek form. The problem arose because of comments in the writings of early church fathers. Irenaeus, Eusebius, and Origen refer to an earlier reference in Papias to the effect that Matthew produced a written Gospel among the Hebrews "in their own dialect" (Morris, *The Gospel According to Matthew*, 12). That led some to conclude that our current Greek version of Mathew is actually a translation of an earlier Aramaic version. No solid evidence of such a Gospel of Matthew in Aramaic exists, nor do copies or fragments exist. Greek scholars are convinced that the present Greek edition of Matthew is an original writing, not a translation of an Aramaic document. Two solutions have been proposed. (1) The reference to Hebrew "dialect" simply indicates that Matthew wrote a "Jewish Gospel" in that it presented Jesus as the Messiah from a Jewish standpoint (Gundry, *Matthew*, 619-20). (2) Matthew wrote earlier tracts and sayings of Jesus in Aramaic before composing his Gospel in Greek. Whatever the case, there is no manuscript evidence of writings by Matthew in Aramaic, but a very large number of manuscripts and fragments of this Greek Gospel by Matthew do exist (Turner, *The Gospel of Matthew*, 6-7).

The Meaning of "Kingdom" in Matthew

The Gospel according to Matthew is preeminently the Gospel of the kingdom. Matthew has been described as the Jewish Gospel, the theological Gospel, the kingly Gospel, etc., but Matthew is above all the Gospel of the kingdom of God, which he labels "the kingdom of heaven." This kingdom emphasis distinguishes Matthew from Mark and Luke as well as from John. This kingdom concept (1) unites Matthew's Gospel with the Old Testament, (2) indicates the purpose for his writing, and (3) drives the logical development of his argument. Matthew presents the life of Christ in relationship to His kingship and to His kingdom program. The person of the King is inseparably united with the kingdom He came to offer. This emphasis on the King and His kingdom in Matthew is supported by at least three lines of evidence.

The first line of evidence is the frequency with which Matthew uses the terms *basileus* "king" and *basileia* "kingdom." *Basileus*, "king" occurs twenty-three times in Matthew compared to twelve in Mark, eleven in Luke, and sixteen in John. *Basileia*, "kingdom" is used fifty-six times by Matthew compared to twenty-one by Mark, forty-five by Luke and only five by John. The second line of evidence is Matthew's frequent reference to the Old Testament prophecies regarding the Messiah and his explicit statements that those prophecies were fulfilled in Jesus Christ. Matthew refers to the Old Testament 129 times including 53 citations and 76 allusions. Reference is made to 25 of the 39 Old Testament books. The Gospel of Matthew has thirty-three passages that relate to the Old Testament and Jesus as the Messiah and he uses the fulfillment formula "that it might be fulfilled" eleven times (Scroggie, *A Guide to the Gospels*, 270-78). A third line of evidence is the logical argument of the Gospel of Matthew itself. Christ's words and works as the messianic King provide the key that unlocks the argument of Matthew. The following synthesis traces that argument. But first it is necessary to answer the question, what is the meaning and nature of the kingdom as it appears in Matthew? Scripture uses the term "kingdom" in four ways (in addition to the kingdom of darkness over which Satan rules).

(1) **The eternal kingdom** embraces everything God has created and exists from eternity past to eternity future. *Yours, O LORD, is the greatness and the power and the glory and the victory and the majesty, indeed everything that is in the heavens and the earth; Yours is the dominion, O LORD, and You exalt Yourself as head over all* (1 Chronicles 29:11). Matthew is not referring to the eternal kingdom since it has just now

"come near" and thus was not present earlier. Some people are outside and may not enter the kingdom (5:20: 7:21; 18:3). Further, Matthew records Jesus' declaration that the kingdom will be taken away from that unbelieving generation of Israel to whom it is offered (Matthew 21:43). The eternal kingdom is always present and includes everything and everyone without exception. *The LORD has established His throne in the heavens, and His sovereignty rules over all* (Psalm 103:19).

(2) **The Davidic/messianic kingdom** was an earthly kingdom promised to David, and will ultimately be fulfilled in the Messiah who will rule over Israel and bring both judgment and blessing to the nations (Genesis 17:6, 16; 49:8-12; 2 Samuel 7:12-16). This literal, earthly kingdom receives much attention in the Old Testament prophets (Isaiah 11:1-2; 35:1-10; 40:1-5; 52:7-10; 61:1-2; Jeremiah 23:23:5-8; 30:4-11; 33:14-22; Ezekiel 34:23-31; 36:23-27; 37:24-28; 39:25-29; Daniel 2:35, 44-45; 7:13-14; etc.). It was this Davidic kingdom that was announced to Mary by the angel. *And behold, you will conceive in your womb and bear a son, and you shall name Him Jesus. He will be great and will be called the Son of the Most High; and the Lord God will give Him the throne of His father David; and He will reign over the house of Jacob forever, and His kingdom will have no end* (Luke 1:31-33).

Throughout the Gospel of Matthew Jesus is presented as the Davidic king. At His birth Jesus is designated King of the Jews by the magi from the east (2:1-2), Jesus confirms that designation at His trial before Pilate (27:11), and at His death the sign placed over the cross proclaims, "This is Jesus, the King of the Jews" (27:37). Matthew's parables of the kingdom in chapter 13 are the most extensive treatment of the course of the kingdom during the present age in light of Israel's rejection. The cross does not represent defeat for the King or destruction for the promised kingdom because Jesus is raised from the dead and announces to the disciples, *all authority has been given to Me in heaven and on earth* (28:18). Jesus will one day return as King to establish the kingdom (25:31-46; 26:64). In the meantime the gospel of the kingdom will be preached in the whole world (24:14).

Daniel had prophesied that Israel's bondage to Gentile kingdoms would end when the Messiah comes to judge and to rule the nations. *I kept looking in the night visions, and behold, with the clouds of heaven One like a Son of Man was coming, and He came up to the Ancient of Days and was presented before Him. And to Him was given dominion, Glory and a kingdom, that all the peoples, nations and men of every language might serve Him. His dominion is an everlasting dominion which will not pass away; and His kingdom is one which will not be destroyed* (Daniel 7:13-14). Centuries of oppression had created in Israel an expectation for that kingdom. Unfortunately their understanding of the kingdom was seriously flawed.

Moses had warned Israel that rebellion against God would bring exile among the nations (Leviticus 26:14-39; Deuteronomy 28:15-68). Only when they repented would God gather them from among the nations, return them to the land, and restore them to their place of blessing. *If they confess their iniquity and the iniquity of their forefathers, in their unfaithfulness which they committed against Me, and also in their acting with hostility against Me—I also was acting with hostility against them, to bring them into the land of their enemies—or if their uncircumcised heart becomes humbled so that they then make amends for their iniquity, then I will remember My covenant with Jacob, and I will remember also My covenant with Isaac, and My covenant with Abraham as well, and I will remember the land* (Leviticus 26:40-42). The exile became a reality, and in Jesus' day Israel was still living under Gentile rule.

For centuries the prophets' call to repentance had fallen on deaf ears. *I have spoken to you again and again; yet you have not listened to Me. Also I have sent to you all My servants the prophets, sending them again and again, saying: "Turn now every man from his evil way and amend your deeds, and do not go after other gods to worship them. Then you will dwell in the land which I have given to you and to your forefathers; but you have not inclined your ear or listened to Me"* (Jeremiah 35:14-15). The messianic kingdom involved a spiritual transformation; it required repentance and a changed heart (Jeremiah 31:31-34; Ezekiel 18:30-32; Hosea 14:1-2; Joel 2:12-13, 32; Zechariah 12:9-13:1). John the Baptist and Jesus continued that prophetic call for Israel to repent (Matthew 3:2; 4:17). This was the precondition for entering the kingdom. But again the call to repentance fell on deaf ears (Matthew 13:13-15).

Israel had been in exile to Gentile nations for over six centuries. They longed for the promised deliverance from Gentile rule but refused to recognize that the kingdom had a spiritual basis and required repentance (Deuteronomy 30:1-10; John 6:14-15). Jesus offered the messianic kingdom to Israel but they rejected Him and thus the kingdom He offered. They failed to understand the numerous prophecies that spoke of the suffering of the Messiah. The cross and the crown were both essential to the work of the Messiah (Psalm 22; Isaiah 53; Daniel 9:24-26; Zechariah 12:10, 13:1). Israel's rejection of Jesus as the Messiah was tragic but not unforeseen for it resulted in the postponement of the Davidic kingdom (Matthew 21:42-44). Rejection did not mean the termination or withdrawal of the kingdom (Matthew 26:64). Jesus lamented Israel's persistent failure to heed the prophets' call to repent (Matthew 23:37-39). It was this Davidic/messianic kingdom that the disciples (indeed all Israel) anticipated (Matthew 11:3; 20:20-28; John 6:15). After Jesus' death, burial, and resurrection the disciples still anticipated that the messianic kingdom would be restored to Israel and were assured that it would come, but not at that time (Acts 1:6).

Israel wanted the political and material blessings of the messianic kingdom but was unwilling to repent, which was the requirement for entrance into that kingdom (Matthew 3:2; 21:32). Entrance into the messianic kingdom required entrance into another, broader kingdom: the spiritual or soteriological kingdom. The two kingdoms are related but they are not synonymous. The Davidic/messianic kingdom was postponed because of Israel's rejection of the Messiah and will not be established until Israel repents and receives Jesus as the Messiah.

Because that kingdom will be established in the future when Jesus returns to earth, it is often identified separately as the **millennial kingdom** but it is the same kingdom Israel rejected. This is the focus of the Lord's Prayer in Matthew 6:9-10. *Our Father who is in heaven, Hallowed be Your name. Your kingdom come. Your will be done, on earth as it is in heaven.* This is the kingdom proclaimed in heaven at the consummation of the age. *Then the seventh angel sounded; and there were loud voices in heaven, saying, "The kingdom of the world has become the kingdom of our Lord and of His Christ; and He will reign forever and ever"* (Revelation 11:15). This kingdom will be established when Jesus returns to the earth in fulfillment of Daniel's prophecy (Daniel 7:13-14; Matthew 16:27; 26:64; Revelation 19:11-20:4). The spiritual kingdom continues and includes all who believe whether Jew or Gentile (Matthew 28:20).

(3) **The spiritual (soteriological) kingdom**. Jesus taught that the spiritual kingdom can be entered only by the new birth (John 3:3-8). Nicodemus was puzzled about it, but it was not something new and unique. Jesus was simply repeating Ezekiel's call for a heart relationship to God. *Then I will sprinkle clean water on you, and you will be clean; I will cleanse you from all your filthiness and from all your idols. Moreover, I will give you*

19

a new heart and put a new spirit within you; and I will remove the heart of stone from your flesh and give you a heart of flesh. I will put My Spirit within you and cause you to walk in My statutes, and you will be careful to observe My ordinances (Ezekiel 36:25-27). As the Messiah, Jesus did not come simply to restore Israel's political kingdom; He came to establish the promised messianic kingdom that involved a heart relationship with God, that is, entrance into the spiritual kingdom (Ezekiel 18:30-32). The spiritual kingdom is that kingdom into which all believers have entered by faith in the Lord Jesus Christ. *For He rescued us from the domain of darkness, and transferred us to the kingdom of His beloved Son, in whom we have redemption, the forgiveness of sins* (Colossians 1:13-14). This is the kingdom that the apostles preached (Acts 8:12; 19:8; 28:23) and wrote about (1 Corinthians 15:30; Galatians 5:21; 1 Timothy 2:12; Revelation 1:6).

(4) **The mystery form of the kingdom**. Following the rejection of Jesus by Israel's leaders (12:38-45) Matthew records Jesus' parabolic teaching regarding the kingdom (13:1-52). This answers a critical question, What will happen to the kingdom now that the King has been rejected? Much discussion and debate have not resulted in unanimity regarding the present form or status of the kingdom that Jesus revealed here in Matthew 13. But it is not a new or different kingdom since Jesus uses the same term "kingdom of heaven" that He has used repeatedly throughout His ministry (4:17, 23; 9:35). However, He introduced the revelation as "the mysteries of the kingdom," prompting many to call it "the mystery form of the kingdom." That may lead to some misunderstanding.

"Mystery" refers to something previously not made known rather than to something mysterious. Paul defines a mystery thus, *the mystery which has been hidden from the past ages and generations, but has now been manifested to His saints, to whom God willed to make known what is the riches of the glory of this mystery among the Gentiles, which is Christ in you, the hope of glory* (Colossians 1:26-27). John Walvoord explains,

"A mystery truth, accordingly, has two elements. First, it has to be hidden in the Old Testament and not revealed there. Second, it has to be revealed in the New Testament. It is not necessarily a reference to a truth difficult to understand, but rather to truths that can be understood only on the basis of divine revelation. The Old Testament reveals, in clear terms, the earthly reign of Christ when He comes as King to reign on the throne of David (which truths are not mysteries). Matthew 13 introduces a different form of the kingdom, namely the present spiritual reign of the King during the period He is physically absent from the earth, prior to His second coming. The mysteries of the kingdom, accordingly, deal with the period between the first and second advent of Christ and not the millennial kingdom which will follow the second coming" (*Matthew: Thy Kingdom Come*, 97).

Key Verse
The record of the genealogy of Jesus the Messiah, the son of David, the son of Abraham (Matthew 1:1).

Message of Matthew

Presentation of the King (1:1-4:11). Jesus is the man born to be King. A King must have a genealogy. Jesus is identified as the Messiah in the very first verse and His genealogy is traced to David and to Abraham. God's covenant with David promised a messianic King whose reign will be eternal (2 Samuel 7:11-16; Psalm 110). His covenant with Abraham promised a nation, a land, and a seed through whom both Israel and the nations will be blessed (Genesis 12:1-3). Matthew sees these promises as consummated by and through Jesus Christ, the Messiah, as foretold by the prophets. Jesus is the rightful King of Israel (1:1-17) and the virgin-born Son of God (1:18-25) as predicted by Isaiah (7:14; 9:6-7). The New Covenant God promised (Jeremiah 31:31-34; Ezekiel 36:25-27) requires regeneration and forgiveness of sins. These kingdom essentials are preached by John the Baptist and are provided through Jesus, who is Savior and Immanuel, God with us (1:18-25). Sin was originally introduced into human experience through Satan's tempting and Satan appears prominently in Matthew in the temptation of Jesus.

The opposition of the false kingdom that was introduced in Genesis 3 appears in the person of the usurper Herod, who attempts to slaughter the newborn King (Matthew 2:1-23) and later in the person of Satan, who seeks to tempt Jesus by offering Him a counterfeit kingdom (4:1-11). However, two signs of kingdom power are revealed to counter this dark picture: (1) the newborn King is worshiped and His kingship recognized by magi from Gentile nations (2:1-12). This reveals the relationship of Gentiles to the kingdom as recipients of blessing through the Messiah and is also a foreshadowing of Israel's rejection and crucifixion of her King. (2) The providence of God is revealed as He delivers the King from the forces of Satan; Herod dies and the King lives (2:12-23)! God's omnipotent working on behalf of the kingdom is made evident in direct fulfillment of Old Testament prophecies.

21

The Baptism and Temptation of Jesus

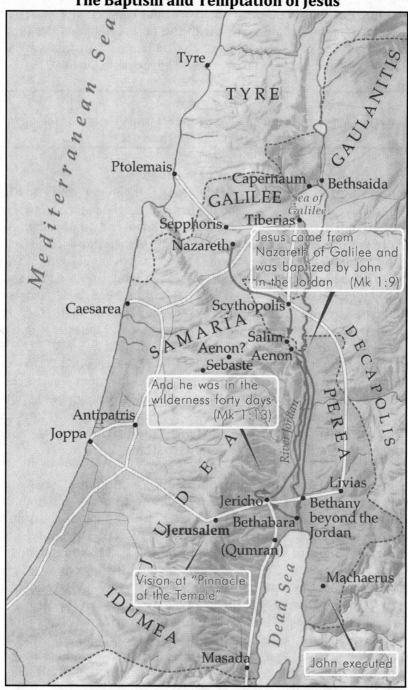

Copyright by Carta Jerusalem, Used by permission

John the Baptist's arrival on the scene marks the arrival of Messiah's forerunner (Malachi 3:1-7). The kingdom of heaven is "at hand," that is, the kingdom is present in the person of the King (3:1-12). John preaches repentance, the divine requirement for the nation to enter the kingdom. John is not offering the kingdom; he is introducing the King who will Himself offer the kingdom. The baptism of Jesus (3:13-17) serves to identify Him with the message of John. Jesus is the King, the personification of John's message that the kingdom is at hand. The messianic King has come! Satan's kingdom immediately opposes the King's herald in the person of the Pharisees and Sadducees (3:7-12). The stakes are high! Satan personally attacks the King who proves His right to rule by overcoming Satan's temptations (4:1-11).

Proclamation of the King (4:12-7:29). From the temptation of Jesus Matthew moves immediately to John's imprisonment, which shows the activity of the false kingdom (4:12-16). The fight is on! Jesus takes up the same message as that of John, except that now the King is offering the kingdom (4:17). The new work of the King calls for men to whom authority and responsibility can be delegated, so Jesus begins to call His disciples (4:18-22). The character of the Davidic (millennial) kingdom will involve great physical as well as spiritual renovations, hence Jesus' power to heal and defeat Satan's demons is demonstrated (4:23-25).

The Sermon on the Mount is the throne speech of the messianic King (chaps. 5-7). The Sermon on the Mount presents the means of entrance or the prerequisite of entrance into the kingdom. The former revelation of God's righteousness, the Law of Moses, is expounded by Christ, the King, to show that the righteousness required for entrance into the kingdom is absolute, is not attainable by works as taught by the Pharisees (5:17-20), and can be found only in the Messiah (5:48). This is the righteousness imputed to Abraham when he believed (Genesis 15:6) and is now being offered by Christ to all who will believe and ask (7:7-14). The character of the citizens is revealed based on their reception of the new heart promised in the New Covenant and now offered by Christ (5:3-12). The kingdom Christ offered was not a "spiritual" or mystical kingdom as frequently understood. Instead it was the kingdom promised before by the Old Testament prophets (Jeremiah 31; Ezekiel 36). Since rejection is evident (5:12) there is a present ministry for the remnant as salt and light (5:13-16).

Matthew 5:17-7:6 addresses the question of the King's relationship to the Mosaic Law (5:17-20) and explains the absolute righteousness required by the King in His kingdom (5:21-48). The conduct of the citizens is diametrically opposite to the hypocrisy of the Pharisees (6:1-7:6). God's righteousness is absolute and citizens of the kingdom can be perfectly holy as God is but only by the imputation of God's righteousness (5:48). Those who ask God for His righteousness to be imputed to them will receive it (7:7-14). Immediately following this Sermon on the Mount a leper comes to Jesus, asks and receives cleansing (8:1-4). Concluding the announcement of the kingdom and its explanation an appeal is made. Repentance is necessary and a decision is required. Two roads (7:13-14), two trees (7:15-20), two claims (7:21-23), and two houses (7:24-27) illustrate the need to decide and the consequences of their response to the King's invitation.

Power of the King (chaps. 8-10). Following Jesus' exposition of the kingdom and the means of entrance into it, Matthew introduces the miracles of Christ as authentication for the offer of the kingdom. The King grants cleansing to the leper (8:1-4), healing to the Gentiles (8:5-13) and to a woman (8:14-15), and release to the demon possessed (8:16-17). The miracles prove that Jesus has the power to do the works that the Old Testament prophets said the Messiah would do (8:17). Latent in this is the rejection of the King and the kingdom seen in the failure of the priests to come to Jesus and in the needy to whom Christ ministers. The miracles of this section of Matthew do more than authenticate; they reveal by illustration the character of the Davidic kingdom being offered by Christ. There will be cleansing (8:1-4), healing (8:5-17), unhindered obedience to the King (8:18-22), controlled nature or elements (8:23-27), binding or annulling of demonic power (8:28-34), forgiveness and restoration (9:1-8), sovereign authority (9:9-17), and victory over death (9:18-26), blindness (9:27-31), and the demons of Satan's kingdom (9:32-34).

Jesus turns His attention and the eyes of His disciples to the needs of the masses of people and the harvest of souls that calls for workers (9:35-38). Jesus has compassion for them and commissions twelve apostles to herald the kingdom message throughout Israel. *Jesus summoned His twelve disciples and gave them authority over unclean spirits, to cast them out, and to heal every kind of disease and every kind of sickness* (10:1). His authority is delegated to them and they are empowered to do the work of the kingdom just as Jesus has been doing it. The compassionate Christ is making a concerted effort to spread the good news and sends His disciples to reap in the waiting harvest within Israel (9:37-38). *These twelve Jesus sent out after instructing them: "Do not go in the way of the Gentiles, and do not enter any city of the Samaritans; but rather go to the lost sheep of the house of Israel. And as you go, preach, saying, 'The kingdom of heaven is at hand'* (10:5-7). These instructions form the second major discourse recorded by Matthew (10:5-42). Opposition to the Messiah is growing within Israel. It is fueled by the hatred and religious hypocrisy of the Pharisees and the scribes. Thus far in Matthew there have been strains of opposition, but later in the next segment the writer shows the progressive development of that opposition.

Progressive opposition to the King (11:1-16:12). That there is a false kingdom and that it is in a violent, life-and-death struggle against God's sovereign authority is no new revelation. However, this may be misunderstood and so Matthew now turns to the theme of rejection to show its course and its completeness. Already the forerunner, John, has been imprisoned and bears defending by the King (11:2-19). Considering the gathering gloom of unbelief and rejection, a denunciation is in order (11:20-24) and an invitation to the oppressed in Israel is necessary (11:25-30). The King will provide rest and peace in His kingdom. Israel must choose between the yoke of the Messiah or remain under the iron yoke of Gentile oppressors. *Come to Me, all who are weary and heavy-laden, and I will give you rest. Take My yoke upon you and learn from Me, for I am gentle and humble in heart, and you will find rest for your souls. For My yoke is easy and My burden is light* (11:28-30).

The occasion of the controversy may vary and seem to be insignificant (12:1-8), but the opposition is real (12:9-14), and violent (12:14), in contrast to Messiah's unassuming manner (12:15-21). The climax of the opposition comes in 12:22-24 with the blasphemous accusation that Jesus is in league with Beelzebub, the prince of demons. The significance of this charge is that the Messiah who has come and who has offered the promised kingdom is accused of being energized by Satan, the very one whose sin occasioned God's redemptive plan and kingdom program. Thus the theocratic kingdom in the person of its King is repudiated by being identified with its opposing counterpart, the satanic kingdom. The King's defense is complete (12:25-37), but falls on deaf ears. These unbelieving leaders only raise the cry for another sign (12:38). In the place of a sign Jesus gives the promise of the resurrection as proof of Messiah's person and as a warning of certain and severe judgment on unbelieving rejecters

(12:39-45). Having been rejected by the leaders of Israel the King now repudiates natural or traditional relationships (12:46-50).

The rejection of the King and His kingdom will lead to the cross but not until the Messiah is formally presented and officially rejected in Jerusalem. Matthew now addresses a critical question, "If the Messiah is rejected by His own nation, Israel, what will happen to the kingdom He has been offering?" In the parables of Matthew 13 Jesus explains the kingdom program during the interadvent (church) age. This chapter is often referred to as "the mystery form of the kingdom," not because it is mysterious or obscure but because it is new revelation concerning the church age, something previously not made known (Romans 16:25-27; Ephesians 1:9-10; 3:1-12).

Matthew chapters 1-12 deal primarily with the Davidic or millennial form of the kingdom. There is relatively little difficulty following the course of the kingdom thus far. Matthew 13:1 begins a section of the Gospel in which it is more difficult to trace the kingdom concept. Now there are two aspects in view: One is the Davidic/messianic form of the kingdom as offered by Christ (11:28-30), rejected by Israel (11:38-45), and awaiting a future establishment (24:30-31). The other aspect is the mystery form, the present manifestation of the kingdom during the interadvent or church age. A distinction at this point is helpful.

In Matthew chapters 13-23 when the kingdom is being offered or rejected the Davidic/messianic (millennial) form is in view. However, after the blasphemous charge of the religious authorities (12:24) when Christ is teaching His disciples concerning the kingdom, generally the interadvent form of the kingdom is in view. Specifically, the parables of Matthew 13 reveal that the kingdom will have a new, unforeseen manifestation in view of the rejection. There will be a sowing, kingdom activity, a counter-sowing, false-kingdom activity, and phenomenal growth of the kingdom including both Jews and Gentiles, with a separating judgment at the end of the age. The millennium is not referred to directly in the conclusion, though the effect of judgment on the rejecters is told. Jesus' parables regarding the kingdom are focused on the interadvent or church age and climax in the final judgment when the messianic kingdom will come on earth.

The departure of Christ is a strategic movement (13:53). The narrative turns abruptly from the parabolic teaching in view of Jesus' rejection to focus on Israel's continued unbelief and rejection (13:54-58). The death of the forerunner is a harbinger of the Messiah's approaching death (14:1-12). The rejected King, if He has not failed, must be able to meet the needs of His own in the kingdom (14:13-36). Once again the rejecters appear on stage as the Pharisees repeat their willful unbelief (15:1-2), and following a stinging denunciation of such hypocrisy (15:3-20), Jesus turns to the Gentiles to show that the Messiah will bless the Gentiles not only as Israel's Messiah in the millennium but also as the omnipotent Lord in the interadvent age (15:21-39). The Pharisees appear on stage in seesaw fashion as rejecters of the kingdom and the King who offered it (16:1-12).

Jesus' Ministry in Gentile Territory

Copyright by Carta Jerusalem, Used by permission

Preparations by the King in light of His rejection (16:13-20:34). Turning to His own, the children of the kingdom, Christ now instructs them by the revelation of His person (16:13-16), and His program (16:17-

27

18). The church is seen for the first time in Matthew as comprising the bulk of time during the interadvent age. The church is not an alternative to or a replacement of the Davidic kingdom that Jesus offered. Jesus' transfiguration is the strongest evidence of the millennial kingdom in this section. The revelation of Jesus' glory (17:1-12) is a miniature picture of the King in His kingdom. Such a revelation is in direct contrast to the condition of Israel as impotent (17:14-21) and emphasizes the fact spoken by Zechariah (12-14) that the establishing of the messianic kingdom necessitated a turning or repentance on the part of Israel. The large section that follows (Matthew 17:22-20:34) is devoted to Jesus' instruction of the disciples in view of the King's rejection. These chapters include a wide range of subjects such as the Messiah's betrayal (17:22-23), the disciples' privileges as sons (17:24-27), true greatness and humility (18:1-9), the value of the lost individual (18:10-14), the right way to handle offences (18:15-35), divorce and children (19:1-15), and the cost and reward of following Christ (19:16-20:28). Jesus is now approaching Jerusalem. The last event before His formal presentation and rejection is the healing of two blind men at Jericho (20:29-34). This miracle illustrates the authority of the King in His kingdom and also that Israel, blinded by unbelief, stands desperately in need of the light of Messiah. The blind know that Jesus is the Messiah, the Son of David, but Israel remains blind and refuses to believe.

Presentation and official rejection of the King (chaps. 21-25). The entrance of Christ into Jerusalem with His ardent followers is the final and official offer of the kingdom in Matthew. The king enters Jerusalem in keeping with Old Testament prophecy (21:1-8 with Zechariah 9:9) and the crowd proclaims His kingship (21:9-11). Their cry is a messianic declaration. The King who is the rightful heir to David's throne officially offers the Davidic kingdom. The authority of the Messiah over the temple is demonstrated in a trilogy of messianic acts (21:12-14). However, the opposition of unbelief is aroused and the chief priests, with indignation, reject the King and His offered kingdom (21:15-17). The result of this final rejection is seen in the withering of the fig tree (21:18-22). Israel had been chosen and cared for like the fig tree but had produced no fruit (Isaiah 5:1-7; Jeremiah 24:1-10). The Messiah has come and has found no fruit of repentance in the nation only empty promise. The cursing of the fig tree represents the irreversible judgment on that generation. The rejection of the King and the kingdom is complete. The rejection was previewed in 21:15 but is now fully expounded (21:23-23:29).

Jesus' Journey to Jerusalem

A map showing Jesus' journey to Jerusalem with the following labeled locations and regions:

Bodies of water and regions: Mediterranean Sea, TYRE, GALILEE, Sea of Galilee, GAULANITIS, DECAPOLIS, SAMARIA, PEREA, JUDEA, River Jordan

Cities and places: Tyre, Caesarea Philippi, Ptolemais, Capernaum, Gennesaret, Tiberias, Sepphoris, Nazareth, Mt. Tabor, Hippus, Gadara, Dor, Caesarea, Scythopolis, Ginae, Samaria-Sebaste, Apollonia, Antipatris, Joppa, Gadora, Lydda, Abila, Bethphage, Jerusalem, Bethany, Jericho

Callout boxes:
- Samaritans refuse to receive Jesus; some healed
- Jesus passes between Samaria and Galilee
- Jesus heals blind Bartameus, and leads Zacchaeus the tax collector to repentance
- Jesus stays with Martha and Mary

Copyright by Carta Jerusalem, Used by permission

The chief priests question the Messiah's authority, but are soundly defeated and put to silence by a series of three parables (21:23-22:14). The parable of the two sons establishes their responsibility for rejection (21:23-32). The second, the parable of the wicked husbandmen, explains the course of the rejection and the consequent judgment (21:33-46). The chief priests are ensnared into condemning themselves by their interpretation of the parable (21:40-42). A significant feature of this section is the reciprocal rejection of that generation by Christ. *Therefore I say to you, the kingdom of God will be taken away from you and given to a people, producing the fruit of it* (21:43).

The kingdom concept in Matthew 21:43 is dependent on one's interpretation of "you" and of *ethnos* "people," "nation," or "generation." The people addressed by Jesus were the leaders of the nation Israel. Their rejection of Jesus as the Messiah was an official rejection committed by representatives of the nation of Israel. The kingdom Jesus offered was the Davidic kingdom God promised to the nation Israel. It was a literal earthly kingdom with a throne and a king ruling over the nation. God declared on oath that He would not take the kingdom away from David's descendants (2 Samuel 7:12-17; 2 Chronicles 6:15-17) and that Israel will always exist as a nation (Jeremiah 31:36-37). Thus the Davidic kingdom could not be eliminated or be given to a Gentile nation. It could not become a spiritual, nonliteral earthly kingdom in light of the extensive promises of the Old Testament. The church is not a replacement for the Davidic/messianic kingdom. The Davidic (millennial) kingdom was being taken from that generation of Israel and will be given to the future generation that manifests repentance. Jesus' repeated statements indicate that He will return to establish His kingdom on earth (Daniel 7:13-14 with Matthew 16:27-28; 24-25; 26:64) and are in keeping with the question asked by the disciples after Jesus' resurrection (Acts 1:6).

The third parable, that of the marriage feast (22:1-14), reveals that the kingdom will have guests in spite of the rejection of the bidden ones in Israel. As confirmation of their guilt the Pharisees, the Herodians, and the Sadducees as separate groups each demonstrate their rejection of the kingdom offer (22:15-46) and Jesus scathingly denounced them as hypocrites (23:1-36). The finality of Israel's rejection of Jesus as the Messiah and the coming destruction of Israel and Jerusalem by the Roman army are graphically unfolded as Jesus weeps over Jerusalem and what might have been (23:37-39). Israel's house, that is, the nation Israel, is left desolate and the Davidic/messianic kingdom is postponed until the nation repents. The mystery form of the kingdom is administered today through the church and not through Israel. But Israel is not cast away. Paul argues strongly for the future salvation of Israel (Romans 11:25-29).

The Olivet Discourse is the most complete revelation in the four Gospels of the return of the King and the coming judgment (chaps. 24-25). Like the Sermon on the Mount this section merits detailed analysis and careful exposition. The temple, the center of national life for Israel, is doomed to destruction (24:1-2). This occasioned the interest of the disciples in the establishment of the Davidic kingdom. That the form of the kingdom in view is the millennial form is seen by the term, "the end of the age" (Daniel 12:9). Four events are unfolded in the Olivet discourse that are preparatory for the establishment of the Davidic kingdom: (1) the sign of the tribulation (24:9-28 with Daniel 9:26-27), (2) the coming of the Messiah, the Son of Man (24:29-30 with Daniel 7:13-14), (3) the regathering of the dispersed nation Israel (24:31), and (4) the judgment separating believers from unbelievers both in Israel (25:1-30) and among the Gentiles (25:31-46). A concluding exhortation to watchfulness is given in view of the King's return (24:32-51). The Olivet Discourse is related to the future institution of the millennial or Davidic form of the kingdom.

Passion of the King (chaps. 26-27). The reader is taken rapidly in panoramic fashion from the Davidic kingdom as offered and its rejection to the broader base of the Abrahamic covenant and the Seed, the promised One, who will bring the blessing of redemption. This movement is tied logically to the opening statement of Matthew (1:1) and follows the unusual order found there, first David's son then Abraham's son. First, the King as David's Son has offered the kingdom. Now as the crucified Savior, Abraham's seed, He will offer the blessings of salvation. In the Old Testament the Messiah was portrayed both as the lion of the tribe of Judah (Genesis 49:8-12) and also as the Passover lamb (Isaiah 53:1-12). The previous intrigue continues (26:1-5), but the discordant notes of rejection and fear are struck more often (26:6-63). Jesus is worshiped and anointed for His coming crucifixion with a very costly ointment (26:6-13) but betrayed by Judas for the mere price of a slave (26:14-16). The Messiah and His disciples participate in the last Passover and initiate the Lord's Supper (26:17-35). The blood Jesus sheds on the cross becomes the saving grounds on which the New Covenant is instituted. *This is My blood of the covenant, which is poured out for many for forgiveness of sins. But I say to you, I will not drink of this fruit of the vine from now on until that day when I drink it new with you in My Father's kingdom* (26:28-29). The basis of the

31

millennial kingdom is Messiah's work at Calvary, and when the Messiah returns in triumph the Davidic kingdom will be established on earth.

Jesus' agonizing prayer in Gethsemane reveals the horror of the cross (26:36-46). The sinless Son of God, the Messiah, the Lamb of God, is slain for the sins of the world (Isaiah 52:13-53:12). His trial before the Sanhedrin is a mockery of religious justice (26:57-68). His trusted followers, including their spokesman Peter, abandon the Messiah and in doing so they fulfill the word of the prophets (Matthew 26:31; 27:69-75; Zechariah 13:7). The time of repentance is past for the nation and for His betrayer Judas (27:1-10). Guilt for the crucifixion of the Messiah is universal as the Gentile ruler, Pilate, sentences Jesus to death by crucifixion (27:11-26). But this condemned One is the King. This is seen in Jesus' own words (26:64; 27:11), in the mockery of the soldiers (27:27-31), and in the accusation written over His cross (27:37). But Jesus is also the Savior. The hope of the entire world rests on and flows from His death on the cross. Darkness shrouds the agony of Jesus, the Son of God and Savior of the world as He dies on a Roman cross (27:32-56). The death of the Messiah ripped forever the veil in the temple that separated man from God (27:51). Jesus is hastily buried in a tomb and heavily guarded in a vain attempt to ensure that He remains in the grave (27:57-66). As in His life and ministry, so in His death, burial, and resurrection Jesus fulfilled Old Testament prophecy (Isaiah 53:1-12).

Proof of the King (chap. 28). The resurrection of Jesus validates His claim to be the Messiah (Psalm 16:10; Acts 17:30-31; Romans 1:4). Jesus foretold His resurrection as well as His crucifixion and His word is perfectly fulfilled (12:38-40; 16:21; 17:9, 23; 20:18-19; 27:63). Thus Jesus' person, His power over death, His foreknowledge of the future, His truthfulness, and His absolute authority in heaven and on earth are proved beyond doubt. Matthew's record of the resurrection is brief but important. Jesus is worshiped and all doubt removed from the minds of the disciples (Matthew 28:1-17). The resurrection of Christ is a reality, an indispensable truth, and the foundation for the establishment of the postponed Davidic kingdom. It is the declaration by the Father of Jesus' divine Sonship (Romans 1:4). No Satanic opposition can prevent the resurrection (Matthew 27:62-66) or distort the truth of this divine authentication (28:11-15).

Matthew's Gospel closes with the great commission (28:16-20). The basis of the commission is the absolute authority of the risen Messiah both in heaven and on earth. The commission is a clear statement of the Trinity as the Father, Son, and Holy Spirit are all engaged in the disciple-making ministry to which the disciples (apostles) are being commissioned. *All authority has been given to Me in heaven and on earth. Go therefore and make disciples of all the nations, baptizing them in the name of the Father and the Son and the Holy Spirit, teaching them to observe all that I commanded you; and lo, I am with you always, even to the end of the age* (Matthew 28:18-20).

Outline

I.	Presentation of the King	1:1-4:11
	A. Genealogy: His legal right to rule	1:1-17
	B. Birth: His Divine right to rule	1:18-25
	C. Authentication: recognition by Gentiles	2:1-12
	D. Preservation: Early opposition to His rule	2:13-23
	E. Presentation: Confirmation of His right to rule	3:1-17
	F. Testing: His moral right to rule	4:1-11
II.	Proclamation of the King	4:12-7:29
	A. Inauguration of the King and His kingdom offer	4:12-25
	B. Portrait of citizens in the kingdom	5:1-16
	C. Principles for life in the kingdom	5:17-48
	D. Practices of life in the kingdom	6:1-7:12
	E. Proof of life in the kingdom	7:13-29
III.	Power of the King	8:1-10:42
	A. Power to heal infirmities	8:1-17
	B. Power to deny entrance into the kingdom	8:18-22
	C. Power over nature, demons, and sin	8:23-9:8
	D. Power to call sinners into the kingdom	9:9-17
	E. Power over death, blindness, and demons	9:18-34
	F. Power to appoint ambassadors	9:35-10:42
IV.	Progressive Opposition to the King	11:1-16:12
	A. The King's assessment of that generation	11:1-19
	B. The King's denunciation of unrepentant cities	11:20-24
	C. The King's appeal to accept His yoke	11:25-30
	D. The King's enemies persist in rejecting Him	12:1-21
	E. The King's enemies commit blasphemy	12:22-50

F.	The King's program in light of His rejection	13:1-52
G.	The rejection of the King by His own people	13:53-58
H.	The murder of the King's ambassador by Herod	14:1-12
I.	The King's ministry to the believing remnant	14:13-36
J.	The King exposes the hypocrisy of His enemies	15:1-20
K.	The King invites Gentiles to enter the kingdom	15:21-39
L.	The King warns against His enemies' teaching	16:1-12

V.	Preparations by the King in Light of His Rejection	16:13-20:34
A.	The King's revelation of the church	16:13-20
B.	The King's revelation of His death in Jerusalem	16:21-28
C.	The King's revelation of His glory	17:1-21
D.	The King's revelation of His betrayal	17:22-23
E.	The King's teaching of His appointed apostles	18:1-20:28
F.	The King opens blind eyes in a blind nation	20:29-34

VI.	Presentation and Official Rejection of the King	21:1-25:46
A.	The King's triumphal entry in Jerusalem	21:1-11
B.	Purification of the temple by the King	21:12-17
C.	Judging the fig tree: Israel's failure to repent	21:18-22
D.	The messianic King silences His enemies	21:23-22:46
E.	The King announces Israel's coming judgment	23:1-39
F.	The King reveals the plan for His return	24:1-25:46

VII.	Passion of the King	26:1-27:66
A.	The plot of the authorities against the King	26:1-5
B.	The King anointed in anticipation of His death	26:6-13
C.	The King betrayed by one of His own (Judas)	26:14-16
D.	The King shares the Passover with His own	26:17-35
E.	The King's prayer and arrest in Gethsemane	26:36-56
G.	The King's trial before religious authorities	26:57-75
H.	The King's betrayer commits suicide	27:1-10
I.	The King's trial before the civil authorities	27:11-26
J.	The King's humiliation and death by crucifixion	27:27-56
K.	The King's burial in a guarded tomb	27:57-66

VIII.	Proof of the King's Right to Rule the Kingdom	28:1-20
A.	The resurrection of the King	28:1-4
B.	The appearance of the King to His followers	28:5-10
C.	Enemies attempt to conceal His resurrection	28:11-15
D.	The King's commission to His ambassadors	28:16-20

Bibliography

Blomberg, Craig. *Matthew.* New American Commentary. Nashville: Broadman and Holman, 1992.

Carson, D. A. "Matthew," in *The Expositor's Bible Commentary.* Vol. 9. Rev. ed. Zondervan Publishing House, 2010.

Carson, D. A., Douglas J. Moo, and Leon Morris. *An Introduction to the New Testament.* Grand Rapids: Zondervan Publishing House, 1991.

Edersheim, Alfred. *The Life and Times of Jesus the Messiah.* 2 vols. Grand Rapids: Wm. B. Eerdmans Publishing Co., 1959.

Gaebelein, Arno C. *The Gospel of Matthew.* New York: Loizeaux Brothers, 1961.

Glasscock, Ed. *Matthew.* Moody Gospel Commentary. Chicago: Moody Press, 1997.

Gundry, Robert H. *Matthew.* Grand Rapids: Wm. B. Eerdmans Publishing Co., 1994.

Guthrie, Donald. *New Testament Introduction.* Downers Grove, IL: InterVarsity Press, 1990.

Hiebert, D. Edmond. An *Introduction to the New Testament.* Vol. 1. Chicago: Moody Press, 1975.

Morris, Leon. *The Gospel According to Matthew.* Pillar New Testament Commentary. Grand Rapids: Wm. B. Eerdmans Publishing Co., 1992.

Plummer, Alfred. *An Exegetical Commentary on the Gospel According to S. Matthew.* Grand Rapids: Wm. B. Eerdmans Publishing Co., 1960.

Toussaint, Stanley D. *Behold the King: A Study of Matthew.* Grand Rapids: Kregel Publications, 1980.

Turner, David L. *The Gospel of Matthew.* Cornerstone Biblical Commentary. Carol Stream, IL: Tyndale House Publishers, 2005.

Scroggie, W. Graham. *A Guide to the Gospels.* London: Pickering & Inglis, 1962.

Walvoord, John F. *Matthew: Thy Kingdom Come.* Chicago: Moody Press, 1974.

Wenham, David, and Steve Walton. *Exploring the New Testament: A Guide to the Gospels and Acts.* Downers Grove, IL: InterVarsity Press, 2001.

Mark: The Son of God Became a Servant, a Ransom for Sin

Key verse: 10:45, the Son of Man did not come to be served, but to serve, and to give His life a ransom for many.

Key Words
Immediately,
Son of Man,
Evil spirits,
Disciples,
Gospel

Logical progression	
Initiation of the Son's Servant ministry: 1:14-45	**Presentation of the Son of God** — 1:1
Servant's ministry stirs controversy 2:1-3:12	1:14 *Jesus came into Galilee, preaching the gospel of God*
Servant's ministry in light of rejection 3:12-8:26	**Person and Work of the Son as the Suffering Servant**
Teaching disciples: 8:27-9:50	**Pivot: Peter's confession** — 8:27 *He went to Caesarea Philippi: teaching He must be killed, rise*
Journey to Jerusalem 10:1-52	
Official rejection 11:1-13:37	**Passion of the Son of God as the Suffering Servant**
Trial and death 14:1-15:47	
Resurrection 16:1-20	16:20

Mark
AD 63-67
Purpose: to explain the gospel of Jesus, the Son of God, the ransom for sin, to Romans

MARK

The beginning of the gospel of Jesus Christ, the Son of God (Mark 1:1).

For even the Son of Man did not come to be served, but to serve, and to give His life a ransom for many (Mark 10:45).

Mark is the "blue-collar Gospel," the "on-the-go" Gospel. It is a fast-paced report of the life of Jesus Christ much like today's evening news. The word *euthus* ("immediately") occurs forty-two times. The stress is on Jesus' works rather than His words. The language of Mark reflects the Greek spoken in the marketplace rather than in the universities of the day. But Mark is not "Jesus Lite." It is not a "Reader's Digest Condensed" version of Jesus' life and labor or the sixty-second "sound bite" that highlights major events in news broadcasts. Mark was "a skilled artist and theologian" (Edwards, *The Gospel According to* Mark, 3). The Gospel of Mark is an evangelistic treatise designed to prove that Jesus Christ is the Son of God who has come as the Suffering Servant promised in the Old Testament. It is the gospel, the good news, that Jesus is the Savior of all who believe. Jesus' very first words are an urgent invitation. *The time is fulfilled, and the kingdom of God is at hand; repent and believe in the gospel* (Mark 1:15). Almost half of the book deals with Jesus' substitutionary death, a much larger percentage than the other Gospels.

The "least has become the greatest." Judging by the small number of references to the Gospel of Mark in the early church fathers and the absence of commentaries they wrote on the book, one might conclude that Mark was the "least" of the four Gospels. It received less attention among the church fathers than the other three Gospels, though from the beginning the Gospel of Mark was accepted as inspired and was placed alongside the other Gospels as authoritative. In recent years the roles have been reversed. Mark has become the most studied and emphasized of the four Gospels. The early church fathers considered that Mark was written after Matthew and Luke and was to a large extent dependent on them, but most modern scholars argue the opposite. It is now commonly held that Matthew and Luke both depended on and used Mark's Gospel extensively in writing their Gospels.

Mark's arrangement and reporting of events is now considered the foundation for any systematic treatment of the life of the Lord Jesus Christ. According to Hiebert, "In the ancient church, the Gospel of Mark, the shortest and simplest of the four Gospels, did not command the attention received by the other three. Since it was commonly regarded as a mere abbreviation of the First Gospel, Mark did not elicit the popularity enjoyed by the more comprehensive Matthew. But the views of modern critical scholarship have terminated this comparative neglect of the Second Gospel and have catapulted it into the limelight of scholarly interest and critical study. It is no longer held to be an abridgment of a fuller account but is accepted as an independent work, complete in itself, written with a specific purpose, and eminently suited for an initial study of the gospel story" (*The Gospel of Mark*, 1).

Author

The Gospel of Mark is anonymous as are all of the four canonical Gospels, but the support of the early church fathers for Mark as author was universal. The superscription, *euangelion kata Markon,* "the gospel according to Mark," appears in all the early manuscripts. Mark was consistently identified as the author in the writings of Papias, Justin Martyr, *The Anti-Marcionite Prologue,* Irenaeus, Clement of Alexandria, and Eusebius. The apostle John may be the earliest witness to Mark as the author (if he is "the elder" in Eusebius). The writings of John's disciple, Papias (AD 70-140), are preserved in the quotation that appears in Eusebius's *Ecclesiastical History.*

"The elder said this also: Mark, who became Peter's interpreter, wrote accurately, though not in order, all that he remembered of the things said or done by the Lord. For he had neither heard the Lord nor been one of his followers, but afterwards, as I said, he had followed Peter, who used to compose his discourses with a view to the needs of his hearers, but not as though he were drawing up a connected account of the Lord's sayings. So Mark made no mistake in thus recording some things just as he remembered them. For he was careful of this one thing, to omit none of the things he had heard and to make no untrue statements therein" (Eusebius, *Ecclesiastical History,* 3.39.15).

Few scholars question the authorship by John Mark or the apostolic connection with Peter in Rome. John Mark is mentioned eight times in the New Testament though never in the Gospels. He is first mentioned in Acts when his mother opened their home in Jerusalem as the meeting place for the early church (Acts 12:12-17). It must have been a large home to accommodate the gathering of believers and employ servants. Peter may have led him to faith in Christ since Peter later called Mark his "son" (1 Peter 5:13). He probably believed in Christ at an early age and may have known Christ personally. Mark's report of the young man who fled naked at Jesus' arrest in Gethsemane has the marks of an autobiographical note (Mark 14:51-52).

The church fathers always associated Mark with Peter. However, Mark also had a significant ministry connection with his cousin, Barnabas, and with Paul. He accompanied them when they returned to Antioch from their ministry in Jerusalem (Acts 12:25) and traveled with them on their first missionary journey. For some unrecorded reason Mark deserted the church-planting team of Paul and Barnabas and returned to Jerusalem (Acts 13:13). Mark's desertion was a deep disappointment to Paul and resulted in the breakup of the effective ministry team (Acts 15:36-40). The estrangement between Paul and Mark was only temporary as Mark was with Paul during Paul's imprisonment in Rome (Colossians 4:10). His true character and value in ministry are evident when Paul faces martyrdom in a prison in Rome and requests Mark's presence. *Pick up Mark and bring him with you, for he is useful to me for service* (2 Timothy 4:11).

Audience
The Gospel of Mark was probably written in Rome and for a Roman audience. Mark ministered in Rome with Paul (Colossians 4: 10) and with Peter (1 Peter 5:13). Papias associated Mark with Peter in Peter's final days there and early church fathers echoed that understanding. Added support comes from (1) the probability that Peter was martyred in Rome, (2) the use of Latin loan words rather than Greek terms (7:4; 12:14; 15:16), (3) the explanation of Jewish customs indicates a Gentile audience unfamiliar with Jewish religious practices (7:3-4; 12:41-42; 14:12; 15:42), and (4) the specific mention of Rufus (15:21) who is apparently a member of the church at Rome (Romans 16:13).

Date
Determining the date for the writing of the Gospel of Mark is difficult. The synoptic problem is one major factor but so also is the relationship of Mark to Peter's martyrdom. Eusebius indicated that Peter was still living and active when Mark wrote this Gospel. "When Peter had preached the word publicly in Rome and announced the gospel by the Spirit, those present, of whom there were many, besought Mark, since for a long time

he had followed him and remembered what had been said, to record his words. Mark did this, and communicated the gospel to those who made a request of him. When Peter knew of it, he neither actively prevented nor encouraged the undertaking" (Eusebius, *Ecclesiastical History* 6.14.6-7). However, Irenaeus wrote that Mark's Gospel was transmitted after the "exodus" of Peter and Paul in Rome. That is understood to be a reference to their martyrdom. The question then is, did Mark write his Gospel before or after the death of Peter? Irenaeus refers to the "transmission" of the Gospel and that may indicate its distribution not its composition. The range of dates is minor either way.

Roman history and Christian tradition indicate a date of AD 64 for Peter's martyrdom and AD 67 for Paul's martyrdom under the persecution of Christians instigated by Nero. A terminal date of AD 70 is likely since Mark makes no mention of the destruction of Jerusalem that occurred in that year. After an extensive review of the evidence, Edwards concludes, "In summary, although none of the foregoing arguments and evidence is conclusive in itself, a combination of external and internal data appears to point to a composition of the Gospel of Mark in Rome between the great fire in 64 and the siege and destruction of Jerusalem by Titus in 70, that is, about the year 65" (*The Gospel According to Mark*, 9). This date does enter into the synoptic debate. Scholars arguing for Markan priority sometimes propose an earlier date for the writing of Mark or place the writing of Matthew and Luke after the destruction of Jerusalem in AD 70.

Purpose

Mark's purpose was primarily evangelistic but with a pastoral emphasis. His topic sentence emphasizes the good news concerning Jesus Christ, *The beginning of the gospel of Jesus Christ, the Son of God* (Mark 1:1). The first half of Mark's Gospel is devoted to proving the identity of Jesus Christ as the Son of God in the face of intense opposition. He achieves that through a series of confessions, twice by the Father Himself (1:11; 9:7), frequently by evil spirits (1:24; 3:11; 5:7), by Peter (8:29), and finally, by the Roman centurion (15:39). The emphasis on Jesus as the Son of God coincides with Mark's emphasis in the second half on Jesus' suffering as the fulfillment of God's redemptive plan. There are seven passion predictions and all occur in the last half of Mark (8:30-33; 9:30-32; 10:32-34, 45; 12:1-12; 14:3-9, 22-31). "The key to the understanding of Mark's portrayal is his deliberate contrast between the personal dignity of Jesus as the Son of God and the stark experiences of suffering and rejection which He voluntarily accepted. The portrait contains a remarkable blend of matchless strength and amazing submission, of the achievement of glorious victory through apparent defeat" (Hiebert, *The Gospel of Mark*, 11).

Writing for a Roman audience Mark presents Jesus as the Son of God who has come as the Suffering Servant to be a ransom for sinners just as promised in the Old Testament prophets. *For even the Son of Man did not come to be served, but to serve, and to give His life a ransom for many* (Mark 10:45). He is also writing to encourage Roman Christians suffering under the brutal persecution of Nero. Christians became the scapegoat for a disastrous fire in AD 64 that devastated Rome. Roman historian Tacitus wrote, "But neither human help, nor imperial munificence, nor all the modes of placating Heaven, could stifle the scandal or dispel the belief that the fire had taken place by order. Therefore, to scotch the rumour, Nero substituted as culprits, and punished with the utmost refinements of cruelty, a class of men, loathed for their vices, whom the crowd styled Christians. Christus, the founder of the name, had undergone the death penalty in the reign of Tiberius, by sentence of the procurator Pontius Pilatus, and the pernicious superstition was checked for a moment, only to break out once more, not merely in Judaea, the home of the disease, but in the capitol itself, where all things horrible or shameful in the world collect and find a vogue" (Tacitus, *Annals* 15.44).

Peter and Paul were not the only casualties of Nero's violence. The catacombs beneath Rome bear eloquent testimony to the suffering of Christians in Rome. Mark points these believers to the example of Jesus Christ, the Son of God, who suffered at the hands of unbelieving men, secured salvation and forgiveness for sinners through the cross, and triumphed over death. Those who would follow Christ are entering the "way of the cross" (8:34-38). It is also the way of triumph and eternal life. Mark stresses the theme of discipleship and another purpose for his Gospel is to provide believers a pattern for following Jesus. He is candid in reporting the shortcomings of the disciples (4:11-13; 6:52; 8:14-21) as well as the cost of following Christ (8:34-38; 10:17-31). Mark is the only Gospel writer to mention that the disciples didn't have time even to eat (3:20; 6:31). Following Jesus is not for the fainthearted!

Distinctive Features
Action orientation. Mark's Gospel has a kind of breathless quality. The writer seems to be in a hurry and yet the narrative is deliberate. Mark uses the word *euthus* ("immediately") more often (forty-two times) than the other three Gospel writers combined. Jesus seems always on the move and

always surrounded by crowds. He had to apply special effort to find time alone (1:35). Jesus' works appear more prominent than His words. Mark refers often to Jesus' teachings but he seldom records what Jesus taught. Mark records only two extended discourses by Jesus, His parables (4:1-34), and His end-times teaching on the Mount of Olives (13:1-37). Miracles are prominent. Mark is much shorter than the other Gospels but contains the same number of miracles as Matthew and Luke.

> "The gospel of Mark is a succinct, vivid, and action-packed account of the ministry, suffering, death, and resurrection of Jesus Christ. Jesus appears suddenly on the scene as the mighty and authoritative Messiah and Son of God, teaching with great authority, driving out demons, healing the sick, and even raising the dead. He calms the sea with a word and feeds the multitudes with a few loaves and fish. This person is truly God's Messiah, the promised Savior! ... Mark presents the narrative in an appealing way; he tells the good news about Jesus Christ so simply that a child can understand it" Walter W. Wessel, "Mark," in *The Expositor's Bible Commentary*, 673).

Gospel emphasis. Mark's Gospel opens with *euangelion*, the gospel or "good news" of Jesus Christ. What follows is the good news about or concerning Jesus Christ. This word occurs seven times in Mark (eight counting the disputed ending) compared to just four times in Matthew and never in Luke and John. Jesus is the subject of the gospel but He is also the One proclaiming the gospel (1:14, 15).

Messianic secrecy. For a Gospel aimed at evangelism it is striking to read the many exhortations by Jesus that others not spread the news (1:43-45; 5:43; 7:36; 8:26). The appeal to secrecy is more prominent in Mark than in any other Gospel. Peter's confession is the pivotal event in Mark and yet the disciples are instructed not to broadcast it. *He warned them to tell no one about Him* (8:30). It is not difficult to understand why evil spirits were forbidden to speak (1:25, 34; 3:12), but why muzzle the disciples? The likely answer to the element of secrecy is that miraculous healings drew crowds that hindered His ministry (1:45) and led to false messianic expectations. "Jesus doubtlessly used the command to silence to protect himself from false messianic expectations. ... he eschewed militaristic methods of effecting his kingdom. Not the warrior's sword but the servant's towel, as foretold by the prophet Isaiah, was the model he embraced" (Edwards, *The Gospel According to Mark,* 19).

Abrupt, disputed ending. Scholars have long puzzled over the ending of the Gospel. The earliest manuscripts do not contain Mark 16:9-20 though the verses appear in most later manuscripts. According to John Grassmick, "The last 12 verses of Mark (16:9-20) known as "the longer ending of Mark" constitute one of the most difficult and most disputed textual problems in the New Testament" ("Mark," 193). The two major Uncials, the Vaticanus and the Sinaiticus end at Mark 16:8. *They went out and fled from the tomb, for trembling and astonishment had gripped them; and they said nothing to anyone, for they were afraid* (16:8). Guthrie observes, "It must be admitted that it is strange to find a gospel, a book of good news, ending with a note of fear" (*New Testament Introduction*, 91). Irenaeus attests to 16:9-16 being part of the Gospel, and he notes that without these verses Mark appears to be unfinished. The promised immunity of believers to snake bites and poison have led to extreme behavior among some Christians. It must be asked if these promises are intended only for the disciples in the apostolic period or are permanent and universal promises for all believers.

There are several lines of evidence supporting the inclusion of Mark 16:9-20. (1) Mark began with "the good news of Jesus Christ the Son of God" and it is strange that he would end his Gospel with women fleeing from the tomb and saying nothing to anyone because they were afraid. (2) The longer ending (16:9-20) appears in the majority of later manuscripts and also in early versions (translations) of Mark. (3) It was quoted or included by some church fathers in the second century indicating an early existence. (4) Verse 8 ends with the Greek preposition *gar*, "for," an odd and grammatically unusual way to end the Gospel. (5) Mark has repeatedly reported Jesus' passion predictions and taken care to show their fulfillment. Jesus promised that after His resurrection He would meet the disciples in Galilee (14:28) and the messenger at the tomb repeated that promise (16:7). It would be strange for the author to omit proof of what he has stated clearly and recently.

Arguments against the inclusion of Mark 16:9-20 are substantial. (1) There is an abrupt change of subject from the women in verse 8 to Jesus in verse 9. (2) These verses are missing in the two earliest and best manuscripts. (3) More than one-third of the words in the longer ending are considered "non-Markan," that is, they do not appear elsewhere in Mark or are used with a different meaning. (4) The signs promised to believers seem out of character with the rest of Mark and with the other Gospels. The role of the disciples in casting out demons and healing the sick is mentioned briefly (3: 15; 6:13), but there is no precedent for surviving poisonous snakebites and drinking deadly poison (16:18). (5) The literary style of these verses differs from the remainder of the Gospel suggesting a different author. According to Walter W. Wessel and Mark L. Strauss "there is overwhelming evidence—both internal and external—that vv. 9-20 were not composed by Mark" ("Mark," 984).

If the longer ending was not part of original manuscript we are left to ponder whether Mark intended to end his Gospel as abruptly as he did in verse 8 or whether a portion of his original manuscript was lost. Scholars are divided on that issue but have put forth a number of proposals as demonstrated in *Perspectives on the Ending of Mark: 4 Views*, edited by David Alan Black. Darrell L. Bock offers this summary. "Whatever view one has on this issue, there is no central teaching of the Christian faith at stake in which view is chosen. Obviously, if the Long Ending is taken as original, then everything presented there is taught. ... As instructive and interesting as this problem is, we should not make more out of the debate than what it deserves. The long and the short of it is this: whatever choice we make, it should not significantly alter our faith" (*Perspectives on the Ending of Mark: 4 Views*, 141).

Confessions. Mark declares in his opening statement that Jesus is the Son of God, and he validates this point with a series of confessions throughout the book. (1) At Jesus' baptism the Father declares, *You are My beloved Son, in You I am well pleased* (1: 11). (2) Evil spirits confess that Jesus is God but are ordered to remain silent (1:24-25; 3:11-12; 5:7-8). (3) Peter's confession that Jesus is the Christ marks the turning point in the narrative (8:29). (4) At the transfiguration the Father again declares, *This is My beloved Son, listen to Him!* (9:7). (5) The final confession is by a Roman centurion at the crucifixion (15:39).

Conflict. Mark is writing about the gospel, the good news that Jesus, the Son of God, has provided salvation through His death as a ransom for sin (1:1; 10:45). How did the Son of God end up dying on a cross? Mark records a series of confrontations between Jesus and the religious leaders of Israel that result in His trial and crucifixion. Conflict abounds throughout the book. The theme of rejection is sounded even before Jesus begins His ministry when His forerunner, John the Baptist, is imprisoned (1:14). This is followed by thirteen separate incidents where Jesus clashes with the Jewish establishment, particularly the religious authorities. The intensity of the opposition grows as the cross looms nearer.

1. Jesus' authority to forgive sin is challenged by Scribes	2:1-12
2. His association with sinners is challenged by Pharisees	2:13-17
3. Jesus' disciples' neglect of fasting is challenged	2:18-22
4. Jesus' disciples' Sabbath actions are challenged	2:23-28
5. Jesus' healing a man on the Sabbath is challenged	3:1-6
6. Jesus' critics make a blasphemous accusation	3:20-34
7. Jesus' own hometown people take offense at Him	6:1-6
8. His observance of Jewish traditions is challenged	7:1-23
9. His feeding of 4,000 is ignored and a sign is requested	8:1-10
10. Jesus' teaching on marriage and divorce is challenged	10:1-12
11. His right/authority to cleanse the temple is challenged	11:15-19
12. His teaching silences critics who then plan His death	12:1-12
13. Jesus' critics unite in their effort to destroy Him	12:13-27

Passion predictions. As Jesus journeys to Jerusalem and His attention focuses on preparing the disciples for the cross, Mark records at least seven references Jesus makes to His rejection, death, and resurrection (8:30-33; 9:30-32; 10:32-34, 45; 12:1-12; 14:3-9, 27-28). Most of these passion predictions are very direct. For example, *He began to teach them that the Son of Man must suffer many things and be rejected by the elders and the chief priests and the scribes, and be killed, and after three days rise again. And He was stating the matter plainly* (8:31-32). Other predictions are evident but are contained in a parable (12:1-12), in His symbolic anointing (14:3-9), and in His Passover teaching (14:22-28). All these passion predictions are found in the second half of the Gospel of Mark.

Jesus' Predictions of His Death and Resurrection	
1st prediction: Religious authorities will kill Him	8:30-33
2nd prediction: He will rise again after three days	9:30-32
3rd prediction: He will be handed over to the Gentiles	10:32-34
4th prediction: His death will be a ransom for many	10:45
5th prediction: Parable reveals His death as prophesied	12:1-12
6th prediction: Anointing anticipated His death	14:3-9
7th prediction: Shepherd will be stricken, sheep scattered	14:20-28

Structure

The structural markers evident in Matthew are less noticeable in Mark. But that does not mean there is no structure. The Gospel of Mark is logically divided into two major sections by the confession of Peter that Jesus is the Christ (8:29). The first half of Mark focuses on the person of Jesus as the Son of God, and the second half focuses on the passion of Jesus as the Suffering Servant of Isaiah 53. The eight predictions of Jesus' passion all occur after Peter's confession. A logical connection can be seen between the beginning of Jesus' ministry (1:14) and the beginning of Jesus' teaching regarding the cross. *And He began to teach them that the Son of Man must suffer many things and be rejected by the elders and the chief priests and the scribes, and be killed, and after three days rise again* (8:31).

Geographical markers. There are several geographical markers and a pronounced geographical progression in the Gospel. The focus is on Galilee in the first half of Mark and on Jerusalem in the second half. Within the first half (1:14-8:29) the report of John the Baptist's imprisonment by Herod marks the beginning of Jesus' ministry inside Galilee. *Now after John had been taken into custody, Jesus came into Galilee, preaching the gospel of God* (1:14). Mark returns to that theme with the extended report of John's martyrdom by Herod (6:14-29) and follows it with Jesus' ministry outside Galilee (6:30-9:32). Peter's confession follows immediately after the geographical shift to Caesarea Philippi (8:27-30). After a brief return to Galilee (9:33-50) Jesus begins His journey to Jerusalem and the cross (10:1-16:8).

Key Verse

For even the Son of Man did not come to be served, but to serve, and to give His life a ransom for many (Mark 10:45).

Message of Mark
Presentation of the Son of God as the Suffering Servant (1:1-13). *The beginning of the gospel of Jesus Christ, the Son of God* (1:1). The brevity and simplicity of Mark's introduction belies its profound truth and rich connection with the Old Testament. The term "gospel" is the "good news" to be announced by a prophetic messenger as promised in Isaiah (40:1-9). Mark will draw deeply and often from the promises contained in Isaiah. The good news he announces is the arrival of the Suffering Servant of Isaiah 52:7-53:12. With these few words Mark has declared the uniqueness of Jesus' person as the Son of God and His redemptive work as the Suffering Servant. Jesus is introduced as "the Christ," that is, the Anointed One, the Messiah promised in the Old Testament (Psalm 2:1-2). He is the Son of God, a bold claim for one who is also man; that too is drawn from Psalm 2:7. The identification of Jesus as the Son of God appears like bookends (1:1 with 15:39). Mark is writing to and for Christians in Rome and appropriately climaxes his Gospel record with the

declaration of a Roman centurion at the crucifixion of Jesus. *"Truly this man was the Son of God!"* (15:39).

A servant needs no genealogy and Mark gives none. He launches immediately into the ministry of John the Baptist as the promised messenger and Jesus, the Christ, as the good news promised in Isaiah. John preaches in the wilderness as Isaiah prophesied (Isaiah 40:3) and calls people to repentance for the forgiveness of sins (Mark 1:4-8). The Spirit descends on Jesus when He is baptized (1:9-10) affirming that He is the Messiah, the Suffering Servant, as Isaiah had predicted. *Behold, My Servant, whom I uphold; My chosen one in whom My soul delights. I have put My Spirit upon Him; He will bring forth justice to the nations* (Isaiah 42:1). The Father declares, *"You are My beloved Son, in You I am well-pleased"* (1:11). Jesus is "immediately" (Mark's favorite word) driven into the wilderness by the Spirit and emerges triumphant from His conflict with Satan at the temptation (1:12-13). That introduces the recurring theme of conflict in Mark's Gospel but also signals the ultimate triumph of the Son of God. Following this brief but powerful introduction, Mark notes the arrest of John the Baptist and proceeds abruptly to the public ministry of Jesus. Mark will maintain this breathtaking pace throughout the Gospel.

Person and Work of the Son as the Suffering Servant (1:14-8:26).

Initiation of the Servant's ministry (1:14-45). John is arrested, foreshadowing the opposition to Jesus that leads to the cross. Isaiah's prophecies are reflected in Jesus' call for the people of Israel to repent and believe (Isaiah 59:20) and in the Galilean location of His ministry (Isaiah 9:1-7). Jesus' authority is evident in His enlistment of disciples (Mark 1:16-20), in His teaching (1:21-22), in His power over unclean spirits (1:23-28), and in the healing of the deformed and diseased (1:29-45).

The Servant's ministry stirs controversy (2:1-3:12). Mark records a series of five controversies between Jesus and the religious authorities. They challenge (1) His right to forgive sin (2:1-12), (2) His association with sinners (2:13-17), (3) His disciple's neglect of religious tradition (2:18-22) and (4) Sabbath rituals (2:23-28), and (5) His own claim to be "Lord of the Sabbath" (2:28-3:6). Many are healed and Mark's "summary" account (3:1-12) authenticates Jesus in His person and work as the Son of God who has come to be the Suffering Servant. Demons are commanded to be silent regarding Jesus' identity and mission but not so the disciples (3:13-19).

The Baptism and Temptation of Jesus

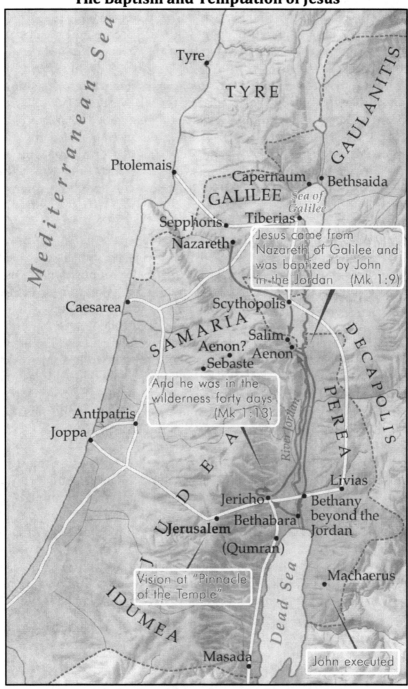

Copyright by Carta Jerusalem, Used by permission

The Servant's ministry in light of His rejection (3:13-8:26). Matthew does not arrive at the religious authorities' blasphemous accusation against Jesus until his twelfth chapter. Mark arrives there already in chapter 3! The blasphemous accusation of the Scribes (3:20-30) and the rejection of Jesus by "His own" (3:31-35) is a pivotal event in Mark. Jesus begins to publicly teach the crowds using parables while instructing the disciples privately (4:1-34). Jesus further reveals His identity by calming a storm on the sea (4:35-41) and delivering a demonized man from chains (5:1-20). The disciples ask, *"Who then is this, that even the wind and the sea obey Him?"* They needed only to refer to Psalm 107 for the answer. Jesus' deity is demonstrated in these events. It is the Lord God who releases captives from chains (Psalm 107:10-16) and who calms the raging sea (Psalm 107:23-32).

Jesus' miracles in Galilee authenticate His identity as the Son of God and His redemptive mission (5:21-43) but He is rejected by His own people and in His own hometown of Nazareth (6:1-6). The opposition intensifies as the forerunner of the Messiah, John the Baptist, is martyred (6:14-32). Feeding 5,000 men (6:33-44), walking on a stormy sea (6:45-52), and healing all manner of diseases is met with faith in the Gentile territory of Galilee (6:53-56) but not in Jerusalem. Mark's record of Jesus' ministry has focused on Galilee but his attention is about to shift to Jerusalem where the cross awaits Jesus (7:1-23). Mark frequently quotes the Old Testament in the remaining chapters in order to demonstrate that the cross is part of God's redemptive plan and not a mark of defeat. The Servant must suffer death on the cross in order to provide salvation (Isaiah 53).

Rejection by Israel's leaders from Jerusalem leads to Jesus' ministry in Gentile territory (7:24-37) where He feeds 4,000 men (8:1-10). Jesus heals a blind man living in the midst of a nation that remains blind and in darkness (8:11-26). Mark introduced his first major division on Jesus' person and work (1:14-8:26) with a geographical marker. *Now after John had been taken into custody, Jesus came into Galilee, preaching the gospel of God* (Mark 1:14). Another geographical marker introduces his second major division (8:27-15:20). *Jesus went out, along with His disciples, to the villages of Caesarea Philippi* (8:27). Jesus' ministry changes with the change in location.

Jesus' Ministry in Gentile Territory

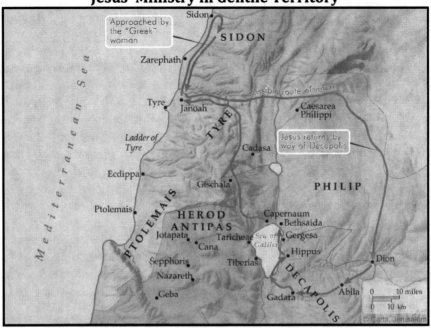

Copyright by Carta Jerusalem, Used by permission

The Passion of the Son of God, the Suffering Servant (8:27-16:20)
Teaching the disciples in anticipation of His suffering (8:27-9:50).
Peter's confession, *You are the Christ* (8:29) is the pivotal point in Mark's narrative. It is followed immediately by the first of at least seven passion predictions given by Christ to prepare the disciples for His crucifixion. *He began to teach them that the Son of Man must suffer many things and be rejected by the elders and the chief priests and the scribes, and be killed, and after three days rise again* (8:31). The disciples are called to follow Him on the "way of the cross," *whoever wishes to save his life will lose it, but whoever loses his life for My sake and the gospel's will save it* (8:34-38). The next event is the transfiguration (9:1-13). The timing is strategic. The cross looms on the horizon but the transfiguration gives the disciples a glimpse of Jesus' inherent glory when He returns in triumph as the King. In the meantime the disciples must learn the importance of prayer and dependence on Him for the ministry of the gospel (9:14-29). The cross is not the end. Jesus' next passion prediction focuses on His resurrection. *The Son of Man is to be delivered into the hands of men, and they will kill Him; and when He has been killed, He will rise three days later* (9:31). The disciples are taught that greatness is measured by servanthood, sin is serious, and judgment is real (9:33-50).

Teaching amidst controversy on His journey to Jerusalem (10:1-52). Conflict has never been far away but now it takes center stage in Mark's narrative. Hostile Pharisees raise the issue of divorce under Mosaic Law (10:1-12). The hypocrisy of the Pharisees is in sharp contrast to the faith of children who are welcomed by Jesus (10:13-16). A self-righteous young man balks at the "cost" of following Christ (10:17-27) providing a teachable moment for the disciples. They will receive far more than they leave behind to follow Christ (10:28-31). Another passion prediction reveals the role of the chief priests and scribes. *Behold, we are going up to Jerusalem, and the Son of Man will be delivered to the chief priests and scribes; and they will condemn Him to death and will hand Him over to the Gentiles. They will mock Him and spit on Him, and scourge Him and kill Him, and three days later He will rise again* (10:34). The disciples profess to be able to follow Him all the way to the cross but are still debating among themselves which of them is the greatest (10:35-44). Jesus uses this teaching moment to explain to the disciples the reason He, the Son of God, has become the Suffering Servant. It is the central thesis of Mark's Gospel. *For even the Son of Man did not come to be served, but to serve, and to give His life a ransom for many* (10:45).

Jesus' journey to Jerusalem takes Him through Jericho where Bartimaeus, a blind man, cries out for help (10:46-52). Bartimaeus is physically blind but not spiritually. He addresses Jesus as "Son of David," a messianic title (Isaiah 9:6-7; Mark 12:35-37). Matthew, Mark, and Luke all record this miracle and the use of this messianic title. It is a strategic event in the life of Christ as He heals a man who is physically blind while He is rejected by a nation that is spiritually blind.

Official presentation and rejection of the Son in Jerusalem (11:1-13:37). Jesus enters Jerusalem riding on a colt in the same way David had presented his son, Solomon, as Israel's king (1 Kings 1:33) and as Zechariah foretold the Messiah's arrival. *Rejoice greatly, O daughter of Zion! Shout in triumph, O daughter of Jerusalem! Behold, your king is coming to you; He is just and endowed with salvation, humble, and mounted on a donkey, even on a colt, the foal of a donkey* (Zechariah 9:9). Messianic acclaim greeted Jesus as He entered Jerusalem (11:1-11). Israel is portrayed as a fig tree (Isaiah 28:4; Amos 8:1-2; Luke 13:1-9) and the judgment of the barren fig tree by Jesus is symbolic of Israel's failure to provide the necessary fruit of repentance (11:12-14).

52

Jesus' Journey to Jerusalem

Tyre

Caesarea Philippi

TYRE

GAULANITIS

Mediterranean Sea

Ptolemais

Capernaum

Gennesaret

GALILEE

Sea of Galilee

Tiberias

Sepphoris

Hippus

Nazareth

Mt. Tabor

Gadara

Dor

Samaritans refuse to receive Jesus; some healed

Jesus passes between Samaria and Galilee

DECAPOLIS

Caesarea

Scythopolis

Ginae

SAMARIA

Samaria-Sebaste

River Jordan

PEREA

Apollonia

Jesus heals blind Bartameus, and leads Zacchaeus the tax collector to repentance

Antipatris

Gadora

Joppa

Jesus stays with Martha and Mary

Lydda

JUDEA

Abila

Jericho

Bethphage

Jerusalem

Bethany

Copyright by Carta Jerusalem, Used by permission

The chief priests take exception to Jesus' cleansing of the temple and seek to destroy Him (11:15-26). They recognize themselves as the offenders in Jesus' parable of the vineyard (12:1-12). The chief priests are not friends with the Pharisees, Herodians, and Sadducees but they join forces in their determined effort to have Jesus killed (12:13-44). Their repeated attempts to entrap Jesus fail but their determination grows. Mark is showing how Jesus' prediction of His death (10:34) is being fulfilled. The rejection of Jesus as the Messiah, the rightful Davidic King, is official. Jesus declares that the temple will soon be destroyed (13:1-2). Sitting on the Mount of Olives, Jesus explains privately to the disciples the course of events that will follow His death (13:3-13) and will precede His return (13:14-37).

The sacrificial suffering of the Son (14:1-15:47). The Passover is at hand and Mark records two contrasting but connected events. The chief priests seek to seize Jesus by stealth and kill Him (14:1-2). Meanwhile, in a home in Bethany, a woman pours a very costly perfume on Jesus' head (14:3-9). The disciples call it a "waste," but Jesus says it is in preparation for His death. The two incidents are linked by the decision of Judas Iscariot to go to the chief priests to betray Jesus and thus precipitate His death (14:10-11). During the Passover celebration (Mark 14:12-31) Jesus explains that His blood will initiate the New Covenant. That covenant was promised to the nation Israel and will yet be fulfilled when Israel repents (Isaiah 42:6; 49:8; Jeremiah 31:31-34; Ezekiel 16:60-63; 37:24-28). Until that time, all who believe in Jesus receive the blessings and benefits of that New Covenant (Hebrews 7:22; 8:6; 9:15, 23-28). Jesus also reveals that one of the disciples now seated with Him will betray Him and that the others will abandon Him.

The scene shifts briefly to the Mount of Olives where Jesus prayerfully submits to His heavenly Father and to the suffering of the cross (Mark 14:32-42). The disciples sleep while Jesus agonizes over His impending death on behalf of sinners. The Mount of Olives was well known to Judas as it had provided a place of rest for Jesus and His disciples on other occasions. The place of prayer and renewal becomes a place of betrayal. The chief priests wanted to arrest Jesus "with stealth" and acted under the cloak of darkness (14:43-52). Jesus' disciples *all left Him and fled* as He had predicted. Mark notes that *a young man was following Him, wearing nothing but a linen sheet over his naked body; and they seized him. But he pulled free of the linen sheet and escaped naked* (14:51-52). We are left with the intriguing possibility that the young man was the author, John Mark himself.

The trial of Jesus before the Council of priests was in violation of the very Law they claimed they were protecting, it was held at night and relied on false testimony (14:53-60). The contrived evidence proved insufficient and the high priest asked Jesus directly *"Are You the Christ, the Son of the Blessed One?"* (14:61). Jesus answers in the affirmative. *And Jesus said, "I am; and you shall see the Son of Man sitting at the right hand of Power, and coming with the clouds of heaven"* (14:62). He is the Messiah promised in the enthronement Psalm 110 who will return in power to bring judgment (Daniel 7:13). Evidence presented in Mark's Gospel fully substantiates Jesus' claim but is ignored and the religious leaders beat and abuse Jesus (14:63-65). Mark, associate of the apostle Peter, does not shy away from recording Peter's threefold denial of Jesus (14:66-72). Peter's denial fulfills Jesus' earlier prediction (14:29-31).

Jesus has given many predictions regarding His crucifixion and they now find fulfillment. The Council turns Jesus over to Pilate, the Roman official who has authority to impose the death sentence they seek (15:1). Mark only briefly records the trial before Pilate (15:2-5). Pilate asks *"Are You the King of the Jews?"* and Jesus answers, *"It is as you say."* Pilate accepts that "confession," but in an attempt to avoid full responsibility he allows the crowd to decide who is crucified, Jesus or Barabbas, a convicted murderer. Pilate knows that the chief priests have handed Jesus over to him out of envy yet he allows them to stir up the crowd to insist on the crucifixion of Jesus' and the release of Barabbas (15:6-15). The entire cohort of Roman soldiers joins in mocking Jesus, acclaiming, *"Hail, King of the Jews!"* The mockery involved striping Him naked, clothing Him with an imitation "royal" robe, placing a "crown" of thorns on His head, savagely beating His head, and spitting on Him. The beating was so brutal that Jesus was too weak to carry His own cross, as was the Roman custom (15:16-21).

The crucifixion occurred at a place called Golgotha because it resembled a skull. Mark's description of the crucifixion is graphic but brief (15:22-41). Soldiers gamble over His clothing, the chief priests taunt *He saved others; He cannot save Himself.* The horror of the cross is evident when darkness descends over the scene and Jesus cries out *My God, My God, why have You forsaken Me?* The true meaning of Jesus' death is indicated when the veil of the temple that separated man from God is ripped in two from top to bottom, signifying that the way of access was now open to God. The confession of the Roman centurion confirms Mark's central theme. *Truly this man was the Son of God!* Jesus is hurriedly buried in a borrowed tomb but that is not the end (15:42-47). The promised resurrection awaits!

Proof of Jesus' person and gospel by His resurrection (16:1-20). The burial of Jesus was hurried prohibiting the usual burial procedures. The eagerness of Jesus' friends is evident as the three women arrive at the tomb very early on Sunday, the first day of the Jewish week. They come prepared to anoint Jesus body with spices and find that the heavy stone used to seal the tomb has been rolled away. On entering the tomb the women are amazed to see a young man, whose white robe suggests a heavenly origin. He has startling news. *Do not be amazed; you are looking for Jesus the Nazarene, who has been crucified. He has risen; He is not here; behold, here is the place where they laid Him* (16:6). The women are instructed to announce Jesus' resurrection to the disciples and especially to Peter. Instead *they went out and fled from the tomb, for trembling and astonishment had gripped them; and they said nothing to anyone, for they were afraid* (16:8). The two best and earliest manuscripts of the Gospel of Mark end at this point. However, the longer ending (16:9-20) appears in most later manuscripts and translations of Mark. Mark's proof of Jesus' resurrection is the effect His appearance has on the skeptical disciples (16:8-14). The post-resurrection appearances of Jesus are sufficient to prove that Jesus is alive just as He promised. The disciples and Peter are assured that Jesus has not abandoned them though they had abandoned Him at His arrest and trial. On the contrary, Jesus renews their commission to continue His gospel ministry. *Go into all the world and preach the gospel to all creation* (16:15).

Outline

I. Presentation of the Son of God as the Suffering Servant   1:1-13
   A. Thematic title: the Gospel of the Son of God   1:1
   B. Prophetic introduction of the Son   1:2-8
   C. The Father's authentication of the Son   1:9-11
   D. Validation of the Son in His victory over Satan   1:12-13

II. Person and Work of the Son as the Suffering Servant   1:14-8:26
   A. Initiation of the Servant's gospel ministry   1:14-45
      1. Arrest of John signals opposition to His gospel   1:14a
      2. His call to repentance and faith in the gospel   1:14b-15
      2. His call to men to share the work of the gospel   1:16-20
      3. His authoritative teaching, power over demons   1:21-28
      2. His power to heal all kinds of diseases   1:29-34
      3. His gospel proclamation permeates Galilee   1:35-39
      4. His gospel demonstrated by cleansing a leper   1:40-45

B. The Servant's ministry stirs controversy 2:1-3:12
   1. Healing a paralytic and forgiving sin 2:1-12
   2. Calling Levi, a tax collector to follow Him 2:13-17
   3. Explaining His disciples' neglect of fasting 2:18-22
   4. Declaring His authority over the Sabbath 2:23-28
   5. Demonstrating His authority over the Sabbath 3:1-6
   6. Summary of His ministry in light of opposition 3:7-12
C. The Servant's ministry in light of His rejection 3:13-8:26
   1. Apostles are appointed as opposition grows 3:13-19
   2. Opponents make a blasphemous accusation 3:20-34
   3. Servant's parables in light of His rejection 4:1-34
   4. His person and power revealed in a storm 4:35-41
   5. His power revealed over Satan's kingdom 5:1-20
   6. His power displayed over death and disease 5:21-43
   7. His person questioned and rejected by His own 6:1-6
   8. His gospel ministry carried on by His apostles 6:7-13
   9. Opposition leads to murder of His forerunner 6:14-29
   10. His compassion in feeding 5,000 men 6:30-43
   11. His person and power demonstrated in a storm 6:44-52
   12. Summary of His ministry in light of rejection 6:53-56
   13. His rejection exposed, confirmed prophetically 7:1-23
   14. His gospel confirmed by the faith of Gentiles 7:24-37
   15. His gospel extended to all by feeding Gentiles 8:1-10
   16. The warning in light of the nation's rejection 8:11-21
   17. Healing one blind man living in a blind nation 8:22-26

III. The Passion of the Son of God as the Suffering Servant 8:27-16:20
   Peter's confession: Turning point of the narrative 8:27-30
A. Teaching disciples in anticipation of His suffering 8:30-9:50
   1. The call to follow Him in the "way of the cross" 8:34-38
   2. His future glory displayed in the transfiguration 9:1-13
   3. Disciples must depend on Him in ministry 9:14-29
   4. Disciples taught that greatness is servanthood 9:33-37
   5. Disciples taught seriousness of sin, judgment 9:38-50
B. Teaching and conflict on His journey to Jerusalem 10:1-52
   1. Teaching Pharisees on marriage and divorce 10:1-12
   2. Teaching disciples on the value childlike faith 10:13-16
   3. Teaching seekers on the cost of following Him 10:17-27
   4. Teaching disciples on the cost of following Him 10:28-31
   5. Teaching disciples that service is greatness 10:35-44
   6. Healing a blind man in a nation of blind men 10:46-52

C. Formal presentation and rejection in Jerusalem 11:1-13:37
   1. His entry is met with messianic acclaim 11:1-10
   2. His judgment of the barren fig tree (Israel) 11:12-14
   3. His claim of ownership by cleansing the temple 11:15-19
   4. His lesson for disciples on faith and forgiveness 11:20-26
   5. His right to cleanse the temple is challenged 11:27-33
   6. His parable of judgment after rejection by Israel 12:1-12
   7. His critics unite in an effort to destroy Him 12:13-27
   8. His critics silenced by His use of Scripture 12:28-34
   9. His condemnation of hypocrisy of the leaders 12:35-40
   10. His commendation of faith/giving by a widow 12:41-44
   11. His revelation of end-time events at His return 13:1-37
D. Sacrificial suffering of the Son fulfills prophecy 14:1-15:47
   1. His enemies secretly plan His death 14:1-2
   2. His death memorialized by His anointing 14:3-9
   3. His betrayal by Judas to Israel's leaders 14:10-11
   4. His betrayal and abandonment is announced 14:12-31
   5. His submission to the Father in the garden 14:32-42
   6. His betrayal by Judas and His armed arrest 14:43-52
   7. His mock trial before religious authorities 14:53-65
   8. Peter's threefold denial as He predicted 14:66-72
   9. His crucifixion decided in a trial before Pilate 15:1-15
   10. His humiliation and abuse by Roman soldiers 15:16-21
   11. His agonizing death on the cross 15:22-41
   12. His burial in a borrowed tomb 15:42-47
E. Proof of His person and gospel by His resurrection 16:1-20
   1. Evidence of the open and empty tomb 16:1-5
   2. Validation by the angelic announcement 16:6-8
   3. Validated by post-resurrection appearances 16:9-13
   4. Disciples commissioned to continue His work 16:14-18
   5. Ascension/enthronement of the triumphant Son 16:19
   6. Gospel ministry continues through the disciples 16:20

Bibliography

Barbieri, Louis. *Mark.* Moody Gospel Commentary. Chicago: Moody Press, 1995.

Black, David Alan, ed. *Perspectives on the Ending of Mark: 4 Views.* Nashville: B & H Academic, 2008.

Bock, Darrell L. *The Gospel of Mark*. Cornerstone Biblical Commentary. Carol Stream, IL: Tyndale House Publishers, 2005.

Carson, D. A., Douglas J. Moo, and Leon Morris. *An Introduction to the New Testament*. Grand Rapids: Zondervan Publishing House, 1991.

Edersheim, Alfred. *The Life and Times of Jesus the Messiah*. 2 vols. Grand Rapids: Wm. B. Eerdmans Publishing Co., 1959.

Edwards, James R. *The Gospel According to Mark*. Pillar New Testament Commentary. Grand Rapids: Wm. B. Eerdmans Publishing Co., 2002.

France, R. T. *The Gospel of Mark*. New International Greek Testament Commentary. Grand Rapids: Wm. B. Eerdmans Publishing Co., 2002.

Grassmick, John D. "Mark." In *The Bible Knowledge Commentary: New Testament*. Edited by John F. Walvoord and Roy B. Zuck. Wheaton, IL: Victor books, 1983; reprint, Colorado Springs, CO: Cook, 1996.

Guthrie, Donald. *New Testament Introduction*. Downers Grove, IL: InterVarsity Press, 1990.

Hiebert, D. Edmond. An *Introduction to the New Testament*. Vol. 1. Chicago: Moody Press, 1975.

_____. *The Gospel of Mark: An Expositional Commentary*. Greenville, NC: Bob Jones University Press, 1994.

Scroggie, W. Graham. *A Guide to the Gospels*. London: Pickering & Inglis, 1962.

Swete, Henry Barclay. *The Gospel According to Mark*. Reprint. Grand Rapids: Wm. B. Eerdmans Publishing Co., 1978.

Wenham, David, and Steve Walton. *Exploring the New Testament: A Guide to the Gospels and Acts*. Downers Grove, IL: InterVarsity Press, 2001.

Wessel, Walter W., and Mark L. Strauss. "Mark," in *The Expositor's Bible Commentary*. Rev. ed. Vol. 9. Grand Rapids: Wm. B. Eerdmans Publishing Co., 2010.

60

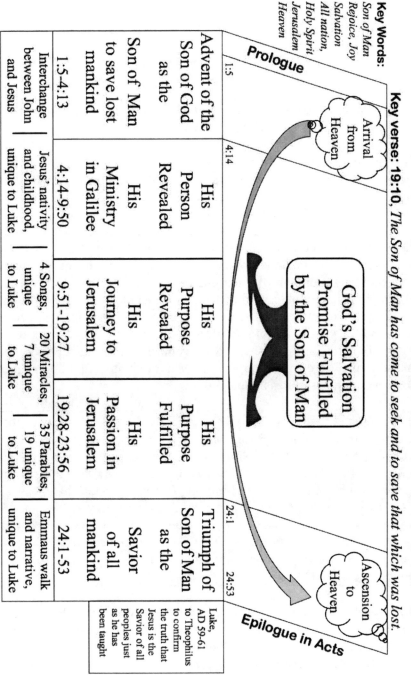

LUKE

The Son of Man has come to seek and to save that which was lost
(Luke 19:10).

Luke is everyman's Gospel, the good news of salvation for all humanity regardless of gender, social status, ethnicity, or position. Heaven reverberates with rejoicing as the lost come to Jesus. Luke presents Jesus as the perfect man, the last Adam through whom God will provide salvation. Though descended from David and destined to sit on the throne of David, Jesus is descended from Adam and able to reverse sin's curse that came through Adam. Salvation is the primary theme of the Gospel of Luke, and that salvation is for all nations beginning with Israel. As Luke's presentation of Jesus unfolds, people from all walks of life are drawn to the Savior and they are never disappointed. Together with the sequel in Acts, Luke records God's provision of salvation, His plan for that salvation to be declared to all people and nations, and the remarkable spread of that good news in the face of determined opposition. What begins in Bethlehem goes global on earth and resonates in heaven.

"Luke is the Gospel that reveals the heart and mind of Jesus. It is here that we see how God cares for the sinner, the poor and the despised, the ones the text calls 'tax collectors and sinners.' Luke reveals how God cares for people who normally despise one another. Here Luke sets the table for the message of reconciliation and the possibility of healthy relationships, even across ethnic lines that should be the result of a response to the gospel. Here we see Jesus relating in a healthy way with those of different gender, valuing their contribution to the work of God. If believers wish to know what God would have us do in forming relationships and values, Luke is a beautiful port for reflective pause" (Darrell L. Bock, *Luke*, 24).

God's love for lost humanity permeates the Gospel of Luke. A chorus of angels burst into song at the happy announcement that God's One and Only Son, Jesus, has been born in Bethlehem. *I bring you good news of great joy which will be for all the people; for today in the city of David there has been born for you a Savior, who is Christ the Lord* (2:10-11). That is joyous good news for all people, as heaven declares (1) the perfect humanity of

Jesus (He has been born on earth), (2) His divine nature as *Lord* (Yahweh of the Old Testament), (3) His office as the *Christ*, the Anointed One promised for centuries by God's prophets, and (4) His mission, to be the *Savior* of all humanity. Zechariah sings a song of praise in recognition of God's redemptive plan (1:67-79), the aged Simeon praises God for His salvation and declares that it is for all people (2:29-32), the prophetess, Anna, proclaims salvation to all who will listen (2:38), and all heaven rejoices when even one sinner repents (15:7, 10).

Author

External evidence. This Gospel, like all the others, is anonymous. However, the earliest copies of the Gospel contain the heading, *euangelion kata Lukan* ("according to Luke") and no doubt was voiced in the early church regarding the identity of the author. The authenticity of the Gospel of Luke and its authorship by the man whom Paul called "the beloved physician" were endorsed by the major church fathers. The Anti-Marcionite Prologue to the Gospel, the Muratorian Canon (AD 160-200), Irenaeus (AD 185), Tertullian, Clement of Alexandria, and Origen all identified Luke as the author of the Gospel. "The testimony of all the early witnesses not only named Luke as the author of the third gospel but also asserted that he wrote Acts. This testimony of the Lucan authorship of the third gospel comes from all parts of the Christian world. The author is uniformly identified as a physician and companion of Paul" (Hiebert, *An Introduction to the New Testament*, I:117). According to Guthrie, "at no time were any doubts raised regarding this attribution to Luke, and certainly no alternatives were mooted. The tradition could hardly be stronger, but some scholars attach little importance to it" (*Introduction to the New Testament*, 114).

Internal evidence. Luke and Acts evidence a common authorship. (1) They begin with the same prologue. (2) They are dedicated to the same individual, Theophilus. (3) They are similar in language and style. (4) They have a common theme (the plan of God for the salvation of humanity, both Jew and Gentile). (5) They employ a common geographical progression (beginning with a Roman context in Luke, progressing to the cross and resurrection in Jerusalem and radiating out again to the final chapter of Acts in Rome). (6) They show the same attention to historical data. (7) They exhibit the same qualities of universalism with strong concern for individuals (women, rich and poor, Samaritans, Roman officials, Gentiles, etc.). "It may safely be concluded that the evidence is very strong linking the two books as the work of one man, a conclusion which few modern scholars would dispute" (Guthrie, *Introduction to the New Testament*, 116).

The man Luke. Readers of the New Testament are familiar with Luke but surprised to discover that He is named only three times in the New Testament (Colossians 4:14; Philemon 24; 2 Timothy 4:11). Luke is well known because of his association with the apostle Paul and his authorship of the Gospel and Acts, but one can only speculate on the details of his background and conversion. The reliability of the biographical sketch contained in the *Anti-Marcionite Prologue* (AD 160-80) to the Gospel of Luke has been debated but it represents the traditional understanding of Luke's identity. "Luke is a man from Antioch, Syria, a physician by profession. He was a disciple of the apostles, and later accompanied Paul until his martyrdom. Having neither wife nor child, he served the Lord without distraction. He fell asleep in Boeotia at the age of eighty four, full of the Holy Spirit. Moved by the Holy Spirit, Luke composed all of this Gospel in the districts around Achaia although there were already Gospels in existence—one according to Matthew written in Judea and one according to Mark written in Italy" (quoted in Hiebert, *An Introduction to the New Testament*, I:117-18).

Paul calls Luke "the beloved physician" and there is no reason to doubt Luke's medical profession or his devotion to the apostle. Luke was evidently a Gentile. In Colossians Paul differentiates between fellow workers who are *from the circumcision* and others who are not (4:10-11). Luke is listed among the later along with Epaphras and Demas (4:12-14). From the "we sections" of Acts (16:10-17; 20:5-21:18; 27:1-28:16) we are able to reconstruct some of Luke's travels with Paul. Second Timothy 4:11 and Philemon 24 indicate that Luke was with Paul during his first Roman imprisonment. When and where Luke was converted is unknown. Judging from his prologue to Luke and Acts Luke was a second-generation believer and depended on sources for his information regarding the life and work of Jesus. His commitment to careful research, the abundance of written accounts, and the availability of eyewitnesses gave Luke ample information that could be checked for reliability. The language of Luke and Acts indicates that Luke was well educated and wrote with consummate skill.

Luke: Biography, History, or Theology?

"Luke-Acts has been labeled the storm center of modern New Testament study, not least because of the questions raised about the historical reliability of its author" (Pate, *Luke*, 23). In the preface to his Gospel Luke explains that his writing is based on thorough research of reliable existing documents and interviews with eyewitnesses. He claims historical validity for his Gospel and also later for the second volume, the book of Acts. In his exegesis of Luke's preface Marshall states, "Luke's purpose was to give an historical account which would form the basis for a sound Christian faith on the part of those who had already been instructed, perhaps imperfectly and incompletely, in the story of Jesus. Throughout the preface there is a stress on the historical accuracy of the material presented" (*The Gospel of Luke*, 40). (For a thorough discussion of Luke as historian and theologian see J. Howard Marshall, *Luke: Historian and Theologian*).

Luke was a careful researcher with an eye to detail and a commitment to accuracy as evidenced by his historical documentation. *In the fifteenth year of the reign of Tiberius Caesar, when Pontius Pilate was governor of Judea, and Herod was tetrarch of Galilee, and his brother Philip was tetrarch of the region of Ituraea and Trachonitis, and Lysanias was tetrarch of Abilene, in the high priesthood of Annas and Caiaphas, the word of God came to John, the son of Zacharias, in the wilderness* (Luke 3:1-2). Scholars have recently debated whether Luke was an avid theologian who accommodated history to suit his purpose or was primarily a historian with a theological interest. The fairest assessment is that Luke was both a reliable historian and a diligent theologian. "Luke's historical perspective is not subordinate to his theological concerns. Rather, the two go hand in hand. Luke is both historian and theologian, and in that order. This means that Luke is fully trustworthy as a historian of the life of Christ. Therefore, to read the third gospel is to encounter the authentic, historical Jesus" (Pate, *Luke*, 27).

Luke's integrity has been amply demonstrated by archaeological evidence. Sir William Ramsey, a skeptic trained in the Tubingen School of criticism, set out to disprove the historical accuracy of Luke's Gospel and ended up being one of its most ardent defenders. After comparing Luke with Roman historical data He concluded, "The present writer takes the view that Luke's history is unsurpassed in respect of its trustworthiness" (*The Bearing of Recent Discovery on the Trustworthiness of the New Testament*, 81). According to Morris, "His writings, and more particularly Acts, have been subjected to a very close scrutiny. They have been compared with those of other early writers and the results of archaeological research have been taken into account. While it would not be true to say that all the problems have been solved, there is widespread recognition that Luke is a reliable historian. His theological purpose is real. We should not miss it. But his theology does not run away with his history" (*Luke*, 36).

Date

If Luke composed the book of Acts while he was with Paul in Rome (AD 61-63), then he probably wrote his Gospel during the preceding two years that Paul was imprisoned at Caesarea (AD 59-61). However, the Markan priority view seems to require a later date. If Luke utilized the Gospel of Mark as one of his primary sources, a date after AD 70 is often suggested since a date for the composition of Mark before AD 60 is difficult to support (Pate, *Luke*, 20-21). This late date raises questions regarding Luke's reference to Jesus' prediction of Jerusalem's fall and also the close of Acts. As Jesus entered Jerusalem He announced, *the days will come upon you when your enemies will throw up a barricade against you, and surround you and hem you in on every side, and they will level you to the ground and your children within you, and they will not leave in you one stone upon another, because you did not recognize the time of your visitation* (Luke 19:43-44). Some scholars see that as so literal and detailed when compared with Mark's record that Luke must have written it after the destruction of Jerusalem in AD 70. In that case it is only disguised as a prophecy and Luke's credibility as an accurate historian is cast in doubt. But it is prophetic and a date before AD 70 for the writing of Luke is preferable. Likewise, if Luke wrote Acts after Paul's martyrdom (AD 67) we must explain why he chose not to mention the persecution under Nero (AD 64-68) or Paul's final years of ministry and his death. One proposal is that Luke wrote his Gospel almost simultaneously with that of Mark. Even if one holds to the priority of Mark, a date in the early 60s for the writing of the Gospel of Luke is possible and is well supported by the evidence (Morris, *Luke*, 24-28).

Audience

The Gospel of Luke was written for the immediate benefit of an individual, Theophilus, but is intended for a wider audience. Theophilus means "friend of God" and was likely a certain individual not a generic title for Christians. Theophilus is called "most excellent" indicating that he was a person of high social standing. He may have been the benefactor who supported Luke as he traveled with Paul. The larger intended audience of Luke-Acts was evidently Gentile. (1) Luke uses Greek words in place of Aramaic ("teacher" replaces "rabbi"). (2) He explains Jewish customs and locations that would be unnecessary for a Jewish audience. (3) Luke does not stress the fulfillment of Old Testament prophecy, as does Matthew, and references to the Old Testament occur primarily in Jesus' discourses. (4) Coordination of events in the life of Christ with Roman history points to a Gentile audience for whom that would be meaningful validation. (5) Roman officials are presented in a fairly sympathetic light, suggesting a Gentile rather than a Jewish audience.

Purpose

The preface reveals both the purpose and the methodology of Luke's Gospel. *Inasmuch as many have undertaken to compile an account of the things accomplished among us, just as they were handed down to us by those who from the beginning were eyewitnesses and servants of the word, it seemed fitting for me as well, having investigated everything carefully from the beginning, to write it out for you in consecutive order, most excellent Theophilus; so that you may know the exact truth about the things you have been taught* (Luke 1:1-4). Luke's primary purpose was to assure Theophilus that the things he had been taught about Jesus Christ were true. The purpose for the Gospel should not be separated from the companion volume, the book of Acts. They are a set. Taken together Luke's purpose is to provide a reliable record of salvation history that begins with the birth of Jesus, climaxes in Jesus' crucifixion, resurrection, and ascension, and radiates out to the whole world through the witness of the apostles in the companion volume of Acts.

> "The great thought Luke is expressing is surely that God is working out his purpose. This purpose is seen clearly in the life and work of Jesus, but it did not finish with the earthly ministry of Jesus. It carried right on into the life and witness of the church" (Morris, *Luke*, 15).

The purpose of the Gospel alone is to document the fulfillment of God's salvation plan for all humanity through Jesus Christ. Luke opens with the birth of Jesus as Savior, explains His mission to provide salvation through His death, burial, and resurrection, and ends with Jesus' declaration that God's salvation plan has been fulfilled. *"These are My words which I spoke to you while I was still with you, that all things which are written about Me in the Law of Moses and the Prophets and the Psalms must be fulfilled." Then He opened their minds to understand the Scriptures, and He said to them, "Thus it is written, that the Christ would suffer and rise again from the dead the third day"* (Luke 24:44-46). Luke then transitions to Acts with Jesus' mandate for the disciples, *that repentance for forgiveness of sins would be proclaimed in His name to all the nations, beginning from Jerusalem. You are witnesses of these things. And behold, I am sending forth the promise of My*

Father upon you; but you are to stay in the city until you are clothed with power from on high (24:47-49).

Distinctive Features

Universality of salvation. Salvation is the primary theme of the Gospel of Luke, and that salvation is for all people. This is evident from a word search of "salvation" and its companion terms in the New Testament. Luke is the only Synoptic Gospel writer to call Jesus, "Savior" *soter*, and he does so twice (1:47; 2:11) and twice also in Acts (5:31; 13:23). Salvation, *soteria* and *soterion* occur six times in Luke (1:69, 71, 77; 2:30; 3:6; 19:9), but never in Matthew or Mark, and only once in John (4:22). Save, *sozo* occurs more often in Luke than in any other Gospel. When combined with Acts it occurs 30 times. That reflects a Pauline influence as it appears 29 times in Paul's epistles and only 11 times in the other epistles and Revelation combined.

Salvation is the central theme of the Gospel and Luke 19:10 is the key verse. *The Son of Man has come to seek and to save that which was lost.* "God's love is for all people and his salvation reaches far and wide" (Morris, *Luke*, 38). Salvation comes first to Israel (1:69, 71, 77) but is for all people (2:29-32). The universality of that salvation is evident from the angel's announcement, *I bring you good news of great joy which will be for all the people; for today in the city of David there has been born for you a Savior, who is Christ the Lord* (2:10-11). The theme of universality is evident when the genealogy is traced all the way back to Adam (3:37). It is further demonstrated in the inclusiveness of those to whom the message of salvation is given: a Roman centurion (7:1-10), a widow (7:11-17), tax collectors (7:29), an immoral woman (7:36-50), Samaritan towns (9:51-54), a Samaritan leper (17:11-19), and a demonized Gentile (8:26-39). In response to the question, *Lord, are there just a few who are being saved?* Jesus revealed the universal impact of the gospel. *They will come from east and west and from north and south, and will recline at the table in the kingdom of* God (13:22-30). After His resurrection Jesus announced *that repentance for forgiveness of sins would be proclaimed in His name to all the nations, beginning from Jerusalem* (24:47).

Travel narrative. The Luke-Acts narrative follows a geographical progression centered in Jerusalem. Herod, a Roman representative, is the first person mentioned in Luke, and the setting is the temple in Jerusalem (1:5). From the context of Jerusalem in the Roman Empire (3:1) Luke's narrative advances geographically to Jesus' ministry in Galilee (3:2-9:50).

Peter's confession (9:20) marks a turning point as Jesus begins to reveal to the disciples that He will be rejected and killed in Jerusalem (9:22-50). *When the days were approaching for His ascension, He was determined to go to Jerusalem* (9:51). Luke's transitional statement looks beyond the crucifixion in Jerusalem to Jesus' ascension. The ascension of Jesus into heaven closes the Gospel (24:50-53) and opens the book of Acts (1:1-11). From that pre-announcement Luke traces Jesus' ministry on His journey to Jerusalem (9:51-19:27) and explains His arrest, crucifixion, and resurrection in Jerusalem (19:28-24:49).

Luke records Jesus' post-resurrection ministry in Jerusalem but does not report the Galilean appearances, as do Matthew and John. Readers are prepared for the second volume with Jesus' statement of His plan *that repentance for forgiveness of sins would be proclaimed in His name to all the nations, beginning from Jerusalem. You are witnesses of these things. And behold, I am sending forth the promise of My Father upon you; but you are to stay in the city until you are clothed with power from on high* (24:47-49). The opening of Acts (1:1-11) mirrors the close of Luke. The geographical narrative is then reversed as the narrative moves from Pentecost (1:12-2:47) and the spread of the gospel in Jerusalem (chaps. 3-7), back to Judea and Samaria (chaps. 8-12) and on to the city of Rome (chaps. 13-28). The ascension of Jesus from Jerusalem provides the axis on which the Luke-Acts geographical narrative turns. The narrative moves up to Jerusalem and then out from Jerusalem.

Prayer, praise, and rejoicing. The Gospel opens with an emphasis on prayer. Worshipers are praying while Zechariah burns incense in the temple (1:10). John's birth is an answer to Zechariah's prayer (1:13). The prophetess Anna is worshiping, fasting, and praying continuously in the temple (3:37). Luke records seven instances of Jesus praying that are not recorded in any other Gospel. They occur at strategic times. Luke alone records that Jesus spent the entire night in prayer before calling the disciples. *It was at this time that He went off to the mountain to pray, and He spent the whole night in prayer to God. And when day came, He called His disciples to Him and chose twelve of them, whom He also named as apostles* (6:12). Jesus taught the disciples about prayer both directly (11:1-4) and through parables (11:5-13; 18:1-14), and exhorted them to pray (22:40, 46). Jesus prayed for Peter (22:31) and for His enemies (23:34) (Morris, *Luke*, 50).

Songs of worship and praise permeate the Gospel. Luke alone records the four songs related to the nativity of Jesus: Mary's *Magnificat* (1:46-55), the *Benedictus* of Zechariah (1:68-79), the *Gloria in Excelsis* of the angels (2:14), and the *Nunc Dimittis* of Simeon (2:29-32). "Luke is the gospel of song and thanksgiving" (Hiebert, *An Introduction to the New* Testament, 3:141). "Praise" and "praising" appear eighteen times in Luke compared to five times in Matthew and only once in Mark. Joy and rejoicing resonate throughout Luke. "Joy," and "rejoice" occur twenty times in Luke compared to twelve times in Matthew and only three times in Mark. Rejoicing in heaven and on earth marks the parables of chapter 15. "This Gospel finishes, as it had begun, with rejoicing (24:52; *cf.* 1:14)" (Morris, *Luke*, 50).

Holy Spirit. Pentecost is not the beginning of Luke's emphasis on the Holy Spirit. Luke relates the activity of the Holy Spirit as frequently as Matthew and Mark combined. "Luke has more to say about the Spirit in his Gospel than does any of the other Evangelists. This forms a bond of continuity. Both in the ministry of Jesus and in the life of the early church the Spirit of God is at work" (Morris, *Luke*, 49-50). More important than the number of occurrences (seventeen) is the role the Spirit plays in the life of Jesus and His disciples. The virgin birth of Jesus is brought about by the Holy Spirit (1:35); Jesus is led by the Spirit (4:1); He is always "full of the Spirit" (4:1; 10:21); and His ministry is empowered by the Spirit (4:14, 18). John the Baptist, Elizabeth, Zechariah, and Simeon are filled with the Holy Spirit (1:15, 41, 67; 2:24-27). Blasphemy against the Holy Spirit will not be forgiven (12:10).

Literary features. The Gospel of Luke is the longest book of the New Testament. The Luke-Acts narrative comprises twenty-eight percent of the New Testament, making Luke its most prolific author. The prefaces to Luke and Acts indicate that he was a thorough researcher, well informed on both Roman history and Jewish customs, and committed to uncovering and recording only the truth. Luke was a well-educated man, thoroughly at home in the Greek language, and he possessed an unusually wide vocabulary. Approximately eight hundred words in the Luke-Acts narrative appear nowhere else in the entire New Testament (Hiebert, *An Introduction to the New Testament*, 146).

Theme and Structure

Luke's thesis is that Jesus Christ, the Son of Man, is the Savior of all men. Luke declared his purpose for writing the Gospel in his preface. He set out

70

to give Theophilus a carefully documented account of the life of Jesus Christ so that he would know with certainty the things he had been taught concerning Jesus Christ. His evidence is presented logically throughout the Gospel and the resulting impact is continued in the second volume, the book of Acts. Luke is a difficult Gospel to outline but salvation history is the central theme. Geographical progression is significant in Luke and is used as a means of advancing his argument. Luke focuses on Jerusalem in both the Gospel and the book of Acts. In the Gospel the action leads up to and reaches a climax in Jerusalem. In Acts the action begins in Jerusalem and proceeds out to the ends of the earth. Rome serves as bookends for both Luke and Acts.

Key Verse
The Son of Man has come to seek and to save that which was lost
(Luke 19:10).

Message of Luke

Prologue (1:1-4). Luke approaches his Gospel with the precision of a surgeon, the concern of a theologian, and the inquisitiveness of a historian. He has *investigated everything carefully* and is writing *an orderly account.* His sources are *eyewitnesses* and include both written accounts and personal interviews. Luke's purpose is to provide Theophilus with the kind of verifiable information that will enable him to *know the exact truth about the things you have been taught.*

Advent of the Son of God as Son of Man (1:5-4:13). Luke's birth and childhood narratives are unique among the four Gospels. He interchanges between John the Baptist and Jesus giving details that show the heavenly origin of Jesus yet focus on His humanity. The angel, Gabriel, announces two births, both of which fulfill Old Testament prophecies. The birth of John the Baptist (1:5-25) fulfills Malachi's prophecy that "Elijah" would come to prepare the way for the advent of the Messiah (Malachi 4:5). Jesus is the Messiah and His birth (Luke 1:26-38) fulfills Isaiah's prophecy. *Therefore the Lord Himself will give you a sign: Behold, a virgin will be with child and bear a son, and she will call His name Immanuel* (Isaiah 7:14). Luke connects the two births by recording the visit of Mary to Elizabeth (Luke 1:39-45). Mary's song of exaltation, the Magnificat (1:46-56) is the first of four nativity songs that are unique to Luke. Luke records the two births in considerable detail. John's birth (1:57-66) is accentuated by a second hymn of praise. Zechariah's *Benedictus* (1:67-80) declares that John will be *the prophet of the Most High, the Sunrise,* (the Messiah).

71

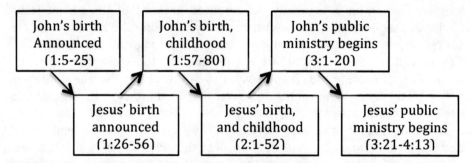

John will go *before the* L*ORD to prepare His ways; to give to His people the knowledge of salvation by the forgiveness of their sins* (1:76-77). Luke is thus introducing His theme of salvation through Jesus. The birth of John is relatively private but not the birth of Jesus (2:1-20). His birth in Bethlehem is accompanied by a spectacular display in the heavens, announced to shepherds by an angel, and heralded by a massive choir of angels singing the *Gloria in Excelsis* (2:13-14). The sheep being guarded by the shepherds are likely destined for sacrifice in Jerusalem and Luke's theme of salvation is amplified by the angel's announcement. *Do not be afraid; for behold, I bring you good news of great joy which will be for all the people; for today in the city of David there has been born for you a Savior, who is Christ the Lord* (2:10-11).

The universality of God's salvation plan is evident when Jesus is presented in the temple at Jerusalem (2:21-38). Two witnesses, Simeon and Anna, highlight the theme of salvation. Simeon's eulogy, *Nunc Dimittis* (now dismiss), emphasizes the universal nature of the salvation to come through Jesus. *For my eyes have seen Your salvation, which You have prepared in the presence of all peoples, a Light of revelation to the Gentiles, and the glory of Your people Israel* (2:30-32). Simeon also declares that violent conflict awaits the Savior, particularly within Israel (2:34-35). Anna broadcasts hope to all *who were looking for the redemption of Jerusalem* (2:38). Jesus' appearance in the temple In Jerusalem at the age of twelve (2:39-52) is unique to Luke. Jesus claims that God is His Father, demonstrating His self-awareness as God (2:49), and at the same time His humanity as He *continued in subjection* to His earthly parents (2:51). Luke's Gospel begins and ends in Jerusalem but his record of Jesus' ministry focuses on Galilee (4:14-9:50) and later on Perea and Samaria (9:51-19:27) as Jesus makes His way to Jerusalem and the cross (19:28-23:56).

The third narrative link between John and Jesus is in the initiation of their public ministries. After thirty years of "silence" *the word of God came to John, the son of Zacharias, in the wilderness* (3:2). Luke establishes the chronology by identifying seven Roman officials and Jewish religious leaders in power at that time (3:1-3). John's ministry is tied to Isaiah's promise of salvation through the Messiah (Isaiah 40:3-5) and is located in the wilderness along the Jordan River not in Jerusalem. It attracts crowds but also opposition. John exposes the hypocrisy of Israel and calls the nation to repent in anticipation of the arrival of Jesus, the Messiah (Luke 3:4-18). His denunciation of evil arouses the ire of Herod and results in John's arrest (3:19-20). Luke's narrative now shifts from the prophetic forerunner to the Messiah, from John the Baptist to Jesus at Jesus' baptism (3:21-22).

Jesus begins His ministry at *about thirty years of age* (3:23). Luke has already established the deity of Jesus as the *Son of the Most High God* (1:32-35) and as *Christ the LORD* (2:11), now he establishes the genuine humanity of Jesus as Savior by tracing His genealogy back to Adam (3:23-38). To be the Savior of lost humanity Jesus must be both God and man. Through His virgin birth Jesus, the Son of God, has become the perfect man (1:31-35). The deity and humanity of Jesus are united in the Messianic title "Son of Man" (Daniel 7:13). Jesus refers to Himself as "the Son of Man" twenty-six times in Luke. "Son of Man" unites Jesus' mission as Savior at His first advent (Luke 9:22; 18:31-33; 19:10) with His return as Sovereign to judge (Psalm 110:1; Luke 21:27; 22:27; Revelation 1:7).

To fulfill His mission as Savior of fallen humanity Jesus must defeat Satan, the author of sin in humanity (Genesis 3). The Holy Spirit leads Jesus into the wilderness where He triumphs over the threefold temptation of Satan (4:1-13). *When the devil had finished every temptation, he left Him until an opportune time* (4:13). Jesus' ultimate triumph over Satan will come at the cross but is evident throughout Luke as He drives out demons (11:14-26).

The Baptism and Temptation of Jesus

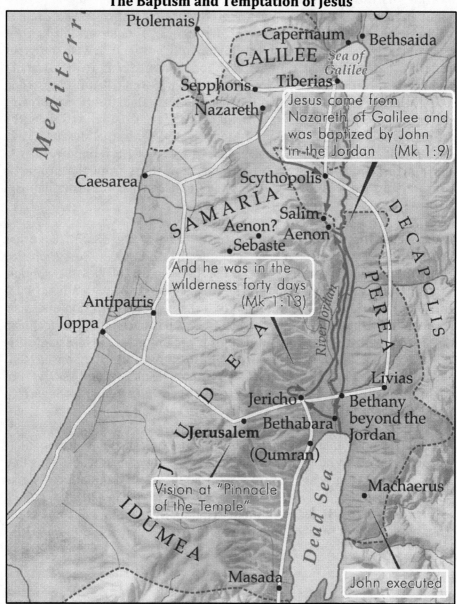

Copyright by Carta Jerusalem, Used by permission

The Ministry of the Son of Man to Men (4:14-19:27)

How does the Son of God become the Savior of lost humanity? How does the King destined to wear David's crown end up on a cross in David's city, Jerusalem? How does the joyful worship that greeted Jesus at His birth turn into the hate filled taunting of the cross? Luke will trace that process through Jesus' public ministry.

Ministry in Galilee: Jesus reveals His person (4:14-9:50). Luke refers very briefly to Jesus' early ministry in Galilee noting that He is *praised by all* (14:14-15), but chooses to "fast forward" to Jesus' ministry in the synagogue at Nazareth where He meets with violent opposition (4:16-30). Jesus is no stranger to the synagogue there and is given the scroll of Isaiah to read and make comments. His choice of passages is strategic. Isaiah 61:1-2 describes the work of the Messiah and Jesus boldly claims, *today this Scripture has been fulfilled in your hearing* (Luke 4:21). The people of Nazareth approve His speech but want to see miracles like those He performed in Capernaum. Acclaim turns to rage when Jesus reminds them of Israel's past unbelief and says salvation is for Gentiles not just for Israel (4:24-27). Their attempt to kill Him fails but the theme of rejection and death has been introduced. Luke alternates between Jesus' ministry to men that involved miracles and His calling and equipping of the disciples.

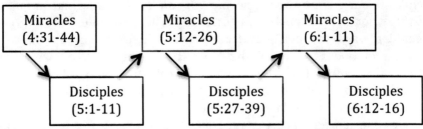

Miracles validate Jesus' claim to be the fulfillment of Isaiah 61 (Luke 4:18-19). His identity as the man from Nazareth, the Holy One of God, and the Christ is confessed by demons (Luke 4:31-44). The miraculous catch of fish elicits Simon's personal confession and results in Simon, James, and John being commissioned as "fishers of men" (5:1-11). The healing of a leper (5:12-15) draws multitudes to Jesus and necessitates His withdrawal to the wilderness to find opportunity to pray (5:16). Another crowd assembles, but this time it is a crowd of critics. Pharisees and scribes *come from every village of Galilee and Judea and from Jerusalem* and the stage is set for confrontation (5:17). Jesus heals a paralytic as proof that He has authority to forgive sin (5:18-26). *But, so that you may know that the Son of*

Man has authority on earth to forgive sins—He said to the paralytic—"I say to you, get up, and pick up your stretcher and go home" (5:24).

The Pharisees continue their opposition when Jesus calls Levi (Matthew) to join the disciples and accepts Levi's invitation to a "big reception" in his home (5:27-29). They take exception to Jesus eating with "sinners" and allowing His disciples to enjoy the reception rather than engage in fasting like the Pharisees (5:30). Luke's theme of salvation is evident when Jesus replies *I have not come to call the righteous but sinners to repentance* (5:32) and announces the new order, *new wine must be put into fresh wineskins* (5:33-39). Evidence of the new order follows when Jesus' disciples pluck grain and eat it on the Sabbath (6:1-4). Jesus reveals His identity by claiming *the Son of Man is Lord of the Sabbath* and provides proof of the new order by healing a man with a withered hand on the Sabbath (6:1-11). The Pharisees respond with rage and the threat of death just as the synagogue crowd did in Nazareth (4:28-29). The growing threat against Jesus provides the background for Jesus' intense time of prayer leading to the appointment of the twelve disciples to become His apostles (6:12-16).

Jesus' "Sermon on the Plain" (6:20-49) is delivered to *a large crowd of His disciples, and a great throng of people from all Judea and Jerusalem and the coastal region of Tyre and Sidon* (6:17-19). The beatitudes (6:20-38) are directed toward the disciples (6:20) and call for them to reflect the character of God as "sons of the Most High." The parable that follows includes the crowd of seekers as well and calls for genuine heart change (6:39-45). Jesus' extended discourse climaxes with His call for the hearers to make a commitment. Many in the crowd were calling Him "Lord" but had not experienced a heart change. Those that hear Jesus' words but do not act on them (do not believe) are like the man who built his home without a foundation and faced ruin when the flood (judgment) brought destruction (6:46-49).

Two miracles illustrate the importance and power of "hearing Jesus' words." The Jewish elders praise the Roman centurion for his **works** on behalf of Israel but Jesus commends him for his **faith**. *I say to you, not even in Israel have I found such great faith* (7:9). The centurion believes in the person of Jesus and in the power of Jesus' words. *Just say the word, and my servant will be healed* (7:7). The centurion sought Jesus and his faith was rewarded (7:1-10). In the second miracle it is Jesus doing the seeking. He travels twenty miles to Nain where a widow grieves the loss of her only son (7:11-17). At Jesus **word** her dead son is restored to life.

Luke draws this section to a close with an inclusion, that is, repetition of a common feature at each end of a narrative. The arrest of John the Baptist (3:20) signaled the beginning of Jesus' public ministry and Luke turns his attention once again to John as he concludes the report of Jesus' ministry in Galilee (7:18-35). John has been languishing in prison. He has heard second hand reports of Jesus' ministry and sends his disciples to ask Jesus a crucial question, *Are You the Expected One, or do we look for someone else?* (7:20). Jesus began His ministry in the synagogue at Nazareth by claiming that He was fulfilling Isaiah's prophecy of the Messiah (Luke 4:18-21 with Isaiah 61:1-2). Jesus once again quotes Isaiah and assures John that Isaiah's prophecy has been fulfilled. John's disciples arrive providentially with their question at the same time Jesus is performing the miracles promised by Isaiah (Isaiah 35:5; 61:1-2 with Luke 7:21-22).

Jesus' commendation of John unites the two men in their ministry and in their rejection by Israel's religious leaders (Luke 7:24-28). The lines are sharply drawn. *When all the people and the tax collectors heard this, they acknowledged God's justice, having been baptized with the baptism of John. But the Pharisees and the lawyers rejected God's purpose for themselves, not having been baptized by John* (7:29-30). John and Jesus have been rejected by that generation (7:31-35) and the stage is set for both John and Jesus to be killed. Herod will behead John (9:7-9) and Jesus will begin His journey to Jerusalem and the cross (9:22, 44).

Simon the Pharisee and an "immoral" woman (7:36-39) illustrate the divided reaction to Jesus. Jesus' parable of the two debtors reveals the hostile heart of Simon who is not forgiven and the broken heart of the woman who hears Jesus say, *your sins have been forgiven. Your faith has saved you; go in peace* (7:40-50). One of the unique features of Luke's Gospel is his emphasis on women. Jesus healed many women and they in turn provided support for Him and His disciples in Ministry (8:1-3). Jesus' parables of the sower (8:4-15) and the lamp (8:16-18) are given in light of the divided response to His ministry. Even His own family fails to comprehend the import of His words and Jesus declares *My mother and My brothers are these who hear the word of God and do it* (8:19-21). The series of miracles that follows highlights the faith response of diverse individuals as Jesus prepares the disciples to continue His redemptive ministry (8:22-9:17).

The disciples have much to learn about the identity of Jesus. Jesus calms the storm on Galilee (8:22-25) prompting them to ask, *"Who then is this, that He commands even the winds and the water, and they obey Him?"* Their faith is still developing and this miracle equates Jesus directly with the work of the LORD in Psalm 107:23-32. The healing of the demonized man in the Roman territory of the Decapolis (ten cities) is a further demonstration that Jesus is one with the LORD of the Old Testament (8:26-39 with Psalm 107:10-22). The importance of faith is evident as the twelve-year old daughter of a synagogue official is restored to life and a woman is healed from a hemorrhage that had plagued her for twelve years (8:40-56). The twelve disciples have witnessed Jesus at work and are now given power and authority to go out on their own as Jesus' ambassadors (9:1-6). Jesus' final miracle in this section is the feeding of 5,000 men at Bethsaida and again He uses the occasion to train the disciples (9:10-17).

The martyrdom of John the Baptist by Herod sounds an ominous note (9:7-9) and prepares the reader for a major shift in Jesus' ministry. Jesus' ministry in Galilee has revealed His identity as the Son of Man and He elicits a report from the disciples. *"Who do the people say that I am?"* (9:18). The public perception falls short of Jesus' true identity, but Peter's confession is a fitting climax to Jesus' self revelation. Jesus is *the Christ of God* (9:20). Jesus has intimated that He will be put to death but now He declares it openly to the disciples. *The Son of Man must suffer many things and be rejected by the elders and chief priests and scribes, and be killed and be raised up on the third day* (9:22). He will one day return in glory but in the meantime those that follow Him must live in the shadow of the cross (9:23-27). Three disciples, Peter, James, and John are given a glimpse of Jesus' glory at the transfiguration (9:18-36). They prefer to bask in that glory with Jesus but are promptly thrust into the spiritual battle that is to mark their life after Jesus has returned to heaven (9:37-45). The contrast is striking. The cross is uppermost in Jesus' thinking but not in the minds of the disciples as they debate which of them is the greatest (9:44-50).

Journey to Jerusalem: Jesus reveals His purpose (9:51-19:27). Luke's narrative abruptly shifts from Jesus' ministry in Galilee (4:14-9:50) to His journey to Jerusalem (9:50-19:27). *When the days were approaching for His ascension, He was determined to go to Jerusalem* (9:51). Jesus has revealed His person, now He will reveal His purpose. A Samaritan village refuses to provide hospitality and Jesus uses the occasion to declare His mission. *The Son of Man did not come to destroy men's lives, but to save them* (9:52-56). Following Christ is not for the fainthearted and "wannabe" disciples turn away (9:57-62). However, a harvest awaits and seventy disciples are commissioned to go ahead of Jesus and announce the arrival of the kingdom of God in the person of Jesus, the Messiah (10:1-24). *All things have been handed over to Me by My Father, and no one knows who* *the Son is except the Father, and who the Father is except the Son, and anyone to whom the Son wills to reveal Him* (10:22). The teaching and testing continues when a lawyer puts Jesus to the test only to find himself put to the test and convicted by Jesus' parable of the Good Samaritan (10:25-37). Mary and Martha serve as a reminder that work does not take the place of worship in the life of a disciple (10:38-42). Prayer has been an integral part of Jesus' life and the disciples are taught how to pray (11:1-13).

Opposition against Jesus erupts when the authorities test Him, seeking yet another sign and making the blasphemous accusation that He is in league with Satan (11:14-17). Jesus effectively refutes their charge (11:18-28) and counters with His own charge against *this wicked generation.* Nineveh was spared when they repented and will stand to condemn this unrepentant generation. The only sign this wicked generation will receive is the sign of Jonah, referring to Jesus' resurrection (11:29-36). Jesus follows with a scathing denunciation of the Pharisees for their hypocrisy (11:37-44) and turns the tables on a religious lawyer who takes offense (11:45-52). The opposition intensifies as the Pharisees and scribes plot against Him (11:53-54).

Jesus' critics will end up killing Him and the disciples are warned to avoid the hypocrisy of the Pharisees and to remain faithful even in the face of death (12:1-12). God does not forget the tiny sparrow and will certainly not forget them. They are not to be preoccupied with wealth, or the lack of it, like the man in the crowd (12:13-34). *But seek His kingdom, and these things will be added to you. Do not be afraid, little flock, for your Father has chosen gladly to give you the kingdom. ... For where your treasure is, there your heart will be also* (12:31-34). A day of judgment awaits and the disciples are to be working, waiting, and watching in anticipation of Jesus' return (12:35-48). Jesus has come this time to bring life and peace but in that day He will come to bring division and judgment (12:49-59).

Jesus is *passing through from one city and village to another, teaching, and proceeding on His way to Jerusalem* (13:22) and much of His teaching is given in parables that expose the rejection of those in authority and invite others to believe (13:1-16:31). The parable of the fig tree (13:1-9) warns the nation of judgment, a warning unheeded by Jesus' opponents (13:10-17). The parables of the mustard seed and the leaven teach that the kingdom will grow in spite of Israel's rejection (13:18-21). Salvation is entered through the narrow door of faith but multitudes from every part of the globe will enter (13:22-30). The threat of Herod cannot deter Jesus from His journey to Jerusalem where He must die (13:31-35). The parables of guests at a dinner are delivered before Jesus' critics in a Pharisee's home (14:1-24). Those who would follow Christ must count the cost of discipleship (14:25-35). Jesus gives three parables, the lost sheep, the lost coin, and the lost son to explain to His critics why He eats with sinners (15:1-32). Heaven rejoices when a sinner repents even if the Pharisees and scribes do not! The Pharisees are *lovers of money* and their hypocrisy (16:14-18) is exposed in the parables of the unrighteous steward (16:1-17) and the rich man and the beggar named Lazarus (16:19-31).

Jesus' teaching demands a measure of faith and the disciples wisely request, *increase our faith!* (17:1-5). Faith has great power, but obedience is at the heart of their mission (17:6-10). The lessons of faith and obedience are illustrated when ten lepers are healed but only one returns to give thanks (17:11-21). In keeping with Luke's theme that salvation is for all, it is a Samaritan with saving faith. Jesus' discourse and parables on the return of the Son of Man (17:22-37) are in response to the inquiry of a Pharisee about the signs heralding the arrival of the kingdom of God (17:20). He warns that the Son of Man will come suddenly bringing judgment to those that are not prepared. The parable of the unrighteous judge (18:1-8) teaches the disciples to be patient and persistent in prayer. The parable of the tax collector and the Pharisee praying at the temple (18:9-14) is directed at the self-righteous and Jesus' reception of infants teaches that faith is the key to entering the kingdom (18:15-17). Riches keep a wealthy ruler from entering the kingdom (18:18-27) prompting Peter to think about the business he left behind (18:28-30). He is assured that he will receive far more than he has given up to follow Christ.

Jerusalem is on the horizon when Jesus gives the twelve disciples a graphic account of the suffering awaiting Him there. *Behold, we are going up to Jerusalem, and all things which are written through the prophets about the Son of Man will be accomplished. For He will be handed over to the Gentiles, and will be mocked and mistreated and spit upon, and after they have scourged Him, they will kill Him; and the third day He will rise again* (18:31-33). Unfortunately the disciples do not grasp the meaning of His prediction or of the Old Testament Scriptures that are to be fulfilled. They do believe but remain partially blind. The blind beggar at Jericho is contrasted with the partially blind disciples and the totally blind leaders of Israel (18:35-43). The beggar is physically blind but spiritually seeing as He shouts out, *Jesus, Son of David, have mercy on me!* He recognizes Jesus as the Messiah and his faith is rewarded. *Receive your sight; your faith has made you well.*

Jesus' Journey to Jerusalem

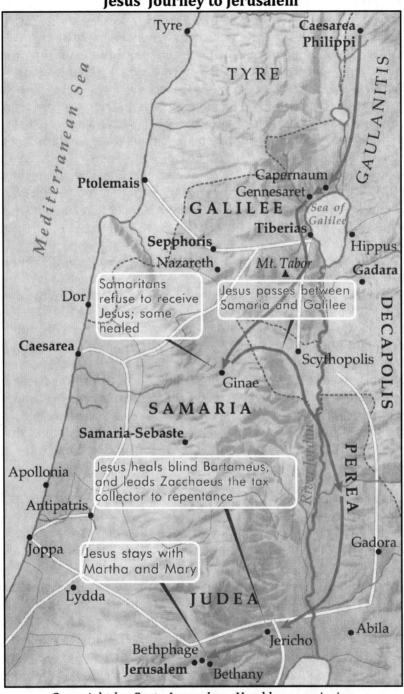

Copyright by Carta Jerusalem, Used by permission

Jesus accepted the hospitality of Levi, a tax collector, when He began His ministry in Galilee and He now requests the hospitality of Zacchaeus, another tax collector, and declares, *today salvation has come to this house.* (19:1-10). The theme Luke has been developing throughout the Gospel is embodied in Jesus' statement of His purpose for coming. *For the Son of Man has come to seek and to save that which was lost* (19:10). The crowd has rejected Jesus as the messianic king yet is looking for an immediate introduction of the kingdom of God (19:11). Jesus answers their false expectation with the parable of a nobleman who goes to a distant country to receive a kingdom (19:11-27). His citizens hate him and request that he not return but the nobleman does receive the kingdom and returns to judge his enemies and reward his loyal servants. Jesus is clearly that nobleman who is about to go away to receive a kingdom and who will one day return to judge the citizens that have rejected Him.

Sacrifice of the Son of Man on behalf of men (19:28-23:56.). Jesus' arrival in Jerusalem is bittersweet (19:28-44). It is called "the triumphal entry" but could just as well be called "the tearful entry." The shout of acclamation from the crowd contrasts with Jesus' tears as He weeps over Jerusalem. The disciples recognize that Jesus' entry on a colt fulfills the Messianic prophesy of Zechariah (Zechariah 9:9) and their shout heralds the arrival of Israel's King. *Blessed is the King who comes in the name of the LORD* comes from the enthronement Psalm (118:26) and the second part of their shout of acclamation has been heard before! *Peace in heaven and glory in the highest* was the anthem of the angels that announced Jesus' birth (Luke 2:14). Jesus weeps over Jerusalem because the city has rejected His invitation to repent (Psalm 118:22) and will be destroyed by the Roman army in AD 70.

It is **Monday** of the final week of Jesus' life on earth. The temple in Jerusalem has become a market place instead of a place of prayer (19:45-48) and Jesus asserts authority over the temple when He drives out the merchants. The chief priests and leaders of the nation challenge His authority but are silenced by their own guilt (20:1-8). Jesus' parable of the vineyard (20:9-18) echoes the sermon Jeremiah preached in Jerusalem six centuries earlier (Jeremiah (2:1-21). Like the tenants in the parable, Israel is going to kill the Son who has come to claim His inheritance. The crowd acclaimed Jesus as the Messiah of Psalm 118:26, but Jesus quotes the preceding verse indicating that His rejection comes before His enthronement as King. *The stone which the builders rejected has become the chief corner stone* (Psalm 118:22).

The religious authorities have already reached a verdict, Jesus must die, but they need an accusation that will satisfy the Roman rulers that control the death penalty (20:19-20). It is **Tuesday** and Jesus' teaching ministry centers in the temple. One after another authorities confront Jesus seeking a chargeable offence. The chief priests raise a sensitive issue about Jews paying taxes to Caesar but fail to entrap Him (20:21-26). The Sadducees pose a hypothetical question about the resurrection of the dead (which they deny) and are silenced by Jesus' use of the Scriptures (20:27-44). The scribes lack the courage to challenge Him further and Jesus seizes the opportunity to warn His disciples about their hypocrisy (20:45-47).

The temple is a showcase for the ostentatious giving of the rich but Jesus commends the sacrificial giving of a widow (21:1-4). Many admire the temple for its architectural beauty but Jesus warns that it will soon be destroyed (21:5-9). That prompts a question about end-time events that Jesus answers by drawing on the prophets of the Old Testament (Luke 21:10-24 with Isaiah 63:4, 18; Daniel 8:13, 19; 9:24-27). The Son of Man is going to be killed in Jerusalem but He will return in triumph (21:25-28). The parable of the fig tree is an appeal to be prepared and a warning that all will have to *stand before the Son of Man* (21:29-38). This discussion likely occurred on **Wednesday**.

The Passover is an annual event when the sacrificial lamb is slain. Jesus will be slain at the same hour on Friday but celebrates the Passover on **Thursday** evening with His disciples (22:1-13). The Passover looks back to Israel's redemption in the exodus but also looks forward to Jesus' return to establish His kingdom on earth (22:14-16). The unleavened bread and the cup are representative of His body that will be crucified for them and His blood that will be poured out on their behalf (22:17-20). The betrayer, Judas, is among them but not detected by the other disciples as they are arguing over which of them is greatest (22:21-24). The love and grace of Jesus is evident when He gently corrects them and then promises that their faith will not fail and that they will rule with Him in His kingdom (22:25-32). Simon Peter vows that he is prepared to die with Jesus and vehemently denies that he will deny Christ that same night (22:33-38). Little did he realize how wrong he was!

The Mount of Olives often provided a refuge for Jesus and the disciples but tonight it would be a place of agonizing prayer for Jesus (22:39-46) and of betrayal by Judas. The chief priests have paid Judas to betray Jesus and he does it under cover of darkness, with a traitorous kiss, and accompanied by a mob (22:47-53). The disciples are prepared to defend Jesus with a sword but Jesus puts a stop to it and even restores the severed ear of a servant to the high priest. Events move rapidly from the garden to the cross. The trials are a travesty of both Roman and Jewish justice. Peter denies being associated with Jesus three times and is brought to tears when Jesus looks directly into his eyes (22:54-62).

Jesus is beaten and mocked by the guards as they pass the night hours before the trial (22:63-65). Luke's account of the religious trial is brief. The Sanhedrin hastily gathers at dawn and insists that Jesus declare Himself as the Christ (22:66-67). Jesus is "convicted" on the basis of His own confession. *If I tell you, you will not believe; and if I ask a question, you will not answer. But from now on the Son of Man will be seated at the right hand of the power of God. And they all said, "Are You the Son of God, then?" And He said to them, "Yes, I am"* (22:67-70). The deceitfulness of the Sanhedrin is evident as they transfer Jesus to Pilate's jurisdiction. They are seeking the death penalty and Jesus' claim to be the Son of God is not punishable by death under Roman law so they distort the accusation to one of treason against Rome. *And they began to accuse Him, saying, "We found this man misleading our nation and forbidding to pay taxes to Caesar, and saying that He Himself is Christ, a King"* (23:2).

Pilate is weak and indecisive. He finds *no guilt* in Jesus but does find a way out of the dilemma by transferring Jesus to Herod who is in Jerusalem and has jurisdiction over Galilee (23:1-7). Herod had been hoping to meet Jesus and to see Him perform a miracle but he yields to the will of the chief priests. Jesus suffers further beating and humiliation before being returned to Pilate (23:8-12). Herod and Pilate are brought together and their mutual animosity ended at Jesus' expense! Pilate declares Jesus' innocence a second and a third time but yields to the demands of the chief priests, releases Barabbas, and condemns Jesus to death (23:13-23). The chief priests have demanded that Jesus be crucified and Pilate *delivered Jesus to their will* (23:24-25).

Jesus is going to the cross willingly (23:26-32). The charge over His cross reads, "This is the King of the Jews" yet Jesus thinks of others not of Himself. He knows the fate awaiting Jerusalem and urges the women lamenting His death to weep for themselves and for their children instead (Isaiah 2:19-20; Revelation 6:16). His first words from the cross are not for Himself but for those who are crucifying Him. *Father, forgive them; for they do not know what they are doing* (23:34). People gaped at Him, rulers sneered at Him, soldiers mocked Him, a criminal on another cross-hurled abuse at Him (23:33-39), yet Jesus had words of forgiveness and hope for the penitent thief on the third cross. *Truly I say to you, today you shall be with Me in Paradise* (23:40-43).

It was a dark hour for humanity; even the sun was obscured, but it was an hour of triumph in heaven. The temple veil that separated men from God was suddenly ripped apart from top to bottom (23:44-45). Jesus' final words from the cross were a cry that His mission was complete. *Father, into Your hands I commit My spirit* (23:46). The reaction of witnesses to Jesus' death was varied. The centurion praised God and affirmed *certainly this man was innocent.* The once hostile crowd left *beating their breasts* (23:47-49). The approach of the Sabbath made it urgent to arrange a burial. Joseph, a member of the Sanhedrin who had not consented to their condemnation of Jesus received permission from Pilate and placed Jesus' body in a newly prepared tomb. The women who had come from Galilee with Jesus made plans to return to the tomb after the Sabbath. They prepared spices and perfumes not anticipating the resurrection (23:50-56).

Triumph of the Son of Man: His resurrection and ascension (24:1-53). Jesus has made the necessity of the cross and His resurrection clear to the disciples but that truth will be doubly reinforced. First, the angels remind the women at the empty tomb, *Why do you seek the living One among the dead? He is not here, but He has risen. Remember how He spoke to you while He was still in Galilee, saying that the Son of Man must be delivered into the hands of sinful men, and be crucified, and the third day rise again* (24:5-7). Jesus had told the disciples that He would rise again on the third day but the women were perplexed to find the tomb empty. They were not the only followers of Jesus to be surprised by Jesus' resurrection! The women reported the empty tomb and the message of the angels to the apostles (24:8-10), but their report sounded like nonsense to the apostles. Peter had to see the empty tomb for himself (24:11-12).

Luke is the only Gospel writer to record the encounter between the disciples and Jesus on the road to Emmaus (24:13-17). It is profoundly important to both the argument of Luke and to our understanding of the connection between the Old and New Testaments. The two disciples were perplexed by all the events in Jerusalem over the past three days (24:18-24). Their understanding of the Messiah promised in the Old Testament did not include His rejection, crucifixion and resurrection. *But we were*

85

hoping that it was He who was going to redeem Israel (24:21). They had not grasped the significance of the Passover and the promises of a Savior who would die for sinners. Jesus offers a mild but stinging rebuke. *O foolish men and slow of heart to believe in all that the prophets have spoken! Was it not necessary for the Christ to suffer these things and to enter into His glory?* (24:25-26). They failed to understand that the events in Jerusalem were in fulfillment of Moses and the prophets. Believers of every generation have wished they could have joined those disciples on that Emmaus walk as Jesus opened the Scriptures to them. *Then beginning with Moses and with all the prophets, He explained to them the things concerning Himself in all the Scriptures* (24:27). They recognized Jesus when He broke bread with them but He vanished as suddenly as He had come to them. They hurried back to Jerusalem and the apostles to confirm that Jesus had risen and to share the new understanding of Jesus' death and resurrection (24:28-35).

Jesus continued to appear to the disciples over a span of forty days. His resurrection body was such that they could touch Him and He could eat before them (24:36-43). Jesus taught the larger group of disciples as He had the two on the Emmaus road. Jesus' concluding seminar reminds the disciples (and Luke's readers) that all that has transpired is part of God's remarkable salvation plan for humanity. *These are My words which I spoke to you while I was still with you, that all things which are written about Me in the Law of Moses and the Prophets and the Psalms must be fulfilled. Then He opened their minds to understand the Scriptures, and He said to them, "Thus it is written, that the Christ would suffer and rise again from the dead the third day, and that repentance for forgiveness of sins would be proclaimed in His name to all the nations, beginning from Jerusalem"* (24:44-47).

This is the first of two volumes that Luke intends to write and he closes the Gospel with the theme that will open the book of Acts. *You are witnesses of these things. And behold, I am sending forth the promise of My Father upon you; but you are to stay in the city until you are clothed with power from on high* (24:48-49). Jesus has come from the Father in heaven and has completed his mission to provide salvation for all who believe regardless of ethnicity, gender, age or social standing. Jesus ascends to heaven leaving behind a joyful group of disciples equipped and motivated to take the good news of salvation to all humanity (24:50-51). Angels first announced the good news of a Savior at Jesus' birth (2:10-14). Now the apostles will broadcast the good news of the Savior, beginning in Jerusalem (24:52-53).

Outline

I. Prologue	1:1-4

II. Advent of the Son of God as Man (from heaven)   1:5-4:13
- A. Birth announcement of His forerunner, John   1:5-25
- B. Birth announcement of Jesus, the Son of God   1:26-56
  - The *Magnificat*, Mary's hymn of worship   1:46-56
- C. Birth narrative of John the Baptist   1:57-80
  - The *Benedictus*, Zacharias's prophetic hymn   1:67-80
- D. Birth narrative of Jesus   2:1-52
  - The *Gloria in Excelsis* of the angelic choir   2:14
  - The *Nunc Dimittis*, Simeon's hymn   2:29-32
- E. Initiation of John's ministry as forerunner   3:1-20
  1. Historic connections of John's ministry   3:1-2
  2. Prophetic connection and message of John   3:3-17
  3. Arrest and imprisonment of John by Herod   3:18-20
- F. Initiation of Jesus' ministry as Savior   3:21-4:13
  1. Baptism of Jesus: authentication as God   3:21-22
  2. Genealogy of Jesus: authentication as man   3:23-38
  3. His Temptation: authentication as Savior   4:1-13

III. Ministry of the Son of Man to Men   4:14-19:27
- A. Ministry in Galilee: Revealing His person   4:14-9:50
  1. Presentation and rejection in Nazareth   4:14-30
  2. Demonstration of power at Capernaum   4:31-44
  3. Enlistment of disciples in light of rejection   5:1-11
  4. Demonstration of authority to forgive sin   5:12-26
  5. Call of Levi leads to conflict with Pharisees   5:27-39
  6. Demonstration of authority over Sabbath   6:1-11
  7. Calling and commissioning twelve apostles   6:12-16
  8. Training the twelve in light of His rejection   6:17-49
  9. He is rejected in spite of miracles as proof   7:1-8:56
  10. Proclamation of the gospel by the disciples   9:1-17
  11. Revelation of His person (transfiguration)   9:18-50
- B. Journey to Jerusalem: Revealing His purpose   9:51-19:27
  1. Preparation of the disciples for His death   9:51-62
  2. Seventy sent out on His final mission   10:1-24
  3. Teaching in the face of testing/trusting   10:25-11:13
  4. Rejection/blasphemy by religious leaders   11:14-36
  5. Resulting judgment is announced   11:37-54
  6. Instruction of disciples following rejection   12:1-59

7.	Instruction through parables	13:1-16:31
8.	Instruction regarding faith and service	17:1-10
9.	Rejection contrasted with reception	17:11-21
10.	Revelation of His return to earth to judge	17:22-37
11.	Teaching on preparedness for His return	18:1-30
12.	Revelation of His death in Jerusalem	18:31-34
13.	Blindness and belief in Israel	18:35-19:27

IV. Sacrifice of the Son of Man on Behalf of Men — 19:28-23:56
- A. Presentation in Jerusalem (Sunday) — 19:28-44
  - 1. Triumphal entry into Jerusalem — 19:28-40
  - 2. Tearful lament over Jerusalem — 19:41-44
- B. Possession of the temple (Monday) — 19:45-48
- C. Rejection by Israel's leaders (Tuesday) — 20:1-47
  - 1. Chief priests challenge His authority — 20:1-18
  - 2. Herodians question Him on paying taxes — 20:19-26
  - 3. Sadducees challenge Him on resurrection — 20:27-40
  - 4. Religious authorities are rebuked — 20:41-47
- D. Revelation of His return (Wednesday) — 21:1-38
- E. The Passover with His disciples (Thursday) — 22:1-38
- F. Prayer, betrayal, and arrest in Gethsemane — 22:39-65
  - 1. His prayer of submission to the Father — 22:39-46
  - 2. His betrayal by Judas, a trusted disciple — 22:47-53
  - 3. His arrest by a religious mob — 22:54-65
- G. Religious trial before the Sanhedrin (Friday) — 22:66-71
- H. Civil trial before Pilate and Herod — 23:1-32
- I. Crucifixion in fulfillment of His purpose — 23:33-56

V. Triumph of the Son of Man for Men (ascension) — 24:1-53
- A. Resurrection fulfills His redemption plan — 24:1-12
- B. Revelation to disciples on the road to Emmaus — 24:13-35
- C. Confirmation by appearances in Jerusalem — 24:36-43
- D. Commission of disciples to proclaim salvation — 24:44-49
- E. The Ascension: Triumphant return to heaven — 24:50-53

Bibliography

Bock, Darrell L. *A Theology of Luke and Acts*. Grand Rapids: Zondervan Book House, 2012.

____. *Luke 1:1-9:50. Luke 9:51-24:53.* Baker Exegetical Commentary on the New Testament. Grand Rapids: Baker Books, 2004.

____. *Luke.* IVP New Testament Commentary Series. Downers Grove, IL: InterVarsity Press, 1994.

____. *Luke.* The NIV Application Commentary. Grand Rapids: Zondervan Book House, 1996.

Evans, Craig A. *Luke.* New International Biblical Commentary. Vol. 3. W. Ward Gasque, ed. Peabody, MA: Hendrickson Publishers, 1990.

Green, Joel B. and Scot McKnight, Eds. *Dictionary of Jesus and the Gospels.* Downers Grove, IL: InterVarsity Press, 1992.

Guthrie, Donald. *New Testament Introduction.* Downers Grove, IL: InterVarsity Press, 1990.

Hiebert, D. Edmond. *An Introduction to the New Testament.* Vol. 1. Chicago: Moody Press, 1975.

Liefeld, Walter L., and David W. Pao. "Luke." In *The Expositor's Bible Commentary.* Vol. 10. Rev. ed. Tremper Longman III and David E. Garland, Eds. Grand Rapids: Zondervan Publishing House, 2007.

Marshall, I. Howard. *Luke: Historian & Theologian.* Downers Grove, IL: InterVarsity Press, 1988.

____. *The Gospel of Luke.* The New International Greek Testament Commentary. Grand Rapids: Wm. B. Eerdmans Publishing Co., 1983.

Morris, Leon. *Luke: An Introduction and Commentary.* Tyndale New Testament Commentaries. Grand Rapids: Wm. B. Eerdmans Publishing Co., 2002.

Nolland, John. *Luke 9:21 - 18:34*. Word Biblical Commentary. David A. Hubbard and Glenn W. Barker, Eds. Dallas: Word Books, 1989.

Scroggie, W. Graham. *A Guide to the Gospels*. London: Pickering & Inglis, 1962.

Wenham, David, and Steve Walton. *Exploring the New Testament: A Guide to the Gospels and Acts.* Downers Grove, IL: InterVarsity Press, 2001.

John: The Son of God, the Word, Became Flesh

Key verse: 20:31, ... written so that you may believe that Jesus is the Christ, the Son of God ... have life in His name

Key Words:
Eternal Life,
Father, Son,
Believe,
Truth,
Light,
Know

	1:1-18	1:19		4 / 5		12 / 13	17 / 18		21
	Prologue	Presentation to individuals leads them to believe		Presentation to multitudes leads some to believe, but His own will not believe		Preparation of the disciples in light of the rejection	Passion of the Son, death on the cross = resurrection triumph		

Behold the Lamb of God

The Son of God Gives Eternal Life to All Who Believe

It is finished!

Seven "Signs"	Seven Discourses	Seven "I am" Statements	John, at Ephesus, AD 85-95 Universal audience
Turning water into wine, 2:1-11	Son of God is the Savior, 3:1-21	I am the **bread** of life, 6:35	
Healing nobleman's son, 4:43-54	Son is the living water, 4:1-26	I am the **light** of the world, 8:12	
Healing man at Bethesda, 5:1-18	Son is one with the Father, 5:17-47	I am the **door** of the sheep, 10:7, 9	
Feeding the 5,000 men, 6:1-14	Son is the bread of life, 6:22-59	I am the good **shepherd**, 10:11, 14	
Walking on the water, 6:15-21	Son is the light of the world, 8:12-59	I am the **resurrection** and the life, 11:25	
Healing a man born blind, 9:1-41	Son is the good shepherd, 10:1-21	I am **the way, the truth, the life**, 14:6	
Raising Lazarus to life, 11:1-57	Son is the way, truth, life, 14:1-16:35	I am the **true vine**, 15:1, 5	

91

JOHN

Therefore many other signs Jesus also performed in the presence of the disciples, which are not written in this book; but these have been written so that you may believe that Jesus is the Christ, the Son of God; and that believing you may have life in His name (John 20:30-31).

John stands alone among the four Gospels. Jesus Christ is the subject of all four portraits but John paints with the most brilliant colors and bold brush strokes. The result is a unique portrait that highlights Jesus as the Son of God and His relationship with the Father while still maintaining His genuine humanity. John is considered the theological Gospel primarily because of its Christology, but it is rich in other doctrines as well.

Author

The fourth Gospel was written by the apostle "whom Jesus loved" (20:20-24). Internal and external evidence alike points to John, the brother of James, as author. The church fathers credited the apostle John with the writing and the designation "according to John" appears in all the early manuscripts. Irenaeus is the earliest witness (AD 185), "Afterwards, John, the disciple of the Lord, who also leaned upon His breast, did himself publish a gospel during his residence at Ephesus in Asia" (Irenaeus, *Against Heresies,* 3:1.1). In his *Ecclesiastical History* Eusebius (AD 324) wrote in defense of the apostle John, "His Gospel, which is known to all the churches under heaven, must be acknolwedged as genuine. ... But of the writings of John, not only his Gospel, but also the former of his epistles, have been accepted without dispute both now and in ancient times."

The author is self-described as *the disciple whom Jesus loved* and is writing as an eyewitness. *This is the disciple who is testifying to these things and wrote these things, and we know that his testimony is true* (21:24). Scholars have recently disputed authorship by John, arguing that John would not have claimed such a title for himself. Since Lazarus is described by Mary and Martha as *the one whom You love* (John 11:3) some have suggested that Lazarus was the author. However, Lazarus does not fit the self-description of the author within the Gospel and is not named in any early external sources. Another view takes a reference to John the elder in the writings of Papias to suggest that there were two men named John at Ephesus and that the author of the Gospel is John, the elder. These and other objections to identifying the author as the apostle John have been satisfactorally answered. Westcott is largely ignored today but his defence of Johanine authorship has never been refuted. He gives extensive internal evidence and concludes, "As far therefore as indirect internal evidence is concerned, the conclusion toward which all the lines of inquiry converge remains unshaken, that the fourth Gospel was written by a Palestinian Jew, by an eye-witness, by *the disciple whom Jesus loved,* by John the son of Zebedee" (Brooke Foss Westcott, *The Gospel According to St. John*, xxiv-xxv).

Relation to the Synoptic Gospels

The synoptic Gospels have come under critical scrutiny because of their similarities but the Gospel of John has been scrutinized because of its differences. John stands alone among the Gospels, not because it contradicts them but because it omits so much of the material the synoptics share in common and because John contains so much material not found in Matthew, Mark, and Luke. The differences of John from the synoptics should not be emphasized to the exclusion of their similarities. All four Gospels affirm both the deity and the humanity of the Lord Jesus Christ. All four Gospels focus on the cross and the resurrection of Jesus as climactic and essential to the purpose of His ministry on earth. All include the promise of Jesus' return. All record the calling and equipping of the twelve disciples.

John's "omissions." The Gospel of John contains no reference to the birth, baptism, temptation, or transfiguration of Christ that the other Gospels feature prominently. John omits the Sermon on the Mount and the Olivet Discourse. There are seventy parables in the synoptics but none in John. John is almost silent about the ministry of Jesus in Galilee that the other Gospels treat extensively. The early Galilean ministry that John does record is not recorded in the synoptics. There are thirty miracles of Jesus recorded in the synoptics only two of which are recorded by John.

John's "additions." John's prologue is unique in its treatment of the preexistence of Jesus as the Son of God (1:1-18). That explanation is implied but not explicit in the synoptics. There are seven "I Am" statements that are strategic to John's argument but absent from the three synoptic Gospels. Several extended discourses by Jesus appear in John that do not appear in Matthew, Mark, and Luke including, Jesus' conversations with Nicodemus (3:1-21) and the woman of Samaria (4:7-26), His defense before "the Jews" (5:19-47), the discourse on the "bread of life" (6:26-59), His defense and discourse on the "light of the world" before the Pharisees in Jerusalem (8:12-59), the "good shepherd" discourse (10:1-18), and the upper room discourse with the twelve disciples (chaps. 13-16). Only John records Jesus' prayer in the upper room (17:1-26). John records five miracles that do not appear in the synoptics: turning water into wine (2:1-11), healing the nobleman's son (4:43-54), healing the paralytic at the Pool of Bethesda (5:1-23), restoring the sight of a blind man in Jerusalem (9:1-41), and raising Lazarus from the dead (11:1-44).

Conclusion. John compliments but does not contradict the three synoptic Gospels. He may be familiar with them but it is difficult to prove a direct connection such as is seen between Mark, Matthew and Luke. There are no identical verbal passages. The language of John does not indicate that the author used the other Gospels as sources but that does not argue that he was ignorant of their existence. It only shows that he wrote independently. A suggestion that John wrote to correct the other Gospel accounts lacks support. It seems best to view John as complimenting the synoptic Gospels by providing information and emphases that were not essential to their purpose. John is writing for an evangelistic purpose, for a different audience, addressing different issues and is writing later than Matthew, Mark, and Luke.

Occasion and Date

The witness of the early church fathers is almost unanimous in assigning the writing to John's ministry in Ephesus and relating it to the book of Revelation. "The Ephesian origin of the Gospel is in full accord with the traditional view concerning the origin of the Johannine epistles. An Ephesian origin is demanded by the book of Revelation. The contents of the fourth Gospel are consistent with this tradition" (D. Edmond Hiebert, *An Introduction to the New Testament*, 1:220). Determining the date for the writing is not quite as easy. Some have attempted to place the writing in the second century as a polemic against Gnosticism, but manuscript evidence refutes that. Two fragments of papyrus dated to the early second century contain parts of the Gospel indicating that it was already in circulation as far away as Egypt (Guthrie, *Introduction to the New Testament*, 282). Irenaeus said that John continued to live at Ephesus until the time of the Roman emperor Trajan (AD 98-117). The most likely date for the composition of the Gospel of John is between AD 85 and 98.

Distinctive Features

Christology. John's primary contribution to gospel literature is his presentation of the incarnation of Jesus, the Son of God, as the Son of man. Both the deity and the humanity of Christ are declared in the prologue. *In the beginning was the Word, and the Word was with God, and the Word was God. He was in the beginning with God.... And the Word became flesh, and dwelt among us, and we saw His glory, glory as of the only begotten from the Father, full of grace and truth* (1:1-2, 14). The intimate relationship between the Father and the Son, their oneness as God, and their eternal and separate existence as persons are repeatedly invoked (1:34; 3:16; 8:16, 42, 54-56; 10:25-30; 13:1-3; 14:6-11; 17:1-8, etc.). The Trinity is also made clear through references to the cooperative ministries of the Father, the Son, and the Holy Spirit (14:15-17, 26; 15:26-27; 16:7-16). The "I Am" claims of Jesus add further details.

Jesus' "I am" statements. John records seven dramatic claims made by Jesus that indicate His self-awareness of His deity and serve as the theme for His discourses.
1) *I am the bread of life* (6:35), follows His feeding of the 5,000.
2) *I am the light of the world* (8:12), introduces His defense of His deity.
3) *I am the door* (10:9), is Jesus' claim to be the only means of access to the Father.
4) *I am the good shepherd* (10:11), declares His sacrifice and love for His sheep.
5) *I am the resurrection and the life* (11:25), reveals His authority over death.
6) *I am the way, the truth, and the life* (14:6), states His exclusive claim as Savior.
7) *I am the true vine* (15:1), declares His continued role in the lives of believers.

Miracles as signs. John is fully aware of the multitude of miracles performed by Jesus (20:30; 21:25), but he deliberately selects just seven and labels them as σημεῖα, "signs." "σημεῖον as an event with special meaning was inevitably an unusual or even miraculous type of occurrence, and in a number of contexts σημεῖον may be rendered as 'miracle.' Certainly that is the referent of the term σημεῖον in Jn 2:23 (πολλοὶ ἐπίστευσαν εἰς τὸ ὄνομα αὐτοῦ, θεωροῦντες αὐτοῦ τὰ σημεῖα ἃ ἐποίει 'many believed in him as they saw the signs he did'). For the Gospel of John, however, a σημεῖον is not simply a miraculous event but something that points to a reality with even greater significance" (J. P. Louw, and E. A.

Nida (1996). *Vol. 1: Greek-English Lexicon of the New Testament: Based on Semantic Domains* (electronic ed. of the 2nd ed., 442). John uses the term "sign" twenty-one times and records five miracles that do not appear in the synoptic Gospels. Though few in number the miracles in John are strategically chosen to provide proof *that Jesus is the Christ, the Son of God* (20:31).

Discourses. John selects discourses of Jesus that relate to his evangelistic purpose. The discourses often occur in the context of a miracle and explain how that miracle functions as a sign to prove that Jesus is the Son of God. Jesus' discourse on "the bread of life" follows the feeding of the 5,000 (6:26-59). His discourse on the "light of the world" (8:12-59) is delivered before a hostile audience and is followed by the healing of a man born blind (9:1-41). In this case John uses the miracle to demonstrate the point of Jesus' discourse highlighting the blindness of the Pharisees. *Those of the Pharisees who were with Him heard these things and said to Him, "We are not blind too, are we?" Jesus said to them, "If you were blind, you would have no sin; but since you say, 'We see,' your sin remains"* (9:40-41). John follows that miracle and message on Jesus' claim to be "the light of the world" with the discourse on "the good shepherd" (10:1-18) in which Jesus claims to be the faithful shepherd who gives His life for the sheep in contrast to the thief and the hireling (Pharisees) who victimize the sheep. Other discourses are directly evangelistic as Jesus explains the way of salvation to individuals such as the seeking Pharisee, Nicodemus (3:1-21), and the adulterous Samaritan woman (4:7-26).

The Upper Room Discourse is Jesus' longest discourse and contains Jesus' instructions to the twelve disciples on a wide range of subjects (chapters 13-16). This teaching is found only in John and reveals (1) the servant nature of the disciples' service and their need for cleansing (13:1-17), (2) their future home in heaven (14:1-7), (3) the inter-advent ministry of the Holy Spirit (14:15-31), and (4) the indwelling presence of the Father, Son, and Holy Spirit following Jesus' triumphant return to heaven (15:1-16:16). Jesus' prayer in John 17 is unparalleled in the Gospels. It is Jesus' discourse with His heavenly Father on the eve of the crucifixion. It is a passionate request to the Father and also a strategic announcement of the true significance of the cross. *Father, the hour has come; glorify Your Son, that the Son may glorify You, even as You gave Him authority over all flesh, that to all whom You have given Him, He may give eternal life. This is eternal life, that they may know You, the only true God, and Jesus Christ whom You have sent. I glorified You on the earth, having accomplished the work which You have given Me to do. Now, Father, glorify Me together with Yourself, with the glory which I had with You before the world was* (17:1-5). Though He was fully aware of the agony that the cross represented, Jesus' concern was for the disciples and for all who would believe through their witness, including those of us reading the Gospel of John today (17:9-26). Eighty percent of Jesus' prayer is for others instead of Himself! What encouragement this must have given the disciples as they faced the future without the physical presence of the Savior they had known, loved, and followed for the past three years!

Theme and Structure

The central idea of the Gospel is evident in John's purpose statement. *These have been written so that you may believe that Jesus is the Christ, the Son of God; and that believing you may have life in His name* (John 20:31). However, the structure of the Gospel is not easy to identify. There are chronological and geographical markers but they do not reveal a pattern, as they do in Mark and Luke. But there is a logical progression. The prologue (1:1-18) introduces the subject; Jesus is the Son of God and has become flesh in order that He might provide salvation. Jesus' early ministry is centered in Galilee and involves signs (miracles) that prove that He is the Son of God who has come as the Messiah (the Christ) (1:19-4:54). The discourses in this section are evangelistic and with individuals, Nicodemus and the Samaritan woman.

The central section (chaps. 5-10) focuses on Jerusalem and reveals the intense opposition to His claims as the Son of God. The signs and discourses in this section represent Jesus' claim to be the Son of God in the public arena, particularly before the hostile Pharisees. As Jesus presses His claim to be the Son of God, there are repeated attempts to take His life (5:18; 7:25, 32; 8:59; 10:39; 11:8, 53; 12:10). The theme of belief is woven prominently into the narrative along with this growing unbelief. "Believe" or "believed" occurs twenty-eight times in these chapters but it is usually used with reference to those who do not believe (5:38; 6:36; 7:5; 8:45; 10:25).

The resurrection of Lazarus (chap. 11) marks the turning point In John's Gospel. After this the Sanhedrin plots Jesus' death (11:45-57). John refers to but does not record Jesus' Perean ministry (11:54), which Luke records in considerable detail. Instead, John introduces Jesus' triumphal entry into Jerusalem and the final week of His life (Chaps. 12-17). Jesus now declares that His "hour has come" (12:23; 13). There is a "count down" to the cross as John marks the days until the crucifixion (12:1, 12; 19:14, 31). The arrest, trials, and crucifixion reveal the import of Jesus' statement that His "hour has now come" (chaps. 18-19). The trials include the religious trial before the Sanhedrin led by the high priest and the trial before Pilate.

John's report of Jesus' resurrection (chap. 20) and His appearances to the disciples (chap. 21) is the most extensive in the four Gospels. While the great commission is not included, Jesus has already made that mandate clear to the disciples in His Upper Room Discourse. The personal interchange between Jesus and Peter makes it clear that the time Jesus has spent with the disciples has been well invested. Peter is commissioned to "shepherd My sheep" (21:15-17) reminding him (and us) that those that believe are Jesus' sheep and need to be fed and shepherded. Whether the final two verses were written by John himself or added by someone else, they provide a fitting conclusion. "The last two verses look like a conclusion written by someone other than the author of the preceding. The conclusion brings in a number of people to authenticate what has been written. They can say, 'We know that his testimony is true'" (Leon Morris, *The Gospel According to John*, 775).

Key Verses

Therefore many other signs Jesus also performed in the presence of the disciples, which are not written in this book; but these have been written so that you may believe that Jesus is the Christ, the Son of God; and that believing you may have life in His name (John 20:30-31).

Message of John

Prologue: Incarnation of the Son of God (1:1-18). John begins with the eternality of Jesus as the Son of God and emphasizes His co-existence and co-equality with God the Father. As in the book of Genesis, there is nothing before or outside of God. He is the first cause and the creator of everything. Jesus is introduced as the divine Word, the *logos*. John gives no genealogy because God has none. He gives no birth narrative, but makes the incarnation clear. The eternally existing Son of God has become man. *The Word became flesh, and dwelt among us, and we saw His glory, glory as of the only begotten from the Father, full of grace and truth* (John 1:14). The Son of God is Life and Light. *In Him was life, and the life was the Light of men* (1:4). As the Light, the Son shined in darkness but the darkness did not comprehend (master) it (1:5). John thus introduces the conflict of the Son with unbelief, a theme he will weave throughout his Gospel.

John the Baptist is introduced abruptly, in much the same way as Jesus; there is no birth narrative for him. The Gospel is about God and what is important about John is that he is *sent from God* (1:6). The theme of believing is likewise introduced through John. He is a witness to the Light *so that all might believe through him* (1:7). The Son entered the world that He created and yet He was not recognized and received by that which He created. To those that did receive Him, the Son *gave the right to become children of God, even to those who believe in His name, who were born, not of blood nor of the will of the flesh nor of the will of man, but of God* (1:12-13). The two themes of belief and rejection are woven throughout the Gospel and John will explain in the next segment how some individuals did receive Him (1:19-4:54).

The prologue of John concludes with the testimony of both John the Baptist and John, the author and apostle (1:14-18). John the Baptist testified to the preexistence and preeminence of the Son. The Word that was and is God has become flesh and has "tabernacled" among men. John, the author, is among those that have personally seen His glory and experienced the fullness of His grace. Grace and truth have been realized (incarnated) through Jesus Christ and John has gotten almost to the end of the prologue before he actually names Jesus Christ! No one has ever seen God but Jesus Christ who is God, the unique and only One, and who is in the very bosom of the Father, has exegeted (made real and visible) the invisible God (1:18).

Presentation to Individuals Leads to Believing (1:19-4:54)
John's testimony concerning Jesus (1:19-34). John's Gospel focuses on Jesus' ministry in Jerusalem and the opposition He encounters there. Antagonism is evident early when an official delegation of priests and Levites is sent by the Pharisees in Jerusalem to interrogate John the Baptist in the wilderness. In response to their interrogation John makes it clear that he is not the Christ or even Elijah, but he is the forerunner of the Messiah as predicted by Isaiah (Isaiah 40:3). He is baptizing those that repent in water but the Messiah who is about to come will baptize those that believe with the Holy Spirit (1:18-28). When Jesus appears the next day John declares, *Behold, the Lamb of God who takes away the sin of the world!* (1:29). Isaiah had portrayed the Messiah as the sin bearing Lamb to be slain on behalf of sinners (Isaiah 53). John the Baptist proclaims that Jesus is the long awaited Lamb, the Passover Lamb (Genesis 3:21; Exodus 12:1-30). John recognized Jesus as the Messiah when he saw the Spirit descending on Him at His baptism (Isaiah 42:1) and declared, *this is the*

Son of God, identifying Jesus directly with the Messiah of Psalm 2:7 (John 1:34).

The testimony of the first disciples concerning the Son (1:35-51). John sees Jesus approaching on the following day and again declares, *Behold, the Lamb of God!* The first disciples Jesus attracts are two men that have been following John. John has testified that Jesus is the Christ and one of the two men, Andrew, testifies to his brother Simon, *"We have found the Messiah"* (1:41). Peter promptly becomes a disciple and is joined by Philip as they make their way to Galilee. Philip summons Nathanael who adds another testimony to Jesus' identity. *Rabbi, You are the Son of God; You are the King of Israel* (1:49). These early disciples are examples of those that receive Jesus (1:12) and validate John's identification of Jesus as the Son of God, the Messiah.

The presentation of the Son as Creator (2:1-12). The scene shifts from the wilderness to a wedding in Cana of Galilee where Jesus, His mother, and His disciples are invited guests. John introduces the wedding scene and wine for a reason. The prophet Joel declared that God's judgment had destroyed the harvest, cut off the supply of wine for drink offerings, and removed joy from mankind (Joel 1:8-12). He called for the nation to repent (Joel 2:12-14) and promised that when they did repent the LORD would remove their reproach and send new wine (Joel 2:18-19; Amos 9:11-15; Zechariah 9:9, 16-17). He would also pour out His Spirit (Joel 2:27-28-29). The nation has not yet repented and Jesus advised His mother that His "hour has not yet come." Nevertheless Jesus turns the water into wine to demonstrate that the promised Messiah is here and is calling Israel to repent. John identifies turning water into wine as the beginning of the "signs" Jesus did. Through this miracle He *manifested His glory and His disciples believed in Him* (2:11).

The presentation of the Son of God to individuals (2:13-4:54). John records a series of personal encounters between Jesus and individuals. Each occurs in a different geographical location. Jesus' first encounter is in **Jerusalem** with the Pharisee, Nicodemus and leads to His discourse on the new birth (3:1-36). Jesus journeys to Jerusalem as the Passover approaches where He finds the temple functioning as a market place (2:13-25). His actions and words were dramatic. He made a whip and drove the merchants out, overturning their tables and ordering, *Take these things away; stop making My Father's house a place of business.* Jesus thus declared He was God's Son and asserted authority over the temple. He responded to the request of "the Jews" for a sign as proof of His authority by predicting His own resurrection (2:19). Jesus also did other unnamed "signs" with the result that *many believed in His name.*

Nicodemus, a ruler of the Jews, came to Jesus under the cover of darkness, an indication of unbelief and opposition in John (1:5). Nicodemus attested to the divine source of the signs, but Jesus turned the conversation to the significance of the signs, and to the need for individuals and the nation to have a new birth (3:1-8). Ezekiel promised that the Messiah would cleanse the nation with water, give them a new heart, and put His Spirit within them (Ezekiel 36:24-28) resulting in the rebirth of the nation (Ezekiel 37:14, 23, 33). Nicodemus was a teacher in Israel yet he did not understand his need for the new birth or that it came through believing in the one and only Son of God who has come from heaven (John 3:9-13). Jesus revealed to Nicodemus that He, the Son of Man, the promised Messiah, will be *lifted up,* that is, crucified (as in 8:28; 12:34) *so that whoever believes will in Him have eternal life* (3:14-15). The words that follow in 3:16-21 may be John's explanation of the import of Jesus' words to Nicodemus. The Son has come this time to save not to judge, however, the one who does not believe is already under judgment (3:16-21).

The second encounter occurs in **Judea** between Jesus and John the Baptist (3:22-36). They do not meet together but their ministries are intertwined as they preach and baptize in the wilderness of Judea (3:22-30). John's disciples are concerned about the growing popularity of Jesus but John himself is full of joy. He has been sent by God to introduce the Messiah and like a friend of the bridegroom he rejoices to know that Jesus, the "bridegroom," has arrived on the scene. John has not yet been arrested but sees his role as diminishing in favor of the ministry of Jesus. *He must increase, but I must decrease.* The author John may have added the explanation that follows as a commentary (3:31-36). It contains a wealth of teaching concerning Christ: He is the Son of God from heaven, speaks the words of God, gives the Spirit, is loved by the Father, has authority over all things, and determines the destiny of all mankind.

The third encounter occurs in **Samaria** as Jesus passed through on His way back to Galilee (4:1-45). Samaria lay between the Jewish territory of Judea and the mixed Jewish—Gentile area of Galilee but was avoided by Jewish travelers. Jesus elected to travel this unlikely route to meet an unlikely individual, a Samaritan woman.

101

Jesus' Visits to Jerusalem as Recorded by John

Ptolemais

Mediterranean Sea

Gennesaret
Jotapata

Capernaum

Sea of
Galilee

GALILEE

Sepphoris

Tiberias

Hippus

Nazareth

Gadara

Dor

Mt. Tabor

River Jordan

After two days he
departed to Galilee
(Jn 4:43)

Caesarea

Scythopolis

Pella

After this there was
a feast of the Jews,
and Jesus went up
to Jerusalem
(Jn 5:1)

Ginae

Salim

Meets Samaritan
woman at well
(Jn 4:7-38)

Sebaste
Mt. Gerizim

SAMARITANS

Sychar

PEREA

Apollonia

Antipatris

Anuatha
Borcaeus

Stayed with the
disciples here
(Jn 11:54)

Joppa

The Passover... was
at hand, and Jesus
went up to Jerusalem
(Jn 2:13)

JUDEA

Gadora

Lazarus raised
from the dead
(Jn 11:1-44)

Lydda

Ephraim

Jamnia

Emmaus

Jericho

Abila

Jerusalem

Bethany

Bethabara

Healing at pool of
Bethesda
(Jn 5:1-17)

It was the feast
of the Dedication
at Jerusalem
(Jn 10:22)

0   10 miles

0   10   20 km

© Carta, Jerusalem

Copyright by Carta Jerusalem, Used by permission

Sychar had historical significance as the area purchased by Jacob and given to his son Joseph (Genesis 33:19; 48:22). The well became the setting for Jesus' second discourse, His discourse on the water of life (John 4:7-38). He broke social conventions by speaking with the Samaritan woman and offered her living water that brings eternal life (4:7-14). Jesus graciously drew a confession from the woman and led her to the recognition that He is the promised Messiah (4:15-26). Jesus has "harvested a soul" and reminded His disciples that the fields were "white for harvest" (4:27-38). A spiritual harvest has already occurred in Samaria as the woman shared her encounter with Jesus (4:39) and the harvest continued when Jesus accepted the invitation of the Samaritans to stay in their village. John's editorial comment that Jesus is not honored in Judea, His own country, but is received by Samaritans and Galileans, links this encounter with a believing woman in Samaria and the following encounter with a believing official in Galilee (4:40-45).

The fourth encounter occurred in **Galilee**, where a royal official pleaded with Jesus to heal his dying son (4:46-54). The designation "royal" may indicate a person of royal ancestry or perhaps someone in the service of Herod Antipas who governed Galilee at this time (Robert H. Mounce, "John," 418-19). Jesus is in Cana, scene of His first sign and the official came to him from Capernaum about 20 miles away. Jesus has recently been in Jerusalem where the Jews asked for a sign but did not believe (2:17-18) and His first response to the distraught father suggests that the official was Jewish. *Unless you people see signs and wonders, you simply will not believe* (4:48). The father persisted in his request and took Jesus at His word when He said, *Go; your son lives.* His servants met him as he returned home with the news that his son was healed at the very same hour when Jesus declared *your son lives.* The result of this "second sign" was that the official believed along with his entire household (4:53-54).

Presentation to Multitudes Leads to Opposition (5:1-12:50)
The heart of John's Gospel highlights Jesus' ministry to multitudes and contrasts the response of belief with the growing opposition of unbelief. Jesus' discourses are interwoven with His signs and serve to authenticate the claims. Jesus' discourse claiming equality with the Father Who has given the Son authority to judge follows His healing of the lame man at the pool of Bethesda (5:1-47). Jesus' discourse on the bread of life follows His feeding 5,000 men (6:1-58). Giving sight to a man that was born blind validates Jesus' claim to be the light of the world (8:12-9:34). The resurrection of Lazarus (11:1-44) is imbedded between Jesus' discourse

103

on the good shepherd (10:1-18) where He claims authority to give eternal life, and the upper room discourse (14:1-8) where He claims to be the way, the truth, and the life. The opposition comes from the Pharisees and the chief priests, whom John identifies as "the Jews," (5:16-18; 7:32; 8:13; 9:22; 12:42), grows in intensity, and climaxes in the official plot of the Sanhedrin to kill Jesus (11:45-53).

Opposition in Jerusalem (5:1-47). Jesus returned to Jerusalem where He healed a lame man at the pool of Bethesda (5:1-17). John identifies Jesus' presence in Jerusalem for three other Passover feasts (2:23; 6:4; 11:55) but this miracle occurred at an unspecified feast and on the Sabbath. The man was helpless and had been an invalid for 38 years. At Jesus' command, *Get up, pick up your pallet and walk,* he was immediately healed. "The Jews" began persecuting Jesus for healing the man on the Sabbath (5:16) and sought to kill Him for claiming to be equal with God (5:17-18). It is ironic that they were free to plan murder on the Sabbath but would not allow Him to heal on the Sabbath. This third sign is followed by Jesus' third discourse in which He claimed to be co-equal with God (5:19-32). Jesus was working in consort with the Father and shared the Father's prerogative to give life, to raise the dead, and to execute judgment. He cited four witnesses to support His own claim, John the Baptist (5:33-35), the works He has done (5:36), the Father (5:37-38), and finally, the Scriptures (5:39-47). *If you believed Moses, you would believe Me, for he wrote about Me. But if you do not believe his writings, how will you believe My words?*

Opposition in Galilee 6:1-71). The fourth sign Jesus performed occurred in Galilee "near the Passover" and the crowd that followed Jesus was made up of "sign seekers" (6:1-4). This is the only one of Jesus' 35 miracles that is recorded in all four Gospels. Several months have likely passed since the miracle and discourse of chapter 5. From the synoptic Gospels we learn that Herod Antipas has beheaded John the Baptist (Matthew 14:1-20; Mark 6:14-43). Jesus feeds 5,000 men plus women and children by multiplying five barley loaves and two fish (6:5-11). The disciples served the crowd and gathered twelve baskets of leftovers after everyone is satisfied (6:12-13). The crowd acclaimed Jesus as "the Prophet" Moses promised would come (Deuteronomy 18:14-22). They wanted to make Jesus their king for selfish reasons and were willing to resort to force (6:14-15). The fickle nature of the crowd was evident in their response to Jesus' discourse on the bread of life that followed (6:26-58).

Jesus' fifth sign, walking on the water (6:16-25), is for the benefit of the disciples but noticed by the sign-seeking crowd. Jesus is developing the faith of His disciples but many of His would-be disciples turn away from following Him at the conclusion of His discourse on the bread of life (6:59-66). Jesus' fourth discourse was challenging to the curious crowd and perplexing to His disciples. The crowd ate the bread and fish but they asked for yet another sign like the manna their fathers ate in the wilderness. Jesus reminded them that their fathers ate the manna in the wilderness and died, whereas He is the true bread from heaven that gives life. *I am the living bread that came down out of heaven; if anyone eats of this bread, he will live forever; and the bread also which I will give for the life of the world is My flesh* (6:51).

The discourse on the bread of life is about believing (6:29) but the crowd stumbled over Jesus' language (6:52-60). *Truly, truly, I say to you, unless you eat the flesh of the Son of Man and drink His blood, you have no life in yourselves* (6:53). Many of His "disciples" withdrew from following Jesus at this point because they did not believe (6:61-66). The twelve original disciples remain with Jesus though one of them, Judas, is destined to betray Him (6:67-71). Peter voices the faith and resolve of the eleven in his confession. *Lord, to whom shall we go? You have words of eternal life. We have believed and have come to know that You are the Holy One of God* (6:68-69).

Opposition at the Feast of Booths (7:1-10:21). Jesus avoided traveling in Judea where "the Jews" (referring to the religious leaders, since all in Judea are Jews) were seeking to kill Him (7:1-2). Jesus' own brothers had not yet believed and they urged Jesus to "go public" with His works (7:1-5), but Jesus knew His "time is not yet here" (2:4; 7:6, 8, 30; 8:20). He knows precisely when the time will come for Him to go to the cross (13:1; 17:1). John reports extensively on Jesus' ministry in Jerusalem before, during, and after the feast of Tabernacles (7:10-10:21). Jesus is secretly present in Jerusalem **before** the feast (7:10-13) and begins to speak openly in the temple **during** the feast (7:14-36). It was the **last day** of the feast when Jesus invited the people to believe in Him and receive "living water" (7:37-39). The crowd was confused and divided on whether He was the Christ, and they feared the authorities. In spite of the confusion in the crowd many did believe (7:31). The authorities sent officers to arrest Jesus but they returned empty-handed and were rebuked by the belligerent Pharisees (7:32, 44-49). Nicodemus met with the same scorn from his fellow Pharisees when he tried to intervene (7:50-52).

The encounter between Jesus, the Pharisees, and the adulterous woman (8:1-11) does not appear in the earliest and best manuscripts and is not generally accepted by protestant scholars as canonical. It may be a genuine historical record of Jesus' encounter but should not be used as a source of doctrine given its uncertain textual support.

Jesus' discourse on the Light of the world (8:12-58) is closely connected with the Feast of Booths (tabernacles) (7:2). On the eighth day of the festival, at evening, the city of Jerusalem was bathed in light when lamps were lighted in the women's court of the temple. The lights reminded the people of the pillar of fire that signaled the presence of the LORD God in their midst as they journeyed through the wilderness. Jesus was asserting His co-equality with the Father when He claimed to be the Light of the world. *I am the Light of the world; he who follows Me will not walk in the darkness, but will have the Light of life* (8:12). The Pharisees took exception to Jesus' claim and entered into an intense debate (8:13-30) that climaxed with Jesus' prediction of the cross where they will *lift up the Son of Man* (8:28). Many believed in spite of the opposition and Jesus promised that those that believe would know the truth and be set free from slavery to sin by the truth (8:31-38). The debate raged on when the Pharisees' claimed that Abraham was their father and Jesus countered with the charge that their father was the devil because they did not believe His word (8:39-47). Twice "the Jews" made the blasphemous charge that Jesus has a demon (8:48, 52). They recognized that when Jesus said *before Abraham was born, I am,* He was claiming to be Yahweh the I AM of the Old Testament (8:49-58), a claim they considered to be blasphemy, so they picked up stones to stone Him to death (8:59).

The healing of a man that was born blind (9:1-34) validates Jesus' claim that He is the Light of the world (8:12). The disciples associated the man's blindness with sin but Jesus turned it into a sign demonstrating that He is the Light of the world (9:1-5). The opposition of the Pharisees continued as they interrogated the man and his parents to find out who healed him (9:6-27). The man's spiritual sight developed throughout the interrogation until he declared that the one who healed him must be from God (9:28-34). The man was "put out" by the Pharisees who had decreed that anyone confessing that Jesus is the Christ would be barred from the synagogue. Jesus sought the man out and revealed to him that He is the Messiah, the Son of Man (9:35-41). The blind man's journey to the Light was now complete as he confessed, *Lord, I believe.* In stark contrast, Jesus confirmed the blindness of the Pharisees. *If you were blind, you would have no sin; but since you say, 'We see,' your sin remains.*

Jesus' discourse on the good shepherd (10:1-18) begins with an illustration of a sheepfold and contrasts the true shepherd with a thief (10:1-5). The true shepherd enters by the door, calls his sheep by name, and leads them out. His audience failed to understand so Jesus explained the lesson of the parable (10:6-18). He is both the door to the sheepfold (10:7) and the good shepherd (10:11). "Life" in John's Gospel is eternal life and the "abundant life" Jesus promised here is eternal life, not "more stuff," or "the good life" (10:10).

The shepherd motif has deep roots in the Old Testament. Jacob acknowledged God as "the Shepherd, the Stone of Israel" (Genesis 49:24). Isaiah said, "like a shepherd He [the Messiah] will tend His flock" (Isaiah 40:11). Jeremiah predicted that the LORD would gather Israel, keep them like a shepherd keeps his flock, and make a new covenant with them (Jeremiah 31:10, 31). Ezekiel said the Messiah would search for His sheep, gather them from the nations, restore them to the land, care for and feed them, and give them rest (Ezekiel 34:11-15). *Then I will set over them one shepherd, My servant David, and he will feed them; he will feed them himself and be their shepherd* (Ezekiel 34:23). Micah prophesied that the Messiah would be born in Bethlehem and that He would shepherd His flock (Micah 5:2-4). Jesus is the promised shepherd! He is going to the cross willingly to lay down His life for the sheep (John 10:11, 15, 17-18). He will be crucified by unbelieving adversaries but has authority to lay down His life and to take it up again, foreshadowing both His death and His resurrection. The audience was divided with many claiming "He has a demon" but others citing the opening of the blind man's eyes as evidence to the contrary (10:19-21).

Opposition at the Feast of Dedication (10:22-42). The Festival of Lights, Hanukkah, commemorated the deliverance of the Jews from Antiochus Epiphanes and the rededication of the temple under Judas Maccabeus in 164 B.C. The shepherd theme continues when Jesus appears in the temple and the authorities insist that He openly declare whether He is the Christ (10:22-30). Jesus has already made His Messianic identity clear but they *are not of His sheep* and do not believe. His claim to be one with the Father removed all doubt so "the Jews" sought to stone Him for blasphemy (10:31-33). Jesus has been sent by the Father, is doing the works of the Father, and rightfully claims, *I am the Son of God* (10:34-38). He eluded

107

their repeated efforts to stone Him and left for the Jordan where He and John were baptizing. Many followed and believed in Him as He left Jerusalem (10:39-42).

Opposition at Bethany (11:1-57). Raising Lazarus from the dead marks the turning point in John's Gospel. Jesus has claimed to be the Life, to have authority to give eternal life to all who believe, and to raise the dead (5:21-29). His final sign before the cross is raising Lazarus from the grave. Bethany was a village located two miles from Jerusalem. Jesus was ministering "beyond the Jordan" when He learned that Lazarus was seriously ill (11:1-3) but delayed two days before making the journey, during which time Lazarus died (11:4-7). The delay was intentional so that the disciples *may believe*. The disciples cautioned Jesus about going because of the recent attempts on His life in Jerusalem but were prepared to go with Him even if it meant death (11:8-19). First Martha and then later Mary met Jesus as He neared Bethany and voiced the same lament, *Lord, if You had been here, my brother would not have died* (11:21, 32). Jesus made one of His seven I AM statements to Martha. *I am the resurrection and the life; he who believes in Me will live even if he dies.* (11:25). Lazarus came out of the tomb at the command of Jesus but the effect of the sign on the crowd was mixed (11:38-46); many believed, others reported it to the Pharisees in Jerusalem. Jesus withdrew temporarily from His public ministry while the Sanhedrin gathered in council and made plans to kill both Jesus and Lazarus (11:47-57).

Opposition in Jerusalem (12:1-50). John now begins a "count-down" to the cross (12:1). Jesus returned to Bethany six days before the Passover, the day of His crucifixion and was the guest of honor at a dinner that Mark says occurred in the home of Simon the Leper (Mark 14:3). John records that Lazarus was reclining at the table with Jesus and Martha was serving (John 12:2). It was customary for a servant to wash the feet of the guest but it was Mary, sister of Lazarus, who performed that service. The home was filled with fragrance as Mary anointed Jesus' feet with a very costly perfume and wiped it with her hair (12:3). Judas Iscariot objected and John inserts the explanation that Judas is the one who will betray Jesus and thus revealed his thieving nature (12:4-6). Jesus was aware that He would be crucified at the Passover in Jerusalem and explained that Mary's anointing was in anticipation of His burial (12:7-8). John uses this incident to unite the betrayal by Judas and the plot of the chief priests to put Jesus to death.

Jesus entered Jerusalem precisely as Zechariah the prophet said the Messiah would enter the city (Zechariah 9:9) and the crowd acclaimed

Him as the Messiah, the King of Israel (12:13). The words they shouted were from a messianic enthronement Psalm (Psalm 118:26), but the disciples did not understand the implications until after the resurrection and ascension of Jesus (John 12:16-19). The request of devout Greeks to see Jesus (12:20-22) signaled the rejection of the Son of God by His own people (1:11-12) and the extension of the message of salvation to the Gentile world of seekers (10:16). Jesus previously said "My hour has not yet come," but with the arrival of the seeking Greeks He announced, *the hour has come for the Son of Man to be glorified* (12:23-26).

Jesus prayerfully submitted to the Father as He prepared for His death on the cross and the voice of the Father confirmed that the cross is part of the divine plan (12:27-36). Jesus' words in this passage are freighted with meaning. The judgment of sin will fall on Him on the cross yet the judgment is really "on the world." He will be "lifted up from the earth" signifying death by crucifixion (a Roman execution) not by stoning (a Jewish penalty for blasphemy). The crowd did not understand the twofold ministry of the Messiah as the Lamb of God who would take away the sin of the world (1:29 with Isaiah 53) and the King who will come to judge (9:39; 12:31; 16:11).

The themes of darkness and light, of life and death, of belief and unbelief permeate John's Gospel and in the shadow of the cross Jesus continued to invite all to believe. *While you have the Light, believe in the Light, so that you may become sons of Light* (12:36). Jesus performed messianic signs in their midst and spoke the words the Father gave Him to speak, but the nation remained blind just as Isaiah prophesied (12:37-43 with Isaiah 6:10). His words are eternal life and the unbelieving will be judged at the last day by the very words they have rejected (12:44-50).

Preparation of the Disciples for the Son's Departure (13:1-17:26)
The Upper Room Discourse is unique to John, but it is not entirely a discourse, it includes Jesus' interaction with His disciples (chap. 13), and His prayer on behalf of the disciples (chap. 17). It may also not be entirely in the upper room. Jesus said, *Get up, let us go from here* (14:31), but continued His instructions for the disciples (chaps. 15-16), and prayed to the Father (chap 17) before John records their departure for the Mount of Olives (18:1). One marked feature is Jesus' awareness that "His hour has come." Three times John has recorded that "His hour has not yet come" (2:4; 7:30; 8:20) and three times it is stated, "His hour had come" (12:23; 13:1; 17:1). Jesus' self-awareness is evident in John's introduction (13:1-4).

Jesus knows (1) that His hour has come, (2) that Judas Iscariot will betray Him, and (3) that the Father has given all things into His hands. That knowledge makes His unfailing love for the disciples (13:1) and His action of washing their feet (13:5-17) all the more striking.

Preparation in the upper room (13:5-14:31). Washing the feet of a guest was common practice and was usually performed by a servant (Genesis 18:3-5; 1 Samuel 25:41; Luke 7:38, 44). However, there were no "servants" among the disciples. They were debating which of them was the greatest and Jesus now taught them two important lessons. (1) They need daily cleansing from the defilement of sin (John 13:7-10). (2) They need to function as servants not as masters (John 13:12-17). Jesus excluded one of the disciples when He declared them "clean" (13:10-11).

Following His washing their feet Jesus openly predicted His betrayal by Judas so that the other disciples would believe (13:18-20). Judas must have been so much like the other disciples that they did not suspect him even when He was given the morsel of bread (13:21-30). It is noteworthy that *it was night* when Judas went out because Jesus has frequently contrasted light with darkness and day with night. The departure of Judas is a sign that the cross is imminent. *Now is the Son of Man glorified, and God is glorified in Him* (13:31-33). Jesus now issued a "new" commandment to the disciples that they love one another, a commandment that He repeats several times for emphasis (13:34-35). Judas is not the only disappointment among the disciples! Simon Peter confidently asserted *I will lay down my life for You,* though he would deny Christ three times before the night was over (13:36-38).

Jesus had much to teach the disciples about their life and ministry following His departure (14:1-16:33). The disciples were troubled by the thought of Jesus leaving them but were assured that they will be reunited with Him in a place that He will be preparing for them (14:1-4). Jesus' statement, *I am the way, and the truth, and the life; no one comes to the Father but through Me* (14:6) is a declaration that He is the one and only means of access to God the Father. This claim makes Christianity exclusive and renders all other religions inadequate as a means of securing heaven. The disciples wanted more evidence to bolster their faith and Jesus' disappointment was evident as He reminded them that they have sufficient proof because His words and works are those of the Father (14:7-11). Jesus' unfailing love for them was evident when He promised that they would do greater works after His departure and that the Father would grant whatever they ask in His name (14:12-15).

Jesus was confident regarding the future performance of the disciples because they would soon experience the enabling power of the Holy Spirit (14:16-26). Jesus' teaching on the role of the Holy Spirit is one of the great contributions of the Gospel of John. The promises in John were directed specifically to the apostles, but the book of Acts and the Epistles reveal that the Holy Spirit indwells, enables, and gifts all believers. The Holy Spirit will (1) be sent by the Father (and the Son) in the name of Jesus, (2) be their "helper," (which may be translated as comforter, counselor, or advocate), (3) permanently indwell them along with the Father and the Son, (4) teach them "all things" and guide them into all the truth, (5) enable them to remember Jesus' words, (6) bear testimony about Jesus, (6) convict the world of sin, righteousness and judgment, (7) disclose the future, and (8) glorify the Son (14:16-26; 16:5-15).

Instruction regarding the disciples' future (15:1-16:33). The Upper Room Discourse continued, perhaps as Jesus and the disciples made their way to the Mount of Olives and the garden of Gethsemane (14:31), but more likely while they were still in the upper room (18:1). Jesus instructed the disciples on their new relationships following His return to the Father. (1) Their changed relationship with Him (15:1-11). (2) Their relationship with each other (15:12-17). (3) Their relationship to the world (15:18-16:4). (4) Their relationship with the Holy Spirit (16:5-15).

The new relationship between the disciples and Christ will be vital and intimate, like a branch attached to the life-giving vine (15:1-5). They will glorify Him as they bear much fruit through abiding in (depending on) Him (15:6-8). They will be filled with joy after His departure, knowing that His love for them is unchanging (15:9-11). The disciples are to love one another, a command that Jesus repeated four times (13:34-35; 15:12, 17). Loving one another is the "badge of identification" of Jesus' disciples (13:35) and true love is sacrificial (15:13). There must be love among Jesus' disciples, but they should not expect to find love in the world. In fact, they will be hated by the world and persecuted because they bear witness for Jesus (15:18-16:4). They will be put out of the synagogue and even killed by adversaries who think they are doing a service to God, but who do not know either the Father or the Son. The Holy Spirit will be their source of strength for the turbulent days ahead (16:5-15). The disciples continue to be puzzled about Jesus' departure. They will be overwhelmed with grief at His death (16:16-19), but their weeping will be replaced with irrepressible joy at His resurrection and ascension to the Father (16:20-22).

Jesus' prayer of intercession for the disciples (17:1-26). Jesus' prayer in the upper room has a threefold focus. (1) His prayer for Himself was for the restoration of the glory He previously shared with the Father now that He has accomplished His mission on earth (17:1-5). (2) His prayer for the disciples was that they would be protected from the evil one and sanctified by the Father (17:6-19). (3) His prayer for the future generations of believers was that they would be one (17:20-26). Jesus said that others would *believe in Me through their* [the apostles] *word,* referring to the words of the apostles recorded in the Scriptures of the New Testament.

The Passion of the Son: His Death and Resurrection (18:1-21:24)

The betrayal and arrest of the Son of God (18:1-11). The garden where Jesus and the disciples intended to spend the night was well known to Judas and its seclusion provided the secrecy the chief priests were seeking (Mark 14:1-2). Their dislike for the Roman army was set aside and their hatred for Jesus revealed when they brought an entire cohort of Roman soldiers (about 600) to arrest Jesus (18:1-3). Jesus, *knowing all the things that were coming upon Him,* approached them and identified Himself as the person they were seeking (18:4-9). Jesus made no attempt to resist but Peter did as he cut off the right ear of Malchus, a servant of the high priest (18:10-11).

The trials of the Son of God (18:12-19:16). The trials of Jesus made a mockery of Jewish and Roman law. They were held at night, involved false and changing charges, and relied on false witnesses. The first trial was before Annas, father-in-law to Caiaphas the high priest. No witnesses were called and Jesus was struck in the face in violation of Jewish Law (18:12-24). Only one of the disciples followed Jesus into the trial chamber, probably John himself. Peter remained nearby but denied Jesus three times during this trial before Annas (18:15-18, 25-27). John mentions a trial before Caiaphas (18:24, 28) but does not record the proceedings of that trial. Most of John's report focuses on Jesus' trial before Pilate (18:29-19:15).

There is a glaring contradiction between the murderous intent of the chief priests and their pious refusal to enter the Praetorium (the Roman governor's residence) lest they be defiled and unable to keep the Passover (18:28). They had no civil charge to bring but were determined to see Jesus crucified, a death that only Roman authorities could impose (18:29-32). Pilate was left to conduct his own inquiry and appeared indifferent and annoyed by the process (18:33-38). Jesus is a king but His kingdom is not a political one. The chief priests did not acknowledge that Jesus was the Messiah, their King, and Pilate did not realize that one day Jesus would crush the Roman Empire as the smiting stone of Daniel 2:44-45 and the Ancient of Days of Daniel 7:22. Pilate was forced to go back and forth between Jesus and the accusers who refused to enter the trial chamber. Twice Pilate declared, *I find no guilt in Him,* yet he did not uphold Roman law by releasing Jesus. Instead Pilate offered Jesus' accusers a choice of prisoners to be released and they insisted that he release a robber, Barabbas, rather than Jesus (John 18:38-40).

Roman justice was again compromised when Pilate had Jesus scourged and allowed the soldiers to abuse the prisoner he twice declares innocent (19:1-3). Pilate brought the abused and bleeding Jesus out to His accusers, perhaps thinking they would relent when they saw Jesus (19:4-5). The chief priests instead cried out, *Crucify, Crucify,* and raised a new charge against Jesus. *He made Himself out to be the Son of God* (19:6-7). The thesis of John's Gospel is that Jesus is the Christ, the Son of God (20:31) and that truth now becomes the basis of Jesus' rejection (19:7). Pilate was fearful but appears weak and helpless in the face of Jesus' accusers (19:8-11). He gave in to them when they charged, *if you release this Man, you are no friend of Caesar; everyone who makes himself out to be a king opposes Caesar.* The great crowd that escorted Jesus into Jerusalem on the first day of the week acclaimed Him as the King of Israel (12:12-13). Now, within the same week, their leaders cry out, *Away with Him, away with Him, crucify Him! We have no king but Caesar* (19:12-15). Jesus' own people have rejected Him (1:11-12). It was six in the morning when Pilate handed Jesus over to the executioners (19:16). The Light of the world has been tried under cover of darkness.

The crucifixion of the Son of God (19:17-42). Jesus was crucified just outside the walls of Jerusalem on a notorious hill named Golgotha, the Place of the Skull. The conflict between Pilate and the chief priests was not over. The Jewish leaders rejected Jesus as their king and Pilate appears vindictive when he placed a sign on the cross over Jesus' head. JESUS THE NAZARENE, THE KING OF THE JEWS (19:19). The crucifixion was part of God's predetermined plan and fulfilled Old Testament prophecies. (1) He was despised and rejected by His own (19:21 with Isaiah 53:3). (2) Jesus accepted His death silently and without protest (19:18 with Isaiah 53:7). (3) The soldiers divided His garments among themselves and gambled over His cloak (19:23-24 with Psalm 22:18). (4) They gave Jesus sour wine (vinegar) for His thirst (19:28-29 with Psalm 69:21). (5) They broke the legs of the two men crucified with Jesus to hasten their death but did not break Jesus' legs since He was already dead (19:36 with Exodus 12:46; Psalm 34:20). (6) They pierced His side with a spear to confirm His death (19:37 with Isaiah 53:5; Zechariah 12:10). (7) He died alongside the wicked and was laid in a rich man's tomb (19:18, 41 with Isaiah 53:9).

Jesus spoke few words while dying on the cross but they were profoundly important. He was the eternal Son of God but was concerned for Mary His birth mother. He demonstrated His love for Mary as well as His confidence in the apostle John when He transferred Mary's future care to John. Jesus' last word from the cross was, Τετέλεσται, *it is finished!* It was a shout of triumph not a cry of defeat (19:30). Τετέλεσται has been discovered on a Roman tax document indicating the taxes were "paid in full." The last word of Jesus from the cross was a proclamation that by His death He had paid the full price of redemption. The announcement of John the Baptist has been fulfilled. *Behold, the Lamb of God who takes away the sin of the world* (1:29). The reality of Jesus' death on the cross was proved by the soldiers who left His legs unbroken but pierced His side instead, and by Joseph of Arimathea and Nicodemus who prepared His body for burial (19:38-42).

The resurrection of the Son: proof of His deity (20:1-10). The empty tomb was proof that Jesus had risen from the dead. Mary Magdalene arrived early on Sunday morning and discovered that the tomb was standing open. She immediately summoned Peter and John (the disciple whom Jesus loved) (20:1-3). John was first to arrive at the tomb but Peter was the first to enter the tomb and to see the empty linen wrappings (20:4-7). Jesus told the disciples that He would rise again on the third day (2:19-22) but they did not understand or believe until they saw the empty tomb (20:8-10).

The appearances of the Son: proof that He lives (20:11-21:23). Jesus appeared to the disciples over a period of time and in a variety of settings as proof that He was alive. His first appearance was to Mary Magdalene at the tomb (20:11-18). Jesus' resurrection body was so real that she could "cling to Him." Jesus appeared to the disciples that Sunday evening as they gathered behind locked doors (20:19). Walls were not an impediment to

His resurrection body. Jesus imbued them with the Holy Spirit until they received the full-orbed ministry of the Spirit at Pentecost. The Father has given "all things into the Son's hands" (3:35; 13:3) and has given Him *authority over all flesh* that *He may give them eternal life* (17:2). The death of Christ, the Lamb of God, on the cross is the only basis for receiving forgiveness and eternal life. The apostles will be proclaiming Jesus' words with the result that others will believe and their sins will be forgiven (20:20-23). Thomas was not among the disciples that first Sunday evening and earned the nickname, "doubting Thomas," because he doubted their reports about Jesus' resurrection (20:24-26). That changed eight days later when Jesus appeared in the same locked room. Thomas must have been shocked when Jesus quoted Thomas's own words and offered him the tangible proof he required (20:27). Thomas believed, but Jesus declared those blessed who believed the word of the apostles without the physical proof that Thomas had received (20:29).

The purpose statement of John's Gospel (20:30-31). The confession of Thomas is a fitting place for John to introduce the thesis of his Gospel. He set out to prove that Jesus is the Son of God and that believing in Him is the only way to the Father. He selected only seven of the many miracles Jesus performed and only a small portion of the many words Jesus spoke. However, John has presented irrefutable proof that Jesus is the Son of God and has given ample reason for the reader to believe. The words and works of Jesus convinced the disciples that He was the Son of God. As one of the eyewitnesses, John has written this Gospel so that all who read it may believe and receive eternal life. *Therefore many other signs Jesus also performed in the presence of the disciples, which are not written in this book; but these have been written so that you may believe that Jesus is the Christ, the Son of God; and that believing you may have life in His name* (20:30-31).

The Son's final appearances in Galilee (21:1-23). The disciples need no further proof that Jesus is alive but they do need a reminder that Jesus has commissioned them to represent Him in the harvest fields (4:34-38). The Father has sent Jesus into the world and He is now sending the disciples into the world to continue His work (17:18-21). They abandoned Jesus in the night of His trial and might wonder if their commission remained valid. Jesus assured them that it did. They received a powerful lesson when their effort at fishing proved futile until Jesus appeared (21:1-8). It reminded them that they, the branches, cannot bear fruit apart from Him as the vine (15:1-8). Peter denied Jesus three times before a charcoal fire (18:18-27) and standing again before a charcoal fire he affirmed his love for Christ three times and was commissioned to *Shepherd My sheep* (21:9-17). Peter was to follow Christ though a cross also awaited him (21:18-19). John has written as a reliable eyewitness and He or another writer concludes, *Therefore many other signs Jesus also performed in the presence of the disciples, which are not written in this book; but these have been written so that you may believe that Jesus is the Christ, the Son of God; and that believing you may have life in His name* (21:24-25).

Outline

I.	Prologue: Incarnation of the Son of God as Man	1:1-18
	A. The essence of the Son of God as the Word	1:1-5
	1. His deity: co-existence with the Father	1:1-2
	2. The Son's preincarnate work in creation	1:3
	3. The Son's preemninence as life and light	1:4-5
	B. The appearance of the Son to the world	1:6-13
	1. John's witness that He is the true Light	1:6-9
	2. The Son is not received by His own	1:10-11
	3. Those that believe become children of God	1:12-13
	C. The exposition of the Son as the Word	1:14-18
	1. The incarnation: the Word became flesh	1:14-15
	2. Grace and truth are incarnated in the Son	1:16-18
II.	Presentation to Individuals Leads to Believing	1:19-4:54
	A. The testimony of John the Baptist	1:19-34
	1. The testimony of John about himself	1:19-28
	2. The testimony of John about Jesus	1:29-34
	B. The testimony of the first disciples	1:35-51
	C. The presentation of the Son as Creator: **1st sign**	2:1-11
	1. The sign: the Son turns water into wine	2:1-10
	2. The effect: the disciples believe	2:11
	D. The presentation of the Son to individuals	2:12-4:54
	1. Presentation in Jerusalem	2:12-3:21
	a. The Son cleanses the temple	2:12-16
	b. Effect: "Jews" reject, but many believe	2:17-25
	c. **1st discourse**: Nicodemus, Son is Savior	3:1-21
	2. Presentation in Judea	3:22-36
	a. Witness of John the Baptist	3:22-30
	b. Explanation by the author, John	3:31-36
	3. Presentation in Samaria	4:1-42
	a. **2nd discourse**: woman, "water of life"	4:1-26
	b. Explanation to the disciples	4:27-38

    c. Effect: many Samaritans believe — 4:39-42
   4. Presentation in Galilee — 4:43-54
     a. **2ⁿᵈ sign**: healing a nobleman's son — 4:43-52
     b. Effect: nobleman and his family believe — 4:53-54

III. Presentation to Multitudes Leads to Opposition — 5:1-12:50
 A. Opposition in Jerusalem at "a feast" — 5:1-47
   1. **3ʳᵈ sign**: healing the invalid man — 5:1-15
   2. Effect: persecution by the Jews — 5:16-18
   3. **3ʳᵈ discourse**: claims equality with God — 5:19-30
       The fivefold authenticating witness — 5:31-47
     a. The witness of the Son Himself — 5:31
     b. The witness of John the Baptist — 5:32-35
     c. The witness of the Son's works — 5:36
     d. The witness of the Father Himself — 5:37-38
     e. The witness of the Scriptures (Moses) — 5:39-47
 B. Opposition in Galilee "near the Passover" — 6:1-71
   1. **4ᵗʰ sign**: feeding the 5,000 men — 6:1-14
   2. **5ᵗʰ sign**: walking on the water — 6:15-21
   3. **4ᵗʰ discourse**: Jesus is the bread of life — 6:22-59
   4. Effect: many turn back; some believe — 6:60-71
 C. Opposition in Jerusalem at the Feast of Booths — 7:1-10:21
   1. In Galilee: <u>before</u> the Feast — 7:1-9
   2. In Jerusalem secretly: <u>before</u> the Feast — 7:10-13
   3. In Jerusalem openly: <u>during</u> the Feast — 7:14-36
     a. Claims His authority is from the Father — 7:14-30
     b. Effect: many believe, crowd is puzzled — 7:31-36
   4. In Jerusalem <u>on the last day</u> of the Feast — 7:37-53
     a. The Son gives the Spirit, living water — 7:37-39
     b. Effect: some believe, leaders do not — 7:40-53
   5. In Jerusalem <u>after</u> the Feast of Tabernacles — 8:1-10:21
     a. The woman caught in adultery — 8:1-11
     b. **5ᵗʰ discourse**: the "light of the world" — 8:12-58
     c. Effect: Jews seek to stone Him — 8:59
     d. **6ᵗʰ sign**: healing a man born blind — 9:1-34
     e. Effect: man believes, Pharisees do not — 9:35-41
     f. **6ᵗʰ discourse**: "the Good Shepherd" — 10:1-18
     g. Effect: the Jews are divided — 10:19-21
 D. Opposition at the Feast of Dedication — 10:22-42
   1. Jesus openly declares His Sonship — 10:22-30
   2. Effect: adversaries try to stone Him — 10:31-42

E. Opposition to the Son at Bethany	11:1-57
1. **7th sign**: raising Lazarus from death to life	11:1-44
2. Effect: unbelief, Sanhedrin plots to kill Him	11:45-57
F. Opposition to the Son in Jerusalem	12:12-50
1. Mary anoints Jesus, anticipating His death	12:1-8
2. Sanhedrin plans to kill Lazarus and the Son	12:9-11
3. The Son enters Jerusalem as prophesied	12:12-19
4. The Son predicts, prepares for His death	12:20-36
5. Jews confirm their unbelief as prophesied	12:37-50
IV. Preparation of the Disciples for His Departure	13:1-17:26
A. Instruction of the disciples in the Upper Room	13:1-14:31
1. Lesson on servanthood: washing their feet	13:1-17
2. Predicting His betrayal by Judas	13:18-30
3. **7th discourse**: in the Upper Room	13:31-14:31
a. Announcing His death, return to glory	13:31-33
b. A new commandment: love one another	13:34-38
b. Promise of a home with Him in heaven	14:1-8
c. The call for the disciples to believe	14:9-15
d. Promise of the advent of the Holy Spirit	14:16-31
B. Instruction regarding the disciples' future	15:1-16:33
1. Their future relationship with the Son	15:1-17
2. Their future relationship to the world	15:18-16:4
3. Their relationship with the Holy Spirit	15:26-16:15
4. His coming departure from them	16:16-28
5. Effect: disciples understand and believe	16:29-33
C. Prayer of intercession for the disciples	17:1-26
1. Prayer of commitment to the Father	17:1-5
2. Prayer for the protection of the disciples	17:6-19
3. Prayer for future believers	17:20-26
V. Passion of the Son of God; His death, resurrection	18:1-21:24
A. The final rejection of the Son by the officials	18:1-19:16
1. The arrest of the Son of God	18:1-11
2. The trials of the Son of God	18:12-19:16
a. First Jewish trial before Annas	18:12-23
Peter's 1st denial	
b. Second Jewish trial,	18:24-27
Peter's 2nd and 3rd denials	
c. First Roman trial before Pilate	18:28-38
d. Second Roman trial before Pilate	18:39-19:16

B. The crucifixion of the Son of God	19:17-37
1. The crucifixion of "the King of the Jews"	19:17-22
2. The abuse by the Roman soldiers	19:23-24
3. The care of the Son for His birth mother	19:25-27
4. The Son dies; His work is accomplished!	19:28-37
C. The burial of the Son of God: proof of His death	19:38-42
D. The resurrection of the Son: proof of His deity	20:1-10
1. The evidence of the empty tomb	20:1-8
2. The effect: the disciples believed	20:9-10
E. The appearances of the Son: proof He lives	20:11-21:23
1. Appearing to Mary Magdalene	20:11-18
2. Appearing to the disciples	20:19-29
3. The author's purpose statement	20:30-31
4. Appearing to the disciples in Galilee	21:1-14
5. The Son reinstates Peter to service	21:15-23
F. John's concluding witness to the Son of God	21:24-25

Bibliography

Blomberg, Craig. *The Historical Reliability of John's Gospel*. Downers Grove, IL: InterVarsity Press, 2002.

Blum, Edwin A. "John." In *The Bible Knowledge Commentary: New Testament*. Edited by John F. Walvoord and Roy B. Zuck. Wheaton, IL: Victor Books, 1983; reprint, Colorado Springs, CO: Cook, 1996.

Carson, D. A., Douglas J. Moo, and Leon Morris. *An Introduction to the New Testament*. Grand Rapids: Zondervan Publishing House, 1991.

Edersheim, Alfred. *The Life and Times of Jesus the Messiah*. 2 vols. Grand Rapids: Wm. B. Eerdmans Publishing Co., 1959.

Green, Joel B., and Scot McKnight, Eds. *Dictionary of Jesus and the Gospels*. Downers Grove, IL: InterVarsity Press, 1992.

Guthrie, Donald. *New Testament Introduction*. Downers Grove, IL: InterVarsity Press, 1990.

Hiebert, D. Edmond. *An Introduction to the New Testament*. Vol. 1. Chicago: Moody Press, 1975.

Kostenberger, Andreas J. *John*. Baker Exegetical Commentary on the New Testament. Grand Rapids: Baker Academic, 2004.

Kruse, Colin. *John*. Tyndale New Testament Commentaries. Grand Rapids: Wm. B. Eerdmans Publishing Co., 2004.

Laney, J. Carl. *John*. Moody Gospel Commentary. Chicago: Moody Press, 1992.

Morris, Leon. *The Gospel According to Matthew*. New International Commentary on the New Testament. Rev. ed. Grand Rapids: Wm. B. Eerdmans Publishing Co., 1995.

Mounce, Robert H. "John." In *The Expositor's Bible Commentary*. Rev. Ed. Vol. 10. Grand Rapids: Zondervan Publishing House, 2007.

Scroggie, W. Graham. *A Guide to the Gospels*. London: Pickering & Inglis Ltd., 1962.

Tenney, Merrill C. *John: The Gospel of Belief*. Grand Rapids: Wm. B. Eerdmans Publishing Co., 1948.

Westcott, Brooke Foss. *The Gospel According to St. John*. Grand Rapids: Wm. B. Eerdmans Publishing Co., 1962.

Acts: The Ongoing Witness of Jesus Christ

Key verse: 1:8, *but you will receive power when the Holy Spirit has come upon you; and you shall be my witnesses…*

Key words: Jesus/Lord, Resurrection, Holy Spirit, Witnesses, Apostles, Preached, Church, Increased

Holy Spirit = Power = Witness

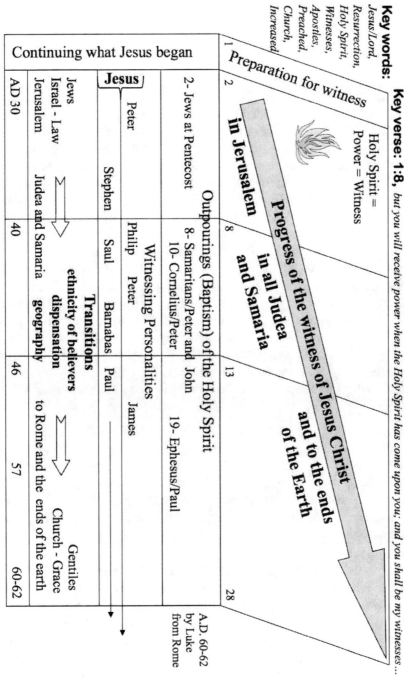

Continuing what Jesus began					
1	2	8	13	28	
Preparation for witness					
	2- Jews at Pentecost	Outpourings (Baptism) of the Holy Spirit 8- Samaritans/Peter and John 10- Cornelius/Peter	Witnessing Personalities 19- Ephesus/Paul		A.D. 60-62 by Luke from Rome
	in Jerusalem	in all Judea and Samaria		and to the ends of the Earth	
Jesus	Peter	Stephen	Philip	Peter	Barnabas	Paul	James	
				Transitions ethnicity of believers dispensation geography		
	Jews Israel - Law Jerusalem	⇒		Gentiles Church - Grace to Rome and the ends of the earth	
AD 30	40		46	57	60-62

Progress of the witness of Jesus Christ

121

ACTS

"Between the ministry of the Lord Jesus Christ and the church as it emerged into the full current of history there is a tremendous gap. How did it happen that the followers of Jesus, who were obscure provincial Galileans and Judeans, became world figures? What changed the timidity that drove these men to denial and flight at the crucifixion into a boldness that made them stalwart apologists for the new faith? How did preachers who were confessedly "unlearned and ignorant men"(Acts 4:13) make such an impact on the world that they created an entirely new culture that reshaped the face of all Western civilization? What was the origin of the theological truths contained in the New Testament and preached by the early missionaries? How is the teaching of the Epistles related to the teaching of the Gospels? How did it happen that a movement that began among Jews, that centered in a Jewish Messiah, and that was founded on the Jewish Scriptures became a religion espoused largely by Gentiles, as it is today? These and similar questions are answered by the book of Acts, which is the only existing link between the ministry and teaching of Christ and the Christianity that appears full-blown in the epistles of Paul and of the other New Testament writers" (Tenney, *New Testament Survey*, *231*).

"Acts is the church's standard textbook on the first three decades of its history and its ageless global task of evangelization. The Bible student of this generation has the unique privilege of viewing the church from two opposite vantage points— that of the church's beginnings, as narrated in Acts, and that of its end times, as recorded by the daily newspaper. Any alert Christian cannot but be concerned over the comparisons he is compelled to make" (Jensen, *Acts: An Inductive Study*, 7).

Acts: The Hinge of New Testament History

The Book of Acts is the indispensable link between the Gospels and the Epistles, between the historical foundation of Christianity and its doctrinal superstructure. "The importance of this book cannot be exaggerated. ... It serves admirably as a link between the records of Jesus and the apostolic correspondence. In many ways the Epistles are not fully intelligible until they are read against the background of the book of Acts" (Guthrie, *New Testament Introduction*, 351). Acts is the only historical book of the New Testament and the only record we have of the progress of the gospel proclamation that followed the death, burial, and resurrection of Jesus Christ. Acts is our only record of the birth of the Christian church and its expansion across the entire Mediterranean region. It is our only record of the conversion and career of the apostle Paul and his church-planting missions.

Acts: A Book of Transitions

The Gospels, which are set in the small territory of Judah and the presence of a few Roman officials, are our only contact with the Gentile world. These four books record the life, death, and resurrection of Jesus Christ in an almost exclusively Jewish context. In the Epistles we are in Mediterranean cities, in a predominantly Gentile world, in churches not synagogues, and with Paul and other characters we do not meet in the Gospels. The book of Acts records how these and many other transitions came about.

Jesus Christ. Acts takes us from the incarnate and visible Jesus to the ascended Christ who is invisible yet present in the lives and in the proclamation of the disciples. Before Jesus dwelt with the disciples; now He dwells within them (Luke 24:45-49; Acts 1:1-11; 2:22-36; 3:11-26; 4:8-12; 23:11; 1 Corinthians 12:12-27; Galatians 2:20).

Religious. The book of Acts records the transition from Judaism to Christianity, from the temple and the synagogue to the marketplace and the church. The church is mentioned only three times in Matthew and nowhere else in the Gospels. In the Gospels the church is undefined and still in the future (Matthew 16:18). In the Epistles the church occupies center stage (Luke 20:9-19; Acts 4:1-22; 7:51-53; 28:23-31; Ephesians 3:8-11; 1 Thessalonians 1:1).

Leadership. In Acts we transition from Jesus as the source of the preaching to Jesus as the subject of the preaching and from Jesus exercising authority over the apostles to the apostles exercising authority as His representatives (Matthew 11:1-6; 28:16-20; John 13:3; 16:1-16; Acts 1:1-8; 15:1-29; 1 Corinthians 5:3-5; 2 Corinthians 10:8).

National. Attention shifts from Israel to the nations in Acts. The call to repentance and the offer of salvation that was first delivered to Israel now goes global (Matthew 10:5-10; 15:21-28; Luke 13:22-30; Acts 1:8; 9:15-16; 10:1-11, 18; 14:27; 22:21; 28:28). God is not abandoning Israel but He is extending the offer of salvation to all peoples, languages, and nations (17:29-31; Romans 11:1-32; Revelation 7:9).

Geography. In the Gospels all action gravitates toward Jerusalem but in Acts the activity radiates out from Jerusalem. Acts is structured around the geographical progression of the witness from Jerusalem to the remotest part of the earth (1:8). In the Gospels Rome impacts Jerusalem, but in Acts Jerusalem impacts Rome (Luke 13:34-35; 19:41-44; 21:24; Acts 1:8; 8:1-8, 26; 10:19-22; 13:1-5; 23:11; 28:28-31).

Dispensation. Acts moves the focus from Israel's kingdom and the Law to the universal church and grace. The kingdom is mentioned 128 times in the four Gospels but only eight times in Acts and 20 times in all the Epistles. (Matthew 4:23; 12:28; 21:42-46; Luke 17:20-25; Acts 1:6-8; 3:17-26; 15:1-29; 28:23-31). Jesus' disciples live under the Law in the Gospels and in the Epistles they are set free from the Law (Romans 7:1-6; 8:1-4; Galatians 3:14, 21-25; Ephesians 3:1-13).

Personalities. The band of witnesses grows from twelve to 120, then to 3,000, and finally beyond numbering (Acts 1:15; 2:41; 4:4; 6:1; Revelation 5:9). Witnessing personalities shift from Jesus to Peter to Paul (Matthew 16:15-20; Luke 22:31, 32; John 21:1-3, 15-21; Acts 1:15; 2:11; 5:12-16; 13:1-3; 15:7, 12).

Holy Spirit. The role of the Holy Spirit moves from promise to presence and from occasional intervention to permanent indwelling and directing. Where Jesus once taught and directed the activity of the disciples, now the Holy Spirit guides their movement and gives them power in their ministry (John 14:16-17; 16:5-16; Luke 24:45-49; Acts 1:8; 2:1-4; 5:32; 13:2, 52; 16:6-7).

> "The first Christian generation clearly formed a transitional period from the age of law to the era of the gospel. No one woke up the day after Pentecost to hear a Jerusalem town crier announcing the end of the old covenant and the inauguration of the new. The differences that Jesus made through his life, death, and resurrection only gradually dawned on his followers. Parallel to this development was the transformation of Jesus' first group of disciples from an exclusively Jewish sect centered in Jerusalem to one that a generation later had become a dominantly Gentile movement scattered throughout the Roman Empire" (Blomberg, *From Pentecost to Patmos*, 10).

Title

The original manuscript of Acts apparently did not have a title. Acts was clearly intended to be a companion volume to the third Gospel (Luke 1:1-4; Acts 1:1), and so as part of an ongoing record it needed no separate title. However, no doubt or confusion exists about the commonly used title "Acts." "Without exception it is designated *Acts (Praxies)*, or some expansion thereof in all Greek manuscripts, the versions, and the Church Fathers. The Greek manuscripts have the title in various forms, 'Acts' or 'The Acts,' 'Acts of Apostles' or 'Acts of the Apostles,' and even 'Acts of the Holy Apostles'" (Hiebert, *An Introduction to the New Testament*, 1:247).

"The Acts of..." was a common designation in the Hellenistic age for a literary work describing outstanding individuals. Fitzmyer notes, "The ancient title **Praxeis** was a term designating a specific Greek literary form, a narrative account of the heroic deeds of famous historical or mythological figures" (*The Acts of the Apostles*, 47). The book could most appropriately be called "The Acts of The Holy Spirit" because the Holy Spirit is the source of the power and the central force in the extension of the witness. Further, not all the acts or all the apostles are recorded in Acts. In view of this fact it is entirely appropriate to speak of this book simply as "The Acts" or more fully as "The Acts of the Apostles."

Author

Internal and external evidence alike clearly point to Paul's companion, the physician Luke, as the author of the third Gospel and Acts. This view was universally held by the church from the second century onward, but has been vigorously challenged by some critical scholars in recent times. Explanations put forward have failed to discredit the internal and external evidence that supports the traditional view. Thorough research by scholars has affirmed the credibility of the traditional Lukan authorship of both Luke and Acts. "It would be difficult to find a book in the whole range of ancient literature concerning which a stronger case can be made in support of a traditional authorship" (Blaiklock, *The Acts of the Apostles*, 14). "Today, the virtual consensus of critical opinion is that the third gospel and Acts come from the same hand and were intended to form a single work on the beginnings of Christianity. The common modern designation 'the Luke-Acts narrative' recognized this unity of plan and purpose for the third gospel and the Acts of the Apostles" (Hiebert, *An Introduction to the New Testament*, 1:119). There is substantial internal and external evidence to support the traditional view that Luke, Paul's coworker and physician, authored both the third Gospel and Acts.

External Evidence. Irenaeus explicitly named Luke as the author of both the third Gospel and the book of Acts in his book *Against Heresies* (A.D. 185). He explained in detail the sections of Acts where the author uses the first person plural "we" and identified Luke as the author and traveling companion of Paul. Luke is also mentioned as the author in the *anti-Marcionite prologue* to Luke (c. A.D. 150-180) and in a fragment of the *Muratorian Cannon* (c. A.D. 160-200). Clement of Alexandria quoted the book of Acts in his *Stomatan* (A.D. 150-215) and attributed its writing to Luke. Later church leaders such as Tertullian, Origen, Eusebius, and Jerome also affirmed Lukan authorship (Polhill, *Acts,* 22-23).

Internal Evidence. Multiple lines of evidence support the common authorship of Luke and Acts. Both Acts and Luke share a common opening statement. The author speaks in the first person as a historian (Luke actually wrote 27 percent of the New Testament!). The Theophilus addressed in the opening words of Acts is undoubtedly the same as the Theophilus to whom the Gospel of Luke is dedicated. The author refers to an earlier volume and introduces Acts as a second companion volume (1:1). Acts is similar in language, style, and structure to Luke. The end of Luke dovetails perfectly with the beginning of Acts. Together they form a seamless narrative. Acts begins where Luke ends with the postresurrection witness mandate (Luke 24:48-49; Acts 1:4-8). Each is the length of a papyrus scroll. This symmetry is not accidental. Peculiarities shared by Luke and Acts point to unity of authorship. These include (1) The appearance of Jesus before Herod Antipas (Luke 23:8-12; Acts 4:27), (2) The post-resurrection appearance of Jesus in Jerusalem (Luke 24:49; Acts 1:4), (3) The post-resurrection promise of the Holy Spirit's coming (Luke 24:49; Acts 1:8), and (4) Common features such as interest in Gentiles, Jesus interest in women, the worldwide focus of witness, and the apologetic emphasis.

The author was Luke, the companion of Paul. The "we" sections found in the Pauline section of Acts point to an eyewitness and coincide with Luke's companionship (Acts 16:8-17; 20:5-21:18; 27:1-28:16). The prologues of both Luke and Acts indicate that the author was a careful researcher and historian for the earlier portions and an eyewitness of later events, which he recorded. The objective and detailed descriptions are those of an eyewitness. The epistles corroborate Luke's presence and relationship to Paul as his "beloved physician" (Colossians 4:14; Philemon 24; 2 Timothy 4:11). Luke is not named in the "we" narratives when other companions of Paul are listed (Silas, Timothy, Tychicus, etc.). The authorship of Acts is addressed very effectively in the following works: F. F. Bruce, *The Acts of the Apostles*, 2-9; D. A. Carson, Douglas J. Moo, and Leon Morris, *An Introduction to the New Testament*, 111-21, 181-94; Donald Guthrie, *New Testament Introduction*, 113-25, 383-98; and D. Edmond Hiebert, *An Introduction to the New Testament*, 1:114-30, and 1:248-54.

Historicity

Given its uniqueness as a record of the primitive church and the abundance of historical references, it is not surprising that the historicity of Acts has been scrutinized and challenged. However, an abundance of archaeological and historical research has confirmed rather than discredited the historicity of Acts. Most notably, archaeologist and historian Sir William Ramsey set out to discredit its historicity, but he ended up being its most ardent supporter (*St. Paul the Traveler and Roman Citizen*, 19). Ramsey has demonstrated that Luke was a remarkably accurate historian. Guthrie concludes, "The Era has now passed when the historicity of Acts can with any plausibility be wholly discredited" (*New Testament Introduction*, 371).

Luke's claim to have conducted personal interviews and carefully examined sources of information is unique among New Testament writers and is substantiated by a careful analysis of his writings. Students of the synoptic Gospels agree that Luke reports the sayings and speeches of others faithfully (Bruce, *The Acts of the Apostles*, 18). Luke follows the standards of the classical historians such as Thucydides. "He relates the story of Christianity to imperial history as no other NT writer does" (Bruce, *The Acts of the Apostles*, 15). Luke shows detailed knowledge of the rights and privileges of Roman citizens and of Roman legal procedures. The voyage and shipwreck narrative is authentic and a classic description of both regional weather and sailing vessels.

Date

Attempts have been made to date the book late in the first century and even well into the second century based on the rejection of the Lukan authorship and the eyewitness nature of Acts. The identity of the author of Acts strongly influences the decision regarding the date of its writing. Based on the conclusion that Luke is the author of Acts and drawing on historical evidence within the book, a date of A.D. 60-62 is probable. (Timelines of events in Acts are included on pages 19 and 20.) Hiebert notes, "there is no firm early tradition to offer guidance concerning the dating of Acts" (*An Introduction to the New Testament,* 1:259). If external authority for the date is lacking, there is ample internal and historical information. Bruce concludes, "There is, indeed, adequate evidence for the view that Luke gathered or set in order much of the material for both parts of his history in Palestine between 57 and 59, that other material was added in Rome, the complete Gospel (= Book I) sent to Theophilus c. A.D. 61, and Acts (= Book II) not very long afterwards" (*The Acts of the Apostles,* 14).

Evidence supports an early date of A.D. 61. (1) The earliest possible date for the writing is Paul's two-year imprisonment in Rome and that can be established as A.D. 60-62. (2) The abrupt ending of the book argues strongly for a date at or shortly after Paul's imprisonment in Rome. "A significant number of scholars have thought that the book of Acts furnishes one piece of evidence that determines a relative firm and exact date for the book: its abrupt ending. ... The explanation of the ending of Acts that is most popular today is that Paul's arrival in Rome and his unhindered preaching of the gospel in the capital of the Empire bring the book to its intended conclusion" (Carson, Moo, and Morris, *An Introduction to the New Testament,* 192-93). (3) The tolerant attitude of Roman officials toward Christianity and absence of reference to the Neronian persecution of 64-65 suggest an early date. (4) Silence about the fall of Jerusalem in A.D. 70 would be strange given Luke's focus on Jerusalem. That argues for a date prior to 70. (5) Acts contains no premonition of Paul's death, which apparently occurred under Nero (A.D. 65-68). (6) Luke shows little or no acquaintance with Paul's epistles, which suggests that Acts was published before Paul's letters were collected into a unified corpus. (7) The primitive character of the subject matter and theological language are those prevalent in the earliest period of church history. The codifying of doctrine so evident in the second century is clearly lacking in Acts. (8) Issues prominent in the book were of urgent interest in the church before the fall of Jerusalem and the dispersion of the Jews, but they lost their importance soon afterward. (9) There is no reference to Paul's intended visit to Spain (Romans 15:24) which church tradition indicates was accomplished. The Pastoral Epistles relate travels and ministry that cannot be accommodated within the record of Acts. It is best explained by the release of Paul from his first Roman imprisonment, a period of ministry in both east and west and a second imprisonment culminating in Paul's execution at Rome. Acts was most likely written before that ministry and Paul's second imprisonment (Guthrie, *New Testament Introduction,* 356-59). We may safely conclude, "The evidence for an early date seems more convincing than that for a later time. And while it comes short of complete proof, it should be accepted" (Carson, Moo, and Morris, *An Introduction to the New Testament,* 117).

Audience and purpose

Acts, like the Gospel of Luke, is addressed to an individual named Theophilus, "dear to God," or "lover of God." Theophilus was most likely an individual and perhaps even a patron who had supported Luke in his ministry with Paul (Carson, *An Introduction to the New Testament,* 195). Beginning with Origen it was common to treat Theophilus as symbolic of all who were "lovers of God." "It is almost certain that Luke had a broader audience than one individual in mind. Just who made up Luke's intended audience can be determined only after we have identified his purpose in writing" (Carson, *An Introduction to the New Testament,* 195).

The primary purpose for Acts is apparently the same as that stated in the preface to Luke's Gospel, *so that you may know the certainty of the things you have been taught* (Luke 1:4). Luke's primary purpose in writing was historical. He sought to provide a systematic, historically reliable record of the birth and spread of Christianity from its roots in the birth of Jesus, its foundation and source, to its spread to Rome through the witness of the apostles and Paul. The following aims are joined together to achieve Luke's central purpose to provide a reliable history for the origin and spread of the Christian faith. (1) Document the spread of Christianity from the crucifixion of Christ in Jerusalem to its arrival in Rome, the center of world government. (2) Explain the centrality and continuity of the work of Jesus Christ within the church. Acts is all about the ongoing witness of Jesus Christ (Acts 1:1, 8). (3) Demonstrate the unifying role of the Holy Spirit in the extension of the church following Christ's resurrection (Bruce, *The Acts of the Apostles,* 30). (4) Explain the divine origin of the church and the Christian faith as evidenced by its extension in the face of determined opposition. (5) Show the supernatural nature of the Christian faith as evidenced by the continued miracles under the apostles. (6) Vindicate the mission and methods of the church before its Jewish opponents and document the rejection of Christianity by the leaders of Judaism. (7) Explain the origin and nature of the church and its pervasive growth for the benefit of questioning Roman authorities (24:10-16; 26:1-3). (8) Provide an apologetic for the developing Gentile nature of the church, the shift of its focus from Jerusalem, and its transition from its roots in Judaism to a universal faith. (9) Provide an apologetic for Paul by authenticating his apostleship and documenting his contribution to the Christian faith.

Theme and Organizing Principle of Acts

The central idea of Acts is the continued work and witness of Jesus Christ through the apostles (1:8). The Holy Spirit, through Luke, skillfully weaves together multiple strands of ideas, actions, and people to form this single cord. Acts exhibits remarkable unity and continuity of thought while at the same time developing these parallel ideas.

The **centrality of Jesus Christ** as both the source and the subject of the witness is carefully maintained throughout the book (1:1). Jesus is the suffering Servant (3:13, 26; 4:27, 30) and also the risen Lord (2:32-36). He is the Messiah promised in the Old Testament (3:17-26). He is also the triumphant One who will return to judge (17:31).

The **presence and power of the Holy Spirit** explains the supernatural nature of the witness (1:8; 2:4; 4:31). Advances into new areas are prompted by the Spirit and are confirmed by the outpouring of the Holy Spirit (8:17; 10:44; 11:15; 13:2; 16:6-8).

The **extension of the church** from Jew to Gentile and from Jerusalem to Rome is mapped out by the Holy Spirit and yet marked by **apostolic witness**. Peter is the principal spokesman in the first half (chaps. 1-12) but others are significantly involved; Philip takes the gospel to the Samaritans (chap. 8), and James presides over the Jerusalem council (chap. 15). Attention shifts later to Paul as *one abnormally born* (Acts 9:15-16; 1 Corinthians 15:8). Though the attention shifts from Peter to Paul, both men appear together before the Jerusalem council to support the inclusion of Gentiles in God's redemptive plan (Acts 15).

Opposition arises immediately from the officials of Judaism (Acts 3) and persists through to Paul's imprisonment at Rome. The supernatural growth and triumph of the gospel occurs against the background of determined opposition, but this persecution is actually used by the Spirit of God to further the witness (8:2-4).

Geographical progression provides the structural framework of Acts. The progress of the witness mandated at the outset by the risen Christ (1:8) is traced throughout the narrative. The outline of the book of Acts follows this geographical progression from Jerusalem, to Judea and Samaria, and to the ends of the earth.

Progress reports occur frequently throughout Acts, keeping both the central idea and the success of the witness in clear focus (2:42-47; 4:32-37; 6:7; 9:31; 12:24-25; 16:4-6; 19:17-20; 28:25b-29).

Speeches are an integral part of the Acts narrative. Fernando notes, "Acts has thirty-two speeches (excluding short statements), which make up 25 percent of the narrative" (*Acts,* 28). While only a digest of these speeches, Luke's record is accurate and true to the original message.

Key verse and organizing principle: Acts 1:8
But you will receive power when the Holy Spirit has come upon you; and you shall be My witnesses both in Jerusalem, and in all Judea and Samaria, and even to the remotest part of the earth.

The word "witness" and the preaching, teaching, miracles, and other works effecting that witness occur throughout Acts as the unifying principle. Predicted in the Old Testament and commissioned by Christ, the witness began in Jerusalem (chaps. 1-7), extended throughout Judea and Samaria (chaps. 8-12), and arrived at Rome on its way to the remotest part of the earth (chaps. 13-28). The abrupt ending of Acts is intentional and meaningful. The witness of Jesus Christ did not end with the Gospels nor does it end with Acts. Luke clearly intended for his readers to understand that the witness of Jesus Christ would continue after Paul and would reach beyond Rome.

Message

Luke uses the mandate given by Christ in Acts 1:8 as the outline for the narrative. After recording the necessary preparation for the witness: the Holy Spirit is to be given at Pentecost (1:1-26), Luke documents the geographical progress of the witness (chaps, 2-28), first in Jerusalem (chaps. 2-7), then in Judea and Samaria (chaps. 8-12), and finally to the ends of the earth (chaps. 13-28). But Rome is not the end of the earth! The book of Acts does not have a formal ending because the witness of Jesus Christ is to continue until He returns in the same way as He has been taken up into heaven (1:11). The supernatural spread of the witness from Jerusalem to the ends of the earth is marked by a series of progress reports that are logically and strategically placed in Acts. The following attempt to trace Luke's argument is built around the geographical outline given in Acts 1:8 and eight progress reports incorporated in Luke's historical narrative. (Blomberg lists six such "summary statements" in *From Pentecost to Patmos*, 18).

Preparation for the Witness (1:6-26)

Introduction: Luke's resumptive prologue (1:1-5). The Gospel of Luke and the book of Acts form a seamless narrative. Both contain a similar purpose statement. Both identify Theophilus as the intended recipient. Acts briefly summarizes the post-resurrection events recorded in Luke including Jesus' command to wait in Jerusalem and His promise of the Holy Spirit (1:1-5). In this preface Luke makes it clear that Acts is a continuation of the work and witness of Jesus Christ in action and word. That work and witness **commenced** at the incarnation (Luke 2:11), **climaxed** in the crucifixion and resurrection (24:26) and is now **continued** through the church (Acts 1:1).

Luke's Gospel closes rather abruptly. He records Christ's declaration of what will happen next, the message of repentance and forgiveness will be preached *to all nations, beginning at Jerusalem*, the disciples will be witnesses *of these things*, and they are to wait in Jerusalem to receive the power promised by the Father. Following the ascension of Christ the disciples return to Jerusalem as instructed to await the arrival of the Holy Spirit (Luke 24:45-53). Anticipating a second volume, Luke's Gospel does not explain "how" these events will play out, when the disciples will receive the power or how the message will proceed from Jerusalem to all nations. Acts 1:1 reminds us that the Gospel record is not the end but only the beginning of this ongoing work and witness of Jesus Christ. The gospel of repentance and forgiveness of sins will now be preached to all nations and it will begin in Jerusalem. Acts will trace the fulfillment of the promise and the mandate given to the disciples by the risen Christ in the Gospel of Luke.

Statement of the purpose and plan for Acts (1:6-11). The disciple's question reveals that they are still focused on Israel's anticipated messianic kingdom and unsure of what is in store for them. Jesus does not contradict their expectation that the kingdom promised to Israel is to be fulfilled, but He informs them that God the Father alone will determine when that promise to Israel will be fulfilled. Instead, Jesus refocuses their attention on His plan for them to be His witnesses on a global scale (1:8). He states that the Holy Spirit's coming on them to provide power makes clear His mandate that they will be His witnesses in an ever-expanding

132

circle of ministry. As Jesus ascends into heaven from the Mount of Olives, two angelic messengers remind the disciples that Jesus will one day return visibly in the same way He has departed from them (Zechariah 14:3-4).

Preparation of the disciples for witness (1:12-26). In obedience to Jesus' instructions, the disciples returned to Jerusalem to await the promised coming of the Holy Spirit (Luke 24:49). Peter appears as the spokesman of the disciples gathered in the upper room for prayer. Recognizing the prophetic significance of Judas' betrayal and suicide, Peter leads the group in the election of a replacement for Judas (1:15-26) and Matthias is chosen. Luke significantly identifies the twelve as "apostles." They have been called apostles only once in each of the other three Gospels which use the term "disciples." It is Luke's way of highlighting their mission as witnesses or "sent ones." The stage is now set for the arrival of the Holy Spirit and the initiation of their witness.

The Witness in Jerusalem (2:1-7:60)
The witness begins at Pentecost (2:1-47). The arrival of the Holy Spirit at Pentecost marks the inception of the witnessing program and the birth of the church (this is the first of twenty-four references to the "church" in Acts). Luke has explained the source of the power and the strategy by which the witness will be extended to all nations (1:8). The disciples have waited at Jerusalem as instructed (1:12-26). The Holy Spirit now comes on them at Pentecost (2:1-13) with the result that after Peter's sermon many believe (2:14-41). These believers come from *every nation under heaven* (2:5-12). Luke now pauses to describe the vitality of the newly formed church (2:42-47). This **first progress report** (2:47) follows the coming of the Holy Spirit and signals both the birth of the church and the launch of the witness in Jerusalem just as Jesus had promised and mandated (1:8).

The witness prospers and persists amid opposition (chaps. 3-7). Peter and John lead the next phase of the witness in Jerusalem (3:1-4:31). Peter witnesses to a crowd drawn together by the miraculous healing of a crippled beggar (3:1-26). The effective appeal of the message concerning Jesus Christ is evidenced by the fact that five thousand men believed (4:4). Threatened by this, the Sanhedrin set out to block the witness (4:1-22). The attempt of official Judaism to stop the spread of the witness fails and results in rejoicing and intense prayer by the growing band of believers (4:23-30). These religious authorities are entrenched in Jerusalem and the power of the Holy Spirit is evident as this opposition is overcome. The stage is now being set for the expansion of the witness outside Jerusalem, and the opposition will play a key role in that next step.

The **second progress report** (4:31-35) demonstrates that opposition from outside the church cannot defeat the witness of Jesus Christ and reveals the unique quality of life within the community of believers. Luke uses this occasion to introduce Barnabas (4:36-37). Noted here for his generosity, Barnabas will later figure in the conversion of Paul (9:26-31), in the extension of the witness among Gentiles (11:19-30), and will partner with Paul in the third phase of the witness (13:1-14:28). Not all opposition comes from outside the church. The progress report also reveals Luke's transition to the next part of the narrative, the opposition to the witness that comes from within the church itself.

The pretense of generosity by Ananias and Sapphira (5:1-11) stands in stark contrast to the generous sharing by many believers of their personal property to alleviate the needs of fellow believers (4:32-35). Divine judgment in the form of physical death leads to purity within the church, to awe by all observers, to the further spread of the witness (5:12-16), and thus to the renewed opposition of the Sanhedrin (5:17-42).

Luke uses the literary method of interchange by moving between external and internal conditions to explain the spread of the witness. Shifting once again to outside opposition, the apostles are arrested, miraculously released and then rearrested by authorities in Jerusalem (5:17-32). Only the intervention of Gamaliel (5:33-39) spares the apostles from death. Flogging does not deter the witness as the apostles continue preaching Jesus as the Christ (5:40-42). Reverting once again to the internal conditions, Luke notes that growth of the witness brings with it the potential to divide the church along ethnic lines, pitting Hebraic against Hellenistic (Gentile) believers (6:1-6).

The **third progress report** (6:7) follows Luke's recording of the fact that not even deception and divisive problems within the church can thwart the progress of the witness (5:1-6:5). Like external opposition, the Holy Spirit overcomes internal corruption. A chord is struck that will be repeated often, *The Word of God kept on spreading.*

The martyrdom of Stephen (6:8-7:60) provides the literary bridge from the witness in Jerusalem (chaps. 2-6) to the witness in Judea and Samaria (chaps. 8-12). It also serves to introduce an ardent young antagonist to the witness, Saul, who is destined to become its leading voice (chaps. 13-28). The opposition to the witness comes from false witnesses who have been recruited by the Sanhedrin (6:8-15). They charge that Stephen speaks for Jesus and against the temple and the Law of Moses. Stephen's defense is a masterful review of Israel's persistent opposition to Moses and the prophets and climaxes with the charge that they have murdered the "Righteous One" whose coming Moses and the prophets had announced (7:1-53). The determined opposition of religious authorities based in Jerusalem results in the implementation of the second phase of the witness, namely, its expansion into the surrounding territories of Judea and Samaria.

The Witness in Judea and Samaria (chaps. 8-12)

Persecution scatters the Jerusalem church (8:1-4). Luke weaves together these two themes of external and internal obstacles into the explanation of how the witness spreads to Judea and Samaria. Steven, one of the seven men chosen to solve the internal problem, becomes the first martyr at the hands of the external opposition. His witness infuriates the religious authorities in Jerusalem who stone him to death (6:8-7:60). Luke introduces Saul (Paul) as a prominent instigator in this rising tide of persecution (8:1-3). The persecution that follows the martyrdom of Stephen scatters the church from Jerusalem (8:4) and signals the move of the witness out from Jerusalem. Persecution intended to defeat the witness is actually the catalyst used by the Spirit of God to initiate the planned extension of the witness to "all Judea and Samaria."

The witness of Philip in Samaria (8:5-40). The witness of Philip, another of the deacons chosen earlier (6:1-7), extends the witness to Samaritans (8:5-13) and to an Ethiopian (8:25-40). The outpouring of the Spirit at Samaria confirms that this step is in keeping with Christ's promise (1:8) and in harmony with the birth of the church at Jerusalem (8:14-17). Confirmation through Peter and John demonstrates the role of the apostles and the unity of the church as it embraces other races and cultures. This foreshadows the extension of the witness to Gentiles to be initiated later by Peter (10:1-11:18), championed by Paul (11:19-30), and confirmed by the Jerusalem council (15:1-35).

The conversion and witness of Saul, that is, Paul (chap. 9). Luke has introduced Saul as an antagonist to the witness and now records the conversion of Saul/Paul who later becomes the leading witness of Jesus Christ (9:1-30). Paul's conversion is so important to the extension of the

135

witness that Luke records Paul's conversion testimony three times (chaps. 9, 22, and 26). One event, the martyrdom of Stephen, ties this together with the witness in Jerusalem and signals the extension of the witness into two distinct areas, "Judea and Samaria," and "the ends of the earth (Gentiles)." The conversion of Saul, the chief instigator of the persecution, marks a turning point in the narrative and ushers in a new period of quiet and growth for the church. Luke now pauses and gives a **fourth progress report** (9:31) to mark the spread of the witness to Judea and Samaria.

The witness extends to Gentiles through Peter (10:1-11:18). Peter now opens the door of witness to the Gentiles though it faces initial resistance. The personal revelation of Jesus Christ to Saul reflects the centrality of Christ to the witness in Acts and also serves to predict the coming expansion of the witness to Gentiles (9:5-16). Paul is to be Christ's special ambassador to the Gentiles (9:15), but first the task of opening the door of salvation for the Gentiles falls to Peter (Matthew 16:19; Acts 11:15-18; 15:8). It is Christ Himself who initiates this extension of the witness to Gentiles in a vision given to Peter (9:32-10:48). Cornelius is a Gentile but a devout (God-seeking) man. His salvation and the confirming outpouring of the Holy Spirit mark the opening of the door to the Gentile witness. Luke is careful to note that it is the Lord Jesus Christ and the Holy Spirit who initiate this step and who select Peter as the human agent. That this represents a departure from the past is evident by the need for Peter to explain the event to the church at Jerusalem (11:1-17). The conclusion of the Jerusalem church underscores the unity of the church and the strategic nature of the event. *So then, God has even granted the Gentiles repentance unto life* (11:18).

The witness expands among Gentiles in Antioch (11:19-30). Luke uses the declaration by the Jerusalem church as a transition statement, uniting it with a look back at the martyrdom of Stephen (11:19) to turn the focus to the spread of the witness among the Gentiles under the leadership of Paul (11:19-30). Attention shifts from Caesarea, a seaport marking the outer boundary of Judea, to Antioch, a Gentile city outside the circle of Jewish culture, and from the witness of Peter to that of Paul. The establishment of a Gentile church at Antioch (11:19-26) is an expansion of the witness, not a break from the past as the Jerusalem church through Barnabas confirms. As earlier, Barnabas again is the link connecting the Jerusalem church and Paul in the expansion of the witness (9:26-30). Antioch will become the sending church as the witness advances from Judea and Samaria toward the ends of the earth.

The witness climaxes in Jerusalem amid persecution (chap. 12). This "shift of the center of gravity" to Antioch coincides with the intensified persecution of the church in Jerusalem (12:1-23). Herod's execution of James, the brother of John, and his attempt to execute Peter show how determined the opposition was to the witness. By contrast, the miraculous release of Peter from prison and the death of Herod by God's judgment validate the supernatural nature of the church. The door that appears to be closing in Jerusalem is about to open wide for the witness to extend *to the uttermost part of the earth*. Luke pauses to take inventory and provides his **fifth progress report**. *But the Word of God continued to increase and spread* (12:24).

Witness to the Uttermost Part of the Earth (chaps. 13-28)

The stage is now set for the next major expansion of the witness and for the fulfillment of Christ's calling in the life of Paul (9:15). The gospel has already extended to the Gentiles through Peter, and a Gentile-oriented church has been planted at Antioch with the approval of the Jerusalem church. The witness that pervaded Jerusalem (chaps.1-7) has now spread throughout Judea and Samaria (chaps. 8-12). The Holy Spirit has prepared the way for the next major expansion of the witness that will take it to the ends of the earth (chaps. 13-28). Paul's three church-planting missions to the Gentiles will provide the framework for this expansion. Luke's sixth progress report will not occur until the witness has pervaded all of Asia Minor and is poised to cross over to the European continent (16:5).

First mission of Paul and Barnabas to Gentiles (chaps. 13-14). A strategic shift is evident in this next expansion of the witness. While it is still the Holy Spirit who sets apart Barnabas and Saul to extend the witness to the ends of the earth (13:2), it is the predominantly Gentile church at Antioch that is given the responsibility to commission them as witnesses. The witness that was spread from Jerusalem to Judea and Samaria by persecution (8:1) is again persecuted (12:1) and is now launched by the Holy Spirit and prayer on a mission that will finally reach Rome on its way *to the uttermost part of the earth*. The church at Antioch now becomes the witnessing center and the sending church.

Paul and Barnabus witness first on the island of Cyprus and then in Pisidian Antioch (chap. 13). Luke uses this to introduce his readers to Paul's ministry strategy. (1) Paul witnesses first in the synagogue on the Sabbath where he finds those with prepared hearts (13:5, 14; 14:1); (2) Paul reasons from the Old Testament Scriptures to prove that Jesus is indeed the Messiah (13:15-41); (3) many believe the message, both Jews and God-fearing Gentiles (13:42-44); (4) Jewish leaders, prompted by jealousy, oppose the witness (13:45; 14:2, 19); (5) denied the use of the synagogue, Paul and Barnabus move to the marketplace and continue to expand the witness among the Gentiles (13:46-49); (6) persecution arises from the Jewish sector and the missionaries are forced to move on to another city (13:50-52). This pattern will be repeated in city after city and soon the number of Gentile believers will eclipse that of believing Jews.

Churches are planted in Pisidian Antioch (13:13-52), Iconium (14:1-7), Lystra (14:8-18), and Derbe (14:19-20), but determined opposition meets every advance of the witness: At Paphos a Jewish sorcerer seeks to prevent the Roman proconsul, Sergius Paulus, from believing (13:6-12); in Pisidian Antioch Jews and prominent citizens expel the apostles from their region (13:50); in Lystra pagan idolaters seek to offer sacrifice to Paul and Barnabus as if they were gods (14:11-18) and then join the mob that stones Paul and leaves him for dead (14:19). Throughout these ordeals the apostles remain filled with joy and with the Holy Spirit (13:52).

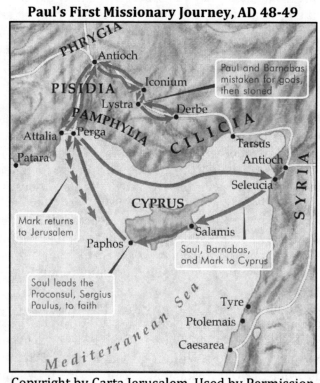

Copyright by Carta Jerusalem, Used by Permission

Paul and Barnabas then retrace their journey, encouraging the new congregations, challenging them to be firm in their faith, and warning them that hardships are to be expected (14:21-25). The new churches are not left leaderless because elders are appointed in each church. Returning to the sending church at Antioch, Paul and Barnabas *reported all that God had done with them and how He had opened the door of faith to the Gentiles* (14:27). It remains for the church at Jerusalem to again confirm that this is part of Christ's plan for the witness to spread beyond the city of Jerusalem and the borders of Judea and Samaria to include Gentiles in the uttermost part of earth. The Jerusalem council serves to unite this new expansion of the witness to Gentiles outside of Judah with the founding church. All believers stand united in Christ.

The council at Jerusalem confirms the witness to Gentiles (15:1-35). The church at Jerusalem had already concluded that God *has granted to the Gentiles also the repentance that leads to life* (11:18). With this rapid growth there now remains no doubt that God has *opened the door of faith to the Gentiles* (14:27). But determined opposition by a Pharisaic party raises questions about the nature of the gospel message and poses a serious threat to the unity of the church and its spread among the Gentiles (15:1). Paul's letter to the "churches in Galatia" (Galatians 1:2) was probably written to the churches founded on this first mission and reflects the impact of this controversy on the young church (Galatians 1:6-9). Paul and Barnabas are delegated to take the matter to the church at Jerusalem (15:2-5).

The council in Jerusalem carefully examines the evidence, listens patiently to all sides, traces the progress of the gospel, and grapples with the significance of the growing Gentile nature of the church. Peter and Paul share the same strong conviction that God has extended the witness to Gentiles through them and has confirmed it by the gift of the Holy Spirit (15:6-12). Speaking for the council, James confirms that salvation in Jesus Christ is for Jew and Gentile alike (15:13-21). An official letter confirms this landmark decision and adds new impetus to the witness to Gentiles (15:22-35). The Jerusalem council thus confirms that there is only one church and only one way of salvation, by grace through faith in Christ without the works of the Mosaic Law. The church began among Jews at Jerusalem and is now growing among Gentiles on its way to the ends of the earth.

Throughout the remainder of Acts Paul will continue his strategy of witnessing first to the Jews, giving them an opportunity to believe in Christ. Persistent rejection by official Judaism will confirm Luke's argument that the rejection of Jesus as the Messiah by Judaism led to the crucifixion of Christ and now it is that same rejection that leads to the growth of the church among Gentiles. Luke marks this milestone with a **sixth progress report.** *So the churches were being strengthened in the faith and increasing in numbers daily* (16:5).

The second mission of Paul to Gentiles (15:36-18:22). Conflict between Paul and Barnabas disturbs but does not defeat the outward expansion of the witness (15:36-40). Paul's break with Barnabas and John Mark is not permanent, but the remainder of Acts focuses solely on Paul. New associates like Silas, Timothy, and Titus now become his traveling companions (16:1-5). The Macedonian call is a dramatic step forward (16:6-10). The witness now spreads to Europe and is well on its way to *the ends of the earth*. In his second mission to the Gentiles (15:36-18:22) Paul's strategy of concentrating on cities of influence becomes evident. His itinerary takes him along the highway linking the major cities of the Roman Empire. Churches are established in Philippi, Thessalonica, Berea, Corinth, and Ephesus (to name a few). Luke's record of Paul's ministry in these centers forms the background for the letters Paul later writes to these churches.

Paul's ministry at Philippi begins quietly among women of faith gathered for prayer but escalates rapidly with the deliverance of a demon-possessed woman (16:11-21). Paul and Silas are arrested and beaten, but this only furthers the spread of the witness (16:22-40). Though compelled to leave, the church that has taken root in Philippi will flourish and become a major source of support for Paul and be the recipient of one of his most uplifting letters (Philippians 4:10-20). At Thessalonica he finds prepared hearts in a synagogue but even more among Gentiles (17:1-9). Jealous Jewish leaders incite a mob, and once again Paul is forced to move on leaving behind a young but vibrant church. His ministry in Berea is fruitful, but it is cut short as opposition follows him and forces another early departure (17:10-15).

Alone at Athens, Paul gives his most eloquent and thought-provoking message, but he finds the intellectual climate hostile and the people less responsive (17:16-34). There seems to be a declining level of response to the message as Paul has moved from Philippi to Athens and Paul begins a new ministry at Corinth on a somewhat subdued note (18:9). Tentmaking with Jewish expatriates Priscilla and Aquila, encouraging reports from Timothy and Silas (from Thessalonica and Berea respectively), and most of all the personal appearance of the Lord, lead to an extended ministry in Corinth (18:1-11). After another eighteen months Jews again stir up trouble and Paul feels obliged to move on, returning as he always does to the sending church at Antioch after brief stops in Ephesus and Caesarea (18:12-22).

Paul's Second Missionary Journey, AD 50-52

Copyright by Carta Jerusalem, Used by Permission

The third mission of Paul to Gentiles (18:23-21:16). Luke passes over this "furlough" time in Antioch (18:22) and Paul is soon launched on his third mission. Paul stopped briefly in Ephesus on the way back to Antioch and promised to return (18:19-21). He now makes good on that promise, stopping along the way to encourage the churches planted on his first and second missions (18:23). Apollos, a Jewish convert noted for his eloquence, precedes Paul in Ephesus and is more fully informed in the

141

faith by Priscilla and Aquila whom Paul had left in that city (18:24-28). Apollos then goes on to Corinth where his eloquence will attract a following that threatens to divide the church (1 Corinthians 3:1-23). One possible reason for Luke's mention of Apollos is that he may have been the one who imperfectly instructed the disciples of John that Paul encounters on his arrival in Ephesus (Acts 19:1-7). The outpouring of the Holy Spirit (the fourth recorded in Acts) confirms the witness to the disciples of John the Baptist, draws in the last of the pre-Pentecost believers, and also confirms the apostolic ministry of Paul.

Three months of ministry in the synagogue ends when Jewish authorities oppose Paul's message. Relocating to the school of Tyrannus next door, Paul enjoys two years of ministry that may well be his longest stay in one city. So effective is the ministry that *all who lived in Asia heard the word of the Lord, both Jews and Greeks* (19:8-10). Miracles are a unique feature of Paul's ministry in Ephesus, leading to the burning of books of magic by new believers (19:11-20). Luke's **seventh progress report** climaxes Paul's ministry at Ephesus and summarizes the Spirit-led extension of the witness to the European continent. *So the Word of the Lord was growing mightily and prevailing* (19:20).

Paul's ministry in Ephesus appears finished as he *purposed in the Spirit to go to Jerusalem* but Paul's ultimate goal is Rome (19:21). Luke includes Paul's purpose statement to signal the next major movement in the historical narrative. The balance of Acts (21:17-28:31) will record Paul's final witness in Jerusalem that takes him on to Rome. Paul leaves Ephesus only after Demetrius and other silversmiths cause a riot (19:23-41). Here the Christian faith is labeled "the Way." Because Paul's focus is now on Jerusalem and eventually Rome, Luke only briefly records his extended ministry in Macedonia and Greece including two visits to Corinth (1 and 2 Corinthians and Romans are written during this time) devoting more time to Paul's journey to Jerusalem (20:1-16) and his final report to the Ephesian elders who met him at Miletus (20:17-37). Paul's farewell message to them is a warm and moving defense of his motives and ministry.

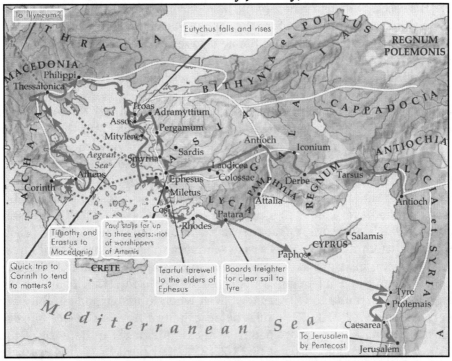

Copyright by Carta. Jerusalem, Used by Permission

Undeterred by the warning that the Jews would arrest him and hand him over to the Gentiles (21:1-16), Paul makes his fifth and final visit to Jerusalem (21:17). Lest we think that the gospel has failed to bear fruit in Jerusalem and among the Jews, Luke records that *many thousands there are among the Jews of those who have believed* (21:20). But opposition of Judaism that began at Pentecost continues to follow the witness. Its final act is to attempt to destroy Paul as the leading witness for Jesus Christ. (21:27-36).

Paul's arrest and witness in Jerusalem (21:17-23:35). Paul's plan to visit Rome (19:21) is now confirmed by the Lord himself (23:11). God used the circumstances of a Jewish plot on Paul's life and the desire of the Roman authorities to maintain order as the means of extending Paul's witness to Rome. The last portion of Acts records Paul's witness as a prisoner on the road from Jerusalem to Rome. These chapters highlight a series of **six messages** Paul delivers in defense of the gospel of Jesus Christ and in defense of his apostolic ministry.

1. Paul's first defense is before a mob in Jerusalem (21:37-22:21).
2. His second defense is before the Sanhedrin (23:1-10).
3. A third is in Caesarea before the Roman governor, Felix (24:1-27).
4. His fourth defense is before the new governor, Festus (25:1-12).
5. A fifth is before king Agrippa and his wife Bernice (26:1-32).
6. Paul's final defense is in Rome before Jewish leaders (28:17-28).

Paul's witness as a prisoner in Caesarea (chaps. 24-26). Paul's accusers arrive from Jerusalem and include Ananias, the high priest. Ananias' presence demonstrates how seriously they view the case. Their charges before Governor Felix are false and are readily refuted by Paul (24:1-21). Felix is familiar with "the Way," and he and his wife Drusilla, a Jewess, repeatedly summon Paul and listen to his message concerning Jesus but he never comes to a personal decision (24:22-27). When Festus arrives, Paul's accusers repeat their accusations but offer no proof (25:1-8). Their attempt to have Paul's case sent back to Jerusalem for trial forces Paul to claim his right as a Roman citizen to appeal to Caesar (25:9-12), which results in Paul being transferred to Rome for trial. Paul has yet another opportunity to witness for Christ when King Agrippa and his wife Bernice arrive (25:13-22). Paul's defense before Agrippa is the longest, most passionate, and most cogent of his six messages in defense of the witness concerning Jesus (25:23-26:32). Luke records the private conversation among the Roman officials that conclude Paul has not committed an offense against Roman law but yet must be transferred to Rome because he has appealed to Caesar. Thus Paul will now make his intended journey to Rome after two years of imprisonment in Caesarea.

Paul's witness on the voyage to Rome (27:1-28:15). Naval authorities have noted the historical accuracy with which Luke documents Paul's ill-fated voyage to Rome. It is probably the most dramatic event of Paul's missionary exploits (27:1-44). Neither shipwreck nor venomous snakes can thwart God's plan for Paul to carry the witness to Rome. Instead, these near tragedies open the opportunity to evangelize the Roman soldiers, the crew of the ship, and the entire island of Malta (28:1-15).

Paul's witness as a prisoner in Rome (28:16-31). So much importance has been attached to Paul's witness in Rome that we are surprised by the brevity of Luke's account of the two years Paul spends there as a prisoner. But it is an essential and appropriate conclusion to the argument of the book of Acts.

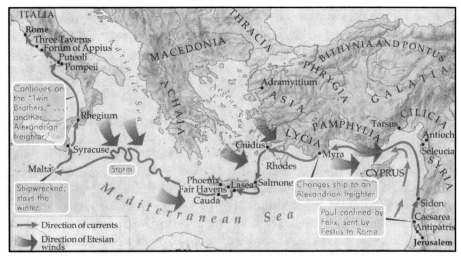

Copyright by Carta Jerusalem, Used by Permission

The Jewish delegation seems unaware of what has transpired in Jerusalem and Caesarea. Drawing on the Old Testament, Paul seeks to persuade them that Jesus is the Messiah spoken of by Moses and the prophets (28:23-24). Their refusal to believe prompts Paul to cite the prophecy of Isaiah foretelling their hardheartedness (28:25-27). This marks the official and final rejection of the witness of Jesus recorded in Acts. With that Paul announces that God will now send the good news of salvation through Jesus Christ to the Gentiles who will listen. The official rejection of the witness concerning Jesus does not spell the end or indicate defeat of the witness. Rather, it signals a new beginning when Paul declares, *God's salvation has been sent to the Gentiles, and they will also listen* (28:28).

An **eighth progress report** (28:28-31) concludes the book of Acts. The witness of Jesus Christ has now reached Rome through Paul! Rome is the seat of government and the staging ground for the later spread of the witness to the remotest parts of the earth. The limited freedom Paul enjoys as a prisoner of Rome will change under Nero (A.D. 64-68). But prison chains do not prevent him from witnessing to his Roman guards or from writing letters to congregations in Ephesus, Philippi, and Colosse as well as to his dear friend, Philemon.

Conclusion and the unfinished nature of Acts. Paul has carried the witness and work of Jesus Christ forward but it does not depend on nor does it end with the greatest of the apostles. Luke (more properly, the Holy Spirit) deliberately ends Acts without recording the martyrdom of

Paul or the continued spread of Christianity around the globe. After all, Acts is about Jesus, not Paul. Paul's release from prison, his ministry in Asia Minor and Spain, and his execution in Rome, are yet in the future. During this brief but productive time Paul will also author pastoral letters to his young coworkers, Timothy and Titus.

Luke has accomplished his purpose of documenting the spread of the witness from Jerusalem, through Judea and Samaria and on to the uttermost part of the earth (1:8). What Jesus began, He has effectively continued through the apostles. But the witness does not end with Acts. It will not end until the same Jesus who commissioned the witness returns to mark its triumphant completion (1:7-11). This **final progress report (28:30-31)** serves notice that neither the determined opposition of official Judaism nor a Roman prison can prevent the witness from spreading. Acts is hardly an "unfinished symphony" for the declared purpose of Jesus in Acts 1:8 has been accomplished. Yet the witness is destined to continue around the globe and across the centuries. It will continue its advance until Jesus returns.

Timeline for Acts, Paul's Ministry, and Paul's Epistles

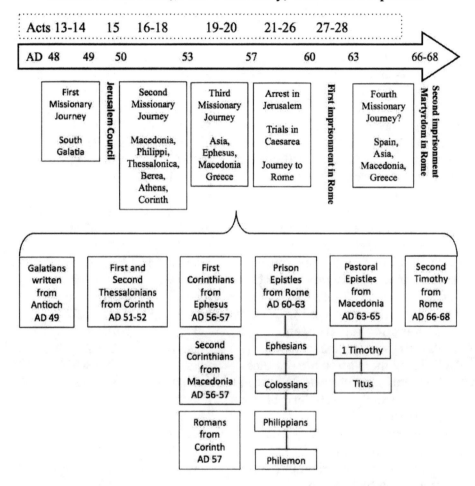

Chronology of Acts and the Ministry of Paul

Event	Scripture	Date
Public ministry of Jesus	Luke/Acts	c. A.D. 27-30
Crucifixion and ascension	Luke/Acts	A.D. 30
Pentecost = church founded	Acts 2	A.D. 30
Death of Stephen/persecution	Acts 6-8	c. A.D. 32-35
Paul's conversion	Acts 9	c. A.D. 32-35
Paul in Damascus	Acts 9	A.D. 35-37
Paul's **first** Jerusalem visit	Acts 9	A.D. 37
Peter's witness to Cornelius/Gentiles	Acts 10	A.D.40-41
Founding of church at Antioch	Acts 11	A.D. 41
Paul at Antioch	Acts 11	A.D. 42-43
James, son of Zebedee, martyred	Acts 12	c. A.D. 41-43
Famine in Jerusalem	Acts 11	A.D. 44-45
Paul's **second** Jerusalem visit	Acts 11	A.D. 44-45
Paul's **first mission** to the Gentiles	Acts 13-14	A.D. 46-48
*Galatians written from Antioch?	Acts 14	A.D. 48-49
Jerusalem council; Paul's **third** visit	Acts 15	A.D. 50
Paul's **second mission** to the Gentiles	Acts 15-18	A.D. 50-52
*1, 2 Thessalonians written	Acts 18	A.D. 51-52
Paul's **fourth** Jerusalem visit	Acts 18	A.D. 52
Paul's **third mission** to the Gentiles	Acts 18-21	A.D. 53-57
*1, 2 Corinthians, Romans, written	Acts 18-21	A.D. 54-57
Paul's **fifth** (final) visit to Jerusalem	Acts 21	A.D. 57
Paul's arrest in Jerusalem	Acts 21-23	A.D. 57
Paul's imprisonment in Caesarea	Acts 23-26	A.D. 57-59
Paul's voyage to Rome	Acts 25-27	A.D. 59
Paul's (first) imprisonment in Rome	Acts 28	c. A.D. 60-63
*Acts written by Luke in Rome		A.D. 60-62
*Ephesians, Colossians, Philippians, **Philemon, written from prison**	Acts 28	A.D. 60-62
Paul's release from prison		c. A.D. 62-63
Paul in Asia Minor, Spain		c. A.D. 63-66
*1 Timothy and Titus written		A.D. 63-65
Nero's persecution of Christians		A.D. 64-68
Paul's arrest and imprisonment at Rome		c. A.D. 66-67
*2 Timothy written from prison		c. A.D. 66-67
Martyrdom of Peter and Paul in Rome		c. A.D. 64-68
Roman war against Jews, destruction of Jerusalem		A.D. 66-70
*Destinations and dates of Paul's letters		

Outline

I. Preparation for witness   1:1-26
- A. Resumptive prologue by Luke   1:1-5
  - 1. Previous and present message of Luke   1:1a
  - 2. Previous and present ministry of Christ   1:1b-5
- B. Statement of the purpose and plan   1:6-11
  - 1. The apostles' question about the kingdom   1:6
    - a. The antecedent: kingdom signs
    - b. The issue: at this time?
  - 2 Jesus' answer   1:7-8
    - a. What it is not   1:7a
    - b. What it is   1:7b
    - c. What it means: power for witness   1:8

Theme and outline: the ongoing witness of Jesus Christ (1:8)
The person: by and about Jesus Christ
The power: the Holy Spirit
The program: you will be My witnesses
The plan: in Jerusalem, all Judea and Samaria, and even to the remotest part of the earth.

  - 3. Jesus' ascension   1:9-11
    - a. Visible, bodily departure   1:9
    - b. Visible, bodily return promised   1:10-11
- C. Preparation of the disciples for witness   1:12-26
  - 1. Waiting prayerfully in Jerusalem   1:12-14
  - 2. Selecting a replacement for Judas   1:15-26
    - a. Scripture fulfilled by Judas's rejection   1:15-20
    - b. Selection of a replacement   1:21-26

II. Witness in Jerusalem   2:1-8:3
- A. Witness begins at Pentecost   2:1-47
  - 1. Power of Pentecost = Holy Spirit present   2:1-13
    - a. Evidence of the Spirit's presence   2:1-4
    - b. Effects of the Spirit's presence   2:5-13
  - 2. Preaching of Peter at Pentecost   2:14-47
    - a. Peter's sermon   2:14-36
    - b. Response to Peter's sermon   2:37-41
    - c. *** First progress report**   2:42-47

B. Witness prospers, persists amid opposition 3:1-7:60
  1. Witness of Peter and John 3:1-4:31
    a. Occasioned by miracle of healing 3:1-10
    b. Explained by Peter's sermon 3:11-26
    c. Opposition of official Judaism 4:1-31
      (1) Arrest of Peter and John 4:1-3
      (2) Acceptance by many 4:4
      (3) Trial before Sanhedrin 4:5-14
      (4) Attempt to prevent the witness 4:15-22
      (5) **Second progress report** 4:23-36
  2. Witness through discipline in the church 5:1-11
    a. Hypocrisy: attack from within 5:1-2
    b. Judgment: eliminating hypocrisy 5:3-10
    c. Witness extended following cleansing 5:11
  3. Witness of apostles under opposition 5:12-42
    a. Witness accompanied by miracles 5:12-16
    b. Imprisonment and release of apostles 5:17-26
    c. Official opposition of Judaism 5:27-40
    d. Witness continued by apostles 5:41-42
  4. Witness through unity in the church 6:1-7
    a. Problem of cultural disharmony 6:1
    b. Solution proposed by apostles 6:2-4
    c. Selection of deacons to solve problem 6:5-6
    d. **Third progress report** 6:7
  5. Witness of Stephen 6:8-7:60
    a. Effectiveness of Stephen's witness 6:8-10
    b. Attack on Stephen's witness 6:11-14
    c. Defense of Stephen 6:15-7:53
    d. Martyrdom of Stephen 7:54-60

III. Witness in Judea and Samaria 8:5-12:25
  A. Persecution scatters the Jerusalem church 8:1-4
  B. Witness of Philip in Samaria 8:5-40
    1. Accompanied by miracles in Samaria 8:4-8
    2. Evidenced by conversion of a sorcerer 8:9-13
    3. Authenticated by the Holy Spirit, 8:14-25
    4. Extended to an Ethiopian 8:26-39
    5. Extended to Caesarea 8:40

150

C. Conversion and witness of Saul — 9:1-31
  1. Commission of Saul against Christ — 9:1, 2
  2. Conversion and witness of Saul (Paul) — 9:3-19a
    a. Revelation of Christ to Saul — 9:3-9
    b. Revelation of Christ to Ananias — 9:10-16
    c. Revelation of Christ in Saul — 9:17-19a
  3. Confession of Saul for Christ — 9:19b-22
  4. Conspiracy against Saul — 9:23-25
  5. Confirmation of Saul by Jerusalem church — 9:26-30
  6. Consequence: **Fourth progress report** — 9:31
D. Witness of Peter extends to Gentiles — 9:32-11:18
  1. Healing of Aeneas at Lydda — 9:32-35
  2. Raising of Dorcas at Joppa — 9:36-43
  3. Conversion of Cornelius at Caesarea — 10:1-43
    a. Vision to prepare Cornelius — 10:1-8
    b. Vision to prepare Peter — 10:9-23a
    c. Witness of Peter to Cornelius — 10:23b-43
  4. Confirmation by the Holy Spirit — 10:44-48
  5. Confirmation by the church at Jerusalem — 11:1-18
    a. Accusation from Judaizers — 11:1-3
    b. Explanation by Peter — 11:4-17
    c. Approval of the church — 11:18

"God has granted to the Gentiles also the repentance that leads to life"
(11:18)

E. Witness expands among Gentiles in Antioch — 11:19-30
  1. Gentile church established at Antioch — 11:19-30
    a. Conversion of Gentiles at Antioch — 11:19-21
    b. Confirmation by the Jerusalem church — 11:22-24
    c. Coming of Saul to Antioch — 11:25-26
    d. Care of Gentiles for Jerusalem church — 11:27-30
F. Witness persecuted in Jerusalem by Herod — 12:1-25
  1. Execution of James by Herod Agrippa — 12:1-2
  2. Arrest of Peter by Herod Agrippa — 12:3-5
  3. Miraculous release of Peter from prison — 12:6-19
  4. Judgment and death of Herod — 12:20-23
  5. Outcome: **Fifth progress report** — 12:24-25

IV. Witness to the Uttermost Part of the Earth 13-28
   A. First mission of Paul and Barnabas to Gentiles 13-14
      1. Paul to witness at Antioch 13:1-3
      2. Witness of Barnabas and Paul in Cypress 13:4-12
         a. Witness in the synagogue 13:4, 5
         b. Reaction: Jewish sorcerer judged 13:6-11
         c. Result: proconsul converted 13:12
      3. Witness in Antioch of Pisidia 13:13-52
         a. Paul's sermon in the synagogue 13:13-41
         b. Response: many Jews believe 13:42-43
         c. Reaction: rejection by official Judaism 13:44-47
         d. Result: church grows among Gentiles 13:48-52
      4. Witness at Iconium 14:1-7
         a. Witness in the synagogue 14:1a
         b. Response: many believe 14:1b
         c. Reaction: opposition by Judaism 14:2-7
      5. Witness at Lystra 14:8-20
         a. Witness through healing of a cripple 14:8-10
         b. Response: witnesses viewed as gods 14:11-13
         c. Rejection of worship by apostles 14:14-18
         d. Reaction: Judaism provokes rejection 14:19a
         e. Result: Paul stoned and left for dead 14:19b-20
      6. Witness at Derbe 14:21a
      7. Churches confirmed on return to Antioch 14:21b-28
         a. Encouraging the new churches 14:21b-22
         b. Appointing elders 14:23-25
         c. Reporting to church at Antioch 14:26-28

* *God...had opened a door of faith to the Gentiles* (14:27)

   B. Jerusalem council affirms inclusion of Gentiles 15:1-35
      1. Dissension caused by Judaizing element 15:1
      2. First discussion: Paul, Barnabas report 15:2-4
      3. Dissension by Judaizers continued 15:5
      4. Second discussion: Peter reports 15:6-21
         a. Extended discussion 15:6, 7a
         b. Peter's argument 15:8-11
         c. Paul and Barnabas's argument 15:12-18
         d. Decision recommended by James 15:19-21
      5. Decision reached/reported by the council 15:22-29
         a. Representatives chosen 15:22

	b. Letter sent to churches	15:23-29
6.	Gentile believers are encouraged	15:30-35
C.	Second mission of Paul to Gentiles	15:36-18:22
1.	Separation of Paul and Barnabas	15:36-40
2.	Strengthening of Gentile churches	15:40-16:6
	a. Silas and Timothy enlisted	15:40-16:3
	b. Result: ***Sixth progress report**	16:4-6
3.	Call to witness in Macedonia	16:7-10
	a. Doors closed by the Holy Spirit	16:7-8
	b. Door opened by Macedonian vision	16:9
	c. Door entered by Paul	16:10
4.	Witness in Philippi	16:11-40
	a. Witness to devout women	16:11-15
	b. Witness through exorcism	16:16-21
	c. Reaction: Paul beaten, imprisoned	16:22-24
	d. Response: Paul released, jailer saved	16:25-34
	e. Result: Paul expelled with apology	16:35-40
5.	Witness in Thessalonica	17:1-9
	a. Witness in the synagogue	17:1-3
	b. Response: many Gentiles believe	17:4
	c. Reaction: Jews provoke riot	17:5-9
6.	Witness in Berea	17:10-15
	a. Witness in the synagogue	17:10
	b. Response: eager acceptance	17:11-12
	c. Reaction: Jews agitate crowd	17:13-15
7.	Witness in Athens	17:16-34
	a. Witness in synagogue, marketplace	17:16-18
	b. Witness at the Areopagus	17:19-31
	c. Response: a few believe	17:32-34
8.	Witness in Corinth	18:1-17
	a. Witness in synagogue	18:1-4
	b. Reaction: Jews opposed	18:5-6
	c. Witness to Gentiles intensified	18:7
	d. Response: many believe	18:8
	e. Witness confirmed by a vision	18:9-11
	f. Result: Jews bring Paul before Gallio	18:12-17
9.	Return to Antioch via Ephesus	18:18-22
	a. Priscilla and Aquila left at Ephesus	18:18-19
	b. Paul promises to return to Ephesus	18:20-21
	c. Paul reports to church at Antioch	18:22

D. Third mission of Paul to Gentiles	18:23-21:16
1. Witness at Ephesus	18:23-19:41
a. Ministry in Galatia	18:23
b. Witness of Apollos at Ephesus	18:24-30
c. Confirmation by the Holy Spirit	19:1-7
d. Witness in the synagogue	19:8
e. Reaction: rejection by Jews	19:9a
f. Result: witness extended to Gentiles	19:9b-12
g. Reaction: Jewish exorcists defeated	19:13-16
h. Result: **Seventh progress report**	19:17-20
i. Witness planned for Rome	19:21-22
j. Riot of idol makers at Ephesus	19:23-41
2. Witness on Paul's return to Antioch	20:1-3
3. Paul's journey to Jerusalem (fifth visit)	20:4-21:16
a. Paul's traveling companions	20:4-6
b. Paul at Troas, Eutychus revived	20:7-12
c. Paul's farewell to Ephesian elders	20:13-38
d. Paul warned of danger in Jerusalem	21:1-16
E. Paul's witness and arrest in Jerusalem	21:17-23:35
1. Meeting of Paul and Jerusalem elders	21:17-26
2. Riot in the temple, Paul seized	21:27-32
3. Paul rescued by Roman officer	21:33-39
4. Paul's defense before the mob	21:40-22:22
5. Paul's claim to Roman citizenship	22:23-29
6. Paul's defense before the Sanhedrin	22:30-23:11
7. Plot of Jews to kill Paul	23:12-22
8. Paul transferred to Caesarea	23:23-35
F. Paul's witness as a prisoner in Caesarea	24:1-26:32
1. Paul's defense before Felix	24:1-27
a. Accusations against Paul	24:1-9
b. Defense of Paul	24:10-21
c. Decision postponed by Felix	24:22-27
2. Paul's defense before Festus	25:1-12
a. Renewed plot on Paul's life	25:1-9
b. Paul appeals to Caesar	25:10-12
3. Paul's defense before Agrippa	25:13-26:32
a. Paul's case brought before Agrippa	25:13-22
b. Paul's defense before Agrippa	25:23-26:23
c. Paul's case transferred to Rome	26:24-32

G.	Paul's witness on the journey to Rome	27:1-28:15
	1. Witness aboard ship	27:1-44
	a. Difficult journey to Fair Havens	27:1-8
	b. Paul's warning ignored	27:9-12
	c. Violent storm at sea	27:13-20
	d. Paul's message of encouragement	27:21-26
	e. Shipwreck and survival	27:27-44
	2. Witness at Malta (Melita)	28:1-10
	a. Through Paul's surviving a snakebite	28:1-6
	b. Through healing of Publius's father	28:7-10
	3. Journey to Rome resumed	28:11-15
H.	Paul's witness as a prisoner in Rome	28:16-31
	1. Paul under house arrest	28:16
	2. Paul's meetings with Jewish leaders	28:17-29
	a. First meeting: Paul reviews his case	28:17-20
	b. Response: professed interest	28:21-22
	c. Second meeting: the gospel explained	28:23
	d. Response: both belief and rejection	28:24-25a
	e. Result: salvation sent to Gentiles	28:25b-29
	3. ***Eighth and final progress report**	28:30-31

* This salvation of God has been sent to the Gentiles; they will also listen (28:28)

Bibliography

Bock, Darrell L. *Acts.* Baker Exegetical Commentary on the New Testament. Grand Rapids: Baker Academic, 2007.

Blaiklock, E. M. *The Acts of the Apostles.* Tyndale New Testament Commentary. Grand Rapids: Wm. B. Eerdmans Publishing Co., 1959.

Blomberg, Craig L. *From Pentecost to Patmos.* Nashville: Broadman & Holman Publishers, 2006,

Bruce, F.F. *Commentary on the Book of Acts.* The New International Commentary on the New Testament. Rev. ed. Grand Rapids: Wm. B. Eerdmans Publishing Co., 1988.

Carson, D.A., Douglas J. Moo, and Leon Morris. *An Introduction to the New Testament.* Grand Rapids: Zondervan Publishing House, 1991.

Chambers, Andy. *Exemplary Life: A Theology of Church Life in Acts.* Nashville: B & H Publishing Group, 2012.

Couch, Mal, ed. *A Bible Handbook to the Acts of the Apostles.* Grand Rapids: Kregel Publications, 1999.

Fernando, Ajith. *Acts.* NIV Application Commentary. Grand Rapids: Zondervan Publishing House, 1998.

Guthrie, Donald. *New Testament Introduction.* Downers Grove, IL: InterVarsity Press, 1990.

Hiebert, D. Edmond. An *Introduction to the New Testament.* Vol. 1. Chicago: Moody Press, 1975.

Jensen, Irving L. *Jensen's New Testament Survey.* Chicago: Moody Press, 1981.

Larkin, William. *Acts.* IVP New Testament Commentary. Downers Grove, IL: InterVarsity Press, 1995.

Longenecker, Richard. "Acts." In *The Expositor's Bible Commentary*. Grand Rapids: Zondervan Publishing House, 1981.

Polhill, John. *Acts.* New American Commentary. Nashville: Broadman & Holman Publishing, 1992.

Rackham, Richard B. *The Acts of the Apostles.* Grand Rapids: Baker Book House, 1964.

Ramsey, William M. *St. Paul the Traveler and Roman Citizen.* Grand Rapids: Kregel Publications, 2001.

Stott, John. *Acts.* Downers Grove, IL: InterVarsity Press, 1990.

Tenney, Merrill C. *New Testament Survey.* Grand Rapids: Wm. B. Eerdmans Publishing Co., 1961.

Witherington, Ben. *The Acts of the Apostles.* Grand Rapids: Wm. B. Eerdmans Publishing Co., 1997.

Background and Pauline Studies

Barrett, C. K. *Paul.* Philadelphia: Westminster John Knox Press, 1994

Bruce, F. F. *Paul.* Grand Rapids: Wm. B. Eerdmans Publishing Co., 1977

Conybeare, W. J. and J. S. Howson. *The Life and Epistles of St. Paul.* Grand Rapids: Wm. B. Eerdmans Publishing Co., 1962.

Dunn, James D. J. *The Theology of Paul the Apostle.* Grand Rapids: Wm. B. Eerdmans Publishing Co., 1998.

Hawthorne, Gerald F., and Ralph A. Martin, eds. *Dictionary of Paul and His Letters.* Downers Grove, IL: InterVarsity Press, 1993.

Hiebert, D. Edmond. *Personalities around Paul.* Chicago: Moody Press, 1973.

Machen, J. Gresham. *The Origin of Paul's Religion.* Grand Rapids: Wm. B. Eerdmans, Publishing Co., 1947.

McRay, John. *Paul: His Life and Teaching.* Grand Rapids: Baker Book House, 2002.

Pate, C. Marvin. *The End of the Age Has Come: The Theology of Paul.* Grand Rapids: Zondervan Publishing House, 1995

Polhill, John B. *Paul & His Letters.* Nashville: Broadman & Holman Publishers, 1999.

Richards, E. Randolph. *Paul and First Century Letter Writing.* Downers Grove, IL: InterVarsity Press, 2004

Winter, Bruce, ed. *The Book of Acts in Its First-Century Setting.* 5 vols. Grand Rapids: Wm. B. Eerdmans Publishing Co., 1993-96

Witherington, Ben. *The Paul Quest.* Downers Grove, IL: InterVarsity Press, 1998.

158

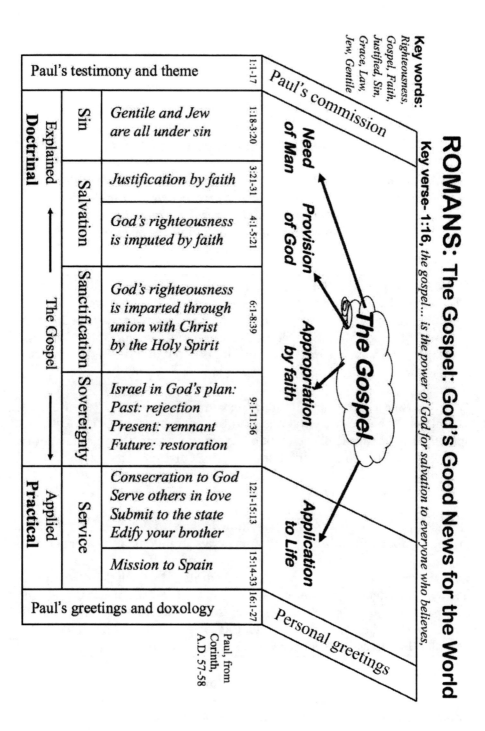

ROMANS

The Gospel: God's Good News for the World

For I am not ashamed of the gospel, for it is the power of God for salvation to everyone who believes, to the Jew first and also to the Greek.
For in it the righteousness of God is revealed from faith to faith; as it is written, "But the righteous man shall live by faith"
(Romans 1:16-17).

"This Epistle is really the chief part of the New Testament and the very purist Gospel, and is worthy not only that every Christian should know it word for word, by heart, but occupy himself with it every day, as the daily bread of the soul. It can never be read or pondered too much, and the more it is dealt with the more precious it becomes, and the better it tastes" (Martin Luther, *Commentary on Romans*, xiii).

"The Reformation was undoubtedly the work of the Epistle to the Romans, as well as of that to the Galatians; and the probability is that every great spiritual revival in the church will be connected as effect and cause with a deeper understanding of this book. ... The Epistle to the Romans is the cathedral of the Christian faith" (Frederick L. Godet, *Commentary on the Epistle to the Romans,* 1).

"The Epistle to the Romans is acknowledged to be one of the most profound books in existence. Its impressive grandeur and impenetrable depths make it one of the most highly prized parts of Holy Scripture. It has very appropriately been termed the Cathedral of the Christian faith. It was not without adequate reason that this matchless epistle was assigned the first position among the Pauline writings in our New Testament Canon. It forms one of the most major bulwarks of evangelical Christianity" (D. Edmond Hiebert, *An Introduction to the New Testament*, 2:163).

The City of Rome

Rome was the largest and most important city of the first century. Its influence extended throughout the entire Mediterranean. Rome had ruled for more than a century. Internal decay was beginning when Paul writes

160

this letter, but Rome was still "the city set on a hill." Rome was the economic hub of a vast commercial empire. Roman-built highways formed a network that adjoined major cities. The claim, "All roads lead to Rome," was true. The city was strategically located both by land and by sea and boasted a large population. An inscription discovered in 1941 gave the population as 4,100,000 in A.D. 14. Commerce attracted people from all across the Roman Empire. The city was a melting pot of cultures and languages. The Jewish population was substantial and exerted both an economic and a religious influence.

The Roman Empire ruled with absolute authority. Roman "peace" was enforced by military power. Commanders were honored and had great authority over the territories they occupied. Still the rule of law prevailed. Government was generally fair and just, but full rights were limited to a small percentage of citizens. Polytheism characterized religion in the city and the diverse population of inhabitants worshiped many foreign deities. Emperor worship was also promoted. The moral bankruptcy of these religions prompted some to turn to the ethical monotheism of the Jews and played a part in preparing the way for the later conquest of Rome by the Christian faith. The official language of Rome was Latin, but Greek was widely used as a cultural and business language. The Greek language provided a common bond for Christians across the Roman empire. When Paul wrote the epistle to the Romans in Greek, it was readily understood (D. Edmond Hiebert, *An Introduction to the New Testament*, 2:163-65).

The Church at Rome
Founding of the church at Rome. The church had already been in existence for many years before Paul wrote this letter to them (Romans 15:33). No one knows the exact date and circumstance of its founding. The epistle to the Romans points to a substantial and well-established church. There have been three prominent attempts to explain the origin of the church. First, Peter founded it. Roman Catholic tradition from the fourth century claimed that Peter established the church during a twenty-five year residence in Rome. The tradition has been disproved and largely rejected, even by the Catholic Church. The difficulties with the theory are many. (a) Peter was still in Jerusalem as late as A.D. 49. His travels had taken him only as far as Antioch by A.D. 51. (b) Ambrosiaster, a fourth-century church father, said that the Romans had embraced the Christian faith without the benefit of direct apostolic ministry (Douglas J. Moo, *The Epistle to the Romans*, 4). (c) Paul claims that he did not build on another man's foundation (15:20). He probably would not have put so much

emphasis on a ministry in Rome if Peter founded the church there. Nowhere else did Paul follow Peter or another apostle in church planting. (d) Paul would surely have mentioned Peter's name if he was, or had been, residing in Rome. Peter's name is absent from Romans and from Paul's later prison epistles written from Rome. (e) It is considered unlikely that Peter arrived in Rome much before his martyrdom there under Nero in A.D. 64. (f) Peter was principally the apostle to the Jews and the church at Rome seems to have had a Gentile majority. The view that Peter founded the church at Rome has little support in history or in contemporary scholarship.

A second view is that Jewish converts returning from the feast of Pentecost founded the church (Acts 2:10). Donald Guthrie and Douglas Moo suggest that the church in Rome began among the Jews and caused great conflict within the Jewish community. Claudius expelled Jews from Rome because they were constantly rioting at the instigation of Chrestus (Acts 18:2). They see this as a reference to Christ and an indication that the gospel had already impacted Rome by A.D. 49 (Douglas J. Moo, *The Epistle to the Romans*, 4-5). Though possible, this explanation also has serious difficulties. (a) The Jews in Jerusalem for the day of Pentecost would not likely have had sufficient teaching to establish a church without further direction from the apostles. The congregation at Rome appeared to be mature and well taught (Romans 15:14, 24). (b) There is no record in Acts of such churches springing up as a result of converts from Pentecost. When Christians were scattered from Jerusalem following Stephen's martyrdom, they witnessed in Judea and Samaria (Acts 8:1-4). The apostles remained in Jerusalem and were careful to send a representative to confirm that witness before a church was recognized (Acts 8:14-17; 11:1-30). Congregations appeared to develop as a result of apostolic initiative and in an ever-widening circle from the base at Jerusalem. (c) The Jews who came to Paul during his imprisonment at Rome (Acts 28) seemed to be hearing the gospel for the first time. There is no indication that conflict existed between the Jewish synagogues and the Christian community. Hiebert suggests that more likely a converted Roman like Cornelius (Acts 10) would have carried the gospel to Rome (*An Introduction to the New Testament*, 2:168-69).

A third and preferred view is that associates of Paul founded the church at Rome. (a) Associates of Paul established congregations in other areas as an extension of his ministry (Acts 19:10; Colossians 1:6-7). (b) Paul had a large following of friends and associates in Rome. He mentions twenty-six

162

people in the church by name (Romans 16:3-16). Paul's comments regarding them indicate that they had shared the gospel ministry with him on other occasions. (c) The people at Rome seemed to look to Paul as their spiritual father. He did not have to defend his apostleship or justify his desire to visit them. (d) Paul's first visit to Rome (Acts 28) occurred about 20 years after he began his first missionary journey. This allowed ample time for some of his co-workers and converts to have settled in Rome. (e) Rome was to the empire what the heart is to the body. The record of Acts and of Paul's letters indicates a great deal of movement on the part of Christians. Commercial travel and convenient transportation increased mobility around the Mediterranean region. Hiebert argues, "Romans 16 shows that a number of Paul's acquaintances had moved to Rome and would be active in the Gospel there. It is safe to say that the self-propagating nature of Christianity carried it to Rome, not on one occasion only, but on different occasions and under varied circumstances. Thus apparently the church at Rome owed its origin to the migration to Rome of Christians from the eastern part of the Empire who had been converted as they came into contact with the Gospel as presented by Paul. Some of these would be Jews and others Gentiles" (*An Introduction to the New Testament*, 2:169).

Conclusion. No one can be dogmatic about when and how the church was planted in Rome. But its founding may have predated Paul's letter and planned visit by a decade. A warm relationship existed between the Christians at Rome and Paul, at least suggesting he was indirectly associated with the church's founding there. His determination to avoid building on another man's foundation (15:20) and his longstanding desire to visit them (1:13) indicates a personal relationship with the church. His desire to strengthen them spiritually and be mutually encouraged with them points to a direct association (1:11-13).

Character of the church at Rome. The church had already been in existence for some time when Paul wrote this epistle (Romans 15:23). The church was widely known and apparently influential (1:8). The church probably consisted of several house churches rather than one large, centrally located congregation. Several such churches are greeted (10:11-15; 16:5). Paul does not address the letter to "the church at Rome" as he does in his Corinthian and Thessalonian epistles. Instead, the letter is addressed to all the individual believers in Rome (Romans 1:7). The congregations appeared to be well taught (15:14). They were sufficiently well established to become a sending church (15:24). Another apostle had not likely visited the churches in Rome (15:20). This might account for the unstructured nature of the church and the absence of reference to church officers (Acts 14:23). The congregations were blessed with a significant number of leaders and a high quality of leadership (Romans 16:16). They understood and utilized spiritual gifts (Romans 12:6-8). The church appears to have been made up of both Jew and Gentile, but there is significant debate about which group, if either, was dominant. Moo says, "Unfortunately, the letter appears to send out mixed signals on this issue" (*The Epistle to the Romans, 9*). (a) In favor of a Jewish majority: Paul directly addresses the Jews (2:17), associates his readers with the Mosaic Law (6:14; 7:1), appeals to Abraham as "our forefather" (4:1), and deals extensively with the place of the Jew in God's plan (chaps. 9-11). (b) In favor of a Gentile majority: Paul includes them among the Gentiles to whom he is called to minister (1:5-6), addresses them directly as Gentiles (1:13; 11:13), and claims to be writing as a priest on behalf of the Gentiles (15:14-16).

Jews must have made up a significant part of the congregation and the Gentiles were thoroughly instructed in matters of Jewish heritage. Whether this was because the gospel had come to them first through Jews, or because they had been "God fearers" prior to their conversion is unclear. Moo concludes, "Along with the majority of commentators, then, we think that Paul addresses a mixed group of Jewish and Gentile Christians in Romans. Some decline to estimate the relative proportion of the two groups, but the considerations advanced above show that Gentile Christians were in the majority, perhaps an overwhelming majority" (*The Epistle to the Romans*, 12-13). There appears to be no major controversy among the believers at Rome. Paul's concluding warning about false teachers is more of a preventive than a corrective instruction (16:17-19). They did need to be more loving (13:8-10) and less judgmental (14:9-18) in their relationships with each other. They also had significant room for growth in unity, respect, and mutual encouragement (14:19-15:7).

Author
Paul's authorship of Romans has been accepted without serious debate. Guthrie does not even deal with the matter of authorship in his introduction. Paul's personality, passion, and theology are easily discernible in Romans. The epistle has been accepted and widely circulated from the beginning. "From Irenaeus onward the references to Romans are full and complete in all church writers; it is uniformly recognized as by Paul and as canonical" (Thiessen, *Introduction to the New*

Testament, 220). The author identifies himself as Paul (1:1). This is substantiated by personal references and claims of apostleship (1:5, 8-13; 15:23-29). The people named (16:3-16) and the places of ministry fit perfectly into Paul's journeys in Acts (Romans 15:23-29 with Acts 20:1-6).

Tertius served as Paul's scribe (amanuensis) but it is doubtful that he had much influence over the choice of words let alone the content. "Ancient authors gave to their amanuenses varying degrees of responsibility in the compositions of their works--from word-for-word recording of what they dictated to quite sweeping responsibility for putting ideas into words. Paul's method in Romans is certainly far toward the 'dictation' end of this spectrum. For the style of Romans is very close to that of Galatians and 1 Corinthians--and we have no evidence that Tertius was involved in the composition of either of these letters (indeed, see Gal. 6:11)" (Moo, *The Epistle to the Romans,* 1-2). Paul was at the height of his ministry and Romans is his *magnum opus.* The gospel of salvation by grace through faith has changed lives throughout the entire Mediterranean region. Twenty years of debate with Pharisaic Judaism and pagan philosophers has enabled Paul to identify the issues and articulate answers. It is a strategic time in Paul's life and in the establishment of the Christian faith. The time was right for this definitive letter to the Romans.

Occasion for writing

Paul makes the occasion for this letter clear, but it hinges on the unity and integrity of the letter. If chapters 15 and 16 are part of the original letter (as the evidence strongly indicates) then the occasion and date of Romans can be fixed with precision. The epistle to the Romans was occasioned by Paul's travel plans (Romans 1:10-13; 15:23-29). The lengthy explanation by D. A. Carson, Douglas J. Moo, and Leon Morris merits inclusion.

"If there is little debate about whether Paul wrote Romans, neither is there about the general situation in which he wrote. According to 15:22-29, three localities figure in Paul's travel plans: Jerusalem, Rome, and Spain. Paul's immediate destination is Jerusalem. As his prayer in 15:30-33 reveals, Paul looked upon this trip to Jerusalem with considerable trepidation. Paul is bringing to the impoverished Jewish Christians in Jerusalem an offering gathered from the Gentile-Christian churches he has planted (15:25-27), and he is uncertain how the offering will be received. He hopes that the offering will be acceptable to the Jewish believers and that this will help cement relations between Jewish and Gentile Christians. But Paul is unsure about this and requests the Roman Christians to pray for this outcome. The second stop Paul plans to make is in Rome, but only as a stopping-off point on his way to Spain (15:24, 28). This is not to minimize the strategic importance of Rome but reflects Paul's sense of calling to 'preach the gospel where Christ (is) not known' (15:20). Paul's gaze is fixed on faraway Spain because the task of initial church planting in the eastern Mediterranean has been completed: 'from Jerusalem all the way around to Illyricum, I have fully proclaimed the gospel of Christ' (15:19). As a result of his first three missionary journeys, thriving churches have been planted in major metropolitan centers throughout this region. These churches can carry on the task of evangelism in their respective areas while Paul pursues his calling in virgin territory" (*An Introduction to the New Testament,* 241).

Phoebe, "a servant of the church which is in Cenchrea," was about to journey to Rome and this provided an excellent opportunity for Paul to have this letter delivered (16:1-2). Cenchrea was the nearby port for Corinth and thus confirms the location for the writing. In addition, Gaius (Romans 16:23), and Erastus (Romans 16:23) are probably identified with the Corinthian church (1 Corinthians 1:14; 2 Timothy 4:20). The moral decay of Corinth provides the backdrop for Paul's description of the sinfulness of all humanity (Romans 1-3). Happily, the problems that plagued the church at Corinth were now resolved and were not apparent in the church at Rome.

Romans was written at a strategic but difficult time in Paul's life. His journey to Jerusalem was fraught with danger (Acts 20:3, 22-24). Paul hoped that the offering he carried for relief of the saints in Jerusalem would be well received, but he anticipated conflict with the Jewish authorities. Paul's announcement to the Ephesian elders that they would never see him again (Acts 20:25) showed the gravity of the situation. The elders wept at that news (Acts 20:36-38) and Paul must have felt something of that pain himself. Guthrie relates the contents and form of the letter to the Romans to the strategic personal situation of Paul. "The apostle had reached a turning point in his missionary career in that his face was turned towards Jerusalem and Rome and he could not be certain what the outcome would be. He therefore casts his mind back and gathers almost unconsciously the fruits of his past work. His mind has been dwelling on many great themes and he now proceeds to write down his conclusions. He may well have chosen to send the results of his meditations to the church at Rome because he foresaw its strategic importance for the future. Or he may have had in mind these maturing thoughts and the occasion to commit them to writing arose with the need to write to the Roman church about his coming visit" (*Introduction to the New Testament*, 410).

Paul had a longstanding burden for the Christians at Rome (Romans 1:8-10). They seemed to look to Paul as their mentor and he felt a keen need to help strengthen them in the faith (1:11). At the same time, Paul felt a need for the mutual encouragement both he and they would receive (1:12). Paul had been prevented from visiting in the past, but the way now seemed open (1:13). He expected a time of harvest in Rome. Spain was virgin territory for the gospel and that was Paul's ultimate destination (15:24, 28). Rome was of vital importance to that mission. Geographically his travels must take him through Rome. More importantly the Christians at Rome had progressed to the point that they could become a sending church. Their prayers, encouragement, and even financial support would help Paul in his next missionary endeavor (15:24-29).

There was also a vital social and theological issue that compelled Paul to write Romans. Though addressed to the Christians at Rome, it is a universal letter for Christians of all times and places. Paul has defended the gospel of salvation by faith against legalistic Judaism in his letter to Galatians. The church is becoming less Jewish and more Gentile. There are important issues to be addressed regarding salvation by faith, the relationship to the Law of Moses, and the place of Israel in God's redemptive plan. Paul addresses these issues with profound depth and clarity in Romans. As Moo explains, "What emerges as especially significant from this sketch of Paul's own situation is that he writes his letter to the Romans at an important transition point in his missionary career. For almost twenty-five years, Paul has planted churches in the eastern Mediterranean. Now he prepares to bring to Jerusalem a practical fruit of that work, one that he hopes will heal the most serious social-theological rift in the early church—the relationship between Jew and Gentile in the people of God. Beyond Jerusalem, Spain, with its 'fields ripe for the harvesting,' beckons. On the way is Rome" (*The Epistle to the Romans*, 3).

Purpose
Paul likely had several purposes in mind when he wrote the letter to the Romans. Which of those purposes dominated is not easy to determine. Paul's travel plans, the need for strengthening the church, resolution of the place of the Jew and Gentile in God's program, and the exact nature and

full extent of the gospel all prompted Paul to write this letter. Each of these issues is addressed in Romans. Moo concludes, "The purpose of Paul in Romans, then, cannot be confined to any one of these suggestions; Romans has several purposes. But the various purposes share a common denominator: Paul's missionary situation. The past battles in Galatia and Corinth; the coming crisis in Jerusalem; the desire to secure a missionary base for his work in Spain; the need to unify the Romans around 'his' gospel to support his work in Spain--all these forced Paul to write a letter in which he carefully rehearsed his understanding of the gospel, especially as it related to the salvation-historical questions of Jew and Gentile and the continuity of the plan of salvation" (*The Epistle to the Romans*, 20-21).

Date

The date for the writing of Romans can be established from the circumstances involved. The epistle was written during the winter that Paul spent in Corinth and before he made his last visit to Jerusalem (Acts 20:1-3 with 2 Corinthians 13). Hiebert, like Conybeare and Howson, dates Paul's three-month ministry in Corinth during the spring of A.D. 58 (*An Introduction to the New Testament*, 2:175). Noting that the spring sailing season was about to begin, he suggests Romans was actually written late in the spring of 58. Others, like Guthrie, are less precise, but agree on a timeframe of A.D. 57-59.

Unity and Integrity of Romans

The authenticity of Romans has been accepted without challenge. However, the rise of higher criticism in modern times led to questions about the unity and hence the integrity of Romans in its present form. Questions center on the last two chapters and whether they were part of the original letter or were added later. Guthrie provides a detailed examination of the issues (*New Testament Introduction*, 412-27). The problem of chapters 15 and 16 stems from the fact that some fragments of Romans end the epistle at chapter 14. There is also some variation in where the doxology (16:25-27) appears. After examining the information Guthrie concludes, "To sum up this mass of textual evidence, it would seem certain that a shorter recension of the epistle was in circulation at one time in its textual history. That this recension was also very early is also probable. But to account for all the variations is by no means an easy matter and a number of explanations have been suggested, which will need to be briefly considered" (*New Testament Introduction*, 418). Variations in the ancient manuscripts have led to several hypotheses.

1. The letter originally ended at chapter 14. Chapters 15 and 16 were added later and may or may not be Pauline. This position has been thoroughly examined and well refuted. This explanation is given little credence today.

2. A shorter version was in circulation. It was prepared either by Paul himself or by others associated with Paul in an attempt to make Romans more "universal" for broader use in the church. Proponents of this view are uncertain whether the original letter contained all sixteen chapters and was shortened, or whether the last two chapters were added to the original letter. Whichever the case, all sixteen chapters are considered genuinely Pauline though not necessarily united.

3. Chapter 16 was a separate letter. Others suggest that chapter 15 was originally a part of the letter, but chapter 16 was actually a separate letter of introduction for Phoebe and was intended for the church at Ephesus. Advocates of this view suggest that Ephesus is a more likely location given the large number of personal greetings in the chapter. They claim Paul was well known at Ephesus and it would be appropriate for him to have many acquaintances there, but it would be improbable at Rome.

4. The doxology was added. Some scholars propose that the doxology (16:25-27) was not part of the original letter. They accept it as genuinely Pauline but claim it was incorporated into the letter at a later date and at varying locations.

5. Marcion deleted these two chapters. Most scholars favor the explanation that Marcion was responsible for deleting the last two chapters from Romans because he objected to its Jewish nature. Origin (A.D. 185-254) and Tertullian (A.D. 160-220) first raised this accusation. "Perhaps the best explanation is also the earliest: that Marcion was responsible for cutting off the last two chapters of the letter. Given his biases against the Old Testament, Marcion may have been unhappy with the Old Testament quotations in 15:3 and 15:9-11 and considered that 15:1 was the most convenient place to make the break (D. A. Carson, Douglas J. Moo, and Leon Morris, *An Introduction to the New Testament,* 246).

Solution. The problem is not as serious as it might first appear. While there is variation in some early manuscripts, the evidence supports the unity and integrity of Romans as we now have it.

1.   The manuscript evidence supports the inclusion of all sixteen chapters in their current form. "Although we have some three-hundred manuscripts of Romans, not one of them, so far as it is uninjured, fails to give the Epistle complete, as we have it today, with the one exception of the final doxology. There are few today who deny the genuineness of these chapters, and still fewer who hold that ch. 15 was not in the original Epistle to the Romans" (Thiessen, *Introduction to the New Testament*, 224).

2.   Most of the oldest manuscripts have the doxology at the end of chapter 16 and only there. Variation in the location of the doxology is largely confined to fragments and to later manuscripts (Hiebert, *An Introduction to the New Testament*, 2:171).

3.   Chapter 15 is an integral part of Romans and a necessary conclusion. It is recognized as Pauline and as an inherent part of the epistle. "Chapter 15:1-13 is the natural sequel to chapter 14. It seems incredible that Paul should have closed the epistle with chapter 14. That Paul wrote chapter 15 is now commonly admitted. But if it was not written in connection with chapter 14, how are we to account for the existence of an independent passage so imminently fitted to be joined to the epistle?" (Hiebert, *An Introduction to the New Testament*, 2:171).

4.   Greetings to and from a long list of individuals in chapter 16 are explainable. Paul had many associates and some would likely have found their way to Rome. "The only epistle to a church which contains greetings to individuals is the one to the Colossians, to whom he was a stranger. Thus in writing to the church at Rome, where he has not yet been, it is but natural that he should send his greetings to the Christians there whom he knew" (Hiebert, *Introduction to the New Testament*, 2:173). No manuscripts end the epistle at chapter 15. Moo insists, "Textually, this theory is on shaky ground from the outset, for there is no single MS of Romans that contains only 15 chaps" (*The Epistle to the Romans*, 8).

Conclusion. These theories do not pose a serious threat to the integrity of the Epistle to the Romans. All sixteen chapters are recognized as Pauline and are best explained as united in the original letter. "We have, then, good grounds for concluding that Paul's letter to the Roman Christians contained all sixteen chapters. ... And we think it likely that 16:25-27 was Paul's own conclusion to this letter" (Carson, Moo, and Morris, *An Introduction to the New Testament*, 247). Hiebert reaches a similar conclusion. "We unhesitatingly conclude that Paul would not terminate the epistle with chapter 14. The textual phenomena are best explained due to later tampering with the text. The balance of evidence seems definitely in favor of Romans 16 as part of the original letter" (*Introduction to the New Testament*, 2:174).

Distinctive Features

Theology. Romans contains the most comprehensive statement of the doctrine of salvation by grace through faith to be found in the New Testament. The sinfulness of mankind, the atoning sacrifice of Christ, justification by faith and faith alone, and the consequent deliverance from sin's power by the Holy Spirit are clearly declared in Romans. Though it is not a systematic theology, the epistle includes important references to Christology, ecclesiology, and eschatology. These doctrines are not extensively treated, but the doctrines of sin and salvation are carefully and fully developed in Romans.

Style and quality. This epistle is the most carefully reasoned and formal of Paul's letters. The literary genre of Romans is difficult to classify. Its genre has been called "diatribe," "treatise," "ambassadorial letter," and "letter essay," to name a few. Personal references in the opening and the greetings at the close mark Romans as a personal letter. However, the careful argumentation, methodical development of subject, and frequent use of questions mark it as a theological treatise. Godet explains, "The Epistle to the Romans is thus, properly speaking, neither a treatise nor a letter; it is a treatise contained in a letter" (Godet, *Commentary on the Epistle to the Romans*, 59). According to Hiebert, "The epistle is characterized by the systematic and logical arrangement of its contents. It is one of the finest pieces of logic ever penned. It is full of originality of thought and is forceful in its presentation" (*An Introduction to the New Testament*, 2:180).

Universality. Universality permeates Romans. One need not eliminate chapters 15 and 16 in order to make this epistle universal. "The outstanding characteristic of Romans is its universalism. It shows that in all times and nations men are sinners. This universal sinfulness of man is traced back to mankind's ultimate oneness in Adam. In the Gospel there is offered a full salvation that is available to all alike, whether Jew or Gentile, on the principle of faith. And this free salvation is treated 'not in its relation to a single soul or even a single church, but in its relation to the creation itself and to every nation in it'" (Hiebert, *An Introduction to the New Testament*, 2:179-80).

171

Old Testament quotations. Paul quotes more often from the Old Testament in this epistle than in all the other epistles combined. Romans has 61 direct quotations and many more indirect allusions to the Old Testament. Paul draws from at least 14 different books of the Old Testament. Isaiah and Psalms are the most frequently quoted (Hiebert, *An Introduction to the New Testament*, 2:181).

Influence. The Epistle to the Romans has been at the heart of the great evangelical revivals of history. Romans was the key to Luther's conversion and subsequently to the Protestant Reformation. According to Johnson, "Great intellects like Augustine, Luther, Calvin, and Edwards have studied Romans only to discover depths beyond their depths. ... It may be because Romans is the greatest treatise on God that has ever been written that the letter has figured prominently in every significant evangelical renaissance in history. Such was the case with Saint Augustine, Luther, and John Wesley. While not a full return to evangelical faith, the more recent work of Karl Barth on Romans, (*Romerbrief,* 1990) broke the stranglehold of liberal theology on the scholarly world and brought some significant return to a biblical theology" (*The Freedom Letter*, 11-12).

Theme

Multiple themes are woven together in the tapestry of the epistle to the Romans, but the gospel, the "good news" of justification by faith through the redemptive work of Jesus Christ, dominates. Opinions as to the unifying theme of Romans have shifted with time. "Opinions about the theme of Romans have tended over time to move the center of attention to the end of the letter. The Reformers, following the lead of Luther, singled out justification by faith, prominent especially in chapters 1-4, as the theme of the letter. At the beginning of this century, however, Albert Schweitzer argued that justification by faith was no more than a "battle" doctrine--a doctrine Paul used only to fight against Judaizers--and that the true theme of Romans is to be found in the teachings of Romans 6-8 about union with Christ and the work of God's Spirit. Romans 9-11 was the next section to take center stage in the debate. ... the history of salvation and of the two peoples, Jews and Gentiles, within this history. Finally, it has been argued that the practical exhortation to unity in 14:1-15:13 is the true heart of the letter" (Carson, Moo, and Morris, *An Introduction to the New Testament*, 253).

All the themes noted above are significant components of Romans, but Luther and the Reformers were closest to the mark. The theme of Romans is the "gospel," the "good news" of justification by grace alone through faith alone in Christ alone. Paul intends to carry the gospel to Spain and it is this gospel that he expounds clearly in Romans. "It is the word 'gospel' that has pride of place in 1:16-17, which is so often (and probably rightly) taken to be the statement of the letter's theme. Moreover, as we have seen, Romans grows out of Paul's missionary situation, which makes natural a focus on that gospel with which Paul had been entrusted by his Lord. Romans, then, is Paul's statement of his gospel" (Carson, Moo, and Morris, *An Introduction to the New Testament*, 254).

Key Verses

For I am not ashamed of the gospel, for it is the power of God for salvation to everyone who believes, to the Jew first and also to the Greek.
For in it the righteousness of God is revealed from faith to faith;
as it is written, "But the righteous man shall live by faith"
(Romans 1:16-17).

Message of Romans

The theme stated by Paul in 1:16-17 is explained in the balance of the letter. The key thoughts Paul develops in his letter are all found in these two verses. Readers are to keep the words *salvation, faith, everyone,* and *live* in mind as they read this letter. Paul is not ashamed of the gospel because of what it is. It is *the power of God for the salvation to everyone who believes.* To justify that high estimate of the gospel Paul explains each element of the gospel.

The need for the gospel: the universal sinfulness of man (1:18-3:20). The universal need of man for salvation is proved conclusively (1:18-3:20). All humanity is *under sin* and therefore *under the wrath of God.* Gentiles (1:18-31) and Jews (2:1-29) alike stand guilty of sin (3:1-20) because they have not heeded God's revelation. Gentiles are condemned by natural revelation even though they are *without the Law.* God has revealed Himself in nature, but they have exchanged the truth of God for corrupt images, and have worshiped the creation rather than the Creator. Jews stand first in guilt because they have God's special revelation in the Law and are *under the Law.* They have heard the Law, but they have not believed it and practiced it. They boast about being Jews and take pride in their circumcision, but are sinners at heart. Both Jews and Greeks (Gentiles) are *without excuse.* All are *under sin.* Sin is a universal problem only God can solve.

The heart of the gospel: justification by grace through faith (3:21-31). *But now*, marks a dramatic change of focus from the sinfulness of all humanity to the gift of redemption through Jesus Christ (3:21). God's righteousness has been revealed. Salvation has been provided through Christ. The heart of the gospel is declared in 3:21-26. In one grand, sweeping paragraph Paul combines the universal sinfulness of man, the harmonizing of the grace and justice of God, the atoning sacrifice of Christ, and justification by faith that results in God's righteousness replacing the sin of those who believe. This is good news for all and eliminates every vestige of religious pride (3:27-31).

The nature of the gospel: imputation of God's righteousness by faith (4:1-5:21). Paul marshals evidence to prove that the gospel is exactly what he has stated. Both the need of man (universal sin) and the provision of God (justification by faith) predate the Jew and Gentile distinction. **Abraham** proves conclusively that God imputes His righteousness to and only to those who believe (4:1-25). Abraham believed God and God imputed (credited) righteousness to him (4:1-22). Abraham was justified (declared righteous) before the Law and circumcision were instituted. He is the father of all who believe, both Jews and Gentiles. Now the benefits of Christ's death and resurrection are credited to all who believe, but only to those who believe (4:23-25). Justification is by grace through faith and results in hope of sharing in the coming glory of God (5:1-2). This hope sustains the believer through the Holy Spirit who indwells them (5:3-5). God amply demonstrated His love by sending His Son to die for sinners while they were helpless to solve their sin problem (5:6-11). Those who believe are saved from the wrath of God that sin requires.

As Abraham is the father of all who believe, Adam is the father through whom sin has become universal. **Adam** proves conclusively that everyone, both Jews and Gentiles, need reconciling and need God's righteousness (5:12-21). The imputation of Adam's sin has created a universal experience of death (5:12-14). By contrast, God's righteousness is imputed to those who believe (5:15-21). *But the free gift is not like the transgression. For if by the transgression of the one the many died, much more did the grace of God and the gift by the grace of the one Man, Jesus Christ, abound to the many* (5:15). Paul makes a startling statement that he defends and explains in the following chapters. *The Law came in so that the transgression would increase; but where sin increased, grace abounded all the more* (5:20).

The effect of the gospel: impartation of God's righteousness (6:1-8:39). Paul has stated that grace has triumphed over sin and faith has displaced works. What are we to say then about the continuing influence of sin and the role of the Law? Does grace mean that a believer can continue in sin? Is he or she under the Law? No! As God's righteousness is **imputed** (positionally and permanently) through faith in Christ's redemptive work, so God's righteousness is **imparted** (practically and progressively) through the believer's union with Christ (6:1-23). Deliverance from the authority of sin is impossible through the Law (7:1-25) but is accomplished in the believer by the power of the indwelling Holy Spirit (8:1-27).

The thought that grace condones sin is anathema. One's responsibility is to submit to the lordship of Christ and experience grace's liberating power (6:11-23). The Law was given by God to expose sin, not to remove sin (7:1-13). The problem with the Law is its impotence; it lacked the power to make the "fleshly" person "spiritual" (7:14-23). Only Jesus Christ can deliver the believer from the continuing influence of the sin nature (7:24-25). What the Law cannot do, the Holy Spirit does in the lives of all who believe, He liberates from the power of sin! (8:1-16). God's salvation is complete. It not only saves from the **penalty** of sin; it also saves from the ongoing **power** of sin. Yet that is not the end of the story. God's salvation will also one day save the believer from the very **presence** of sin (8:18-30). The prospect of eternal glory excites Paul and elicits a response of awe-filled worship (8:31-39). Chapter 8 is the crown jewel of Romans.

> "If the Epistle to the Romans rightly has been called 'the cathedral of the Christian faith,' then surely the eighth chapter may be regarded as its most sacred shrine, or its high altar of worship, of praise, and of prayer. ... Here, we stand in the full liberty of the children of God, and enjoy a prospect of that glory of God which someday we are to share" (Charles Erdman, *The Epistle of Paul to the Romans*, 82).

The response to the gospel: Israel's unbelief and God's plan (9:1-11:32). What about Israel's rejection of Jesus Christ? Where does the Jew stand in this present age of grace? Has God rejected Israel and abandoned His covenant promises to Israel? What is Israel's future in God's plan? Paul addresses these questions systematically in chapters 9-11. Paul's deep love for Israel is unquestioned (9:1; 10:1). *I have great sorrow and unceasing grief in my heart. For I could wish that I myself were accursed,*

175

separated from Christ for the sake of my brethren, my kinsmen according to the flesh (Romans 9:2-3).

Israel's past: Israel's rejection and the fairness of God (9:4-33). How does one account for Israel's failure to believe in Jesus Christ in light of all the privileges they have enjoyed from God's hand (9:4-5)? It is certainly not a failure of God's Word, nor is it injustice on God's part (9:6-18). God is sovereign, but Israel bears the responsibility for their unbelief (9:19-29). Israel has failed to obtain God's righteousness because they pursued it by works, not by faith (9:30-33). In spite of Israel's past privileges, only a "remnant" has believed and experienced God's salvation. By contrast, the Gentiles have believed and thus have received righteousness.

Israel's present: a remnant is being saved through the gospel (10:1-21). God is now saving a believing remnant out of Israel. Faith is indispensable to Israel's salvation. *If you confess with your mouth Jesus as Lord, and believe in your heart that God raised Him from the dead, you will be saved; for with the heart a person believes, resulting in righteousness, and with the mouth he confesses, resulting in salvation* (10:9-10). Both Jew and Gentile are under sin and must come by faith to Jesus Christ. *There is no distinction between Jew and Greek; for the same Lord is Lord of all, abounding in riches for all who call on Him* (10:12). Saving faith comes in response to hearing the gospel; therefore the good news that Jesus is the Savior must be preached, beginning with Israel.

Israel's future: God will prevail and all Israel will be saved (11:1-32). What does the future hold for Israel? Has God rejected Israel? Paul's answer is, definitely not! (11:1). God has not rejected His people (11:2-10). They have not fallen beyond recovery (11:11-24). Rather, the unbelief and fall of Israel is part of God's sovereign plan. Their unbelief has opened the door of opportunity for Gentiles to believe. When God's entire plan is seen, there is no room for arrogance on the part of Gentiles! God is now using and will yet use the salvation of the Gentiles to provoke Israel to jealousy and ultimately to lead Israel to repentance and faith (11:25-32). Israel remains God's chosen and beloved people. God's covenant promises are irrevocable. Israel's hardening is only temporary. When God's plan for the Gentiles reaches its fullness, "all Israel will be saved" (11:25). For both Gentile and Jew, disobedience will give way to God's mercy (11:28-32).

Paul's doxology: the unsearchable riches of God's plan (11:33-36). God's sovereign plan for the salvation of Israel is an awesome display of power wedded to grace. Paul cannot help but pause and express his worship and praise to such a God. This doxology climaxes Paul's explanation of the gospel and is the transition to the practical application of that gospel to the believer's everyday life (12-15).

The application of the gospel: how the righteous live by faith (12:1-15:13). Praise leads to appeal. *Therefore* opens the "practical" section. Paul sums up all he has written in the one word, "mercies," and applies it to the believer's experience. The gospel of salvation by grace through faith that prompted Paul's doxology merits a worshipful response from every believer (12:1-2). All of the exhortations of chapters 12-15 are amplifications of the theme in 1:17, *The righteous shall live by faith.* God's mercy, as expressed in Christ, calls believers to offer their whole being to God as a living sacrifice. They must consciously resist conforming to the world around them. To do this their minds must be renewed so that they can think God's thoughts after Him.

All who believe are now members of Christ's body and gifted to serve one another (12:3-8). Such service is to be prompted by and permeated with love (12:9-21). Living by faith is not confined to the household of faith (12:1-21). Saints are to be submissive to the state as God's established authority (13:1-7). Love does not violate God's Law; rather it fulfills it (13:8-10). Paul now issues a wakeup call (13:11-14). *Do this, knowing the time, that it is already the hour for you to awaken from sleep; for now salvation is nearer to us than when we believed* (13:11). The full and eternal realization of our salvation is near. All who believe should say no to the sinful flesh and avail themselves of the resources of the new life that is theirs in Christ.

The gospel of salvation by grace through faith has brought Jews and Gentiles together in the body of Christ. Christian liberty leaves room for choice in their diversity of customs and cultures (14:1-15:13). Christians should not be judging one another over matters in which God has given them freedom to choose (14:1-12). Rather than demand and flout their rights, they should seek to build up other believers (14:13-21). As faith is the basis of salvation, so faith is the basis of one's choices in everyday life (14:22-23). All believers, whether strong or weak, Gentile or Jew, are to live in unity. But those who are strong in faith should lead the way (15:1-6). Christ Himself has modeled the strong love that serves and unites (15:7-13).

The spread of the gospel: from the Mediterranean to Spain (15:14-33). Paul concludes the body of the letter by explaining his reason for writing so "boldly." God has entrusted Paul with the gospel for the Gentiles (15:14-17). This divine appointment has been fulfilled all across the Mediterranean (15:17-22). Now the time has come for Paul to visit Rome on his way to Spain, the next frontier for the gospel (15:23-33).

The fellowship of the gospel: personal greetings (16:1-24). Phoebe's journey to Rome gives Paul the opportunity to write this letter and also to send personal greetings to a host of Christian friends (16:1-16). A brief warning is in order because false teachers have dogged Paul's path of ministry (16:17-19). All such false teaching comes from Satan and will be crushed under the believer's feet by God's power (16:20). Paul's companions also have friends in Rome and their greetings are added to his own long list (16:21-24).

The ultimate triumph of the gospel: doxology and benediction (16:25-27). This letter to the Romans has been punctuated with doxologies (8:31-39; 11:33-36). This doxology serves as a benediction to the letter (16:25-27). Paul began by calling this message "the gospel of God" (1:1), but he closes by calling it "my gospel" (16:25). God has now revealed this gospel and confirmed it in the "prophetic writings." Paul has faithfully proclaimed this gospel. God's goal is "that all nations might believe and obey Him." Eternal glory is due to this wise God and it will be His forever through Jesus Christ.

Outline

I. The Gospel of God: Paul's Calling to Share It	1:1-17
A. Paul's commission to preach the gospel	1:1-5
B. Paul's greetings to those who have believed	1:6-7
C. Paul's desire to preach the gospel at Rome	1:8-15
D. Statement of the gospel: salvation for all by faith	1:16-17
II. The Need for the Gospel: Universal Sinfulness of Man	1:18-3:20
A. The guilt of Gentiles	1:18-32
1. God's revelation through nature is plain to all	1:18-20
2. Gentiles have rejected God's revelation	1:21-23
3. God has judicially bound them over to depravity	1:24-32
B. The guilt of Jews	2:1-3:8
1. The principles of God's judgment	2:1-16
2. The privilege and peril of the Jews	2:17-3:8

	a. Jews have broken God's revealed Law	2:17-24
	b. Jews have trusted circumcision, not God	2:25-29
	c. God's judgment is fair	3:1-8
C.	The guilt of all whether Jew or Gentile	3:9-20
	1. The accusation: all alike are under sin	3:9
	2. The evidence: all sin in character and conduct	3:10-18
	3. The verdict: whole world is accountable to God	3:19-20

III. The Heart of the Gospel: Justification by Faith — 3:20-31

A.	Universal provision of God's righteousness	3:20-26
	1. Apart from the Law, as prophesied	3:21
	2. Appropriated by faith in Jesus Christ	3:22
	3. Accomplished by the atoning sacrifice of Christ	3:23-25a
	4. Accounts for God's dealing with sinners	3:25b-26
B.	Excludes any boasting since it is by faith for all	3:27-31

IV. The Nature of the Gospel: Imputation of Righteousness — 4:1-5:21

A.	Abraham proves justification is by faith	4:1-25
	1. Righteousness imputed to Abraham by faith	4:1-8
	2. Righteousness imputed before circumcision	4:9-12
	3. Righteousness promised to all who believe	4:13-25
B.	Exultation: the enduring blessings of justification	5:1-11
	1. Peace with God	5:1
	2. Firmly standing in grace	5:2a
	3. Rejoicing in hope of the glory of God	5:2b
	4. Rejoicing in present sufferings	5:3-8
	5. Will be saved from God's wrath	5:9-10
	6. Reconciled to God	5:11
C.	Christ provided justification as a free gift	5:12-20
	1. Universal product of Adam's sin: death	5:12-14
	2. Universal provision of Christ's gift: life	5:15-19
	3. Triumph of life over death, grace over Law	5:20-21

V. The Effect of the Gospel: Impartation of Righteousness — 6:1-8:39

A.	Basis of applied righteousness: union with Christ	6:1-14
	1. The issue: does grace mean a license to sin?	6:1
	2. The answer: definitely not!	6:2a
	3. The explanation: union with Christ	6:2b-10
	4. The application: one must act on this truth	6:11-14
	a. By knowing the truth of union with Christ	6:6,9
	b. By reckoning (accepting) it as true	6:11

	c. By yielding to (acting on) this truth	6:12-14
B.	Effect of applied righteousness: obedience to Christ	6:15-23
	1. The issue: does freedom from Law lead to sin?	6:15a
	2. The answer: definitely not!	6:15b
	3. The explanation: obligation to righteousness	6:16-18
	4. The application: yield in obedience to God	6:19-23
C.	Alternative to grace: enslavement to the Law	7:1-25
	1. Now under Christ not the Law	7:1-6
	2. The Law is holy but can only expose sin	7:7-13
	3. The Law is powerless to overcome sin	7:14-23
	4. The Law points one to Christ who overcame sin	7:24-25
D.	Operation of grace: set free by the Holy Spirit	8:1-17
	1. Freedom from the condemnation of sin	8:1-4
	2. Freedom from the control of sin	8:5-11
	3. Freedom to serve under Christ's control	8:12-17
E.	Goal of justification by faith: glorification	8:8-39
	1. Anticipation of glory in present suffering	8:18-30
	2. Assurance of glory: God's unconquerable love	8:31-39

VI.	The Response to the Gospel: Israel's Unbelief	9:1-11:36
A.	Paul's sorrow over Israel's rejection	9:1-5
B.	Past: Israel's rejection and the fairness of God	9:6-33
	1. Rejection does not mean God's Word has failed	9:6-13
	2. Israel's rejection does not mean God is unfair	9:14-29
	3. Israel's rejection is due to her own unbelief	9:30-33
C.	Present: Israel's ignorance and need for the gospel	10:1-21
	1. Israel is ignorant of the gospel of Christ	10:1-5
	2. Israel's only hope is in the gospel of Christ	10:6-13
	3. Israel needs to hear the gospel	10:14-15
	4. Israel must respond to the gospel with faith	10:16-21
D.	Future: Israel will yet repent and be restored	11:1-32
	1. Israel's rejection is partial	11:1-10
	2. Israel's rejection is not permanent	11:11-24
	3. God has promised that all Israel will be saved	11:25-32
E.	Unsearchable riches of the gospel: a doxology	11:33-36

VII.	The Application of the Gospel: How to Live by Faith	12:1-15:13
A.	The believer's relation to God	12:1-2
B.	The believer's relation to society	12:3-21
	1. Serving others according to one's gift	12:3-8
	2. Serving other believers in love	12:9-13

	3. Showing love in a hostile world	12:14-21
C.	The believer's relation to the state	13:1-10
	1. Submission to established authority	13:1-7
	2. Love toward fellow citizens	13:8-10
D.	The believer's relation to time and Christ's coming	13:11-14
E.	The believer's relation to a weaker brother	14:1-15:13
	1. Do not judge your brother	14:1-12
	2. Do not offend your brother	14:13-23
	3. Accept your brother as Christ has accepted you	15:1-13
VIII.	The Spread of the Gospel: Targeting Spain	15:14-33
A.	Paul's commission to preach to the Gentiles	15:14-16
B.	Paul's Mediterranean mission completed	15:17-22
C.	Paul's commitment to take the gospel to Spain	15:23-29
D.	Paul's request for their prayers	15:30-33
IX.	The Fellowship of the Gospel: Personal Greetings	16:1-24
A.	Commendation of Phoebe	16:1-2
B.	Greetings to Paul's friends in Rome	16:3-16
C.	Warning about false teachers	16:17-20
D.	Greetings from Paul's friends to Rome	16:21-24
X.	Concluding Doxology	16:25-27

Bibliography

Bruce, F. F. *The Epistle of Paul to the Romans.* Tyndale New Testament Commentaries. Grand Rapids: Wm. B. Eerdmans Publishing Co., 1963.

Carson, D. A., Douglas J. Moo, and Leon Morris. *An Introduction to the New Testament.* Grand Rapids: Zondervan Publishing House, 1991.

Cranfield, C. E. B. *A Critical and Exegetical Commentary on the Epistle to the Romans.* International Critical Commentary. Edinburgh: T. & T. Clark, 1979.

Dunn, James D. G. *Romans.* Word Biblical Commentary, 2 vols. Dallas: Word Books, 1988.

Godet, Frederick L. *Commentary on the Epistle to the Romans.* Reprint. Grand Rapids: Zondervan Publishing House, 1956.

Guthrie, Donald. *New Testament Introduction.* Downers Grove, IL: InterVarsity Press, 1990.

Hiebert, D. Edmond. An *Introduction to the New Testament.* Vol. 1. Chicago: Moody Press, 1975.

Johnson, Alan F. *The Freedom Letter.* Chicago: Moody Press, 1974.

____. *Romans.* Everyman's Bible Commentary. Chicago: Moody Press, 2000.

Liddon, H. P. *Explanatory Analysis of St. Paul's Epistle to the Romans.* Grand Rapids: Zondervan Publishing House, 1961.

Lopez, Rene. *Romans Unlocked.* Rev. ed. Springfield, MO: 21st Century Press, 2009.

Luther, Martin. *Commentary on Romans.* Translated by J. Theodore Mueller. Grand Rapids: Zondervan Publishing House, 1954.

Moo, Douglas J. *The Epistle to the Romans.* New International Commentary. Grand Rapids: Wm. B. Eerdmans Publishing Co., 1996.

____. *Romans.* NIV Application Commentary. Grand Rapids: Zondervan Publishing House, 2000.

Morris, Leon. *Romans.* Pillar New Testament Commentary. Grand Rapids: Wm. B. Eerdmans Publishing Co., 1988.

Stott, John. *Romans: God's Good News for the World.* Downers Grove, IL: InterVarsity Press, 1994.

Stiffler, James M. *The Epistle to the Romans.* Chicago: Moody Press, 1983.

Thiessen, Henry C. *Introduction to the New Testament.* Grand Rapids: Wm. B. Eerdmans Publishing Co., 1952.

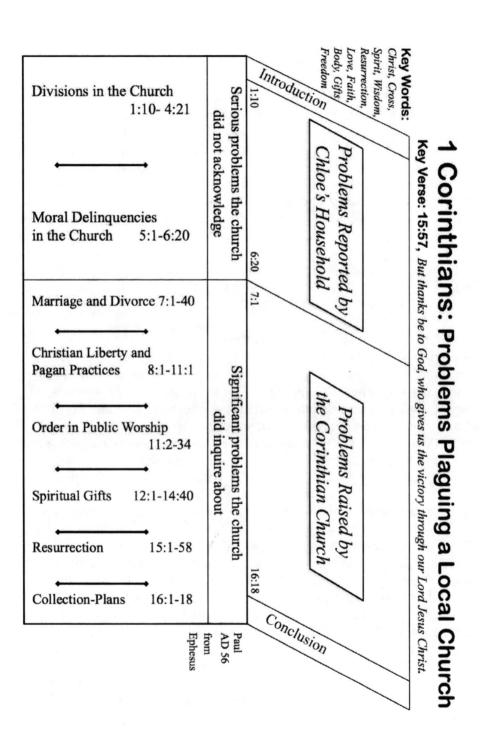

1 and 2 CORINTHIANS

"We possess more detailed information about the actual conditions within the church at Corinth than about any other church in the New Testament. The picture given us of this church shows that even apostolic churches were not perfect churches. Our picture of the Corinthian church is drawn, not by an enemy of the church but by the founder of that church himself, as contained in his two epistles to that church which have been preserved for us. ... The letter also contains a distressing revelation of the interior life of an apostolic church. It forever dissipates the dream that churches founded and nurtured by the apostles were in an exceptional condition of holiness of life or purity of doctrine. Out of the sins and shortcomings of the Corinthian church our sovereign God has seen fit to give us one of the priceless treasures of the New Testament" (D. Edmond Hiebert, *An Introduction to the New Testament,* 2:102, 116).

Author

Acceptance. The Pauline authorship of 1 Corinthians is almost universally accepted. Not even the most ardent opponents of church tradition question the Pauline authenticity of 1 Corinthians. Evidence is very strong for 2 Corinthians as well, but questions have been raised about portions of Paul's second letter. The most frequently and strongly debated section is 2 Corinthians 6:14-7:1. But charges that this and possibly a few other passages in 2 Corinthians are non-Pauline interpolations have not been widely accepted. Pauline authorship of both epistles has strong support from church history and so few opponents from among modern critics that New Testament introductions scarcely mention the issue of authorship.

External evidence. Early church fathers endorsed these letters as authentic and credited them to the apostle Paul. Authentications include these: Clement of Rome (c. 95-97) endorsed Pauline authorship. Polycarp (c. 110-150) quoted from or alluded to both epistles. The Shepherd of Hermas (c. 115-140) contains references to both epistles. Irenaeus (c. 130-202) confirmed Pauline authorship. Later second-century church fathers, such as Justin Martyr, Clement of Alexandria, Tertullian, and Origen, also affirmed Pauline authorship. Church fathers of the third and fourth century demonstrate unbroken support for Pauline authorship. These include Eusebius, Jerome, and Augustine (Geisler, *A General Introduction to the Bible,* 187, 193).

Internal evidence. Internal evidence is equally strong. Paul identifies himself as the author in the opening of both letters and at the close of his first letter (1 Corinthians 1; 16:21; 2 Corinthians 1:1). Paul refers to himself several times in the biographical sections of both epistles (1 Corinthians 1:12, 13; 3:4, 5, 6, 22; 2 Corinthians 10:1). Extensive personal references occur in the "I" sections that are uniquely and exclusively Pauline (1 Corinthians 2:1-5; 4:1-3; 5:9-11; 9:1-6; 2 Corinthians 3:1-3; 4:1-15; 11:1-12:21). The language, vocabulary, and style of both epistles are typically Pauline. References to Paul's ministry among them harmonize with Luke's record in Acts and also with the later hardships recorded in his pastoral letters.

The City of Corinth

Location. Corinth is located atop a narrow Isthmus that connects the Grecian Peloponnesus with the continent. The city benefited from having a gulf on two sides; both with excellent harbors that attracted ships from across the Mediterranean Sea. The city was also well located for military defense. The Acro-Corinth dominated the southern edge of Corinth. This rocky ledge rose almost perpendicularly to a height of over 1,800 feet. The original city of Corinth began on that mountain, but later spread across the plain, linking the mountain with the harbor areas.

History. Corinth was a thriving commercial center in Paul's day. It had a long history, but achieved its greatest influence during the New Testament era. Corinth was a major Greek city and a strong rival to Athens, the cultural center located 45 miles to the east. The city fell to the Romans in 146 B.C. and was completely destroyed. After a century of neglect, Julius Caesar rebuilt the city as a model of Roman architecture and design. The new city was built and inhabited by veterans and freed men in 46 B.C. and prospered as a thoroughly Roman city. Augustus made Corinth the capital of the province of Achaia. It was also the residence of the proconsul, Gallio (Acts 18:12-17). Nero sought to capitalize on the two natural harbors by digging a canal through the narrow Isthmus. In A.D. 66 Nero turned the first sod in a special ceremony and put six thousand Jewish captives to work digging the canal. Work was soon abandoned, but the project was revived centuries later and a four-mile canal completed in A.D. 1881-1893.

Commerce. Two major avenues of trade converged at Corinth, making it a prosperous commercial center. All goods traveling by land and most cargo carried by ships passed through Corinth. The city was near three busy harbors. Hazardous seas to the south of the Peninsula prompted most ships to unload their cargo at one of the two major ports and transfer it overland to another vessel. Almost all trade between Italy and Asia passed through Corinth. The abundance of trade made Corinth a wealthy city. The ancient geographer Strabo said, "Corinth is called 'wealthy' because of its commerce, since it is situated on the Isthmus and is master of two harbors, of which the one leads straight to Asia, and the other to Italy; and it makes easy the exchange of merchandise from both countries that are so far distant from each other" (Hiebert, *An Introduction to the New Testament*, 2:104).

Inhabitants. Roman officials and free men constituted the dominant minority. The population is estimated to have been at least 300,000 and perhaps as many as 600,000. Part of what made the city prosperous was the fact that two-thirds of its inhabitants were slaves. Wealth and poverty existed side by side. A sizable community of Jews was drawn to the city by its business opportunities and contributed to a diverse population that made Corinth a cosmopolitan city.

Culture. Corinth was a multicultural city. Wealth enabled both a transient population and its leading citizens to put their mark on city life. Vice and violence abounded. Extremes of wealth and poverty, freedom and slavery made for a turbulent social life. Shaw describes Corinth thus: "At night its streets were hideous with the brawls and lewd songs of drunken revelry. In the daytime its markets and squares swarmed with Jewish peddlers, foreign traders, sailors, soldiers, athletes in training, boxers, wrestlers, charioteers, racing-men, betting-men, courtesans, slaves, idlers and parasites of every description-a veritable pandemonium!" (*The Pauline Epistles*, 130). Magnificent architecture and gardens graced the city. Corinth was a pseudo-intellectual city. Money could not buy the sophistication of its rival Athens. Unwilling to admit its "poverty" in that field, Corinth prided itself on its knowledge, literature, and art, "yet with the majority this interest was quite shallow and superficial" (Hiebert, *An Introduction to the New Testament*, 2:105). Wealth and abundant leisure time made Corinth the center of athletics and entertainment. The Isthmian Games were held every two years and were second only to the Olympic games as national festivals.

Morals and religion. The city was notoriously corrupt. The word "Corinth" defined depravity in the Roman Empire. To "Corinthianize" meant to engage in drunkenness and debauchery. Greek plays portrayed Corinthians as drunkards. Alcohol abuse and sexual perversion were widespread. Prostitution was actively promoted in both the old and the new city. The original Greek city located on the peak of the Acro-Corinth had a temple to the goddess of love, Aphrodite. A thousand female prostitutes were available for the free use of "worshipers" visiting the temple. A new temple was built in the city to honor the goddess Venus. Though less depraved than the original, it did little to change the city's reputation. Idolatry flourished. Temples were built to Apollo, Poseidon, Hermes, and even a Pantheon or temple of "All the Gods." Foreign cults with their gods and goddesses were made to feel at home. "Money was freely spent in Corinth for sinful pleasures by those who had come for a moral holiday. The flourishing of both eastern and western religions in Corinth furthered rather than hindered its moral corruption" (Hiebert, *An Introduction to the New Testament,* 2:106).

Corinth represented the worst of paganism, but it was there that the Holy Spirit used Paul to plant a church. The dark background of degeneration helps us appreciate the dramatic change that had occurred in the lives of believers at Corinth (1 Corinthians 5:17; 6:9-11). It also helps explain the many deficiencies and serious problems Paul had to address in his letters (1 Corinthians 5:1-1; 6:1-8; 10:7-13). The monotheism and narrow legalism of the Jews stood in stark contrast to the pagan majority. Paul began his ministry in the synagogue (Acts 18:4) and this Jewish element falsely charged Paul with treason against Caesar (18:12-17). The animosity of the pagan population against the Jews was evident when they turned on the Jews and beat Sosthenes, leader of the synagogue. The strongest indication of the depravity of Corinth lies in the fact that it was here that Paul wrote his letter to the Romans during his third missionary journey. The moral depravity and cultural bankruptcy of Corinth can be seen in Paul's description of the natural man in Romans chapter 1. Farrar writes, "East and west mingled their dregs of foulness in the new Gomorrah of classic culture, and the orgies of the paphian goddess were as notorious as those of Isis and Asherah" (*The Life and Work of St. Paul,* 316).

The Church at Corinth
Founding of the church. Paul arrived alone at Corinth after preaching with limited success in Athens (Acts 18:1-18). At first Paul engaged in tent making with Aquila and Priscilla, a Jewish couple that had been ordered out of Rome by Claudius. Paul's preaching ministry began in the Jewish synagogue but was limited to the Sabbath day. Silas and Timothy arrived with encouraging reports from the churches at Berea and Thessalonica. Paul wrote 1 Thessalonians in joyful response (1 Thessalonians 3:6-8).

Strengthened by the arrival of Silas and Timothy, "Paul devoted himself exclusively to preaching." It was at this time or soon thereafter that Paul received an offering from the church at Philippi, probably brought by Silas (2 Corinthians 11:8-9; Philippians 4:15). This intensified ministry to the Jews brought much fruit, but also strong opposition.

Paul left the synagogue and began preaching from the nearby home of Titus Justus, a Greek proselyte to Judaism. Crispus, the ruler of the synagogue, was among the converts (Acts 18:6-8). This relocation of Paul's ministry seems to have opened the door to an increasing number of Gentiles, and the church grew rapidly as these Gentiles responded to the gospel. Paul apparently feared that the Jewish leaders would begin a riot as they had at Thessalonica and Berea (Acts 17:5, 13), thus forcing him to terminate his ministry at Corinth (Acts 18:9). Through a vision, the Lord assured Paul that he would be kept free from harm and would be able to continue his ministry in Corinth, *"for I have many people in this city"* (Acts 18:9-11). Some months later the uprising that Paul anticipated did occur. Hopeful that the new proconsul, Gallio, would be sympathetic, the Jews accused Paul of sedition. They charged Paul with encouraging people to worship God contrary to Roman law (Acts 18:12-17). Gallio saw through the accusation as a religious, not a political issue. Having no interest in such a dispute he dismissed the case. Apparently they refused

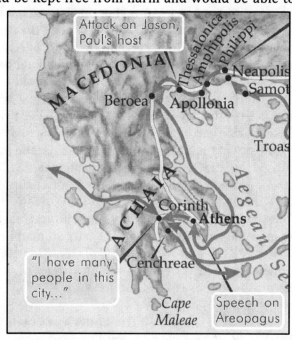

Copyright by Carta Jerusalem, Used by permission

to leave and had to be ejected from the court. In the backlash against the Jews, Sosthenes, ruler of the synagogue, was beaten in front of the court. The reversal of the Jewish attack and the benevolent indifference of Gallio enabled Paul to continue his ministry in Corinth for some time. After a ministry that extended over at least 18 months, Paul left Corinth for Jerusalem, stopping along the way at Ephesus (Acts 18:18-22). Before leaving, Paul initiated a vow and had his hair cut off at Cenchrea, the port city next to Corinth. Priscilla and Aquila traveled with Paul and took up residence in the city of Ephesus. Paul preached in the synagogue at Ephesus briefly and then continued on his way to the sending church at Antioch with a brief stop at Jerusalem. This marked the completion of Paul's second mission to the Gentiles.

Members of the church. Priscilla and Aquila were the first members Paul mentioned. They may have come to faith in Christ prior to leaving Rome, but certainly they grew in their faith through interaction with Paul. The majority of the members were Gentiles with a background in idolatry (1 Corinthians 12:2). Some of the members were Roman citizens or at least had Roman names. The majority of the members were common people with little power or influence (1 Corinthians 1:26-31). There was considerable social and economic disparity as the church included both slaves and freedmen (1 Corinthians 7:21-22; 12:13). Rich and poor brought their social distinctions to the Lord's Supper (1 Corinthians 11:20-22). Early converts were Jews and proselytes at the synagogue, but those saved later came from the dregs of Corinthian society (1 Corinthians 6:9-11).

Problems within the church. Though members of the church at Corinth were new creatures in Christ, old habits died hard. Every imaginable moral and spiritual problem appeared to surface in the church. The flourishing of a church at Corinth demonstrated the power of God to transform the lives of depraved people. The church also demonstrated that the sanctification process, which follows salvation, is by no means automatic or easy. The following list of problems is not exhaustive, but it is sufficient to explain why Paul could openly speak of these believers as "*fleshly*" (1 Corinthians 3:1-3).
1. **Divisiveness**. Personality cults and quarrels abounded (1 Corinthians 1:10-13; 3:3-4).
2. **Pseudo-intellectualism**. They valued the wrong kind of wisdom and for the wrong reasons (1:18-2:16).
3. **Arrogance and boasting**. Pride was a "badge of honor" to some (3:18-23; 4:18-21).
4. **Mean spirited**. They were critical of others and judgmental (4:1-5).
5. **Sexual immorality**. They prided themselves on their tolerance, even condoning incest by a member of the congregation (5:1-13).

189

6. **Petty and vengeful**. They filed lawsuits against fellow believers over the most trivial matters (6:1-8).
7. **Promiscuous**. Some believers still succumbed to prostitution and sexual deviation (6:13-20).
8. **Divorce and troubled marriages**. There were many spiritually divided homes and much confusion about marriage (7:1-40).
9. **Idolatry**. The greed and gluttony associated with idol worship still tempted some believers and perplexed or confused others (8:1-13; 10:6-7).
10. **Self-centeredness**. Rebellious nonconformists maintained their independence and demanded their rights (9:1-27; 10:24).
11. **Drunkenness**. This occurred as the church gathered for the Lord's Supper (11:21).
12. **Preoccupation and pride over spiritual gifts**. They were not lacking in any spiritual gifts but were preoccupied with the gifts themselves, rating some more important or desirable than others, and they competed with each other in the exercise of the gifts that were intended for edification not for self-promotion (12:1-14:35).
13. **Disorderliness**. Chaos and disruption often marked their worship services (14:26-40).
14. **Doctrinal error**. Some apparently expressed doubt about the resurrection of Jesus Christ and hence of the saints (15:12-57).
15. **Harsh and vindictive**. When they did finally discipline a sinning member, they did not know when to stop and how to show forgiveness (2 Corinthians 2:5-11).
16. **Compromise and compliance with unbelievers**. They failed to maintain a biblical separation from sin while reaching out to sinners (2 Corinthians 6:14-7:1).
17. **Others**. At the close of his second letter Paul expressed the fear that his next visit might expose still more sins. To those already identified, he added jealously, outbursts of anger, slander, and gossip.

Background and Occasion of the Corinthian Letters

Paul's visits and letters to Corinth. Reconstructing Paul's contacts with the church at Corinth poses a challenge. References within the epistles indicate that Paul made at least three visits to the city (2 Corinthians 13:1-2). His reference to a *"previous letter"* in 1 Corinthians 5:9-11 and to a *"sorrowful"* letter in 2 Corinthians 7:8-9 indicate that Paul wrote at least three and possibly four letters to the church. He also sent Timothy on a mission to the church that was apparently not completed (1 Corinthians 4:17-21; 16:10-11). Titus, however, did enjoy a very productive visit to the church (2 Corinthians 7:5-16). When these passages are compared with Luke's record in Acts, we suggest the following reconstruction of Paul's ongoing ministry to the church at Corinth.

1. Ephesus becomes the base of operations for three years on Paul's third mission to the Gentiles (Acts 18:23; 19:1-20:1, 31). Apollos travels to Corinth to preach.

2. Paul wrote a letter to the church at Corinth that has not been preserved. That "previous letter" was misunderstood and required clarification (1 Corinthians 5:9-11). Paul's instruction that they not associate with sexually immoral people was meant to refer to other believers, not those outside the church. This letter is not likely our 1 Corinthians (Guthrie, *New Testament Introduction*, 437).

3. Representatives of Chloe's household brought a disturbing report to Paul concerning problems in the church (1 Corinthians 1:11).

4. Timothy was sent to clear up misunderstanding regarding the previous letter and to address the problems mentioned by Chloe's family (1 Corinthians 4:17). Timothy traveled through Macedonia (Acts 19:22) and apparently did not reach Corinth (1 Corinthians 16:10-11). It appears likely that Timothy left for Corinth prior to Paul's writing of our present 1 Corinthians.

5. A delegation arrived from the church at Corinth with a list of questions addressed to Paul (1 Corinthians 7:1; 16:17). Most of 1 Corinthians 7-16 constitutes Paul's written response to those questions. Stephanas, Fortunatus, and Achaicus likely brought a gift to Paul and certainly brought him encouragement.

6. Paul writes the letter we now know as 1 Corinthians in order to clarify their misunderstanding regarding his previous letter and to address the problems exposed by Chloe's report and the questions posed by representatives of the church. The most probable date for the writing of 1 Corinthians is A. D. 55 or 56.

7. Paul made a second visit to the church at Corinth that he describes as "*sorrowful*" (2 Corinthians 2:1-4; 13:2, 10). Luke does not record this visit in Acts. Paul was humiliated before the church and obliged to leave in haste.

8. Paul wrote a "**sorrowful**" letter in the aftermath of the visit (2 Corinthians 2:4). Since the letter was written "*out of much affliction and anguish of heart I wrote to you with many tears*," he was probably not referring to our 1 Corinthians. In all probability this "*sorrowful*" letter has been lost along with the "*previous letter*" referred to earlier (1 Corinthians 5:9).

9. The letter in question may have been sent with Titus. The severity of the letter and the failure of Titus to arrive at Troas as expected added to Paul's distress (2 Corinthians 2:12-13). Joyful comfort replaced Paul's distress when Titus arrived in Macedonia with a positive report from the church (2 Corinthians 7:5-16; Acts 20:1).

10. Paul then wrote 2 Corinthians to encourage the majority with whom he had been reconciled and to defend his apostleship and ministry from a minority group that remained highly critical. Second Corinthians was apparently written from Macedonia (2 Corinthians 7:5-16) and may have followed the writing of 1 Corinthians by just a few months. It had to be written after the spring season and before the winter Paul planned to spend in Corinth (1 Corinthians 16:6-9). Dating the epistle in A.D. 57 depends on identifying the "*winter*" of 1 Corinthians 16:6 with that of Acts 20:3. If these are not the same, then up to 18 months might have elapsed between 1 and 2 Corinthians.

11. Having encouraged the church at Corinth to make good on its plan to provide a generous offering for the church at Jerusalem (2 Corinthians 8-9), Paul then returned to Corinth where he spent the winter, and in spring he began his journey to Jerusalem bearing a love gift from the church at Corinth (Acts 20:1-6).

Date and location of writing. The suggested date for the writing of 1 Corinthians is early in A.D. 56. Second Corinthians followed in late summer or early fall of the same year. The following observations help establish the date and location of writing.

1. A substantial amount of time had to elapse after the founding of the church in order for the problems to become so numerous and serious. Time was also required for Paul to receive information from Corinth and to write a letter to them.

2. First Corinthians had to be written after Apollos had ministered in Corinth (Acts 18:27-19:1; 1 Corinthians 1:12).

3. The letter was also written after Timothy and Paul had sent Erastus from Ephesus to Macedonia (Acts 19:22).

4. The letter must also be dated after Timothy had been given an assignment to visit Corinth following the ministry in Macedonia (1 Corinthians 4:17 with 16:10-11).

5. First Corinthians was probably written from Ephesus near the end of Paul's three-year ministry there. Apparently Paul wrote it early in the spring and shortly before his planned departure at Pentecost (1 Corinthians 16:8). The year was likely A. D. 56.

6. Titus was sent on an important mission to the church at Corinth with instructions to meet Paul via the overland route at Troas (2 Corinthians 2:12-13). When Titus failed to arrive, Paul continued toward Corinth on the famed Roman highway until the two met somewhere in Macedonia (2 Corinthians 7:5-16).

7. Second Corinthians was written from Macedonia following the report of Titus and prior to Paul's third visit to Corinth (13:1). Paul intended to spend the winter in Corinth (1 Corinthians 16:6-7). Since that extended visit was planned for the spring of A.D. 56, it is likely that 2 Corinthians was written in the fall of 56 shortly before Paul fulfilled his plan to settle down for an extended winter stay at Corinth.

8. Paul's letter to the believers at Rome is written during this winter in Corinth. In it he announces his plan to visit them in Rome and also to travel on to Spain (Romans 15:23-29). But first Paul intends to take a gift from the Gentile churches of Achaia and Macedonia to aid the distressed church at Jerusalem (Romans 15:25-27).

9. Paul's plan to sail from Corinth to Syria on his way to Jerusalem was thwarted by Jews plotting against his life (Acts 20:3). Thus he followed the overland route through Macedonia, making stops in Troas and Miletus (Acts 20:4-38).

Paul's Third Missionary Journey, AD 53-57

Copyright by Carta Jerusalem, Used by Permission

1 CORINTHIANS

Distinctives. Among the epistles of the New Testament, only Romans exceeds 1 Corinthians in length. Paul discusses an exceptional range of subjects in this letter. The work of the Holy Spirit in relation to the church, love, spiritual gifts, death, and resurrection, all receive substantial attention along with the many and varied problems that plagued the church at Corinth. "This is the most business-like of all Paul's epistles. He has a number of subjects with which he intends to deal and he sets about them in a most orderly manner" (Guthrie, *New Testament Introduction*, 440). The cross of Jesus Christ is applied to every problem of life. It is the focal point of Paul's preaching, the dividing line between human and divine wisdom, and the grounds of our sanctification.

First Corinthians possesses a simple eloquence. The language of 1 Corinthians is said to be "the simplest and most direct found in Paul's epistles." Hiebert adds, "In this book some of the most sublime passages flow forth without effort as the Apostle pursues his purpose, and that in a letter in which he entirely repudiates all attempts at rhetoric as utterly inconsistent with the simplicity of the gospel (2:1-5). This epistle offers a beautiful illustration of the unconscious character of true eloquence" (*An Introduction to the New Testament,* 2:115-16). The letter is also characterized by unassuming wisdom. Human wisdom is denied, but heavenly wisdom is displayed in both the content and language of 1 Corinthians (1:18-2:16). Paul's writing is methodical at the same time it is impassioned. It is significant that Paul used the best of human wisdom at Athens before preaching the simple gospel at Corinth. He saw through the pseudo-intellectualism of the Corinthians and was resolved that their faith would not *rest on the wisdom of men, but on the power of God* (1 Corinthians 2:5).

Doctrinal significance. Christian theology would be impoverished without this letter. Here Paul teaches on (1) the importance and observance of the Lord's Supper (chap. 11), (2) the nature, use, and abuse of spiritual gifts, particularly tongues and prophesying (chap. 12), (3) the church as the body of Christ; characterized by oneness yet possessing diversity, and formed by the baptizing work of the Holy Spirit (chap. 12), (4) the nature and supremacy of love (chap. 13). Regarding chapter 13 F. F. Bruce says, "Above all, this letter emphasizes the surpassing power and worth of the love of God in human life; Christianity may survive in the absence of many valuable things, but it will die if love is absent" (Bruce, "Corinthians, First Epistle to the," 1:971); (5) the essence of the gospel as the death, burial, and resurrection of Jesus Christ (15:1-11); and (6) the certainty and significance of the resurrection (chap. 15). The central passages for all these vital doctrines are found within this one letter.

Purpose of 1 Corinthians

Paul had several reasons for writing to the church at Corinth. The primary reason was to address the serious problems reported to Paul by members of Chloe's household (1 Corinthians 1:11). (1) Quarrels fueled by personality cults were destroying God's ideal of unity for the church and threatened to divide the church (1 Corinthians 1:10-4:21). (2) Believers in Corinth were indifferent toward the incestuous relationship of a member, something that was scandalous even to pagans (chap. 5). (3) Believers were filing lawsuits against other believers over trivial matters and doing so in pagan courts (6:1-11). (4) Christian liberty was mistaken for a license to sin. This resulted in tolerance toward and even indulgence in the sexual immorality that characterized the pagans of Corinth (6:12-20).

Paul's secondary reason for writing was to answer a series of questions addressed to him by the church. *Now concerning the things about which you wrote* (7:1). These sections begin with *"now concerning"* (*peri de*). The issues involved: marriage (7:1-24); virgins (7:25-40); Christian liberty, particularly meat sacrificed to idols (chaps. 8-10); spiritual gifts (chaps. 12-14), and the collection for the saints in Jerusalem (16:1-4). While the complete formula is not used, it seems likely that they also asked for instruction regarding the Lord's Supper (chap. 11), and for clarification regarding the resurrection (chap. 15).

Paul closes this letter with an explanation of when and why he would visit them personally (16:5-11). Communication had traveled back and forth between Paul and the church numerous times and through a variety of people. He wanted to spend more time with them, but his present ministry at Ephesus was strategic and he felt compelled to remain there longer (16:8-19).

195

Message of 1 Corinthians

Paul strikes the recurring theme of the book in his opening. He states what the church is (1:2-3), what the church has (1:4-7), and why the church exists (1:8-9). As God's church they have been sanctified (set apart for a special purpose) in Christ Jesus and called to practical holiness together with all who have called on Jesus as Savior and thus have accepted His lordship (1:2). Their appalling problems notwithstanding, Paul is thankful for them. The basis of his thanksgiving is not in their performance, but in God's grace and gifting in their lives (1:4-7). Paul leaves no doubt that he is unhappy with their present level of spirituality, but remains confident that they will ultimately be blameless at the coming of Jesus Christ (1:8-9). The Lord Jesus Christ is the source of their salvation and the solution to their problems, and He is named ten times in the first ten verses! With that genuine but guarded statement of thanksgiving, Paul confronts the problems of the church head on.

The book of 1 Corinthians is structured around two reports and the numerous problems that were raised by these reports. Paul's primary purpose was to address these problems, and he does this in a very logical and direct way. The first report is a personal but unofficial report from members of the household of Chloe (chaps. 1-6). The problems reported to Paul involved serious divisions that threatened the very life of the church (1:10-4:21), and scandalous moral delinquencies that threatened the witness of the church (5:1-6:20). The second report was a series of questions brought by an official delegation from the church at Corinth (7:1-16:18). Paul systematically answers each of these inquiries. These formal requests had to do with marriage (chap. 7), food offered to idols (chaps. 8-10), order in public worship (chap. 11), spiritual gifts (chaps. 12-14), the resurrection (chap. 15), and the procedure for a special collection (chap. 16).

Problems Reported by Chloe's Household (1:10-6:20)

Divisions in the church (1:10-4:21). Paul reacts strongly to the divisions in the church (1:13-17) and points them to the centrality of the cross as the cure (1:18-2:16). The congregation was evaluating leaders on a faulty basis and attaching themselves to their favorite leader (1:12). They only needed to look inwardly to be reminded that they themselves were not among the intellectually and socially elite (1:26-31). Paul's ministry among them was empowered by the Spirit and marked by God's wisdom, not man's wisdom, so that their faith would rest solely on the power of God (2:1-15). The divisions at Corinth grew out of their pride in earthly wisdom and are actually evidence of their carnality (3:1-4). The divine remedy is to remember that leaders like Paul, Peter, and Apollos are only God's servants, and that all are accountable to God (3:5-15). They are the temple of God and are indwelt by the Spirit. They belong to Christ and not to Paul, or Apollos, or Cephas (3:16-23). It is wrong to pass judgment on leaders; God will do that and He will judge the motives of the heart (4:1-7). Their arrogance is inappropriate and in contrast to the apostles who are often treated like the dregs of society (4:8-13). Their arrogance will be put to the test when Paul comes to them, but in the meantime they should remember that Paul is their father in the faith and they are admonished to follow his example of servanthood (4:14-21).

Moral delinquencies in the church (chaps. 5-6). A scandalous situation existed in the church, a member was committing **incest,** and the church took pride in their tolerance of this deplorable sin (5:1-8). Stern measures were required. The offender must be expelled. Paul has written to them before about this subject but they misunderstood (5:11). The church may associate with immoral persons on the outside but must not tolerate immorality within the membership (5:9-13). To make certain that the church takes action, Paul closes with an imperative taken straight from the Mosaic Law, *Remove the wicked man from among yourselves* (Deuteronomy 21:21).

Paul progresses immediately to the issue of lawsuits. The cause is not specified. Immorality may be contributing to the frequent **lawsuits** of believer against believer but, whatever the cause, pagan courts were not the solution (6:1-11). Even if a believer wins in the court he has lost in the court of heaven. Paul returns to the theme of immorality and provides the ultimate rationale for sanctified living: they were once just like the pagans but have been sanctified and justified in the name of the Lord Jesus Christ (6:11). The body of a believer is the temple of the Holy Spirit and has been purchased by the sacrifice of Christ. They ought to flee immorality, not indulge in it! The believer's body is the temple of the Holy Spirit, has been purchased at enormous cost, and should be used solely to glorify God to whom it belongs (6:12-20).

Questions Raised by the Corinthian Church (7:1-16:18)
The official delegation from the church at Corinth brought a list of questions for which the church sought Paul's insight. They recognized Paul's apostolic authority even though they were divided in their loyalties between Paul, Apollos, and other leaders. Paul introduces his response to

each of these questions with the formula *now about* (*peri de*). Paul's answers are logical and compelling. In each case he remains focused on what is important and eternal. Paul used some gentle chiding and rebuke, but he always gave a challenge to live up to their high calling in Christ.

Concerning marriage and divorce (chap. 7). The principle enunciated at creation, one man and one woman forming one flesh (Genesis 2:24), remains God's ideal (1 Corinthians 7:1-7). Marriage is not for all and is not necessary, but it is expedient and appropriate for some. The central principle regarding marriage is *each man has his own gift from God* (7:7). In mixed marriages in which one is a believer and the other is not, Paul advocates remaining in the relationship if possible (7:8-16). Marriage is not the only issue, whether a Jew (circumcised) or a Gentile (uncircumcised), whether slave or freedman, *each one is to remain with God in that condition in which he was called* (7:17-24). Christianity is not a mechanism by which we escape problem situations, but a new way of life in which we triumph through them.

Paul addresses another, closely related question the church has voiced: What is a virgin to do regarding marriage (7:25)? Paul does not define *the present distress,* but he argues for a sense of urgency in decision-making (7:26). While this is not a matter of a command from the Lord but of Paul's opinion, it is trustworthy. The present age is passing away, and eternity looms on the horizon. We are to use this world without becoming attached to it. Our focus should always be on pleasing the Lord (7:27-40).

Concerning Christian liberty and pagan practices (chaps. 8-11). Idol worship was rampant in Corinth, and Christians were confused about how far their freedom in Christ allowed them to go. Since idols have no real existence, believers do have substantial freedom in eating food sacrificed to idols. However, idols still represent reality to weak believers. Christian liberty must be tempered with love. Under no circumstances should the exercise of our personal freedom in Christ be the cause for a fellow believer to fall (8:1-13). The Christian life is not about demanding one's rights and exercising one's freedom in Christ. This lesson on liberty is reinforced by the powerful example of Paul himself as he waived his apostolic rights for the benefit of the gospel (9:1-27). Whether eating meat or not eating meat (8:13), whether marrying or remaining single (9:1-5), whether financially supported or self-supported (9:6-14), Paul has not claimed his rights as an apostle. Everything Paul does is for the sake of the gospel (9:15-23). His eye is on the ultimate reward, not the enjoyment of his rights (9:24-27). Paul's example is positive, but this lesson is also reinforced by the negative example from Israel's history (10:1-22).

The book of Numbers is a reminder of Israel's preoccupation with idols, food, and play (10:1-10). We must learn from Israel's example and not think we are immune to failure (10:11-12). God has provided a way for believers to overcome temptation (10:13). Liberty in Christ should not lead to license but to a responsible exercise of our freedom in Christ. *All things are lawful, but not all things are profitable. All things are lawful, but not all things edify. Let no one seek his own good, but that of his neighbor* (10:23-24). We are living under the law of love and should not give offense to unbelieving Jews and Greeks or to fellow believers (10:25-11:1). *Whether, then, you eat or drink or whatever you do, do all to the glory of God* (10:31).

Concerning order in public worship (chap. 11). The church at Corinth was uncertain about what was appropriate for the worship services of the church. Paul's instruction on public worship seems archaic to us in this freewheeling, anything-goes, twenty-first century. Head coverings for women and hairstyles for men are not elements we associate with prayer in public worship. But these were debated issues in Corinth (11:2-16). The issue was divinely established order not supremacy. Likewise, abuse of the Lord's Supper exposed the social divisions that existed in the church. The early church combined the Lord's Supper with a meal, but at Corinth some went hungry while others overindulged and were drunk (11:17-22). It was shameful and did not merit Paul's praise. Paul's antidote is to remind them of the personal revelation he had received from the Lord and had delivered to them regarding the Lord's Supper (11:23-26). Abuse of the Lord's Supper brought severe punishment from God and calls for self-examination as well as restraint when we partake (11:27-34).

Concerning spiritual gifts (chaps. 12-14). In the opening of this epistle Paul has expressed thanksgiving for the giftedness of the Corinthian church (1:4-7). There is also an implied rebuke as the abundance of spiritual gifts and their preoccupation with them was disrupting their worship and hindering their witness to outsiders. In answering this question, Paul provides us with vital teaching on spiritual gifts and on the nature of the church as the body of Christ. The important elements include these facts: (1) The Holy Spirit sovereignly bestows gifts on each and every believer. (2) All believers are united in the body of Christ through the baptizing work of the Holy Spirit. (3) A variety of gifts lead to a variety of ministries. (4) God intended those gifts to be used to edify that body of Christ. (5) All gifts are necessary and should not become a source of pride or division. (6) Love superintends the exercise of gifts and takes supremacy over all. (7) The gift of tongues has become divisive at Corinth and must be regulated in public worship. The gift of tongues was misunderstood and misused at Corinth, which created confusion in public worship (14:1-39). God is a God of order, not confusion. Public worship is for the purpose of evangelism of the unsaved and edification of believers, not for self-expression. *All things must be done properly and in an orderly manner* (14:40).

Concerning the resurrection (chap. 15). The issue of the resurrection may not have been phrased in a question by the church, but it certainly was a problem. Paul devoted extensive space to the matter because it was of critical importance. The resurrection touched at the very heart of the gospel and provided the occasion for Paul to make a definitive statement of the Christian gospel (15:3-4). The cross of Christ is the answer to the sin of Adam, but the resurrection of Jesus Christ is indispensable to the gospel and to our salvation. The resurrection of Jesus Christ is firmly established because of the reliable testimony of many witnesses (15:5-11). If Christ was not raised from the dead, Paul is a false witness, the faith of believers is futile, and believers are still in their sins (15:12-19). If there is no resurrection, there is no hope of heaven and believers are to be pitied. But, Jesus was raised and will come again to abolish death and to rule (15:20-28). Believers should not be distracted by questions about the nature of the resurrection body but should focus on living wisely in anticipation of Christ's return (15:29-49). The resurrection of Jesus Christ assures all believers that they will enjoy immortality and triumph (15:50-58). The fact of Christ's resurrection in the past and the certainty of our resurrection in the future provide the motivation for our present service and the assurance of our future victory.

Key verses
Thanks be to God, who gives us the victory through our Lord Jesus Christ. Therefore, my beloved brethren, be steadfast, immovable, always abounding in the work of the Lord, knowing that your toil is not in vain in the Lord (15:57-58).

Concerning the collection for the saints (16:1-18). The letter concludes on a very personal and practical note. The Corinthian believers' question about the collection for the saints became the occasion for Paul to explain his own absence and announce his plans for spending the winter in Corinth (16:1-18). Given the pervasive disorder and divisions in the Corinthian church, it is noteworthy that Paul concludes the letter with warm greetings (16:19-24). The closing greeting is written by Paul's own hand. The last words of this letter are a confirmation of his abiding love for this problem-filled church. *My love be with you all in Christ Jesus.*

Outline of 1 Corinthians

I.	Introduction	1:1-9
	A. Salutation	1:1-3
	1. The writers	1:1
	2. The readers	1:2
	3. The greeting	1:3
	B. Thanksgiving	1:4-9
	1. The basis	1:4-7
	2. The goal	1:8
	3. The affirmation	1:9
II.	Problems Reported by Chloe's Household	1:10-6:20
	A. Divisions in the church	1:10-4:21
	1. The report to Paul	1:10-12
	2. The reaction of Paul	1:13-17
	3. The reality: the centrality of the cross	1:18-2:16
	a. The cross- the essence of the gospel	1:18-25
	b. The cross- is essential to salvation	1:26-31
	c. The cross- Paul's passion	2:1-5
	d. The cross- revealed by the Spirit	2:6-16
	4. The reason: the carnality of the church	3:1-4
	a. The indictment: their infant diet	3:1-3a
	b. The evidence: their divisions	3:3b-4
	5. The remedy	3:5-4:21
	a. The antidote: understand that:	3:5-4:5
	(1) We are only God's servants	3:5-9
	(2) We are only builders	3:10-15
	(3) You are God's temple	3:16-17
	(4) You are also accountable to God	3:18-23
	(5) God judges our faithfulness	4:1-5
	b. The application	4:6-21
	(1) Arrogance is inappropriate	4:6-8
	(2) Paul's example is the opposite	4:9-13

201

(3) They should imitate Paul	4:14-17
(4) Paul confronts their arrogance	4:18-21
B. Moral delinquencies in the church	5:1-6:20
1. Gross immorality within the church	5:1-8
a. The shameful offence: incest	5:1
b. Their shameful attitude: pride	5:2
c. The stern discipline: expulsion	5:3-5
d. The stinging rebuke	5:6-8
2. The godly church in an immoral world	5:9-13
a. Association without assimilation	5:9-10
b. Expelling evil from within	5:11-13
3. Lawsuits before pagan courts	6:1-11
a. The shameful practice	6:1-6
b. They are saved for something better	6:7-11
4. The sanctity of the believer's body	6:12-20
a. Designed by God to be His temple	6:13, 19-20
b. Destined to be resurrected	6:14
c. Devoted to Christ alone	6:15-17
d. Desecrated by immorality	6:18

III. Problems Raised by the Corinthian Church — 7:1-16:18
- A. Concerning marriage and divorce — 7:1-40
  - 1. Regarding celibacy, sexual abstinence — 7:1-9
    - a. Celibacy is good (for the single) — 7:1
    - b. Abstinence in marriage is not good — 7:2-6
    - c. Marriage and celibacy are both gifts — 7:7
    - d. Marriage may be better for some — 7:8-9
  - 2. Regarding divorce and remarriage — 7:10-24
    - a. Believers should not seek a divorce — 7:10
    - b. If divorced, seek reconciliation — 7:11
    - c. Don't seek to divorce an unbeliever — 7:12-14
    - d. Not bound if the unbeliever leaves — 7:15-16
    - e. Remain as you were when saved — 7:17-24
  - 3. Regarding virgins and widows — 7:25-40
    - a. Singleness is good but not required — 7:25-31
    - b. Singleness aids undivided devotion — 7:32-35
    - c. Marriage is not always preferred — 7:35-40
- B. Concerning liberty and pagan practices — 8:1-11:1
  - 1. Love and the exercise of liberty — 8:1-13
    - a. Liberty should be governed by love — 8:1-3
    - b. God alone is real, idols are not — 8:4-6

	c.	Weak believer may not understand	8:7
	d.	Freedom must not destroy the weak	8:8-13
2.		Paul's example of love and liberty	9:1-27
	a.	Paul's rights as an apostle	9:1-12a
	b.	Paul's reasons for waiving his rights	9:12b-23
		(1) To avoid hindering the gospel	9:12b-14
		(2) To keep the gospel truly free	9:15-18
		(3) To win many to Christ	9:19-23
	c.	Paul's request: run with discipline	9:24-27
3.		Israel's negative example	10:1-13
	a.	Their spiritual privileges	10:1-5
	b.	Their abuse of those privileges	10:6-10
	c.	Their example is a warning to us	10:11-12
	d.	God's provision for the tempted	10:13
4.		The principle of liberty applied to life	10:14-11:1
	a.	Avoid idolatry	10:14
	b.	Christ's sacrifice governs liberty	10:15-22
	c.	Liberty is under the law of love	10:23-11:1

C. Concerning order in public worship — 11:2-34

1.		Regarding prayer and head coverings	11:2-16
	a.	Praise for respecting Paul's teaching	11:2
	b.	The principle of headship	11:3
	c.	The practice of head coverings	11:4-6
	d.	The principle and practice explained	11:7-16
		(1) By the order of creation	11:7-12
		(2) By the pattern of nature	11:13-15
		(3) By the practice of the church	11:16
2.		Regarding the Lord's Supper	11:17-34
	a.	Condemnation of abuses	11:17-22
	b.	Correct way to celebrate	11:23-27
	c.	Consequences of abusing	11:28-34

D. Concerning spiritual gifts — 12:1-14:40

1.		The test for speaking by the Spirit	12:1-3
2.		The unity and diversity of gifts	12:4-11
	a.	One common source: the Spirit	12:4-6
	b.	One common purpose: edification	12:7
	c.	The rich diversity of gifts	12:8-10
	d.	The sovereign distribution of gifts	12:11
3.		The unity and diversity of the body	12:12-31a
	a.	All are baptized into one body	12:12-13
	b.	The body has unity in diversity	12:14-26

c.	The inclusiveness of the body	12:27
d.	The function of gifts in the body	12:28-31a
4.	The supremacy of love in using gifts	12:31b-13:13
a.	The necessity for love	12:31a-13:3
b.	The nature of love	13:4-7
c.	The permanence of love	13:8-13
5.	The proper use of gifts	14:1-40
a.	What matters most is edification	14:1-6
b.	Guidelines for speaking in tongues	14:7-25
(1)	Tongues must edify the church	14:7-12
(2)	Tongues must be interpreted	14:13-19
(3)	Tongues are for the mature	14:20-21
(4)	Tongues are signs to unbelievers	14:22-25
(5)	Tongues must be orderly	14:26-28
(6)	Speakers must exercise control	14:29-33
(7)	Wives to submit to husbands	14:34-35
(8)	Obedience to replace arrogance	14:36-40

E. Concerning the resurrection — 15:1-58
   1. The importance of the resurrection — 15:1-11
     a. It is the grounds of their salvation — 15:1-2
     b. It is the very essence of the gospel — 15:3-8
     c. It is essential to Paul's apostleship — 15:9-11
   2. The argument for the resurrection — 15:12-34
     a. It is essential to the gospel message — 15:12-19
     b. It is essential to God's program — 15:20-28
     c. It is essential to Christian living — 15:29-34
   3. The explanation of the resurrection — 15:35-57
     a. Questions regarding resurrection (How and what kind of body?) — 15:35
     b. Answer: heavenly, not earthly body — 15:36-49
       (1) The analogy of creation — 15:36-41
       (2) The application to resurrection — 15:42-49
     c. Answer: raised at Christ's return — 15:50-57
       (1) Radical change is necessary — 15:50
       (2) Revelation explains the process — 15:51
       (3) Christ will bring transformation — 15:52-57
   4. The assurance provided by resurrection — 15:58

F. Concerning the collection for the saints — 16:1-18
   1. Order and planning in giving — 16:1-4
   2. Intended visit by Paul — 16:5-9
   3. Instructions for Timothy's visit — 16:10-11

4.	Explanation of Apollos' delayed visit	16:12
5.	Exhortation to watchfulness	16:13-14
6.	Acknowledgement of representatives	16:15-18

IV. Conclusion — 16:19-24
- A. Greetings from Paul's companions — 16:19-20
- B. Paul's authenticating signature — 16:21
- C. Paul's warning to false teachers — 16:22
- D. Paul's affirmation of love — 16:23-24

206

2 Corinthians: Christ's Ambassador Answers His Critics

Key verse: 5:20, *Therefore, we are ambassadors for Christ, as though God were making an appeal through us*

	Consolation: Paul's Ministry of Reconciliation	Solicitation: to Grace Giving	Vindication: of Paul's Apostleship
	1 — 7	8 — 9	10 — 13
Key Words	Comfort, confidence, forgive, ministry, glory, trouble	Given, gift, grace, generous	Boast, weakness, apostle, power, fool
Style:	Appealing, explaining, uplifting	Reminding, urging	Warning, refuting
Focus:	Penitent, positive majority	Giving majority	Critical, negative minority
Tone:	Conciliatory, encouraging	Challenging	Defensive, apologetic
Paul's Ministry:	Marked by Glory, Compelled by Christ's love	Integrity Generosity	Suffering, not inferior, Made perfect in weakness

Paul, A.D. 56 from Macedonia

2 CORINTHIANS

Unity and Continuity of 1 and 2 Corinthians

Comparison of 1 and 2 Corinthians. Marked differences between 1 and 2 Corinthians are evident. The tone of 2 Corinthians is sharper and more biting. The businesslike style of 1 Corinthians gives way to abrupt, almost disjointed changes of subject in 2 Corinthians. Divisions were a serious problem in 1 Corinthians but the personalities were all from within the church. In 2 Corinthians the attack is from outside in the form of Judaizers. The Judaizers that prompted the strong outburst of Paul in 2 Corinthians 10-13 are absent in 1 Corinthians. Hiebert concludes, "It is of value and lasting interest to compare the two epistles to the Corinthian church. They are closely related to each other, yet they are very different from each other" (*An Introduction to the New Testament*, 2: 150-51).

The marked difference in style between the two epistles is explainable on the basis of the different situations that occasioned the letters. The remorseful attitude of the majority in the church at Corinth prompted Paul's message of comfort in 2 Corinthians 1-7. At the same time the intrusion of false apostles with their distorted gospel prompted Paul's scathing denunciation in chapters 10-13. The problems that occasioned 1 Corinthians fell between these two "extremes." They called for repentance that was not yet evident, but they did not call for the scathing denunciation that became necessary in the second letter. Scroggie provides an excellent comparison of these two letters by Paul.

> "The First gives insight into the character and condition of the early Churches; the Second, into the life and character of the Apostle Paul. The First is objective and practical; the Second is subjective and personal. The First is systematic; the Second is not. The First is deliberate; the Second is impassioned. The First warns against Pagan influences; the Second, against Judaic influences. The two together are valuable beyond all estimate for an understanding of the problems of first century Christians, and for an appreciation of the greatest missionary of the Christian era" (*Know Your Bible*, 2:142-43).

Continuity of 1 and 2 Corinthians. Commentators often emphasize the contrasts between these two epistles to the neglect of their similarities. A close connection does exist between the two and is staunchly defended by Hiebert (*An Introduction to the New Testament*, 2: 138-41). Not many go as far as Hiebert in claiming that the *sorrowful letter* (2 Corinthians 2:4) is actually 1 Corinthians. However, he does show several passages that closely link the two letters.

Unity of 2 Corinthians. "It is the unity of 2 Corinthians, rather than its authenticity, that is brought into question by the critics" (Hiebert, *An Introduction to the New Testament*, 2: 135). The primary argument of those who deny the unity of 2 Corinthians is the substantial change of tone between chapters 10-13 and the early chapters 1-9. "We are told that the difference in tone between chapters 1-9 and 10-13 makes it impossible to believe that the two parts originally formed one letter. It is asserted that the unity of the epistle as it stands "is psychologically impossible" (Hiebert, *An Introduction to the New Testament*, 2:142). Critics claim that 2 Corinthians is a collage containing the remnants of several previous letters. Tasker explains,

"It has become very fashionable to maintain that the last four chapters are not part of the letter which Paul wrote from Macedonia when he received the good news which Titus brought back from Corinth, but that they formed the closing portion of the 'painful' letter to which reference is made in 2 Cor. vii. 8. Many critics also suppose that the trenchant passage, vi. 14-vii. 1 is out of place in its present context, but belonged originally to the 'previous' letter to which the writer refers in 1 Cor. v. 9. It has also been held, though not so generally, that the section ii. 14-vii. 4 is alien to the context in which it is found, and interrupts what is otherwise a continuous sequence" (*The Second Epistle of Paul to the Corinthians,* 24).

For additional study of the problem of the unity or integrity of 2 Corinthians see D.A. Carson, Douglas J. Moo, and Leon Morris, *An Introduction to the New Testament,* 267-77; Guthrie, *New Testament Introduction,* 444-57; and Tasker, *The Second Epistle of Paul to the Corinthians,* 23-35.

Arguments supporting the unity of 2 Corinthians include the following.
1. Early manuscripts and writings of the church fathers overwhelmingly support unity. "2 Corinthians has come down to us as a single Epistle. In no MS is there any trace of a division at any point in the letter, or

any variation in the arrangement of the material; and in no early Christian writer is there any suggestion that the document is composed of different letters, or that it was not all written at one time to meet one particular situation" (Tasker, *The Second Epistle of Paul to the Corinthians,* 23-24).

2. Conservative scholars have refuted the partition-theory that it is psychologically impossible for the same man to have written both sections at one time, given their differences in tone and style. "That there is a marked change of tone at the beginning of chapter x is evident to every reader of the letter. It is, however, very easy to exaggerate it; and it is very doubtful whether in itself it is sufficient to warrant the theory that the closing chapters belong to another letter" (Tasker, *The Second Epistle of Paul to the Corinthians,* 31).

3. The change in tone and style, which is evident between the three sections of the epistle, is explainable on the basis of changes in the subject matter and purposes of the author. "Rather than summarily rejecting the unity of the epistle, the effort should be made to follow the mind of the Apostle in the composition of it. An attentive reading of the epistle as we have it today leaves one with the impression of an order that is both natural and logical ... when thus read as a whole the gulf between the three sections do not seem to be as impossible as the critics think. The change in tone in the last section is indeed unexpected but not necessarily impossible psychologically for Paul" (Hiebert, *An Introduction to the New Testament,* 2:143).

4. It is probable that 2 Corinthians was written over a period of time, rather than at one sitting. It is a lengthy epistle and covers a wide range of subjects. It is probable that neither of these two epistles was written in a very short period of time and certainly not to address a single issue (Guthrie, *New Testament Introduction,* 457). Paul was dealing with two separate elements within the church at Corinth. The majority had been remorseful over their previous treatment of Paul, enabling him to focus on comfort and forgiveness in the first seven chapters. That was genuine and appropriate for the majority and the primary trust of Paul. However, the appearance of Judaizers claiming to be *super-apostles* posed a serious threat to the future of the church. The minority of people who were swayed are those addressed by Paul in chapters 10-13. "The opponents of Paul, now a minority element, called for a strong self-vindication and a vehement condemnation (chs. 10-11)" (Guthrie, *New Testament Introduction,* 453).

5. Critics lack unanimity in their view of the epistle's unity. Given the uniform support of external evidence and the weight of internal evidence, we can be confident that 2 Corinthians is a single letter written by the apostle Paul. We may conclude with Tasker, "It is therefore our duty to approach the Second Epistle to the Corinthians as a unity, and to attempt to 'see it steadily and see it whole'" (*The Second Epistle of Paul to the Corinthians*, 35).

Distinctive Features of 2 Corinthians

Language and style. This epistle is the most personal of all Paul's letters, indeed of the entire New Testament. "The personal element in it is one of its outstanding features, and is one of its chief values" (Scroggie, *Know Your Bible*, 2:140). Second Corinthians is the least systematic of all Paul's letters. It stands in sharp contrast to the first letter, which, along with Romans, is the most systematic. Frequent and abrupt changes in both subject matter and tone are seen in 2 Corinthians. "Since emotions are not concerned with logical order, it is not surprising that this has been termed the least systematic of all Paul's writings" (Hiebert, *An Introduction to the New Testament*, 2:149). This letter, particularly chapters 10-13, is the most intense, revealing, and emotional of all Paul's writings. Second Corinthians was written during a time of intense emotional stress. "Behind the writing of this Letter was the darkest hour in Paul's life. Evidence of this is seen in such passages as vii. 5; iv. 7-v. 4; vi. 4-10, in addition to the passages already referred to. (2 Cor. i.8-10; ii.3-17)" (Scroggie, *Know Your Bible*, 2:140). Variety of subject matter, combined with intensity, resulted in an epistle rich in unique words. There are 171 Greek words that do not occur in Paul's other epistles. There are also 91 Greek words that do not occur anywhere else in the New Testament (Scroggie, *Know Your Bible*, 2:144-45).

Autobiographical element. This letter contains many details about the life and work of Paul that are not revealed anywhere else. Among the examples are his experience of being caught up into paradise (12:1-4), his *thorn in the flesh* (12:7-9), and the extensive listing of his physical sufferings (11:23-28). Though Paul emphasizes his weakness, he endured hardships like an "iron man." The depth of Paul's self-disclosure reveals the human side of this spiritual giant. "Second Corinthians is the most autobiographical of all Paul's epistles. In it he bears his heart and life as in none of his other writings. This prominent personal element in 2 Corinthians makes it especially valuable for an understanding of the character of the Apostle. Yet its very wealth of personal references creates difficulty for the interpreter" (Hiebert, *An Introduction to the New Testament*, 2:135).

Paul's defense against his many detractors. We are shocked at the meanness and cruelty of the accusations his critics brought against Paul. Paul was charged with being weak and vacillating in his personal character (1:5-2:1; 10:1; 11:21, 30). His speech was called unimpressive and his appearance bordered on the contemptible (2:14-17; 10:10-11; 11:6). Opponents said the message Paul preached was questionable and his intelligence limited. He lacked the kind of wisdom the Corinthians treasured and thought they had (11:16-19; 13:3). The work of Paul was considered mediocre and not noteworthy or successful (3:1-6; 5:12; 7:2; 13:5-8). Some considered Paul a *second-class apostle* whose credentials and impact failed to meet the standard of the Judaizers (5:16-21; 10:12-18; 11:5, 12, 21-23). It was inferred that Paul was greedy and had refused financial support because he was unworthy and incapable of generating support (11:7-10; 12:12-15). The harshness of Paul's letters and his confrontational manner led to a charge that he was unloving (11:11). He was perceived as harsh and vindictive (13:10). His detractors intimated that Paul was manipulative even in the way he worked through associates like Titus and Timothy (12:16-18).

Doctrinal insights. In defending his own ministry, Paul gives a valuable description of the following.
1. The nature and glory of the gospel ministry (2:12-6:10).
2. The contrast between the Mosaic and New covenants and their ministries (3:4-18).
3. The spiritual blindness of the unregenerate in light of the glorious gospel (4:3-6).
4. The sealing ministry of the Holy Spirit in those who believe (1:22; 5:5).
5. The substitutionary death of Christ and our ministry of reconciliation (8:9; 5:14-21).
6. The judgment seat of Christ where a believer's work is judged and rewarded (5:10).
7. Suffering as an avenue of spiritual growth and ministry (1:3-7; 12:7-10).
8. The hope and future life of the believer (5:1-9).
9. The nature of repentance and the need for forgiveness and restoration in the church (2:5-11; 7:8-13).
10. The deceptive character and work of Satan (2:10-11; 4:3-4; 11:3, 13-15; 12:7-9).

11. The grounds and guidelines of Christian stewardship as grace giving (8:1-9:15).
12. The nature of the world and Christian separation (6:14-7:1).

Background and Occasion of 2 Corinthians

Paul's letters and visits to Corinth. A suggested order of events has already been given in the introduction to 1 Corinthians. Hiebert reminds us of the challenge posed by such a reconstruction: "the effort to reconstruct the background for 2 Corinthians is beset by difficulties" (Hiebert, *An Introduction to the New Testament*, 2:138). Guthrie offers a different reconstruction of events from that of Hiebert, but a similar word of caution. "Because of the complicated character of the historical background it is not possible to be quite certain about the dating of these letters, especially 2 Corinthians" (Guthrie, *New Testament Introduction*, 457).

Paul's opponents at Corinth. Paul addresses two divergent elements within the church, and a serious threat from Judaizing opponents outside the church.
1. The majority of the church at Corinth had apparently repented and sought reconciliation with Paul. This is evident from the conciliatory nature of the first seven chapters. Paul expresses a firm confidence in them (1:7; 7:8-16). This majority had dealt with the offender as urged by Paul (2:6). Judging by Paul's warnings in chapters 10-13 the majority was still in danger of being swayed by the false apostles and by the vocal minority.
2. An opposing minority remained in the congregation (10:10). They apparently were mishandling the Word of God (2:17; 4:2-5). They took pride in their own position and derided Paul as *beside himself* (5:12-13). They were the principal objects of Paul's call for self-examination (13:5-10). The disharmony between this vocal minority and the reconciled majority remained a problem (13:11).
3. The most dangerous opposition to Paul and the most serious threat to the church came from outside the church. These Judaizers carried *letters of commendation* probably from Jerusalem (3:1-3; 10:12-18). They were preaching a false gospel (11:3-4), and denying Paul's apostolic authority (11:5, 13-15, 23). By contrast they portrayed themselves or at least their Jerusalem-based heroes as *eminent apostles*. Paul's defense is so intense in chapters 10-13 because of the danger posed by these false teachers (Guthrie, *New Testament Introduction*, 433-35).

213

Date and location of writing. Second Corinthians was written from somewhere in Macedonia after Titus had rejoined Paul and reported on his visit to Corinth (2:12-13; 7:5-16). This letter was written prior to Paul's third visit to Corinth (12:14; 13:1). The anticipated third visit by Paul is probably the extended winter visit Paul had announced in his first letter (1 Corinthians 16:5-7). This coincides with Luke's record in Acts 20:1-3. Second Corinthians was likely sent with Titus to prepare for Paul's later arrival (8:16-9:5; 12:14-18). Paul's reference to *last year* regarding the offering of the church at Corinth does not require the passage of a full year between the two epistles (8:10-12). Guthrie reminds us, "The Macedonian New Year began on 21 September and the civil reckoning of the Jews coincided within a few days. If Paul had written in October he might easily have referred to the preceding Easter as "last year," and 2 Corinthians would then be placed in the autumn of the same year as 1 Corinthians, separated by about seven months. Certain other considerations confirm the probability of this suggestion" (Guthrie, *New Testament Introduction*, 458).

Paul's Third Missionary Journey

Copyright by Carta Jerusalem, Used by permission

Second Corinthians was probably written in the fall of A.D. 56 from either Philippi or Thessalonica. Paul would have arrived in Corinth in December or January and remained there three months before beginning his planned visit to Jerusalem. A plot by the Jews forced Paul to travel overland from Corinth to Jerusalem rather than by ship when the sailing season opened (Acts 20:1-6).

Purposes for the Writing of 2 Corinthians

To console and encourage the majority. This is the first subject Paul deals with in the letter and the one to which he devotes the most space (chaps. 1-7). Paul was clearly distraught over his relationship with the church and anxious to assure them that he accepted their repentance without hesitation or qualification (7:2-16). The word *comfort,* or a variation of it, occurs thirteen times, and all in the first seven chapters. The words *confident* and *confidence* each occur five times. Uppermost in Paul's mind was the restoration of a harmonious relationship with the church as represented by the majority. The first and largest section is intended to comfort the majority (1:3-7:16). Paul accomplishes this by gentle appeals (1:12-14; 3:1-3; 6:1-2; 7:2-4). Comfort is also administered through patient instruction (1:15-2:11). Paul appropriately defines his ministry as one of *reconciliation* (5:18). Thus his ministry is one that brings comfort. Paul speaks at length about his ministry in this opening section. However, he is not defending his ministry with arguments. Rather, he is defining his ministry by explaining it. These chapters are rich in detail on the glory and eternal importance of the gospel ministry (2:14-5:21).

To restore the disciplined member. The majority had taken action on Paul's request for church discipline. Now it was necessary for him to urge that the church accept the offender's repentance and extend forgiveness and comfort lest it give Satan an occasion to launch an attack (2:5-11).

To complete the collection for the saints. Titus is being sent by Paul to arrange for the gift the Corinthians had promised to send to the church in Jerusalem (chaps. 8-9). This offering was important for at least three reasons. **One**, the saints in Jerusalem were in need because of persecution and natural disasters (1 Corinthians 16:1-4; 2 Corinthians 8:13-15; 9:12). **Two**, it was important for the Corinthian church to fulfill a commitment they themselves had made (2 Corinthians 8:10-12). **Three**, it encouraged other believers and confirmed Paul's boasting regarding the generosity of the Corinthians (8:22-9:5). The second section deals with this practical matter of the collection to be taken for the church in Jerusalem (chaps. 8-

9). The Corinthians had eagerly promised to give, and now Paul exhorts them to finish what they have begun. As the first seven chapters provide a valuable description of the gospel ministry, so chapters 8 and 9 provide the fullest and best discussion of Christian stewardship to be found anywhere in the New Testament.

To vindicate Paul's apostleship. The concluding chapters of this letter were clearly written to vindicate Paul's apostolic authority (chaps. 10-13). Whether *those* and *you* are the minority who opposed Paul, or the false teachers themselves, they are clearly a motivating factor for this letter (13:2-10). The intensity and severity of these chapters make it difficult for some to accept them as part of the same letter or written at the same time. However, the presence of false teachers and the perversion of the gospel of Christ are sufficient warrant for Paul to write in this fashion, even if these critics represented only a minority in the church (Hiebert, *An Introduction to the New Testament*, 2:147-48).

To prepare for Paul's third visit. The fact that Paul deals with this matter briefly and in the concluding chapter (13:1-10) does not diminish its importance. Tasker claims, "The dominating purpose of 2 Corinthians is to prepare the readers for Paul's third visit" (*The Second Epistle of Paul to the Corinthians,* 22). Paul had already canceled an earlier visit because of conditions in the church (1:15-17). He wanted to make certain that this visit would be a positive experience, not a negative one for him and for the church (13:10).

With this broad overview, we return to the introduction and to the several ideas that Paul weaves together throughout the epistle. He focuses attention immediately on his personal sufferings and the comfort that flowed from God through Paul to the church at Corinth (1:3-6). The theme of Paul's sufferings appears frequently and extensively in the following chapters (2, 4, 6, 7, and 11). Paul emphasizes his own sufferings as proof of the sincerity of his ministry (2:14-17), and also as proof of his apostleship (11:23-29).

Message of 2 Corinthians
Introduction (1:1-11). The opening salutation of this letter is unusually brief (1:1-2). Paul introduces himself as the author along with Timothy. The church at Corinth to whom the letter is addressed is sparingly introduced. The simplicity of the opening belies the importance and

intensity of what will follow. Paul calls himself *an apostle of Christ Jesus by the will of God* and spends much of the epistle defending that apostleship. Paul's doxology (1:3-4) is focused on God's comfort in the midst of suffering and provides a fitting introduction to the two major sections of the letter. Paul's sufferings are abundant but so also is God's comfort (1:5) Paul's sufferings are for Christ and for the benefit of the Corinthians, and his hope for them is firm because they share in both his sufferings and in his comfort (1:7). Paul's praise is directed to God and commendation for the church at Corinth is absent. That comes later. His love for them is unconditional, but his praise is dependent on their performance and that is still in some doubt (12:20-21). Paul affirms his love for them on several occasions (7:3; 11:11; 12:15). Paul has boasted about the church to others and he would *most gladly spend and be expended for your souls* (12:15).

Comfort through Paul's Ministry of Reconciliation (1:12-7:16)
Paul's explanation of his change of plans (1:12-2:4). Paul appeals for understanding as he explains his reasons for delaying his return to Corinth (1:12-14). It was not vacillation on Paul's part (1:15-22), but a sincere desire to avoid a confrontational meeting that would bring both Paul and the Corinthians sorrow rather than joy (1:23-2:3). His previous letter was written *out of anguish of heart and with many tears* and was intended to express his love for them, not to cause them sorrow (2:4).

Paul's exhortation to forgive the offender (2:5-11). The majority had acted on Paul's previous letter and had disciplined the member guilty of incest (1 Corinthians 5:1-8). Now he had to exhort them to forgive and restore the repentant member. As an apostle, Paul has forgiven the offender; now it is their turn. Satan works when believers withhold forgiveness and love (2:11).

Paul's explanation of his ministry (2:12-5:21). Paul draws on the triumphal procession of a Roman general to explain that his ministry is one of triumph in Christ and is an *aroma of life* both to those who are being saved and to those who are perishing (2:12-17). Some may need letters of commendation from the church but not Paul. The changed lives of the Corinthians are his "living letters of commendation" (3:1-3). His is a new covenant ministry that is marked by glory and it contrasts with the old Mosaic covenant that was marked by fading glory (3:4-13). It is glorious because it brings righteousness not condemnation and because it is growing brighter from glory to glory and is not fading away. The veil still obscures the understanding of unbelieving Jews but has been taken away from those who believe (3:14-16). The Holy Spirit is progressively transforming each believer into the glorious likeness of the risen Christ (3:17-18).

Paul does not lose heart when he suffers because of the glory of the ministry he has received (4:1-6). The power evident in Paul's ministry is from God who has entrusted him with a ministry of life and light. Death is his constant companion, but he is sustained by the knowledge that he will be raised from death because Jesus was (4:7-15). Paul's afflictions, no matter how severe they seem, are light and momentary compared to the eternal glory to be revealed at the resurrection (4:16-18). Paul's hope is firmly fixed on heaven and his ambition is to please the Lord, knowing that he will appear before the judgment seat of Christ (5:1-15). He is Christ's ambassador, calling men to repentance that they might be reconciled to God (5:16-21).

Paul's call to action (6:1-7:1). This is the day of salvation and nothing should be allowed to discredit the gospel ministry (6:1-2). Paul's example of persistence under persecution and absolute integrity ought to serve as their model (6:3-10). The Christians at Corinth must not discredit the ministry of the gospel by becoming like the lost they seek to win (6:11-13). They are the temple of the living God and must not be bound together with unbelievers (6:14-7:1).

Paul's confidence in the Christians at Corinth (7:2-16). Paul has been distressed by the strained relationship with the church at Corinth, but the arrival of Titus and his good report has filled Paul with comfort concerning them (7:2-7). Commendation that was withheld in the opening is now affirmed (7:3-4). He has great confidence in them and is overflowing with joy. His previous letter caused them sorrow, but that sorrow has led them to repentance and has restored their zeal (7:8-13). Titus too has been refreshed and his love for them has increased (7:14-15). Paul closes this first section of the letter by affirming his full confidence in them. *I rejoice that in everything I have confidence in you* (7:16).

Paul's Solicitation to Grace Giving (chaps. 8-9)
The example of generosity by the Macedonian saints (8:1-5). The church at Philippi and probably those of Thessalonica and Berea are the gold standard for grace giving. They have given generously and joyfully out of their own deep poverty (8:1-2). Their giving was willing and sacrificial. They actually begged for the opportunity to participate in the

collection for the saints in Jerusalem (8:3-4). Their generosity flowed from the fact that they had first given themselves to the Lord (8:5).

Paul's appeal to the Corinthians (8:6-15). Generosity is all about grace, and Paul has commissioned Titus to encourage the Corinthian church to follow the example of the Macedonians (8:6-7). Jesus Himself is the prime example of grace giving (8:9). *For you know the grace of our Lord Jesus Christ, that though He was rich, yet for your sake He became poor, so that you through His poverty might become rich.* The Corinthian church initiated the collection for the saints in Jerusalem and now it is time for them to make good on their pledge (8:10-15).

The administration of their gift (8:16-24). Titus has been commissioned along with another brother to ensure that the gift is managed with the utmost integrity. Poor financial management must not discredit the ministry of the gospel so Paul takes every precaution to do what is honorable in the sight of men as well as the Lord. The men Paul is sending have been tested and proved diligent and the Corinthians should openly prove their integrity and love by fulfilling their commitment.

Incentives for grace giving (chap. 9). Paul has finished his appeal and yet feels constrained to give additional encouragement to ensure their positive response. Paul has boasted of their planned generosity and he does not want to arrive with some of those generous believers from Macedonia and find the Corinthians unprepared. Both he and they would be embarrassed (9:1-5). Other incentives for grace giving include (a) the law of the harvest: *He who sows sparingly will also reap sparingly, and he who sows bountifully will also reap bountifully* (9:6); (b) God loves cheerful givers (9:7); (c) God's grace is overflowing to them (9:8-11); and (d) their generosity will have an impact on others (9:12-14). As he did in the first section, Paul ends this appeal to grace giving with a doxology. *Thanks be to God for His indescribable gift!* (9:15).

Paul's Defense of His Apostleship (10:1-13:10)
In this third section Paul "takes off his gloves," as he defends his apostleship (chaps. 10-13). The vindication of his apostleship is not an afterthought. It is intentionally kept until the last. Paul has been driven to defend his apostleship (12:11-12) and does so with unusual vigor and sharpness. Only in Galatians does one find such impassioned arguments as Paul puts forward in these chapters.

The authority of Paul's apostleship (chap. 10). Paul has been accused of being meek in face-to-face encounters but bold in his letters (10:1-2). But Paul's apostleship is as powerful as his words. His apostleship comes with divinely given power that demolishes the speculations of the false teaching and gives him the authority to punish disobedience (10:3-6). Paul's authority was given to him by Christ Himself and is a commission to build up not to destroy (10:7-9). Paul's detractors charge that *his personal appearance is unimpressive and his speech contemptible* (10:10), and they insinuate that he is a second-class apostle not to be compared with the *imminent apostles* (11:5). Paul does not need to commend himself. The results of his ministry are ample proof of his apostleship; after all, he was the one who first brought the gospel to them at Corinth (10:12-18).

The authenticity of Paul's apostleship (11:1-12:13). Paul is jealous for these Christians because he betrothed them as a virgin bride to Christ and Satan is now luring them away from pure devotion to Christ by a false gospel (11:1-4). Paul's sacrificial service to them is further proof of the authenticity of his apostleship (11:5-10). God knows that Paul loves them even if others claim that he does not (11:11). Paul's accusers are false prophets masquerading as apostles when they are really servants of Satan (11:12-15). Paul is loath to boast but his critics and the gullibility of some at Corinth have driven him to it (11:16-21). His Jewish heritage is genuine (11:22). His record as a servant of Christ is unmatched (11:23-33). The list of Paul's suffering is enough to shame the harshest critic! Crowning these hardships is Paul's *daily concern for all the churches* (11:28).

Paul then "boasts" about his visions and revelations from the Lord (12:1). Those revelations of heaven cannot be described in words (12:2-6). So great are those revelations from the Lord that Paul could easily exalt himself, but instead he has been given a *thorn in the flesh, a messenger of Satan to torment me—to keep me from exalting myself* (12:7). His prayer for the removal of the thorn was not granted, but God gave him grace to endure the thorn so that the power of Christ could dwell in him (12:8-10). Paul issues a mild apology for boasting but they have compelled him to do it (12:11-13).

The agenda for Paul's intended visit (12:14-13:10). Paul closes the letter with an announcement of his pending visit and the importance of the church being adequately prepared (12:14-13:10). He remembers his last, painful visit (2:1), and does not wish to repeat that humbling experience (12:20-21). He calls on the believers at Corinth to *Examine* *yourselves to see whether you are in the faith; Test yourselves* (13:5). The exhortation is not born out of doubt, but out of confidence that they will not *fail the test*, but will *do what is right* (13:6-10). If Paul's opening was abrupt and lacking in praise, his closing is permeated with love and good will (13:11-14).

Summary. Paul has taken great pains to preserve the integrity of his ministry. Having introduced the fact early (1:12), he returns to it often (2:17; 4:1-7; 5:9-12; 6:3-4; 7:2; 8:21; 10:1-6; 11:7-12; 13:8-10). Paul must have felt the sting of the attacks against his ministry and cited this abundance of evidence to prove its genuineness. At the same time Paul argues for the equality and genuineness of his apostleship, and he proudly raises the banner of his weakness. It is one of the great paradoxes of Scripture that *God's power is made perfect in weakness* (12:9).

The pressures and problems of Paul's ministry are beyond his ability to endure (1:8-11), and yet they are insignificant in light of the eternal glory that awaits him (4:16-18). To the majority who accept Paul he reminds them that he has *this treasure in jars of clay* (4:7). But to the false apostles and the critical minority of the church, Paul denies any sense of inferiority (11:5-6; 12:11-12). Throughout the letter Paul balances humility with greatness, weakness with strength, and trouble with triumph (2:14-17; 4:1-18). Paul's example teaches that it is important to listen to one's critics but not to let them dictate one's life or determine one's ministry.

Outline of 2 Corinthians

I.	Introduction	1:1-11
	A. Paul's greeting to the church at Corinth	1:1-2
	B. Paul's praise: comfort through suffering	1:3-7
	1. The source of comfort: God	1:3-4a
	2. The purpose: we can comfort others	1:4b-5
	3. The outcome: shared suffering/comfort	1:6-7
	C. Paul's personal example of suffering	1:8-11
	1. The extent: beyond his ability to endure	1:8-9a
	2. The intent: that we might rely on God	1:9b
	3. The outcome: God has delivered us	1:10
	4. The agency: an answer to your prayers	1:11
II	Consolation: Paul's Ministry of Reconciliation	1:12-7:16
	A. Paul's appeal for understanding	1:12-14
	B. Paul's explanation of his change of plans	1:15-2:4

1.	His plans were carefully made	1:15-17
2.	His plans were under God's control	1:18-22
3.	His plans were changed to spare them	1:23-24
4.	His previous visit too painful to repeat	2:1-4

C. Paul's exhortation to forgive the offender — 2:5-11
1. The punishment has been sufficient — 2:5-6
2. It is time to reaffirm your love for him — 2:7-9
3. Paul has already forgiven him — 2:10
4. Satan works if we withhold forgiveness — 2:11

D. Paul's ministry explained — 2:12-5:21
1. It is triumphant in Christ — 2:12-17
2. It is accredited by changed lives — 3:1-3
3. It is a new covenant ministry of glory — 3:4-18
   a. It is competent through Christ — 3:4-6
   b. It brings righteousness — 3:7-11
   c. It removed the veil of separation — 3:12-16
   d. It is liberating because of the Spirit — 3:17
   e. It transforms us into Christlikeness — 3:18
4. It endures into eternity — 4:1-5:10
   a. It is evident to all but the blind — 4:1-6
   b. Its power is evident in suffering — 4:7-15
   c. Its value will be evident in eternity — 4:16-18
   d. Its guarantee is God's Spirit — 5:1-5
   e. Its goal is to please the Lord — 5:6-10
   f. It is compelled by the love of Christ — 5:11-15
   g. It is a ministry of reconciliation — 5:16-21

E. Paul's appeal for action — 6:1-7:1
1. It is urgent — 6:1-2
2. It is exemplified in Paul's life — 6:3-10
3. It is the overflow of a loving heart — 6:11-13
4. It requires separation from the world — 6:14-7:1

F. Paul's high expectation for the church — 7:2-16
1. His confidence in them — 7:2-4
2. His concern for them — 7:5-12
3. Titus' confirmation of them — 7:13-16

III. Solicitation: To Grace Giving — 8:1-9:15
A. The example of generosity by Macedonians — 8:1-5
1. Grace: the source of their generosity — 8:1
2. Poverty: contrasts with their generosity — 8:2
3. Generosity: gave beyond their ability — 8:3

	4.	Privilege: the attitude of generosity	8:4
	5.	Gave themselves: basis of generosity	8:5
B.	The appeal for generosity by Corinthians		8:6-15
	1.	The appeal to excel in grace giving	8:6-8
	2.	Christ is the example of grace giving	8:9
	3.	The advice to finish what they started	8:10-12
	4.	The underlying principle for giving	8:13-15
C.	The administration of their gift		8:16-24
	1.	The integrity of the process	8:16-21
	2.	The integrity of the people	8:22-23
	3.	The integrity of the purpose	8:24
D.	The incentives for generous giving		9:1-15
	1.	The need of keeping their promise	9:1-5
	2.	The law of the harvest	9:6
	3.	The love of God for cheerful givers	9:7
	4.	The example of God's grace giving	9:8-11
	5.	The impact of generosity on others	9:12-14
	6.	The indescribable gift of God	9:15

IV. Vindication: Of Paul's Apostleship 10:1-13:10
- A. The authority of Paul's apostleship 10:1-18
  - 1. Paul's appeal to the church 10:1-6
  - 2. Paul's answer to the critics 10:7-11
  - 3. Paul's appraisal of the charges 10:12-18
    - a. Paul doesn't commend himself 10:12
    - b. We are commended by results 10:13-16
    - c. God's commendation is what counts 10:17-18
- B. The authentication of Paul's apostleship 11:1-12:13
  - 1. Authenticated by Paul's service 11:1-18
    - a. Paul's admonition to the church 11:1-4
    - b. Paul's sacrificial service is proof 11:5-12
    - c. Paul's critics are Satan's servants! 11:13-15
  - 2. Authenticated by Paul's sufferings 11:16-33
    - a. Paul's admonition to the church 11:16-21a
    - b. Paul's lineage is unquestioned 11:21b-23a
    - c. Paul's sufferings are unequaled 11:23b-29
    - d. Paul's weakness is acknowledged 11:30-33
  - 3. Authenticated by Paul's visions 12:1-10
    - a. Paul's revelations are unique 12:1-5
    - b. Revelations balanced by weakness 12:6-10
  - 4. Paul's "apology" for his self-defense 12:11-13

C. The agenda for Paul's third visit 12:14-13:10
    1. His attitude: gladly expended for them 12:14-18
    2. His fear: being grieved by their sins 12:19-21
    3. His warning: won't spare those who sin 13:1-4
    4. His request: that they do what is right 13:5-9
    5. His reason for writing: to build them up 13:10

V. Conclusion 13:11-14
  A. Paul's appeal for appropriate action 13:11
  B. Paul's greeting 13:12-13
  C. Paul's benediction 13:14

Bibliography for 1 and 2 Corinthians

Barnett, Paul. *2 Corinthians.* The New International Commentary on the New Testament. Grand Rapids: Wm. B. Eerdmans Publishing Co., 1997.

Blomberg, Craig. *First Corinthians.* The NIV Application Commentary. Grand Rapids: Zondervan Publishing House, 1995.

Bruce, F. F. *First and Second Corinthians.* Grand Rapids: Wm. B. Eerdmans Publishing Co., 1981.

Carson, D. A., Douglas J. Moo, and Leon Morris. *An Introduction to the New Testament.* Grand Rapids: Zondervan Publishing House, 1991.

Farrar, *The Life and Work of St. Paul.* New York: E. P. Dutton and Co., 1889.

Fee, Gordon. *The First Epistle to the Corinthians.* The New International Commentary on the New Testament. Grand Rapids: Wm. B. Eerdmans Publishing Co., 1987.

Garland, David E. *2 Corinthians.* The New American Commentary. Nashville: Broadman & Holman Publishers, 1999.

Geisler, Norman L., and William E. Nix. *A General Introduction to the Bible.* Chicago: Moody Press, 1971.

Guthrie, Donald. *New Testament Introduction.* Downers Grove, IL: InterVarsity Press, 1990.

Hafemann, Scott. *Second Corinthians*. Grand Rapids: Zondervan Publishing House, 2000.

Harris, Murray J. "2 Corinthians." In *The Expositor's Bible Commentary*. Vol. 11. Grand Rapids: Zondervan Publishing House, 2008.

Hiebert, D. Edmond. An *Introduction to the New Testament*. Vol. 2. Chicago: Moody Press, 1975.

Johnson, Alan F. *1 Corinthians*. Downers Grove, IL: InterVarsity Press, 2004.

MacArthur, John F. *1 Corinthians*. Chicago: Moody Press, 1984.

Martin, Ralph P. *2 Corinthians*. Word Biblical Commentary. Waco, TX: Word Books, 1986.

Morris, Leon. *The First Epistle of Paul to the Corinthians*. Grand Rapids: Wm. B. Eerdmans Publishing Co., 1983.

Scroggie, W. Graham. *Know Your Bible: New Testament*. Vol. 2. London: Pickering & Inglis, 1960.

Thiselton, Anthony. *First Corinthians*. New International Greek Testament Commentary. Grand Rapids: Wm. B. Eerdmans Publishing Co., 2000.

Verbrugge, Verlyn D. "1 Corinthians." In *The Expositor's Bible Commentary*. Vol. 11. Grand Rapids: Zondervan Publishing House, 2008.

Witherington, Ben. *Conflict and Community in Corinth*. Grand Rapids: Wm. B. Eerdmans Publishing Co., 1995.

GALATIANS: Standing Firm for Freedom in Christ

Key Verse– 5:1, *Christ set us free; therefore keep standing firm and do not be subject again to a yoke of slavery*

Key Words:
Christ, Cross,
Gospel, Faith,
Circumcision,
Law/Grace,
Flesh/Spirit,
Liberty,
Free

Introduction	Personal	Doctrinal	Practical
	His Gospel	Paul's Defense of: Justification by Faith	Freedom in Christ
1:1-10	1:11	3:1	5:1 ... 6:18

Anathema to any other gospel!

	Personal	Doctrinal	Practical
	Source of Paul's Gospel By revelation from Jesus Christ Affirmed by the apostles	**Content** of Paul's Gospel Justification is by faith, not by the Law Affirmed by Abraham	**Effect** of Paul's Gospel Faith brings freedom from the flesh Affirmed by the Holy Spirit
	Lives in me! *I am crucified with Christ*	*I am redeemed from a curse by Christ* **Christ:** *Died for me!*	*Lives through me!* *I now fulfill the law of Christ*
	Cannot make a man righteous If righteousness could be gained by the Law, Christ died for nothing!	**The Law:** Came later to lead us to Christ Now that faith has come, we are no longer under supervision of the Law	Brings us back under slavery If you are led by the Spirit, you are not under the Law

By Paul in A.D. 49 from Antioch

The Emancipation Proclamation of Christianity

GALATIANS

"The book of Galatians is one of the shorter epistles of Paul. ...Few books, however, have had a more profound influence on the history of mankind than has this small tract, for such it could be called. Christianity might have been just one more Jewish sect, and the thought of the Western world might have been entirely pagan had it never been written. Galatians embodies the germinal teaching on Christian freedom which separated Christianity from Judaism, and which launched it upward on a career of missionary conquest. It was the cornerstone of the Protestant Reformation, because its teaching of salvation by grace alone became the dominant theme of the preaching of the Reformers. Luther's *Commentary on Galatians* was the reasoned manifesto of the revolt against the Roman ritual and hierarchy, which more than any other single document, revived the knowledge of Biblical truth in the minds of the people. It has been called 'the Magna Charta of spiritual emancipation,' for on its principles is formed the whole faith of a free church" (Merrill C. Tenney, *Galatians: The Charter of Christian Liberty*, 15-16).

"The Epistle to the Galatians is my epistle. To it I am as it were in wedlock. It is my Katherine" (Martin Luther, *A Commentary on St. Paul's Epistle to the Galatians*, iv).

Author

Paul is identified as the author in the opening statement (1:1) and again emphatically at a crucial point in the argument (5:2). Pauline authorship has been almost uncontested. In fact, the Tübingen school that profoundly influenced critical scholarship at the beginning of the nineteenth century regarded Galatians as the standard by which the authenticity of all other so-called Pauline Epistles were to be measured. Paul is identified as the author within the epistle and the personal references and the theology are unmistakably Pauline. Personal references substantiating Pauline authorship, include the following:

1. The author is the founder of the churches and their spiritual father (4:19-20).
2. He was the first to proclaim the gospel in the region (1:8, 11).
3. His ministry in the region involved an illness (4:13).

4. The power of the Holy Spirit was evident in his ministry (3:2, 5).
5. The message was confirmed by miracles (3:5).
6. An intense bond of love existed between the author and these people (4:15-16).
7. The author's eyesight was severely impaired, forcing him to write in a much larger script (4:15; 6:11).
8. The author's credentials are viewed as impeccable and well known (1:13-14).
9. He was an innovator not an echo with regard to the gospel (1:11-12; 2:6).
10. He was an apostle with a special calling to minister among the Gentiles (1:1; 2:7).
11. Early in his career the author was a violent opponent of Christianity (1:23).
12. He received the personal endorsement of the pillars of the Jerusalem church, Peter, James, and John (2:9).
13. He bore the physical scars of persecution for Christ (6:17).
14. The author was a staunch opponent of Judaizing tendencies, even to the point of publicly confronting Peter (2:1-5, 11-14).

Addressees (Destination) of Galatians

North or South Galatia: A Difficult Issue. The authorship of Galatians may have been unchallenged, but the same cannot be said for its destination and the identity of its recipients. The geographical location and identity of the Galatian churches has been intensely studied and debated in the twentieth century. That is surprising, given how much we learn about the recipients from the epistle itself. The problem stems from the fact that the term "Galatia" had two distinct meanings in the New Testament era. "Galatia" referred to the ethnic-geographical region (North) and also to the political region (South). This has spawned controversy between the "North Galatia" theory and advocates favoring the "South Galatia" theory: Paul's ministry took him to both regions, but at different times and apparently with very different results. The issue does not alter the interpretation, but it is important because it affects the time of the writing and the place of Galatians in the Jew-Gentile controversy of Acts 15.

North Galatia. When used in the *ethnographic* sense Galatia designated the territory inhabited by the Celtic people in north-central Asia Minor. These Celtic tribes migrated into the region from ancient Gaul. They attacked and nearly destroyed Rome itself in 390 B.C. The Gauls gave their name to the district, hence "Galatia" (Hiebert, *An Introduction to the New Testament,* 2:72-73). This "Galatia" was located in the mountainous regions of the north. It had no major cities and no significant Jewish population in Paul's day. Paul did not visit the area until he began his second mission to the Gentiles (Acts 16). Even then, Luke only records that *Paul and his companions traveled throughout the region of Phrygia and Galatia* (16:5).

South Galatia. In 189 B.C. the Gauls were subjugated and the area became a province of Rome. The process of conquest and assimilation was completed in 25 B.C. when Augustus declared the region an official Roman province and called it Galatia. That name had been used previously to describe the **people** who had originally come from Gaul, but now Galatia had a ***political*** meaning. As such it referred to the **province** of Galatia, not just the people. Most importantly for our discussion, the province was extended to the south and incorporated parts of Lycaonia, Phrygia, and Pisidia. Paul's first mission to the Gentiles (Acts 13-14) centered in the political entity known as Galatia. In particular, the cities of Lystra and Derbe were scenes of Paul's church planting ministry. The two church-planting ministries of Paul, commonly referred to as his first and second missionary journeys, were separated by at least three years. Most importantly, they also occurred before and after the Jerusalem Council (Acts 15). At that council the church resolved the very issue addressed by Paul in Galatians.

The issue is whether the *churches of Galatia* addressed in the epistle (1:2) are located in the north or the south of the region known as Galatia. The issue regarding the identity of the recipients has given rise to two dominant theories, the North Galatian view and the South Galatian view. The view chosen may not impact our interpretation of the contents of Galatians profoundly, but it does have a major impact on the order of events and the occasion reflected in the epistle. This issue deserves to be addressed in more detail.

Paul's 1st Journey, Ministry in South Galatia, A.D. 48-49

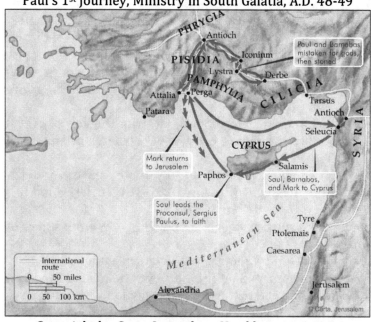

Copyright by Carta Jerusalem, Used by permission

Paul's 2nd Journey, Travels through North Galatia, A.D. 50-51

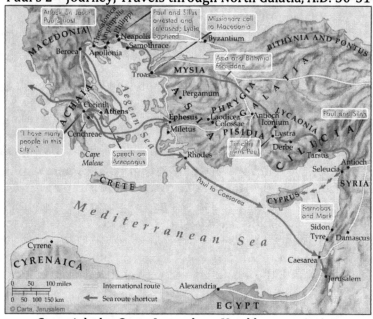

Copyright by Carta Jerusalem, Used by permission

The addressees as described in Galatians. We may not know for certain whether the churches were located in the "North" or the "South," but we do know much about those congregations. As in the case of the author, we glean the character of the addressees from the contents of the epistle.

1. There were several churches not just one (1:2). These churches all had one common problem or disturbance: the infiltration of Judaizers (1:6-7; 5:7-9).
2. The initial contact these churches had with the gospel came through Paul himself (1:8), and the churches were planted by Paul (3:1-3; 4:13-14, 19-20).
3. They had responded enthusiastically to the message and had also embraced the messenger warmly (4:12-15). They revered the apostle as if he were *an angel of God* (4:14).
4. They loved the author enough to be willing to sacrifice their own eyes for him (4:15).
5. They themselves had willingly endured persecution (3:4).
6. They were apparently Gentiles, not Jews, because they had not been circumcised (5:2). Likewise Judaizing tendencies were not a part of their previous experience, but were a new addition (5:7-12).
7. They were familiar with the Old Testament Scriptures (3:6-9).
8. The congregation included at least a minority of Jews (3:26-29).
9. They had been Christians long enough to have matured in their faith, but were still vulnerable to false teaching (5:7-12).
10. The error to which they were falling victim was no slight deviation; rather it was a new and entirely false gospel (1:6-9).

Support for the North Galatia (*Ethnographic*) View. According to this view the churches were located in the ethnographical area known as the original Galatia or North Galatia. This would necessitate a preaching ministry on Paul's second mission to the Gentiles (Acts 16:6), and on his third mission (18:23). The epistle would then have been written later on the third missionary journey (A.D. 53-57) and most probably from either Ephesus or from Corinth. The popularity of the North Galatian view has declined in recent years but has had strong support in early church history and notably by J. B. Lightfoot (*Epistle to the Galatians,* 1-35). Arguments used include the following.

1. This was the universal view of the early church and was largely unchallenged until the beginning of the twentieth century.
2. Paul addressed his letter to the "Galatians" and that was the popular and ethnically acceptable designation for the northern region.

3. Luke uses the term Galatia to refer to the northern region and adds a separate designation for the regions of Pisidia and Lycaonia (Acts 13-14; 14:6).
4. Luke distinguishes between Phrygia and Galatia as two separate districts visited by Paul on his second and third missionary journeys (16:6; 18:23).
5. The characteristics portrayed by the Galatians are those often associated with the Celtic people, "vocal, boastful, quarrelsome, immoral, lovable, exasperating."
6. Luke's expression "traveled throughout" (Acts 16:6; 18:23) at least permits, if not argues for an extensive preaching ministry in the northern district known as Galatia. Further, the fact that doors were shut to the province of Asia and to Bithynia (16:6-7) left Paul no other direction for preaching but to the north (Guthrie, *New Testament Introduction*, 466-67).
7. North Galatia was made up primarily of Gentiles with only a small Jewish population, while the south had more metropolitan areas and a larger Jewish population. This seems to fit with the background of the people as reflected in the epistle.
8. A problem like that confronted in Galatians would more likely have arisen in the north than in the south (where the prominence of Judaism would have forced an early settlement to the debate) (Cole, *The Epistle of Paul to the Galatians*, 18).
9. Notable scholars such as Moffat and Lightfoot have ably defended this view.

Support for the South Galatian (*Political*) View. The South Galatian view is now widely held by conservative scholars. The evidence includes the following.
1. Paul is careful to describe two visits to Jerusalem and identifies Barnabas as accompanying him on the second (1:17-18; 2:1). Paul's second visit to Jerusalem involved the offering for the saints (Acts 11:30). Barnabas accompanied him on that visit (Acts 12:25). (It must be admitted that Paul indicates a private meeting was held with the apostles on the second visit, whereas Acts 11:30 mentions only elders.) Given his care for enumerating Jerusalem visits, it would seem strange for Paul to leave out the visit with Barnabas and the offering they carried for the poor. It is all the more unlikely given the importance Paul attached here to remembering the poor (Galatians 2:10).

233

2. Luke describes the south Galatian ministry in detail and documents the establishment of churches in that region. While he mentions Paul's passing through the north, he does not record a preaching ministry or identify any churches as established in that region.

3. North Galatia is isolated and difficult to reach. It seems unlikely that Paul would travel that far if he was seeking relief from an illness (2:13). William Ramsay has made the most thorough study of the issue and contends that the illness may have been a siege of chronic malaria fever, which prompted him to leave Perga for the highlands of Antioch of Pisidia (*St. Paul the Traveler and Roman Citizen*, 90-92).

4. South Galatia fits best with Paul's strategy of concentrating on cities that were well populated, influential, and had a significant Jewish population. North Galatia possessed few major cities, was less densely populated, and had relatively few Jewish inhabitants.

5. Paul's use of the term "Galatia" differed from Luke's use. Paul seems to favor the use of provincial rather than ethnographic terms. According to Cole, "It is hard to see what common name Paul could have used to cover Pisidians, Lycaonians, etc., other than the provincial name of 'Galatians'" (*The Epistle of Paul to the Galatians*, 18).

6. It is not surprising that the church fathers identified Galatia with the northern district. The province of Galatia of Paul's day was reduced in size and significance in a series of redistributions of its territory by the Roman government in A.D. 74, 137, and 297. "It is not surprising, therefore, that patristic commentators, followed by medieval and Reformation commentators, assumed that Paul addressed his letter to the churches in North Galatia since that was the only Galatia there was in patristic times" (Hansen, "Galatians, Letter to the," 326).

7. One of the most telling arguments favoring the South Galatia view is the number of differences between the Jerusalem Council as recorded in Acts 15 and Paul's description of his second visit to Jerusalem in Galatians 2.

   a. The apostolic decree of Acts 15:22 is not mentioned in Galatians.

   b. The meeting in Galatians 2 appears to have been of a private nature whereas the entire church was assembled in Acts 15.

   c. The focal issue according to Paul in Galatians 2 was the content of his preaching, which the apostles confirmed as accurate. However, the issue in Acts 15 is clearly focused on the Gentiles and whether it was necessary for them to be circumcised in order to be saved and obedient to the Law for continuation in the faith. Since the Jerusalem Council spoke directly to the issue Paul is writing about, it is surprising that he did not mention that council's definitive action on the issue.

8. Galatians contains descriptive details that fit well with Paul's ministry in South Galatia as recorded in Acts 13-14. For example, they received him as *an angel of God* which might well refer to the ascription of deity and the attempt to worship Paul and Barnabas at the Lyconian cities of Lystra and Derbe (Acts 14:6-18). The *physical marks of suffering* (Galatians 6:17) might be a reference to the scars resulting from Paul being stoned and left for dead by the same crowd (Acts 14:19-20). Those who did believe the gospel at that time were Gentiles who had a dramatic conversion from idolatry (Galatians 4:8).

9. Judaizers were clearly operative in the South Galatian region. The disturbance they created there led directly to the Jerusalem Council (Acts 15:1-2). There being few Jews in the northern region, it is unlikely that Judaizers would have sought to extend their influence there, and could not have done so before Paul's ministry there (16:6).

10. After the Jerusalem Council so thoroughly debated the issue of the relationship of Gentiles to circumcision and the Law of Moses it would have been unusual for Judaizers to be effective. The council's decision was so emphatic and communicated so effectively (Acts 15:22-33) that it is difficult to imagine Judaizers having the success described in Galatians.

11. Peter argued so forcefully against the Judaizers in Acts 15 that it is unlikely he would have needed confrontation by Paul later (Gal. 2:11-14). The best time and occasion for Peter's lapse is during the visit of the Judaizers to Antioch before the Jerusalem Council (Acts 15:1).

12. Barnabas is mentioned three times in the book of Galatians and in a way that suggests he was well known to the Galatian churches. Though not required, that would favor the South Galatian view. Barnabas was Paul's companion on the first mission (Acts 13-14) when these churches were planted, but he had separated from Paul before his later ministry (proposed for North Galatia on the second mission in Acts 16:6). No later ministry of Barnabas in North Galatia is recorded.

13. Delegates from South Galatia are mentioned in regard to the offering for Jerusalem (Acts 20:4), but no mention is made of any delegates from North Galatia.

14. Many leading scholars of the twentieth century favor the South Galatia view. These include Wm. M. Ramsay, F. F. Bruce, D. Edmond Hiebert, and Donald Guthrie.

Conclusion. The traditional North Galatian view has substantial and strong support. However, the weight of evidence does seem to favor the South Galatian view. This is further substantiated by the exegesis of the book itself. Galatians appears to have been written early and to churches highly susceptible to attack from Judaizers. These factors point toward South Galatia. Hiebert concludes, "While the evidence for either view is not conclusive, it seems to us that the balance of probability is in favor of the *South-Galatia* theory. ... Fortunately, neither the value of the Epistle or its interpretation is seriously affected by the question. It is not a liberal versus conservative controversy. It is rather a question of historical and biographical interest" (*An Introduction to the New Testament,* 2:80).

Occasion and Date

The date of Galatians depends on one's conclusion regarding its destination. If addressed to the churches of North Galatia, the letter must have been written sometime during Paul's third missionary journey. Many scholars believe that Galatians 4:13 requires two preaching ministries by Paul to the Galatian churches. If that is the case and the recipients are located in North Galatia, the date would have to be toward the end of his third missionary journey (A.D. 53-57).

On the other hand, if the recipients are located in South Galatia, the epistle could have been written before the Jerusalem Council in A.D. 49. If two visits to Galatia are required, it is possible to see these as fulfilled in the outbound ministry of Paul and Barnabas which established the churches and their visit on the return to Antioch when they organized and appointed elders (Acts 14:21-25).

Occasion for the writing of Galatians. The occasion for the writing of Galatians is the disruption of these churches by the teaching of Judaizers. Such an effort is identified in Acts 15 as following Paul's first missionary journey. That activity by Judaizers led to the Jerusalem Council. The council in turn provided a definitive answer and should have made further efforts by the Judaizers unfruitful. If there were indeed churches established in North Galatia on Paul's second and third missionary journeys, it seems unlikely that the Judaizers would be able to draw them away from the gospel of grace as preached by Paul. The entire weight of the church and its leadership had come down on the side of Paul (and Peter). If Judaizers reached that far, the decisions of the Jerusalem Council should have become known there as well. The later one gets in Paul's ministry and the longer the time following the Jerusalem Council, the less likelihood there is of the Judaizers having the kind of impact so evident in Galatians.

Date of the writing. The circumstances seem to favor a date of A. D. 49 for the writing of Galatians. The intense assault on the faith of the Galatians by the Judaizers required an urgent response from Paul. Galatians was probably written from Antioch (Acts 14:28) and before the Jerusalem Council (Acts 15). As Guthrie observes, "The Epistle leaves us in no doubt that the troublers of the church were Jewish Christians who wished to impose Jewish ritual requirements on the Gentile members. ...Acts makes abundantly clear that such Judaizers had been at work in the southern district and that their activity was the immediate cause of the council at Jerusalem" (*New Testament Introduction,* 472).

Nature of the Controversy at Galatia.

The seriousness of the issue confronting the Galatian churches is evident in several ways. First, in the intensity with which Paul writes (1:6; 3:1; 4:12-16). Second, in the absence of any praise or thanksgiving for the readers, an absence unique to Galatians. Third, in the strength of Paul's invectives against the Judaizers, which indicates the importance he attaches to this issue (1:7-8; 3:1-3; 5:12). Fourth, by the fact that Paul wrote the letter by his own hand, with great pain (6:11-17), and also out of a hurt-filled heart (4:12-20; 6:17).

This attack strikes at the very heart of the gospel, the basis on which a person is saved. The Judaizers contradict the good news that the death of Jesus Christ on the cross is the only, essential, effective, and sufficient means of salvation (1:4; 2:16, 21; 4:4, 17-20; 6:14).

This false teaching displaces the gospel of grace with an ineffective gospel of trying to live up to the Law (3:10-14; 5:2-6). Grace is not the interloper in God's plan of salvation! The Law is, for it came 430 years after the promise of justification by faith (3:15-29).

The teaching of the Judaizers misrepresents life under grace. It substitutes obedience of the flesh to the Law of Moses (works) for the crucified flesh (faith) and a life empowered by the Holy Spirit (3:3-5; 4:1-7; 5:1, 16-26).

The Judaizers hypocritically seek to avoid the offence of the cross (persecution occasioned by the cross) by eliminating the cross (6:12-14).

The Judaizers bring the believers into bondage. They were perpetuating the error of the Pharisees that Christ so vehemently condemned (Matthew 23). They brought believers into bondage to the Law and under the domination of the legalizers who interpret the Law (Galatians 4:17-20; 6:13).

Key verse, 5:1
It was for freedom that Christ set us free; therefore keep standing firm and do not be subject again to a yoke of slavery.

Message of Galatians

Galatians is the emancipation proclamation of Christianity, the Magna Charta of the Christian faith. It is our Declaration of Liberty in Christ. Galatians is apologetic in nature. In Galatians Paul defends the gospel of salvation by grace alone, through faith alone, on the grounds of Christ's death alone, resulting in life lived by the Spirit alone. Galatians is a passionate defense of the gospel of salvation by grace through faith in the cross work of Jesus Christ. It has a three-part structure.

First: In the personal section Paul defends the source of the gospel: it is by personal and direct revelation by Christ (chaps. 1-2). The gospel has come to Paul by direct revelation from Christ himself (1:6-12). It is the only true gospel. Its authority comes from its divine source. Though Paul did not receive his gospel from or by human agency, it was confirmed by the apostles at Jerusalem.

Second: In the doctrinal section of Galatians Paul defends the substance of the gospel: justification by faith and faith alone (chaps. 3-4). Only the death of Jesus Christ on the cross is able to bring redemption. Faith, not the works of the Law, is the only ground of salvation (3:11-14). Abraham provides proof that salvation has always been by grace alone through faith alone.

Third: In the practical section Paul defends the application of the gospel: new life in Christ under the control of the Spirit not the flesh (chaps. 5-6). Christ has set us free from the tyranny of sin and the futility of our own self-effort (5:1). We are now able to live by the power of the indwelling Holy Spirit (5:16-26).

Personal Section: Paul's Gospel Defended (chaps. 1-2)

The salutation (1:1-5). Paul's introduction is direct, intense, and confrontational. The abrupt beginning and the absence of words of commendation reveal the seriousness of the problem confronting the Galatian churches. Paul cuts immediately to the heart of the matter. His apostleship was not by human agency, but by direct personal revelation from the risen Christ (1:1). Paul's whole life and ministry rests on the redeeming work of Jesus Christ on the cross (1:4). Paul begins and ends this intensely written letter by focusing on the death of Jesus Christ on the cross (1:4; 6:14-17). At issue is the source and nature of the gospel itself (1:6-10).

The rebuke: they are deserting the true gospel (1:6-10). The unthinkable is happening. Judaizers are attempting to replace the gospel with a different gospel that is no gospel at all! The seriousness of the issue leaves no room for niceties. Paul is shocked that these churches have abandoned the God of grace Himself in order to embrace a gospel that bears no resemblance to the real thing (1:6-7). Anyone, and that includes even angels, who would preach another gospel than that of salvation by faith in the cross of Christ, deserves eternal condemnation (1:8-10).

The source of Paul's gospel (1:11-24). It is the true gospel because it came by direct revelation from Jesus Christ Himself. The gospel preached by Paul did not come through human agency, but by direct, personal revelation from Jesus Christ (1:11-17). God's call to apostleship began with Paul's birth and climaxed in the revelation of Jesus Christ in Paul (1:15-16). Paul's first contact with apostles like Peter and James did not come until three years after his conversion and then it was only a brief acquaintance (1:18-24). The apostles did not determine Paul's gospel, but they did confirm it and rejoiced at Paul's conversion.

The validation of Paul's gospel (2:1-16). The Jerusalem apostles examined and confirmed Paul's gospel. A more definitive meeting occurred between Paul and the apostles in Jerusalem fourteen years later (2:1-10). Even that meeting was private and came at Paul's initiative. Prompted by a revelation from God, Paul submitted his gospel for review by the original apostles. Rather than alter the gospel Paul had already preached for many years, the *pillars* of the church at Jerusalem gave their unqualified endorsement to Paul's apostleship and to the gospel he preached. The acid test came when Paul defended the truth of the gospel against Judaizers while even Peter and Barnabas were swept up in the hypocrisy (2:12-16).

The substance of Paul's gospel (2:15-16). Justification is by faith in Jesus Christ. Having discussed how the true gospel came to him, Paul now proceeds to summarize the content of that gospel (2:15-21). True Jews (by birth) like Paul know that justification is impossible by observing the Law. Paul like other true Jews has put his faith in Jesus Christ because that alone provides justification (2:15-16). *We are Jews by nature and not sinners from among the Gentiles; nevertheless knowing that a man is not justified by the works of the Law but through faith in Christ Jesus, so that we may be justified by faith in Christ and not by the works of the Law; since by the works of the Law no flesh will be justified.* These two verses introduce the matter of justification by faith that Paul will vigorously defend in the heart of this epistle (chaps. 3-4).

The effect of Paul's gospel (2:17-21). The gospel of grace does not promote sin as charged. Paul is well aware of the charge that the gospel of grace promotes sin (2:17). Justification by faith in Christ does not promote sin! Quite the opposite! It provides the means of overcoming sin (2:17-21). In this brief but compelling "pause," Paul is dealing with the issue of sanctification or how we live the Christian life. He will return to that theme when he defends freedom in Christ and explains life in the Spirit (5:1-6:10). The insinuation that salvation by faith promotes sin is a patent lie. Faith leads us to the cross of Christ in "co-crucifixion." Life begins by faith in Christ who died for our sins (1:4), and life continues by faith because the risen Christ now lives in us (2:20). *I have been crucified with Christ; and it is no longer I who live, but Christ lives in me; and the life which I now live in the flesh I live by faith in the Son of God, who loved me and gave Himself up for me.* Faith and freedom in Christ are in harmony with grace! If there was any other way, like keeping the Law, then *Christ died needlessly* (2:21).

Doctrinal Section: Justification by Faith Defended (chaps. 3-4).
Since the Galatians began by faith, why foolishly revert to works (3:1-5)? Just as Paul began the defense of his gospel by declaring its source, so he begins a defense of justification by faith by pointing to the source of the Galatians' salvation (3:1-5). They have received the Holy Spirit and have become partakers of life in Christ by faith, not by the Law. They are foolish to think they can now change the ground rules and finish in the flesh what God has begun in them by His Spirit.

Abraham is proof that justification is by faith, not by the Law (3:6-25). Abraham is the prime example of justification by faith (3:6-9). He believed God and was declared righteous by God as recorded in Scripture (Genesis 15:6). God was thus announcing that He would justify the Gentiles by faith. The gospel that Paul has preached and that they have believed is the fulfillment of God's promise to Abraham: *In you all the families of the earth will be blessed* (Genesis 12:3). Abraham is proof of God's promise that *the righteous will live by his faith* (Habakkuk 2:4). Those who seek righteousness through observing the Law find themselves under a curse instead. The Law is incapable of rendering us acceptable to God (Galatians 3:10-11). But Christ redeemed sin cursed humanity by bearing that curse on the cross (3:13-14). He redeemed us so that the blessing given to Abraham might come to Gentiles. That blessing is only through Christ and is received only by faith. Those who believe also receive the Holy Spirit, a subject that Paul expounds in chapters 5 and 6. The Law was introduced 430 years after Abraham was declared righteous on the grounds of his faith (3:15-25). The Law, not faith, is the interloper. In fact, we were like prisoners under the Law. But the Law does have a legitimate purpose. The Law was added later and was designed to bring us to Christ so that we could be justified by faith (3:19-24). Now that Christ has gone to the cross, faith has found its fruition and *we are no longer under a tutor* (3:25).

Galatians, with all Jews and Gentiles, are one in Christ (3:26-4:7). Whether Jew or Greek, slave or free, male or female, we are all one in Christ Jesus by faith (3:26-4:7). When the time had fully come, God sent forth His Son from heaven to become incarnate as a man, to experience death on the cross, and to redeem those under the Law, and bestow on them the rights of full-grown sons (4:4). Being under the Law was equivalent to being in slavery; being under faith is becoming free. The Galatians are no longer slaves; they are now sons of God, recipients of the Holy Spirit, and heirs of God! They are no longer children under a guardian (the Law); they are sons with all of the rights of sons.

The Galatians are reminded of their pagan past, their early zeal for Christ, and their love for Paul (4:8- 20). Paul has argued for justification by faith by citing their salvation experience and by showing the precedence of Abraham's faith over the Law of Moses. Now he applies that argument by reminding them of their early zeal for Christ, for the cross, and even for Paul himself (4:8-20). If they turn back now, they will be abandoning freedom and returning to slavery. They will also be alienating themselves from Paul as their spiritual father. Such action is unthinkable!

241

Paul is experiencing "labor pains" for them until the likeness of Christ is fully formed in them (4:19).

The analogy of Hagar and Sarah, of Ishmael and Isaac (4:21-31). Paul concludes this doctrinal section and his defense of justification by faith with an illustration. He draws on Abraham's two wives and two sons as an allegory of faith and the Law. Sara and Isaac represent faith and freedom, while Hagar and Ishmael represent Law and slavery (4:21-31). Like Isaac, the Galatian Christians are children of promise who have been persecuted by Ishmael, the children of Law. As Christians they belong in the heavenly not the earthly Jerusalem. As sons of the free woman (4:31) they ought to live free. Paul now turns his attention to defending the freedom of God's sons by faith through the power of the Holy Spirit (5:1-6:10).

Practical Section: Freedom in Christ Defended (5:1-6:10)

Stand firm in the freedom you now have in Christ (5:1-12)! Christ set us free by redeeming us from the curse of the Law. Paul exhorts the churches at Galatia to stand firm in that freedom. The alternative is slavery (5:1). If these Gentile Christians submit to circumcision, *Christ will be of no benefit to you.* The consequences are enormous! They will become obligated to do the entire Law, will be alienated from Christ, and will thus have "fallen from grace" (5:2-6). To place oneself under the Law as a rule of life is to depart from grace as the rule of life. *For in Christ Jesus neither circumcision nor uncircumcision means anything, but faith working through love.* The "agitators" who are confusing them are intruders and are keeping them from obedience to the truth (5:7-12). These agitators are evil like the yeast that God excluded from His offerings and they spread fermentation through the entire church.

Safeguard that freedom with love (5:13-15)! Those who have been justified by faith have been called to freedom but that freedom must never be used as a staging ground for the flesh to indulge its appetites (5:13). Living in the power of the flesh leads to destructive behavior among Christians (5:15) but faith in Christ sets us free from sin and the Law and places us under the law of love (5:14).

The Spirit conquers the flesh and produces spiritual fruit (5:16-26). To live by the Spirit is to live above the appetites of the flesh (5:16). There is constant warfare between the flesh (our old sinful self) and the indwelling Holy Spirit. Those who are united with Christ in His death live under the control of the Spirit and have crucified the flesh with all of its deviant behavior (5:17-21). The fruit of the Spirit now blossoms where the flesh once ruled (5:22-26).

Freedom in Christ leads to life at its best for believers (6:1-10). To live by the Spirit is to live in love toward fellow believers (6:1-10). Compassion replaces criticism. Humility replaces pride. Giving replaces getting. Shouldering responsibility and serving through the seasons of life mark those who live by the Spirit. We reap what we sow, and a harvest of blessing awaits those who persist in the life of faith and freedom!

Conclusion (6:11-18)

This has been a very painful letter written by Paul's own hand (6:11). This has been a difficult letter for Paul to write both physically and emotionally. That is evident from the *large letters* made necessary by his poor eyesight (6:11). Paul has also had to "pluck out his heart" to write this letter to the very same people who once were willing to "pluck out their eyes" for his benefit (4:12-20).

The Judaizers seek to avoid the cross, but Paul embraces it (6:12-17). The true motive of the Judaizers is *simply so that they will not be persecuted for the cross of Christ* (6:12). Paul enthusiastically embraces the cross they seek to avoid (6:14). Paul glories in the cross alone because it is that cross that, by faith, has brought him into the freedom of the sons of God. As Christ bore the marks of Paul's sin in His body on the cross, so Paul now willingly bears the *brand-marks of Jesus* in his body!

Paul calls them brothers and commends them to God's grace (6:18). Paul has expressed guarded optimism that they will respond positively to this letter (5:10). But he offers no words of praise to them. Abandoning faith in Christ and His cross in favor of a gospel of bondage to the Law is too dangerous to be treated lightly. This first letter from the pen of Paul is the Emancipation Proclamation of Christianity. It has been called, "the Magna Charta of Christian Liberty." The book of Acts makes clear that the doctrine of justification by faith and sanctification by the Spirit triumphed over the Judaizers (Acts 15). Fifteen centuries later it triumphed again as the Protestant Reformation proclaimed justification by faith as the only grounds of salvation. Paul's letter to the Galatians was the banner under which the Reformers fought and won that battle. May it serve still as the banner under which we fight the good fight of faith! Let us stand firm in the faith and enjoy the freedom that is ours in Christ!

"The Epistle to the Galatians is spiritual dynamite, and it is therefore almost impossible to handle it without explosions. It has often been so in the history of the Church. The great spiritual awakening of Martin Luther came as he expounded and studied this Epistle, while it was a sermon on Galatians that brought peace of heart to John Wesley. ... At every point it challenges our present-day shallow, easy acceptances and provokes our opposition. It was a controversial letter; and it is vain to expect any commentator, however humble, to avoid controversy when expounding it—especially when the issues are just alive as today" (R. Alan Cole, *The Epistle of Paul to the Galatians*, 11).

Outline

I.	Introduction	1:1-10
	A. The salutation	1:1-5
	1. Paul's apostleship is from God not man	1:1a
	2. Paul's apostleship is with power	1:1b
	3. Paul's letter is endorsed by the church	1:2
	4. The salutation itself	1:3
	5. The essence of the gospel	1:4-5
	B. Paul's reason for writing: Rebuke	1:6-10
	1. They are deserting the God of grace	1:6a
	2. They are deserting the true gospel	1:6b
	3. They are embracing a perverted gospel	1:7
	4. These false teachers are condemned	1:8-9
	5. This letter is not meant to please men	1:10
II.	Personal: Paul's Gospel Defended	1:11-2:21
	A. The source of Paul's gospel: Revealed by Christ	1:11-17
	1. Independent of any human agency	1:11-12a
	2. Personally revealed by Jesus Christ	1:12b-17
	a. Paul's former zeal in Judaism	1:13-14
	b. Paul's call by God's grace from birth	1:15
	c. Paul's call to preach: "Christ revealed in me"	1:16
	d. Paul's years of private incubation	1:17
	B. The substantiation of Paul's gospel	1:18-2:14
	1. Paul's gospel is independent of the	1:18-24
	a. Paul's brief acquaintance with Peter	1:18
	b. The absence of contact with other apostles	1:19
	c. Paul's testimony offered under oath	1:20
	d. Paul was unknown to the churches of Judea	1:21-23
	e. Paul was affirmed by their praise to God	1:24

	2. Paul's gospel was affirmed by other apostles	2:1-10
	a. In a meeting prompted by a revelation	2:1-3
	b. In answer to opponents of freedom	2:4-5
	c. It was examined by pillars of the church	2:6-9
	d. It received their unqualified endorsement	2:10
	3. Paul even opposed Peter's compromise	2:11-14
	a. When even Peter comprised the gospel	2:11-12
	b. When Barnabas joined in the hypocrisy	2:13
	c. Paul held firmly to the truth of the gospel	2:14
C.	The substance of Paul's gospel	2:15-21
	1. Justification is by faith in Jesus Christ	2:15-16
	a. True Jews know what Gentiles do not!	2:15
	b. Justification is not by observing the Law	2:16a
	c. Justification is by faith in Jesus Christ	2:16b
	d. Therefore we have put our faith in Christ	2:16c
	e. Justification is impossible by the Law	2:16d
	2. Sanctification is by faith in Jesus Christ	2:17-21
	a. Faith in Christ does not promote sin!	2:17-18
	b. Faith leads to living for God	2:19
	c. Christ lives within to empower us	2:20
	(1) We were crucified/died with Christ	2:20a
	(2) Christ lives in us	2:20b
	(3) We live by faith in Christ	2:20c
	(4) Christ gave Himself for us	2:20d
	d. Otherwise Christ died needlessly!	2:21
III.	Doctrinal: Justification by Faith Defended	3:1-4:31
A.	Faith is the grounds of their salvation	3:1-5
	1. They are foolish to be bewitched	3:1
	2. They received the Spirit by believing	3:2
	3. They should not now rely on the flesh to finish	3:3
	4. They have suffered for the faith not the flesh	3:4
	5. They have been blessed by faith not the flesh	3:5
B.	Faith was established by promise to Abraham	3:6-9
	1. It was the grounds of Abraham's salvation	3:6
	2. God gave the gospel in advance to Abraham	3:7-8
	3. Those who believe are blessed with Abraham	3:9
C.	Salvation was purchased by Christ on the cross	3:10-14
	1. All who rely on the Law are under a curse	3:10
	2. No one is justified by the Law	3:11a
	3. The righteous live by faith	3:11b

	4.	The Law is not based on faith	3:12
	5.	Christ bore our sins on the cross	3:13
	6.	The redemption promise is ours by faith	3:14
D.		Faith preceded the Law by centuries	3:15-18
	1.	A covenant cannot be altered	3:15
	2.	God made a covenant with Abraham	3:16
	3.	The Law came 430 years after the covenant	3:17a
	4.	The Law cannot replace the covenant	3:17b
	5.	God gave the covenant in grace not Law	3:18
E.		Justification by faith is supported by the Law	3:19-25
	1.	The Law was given later for a purpose	3:19-20
	2.	The Law is not opposed to faith	3:21
	3.	The Law was given to lead us to faith in Christ	3:22-24
	4.	Now we are no longer under the Law	3:25
F.		Faith has set us free from slavery	3:26-4:7
	1.	Sonship is through faith in Christ	3:26-27
	2.	All who believe share alike in that sonship	3:28-29
	3.	Sons are not in subjection like slaves	4:1-3
	4.	God sent his Son to redeem slaves	4:4-5
	5.	God sent his Spirit into our hearts	4:6
	6.	We are no longer slaves, but sons	4:7
G.		Faith must not be compromised by legalism	4:8-20
	1.	To go back is to be enslaved again	4:8-11
	2.	To go back is to abandon their own past	4:12-16
	3.	To go back is to be alienated from Paul	4:17-20
H.		Justification by faith is illustrated by Abraham	4:21-31
	1.	The historical facts	4:21-23
	2.	Abraham's experience as an allegory	4:24-27
	3.	The personal application	4:29-31
IV.		Practical: Freedom in Christ Defended	5:1-6:10
A.		The call to stand firm in freedom	5:1
	1.	Christ set us free for freedom	5:1a
	2.	We are called to stand firm in that freedom	5:1b
	3.	To go back is to be enslaved again	5:1c
B.		The consequences of legalism	5:2-6
	1.	Christ is of no value	5:2
	2.	You are obligated to the Law	5:3
	3.	You abandon grace	5:4
	4.	You miss the one thing that matters	5:5-6

C.	The condemnation of the legalists		5:7-12
	1.	They keep you from maturing in Christ	5:7
	2.	They do not come from God	5:8
	3.	They corrupt and confuse you	5:9-10
	4.	They abolish the offense of the cross	5:11
	5.	They deserve the strongest condemnation	5:12
D.	The condemnation of license		5:13-15
	1.	Freedom is a privileged calling	5:13a
	2.	Freedom is not a platform to indulge the flesh	5:13b
	3.	Freedom produces loving service	5:13c-14
	4.	Freedom prevents destroying each other	5:15
E.	The call to live by the Spirit		5:16-26
	1.	The command: live by the Spirit!	5:16
	2.	The conflict: the flesh against the Spirit	5:17
	3.	The conquest: the Spirit sets us free	5:18
	4.	The characteristics of the sinful nature	5:19-21
	5.	The characteristics of the Spirit-filled life	5:22-26
		a. Fruit that never offends the Law	5:22-23
		b. Crucifixion of the flesh's passions	5:24
		c. Keeping in step with the Spirit	5:25
		d. Keeping clear of conflict with others	5:26
F.	The consequences of living free		6:1-10
	1.	Caring how we treat a sinning brother	6:1
	2.	Carrying each other's burdens	6:2
	3.	Thinking clearly about ourselves	6:3
	4.	Shouldering our own responsibilities	6:4-5
	5.	Sharing freely with others	6:6
	6.	Sowing to please the Spirit	6:7-8
	7.	Keeping on instead of quitting	6:9
	8.	Reaching out to others at every opportunity	6:10

V.	Conclusion		6:11-18
	A.	A handwritten letter from Paul's heart	6:11
	B.	A final warning against the Judaizers	6:12-13
		1. Their motives are false	6:12
		2. Their actions are hypocritical	6:13a
		3. Their boasting betrays them	6:13b
	C.	Paul's personal example	6:14-15
		1. The cross is Paul's only boast	6:14
		2. A new creation is all that counts	6:15

D. The benediction   6:16-18
   1. Freedom in Christ is the true test for a Jew   6:16
   2. Paul bears the brand-mark of Jesus in his body 6:17
   3. The grace of Christ is the true benediction   6:18

Bibliography

Bruce, F. F. *The Epistle to the Galatians: A Commentary on the Greek Text.* New International Greek Testament Commentary. Grand Rapids: Wm. B. Eerdmans Publishing Co., 1982.

Cole, R. Alan. *The Epistle of Paul to the Galatians.* Tyndale New Testament Commentaries. Downers Grove, IL: InterVarsity Press, 1983.

Dunn, James. *The Epistle to the Galatians.* Black's New Testament Commentary. London: A & C, 1993.

Edwards, Mark J. *Galatians, Ephesians, Philippians.* Ancient Christian Commentary on Scripture. Downers Grove, IL: InterVarsity Press, 1999.

Fung, Ronald Y. K. *The Epistle to the Galatians.* New International Commentary on the New Testament. Grand Rapids: Wm. B. Eerdmans Publishing Co., 1988.

George, Timothy. *Galatians.* New American Commentary. Nashville: Broadman & Holman Publishers, 1994.

Gromacki, Robert G. *Stand Fast in Liberty: An Exposition of Galatians.* Grand Rapids: Baker Book House, 1979.

Guthrie, Donald. *New Testament Introduction.* Downers Grove, IL: InterVarsity Press, 1990.

Hansen, G. Walter. "Galatians, Letter to the." In *Dictionary of Paul and His Letters.* Downers Grove IL: InterVarsity Press, 1993.

Hiebert, D. Edmond. An *Introduction to the New Testament.* Vol. 2. Chicago: Moody Press, 1975.

Lightfoot, J. B. *The Epistle of Paul to the Galatians.* London: Macmillan & Co., 1896; reprint, Grand Rapids: Wm. B. Eerdmans Publishing Co., 1971.

Longenecker, Richard. *Galatians.* Word Biblical Commentary. Nashville: Word Publishing Co., 1990.

Luther, Martin. *A Commentary on St. Paul's Epistle to the Galatians.* Reprint. Grand Rapids, MI: Kregel Publications, 1979.

McKnight, Scot. *Galatians.* NIV Application Commentary. Grand Rapids: Zondervan Publishing House, 1995.

Morris, Leon. *Galatians: Paul's Charter of Christian Freedom.* Downers Grove, IL: InterVarsity Press, 1996.

Ramsay, Wm. M. *Historical Commentary on Galatians.* Grand Rapids: Baker Book House, n.d.

Ryken, Philip Graham. *Galatians.* Phillipsburg, NJ: Presbyterian & Reformed Publishing, 2005.

Silva, Moises. *Interpreting Galatians: Explorations in Exegetical Method.* 2nd ed. Grand Rapids: Baker Book House, 2001.

Stott, John R. W. *The Message of Galatians.* Downers Grove, IL: InterVarsity Press, 1986.

Tenney, Merrill C. *Galatians: The Charter of Christian Liberty.* Grand Rapids: Wm. B. Eerdmans Publishing Co., 1950.

Witherington III, Ben. *Grace in Galatia.* Grand Rapids: Wm. B. Eerdmans Publishing Co., 1998.

250

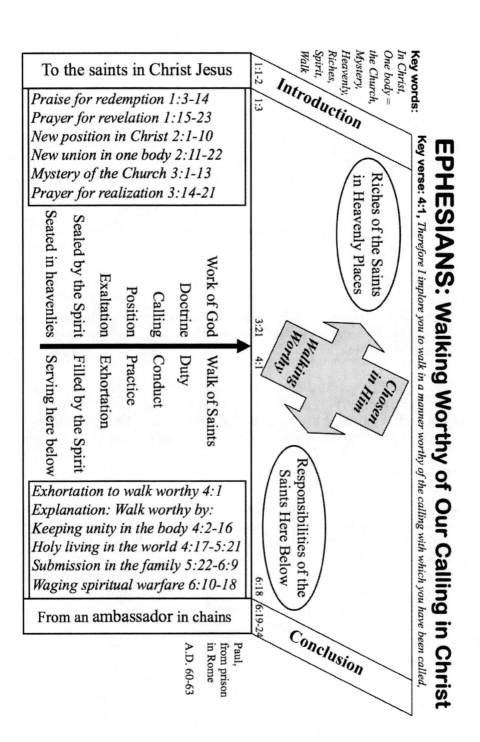

EPHESIANS

Walking Worthy of Our Calling in Christ

> "In the depths of its theology, in the loftiness of its morals, in the way in which the simplest moral truths are based upon the profoundest religious doctrines—the Epistle is unparalleled" (F.W. Farrar, *The Life and Work of St. Paul,*).
>
> "If we would know what the Christian Church is, viewed ideally, we must turn to EPHESIANS, where the revelation is most fully set forth. The unity, the beauty, and the function of the Christian Church are here presented in struggling terms, that is, in language which struggles to express the inexpressible. The Apostle has reached the final note of his music, he has come to the last word of his message, and it is the music and message of *Christ Completed in His Church*" (W. Graham Scroggie, *Know Your Bible: New Testament,* 211-12).

Authenticity and Authorship

Pauline authenticity. The Pauline authorship of Ephesians was accepted by the early church fathers and unchallenged until the rise of modern criticism. "The unanimous position of the ancient Church was to receive this epistle as from the hand of the Apostle Paul" (D. Edmond Hiebert, *An Introduction to the New Testament,* 2:256). According to the International Standard Bible Encyclopedia, "None of the epistles which are ascribed to St. Paul have a stronger chain of evidence to their early and continued use than that which we know as the Epistle to the Ephesians" (Lewis, *International Standard Bible Encyclopedia,* 2:956). A few scholars have challenged the traditional and historical acceptance of the Pauline authenticity of Ephesians. They have claimed that Ephesians was the work of an ardent student of Paul who wrote at a later date. At issue is whether the epistle to the Ephesians is an authentic work of the apostle Paul or a skillful imitation by an admirer of Paul.

Pseudepigrapha. Schleiermacher (1768-1838) cast doubt on the Pauline authorship of Ephesians and his view was adopted by a few scholars such as Moffatt and Goodspeed. Goodspeed claimed that the letter was written by an admirer of Paul at a later date and served as an introduction to the Pauline letters that were being assembled into a collection. According to

252

this view, the letters of Paul had been neglected and the appearance of the book of Acts revived interest in Paul's writings. A student of Paul writing sometime between A.D. 70 and 90 penned Ephesians as the introduction to this Pauline corpus. Against this view is the weight of evidence, both internal and external, favoring Pauline authorship. There is no evidence that Paul's letters were neglected or that Ephesians ever stood at the head of Paul's epistles. Historical evidence is such that it is tempting to brush aside these objections. Most commentaries and New Testament introductions give only brief attention to the critical views. Donald Guthrie is an exception. He says, "Much controversy has surrounded and still surrounds the question of authenticity and the evidence for and against it will need to be examined in some detail" (*New Testament Introduction*, 496). Guthrie devotes 32 pages to a careful examination and refutation of the critical objections.

Evidence for Pauline Authorship

Internal evidence. The author twice identifies himself as Paul and claims to be an apostle of Christ Jesus (1:1; 3:1). He claims to have received special revelation regarding the church in God's plan for the ages (3:1-13). Such a bold claim would have been rejected by the church fathers if the author was not the apostle Paul himself. Ephesians is the most impersonal of all Paul's letters but it is still rich in biographical data. The following texts demonstrate the point.

1:15 - the author has heard of their faith and love.
1:16 - he has been intense and unceasing in his prayers for them.
3:1 - he is a prisoner of Christ Jesus for the sake of Gentiles (4:1)
3:7 - he is a servant of the gospel by the gift of God's grace.
3:8 - he is less than the least of God's saints.
3:13 - he is suffering on behalf of the readers.
4:17 - he exhorts with divine authority.
6:19 - he requests prayer that he will fearlessly declare the gospel.
6:20 - he is an ambassador in chains.
6:21 - Tychicus is a dear brother with personal information.

Literary style. The literary style is unmistakably Pauline. Echoes of Pauline thought and style abound. It is unlikely that an imitator of Paul would have composed a letter containing 90 to 95% of Pauline material (D. A. Carson, Douglas J. Moo, and Leon Morris, *An Introduction to the New Testament*, 306). There are many words that appear in Ephesians that are common to other Pauline epistles but that occur nowhere else in the New Testament.

253

Theological affinities. The church as the body of Christ uniting both Jews and Gentiles is distinctly Pauline (2:11-22; 4:4-16; with 1 Corinthians 12:12-27). So also is the gifting of believers for mutual edification of the church (4:7-16; with 1 Corinthians 12:1-11). Other typically Pauline emphases include the high Christology (1:10, 19-23), the indwelling and enabling ministry of the Holy Spirit (1:13; 5:18), the stress on the believer as "in Christ" and a "new man" (1:3-14; 2:1-10; 3:10-11; 4:20-24), and the preeminence of the cross and the blood of Christ (1:7; 2:13-17). Ephesians is rightly called "the crown of Paulinism" (Guthrie, *New Testament Introduction*, 499).

Colossian parallels. There are striking similarities between Ephesians and Colossians. Out of 155 verses in Ephesians, 78 are parallel to verses found in Colossians (For a list of specific parallel passages see John Eadie, *Commentary on the Epistle to the Ephesians*, xlviii). Some scholars use this as an argument against the authenticity of Ephesians, but it may also support the traditional view of Pauline authorship. Guthrie argues, "If Colossians is a genuine epistle of Paul, and few modern scholars doubt that it is, it's close connection with Ephesians and the patristic assumption that both epistles were genuine raise a strong presumption in favor of Ephesians. In fact the attestation is stronger for Ephesians than for Colossians" (Donald Guthrie, *New Testament Introduction*, 498).

External support for Pauline authorship. Ephesians was widely quoted by church fathers. Clement of Rome, Ignatius, Polycarp, Hermas, Clement of Alexandria, Tertullian, and Irenaeus all quote directly from or make clear references to Ephesians. This epistle appears as a letter of Paul in both the Marcion and Muratorian canons (lists of books considered authentic). There is no indication that anyone in the early church questioned the canonicity of Ephesians. There was some dispute about its destination with Marcion claiming it was written to the Laodiceans but aside from that issue of its destination there was no doubt among the church fathers about the Pauline authenticity of Ephesians (D. A. Carson, Douglas J. Moo, and Leon Morris, *An Introduction to the New Testament*, 312).

Objections to Pauline Authorship

Objections to Pauline authorship discount the external evidence and focus almost exclusively on internal matters. Critical scholars are divided, citing both the similarities and the differences between Ephesians and Paul's other writings as evidence against Pauline authorship. The following is only a brief summary of critical objections and traditional, conservative answers.

Linguistic and stylistic arguments. Some scholars point to the large number of rare words found in Ephesians and suggest that it points to a different author. There are 42 words in Ephesians that occur nowhere else in the New Testament (*hapax legomena*). However, that represents only an average of 4.6 words per page and compares favorably with an average of 5.6 words per page in 2 Corinthians and 6.2 words per page in Philippians, both of which are widely accepted as Pauline (D. A. Carson, Douglas J. Moo, and Leon Morris, *An Introduction to the New Testament,* 308). Critical scholars also charge that the author uses some familiar Pauline words but with different meanings and that there is a slower and more contemplative mood in comparison with Paul's other letters. These differences appear substantial but can be satisfactorily explained. Ephesians contains new and unique concepts regarding the church as the body of Christ, uniting both Jew and Gentile (3:1-13). The author is entitled to use new words in expressing these new thoughts. There is a carefully reasoned style and grandeur in Ephesians that is rivaled only by passages in Romans. Guthrie concludes, "A more important question is whether an imitator would have consciously produced a work with such a style as this, so close to Paul and yet different, so breathing the same atmosphere and yet expressing it in another way. ... If, then, Ephesians is the work of an imitator, the author must have been an extraordinary literary artist" (*New Testament Introduction,* 511).

Literary arguments. One of the main arguments against Pauline authorship is the marked similarity between Ephesians and Colossians. Some argue that it would be impossible for one person to write two letters with such close resemblances. However, these parallels appear less extensive when carefully examined. "There is, in fact, only one passage of any length which can be verbally paralleled in the two epistles, and that concerns Tychicus" (Guthrie, *New Testament Introduction,* 501). A better explanation of these similarities is the fact that these two epistles were written near the same time, sent by the same messenger, and address similar themes. The similarity between Ephesians and Colossians is better explained as the work of one author, Paul himself, than as the product of an anonymous forger. Hiebert explains the similarities and the differences.

"The relationship between Christ and His Church is the dominant theme in both, and the ethical teachings are very much alike. But the differences are as notable as the similarities. The tone of the two stands in marked contrast. In Colossians there are the ringing sounds of spiritual conflict with present antagonists; in Ephesians there is the tranquil and meditative peace of deep reflection. In Colossians everything is definite and local; in Ephesians the presentation is impersonal and lofty in tone. While both deal with the theme of Christ and His Church, each uses a different approach. In Ephesians the major emphasis is on the Church as the Body of Christ, who is the Head, while in Colossians the emphasis is on the person of Christ as the Head of the Church, which is His Body" (Hiebert, *An Introduction to the New Testament*, 2:269).

Historical arguments. Some scholars charge that Pseudepigrapha (forgery- literature that was inscribed with a false name, usually an apostle or church father) was common at the time among Christians. They regard 1 and 2 Peter, Jude, James, Revelation, and the Pastoral Epistles as Pseudepigrapha. However, early Christians vigorously opposed the practice of pseudenomity. Several such works were examined and excluded from Scripture because they were considered spurious. Ephesians and the epistles named above withstood such careful examination and were accorded canonical status by the church fathers.

Doctrinal arguments. Some scholars argue that there are doctrinal differences between Ephesians and other Pauline writings. The differences they cite include: (1) The church is viewed as universal in Ephesians rather than local as in other epistles. (2) The apostles and prophets are said to be the foundation of the church (Ephesians 2:20) in contrast to Christ (1 Corinthians 3:11). (3) Some actions are attributed to Christ in Ephesians (2:16; 4:11) and to God in other epistles (Colossians 1:20; 1 Corinthians 12:28). (4) Marriage seems to hold a more exalted place in Ephesians than it does in 1 Corinthians. "Clearly all of this is subjective. What appears to some as impossible for one mind is for others quite a possibility for such a wide-ranging and inventive mind as Paul's" (D. A. Carson, Douglas J. Moo, and Leon Morris, *An Introduction to the New Testament*, 307).

Conclusion Regarding Pauline Authorship and Authenticity

External evidence argues forcefully for the Pauline authenticity of Ephesians. The early church fathers carefully examined and intensely debated matters of authorship and canonicity. The fact that Ephesians was endorsed early and used widely argues for its integrity. The burden of proof rests on critics to disprove what 2,000 years of scholarly examination have affirmed. Guthrie concludes, "The burden of proof must in any case lie with the challengers since the epistle not only claims to be Pauline but has also been regarded as such by the Christian Church. ... When all the objections are carefully considered it will be seen that the weight of evidence is inadequate to overthrow the overwhelming external attestation to Pauline authorship, and the epistle's own claims" (*New Testament Introduction,* 499, 527).

Destination

A question was raised in the second century regarding the destination of this epistle. Marcion termed the book of Ephesians, "the epistle to the Laodiceans." Tertullian disagreed with Marcion and the vast majority of church fathers followed Tertullian in maintaining that Ephesus was the destination. Scholars have revisited the old debate. Some today hold that the letter was an encyclical, a circular letter to be distributed to a number of churches in the province of Asia. Questions regarding the destination grow out of the following considerations. (1) The words "in Ephesus" (1:1) do not appear in three of the earliest and best Alexandrian Greek manuscripts. (2) The letter is quite impersonal when compared to other Pauline epistles. Paul spent three years ministering in Ephesus (Acts 20:31) yet no individuals are mentioned by name. Further, Paul says he has "heard about their faith in the Lord Jesus" (1:15). That suggests a lack of familiarity with the readers that would not seem to be true of the church at Ephesus. (3) The church in Ephesians is universal and not local. There are no specific problems addressed in the Epistle and the overall impression is one of universality. (D. A. Carson, Douglas J. Moo, and Leon Morris, *An Introduction to the New Testament,* 309-11).

Circular letter proposal. This view suggests that Paul intended the letter to be read in a number of churches and simply omitted the addressee in the original copies and requested Tychicus to fill in the name as he visited each church. Thiessen and Guthrie are among those inclined toward this view. The designation "in Ephesus" resulted from the prominence of that church and the repeated copying of that particular manuscript. This view fits the impersonal and universal nature of the letter. However, there are no ancient manuscripts identifying any other church but that in Ephesus. Each letter would have been hand copied and it is remarkable that none of these other letters survived or appeared later in any manuscript. Also, there are specific references and prayers that would be less appropriate in a circular letter (1:15-16; 3:13).

Evidence in support of Ephesus as the destination. This has been the prevailing view of scholars, both ancient and modern. (1) No other destination is named in any existing manuscripts of the epistle and all but five have the words "in Ephesus." Even the manuscripts that lack "in Ephesus" have "to the Ephesians" in the title over the epistle. (2) The early church fathers accepted the Ephesus destination even though not all had the words "in Ephesus" in their manuscript. (3) The fact that Paul is writing this letter several years after his ministry in Ephesus and near the close of his life may help to explain the universal nature of the letter. As Romans is his *magnum opus* on the gospel, so Ephesians is Paul's *magnum opus* on the church.

Ephesus had been the hub for a church-planting ministry and Paul may well have intended this letter to have the same general use. "In the end we must probably conclude that we do not know for sure for whom the letter was originally intended. The evidence of the great mass of the MSS and the improbabilities of all the other views may drive us back to the view that it was meant for the church at Ephesus. If we feel that the absence of characteristic Pauline expressions of warmth (which would be probable in a letter to a church where he had spent as much time as he did at Ephesus) and of references to concrete situations are significant, then we will probably think of some form of circular. But we are left with difficulties whatever view we adopt" (D. A. Carson, Douglas J. Moo, and Leon Morris, *An Introduction to the New Testament,* 311).

Date

The date for Ephesians is determined by one's view of its authorship and authenticity. As a genuine Pauline letter it must have been written while Paul was a prisoner (3:1; 4:1). The close association with Colossians argues for the same imprisonment. Tradition has uniformly assigned the writing to Paul's first imprisonment at Rome, A.D. 60-63. That timeframe is reliable though the order of the writing of Paul's prison epistles is less certain. In Ephesians Paul gives no hint of his anticipated release from prison as he does in Philippians (1:19-26) and Philemon (vs. 22). This suggests that Paul wrote Ephesians first during the early part of his imprisonment. A date of A.D. 60-63 is likely.

Purpose

The epistle does not contain a purpose statement. There is no specific problem or false teaching addressed in the letter. The travel of Tychicus provided Paul with an opportunity to write (6:21-22). He does address the issue of unity of Jewish and Gentile Christians, but as an established reality, not as a debated issue (2:14-22; 3:6). Paul's extended imprisonment in Caeseara and now in Rome and the growing awareness of his own martyrdom seems to have prompted the writing. "Since Paul was in prison he has clearly had time to reflect and this would well account for the more contemplative mood of the epistle, together with the absence of any tension connected with a specific situation with which he was dealing. His mind dwells on the theme of Christ and the Church, resulting in an exalted Christology and a high appraisal of the privileges of believers in Christ" (Guthrie, *New Testament Introduction,* 535).

The City of Ephesus

Ephesus was the major city of the Roman province of Asia and often designated as the capitol, though Pergamum officially held that title. Wealth and luxury abounded. It was the transfer point for goods traveling by land and sea on the great East-West trade route. Ephesus was the repository of Greek culture, but a melting pot for other cultures as well. Greek philosophy and pagan immorality joined forces. "A Greek colony by extraction, it had become a rendezvous of many nationalities. Its situation on the main thoroughfare from East to West, not unlike that of Venice in the middle ages or of Constantinople today accounts to a large extent for its history. Jew and Gentile rubbed shoulders in its streets, and the ramifications of its mercantile trafficking gave it the motley characteristics of a cosmopolitan mart" (E. K. Simpson, *Commentary on the Epistle to the Ephesians,* 15).

"The chief glory of Ephesus and its top attraction was its magnificent temple, dedicated to its patron goddess. By the Greeks she was called Artemis, by the Romans, Diana. This temple was reckoned as one of the seven wonders of the ancient world. Built of shinning marble, it stood outside the city walls. The temple, facing the East, was erected on a platform about 425 feet by 240 feet and was reached by a flight of fourteen steps. The temple measured 343 feet by 164 feet and had more than a hundred columns about 60 feet high, 36 of which were beautifully carved. In the inner shrine was the image of the goddess, claimed to have fallen from Heaven (Acts 19:35). ... However, when in AD 262 the temple was destroyed by the Goths, its influence had so deteriorated that it was never rebuilt" (Hiebert, *An Introduction to the New Testament,* 2:254).

Ephesus possessed the largest amphitheater in Asia Minor, reputed to seat 50,000 spectators. A stadium was located nearby where athletes competed and wild beasts fought (usually against hapless prisoners like Paul, 1 Corinthians 15:32). Ephesus was the center of magical arts and the hub of idolatry. The record of Paul's ministry in Acts shows how vital and influential false religion was in Ephesus (Acts 19:17-20, 23-34). Ephesus was a city devoted to astrology, sorcery, incantations and exorcisms. Ephesus was at the zenith of its wealth and influence in the first century. A free city under Rome, it had its own assembly and council as well as governor (Acts 19:35-41).

> **The City of Ephesus**
> *Commercial hub of Asia,
> •Transfer point of trade
> *Melting pot of cultures
> *Famed for the temple of Artemis (Roman- Diana)
> * Wealth abounded
> *Free Roman city noted for Greek influence
> *Center of magical arts

Ephesus was located on the banks of the Cayster River. Originally the city was also on the seacoast. However, by Paul's day, silt deposits had built up three miles out from the city. A broad channel needed constant dredging in order to maintain the city's role as a seaport. Ephesus became the focal point of the apostle John's ministry in later years and may well have reinforced his description of the merchandise of "Babylon" (Revelation 18:12-13). In Paul's day Ephesus ranked along with Antioch and Alexandria as one of the three greatest trading centers in the eastern Mediterranean. It was the strategic center of influence in Asia Minor and became the hub for Paul's church planting ministry in that area.

The Church at Ephesus

Paul's first visit to Ephesus was very brief and more in the nature of a field survey to be followed up by later ministry (Acts 18:18-22). Paul preached to the Jews in the synagogue and declared, *I will return to you again, if God wills* (Acts 18:21). Paul's coworkers, Priscilla and Aquila, remained in Ephesus (Acts 18:19) and continued the witnessing begun by Paul, and followed up on converts of Paul's brief ministry. Luke indicates that they were chiefly responsible for explaining the gospel of Jesus Christ more fully to Apollos, a Jew who arrived after Paul had left (Acts 18:24-28). Their ministry seems to have been effective, though perhaps limited in scope.

Paul returned as planned on his third missionary journey (Acts 19:1-10). This was an extended ministry of approximately three years. One of the first and most unique features of this ministry was the baptizing work of the Holy Spirit (19:1-6). Paul encountered believers who had not learned of the advent of the Holy Spirit at Pentecost and thus of the birth of the church. It is the fourth such outpouring of the Holy Spirit in Acts and the only one involving the apostle Paul as the agent. It was a strategic and transitional event. It marked the inclusion of disciples of John the Baptist, the move of Gentiles to center stage, and the endorsement of Paul's ministry alongside that of Peter. Paul's early ministry at Ephesus was aimed at the Jews and focused in the synagogue (19:8-9). After three months, opposition intensified and Paul withdrew along with those who had turned to the Lord Jesus Christ as Messiah. During the next two years Paul carried on a daily preaching and teaching ministry in the lecture hall of Tyrannus. The focal point of his ministry was the Gentile community but many Jews also believed.

Paul's Third Missionary Journey

Copyright by Carta Jerusalem, Used by permission

Ephesus marked a great harvest time in Paul's ministry. The gospel had a broad and powerful impact. *This took place for two years, so that all who lived in Asia heard the word of the Lord, both Jews and Greeks* (Acts 19:10). The gospel struck at the very heart of both the idolatry and the economy of Ephesus (19:17-20). A large number of people believed, renounced their former religion, and publicly burned the mystical scrolls so important to their former religion. *Many also of those who had believed kept coming, confessing and disclosing their practices. And many of those who practiced magic brought their books together and began burning them in the sight of everyone; and they counted up the price of them and found it fifty thousand pieces of silver. So the word of the Lord was growing mightily and prevailing* (Acts 19:18-20). This transformation of the entire community precipitated a near riot and may have hastened Paul's planned departure (Acts 19:21-20:1). Timothy was sent ahead to Macedonia but must have returned later to continue the ministry at Ephesus (Acts 19:22; 1 Timothy 1:3).

The church at Ephesus served as a mother church to other churches across the province and as a central point of ministry. The apostle John spent his later years of ministry in Ephesus and probably returned there after his exile at Patmos. The Ephesian church was the first addressed in John's letters to the churches (Revelation 2:1-7). Thirty years after Paul wrote Ephesians the church had maintained its integrity, but lost some of its earlier zeal. The warning that failure to repent would lead to the removal of the church's "lampstand" (Revelation 2:5) was later fulfilled. The city of Ephesus fell into ruins and the church became a memory. This was a tragic consequence in light of the church's high and holy calling as expressed in Ephesians. It bears remembering that the church in Ephesians is universal not local. The triumph of God's purpose in that universal church is certain (Ephesians 1:10; 3:10-11, 20:21; 5:25-27).

Distinctive Features

Christology. The name of Christ is invoked 49 times in this epistle, exclusive of personal pronouns and other designations. The Father has exalted Christ over the entire universe. *He raised Him from the dead and seated Him at His right hand in the heavenly places, far above all rule and authority and power and dominion, and every name that is named, not only in this age but also in the one to come. And He put all things in subjection under His feet, and gave Him as head over all things to the church, which is His body, the fullness of Him who fills all in all* (1:20-23). Paul's key phrase in Ephesians is "in Christ." It occurs directly or in parallel ("in Him," "in the Lord") at least 36 times (Hoehner, *Ephesians: An Exegetical Commentary,*

262

173). The living union between Christ and the believer is embodied in that one little word "in." It occurs no less than 120 times in the epistle! According to Harrison "it is the biggest word in the book" (Harrison, *His Very Own: Paul's Epistle to the Ephesians*, 14).

Language and style. This letter is noted for its richness of thought and vocabulary. It contains 42 words that occur nowhere else in the New Testament and 39 that occur nowhere else in Paul's epistles. The language is as lofty as the themes addressed. The "hymn of grace" in 1:3-14 is an eloquent song of praise to the triune God. The reader is lifted into the heavenlies with the prayers of Paul as they ascend (1:15-23; 3:14-21). Ephesians is also noted for its long sentences, 1:15-23 is one sentence, as is 3:1-7. It is also rich in synonyms, using four words to denote God's power in just one verse (1:19).

Church. God's high and holy calling for the church is the dominant theme for the first chapters. It is a *holy temple in the Lord* and *a dwelling of God in the Spirit* (2:22). God's unique purpose for the church (1:18-23; 2:6-7; 3:12) will be realized when the church is presented as the bride of Christ in all her radiant perfection (5:25-27). "Clearly the writer wants his readers to catch the splendid vision of one church, thoroughly united in the Lord, though it contains members of various races and is equipped by God to render significant service in this world" (D. A. Carson, Douglas J. Moo, and Leon Morris, *An Introduction to the New Testament*, 315).

Riches and responsibilities of believers. Christians have been blessed with all spiritual blessings in heavenly realms (1:3). God has lavished the riches of His grace on them (1:7-8). They have been chosen in Christ before the creation of the world and predestinated to be to the praise of God's glory (1:4-5, 11-12). They have been saved by grace through faith (2:4-5), raised up, and seated with Christ in heavenly places (2:6). Such a high calling compels believers to live godly, Christ-like lives (4:1). Ephesians is an exquisite blend of doctrine and duty, and of the believer's position in the heavenlies and their practice here below.

Christian home. Life in Christ transforms life in the Christian home. Wives, husbands, children, and even domestic servants all have the opportunity to reflect God's grace (5:22-6:9). Paul's portrait of the Christian family is a welcome change from the fragmented family of the Roman Empire and also of the twenty-first century.

God's wisdom and plan. Paul repeatedly emphasizes God's grand plan for the universe to be placed under the lordship of Christ (1:10, 22). God's purpose in the church is described as a "mystery" specially revealed to Paul. *By revelation there was made known to me the mystery, ... when you read you can understand my insight into the mystery of Christ* (3:2-4). "Mystery" refers to something previously not made known rather than to something mysterious. *To bring to light what is the administration of the mystery which for ages has been hidden in God who created all things* (3:8-9). God has now *revealed to His holy apostles and prophets* a mystery hidden in past generations (1:9; 3:4-9; 6:19). The mystery is the formation of the church as the body of Christ uniting both Jew and Gentile. *The Gentiles are fellow heirs and fellow members of the body, and fellow partakers of the promise in Christ Jesus through the gospel* (3:6). Walvoord explains, "A mystery truth, accordingly, has two elements. First, it has to be hidden in the Old Testament and not revealed there. Second, it has to be revealed in the New Testament. It is not necessarily a reference to a truth difficult to understand, but rather to truths that can be understood only on the basis of divine revelation" (John F. Walvoord, *Matthew: Thy Kingdom Come*, 97).

Spiritual warfare. Believers are seated in heavenly places, but they are also engaged in warfare with spiritual forces of evil (6:10-18). This passage is the most complete and detailed description of spiritual warfare found in the New Testament.

Love. Paul's letter to the Ephesians begins with love (1:4, 6) and ends with love (6:23-24). The word *agape*, "love" occurs more often in Ephesians than in any other book in the New Testament except 1 Corinthians and 1 John. Believers have been predestined in love (1:4) and were the objects of God's great love even when they were still dead in sin (2:4). The love of Christ surpasses knowledge and yet Paul prays that believers would know this love, be rooted and established in it, and grasp its full dimensions (3:17-19). Paul uses the verb form *agapao* nine times in Ephesians and only twenty three times in all his other letters. He uses the noun form *agape* ten times compared with sixty-five times in all his other epistles. Paul's emphasis on the love of God and the believer's love for God was needed at Ephesus. Some thirty years later the apostle John would charge the church with the loss of their first love (Revelation 2:4). (Harold W. Hoehner, "Ephesians," in *The Bible Knowledge Commentary: New Testament*, 2:614).

"Nobody can emerge from a careful reading of Paul's letter to the Ephesians with a privatized gospel. For Ephesians is the gospel of the church. It sets forth God's eternal purpose to create through Jesus Christ a new society which stands in bright relief against the somber background of the old world. For God's new society is characterized by life in place of death, by unity and reconciliation in place of division and alienation, by wholesome standards of righteousness in place of the corruption of wickedness, by love and peace in place of hatred and strife, and by unremitting conflict with evil in place of a flabby compromise with it" (John R. W. Stott, *The Message of Ephesians*, 9).

Theme and Structure

Theme. Ephesians sets forth the high calling of the church as the body of Christ and the holy conduct that should follow. In the first half (chaps. 1-3) Paul's focus is on the riches of the saints in heavenly places in Christ (1:3; 2:6; 3:10). In the second half (chaps. 4-6) Paul's focus is on the responsibility of the saints here below. Both sections open with a statement of the theme.

Key Verses
Blessed be the God and Father of our Lord Jesus Christ, who has blessed us with every spiritual blessing in the heavenly places in Christ (1:3).
Therefore I, the prisoner of the Lord, implore you to walk in a manner worthy of the calling with which you have been called (4:1).

Structure. Parallels and comparisons abound in the two sections of Ephesians. While each is distinct, they cannot be separated from each other. Our high calling in Christ (1-3) demands holy conduct (4-6). Conversely, living in the fullness of the Spirit (4-6) is possible only because we have been made alive in Christ (1-3). Their interrelatedness is evident in the following comparative analysis.

Chapters 1-3	Chapters 4-6
Calling	conduct
Doctrine	duty
Position	practice
Seated in the heavenlies	serving here below
Riches	responsibilities
Salvation	sanctification
United in Christ	keeping the unity
Sealed by the Spirit	filled with the Spirit
Exaltation	exhortation

Message of Ephesians

Introduction (1:1-2). The salutation is short and somewhat formal as Paul seems eager to get to the high praise and prayer that follows (1:3-23). The letter is addressed *to the saints who are at Ephesus and who are faithful in Christ Jesus*, however, the designation "at Ephesus" is absent in the earliest and best New Testament manuscripts. The brevity of the salutation may indicate that Paul intended this letter to be widely circulated among the churches connected with the church at Ephesus. Paul is not suggesting that the addressees are not faithful. The "saints" and the "who are faithful," are one and the same.

The Riches of the Saints in Heavenly Places in Christ (1:3-3:21)

Paul opens the body of the letter with a eulogy to the triune God for the redemption accomplished through Christ (1:3-14) and follows immediately with a prayer that the believers reading this letter would comprehend the full import of the redemption God has provided (1:15-23).

Praise for redemption in Christ (1:3-14). Paul's doxology is directed first to the Father *who has blessed us with every spiritual blessing in the heavenly places in Christ.* Those blessings are accomplished through, (1) the Father's election that predates creation and is the expression of His love, and (2) through His predestination that results in the believer's adoption as sons (1:3-5). This divine blessing is freely bestowed on them *in the Beloved* (1:6) so Paul transitions logically to the work of the Son (1:7-12). Redemption has been accomplished through Christ's blood (1:7-8), has resulted in forgiveness, is appropriate to the fullness of the times (the messianic age when all things will be summed up in Christ), and is in accord with God's predestined plan (1:10-11). The end in view is that the redeemed would be *to the praise of His glory* (1:12). The Holy Spirit is the advance deposit, the guarantor, and pledge that God's redemption plan will be fulfilled for those that believe (1:13-14). This doxology to the triune God is punctuated with the threefold repetition of *to the praise of His glory* (1:6, 12, 14).

Prayer for comprehension of their riches in Christ (1:15-23). Paul's prayer is that believers will comprehend the full extent of the riches they have in Christ. The blessings have been provided by the triune God and are comprehended only through the agency of the Holy Spirit (1:15-17). Paul's prayer for the believer is threefold, that they will grasp: (1) the certainty of the hope they have as a result of God's calling (1:18a), (2) the wealth of the inheritance God has in them as His possession (1:18b), and (3) the greatness of God's power at work in them (1:19). The greatness of God's power was evident in the resurrection, enthronement, and exaltation of Christ (1:20-21). Paul will next explain how that same power has raised the believer from death to life (2:1-7). His prayer climaxes with the exaltation of Christ as head of the church, which is His body (1:22-23).

The new position of the believer in Christ (2:1-10). The dead have come to life! Paul reminds his Gentile readers of their past state. They were formerly under Satan's control and spiritually dead (2:1-3). In Christ they have been made alive. Just as Christ was raised from the dead and is now seated at the Father's right hand, so they, in Christ, have been raised from spiritual death and are seated with Christ in heavenly places (2:4-6). This incredible transformation is a gift, it is achieved by grace and not by any effort or merit of their own. God's purpose is *that in the ages to come He might show the surpassing riches of His grace in kindness toward us in Christ Jesus* (2:7-10). Salvation is by grace through faith. It is not "by" works, but it is "for" good works. Paul introduces the theme of good works and the believer's walk here (2:10) and will develop it fully in the second half of this letter.

The union of Jew and Gentile in one body, the church (2:11-22). Gentiles were formerly outsiders, strangers to God's covenant promises to Israel, without God, and without hope (2:11-12). The cross of Christ changed all that. Now they have been *brought near by the blood of Christ* (2:13). The dividing wall has been broken down and in Christ the two former "enemies" have been made into *one new man* (2:14-18). Gentiles are no longer *aliens* but are now *fellow-citizens with the saints* and are members of *God's household* (2:19). As he so often does, Paul introduces his next topic, the church, using the image of a building. The foundation is the apostles and prophets but the corner stone is Christ Himself. This *one new man* is the church, the body of Christ, and it is a temple in which God dwells by His Spirit (2:20-22). Paul will next explain the church as a new revelation from God (3:1-13), and will again pray that the readers will come to a full understanding of God's incredible plan for them (3:14-21).

The mystery of the church as one body in Christ (3:1-13). Paul has been highly privileged to receive direct revelation from God regarding the church, but he begins by emphasizing that he is *the prisoner of Christ Jesus for the sake of you Gentiles* (3:1). This new revelation is called a mystery, not because it is a cultic secret known only by the initiated, but rather because it is new. It was not revealed previously to the Old Testament prophets as it has now been revealed to Paul and also to the apostles and prophets of the New Testament era (3:2-5). Paul states the "mystery" clearly. *The Gentiles are fellow heirs and fellow members of the body, and fellow partakers of the promise in Christ Jesus through the gospel* (3:6). Paul has been given the high privilege of preaching *the unfathomable riches of Christ* to the Gentiles. The church as the body of Christ uniting Jew and Gentile is new revelation, but it is not an afterthought on God's part. It is in keeping *with the eternal purpose which He carried out in Christ Jesus our Lord* (3:11). Paul is a prisoner but unbowed and unashamed (3:12-13).

Prayer for the realization of the believer's calling in Christ (3:14-21). Paul prayed earlier for the believers to comprehend their riches in Christ (1:15-23). Here he prays for believers to grow to their full potential in Christ. The basis of his prayer is the origin and oneness of "every family" under the Father (3:14-15). It is the One Creator God whose plan is being worked out in the church and only God can assure the fulfillment of His plan. Paul prays that He would strengthen them in the inner man (3:16) with the end in view that they would know and experience the full extent of the love of Christ (3:17-19a), and *be filled up to all the fullness of God* (3:19b). Paul has appealed to the ability of God to achieve His eternal purpose (3:11) and he closes his prayer with a doxology extoling the inexhaustible nature of God's power. *Now to Him who is able to do far more abundantly beyond all that we ask or think, according to the power that works within us, to Him be the glory in the church and in Christ Jesus to all generations forever and ever* (3:20-21).

Responsibilities of the Saints Here Below (4:1-6:18)

Paul's opening exhortation builds on and applies the new position of believers in Christ as members of the church, which is His body. *Therefore I, the prisoner of the Lord, implore you to walk in a manner worthy of the calling with which you have been called* (4:1). The Father sees Christ in us and so should those around us. We are new people in Christ and ought to live accordingly. "Walk" refers to how we live life every day, our lifestyle. The remainder of Ephesians addresses the believer's walk on earth in light of their heavenly calling.

Walk worthy by keeping unity within the body of Christ (4:2-16). Believers do not have to create unity, but they do have to maintain it (4:3). Unity is effected by the Spirit but requires diligence if it is to be preserved. The basis of Paul's appeal is the sevenfold oneness of the church as the body of Christ (4:4-6). This inherent oneness does not mean sameness.

There is a divinely established diversity in the church as the body of Christ (4:7-16). Each and every member of the body is gifted for service to the body (4:7). The risen Christ has sovereignly gifted each believer (4:8-10). Certain gifted persons have been given to the church for equipping the saints to do the actual work of the ministry (4:11-12). The purpose of these gifts is to grow the body into the likeness of Christ through the contribution that each gifted person makes to the wellness of the body, the church (4:13-16).

Walk worthy by holy living before the world (4:17-5:20). Paul opens this section with an exhortation that comes with the authority of the Lord Himself (4:17). He is always careful to provide the basis for his exhortations. In this case he appeals on the grounds of the believer's changed position in Christ (4:17-24). The Gentiles he is addressing (and that includes all of us) are reminded of their past without Christ (4:17-19) and of their life changing encounter with Christ (4:20-21). A new identity calls for a new way of life. The "old self," the person we once were and the way we once lived, is to be laid aside (4:22). The "new self," the person we now are in Christ, is to be "put on" (4:23-24). This is more than a change of wardrobe, it is an inner renewal made possible by the indwelling Holy Spirit (compare Paul's teaching on this in Romans 12:1-2; 2 Corinthians 3:18). The new self is to be Christ-like (4:24).

Paul has reminded his readers of their changed position in Christ and now calls on them to reflect that change in their practice, their day-to-day walk (4:25-5:20). It is a wide-ranging but penetrating call to a new kind and quality of life. Believers must: speak the truth with those around them and have done with lying (4:25), control their anger (4:26-27), be honest, industrious, and generous (4:28), guard their speech to ensure that it is edifying (4:29), avoid sin as it grieves the Holy Spirit (4:30), and replace disruptive behavior with kind, gracious, Christ-like behavior (4:31-32). To "put off" their old behavior, believers must "put on" new behavior by imitating God whose character and actions were perfectly displayed in Christ (5:1-2). Old habits die-hard and Paul repeats his exhortation against being partners with the old ways (5:3-4). The old ways are associated with darkness and bring the wrath of God (5:5-7). Believers are associated with light and should walk like it (5:8-14).

The kind of walk that Paul is describing is impossible by mere self-effort. It is possible under the enablement of the Holy Spirit (5:15-20). This passage is the heart of Paul's exhortation. It is indispensable if one is to walk in a manner worthy of their high calling in Christ. It calls for wise, thoughtful living, for clear understanding of that which is pleasing to God, and above all for living under the control of the Holy Spirit (5:15-18). The Spirit filled life requires submission and dependence on the Spirit on the individual believer's part, but it is not lived in isolation. Believers are to avail themselves of the blessings and benefits of fellowship in the body of Christ. The new life in Christ is a joyful, song-filled life characterized by thanksgiving (5:19-20).

Walk worthy by submission within the family (5:21-6:9). People are often their "natural-self" at home with their family and at work with associates. It is there in the unguarded moments that the "old man," their former self, often appears. Paul calls for the believer to walk worthy by submission to one another, that is, to submit to appropriate authority in relationships (5:21-6:9). Most Bibles place 5:21 at the conclusion of the previous section (4:25-5:20) but it more properly serves as the introduction to the following exhortations regarding submitting to one another (5:21-6:9). Submission is not to "everyone," but is governed by established order within the family and society. All are to submit in fear (respect, reverent trust) of Christ. As we would submit to Christ's loving authority we should submit to those who appropriately have authority over us.

The first and most strategic area of submission is within marriage, between husband and wife (5:22-33). The issue is order not value. The submission of the wife to her husband is in the context of headship and reflective of the submission of the church, the bride of Christ, to Christ (5:22-24). Paul devotes more time and attention to the responsibility of the husband to love his wife sacrificially just as Christ loved/loves the church (5:25-31). The marriage relationship should reflect the loving headship and submission of the church to Christ (5:32-33). Children are to obey their parents in the Lord (6:1-3) and fathers are to train and nurture their children in a way that points them to the Savior (6:4). Slavery was widespread in the world of the New Testament. It was largely an economic arrangement and not racial as in colonial times, but it was still marked by oppression. One may apply it to employee-employer relationships today but should not overlook the fact that the gospel of Christ eventually overcame slavery in the Roman Empire. Paul here calls for those in servant relationships to submit and serve well not out of fear but out of devotion to Christ (6:5-8). Masters are to remember that they have a Master in heaven Who judges without partiality (5:9).

Walk worthy by waging spiritual warfare (6:10-18). The ultimate adversary is the devil and his host of fallen angels (6:10-12). Believers are to "put on" the whole armor of God, that is, avail themselves of the resources God has provided (6:13-17). They are to be *strong in the Lord* and to *stand firm.* They must be wise to the enemy's schemes, vigilant at all times, and diligent in prayer (6:18).

Conclusion. Paul is an ambassador in chains but the gospel is unchained and he requests the prayers of his readers that he will proclaim the gospel boldly (6:19-20). He is more concerned about their welfare than his own and expects that Tychicus will allay any fears they may have on his account (6:21-22). The letter closes with Paul's desire that God's peace and love will be theirs in full measure (6:23-24).

Outline

I. Introduction	1:1-2

II. The Riches of the Saints in Heavenly Places in Christ   1:3-3:21
How God sees believers in Christ in heavenly places
   A. Praise for redemption in Christ   1:3-14
      1. Chosen by the Father   1:3-6
         a. Blessed with every spiritual blessing   1:3
         b. Chosen to be holy and blameless   1:4
         c. Predestined to be adopted as His sons   1:5
         d. Given freely of His glorious grace   1:6
      2. Redeemed by the Son   1:7-12
         a. Redemption through His blood   1:7-8
         b. Revelation of the mystery of His will   1:9-10
         c. Resulting praise of God's glory   1:11-12
      3. Sealed by the Spirit   1:13-14
   B. Prayer for comprehension of their riches in Christ   1:15-23
      1. The basis: report of their faith and love   1:15
      2. The intensity: unceasing thanksgiving   1:16
      3. The addressee: God, the glorious Father   1:17a
      4. The request: for wisdom and comprehension   1:17b
      5. The intent: that believers may know: 1:18-23
         a. The certainty of God's plan for them   1:18a
         b. The riches of God's inheritance in them   1:18b
         c. The greatness of God's power in them   1:19-23
      (Exhibited in Christ's resurrection and enthronement)

C.	The new position of the believer in Christ	2:1-10
	1. Their past state: dead in sin	2:1-3
	2. Their present standing: seated with Christ	2:4-6
	3. God's purpose: display His grace	2:7-10
D.	The union of Jew and Gentile in one body	2:11-22
	1. The former alienation without Christ	2:11-12
	2. The present union with and in Christ	2:13-18
	3. The result: a holy temple in which God lives	2:19-22
E.	The mystery of the church as one body in Christ	3:1-13
	1. The revelation of the mystery to Paul	3:1-5
	2. The statement of the mystery by Paul	3:6
	3. The commission of Paul to preach this mystery	3:7-13
F.	Prayer for realization of the believer's riches	3:14-21
	1. The basis: oneness of the family in the Father	3:14-15
	2. The request: filled with the fullness of God	3:16-19
	a. Strengthened by the Spirit inwardly	3:16-17
	b. Comprehending the love of Christ	3:18-19a
	c. Filled to the measure of the fullness of God	3:19b
	3. The doxology: the transcendent power of God	3:20-21

III.	Responsibilities of the Saints Here Below	4:1-6:18
	How others should see Christ in believers here on earth	
A.	Exhortation: Walk worthy of your high calling	4:1-2
B.	Walk worthy by keeping unity within the body	4:3-16
	1. The appeal: to maintain unity (outward)	4:2-3
	2. The basis: united in the Spirit (inward)	4:4-6
	3. The means: using His gifts to grow His body	4:7-16
	a. Christ has gifted the church for growth	4:7-12
	b. Full maturity in Christ is the goal	4:13-16
C.	Walk worthy by holy living before the world	4:17-5:21
	1. Remembering the believer's changed position	4:17-24
	a. The believer's old unregenerate life	4:17-19
	b. The believer's new life in Christ	4:20-24
	2. Reflecting the change in one's practice	4:25-5:20
	a. Put off the old ways of sin	4:25-32
	b. Put on the new by imitating God	5:1-2
	c. Don't be partners with the old ways	5:3-14
	d. Live wisely by the fullness of the Spirit	5:15-20
D.	Walk worthy by submission in the body of Christ	5:21-6:9
	1. Submit to Christ and to one another	5:21
	2. Wives and husbands: submission and love	5:22-33

3.	Children and parents: obedience and nurture	6:1-4
4.	Servants and masters: obedience and equity	6:1-9
E.	Walk worthy by waging spiritual warfare	6:10-18
1.	The warrior: a call to arms	6:10-11
2.	The warfare: the foe to be faced	6:12
3.	The weapons: the armor God has provided	6:13-18

IV. Conclusion		6:19-24
A.	Personal appeal for prayer	6:19-20
B.	Commissioning of Tychicus	6:21-22
C.	Benediction	6:23-24

Bibliography

Bruce, F. F. *The Epistle to the Ephesians.* London: Pickering and Inglis Ltd., 1961.

Carson, D. A., Douglas J. Moo, and Leon Morris. *An Introduction to the New Testament.* Grand Rapids: Zondervan Publishing House, 1991.

Eadie, John. *Commentary on the Epistle to the Ephesians.* Grand Rapids: Zondervan Publishing House, reprint.

Farrar, F. W. *The Life and Work of St. Paul.* New York: E. P. Dutton and Co., 1889.

Guthrie, Donald. *New Testament Introduction.* Downers Grove, IL: InterVarsity Press, 1990.

Harrison, Norman B. *His Very Own, Paul's Epistle to the Ephesians.* Chicago: Moody Press, 1930.

Hiebert, D. Edmond. An *Introduction to the New Testament.* Vol. 2. Chicago: Moody Press, 1975.

Hodge, Charles. *A Commentary on the Epistle to the Ephesians.* Grand Rapids, MI: Wm. B. Eerdmans Pub. Co., n.d.

Hoehner, Harold. *Ephesians: An Exegetical Commentary.* Grand Rapids: Baker Book House, 2002.

_____. "Ephesians." In *The Bible Knowledge Commentary, New Testament.* Edited by John F. Walvoord and Roy B. Zuck. Wheaton, IL: Victor Books, 1983; reprint, Colorado Springs: Cook, 1996.

Hughes, R. Kent. *Ephesians: The Mystery of the Body of Christ.* Westchester, IL: Crossway books/Good News Publishers, 1990.

Klein, William W. "Ephesians" in *The Expositor's Bible Commentary.* Vol. 12. Rev. ed. Grand Rapids: Zondervan Publishing House, 2006.

Liefeld, Walter L. *Ephesians.* The IVP New Testament Commentary Series. Downers Grove, IL: InterVarsity Press, 1997.

Morris, Leon. *Expository Reflections on the Letter to the Ephesians.* Grand Rapids: Baker Book House, 1994.

Scroggie, W. Graham. *Know Your Bible: New Testament.* London: Pickering & Inglis, 1960.

Simpson, E. K. *Commentary on the Epistles to the Ephesians and the Colossians.* New International Commentary on the New Testament. Grand Rapids: Wm. B. Eerdmans Publishing Co., 1957.

Stott, John R. W. *The Message of Ephesians.* Downers Grove, IL: Inter-Varsity Press, 1979.

PHILIPPIANS: To Live is Christ and to Die is Gain

Key verses, 1:21, *For to me, to live is Christ and to die is gain.* **4:4,** *Rejoice in the Lord always*

Key words:
Christ Jesus,
Joy/Rejoice,
Partnership,
Gospel,
Live/Life,
Consider-
Think

Paul,
from prison
in Rome,
AD 60-63

Christ

Paul, bond-servant of Christ Jesus	Introduction / 1 Our Life	2 Our Pattern	3 Our Goal	4 Our Sufficiency
Aim	To exalt Christ by life or by death	To have the mind of Christ in humility	To know Christ and be like Him	To be content in Christ always
Example	In chains: suffering to advance the gospel	Being poured out as an offering	As we await the Savior from heaven	In the Lord always and in care of others
Rejoicing	Rejoicing that Christ is preached	Rejoicing in sacrificial service	Rejoicing in hope at the resurrection	Rejoicing in the support of saints
Appeals	*Conduct yourselves in a manner worthy of the gospel of Christ*	*Be like-minded and continue to work out your own salvation*	*Live up to what you have already attained, follow my example*	*Rejoice always, pray with thanksgiving, think about true things*
Grace of Christ be with your spirit — Conclusion				

PHILIPPIANS

For to me, to live is Christ and to die is gain (1:21).
Rejoice in the Lord always; again I will say, rejoice! (4:4).

Philippians is the most eloquent of all Paul's letters. It overflows with his joyful devotion to the church at Philippi. Personal references abound. It is written straight from Paul's heart to theirs. Philippians is imbued with the warmth of Paul's spirit and has enjoyed universal acceptance from the earliest days as a genuine letter of the great apostle. It is the most spontaneous and intimate of Paul's letters.

Philippians was one of four letters (with Ephesians, Colossians, and Philemon) written while Paul was a prisoner in Rome (Acts 28). He refers repeatedly to being in chains for the sake of the gospel (1:7, 13, 17), but the rattle of the chains is drowned out by the sounds of joy that mark this short letter. The theme of rejoicing appears sixteen times. Chained day and night to Roman soldiers and facing the possibility of execution under the Emperor, Nero, Paul still knew deep contentment (4:11), was genuinely joyful in the face of death (2:17), and eager that all believers learn to rejoice in the Lord always and in every situation (4:4). Therefore Paul invokes the name of Christ thirty-eight times.

Author
Philippians claims to have been written by Paul and no serious challenges have been made to that claim. Even modern critics have accepted the bulk of the letter as Pauline though they view it as a compilation of two or more letters. Pauline authenticity of Philippians is well supported by the internal and external evidence.

Internal evidence. The letter directly names Paul as the author along with his associate, Timothy (1:1). The circumstances outlined in the book fit what we know of Paul's ministry as recorded in Acts (1:12-26). The author's background as a strict Jew and a Pharisee was uniquely true of Paul (3:4-6). Paul had an intimate relationship with these believers as founder of the church at Philippi, (1:3-8; 2:12; 3:18; 4:14-19). Only Paul could say, *I have you in my heart.* He alone could claim the Philippians as the fruit of his gospel ministry. *Therefore, my beloved brethren whom I long to see, my joy and crown, in this way stand firm in the Lord, my beloved* (4:1). Several of Paul's traveling companions are named in the book. Likewise, there are numerous travel plans that reflect Paul's ministry (1:23-27; 2:19-30). The language and style are Pauline. Comparison with Paul's other letters points clearly to common authorship. Concepts expressed, words chosen, and stylistic features, all bear Paul's imprint.

External evidence. An impressive list of early church fathers drew on Philippians in their own writings including, Clement, Ignatius, Hermas, Justin Martyr, Irenaeus, and Tertullian. Polycarp specifically mentions Paul as the author of the letter. Philippians appears in all the canonical lists including the Marcion and the Muratorian. Hiebert concludes, "No trace of doubt concerning the authenticity of Philippians was ever raised until modern times. The external evidence in its favor is remarkably strong and full" (*Introduction to the New Testament,* 2: 288-89).

Conclusion. Evidence for the authenticity of Philippians is strong, universal, and overwhelming. Donald Guthrie devotes only one paragraph to the issue. "It is hardly necessary to discuss the question of the Epistle's genuineness as the great majority of scholars regard it as indisputable" (*New Testament Introduction,* 545).

Unity and Integrity

The issue. Critics generally accept Pauline authorship, but question whether Philippians is a single letter or a compilation of several letters. This is referred to as "interpolation." These objections to the unity of the epistle generally focus on chapter 3. However, there is no agreement among critics on the exact location of the "breaks," or on their source. The source of the so-called "hymn" in 2:6-11 often forms part of the debate. Critics who argue for these passages as insertions (interpolation) from another source also disagree on whether Paul himself is that source. These critical objections have not gained wide acceptance and are lacking in solid proof.

Support for the unity and integrity of Philippians. Critics cannot agree on where the interpolation begins or ends. If two or more letters were so clearly fused together, one would expect identifiable seams. That is not the case. Vincent concludes, "If the partition theory is admitted, the attempt to fix the dividing lines must be regarded as hopeless in the face of the differences of the critics" (*A Critical and Exegetical Commentary on the Epistles to the Philippians and to Philemon,* xxxii). The abrupt change noted in 3:1-2 can be satisfactorily explained in other ways. Abrupt changes in subject matter and tone are not unique to Philippians. Other letters by Paul contain similar changes (Romans 16:16-19; 1 Thessalonians 2:13-16). Further, the content of chapter three is not as dramatically different from the rest of the epistle as is often charged. It is very difficult to explain why a later scribe would combine two or more letters of Paul or fragments thereof. If an interpolator was seeking to show reverence for Paul, he would more likely have included everything in its original form. The early church universally and warmly accepted Philippians. Given the absence of any doubt by those closest to the writing, the burden of proof clearly rests on modern critics to support their theory. They have failed to do this with any degree of unanimity.

Place and Date of Writing

Place of writing. Philippians was written while Paul was a prisoner. He refers repeatedly to being in chains for the sake of the gospel (1:7, 13, 17). This has been traditionally understood as occurring during Paul's imprisonment at Rome. Some scholars have suggested Paul's imprisonment at Caesarea and a few recent scholars argue in favor of Ephesus even though no Pauline imprisonment is documented for that city. Questions concerning the place of writing go back as far as Origen who said, "Only God knows where Philippians was really written." The majority of conservative scholars support the traditional view that Paul is writing from Rome. When all of the evidence is examined carefully, it seems best to adhere to Paul's imprisonment at Rome as the place and time of writing. The following is offered as support.

1. **Characteristics of Paul's imprisonment**. While he is described as being in chains (1:7, 13, 17), he is free to carry on gospel ministry (1:12-14). He is able to receive visitors and financial support, and to direct coworkers (2:19-30). This accords well with Luke's record in Acts 28.

2. **Uncertain outcome without appeal**. Paul faced a trial that could end in his death (1:19-20, 2:17) or acquittal (1:25; 2:24). The outcome seemed uncertain, but imminent. This was hardly possible in an earlier imprisonment (as proposed for Ephesus) and less likely at Caesarea. God had assured Paul that he would stand trial in Rome (Acts 27:24). Further, there appears no likelihood of appeal in Philippians, whereas Paul always had that right up until his actual appearance before Caesar in Rome.

3. **The praetorian guard and Caesar's household**. The gospel has penetrated the entire palace guard (1:13) and secured converts among Caesar's household (4:22). These references argue strongly for Rome as the location of Paul's imprisonment.

4. **Timothy's presence**. Timothy joins Paul in writing the letter (1:1). Paul also commends Timothy in preparation for a planned visit to Philippi (2:19-23). This seems to accord best with the Roman imprisonment and the later Pastoral Epistles.

5. **Active church**. It is clear from Philippians that others are preaching the gospel and much fruit is being produced (1:12-26). This was the case at Rome and Ephesus, but not likely at Caesarea.

6. **Financial support.** The church at Philippi has heard about Paul's imprisonment and sent Epaphroditus with financial aid (2:25-30; 4:18). Caesarea is unlikely. Paul's stay there was temporary since he was bound for Rome. Ephesus was relatively near Philippi and there is no indication that Paul had a critical personal need while at Ephesus. In fact, he emphasized the collection for the poor in Jerusalem in every letter written around that time and yet makes no reference to such a collection in Philippians.

7. **Paul's planned visit to Philippi**. Paul intends to visit Philippi if acquitted (2:24). While this seems at variance with his intent to carry on ministry in Spain, it is in harmony with the Pastoral Epistles (probably written between a first and second Roman imprisonment) (Gerald F. Hawthorne, *Philippians,* xlvii-xlviii).

Date. The date for Philippians is determined by the place of writing. If Philippians was written from an unrecorded imprisonment at Ephesus, a date of AD 54 to 57 is required (Acts 19). Following a short ministry in Corinth, Paul traveled to Jerusalem and was arrested there. If written during his imprisonment at Caesarea, Philippians would be dated between AD 58 and 60. If written from Rome, as preferred, the date for this letter would be AD 60 to 63. A date of AD 62 is likely since this is the last of Paul's four prison epistles (being preceded by Philemon, Colossians, and Ephesians).

The city of Philippi

Philippi enjoyed a rich history as a Roman city. Philip II, father of Alexander the Great, built it as a fortress city in 358-57 BC. He proudly gave it his own name. It became world famous in 42 BC as the place where Antony and Octavian defeated Brutus and Cassius. Later, in 31 BC Octavian defeated Antony and rebuilt Philippi as a military outpost. It became a colony for Roman soldiers and followers of Antony who were evicted from Italy. Philippi enjoyed the title of *Jus Italicum*, a "free" city. This was the highest privilege enjoyed in the Roman Empire and exempted the citizens from poll and land taxes. The city was built astride the Via Egnatia, the great Roman highway. A spur of this highway linked Philippi with the port city, Neapolis. It was a rich agricultural area and noted for its many springs. The gold that had earlier made the city wealthy was depleted long before Paul's time. Three distinct elements comprised the population. The Romans dominated, though they were not in the majority. Most inhabitants were Macedonians, reflecting the Greek heritage. A small minority of Orientals and transients completed the population. Jews were few in number as evidenced by the absence of a synagogue.

> **The City of Philippi**
> ***356 BC**, built by Philip II, father of Alexander the Great.
> ***42 BC,** Antony and Octavian defeated Brutus and Cassius.
> ***31 BC,** Octavian rebuilt Philippi.
> *Made a "Free City," exempt from taxes.
> a proudly Roman city. *On Egnatian Way, a great Roman highway.

The Church at Philippi

The church was established through the labor of Paul on his second missionary journey (Acts 16:11-40). Silas, Timothy and Luke accompanied Paul at Philippi. Philippi marked a significant turning point in Paul's ministry. After several doors closed at Troas (Acts 16:6-8), Paul received the famous "Macedonian Call" (16:9-10). This movement of the gospel to the European Continent was strategically important for the future of the church. Many were converted at Philippi, but three were prominent in the record of Acts: Lydia, a businesswoman, the Roman jailer, and the demonized slave girl.

The church was born quietly on a riverbank but grew through great conflict (16:13-18). The uproar caused by the deliverance of the demonized slave girl resulted in the arrest of Paul and Silas (16:19-20). There was no formal hearing as required under Roman law, instead the magistrates yielded to the dictates of the mob and ordered the prisoners to be stripped and beaten (16:22-24). A midnight praise service in prison and an earthquake brought the jailer and his family to saving faith (16:25-34). Realizing that they had yielded to mob rule, the magistrates gave orders the next morning for Paul and Silas to be released from prison. At this, Paul appealed to his rights as a Roman citizen and insisted that the magistrates personally escort them from the prison. Paul was looking out for the welfare of the church not merely seeking personal redress.

Paul's Second Missionary Journey

Copyright by Carta Jerusalem, Used by permission

Women enjoyed a high status in Macedonia and were certainly prominent in the church. Lydia was not alone in her generosity or labor. Other women were co-workers with Paul (4:2) and the entire church was marked by frequent and faithful support of Paul (4:10-19). Paul held them up as a model of generosity for the church at Corinth (2 Corinthians 8:1-15). Money was not the only gift Paul received from the church at Philippi. Paul's choice of the term, "koinonia," *fellowship* in the gospel (1:5) highlights the intimacy of their participation. They are part and parcel of his ministry, whether he lives or dies (1:22-26). He visited there at least

281

two more times (2 Corinthians 2:12-13; 7:5-6; Acts 20:6). Paul prayed for them with joy and shared a deep mutual love with this church. *I thank my God in all my remembrance of you, always offering prayer with joy in my every prayer for you all* (1:3-4).

Purpose

Paul's primary purpose for writing the Philippian church was to thank them for the gift they had sent him when they learned of his detention in Rome (1:5; 4:10-19). Philippians is a friendship letter growing out of Paul's deep affection for them (1:7; 4:1). He welcomed the opportunity to write (2:25-28). His heart was overflowing with gratitude and he had many things to communicate. He wrote to update them about his personal condition and the progress of his ministry (1:12-26; 2:24). There was much good news to report. He rejoiced and the gospel advanced, even while he was in chains (1:12-26). He thus demonstrated how to *stand firm in the Lord* (4:1). Paul wanted to encourage the Philippians to persevere in the face of their own experience of persecution and to do so joyfully as did Paul (1:27-30).

There were also some issues to address. He wanted to safeguard them against the seductive reasoning of the Judaizers (3:2-4) and the grace abusers (3:18-19). Paul had much to report about Epaphroditus as well. His illness and recovery, his invaluable service to Paul, and his deep concern for the church at Philippi needed to be expressed (2:25-30). Paul wanted to address the divisions that were beginning to appear within the church (2:1-4, 14). Alongside this was a need for the congregation to grow toward maturity in Christ (3:12-17; 4:4-9). Eternity was just over the horizon for Paul, yet he too was striving to grow in likeness to Christ (1:20-24; 3:7-14). They needed to do the same.

Paul wrote to exhort the Philippians to rejoice regardless of their circumstances (2:18; 3:1; 4:4). His own rejoicing is evident (1:18-20). He desires the same joyful endurance for them. The words "joy" and "rejoice" occur 16 times in Philippians. Paul wanted to reiterate his deep appreciation for their financial support (4:10-20). They had given graciously and repeatedly throughout his ministry. In this regard they stood alone among the churches. Paul had probably expressed his gratitude when the gift first came, but concludes the letter with a heartfelt thank you and an explanation of his contentment whatever his financial condition.

Distinctive Features

Christology. Paul's prison epistles are noted for their Christology, but the most profound passage in all Paul's writings is here in Philippians 2:5-11. It is a simple, but eloquent statement of Christ's equality with the Father, His incarnation, His death and humiliation on the cross, and His exaltation above all creation. While profound in thought, Paul's purpose for including it is ethical, not doctrinal.

Progress of the Gospel. We are surprised to learn that the term "gospel" appears more frequently in this short epistle than in any other of Paul's letters (Gordon D. Fee, *Philippians*, 22). The power of the gospel to transcend every obstacle was evident in Paul's initial ministry at Philippi (Acts 16) and pervades this letter. The gospel can overcome official opposition from Rome, the physical confinement of chains, attacks from extremists on both the left and the right, and even selfish motivation by those who preach! Paul wrote to the church at Rome about the power of the gospel (Romans 1:16-17). Philippians demonstrates that power.

Theme

Joy and rejoicing permeate the book of Philippians. We might well focus on that as the theme for Philippians. The terms "joy" and "rejoice" are found 16 times in Philippians. *Rejoice in the Lord always; again I will say, rejoice!* (4:4). However, the central and unifying theme is actually Christ himself. Paul invokes the name of Christ 38 times, often as Christ Jesus. His passion to make Christ known (1:18) is exceeded only by his passion to know Christ (3:10). Paul's life is summarized and explained by one compelling thought. *For to me, to live is Christ and to die is gain* (1:21).

Key verses,
For to me, to live is Christ and to die is gain (1:21).
Rejoice in the Lord always; again I will say, rejoice! (4:4).

Message of Philippians

Paul gives an account of his present circumstances, while expressing happiness through thanksgiving, prayer, and humiliation for their participation in his suffering (1:1-30); the Philippian congregation must have the "mind of Christ" and continue in unity maintained by humility, Christ being the perfect example (2:1-30), if they are to be happy. This unity is based on the knowledge of Christ, which produces happiness in anticipation of the blessings of complete salvation with Christ (3:1-21);

and, if this is done, the Philippian church will have the happiness and strength of the peace of God (4:1-19).

Paul's prayer for the Philippians (1:3-11). Following the salutation (1:2), Paul prays for the church (1:3-11), thanking them for their fellowship in the gospel, which they had sent via Epaphroditus (vv. 3-5). Paul is confident that God will complete that which He began in their lives (v. 6). His confidence was based in God's continual work, and love (v. 7). Paul longed for fellowship with the Philippians in Christ (v. 8). Furthermore, he longed for the Philippians to mature in "real knowledge" and discernment that would enable them to make wise choices and remain blameless until the day of Christ (vv. 9-11). Prison did not deflect Paul from his desire to know Christ or to make Him known.

Paul's rejoicing in the advance of the gospel (1:12-30). Paul's life provided the pattern of rejoicing for the church and is demonstrated in spite of personal affliction (vv. 12-14), professional rivalry (vv. 15-18), or personal concerns about life and death (vv. 19-26). Paul's example is the basis of his appeal for the Philippians to persevere in their suffering (vv. 27-30). Paul's message in this section is that circumstances help spread the gospel. He related how his circumstances had turned out for the greater progress of the gospel. His imprisonment had actually advanced the cause of Christ (v. 12). The entire praetorian guard (responsible to Rome for prisoners appealing to Caesar) heard the gospel when they were guarding Paul, which resulted in the spread of the gospel (v. 13). Paul's chains also served to advance the gospel by stimulating many others to greater boldness (vv. 14-18). Two attitudes are expressed regarding this situation. There were some who were preaching out of love with courage and fearlessness (v. 14), while others had wrong motives for preaching Christ (vv. 15-18). They seemed to want to outdo Paul's evangelistic ministry while he was limited by imprisonment. Paul disagreed with their motives, but rejoiced that Christ was being proclaimed. For Paul, the success of the ministry transcended personality, and conflict.

Paul had confidence in his release from the bonds of imprisonment (v. 19). However, this does not mean that he was speaking of deliverance from the prison situation, but from distress (v. 17), from any hindrance to the proclamation of Christ (v. 18), and from human life, if God so willed (v. 20). His prayer was that whether by life or death, his existence would simply exalt Christ (v. 21). Paul was confident that he would be delivered for the profit of the Philippians (vv. 22-26). After all, a life lived for Christ was a life given for others (v. 24). Likewise, if the Philippian Church continued in unity of spirit and firm standing in the face of opposition, this would be a sign of God's blessing on them and of His judgment on their opponents (1:27-30). In light of this, Paul exhorted them to be steadfast, fearless, and willing to suffer for Christ, as Christ and Paul had suffered for them (v. 29-30).

Paul's appeal for like-mindedness in Christ (2:1-18). Unity is maintained by humility is the exhortation of 2:1-4. The basis of Paul's appeal is their union with Christ. The four ifs of verse 1 represent conditions that are assumed as true: (1) encouragement from Christ; (2) comfort from His love; (3) fellowship with the Spirit; and (4) tenderness and compassion. The method by which unity is achieved is by right attitudes and actions (vv. 2-4). If the Philippian believers would act on their strong position in Christ they would be united in love, in purpose, in spirit, and would fulfill the apostle's joy (vv. 2 and 4). This would combat conceit and selfish ambition. Humility, for Paul, is the proper evaluation of oneself in the sight of God and others.

> The ancient Greek word κένωσις means an "emptying," from κενός "empty." In Philippians 2:7 "kenosis" is a technical term for the humiliation or humbling of God the Son and His voluntary limiting of the independent exercise of divine attributes during His incarnation.

The perfect example is Christ's self-humbling (2:5-11). The self-humbling (kenosis) of Christ is the perfect example. (1) He was co-equal with God, that is, He was and is God (v. 5). But Jesus did not regard His status of divine equality a prize to be selfishly hoarded (v. 6). (2) He voluntarily took on humanity, in the incarnation God became man, that is, the Creator took on the nature of a creature (v. 7). (3) As "God become man," Christ became obedient to death, that is, He voluntarily absorbed the penalty of man's sin by dying on a cross (v. 8). (4) The result of Christ's humiliation was exaltation by God, the Father (v. 9). (5) One day every knee will bow before Him and every tongue will confess that Jesus Christ is Lord (vv. 10-11; cf. Isaiah 45:23-25). Paul's ideal illustration of humility is Christ's sacrificing himself for others.

By following Jesus' example the church will be able to work out solutions to its own problems (vv. 12-13), but must do so in unity, without murmuring or complaining (vv. 14-18). Paul viewed his life as a "drink offering." Such an offering normally accompanied the burnt and peace offerings (Numbers 15:1-10; 28:7) and was mentioned with the daily offering (Exodus 29:40-41), emphasizing unity and obedience.

Paul's report and recommendation of co-workers (2:19-30). Paul has appealed to the example of Christ Himself but now points to human examples of servanthood in Timothy (vv. 19-23) and Epaphroditus (vv. 25-30). Timothy is an unparalleled example of humble service. He is Paul's son in the faith, is genuinely concerned for their welfare care, and is devoid of self-interest. Paul hoped to send Timothy to them soon. Paul anticipated being released from prison in Rome and also planned to make a personal visit to Philippi (v. 24). Meanwhile he wants to set their mind at ease about their messenger, Epaphroditus (vv. 25-30). He is a brother worthy of honor who has served Paul and the gospel at the risk of his own health. Paul knows they are concerned about reports of Epaphroditus' critical illness and hopes to send him back to them soon along with Timothy. The church ought to welcome Epaphroditus with great joy and honor men like him.

Paul's censure of Pharisaic legalism (3:1-4:1). Paul issues a warning about a continuing threat to their spiritual welfare. Chapter 3 contains exhortations to follow godly patterns, and to rejoice in the Savior because Christ is our expectation. The believer can have no confidence in human achievement. The Lord alone is the focus of rejoicing in achievement (v. 1). Paul warns against spiritual counterfeits that steal away this joy, who present false goals (vv. 2-6). Those who teach false goals, particularly legalistic teachers, violate grace and detract from the all-sufficiency of Christ. Paul is referring to the Judaizers and described them in three ways: (1) They are termed "dogs"(v. 2a), since they cause harm to believers in God's grace; (2) they are "men who do evil,"(v. 2b), since their conduct is sinful; and (3) they advocated "circumcision" as a vital part of Christianity and necessary for salvation (v. 3a), since they were legalistic in creed. Paul emphasized that true circumcision was not of the flesh, but of the heart, and that true Jews are Abraham's descendants by faith, not by the flesh (v. 3b). He uses his own example as a warning against the false goal of trusting in legal righteousness instead of the righteousness of Christ alone (vv. 4-6).

Confidence in human achievement must be replaced by Christ (3:7-11). Paul gave all and gained: (1) the surpassing greatness of knowing Jesus Christ as his Lord; (2) winning Christ as the ultimate prize or treasure; (3)

a position of perfect acceptance in the righteousness of God gained by faith (vv. 8-9); (4) a sharing with Christ in His sufferings; (5) a likeness to His death; and (6) a participation in the resurrection (vv. 10-11). Paul forgot the past, because his goal was continual obedience. Each new experience in life is fresh and powerful for gaining the fruit of righteousness. To describe his Christian walk Paul used the image of a runner stretching for the finish line with hopes of winning the prize (3:12-14).

Paul issues a call to maturity and again appeals for unity (3:15-21). He suggests that if the Philippians did not agree with him, God would correct their views (vv. 15-16). Paul, then, contrasts the enemies of the cross with himself, Timothy, and Epaphroditus (vv. 17-19). The end of the enemies of the cross is contrasted with the end of the Christian (vv. 20-21) All believers share in Christ's past humble state but will also share in His exalted state (3:21; 2:7-9). Although they lived on earth, the Philippian believers were also citizens of heaven. Chapter 4:1 looks back to the previous verses and sums up the entire letter.

Paul's personal notes (4:2-19). In view of their heavenly citizenship and future transformation, believers are to be steadfast in their faith (v. 1). The result of the command to "stand fast" in Christ's sufficiency is that it will heal personal rifts and cause them to "agree with each other in the Lord" (v. 2). It will produce a spirit of helpfulness among believers whose names are in the book of life (v. 3) and produce double joy (v. 4). The point of verse 4 is that rejoicing in anything or anyone other than in Christ and His atoning work of salvation, always decreases joy. A firm stand also generates the "gentleness" of Christ and the expectation of the imminent return of the Lord (v. 5). Gentleness and endurance come from knowing the truth regarding this world and the next; this is real knowledge and discernment (vv. 9-10). Paul called believers to have peace in all circumstances and not to worry (4:6-7). Worry and anxiety implies that God is not involved. The prescription for maintaining God's peace is (1) to guard the mental life (v. 8), and (2) to practice the things that were taught by the apostle and exemplified in his personal contact with them (v. 9).

Paul's gratitude for their gracious giving (4:10-19). The apostle thanks them for the financial support that the Philippians have been sending him (vv. 10, 14). Paul has learned to be content both when his needs are fully met and when he suffers want (vv. 11-13). They have been models of faithfulness and generosity in supporting his ministry (vv. 15-16). Paul makes the point that when the Philippians give to him they are giving to

God, who will meet their own needs and reward them (vv. 17-18). *And my God will supply all your needs according to His riches in glory in Christ Jesus* (v. 19). This oft-quoted verse is a promise to the congregation at Philippi, but an encouragement for all believers and a call to gracious and faithful giving.

Paul's concluding greetings and benediction (4:20-23). Paul's love and his gratitude for them has permeated this letter. No more needs to be said. Greetings to "Caesar's household" and the "saints" (vv. 21-23) conclude this letter. It is a letter from Paul's heart to theirs.

Thematic Outline

I.   Christ Our Life: 1:1-30 –Suffering joyfully to advance the gospel
II. Christ Our Mind: 2:1-30 – Humble toward others, obedient to God
III. Christ Our Goal: 3:1-21 – Looking forward to the resurrection
IV. Christ Our Sufficiency: 4:1-23 – Being content in every situation

Expository Outline

I. Introduction   1:1-2

II. Paul's Prayer for the Philippians   1:3-11
   A. Character of Paul's prayer   1:3-8
      Thankful, joyful, confident, and caring
   B. Content of Paul's prayer   1:9-11
     1. Abounding in real knowledge, discernment   1:9
     2. Blameless until the day of Christ   1:10-11

III. Paul's Rejoicing in the Advance of the Gospel   1:12-30
   A. Gospel advanced through Paul's imprisonment   1:12-14
   B. Rejoicing when the gospel is preached by "rivals" 1:15-18
   C. Rejoicing in Christ whether in life or in death   1:19-26
   D. Appeal for their perseverance in suffering   1:27-30

IV. Paul's Appeal for Like-mindedness in Christ   2:1-18
   A. The appeal; Unity and mutual love in Christ   2:1-4
     1. Basis: union with Christ   2:1
     2. Method: right attitude and action   2:2-4
   B. The example of Christ (*kenosis*: self humbling) 2:5-11
     1. His co-equality with God   2:5-6
     2. His incarnation with humanity   2:7
     3. His obedience to death on the cross   2:8

	4. His exaltation above all by God	2:9
	5. His future acknowledgement by all	2:10-11
C.	The application	2:12-18
	1. Working out God's in-worked salvation	2:12-13
	2. Shining as lights in a perverse world	2:14-15
	3. Holding fast the word of life	2:16-18

V.	Personal Report and Recommendation of Co-workers	2:19-30
A.	Timothy: a "son" of proven worth	2:19-23
B.	Paul's plan to visit	2:24
C.	Epaphroditus: a brother worthy of honor	2:25-30

VI.	Caution regarding Pharisaic legalism	3:1-4:1
A.	Intent of the warning: safeguard for them	3:1
B.	Content of the warning: beware false circumcision	3:2-3
C.	Contrast of Paul's example: confidence in Christ	3:4-14
	1. What Paul's "flesh" had to offer	3:4-6
	2. What Paul has "found-gained" in Christ	3:7-11
	3. What Paul desires to do for (in) Christ	3:12-14
D.	Call to maturity in Christ	3:15-21
	1. By following Paul's example	3:15-17
	2. By forsaking the enemies of the cross	3:18-19
	3. By focusing on their destiny in Christ	3:20-4:1

VII.	Personal Notes	4:2-19
A.	To Euodia and Syntyche	4:2-3
B.	To all believers	4:4-9
	1. To rejoice and pray always	4:4-7
	2. To think on praiseworthy things	4:8
	3. To practice what Paul has preached	4:9
C.	Gratitude for their gracious giving	4:10-19
	1. Paul's contentment in all circumstances	4:10-13
	2. Paul's commendation for their grace giving	4:14-18
	3. Paul's confidence: God will meet their needs	4:19

VIII.	Concluding Greetings and Benediction	4:20-23

Bibliography

Bruce, F. F. *Philippians*. New International Biblical Commentary. Peabody, MS: Hendrickson Publishers, Inc., 1999.

Fee, Gordon D. *Philippians*. IVP New Testament Commentary Series. Downers Grove, IL: InterVarsity Press, 1999.

____. *Paul's Letter to the Philippians*. New International Commentary on the New Testament. Grand Rapids: Wm. B. Eerdmans Publishing Co., 1995.

Garland, David E. "Philippians," in *The Expositor's Bible Commentary*. Vol. 12. Rev. ed. Grand Rapids: Zondervan Publishing House, 2006.

Hawthorne, Gerald F. *Philippians*. Word Biblical Commentary. Rev. Ed. Nashville: Thomas Nelson Publishers, 2004.

Lightfoot, J. B. *Saint Paul's Epistle to the Philippians*. Crossway Classic Commentaries. Reprint. Wheaton, IL: Crossway Books, 1994.

O'Brien, Peter T. *Philippians*. New International Greek Testament Commentary. Grand Rapids: Wm. B. Eerdmans Publishing Co., 1991.

Pentecost, J. Dwight. *The Joy of Living: A Study of Philippians*. Grand Rapids: Zondervan Publishing House, 1974.

Vincent, Marvin R. *The Epistles to the Philippians and to Philemon*. The International Critical Commentary. Edinburgh: T. & T. Clark, 1897.

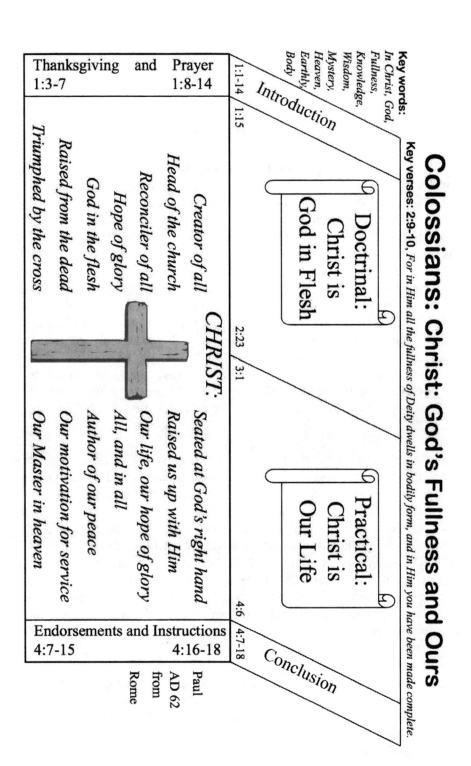

COLOSSIANS

The City of Colossae

Location. Colossae was located in the Roman province of Asia, at the upper end of the Lycus valley. It was part of a trio of cities with neighboring Laodicea and Hierapolis. Laodicea was the chief city of the district and was located 12 miles west in the lower portion of the valley. Hierapolis was located on the north rim of the valley 6 miles from Laodicea. The three cities shared a common culture and industry. Colossae was strategically located. "The city stood on a strategic spot on the important highway from Ephesus to the East in that it occupied the pass that led through the Cadmus range to the east. At this point the Lycus valley becomes a narrow gorge about ten miles long and less than two miles wide, being walled in by great precipices. To the south of the city Mount Cadmus rises to the height of about eight thousand feet. From its lofty heights flow two streams that hemmed in the city on both the eastern and the western side" (Hiebert, An *Introduction to the New Testament*, 2:214-15).

The area surrounding the city was mountainous and volcanic, yet fertile. Large flocks of sheep grazed on the upland pastures and the region was noted for its jet-black wool. Twin natural forces shaped and often dramatically changed the region. The Lycus Valley was the scene of several violent earthquakes. Volcanic-fed streams deposited glacier-like formations of calcium and other chemicals (Lightfoot, *Saint Paul's Epistles to the Colossians and to Philemon*, 2-4). Colossae was located on the major highway that linked ancient Greece with eastern empires. It served as a staging ground for the armies of Xerxes and later of Cyrus in their assaults on Greece. Ephesus, located one hundred miles to the west, was the major shipping and commercial center serving Colossae (Lightfoot, *Saint Paul's Epistles to the Colossians and to Philemon*, 15).

Significance and character of Colossae. Colossae was probably a large and prosperous city in earlier centuries. However, it had declined in size and importance by the time Paul wrote this epistle. Earlier in the first century Strabo described it as "a small town." The city would have remained obscure in Christian history except for the letter Paul wrote to the church at Colossae. It is not among the seven churches of Asia addressed by John in the book of Revelation. The church and the city appear to have already lapsed into obscurity by the close of the first century. Despite its lack of size and significance, Colossae was a rich and prosperous center. Its chief industries centered in its rich, black wool and its dyes. Colossae gave its name (colossimus) to a highly valued purple dye (Lightfoot, *Saint Paul's Epistles to the Colossians and to Philemon*, 4-5). Nearby Hierapolis was famous as a health and vacation resort because of the mineral hot springs. It was also the home of Epictetus, a very influential but pagan moralist. Lightfoot detects the influence of his stoic doctrine in the problems addressed by Paul in Colossians (*Saint Paul's Epistles to the Colossians and to Philemon*, 13).

Colossae was noted more for its mystery religions than for cultic idolatry. Judging by Paul's letter, the city entertained conflicting elements of asceticism and indulgence. The problems addressed by Paul in his letter point to an early, incipient form of Gnosticism. Colossian believers were strongly influenced by the dualism of Greek philosophers that matter is evil and spirit or mind is good. This led some in early Christianity to deny the incarnation of the Lord Jesus Christ. They held that since the physical body is inherently evil, Jesus, as God, could not have had an actual physical body. By contrast, they elevated the mind and the spirit in importance. Whether in pretence or reality, Colossae prided itself on being an intellectual and cultural community.

Population of Colossae. Colossae was a heterogeneous city though the majority of the people were native Phrygians. Greek language and customs prevailed because of heavy migration from Greece. A sizable Jewish population called the trio of cities their home. Paul's reference to circumcision and the Sabbath day indicate a Jewish element within the church. Antiochus the Great (223-187 B.C.) transplanted two thousand Jewish families from Mesopotamia and Babylon into the rebellious region of Phrygia and Lydia (Hiebert, *An Introduction to the New Testament*, 2:217). The influence of Rome and the vigorous commercial activity added a transient and international flavor in spite of the somewhat isolated location of Colossae.

The Church at Colossae
Founding. The church was not established by Paul's direct, personal ministry. Nowhere does he indicate that they heard the gospel directly from him. His knowledge of the church is based on reports he has received

(Colossians 1:4, 8-9). Neither they nor the church at Laodicea had met Paul personally (2:1). The church was established by Epaphras, whom Paul calls *our beloved fellow bond-servant, who is a faithful servant of Christ on our behalf* (1:7). This description by Paul and the fact that Epaphras had traveled all the way to Rome to report to Paul, suggests that he acted as Paul's representative in founding the church. In the companion letter, Philemon, Paul refers to Epaphras as *my fellow prisoner in Christ Jesus* (Philemon 23). Epaphras also joined Paul as a prisoner in Rome. The church at Colossae was likely started during Paul's ministry at Ephesus. Luke does not mention Colossae, but it is probably included in his summary statement, *so that all who lived in Asia heard the word of the Lord, both the Jews and Greeks* (Acts 19:10). Ephesus and Colossae would have been in close and frequent contact making it likely that Epaphras established a church in Colossae at that time. Epaphras was a native of Colossae and may have been responsible for the planting of churches at Laodicea and Hierapolis as well (4:12-13). The church at Colossae would be unknown apart from this letter written by Paul.

Membership. The church was apparently small and predominately Gentile. Lightfoot says, "Without doubt Colossae was the least important church to which any epistle of St. Paul is addressed" (*Saint Paul's Epistles to the Colossians and to Philemon*, 16). The church appears to have been a reflection of its heterogeneous community. It also reflected the speculative, mystery religions present in the community. It lacked the idolatry of Athens, but entertained that same love for philosophy (2:8). The Jewish element in the church was significant, but small, as Paul makes no reference to the Old Testament in the epistle. Along with Epaphras, Colossae was home to Philemon and Onesimus and the church apparently met in the home of Philemon (Philemon 2). A close association existed between the churches as well as the cities of Colossae, Laodicea, and Hierapolis (4:13, 16).

Pauline Authorship and Authenticity of Colossians
External evidence for Pauline authenticity. Early church fathers such as Ignatius, Polycarp, Justin Martyr, Tertullian, and Origen all refer to Colossians. Irenaeus (c. A.D. 130-202) cites its authenticity. So do later writers like Clement, Eusebius, Jerome and Augustine. Pauline authorship was unchallenged until the era of higher criticism. "Until the last century no serious question about Pauline authorship seems to have been raised. Even then questions were raised only by a minority of scholars" (Carson, Moo, and Morris, *An Introduction to the New Testament*, 331). The

294

Christian church through history has consistently maintained Pauline authorship. Hiebert concludes, "The external evidence for the Pauline authorship is all that can be desired" (*An Introduction to the New Testament*, 2:220).

Critical objections to Pauline authorship. Critical attacks on the Pauline authenticity of Colossians began in 1838 with T. Mayerhoff. Critical arguments are based entirely on the language, theology, and style of Colossians. Critical arguments have centered on three major and two minor areas.

1. The first attack is based on the large number of Greek words (55 in all) in Colossians that are not found in Paul's other epistles. To counter this, scholars have pointed to the fact that Paul is using new words because he is addressing a new heresy. Likewise, when compared to other epistles the number of *hapax legomena* is well within the normal Pauline range (Carson, Moo, and Morris, *An Introduction to the New Testament*, 332). Hiebert concludes, "The vocabulary of Colossians is quite what one would expect under the circumstances" (*An Introduction to the New Testament*, 2:221).

2. Some argue that the Christology of the epistle is very much like the Logos doctrine of John (cf. Colossians 1:13-23 with John 1:1-18). Critics say this "cosmic Christ" developed in the late first century and was too advanced for Paul's time. In answer evangelical scholars have pointed out that the passage in Colossians is an expansion of expressions in earlier epistles that are seen as clearly Pauline (1 Corinthians 8:6; Philippians 2:5-11). Lightfoot argues, "The Christology of the Colossian Epistle is in no way different from that of the Apostle's earlier letters" (*Saint Paul's Epistles to the Colossians and to Philemon*, 122). Similarities between Colossians, John, and Hebrews verify that the apostolic authors held a common, high view of the person of Christ.

3. Critics also maintain that Colossians reflects second-century Gnosticism, "The heresy combated in Colossians did not arise until after the time of Paul. This argument proceeds from the assumption that the epistle presupposes the full blown Gnostic systems of the second century" (Hiebert, *An Introduction to the New Testament*, 2:221). Further research has demonstrated that the seeds of later Gnosticism were sown during the first century. The heresy attacked by

Paul was serious, but not identical to later Gnosticism. A few critics have charged that the epistle reflects post-Pauline Catholicism. Guthrie answers this charge briefly but effectively (*New Testament Introduction*, 573-74).

4. Some scholars have charged that one person would never produce two writings as similar as Ephesians and Colossians. That is a strange argument since critics often charge that differences argue for different authors! The differences between the two epistles are substantial, but never contradictory. Similarities can be explained on the basis of an author's consistency and the addressing of common needs. Both Ephesians and Colossians were written at the same time, and to churches in the same area, and to churches established around the same time.

Internal evidence for Pauline authenticity. The difference in vocabulary and style of Colossians is explainable on the basis of new subject matter. The most peculiar features of Colossians are found in the section dealing with the heresy (2:9-15). Critics "do not reckon sufficiently with the fact that a mind like Paul's was capable of adaptation to new situations and to the adoption of new vocabulary and new concepts where older ones do not meet the need" (Carson, Moo, and Morris, *An Introduction to the New Testament*, 334). Guthrie argues that Pauline authenticity "is further supported by the close link between the epistle and Philemon, whose authenticity has been challenged by only the most extreme negative critics" (*New Testament Introduction*, 576). Critics fail to give a reason why a forger would address such a Pauline letter to a church and a town as unimportant as Colossae and how the early church fathers would accept it as authentic, which they obviously did (Carson, Moo, and Morris, *An Introduction to the New Testament*, 334).

Conclusion. The external evidence supporting Pauline authenticity is overwhelming. "There is no shred of evidence that the Pauline authorship of the whole or any part of this epistle was ever disputed until the nineteenth century" (Guthrie, *New Testament Introduction*, 576). The weakness of critical objections and the satisfactory explanation of internal questions enable us to hold with Guthrie "the certainty that Colossians is a genuine work of Paul" (*New Testament Introduction*, 576).

Background and Date

Occasion. Paul's primary reason for writing Colossians was to address the growing threat of heresy that had been reported by Epaphras (1:4, 8). Epaphras had a positive report about the spread of the gospel in the Lycus valley, but he also brought disturbing news about the false teaching that threatened to halt that progress (2:1-5). Probably Epaphras could not cope with the specious arguments and assumed humility of the leader of the false teachers, so he needed the greater wisdom of the apostle (Guthrie, *New Testament Introduction,* 565). A secondary but important reason was the problem of Onesimus returning to his master Philemon in Colossae. Tychicus was traveling with Onesimus and this gave Paul the opportunity and the necessity for writing to Philemon and to the church that met in his home (Colossians 4:7-9) (Hiebert, *An Introduction to the New Testament,* 2:222). Paul was deeply burdened for the churches of the Lycus valley and wanted to encourage them to progress to maturity in Christ (1:28; 3:1-4). Paul wrote Colossians intending it to be read by the church of Laodicea as well (4:16).

Location. Paul is writing from prison and is presently in chains (Colossians 4:3, 10; Philemon 23). The traditional view that Paul is writing from Rome during his first imprisonment is to be preferred. That would have allowed the time necessary for the heresy to take root in the Lycus valley. Philippians and Ephesians, which were probably written during the same imprisonment, provide support for the traditional view. Paul makes reference to the praetorian guard (Philippians 1:13) and sends greetings from *those of Caesar's household* (Philippians 4:22).

Recently scholars have suggested Ephesus or Caesarea as probable locations for the writing of Colossians (Polhill, *Paul and His Letters,* 332-34). However, evidence seems to eliminate both of these cities for the following reasons: (1) There is no record of extended imprisonment for Paul at Ephesus, (2) Onesimus probably would not have fled with Philemon's property to a city located only 100 miles away from Colossae. Contact between Ephesus and Colossae would have made his detection much more likely, (3) Paul did have an extended imprisonment at Caesarea, but he anticipated going from Caesarea to Rome as a prisoner while in Philemon he asks for a room to be prepared in the likelihood of a personal visit (Philemon 22). He would hardly be planning a visit to Colossae and facing imprisonment in Rome at the same time. (4) In addition, Luke is with Paul during this imprisonment as he was in Rome (Acts 28:14-16; Philemon 24), but the record of Paul's imprisonment at

Caesarea is not within the "we" section of Luke's record in Acts (Hiebert, *An Introduction to the New Testament*, 2:206-11).

Date. Colossians was likely written during Paul's first imprisonment at Rome, between AD 60 and 62. Travel was common between Colossae and Rome but was still time-consuming. It is not likely that Epaphras would have learned of Paul's imprisonment and been able to make the journey to report to him until later in Paul's two- year imprisonment (Colossians 1:3-7). That suggests a date near the end of Paul's imprisonment, probably AD 62. The order in which the prison epistles were written is subject to considerable disagreement. Colossians, Philemon, and Ephesians were probably written about the same time since they were dispatched together (Ephesians 6:21-22; Colossians 4:7-9). The order in which they were actually composed is not a major issue. Hiebert puts the writing of Colossians before Ephesians. Most contend that Philippians was the last of the four epistles written during Paul's first imprisonment in Rome.

The "missing" letter to Laodicea. Paul urged the church at Colossae to pass his letter on to the church at Laodicea. Likewise, he directed, *for your part read my letter that is coming from Laodicea* (4:16). Speculation has abounded regarding the identity of this letter. Some have equated it with Ephesians and others with Philemon. A short, obviously forged document was circulated in the medieval church under the label "the letter to the Laodiceans." Guthrie represents most scholars when he concludes, "The most likely solution seems to be that the epistle in question is now lost" (Guthrie, *New Testament Introduction,* 581).

Purposes for Writing Colossians

To refute heretical teaching. The heresy being promoted at Colossae struck at the very core of the Christian faith, the person and work of Christ (1:15-23; 2:8). This teaching would have moved the church away from its foundation in Christ (2:8) with serious consequences (2:18-19).

To encourage the church to progress to maturity in Christ. Paul's opening prayer focuses on their need to grow in knowledge and experience (1:9-14). It also formed the passionate goal of his ministry (1:28-29), and was the content of his exhortation (2:6-7).

To introduce and encourage individuals. Tychicus and Onesimus were more than messengers. In addition to carrying Paul's letters, they were Paul's representatives to inform and to encourage (4:7-9). Paul sought to reassure the church that Epaphras, though now a prisoner with Paul, was well and was still working on their behalf (4:12-13). Finally, a specific request was made that the church encourage Archippus to complete the work he had received in the Lord (4:17).

Nature of the Colossian Heresy

All that is known about the heresy threatening the church at Colossae must be gleaned from this short epistle. That is no easy task. The numerous Jewish elements have led some to associate it with the Essene community and its rigid asceticism. The mysticism and dichotomy between God and matter are suggestive of later Gnosticism. While sharing common features with both, it cannot be limited exclusively to either of these. "It is impossible to determine whether or not this heresy had any coherent form, and we must content ourselves with extracting those particular emphases with which Paul deals and which he immediately recognized as constituting a definite danger to the Christian church" (Guthrie, *New Testament Introduction*, 565-71). Guthrie lists the following elements in the heresy: (1) deviant Christology, (2) philosophical character, (3) Jewish orientation, (4) angel worship, (5) elements of this world (cosmos), and (6) exclusivism. Based on this analysis he concludes, "the heresy was of syncretistic Jewish-Gnosticizing type." Lightfoot provides this analysis:

"The purity of their Christianity is endangered by two errors, recommended to them by their heretical leaders—the one theological, the other practical—but both alike springing from the same source, the conception of matter as the origin and abode of evil. Thus, regarding God and matter as directly antagonistic and therefore apart from and having no communication with each other, they sought to explain the creation and government of the world by interposing a series of intermediate beings, emanations, or angels, to whom accordingly they offered worship. At the same time, since they held that evil resided not in the rebellious spirit of man, but in the innate properties of matter, they sought to overcome it by a rigid ascetic discipline, which failed after all to touch the springs of action. As both errors flowed from the same source, they must be corrected by the application of the same remedy, the Christ of the Gospel. In the Person of Christ, the one mediator between heaven and earth, is the true solution of the theological difficulty. Through the Life in Christ, the purification of the heart through faith and love, is the effectual triumph over moral evil (*Saint Paul's Epistles to the Colossians and to Philemon*, 33-34).

Distinctive Features

The outstanding characteristic of Colossians is its Christology. "The Christology of the epistle is the one central and unifying theme of the whole. Every part of the letter directly or indirectly contributes to this exalted theme and acknowledges Him as all and in all" (Hiebert, *An Introduction to the New Testament*, 2:227). Though Paul mentions Jewish elements like the Sabbath and circumcision, he never refers directly to the Old Testament. The language of the epistle is rich in new vocabulary, lofty in quality, and yet slow and labored in style. Findlay attributes that to Paul's age. It belongs "to the mellow afternoon rather than to the heyday of the apostle's vigor" (Hiebert, *An Introduction to the New Testament*, 2:228). The teaching about the Christian life is exceptionally rich. We have been made *complete* in Christ (2:10). We have *died with Christ to the elementary principles of the world* (2:20). We have been *raised up with Christ,* and our *life is now hidden with Christ in God* (3:1-3). We are now to *put aside* whatever belongs to our *earthly body* (3:5-9). The Christian life is one of laying aside the *old self* and putting on the *new self* (3:9-10). In Christ there is no longer distinction between Greek and Jew, circumcised and uncircumcised, slave and free, *but Christ is all, and in all* (3:11).

Key verses 2:9-10
For in Him all the fullness of Deity dwells in bodily form,
and in Him you have been made complete,
and He is the head over all rule and authority;

Message Of Colossians

The preeminence of Christ is the theme of Colossians. Like two sides of a coin this one theme is expressed in two areas, doctrinal (chaps. 1-2) and practical (chaps. 3-4). The first two chapters focus on the **doctrinal** foundation: all that God is and does is fully resident in the incarnate Christ. Paul refutes the false philosophy that God is good and matter is evil by showing that God has been fully manifest in Christ in the flesh. The false dichotomy between spirit and body, between mind and matter, is immediately and permanently shattered by that truth.

The last two chapters provide the **practical** application: since God's fullness is resident in Christ, completeness (fullness) is realized only in Christ. It is futile to subjugate or abuse the physical body as if it was the source and essence of evil. Rather, in Christ every facet of life is to be brought into submission to the preeminent Christ who lives within (3:1-4). It is in and through His completeness as God incarnate in the flesh that believers find completeness (fullness). As the first two chapters focus on the doctrine of God's fullness residing in Christ, so the last two focus on the believer's duty to become complete (experience fullness) in Christ.

Introduction, (1:1-14). Paul opens his letter with thanksgiving (1:3-7) that the believers at Colossae have *understood the grace of God in truth* (1:6). Epaphras, Paul's fellow servant and a faithful minister of Christ, brought the gospel of grace to the Colossians and he has now informed Paul of their *love in the Spirit* (1:8). This good report prompts Paul to offer a thoughtful and extended prayer (1:9-14) for the Christians at Colossae. They have already *understood* salvation in Christ, but Paul is asking God that they may be *filled with the knowledge of His will in all spiritual wisdom and understanding* (1:9). The proof of their knowledge will be their ability to *walk in a manner worthy of the Lord* (1:10-12). Pleasing God permeates every aspect of life and requires more than a superficial control of the flesh. The power needed to please God comes from Christ's work of redemption. As Christians they have been removed from the domain of darkness and transferred into the *kingdom of His beloved Son* (1:13-14).

Doctrinal Section: The Preeminence of Christ (1:15-2:23)

The mention of Christ and His redemption leads Paul's into an extended treatment of the preeminence of Christ (1:15-2:23). He does this by demonstrating Christ's preeminence in His person and in His work (1:15-23); Christ's preeminence in Paul's ministry (1:24-2:3); and climaxes with warnings of the danger of denying the preeminence of Christ (2:4-23).

Christ is preeminent in His person (1:15-18). Paul emphatically declares both the deity and the humanity of Jesus Christ. Christ is the God become visible (1:15). Christ is the creator of all things (1:16), the sustainer of all things (1:17), the head of the church, the forerunner of the resurrection, and *will come to have first place in everything* (1:18).

Christ is preeminent in His redemptive work (1:19-23). All the fullness of God dwells in Christ. Both His full deity and His genuine humanity are essential to His redemptive work. It is through the *blood of His cross* and *His fleshly body* that Christ has reconciled the Colossians (and other former enemies) to God. Those once alienated from God now have peace with God through faith and will one day be presented to God as holy and without blemish (1:22). Paul has been made a minister of that gospel (1:23), a fact that leads to Paul's discussion of the nature of that ministry.

Christ is preeminent in the ministry of Paul (1:24-2:3). The preeminence of Christ in God's redemptive plan is reflected in the passion and purpose of Paul's ministry (1:24-2:3). Paul is devoting every fiber of his being to the work of bringing each believer up to his or her full potential in Christ (1:28-29). Though he has not seen the readers personally, he is suffering and struggling for their benefit. Paul is laying the foundation for the practical application that will follow later. Believers are destined to be perfectly like Christ in glory and that should be the passion and purpose of their lives here and now.

Warnings against false teaching regarding Christ and the Christian life (2:4-23). Unfortunately not all share Paul's understanding of Christ or his passion for their completion in Christ; hence this extended and pointed warning. First, Paul warns them against **false philosophy** (2:4-15). False teachers threaten to disrupt their progress to completeness in Christ. The primary error of this false philosophy is that it diminishes the person and work of Christ (2:8). The antidote for this false teaching is to understand their position in Christ (2:9-15). Just as the fullness of God dwells in Christ in bodily form, so too the Christian's fullness is to be found only in Christ (2:9-10). Christ has triumphed over the invisible powers that the false teachers are promoting and He has done it through the blood of His cross. Thus Paul declares once again both the full deity and the genuine humanity of Christ.

Paul next warns them against **empty religious ritual, the worship of angels, and asceticism** (2:16-23). Because they misunderstood the person and work of Christ, these false teachers also misunderstood the nature of the Christian life. They advocated religious rituals that were mere shadows and without substance (2:16-17). Because they viewed the physical body as evil, they demeaned the body. Turning from the proper use of the body they worshiped angels and celebrated mystical experiences (2:18) above union with Christ as the believer's head (2:19). These teachings were from men not Christ (2:20-22). This self-made religion was without the power of the indwelling Christ and was unable to restrain the appetites of the old, fallen nature. Harsh treatment of the body did nothing to restrain the sensual indulgence that plagued the body (2:23).

Practical section: The Preeminence of Christ in Life (3:1-4:6)
Having shown the preeminence of Christ and the powerlessness of the false philosophy, Paul now explains clearly how Christians can please this preeminent Christ (3:1-4:6).

The basis of new life: union with the resurrection life of Christ (3:1-4). Just as surely as Christ has triumphed and is now seated at the right hand of God, so surely did believers die to the old life and come alive to the new. They died with Christ to the authority of the old sin principle and have been raised with Christ to new life. They will one day appear with him in glory. Consequently they are now to *set your mind on things above.*

Inwardly believers are to be renewed in the likeness of Christ (3:5-14). They are to consign to death *whatever belongs to our earthly body* (3:5-11). That is the negative side. The positive and complimentary side is that they are also to clothe themselves with what flows from their new life in Christ (3:12-17). That process of inward renewal comes about as they allow the Word of God to permeate their lives (3:16).

Outwardly believers are to reflect Christ's likeness to others (3:15-4:6). As the inward life is being renewed in the likeness of Christ (3:5-14), the outward life then begins to reflect the likeness of Christ (3:15-4:6). Whether engaged in worship with other believers (3:15-17), sharing life in the home (3:18-4:1), or praying and witnessing to outsiders (4:2-6), Christ should be preeminent.

Concluding greetings, instructions, and endorsements (4:7-18). Paul has accomplished his primary purpose for writing. He closes with personal instructions regarding their reception of his messengers and the reading of this letter (4:7-17). Paul's chains weigh heavily on his mind and he concludes with a touching personal request for their prayers on his behalf. *Remember my imprisonment* (4:18).

Outline of Colossians

I.	Introduction	1:1-14
	A. Paul's greeting	1:1-2
	B. Paul's thanksgiving	1:3-8
	1. The basis: their faith, love, and hope	1:3-5
	2. The beginning: gospel learned from Epaphras	1:6-8
	C. Paul's prayer for them	1:9-14
	1. The petition: knowledge of God's will	1:9

303

2. The purpose: a life worthy of the Lord	1:10-a
3. The product:	1:10b-12
a. Fruitful in every good work	1:10b
b. Growing in knowledge of God	1:10c
c. Strengthened in all power to endure	1:11
d. Overflowing with thankfulness	1:12a
4. The power: transferred to the kingdom of Christ	1:12b-14
II. Doctrinal: The Preeminence of Christ	1:15-2:23
A. The preeminence of Christ	1:15-2:3
1. In His person	1:15-18
a. As the visible manifestation of God	1:15
b. As the Creator of all things	1:16-17
c. As the head of the church	1:18
2. In His work	1:19-23
a. Rests on Christ's character as fully God	1:19
b. Results in reconciliation	1:20a
c. Required His blood on the cross	1:20b
d. Realized in the church at Colossae	1:21-23
3. In Paul's ministry	1:24-2:3
a. In his suffering for the church	1:24
b. In his message to the church	1:25-27
c. In his goal for the church	1:28-2:3
B. The warning against false philosophy	2:4-15
1. The reminder of their foundation in Christ	2:4-7
2. The warning against false philosophy	2:8
3. The antidote: God's fullness and ours is in Christ	2:9-15
a. God's fullness is in Christ	2:9-10
b. We are united in and with Christ	2:11-12
c. Our emancipation is through Christ	2:13-15
C. The warning against religious ritual	2:16-17
1. The warning against empty ritual	2:16
2. The antidote: reality is in Christ	2:17
D. The warning against angel worship	2:18-19
1. The warning	2:18
2. The error exposed	2:19
E. The warning against asceticism	2:20-23
1. The warning	2:20-21
2. The error exposed	2:22-23

III. Practical: Christ Is Our Life 3:1-4:6
   A. The basis: Christ is our life 3:1-4
   B. Inward life: renewed in the likeness of Christ 3:5-14
      1. Putting off the old self 3:5-11
      2. Putting on the new self in Christ 3:12-14
   C. Outward life: reflecting the likeness of Christ 3:15-4:6
      1. In the church 3:15-17
      2. In the home 3:18-4:1
         a. Husbands and wives 3:18-19
         b. Children and fathers 3:20-21
         c. Slaves and masters 3:22-4:1
      3. In intercessory prayer 4:2-4
      4. In witness 4:5-6

IV. Conclusion 4:7-18
   A. Endorsements of Paul's messengers 4:7-9
   B. Greetings from Paul's companions 4:10-15
   C. Instructions regarding the letters 4:16
   D. Instructions for Archippus 4:17
   E. Paul's personal request 4:18

Bibliography for Colossians and Philemon

Arnold, Clinton. *The Colossian Syncretism.* Grand Rapids: Baker book House, 1997.

Barclay, John. *Colossians and Philemon.* Sheffield: Academic Press, 1997.

Barth, Markus, and Helmut Blanke. *Colossians.* Anchor Bible. New York: Doubleday, 1994.

____. *The Letter to Philemon.* Grand Rapids: Wm. B. Eerdmans Publishing Co., 2000.

Bruce, F. F. *The Epistle to the Colossians, to Philemon, and to the Ephesians.* Grand Rapids: Wm. B. Eerdmans Publishing Co., 1984.

Carson, D.A., Douglas J. Moo, and Leon Morris. *An Introduction to the New Testament.* Grand Rapids: Zondervan Publishing House, 1991.

Garland, David. *Colossians.* NIV Application Commentary. Grand Rapids: Zondervan Publishing House, 1998.

Guthrie, Donald. *New Testament Introduction.* Downers Grove, IL: InterVarsity Press, 1990.

Hay, David M. *Colossians.* Abingdon New Testament Commentary. Nashville: Abingdon Press, 2000.

Hiebert, D. Edmond. An *Introduction to the New Testament.* Vol. 2. Chicago: Moody Press, 1975.

Lightfoot, J. B. *Saint Paul's Epistles to the Colossians and to Philemon.* 1879. Reprint, Grand Rapids: Zondervan Publishing House, 1961.

Martin, Ernest. *Colossians and Philemon.* Believers Church Bible Commentary. Scottdale, PA: Herald Press, 1993.

Martin, Ralph P. *Colossians and Philemon.* Grand Rapids: Wm. B. Eerdmans Publishing Co., 1981.

Moule, C. F. D. *The Epistle to Colossians and to Philemon.* Cambridge: Cambridge University Press, 1957.

O'Brien, Peter T. *Colossians, Philemon.* Word Biblical Commentary. Waco, TX: Word Press, 1982.

Polhill, John B. *Paul & His Letters.* Nashville: Broadman & Holman Publishers, 1999.

Thompson, Marianne M. *Colossians & Philemon.* Grand Rapids: Wm. B. Eerdmans Publishing Co., 2005.

Walsh, Brian J., and Sylvia C. Keesmaat. *Colossians Remixed: Subverting the Empire.* Downers Grove, IL: InterVarsity Press, 2004.

Wright, N. T. *Colossians and Philemon.* Tyndale New Testament Commentary. Grand Rapids: Wm. B. Eerdmans Publishing Co., 1987.

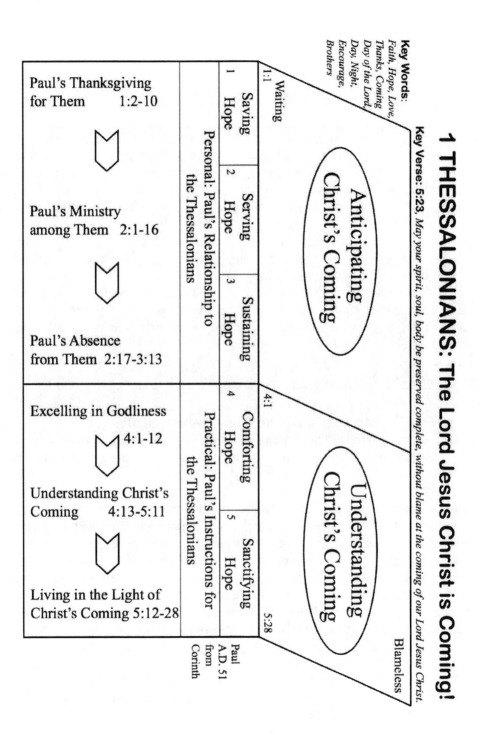

1 and 2 THESSALONIANS

"The Epistles to the Thessalonians are too little studied today. It may be true that they lack the theological profundity of Romans and the exciting controversy of Galatians; but nevertheless their place in Scripture is an important one. No other writing of the great apostle provides a greater insight into his missionary methods and message. Here we see Paul the missionary and Paul the pastor, faithfully proclaiming the gospel of God, concerned for the welfare of his converts, scolding them, praising them, guiding them, exhorting them, teaching them; thrilled with their progress, disappointed with their slowness. Though the continuous exposition of great doctrines is not a characteristic of the Thessalonian writings yet it is fascinating to see how most, if not all, of the great doctrines are present, either by implication or direct mention. When we consider the undoubtedly early date of these letters this is a fact of importance in the history of Christian thought" (Morris, *The Epistles of Paul to the Thessalonians*, 9).

Authorship of the Thessalonian Epistles

Pauline authenticity. The Pauline authorship of 1 Thessalonians has been strongly affirmed by early church fathers and rarely challenged by modern critics. Radical critics challenged Pauline authenticity in the early 19th century, but their arguments have been carefully examined and rejected. Pauline authorship has been almost universally accepted by biblical scholars of the 20th century (Guthrie, *New Testament Introduction*, 588). Hiebert concludes, "It is recognized today that the objections that were advanced against the authenticity of 1 Thessalonians are inadequate or even baseless, and may in fact be arguments in favor of its genuineness. The objections that have been raised are "more than counterbalanced by the tone and character of the Epistle as a whole." An impartial reading of the letter reveals an unmistakable ring of reality which no imitator could ever have attained. ... Modern scholarship has reached practical unanimity concerning its Pauline authorship. Thus Robert and Feuillet can say, "There is no longer any dispute about the authenticity of I Thes, for at the present time it is accepted by all critics as a work of St. Paul" (*The Thessalonian Epistles*, 25-26).

External evidence. The external evidence strongly supports Pauline authorship. Both letters have been accepted as authentic from earliest times and throughout church history (Guthrie, *New Testament Introduction*, 589). Citations or allusions are found in the writings of Ignatius (A.D. 110), Polycarp (c.110-150), and the Didache (c.120-150). Both epistles are named as authentic by Ireneaus (c.130-202). Allusions to both epistles are found in the writings of leading church fathers from the late second century. These include Justin Martyr, Clement of Alexander, Tertullian, and Origen. Both epistles were declared to be genuinely Pauline by leading church fathers of the fourth century. These included Cyril of Jerusalem, Eusebius, Jerome, and Augustine. The Marcion Canon (c.140) and the Muratorian Canon (c.170) include these epistles as genuinely Pauline. The Council of Nicea (c. 325-340) declared these epistles authentically Pauline. Later church councils followed this action also.

Internal evidence. Internal evidence is strong for Pauline authorship of 1 Thessalonians, though internal evidence for the authenticity of 2 Thessalonians is sometimes challenged. However, internal evidence is more than sufficient to support Pauline authorship of it as well as 1 Thessalonians. A careful examination reveals the following facts. (1) The language and style of both letters is unmistakably Pauline. (2) Both epistles clearly identify Paul as the author in the opening. (3) Second Thessalonians is authenticated by Paul's distinguishing signature (3:17). (4) The first person singular and plural are used frequently in both epistles, pointing to Paul's direct involvement in their composition. (5) Numerous personal references reveal the inner character of the apostle and argue for the authenticity of the letters (1 Thessalonians 2:17-3:10; 2 Thessalonians 3:7-10). (6) Circumstances referred to in the epistles fit well with Luke's record of the founding of the church at Thessalonica (Acts 17:1-9). These facts are sufficient to demonstrate both the authenticity and the personal authorship of both epistles by the Apostle Paul.

Alleged discrepancies. Attempts have been made to highlight supposed differences between the two Thessalonian epistles. Suggested discrepancies include: (1) a difference of perspective on eschatology, (2) a more strident tone in 2 Thessalonians, and (3) a distinctive use of the Old Testament in 2 Thessalonians. Guthrie provides a good analysis and answer to these supposed discrepancies (*New Testament Introduction*, 589-99).

The City of Thessalonica

Cicero said Thessalonica was "lying in the lap of the Empire." Lightfoot has called it, "the key to the whole of Macedonia." Paul's strategy was to focus his ministry on cities of influence, and Thessalonica certainly qualified. It was a prominent seaport at the head of the Thermaic Gulf on the Adriatic Sea. The famed Roman highway, the Egnatian Way passed through its walls. Thessalonica was located 100 miles west from Philippi, the scene of Paul's first ministry in Macedonia. Thessalonica was founded about 315 BC. by Cassander and named after his wife, Thessalonica, half-sister of Alexander the Great. Mount Olympus, fabled home of the Greek gods, dominated the horizon. Macedonia was conquered by the Romans in 168 BC. and divided into four provinces with Thessalonica becoming the capital of the second province. The city supported Anthony and Octavian in their war in 42 BC who rewarded their loyalty by designating Thessalonica a "free city." The population of Thessalonica in the days of Paul has been estimated at 200,000. Most of these were native Greeks, but many others were of other national origins. The city was home to Romans, Orientals, and numerous Jews. Thessalonica was a thriving commercial center and thoroughly pagan. One of its poets called it "the mother of all Macedon" (Hiebert, *The Thessalonian Epistles,* 11-13).

> **City of Thessalonica**
> ***315 BC**, founded by Cassander of Greece, named after his wife Thessalonica, half-sister of Alexander the Great.
> ***168 BC,** Conquered by Rome, provincial capitol and center of Macedonia
> ***42 BC,** made a free city by Anthony and Octavian and exempted from taxes.
> *Site of Mt. Olympus
> *On Egnatian Way, the great Roman highway.
> *Called "the mother of Macedonia"

Date and Historical Setting

Founding of the Church at Thessalonica. Paul's ministry at Thessalonica is described by Luke in Acts 17:1-9 and by personal reflections in 1 Thessalonians 1:3-3:8. The arrival of Timothy and Silas at Corinth provide the specific occasion for the writing of Paul's first letter to the Thessalonians (Acts 18:5-6). These epistles, together with Acts, provide one of the most complete and insightful records of life in the primitive church. They are only fully appreciated when studied in light of the following facts.

1. Paul and Silas arrived in Thessalonica after an effective but troubled ministry at Philippi (Acts 16:11-40). Paul was recovering physically from the scourging he received and emotionally from his imprisonment in Philippi (1 Thessalonians 2:2).

2. Luke and Timothy are not mentioned as accompanying Paul to Thessalonica. Perhaps they remained behind to care for the new church at Philippi.
3. In keeping with his custom, Paul began his ministry in the synagogue. Luke records that he proclaimed from the Old Testament Scriptures that Jesus is the promised Messiah. Paul and Silas ministered in the synagogue for three Sabbaths (Acts 17:1-3).
4. Paul's ministry in the synagogue met with initial success. *And some of them were persuaded and joined Paul and Silas, along with a large number of the God-fearing Greeks and a number of the leading women* (Acts 17:4).
5. After only three Sabbaths the synagogue was closed to Paul's preaching and he redirected his ministry toward the Greek community. The length of Paul's ministry at Thessalonica is a significant issue and will be discussed shortly. It is likely that Paul's ministry continued for some weeks if not months, probably from the home of a convert named Jason (Acts 17:5-7). The largest response to the gospel occurred here. At first the believers were "God-fearing Greeks" (Acts 17:4), but evidently most of the later believers at Thessalonica were Greeks who had formerly been idolaters (1 Thessalonians 1:9).
6. Opposition from the Jewish authorities intensified. Unable to locate Paul and Silas, the mob brought Jason before the provincial magistrates. *But the Jews, becoming jealous and taking along some wicked men from the market place, formed a mob and set the city in an uproar* (17:5a). Probably the Jews who were leaders in the synagogue were also among the cities business leaders. They knew whom to enlist in their cause and how to recruit a mob.
7. Paul and Silas were charged with treason against Caesar for claiming that Jesus is king. *They all act contrary to the decrees of Caesar, saying that there is another king, Jesus* (Acts 17:6-7). That charge was a misinterpretation of Paul's teaching regarding Jesus as the Messiah, but it was an effective tool to prompt action by the city officials.
8. Paul and his coworkers had become widely known throughout the Roman Empire and were labeled "troublemakers." The Jews intended it as a derogatory remark but it underscored the effectiveness of Paul's ministry. *These men who have upset the world have come here also* (Acts 17:6).
9. Jason was required to post bond, thus assuring the city officials that he would maintain peace. Apparently Paul and Silas preferred to remain

in spite of the opposition, but they and the brothers did not wish to place Jason in an untenable position (Acts 17:9-10).

10. Paul's ministry at Thessalonica ended abruptly because of the threat to Jason and the other new believers. Paul's departure at night underscores the urgency and the intensity of the opposition (Acts 17:10). Paul did not go willingly; he was "driven out" by the Jews (1 Thessalonians 2:15), who soon pursued him to Berea.

11. Paul and Silas left Thessalonica under cover of darkness and traveled 40 miles west to Berea. Their ministry there proved equally fruitful, but was again disrupted by mob violence. The Thessalonian Jews followed the missionaries and used their business contacts to stir up a riot in Berea (Acts 17:10-13).

12. Paul was anguished over his abrupt departure. He longed to return to Thessalonica, but was thwarted because *Satan hindered us*, most likely by the continued opposition of the Jews (1 Thessalonians 2:17-18).

13. Timothy had now rejoined Paul and Silas at Berea. Probably Timothy stopped briefly in Thessalonica and thus became acquainted with these new converts. Timothy and Silas remained at Berea when Paul was forced to leave (Acts 17:14-15).

14. Other believers escorted Paul to Athens and returned with instructions for Silas and Timothy to join him as soon as possible (Acts 17:15). Paul's anxiety for the church at Thessalonica was unbearable. Twice he said, *I could endure it no longer.* Timothy apparently did arrive in Athens, but was then sent back to Thessalonica to determine how the church was faring and to consolidate the work there (1 Thessalonians 3:1-5).

15. After ministry in Athens, a philosophical and intellectual town (Acts 17:16-34), Paul moved on to the city of Corinth (Acts 18:1-18).

16. Paul's fears were displaced by elation at the good report Timothy brought when he rejoined Paul at Corinth (Acts 18:5; 1 Thessalonians 3:6-10). That report prompted Paul to write the first letter to encourage the believers in their persecution, to explain his absence, and to instruct them regarding the second coming of Jesus Christ and how they should live as they awaited His return.

Paul's Ministry in Macedonia

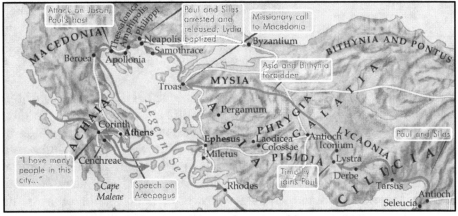

Copyright by Carta Jerusalem, used by permission

Length of Paul's ministry in Thessalonica. Luke mentions three Sabbath days of ministry in the synagogue before opposition of Jewish leaders forced Paul out. That would seem to limit his ministry in the city to just twenty-one days. While it is possible that the church could have been established that quickly, evidence points to the probability that his ministry extended for several weeks or even several months outside the synagogue.

1. Paul frequently turned to the Gentiles and had extensive ministry among them after the initial rejection by the Jews (Acts 13:46; 18:6; 19:8-10).
2. Paul stayed long enough at Thessalonica to pursue his secular trade in tent making (1 Thessalonians 2:9). He must have stayed long enough to occasion need and also to make employment productive.
3. The first converts were Jews and Gentile proselytes (17:4), but these early converts hardly fit the description Paul gives as characteristic of the church at Thessalonica. The church was made up largely of Greeks who had formerly been idolaters (1:4-10). It seems more likely that Paul had an extended and fruitful ministry among the Greeks after his initial preaching in the synagogue.
4. The church at Philippi had sufficient time to send financial support to Paul twice while he ministered at Thessalonica (Philippians 4:16). This would hardly be possible in the space of three weeks.
5. Though the organization of the church is limited, it is clear that enough time passed for leadership to emerge. Some reluctance had already developed on the part of members to accept and encourage such leadership (1 Thessalonians 5:12-15). We may conclude with Hiebert,

"We cannot specify with certainty how long Paul and Silas remained in Thessalonica. It seems preferable to hold that the stay was longer than 3 weeks and that the subsequent period was used to work directly with the Gentiles of the city. The length of this period can only be conjectured" (*The Thessalonian Epistles*, 17).

Date and location of writing. Luke's reference to Gallio as proconsul of Achaia enables us to establish the date of Paul's ministry at Corinth. According to an inscription at Delphi, Gallio likely commenced his duties in the summer of AD 52. The inscription indicates that he addressed questions to the emperor at that time, leading some to suggest his actual appointment was one year earlier. However, the best attested date appears to be mid-summer AD 52. Luke records Gallio's indifference to the accusations raised by the Jews at Corinth (Acts 18:12-17). Though not stated, the hearing before Gallio probably occurred toward the end of Paul's 18 months in the city. This would put the date of Paul's first letter to the Thessalonians around AD 51. Maximum probable range for the dating would be AD 50 and 52.

Some scholars have questioned the order of the Thessalonian letters, preferring to date the second letter before the first. The evidence is not strong for such a view. The second epistle was likely written soon after Paul's first visit to Thessalonica and before his next visit to the city (Acts 20:1-2). "During this period Corinth is the only place where Paul is known to have been with Timothy and Silas and it is reasonable to conclude that 2 Thessalonians was written from there" (Guthrie, *New Testament Introduction*, 603). Paul's second letter to the church at Thessalonica was probably written from Corinth in AD 52. Silas and Timothy are named as co-authors with Paul though the authenticating signature is that of Paul himself (2 Thessalonians 1:1; 3:17).

Paul's Purpose for Writing 1 Thessalonians

Paul's initial and overriding purpose was simply to express his gratitude and excitement at the good report Timothy had brought from the church at Thessalonica (3:6-10). However, Paul also needed to defend his ministry from the slanderous attacks of the Jews. Both his message and his motives were being maligned (1:4-6; 2:1-12). Paul felt compelled to explain his absence and failure to make a return visit. His absence was due to the opposition of Satan and the continued persecution of the Jews, not to a lack of courage or desire on his part (3:17-20). Paul sought to encourage the believers in light of the persecution they were suffering. He did this by comparing their experience to that of the churches in Judea and by describing his intense prayers for them (1:6; 2:14-16; 3:11-13; 5:23-24).

Paul's letter contains no hint of criticism, but he did address areas of need within the congregation. He urged them to excel in godly living (4:1-8) and in love for one another (4:9-12). He also urged them to encourage other believers, particularly their leaders (5:12-15). The most substantial need of the church was for clarification regarding events surrounding the return of Jesus Christ. Believers at Thessalonica apparently anticipated an imminent return of Christ and were concerned about fellow believers who had already died lest they be somehow deprived. Paul wrote to explain more fully the return of Christ for the church (4:13-18), and the relationship of Christians to the day of the Lord (5:1-11). The rapture of the church and the return of Jesus Christ for judgment had been discussed by Paul during his visit. First Thessalonians makes a very important contribution to our understanding of eschatology (doctrine of last things).

> "First and Second Thessalonians are probably Paul's first extant epistles. Indeed, they are among the earliest of all the New Testament writings. Although penned so early these epistles in no way reflect undeveloped, immature teaching, for Paul had been a Christian for seventeen or eighteen years by the time he wrote I Thessalonians, and he had been a missionary for seven or eight years. His theology was fully developed in his mind and tested in his experience before he ever penned an epistle. The Epistles are like finely cut gems. They reflect the depths of theological thought, especially in the area of future things; they mirror the pattern of teaching which the apostle used with new Gentile converts; from every part shine forth the character and conduct of Paul's missionary heart; they sparkle with the brilliance of the captivating power of the gospel of the grace of Christ. They are a joy to read and a delight to study" (Ryrie, *First and Second Thessalonians*, 7).

Theme of 1 Thessalonians

The central theme of the book is the Second Coming of the Lord Jesus Christ. Every chapter climaxes with a reference to that all-important event. That hope sustains them in their suffering, strengthens them in their service, purifies their daily lives, and comforts them in their grief. The truth of Christ's return touches every area of life! Believers are assured that they will be "caught up" (raptured) to meet Christ in the air (4:13-18). They are also assured that they will be spared from the day of the Lord, that time of wrath that will follow the rapture (1:10; 5:1-11). They will then be fully and finally sanctified (3:13; 5:23-24), and they are to live a pure life in the present (4:7). Paul's prayer is that they will be *without blame in holiness before our God and Father at the coming of our Lord Jesus with all His saints* (1 Thessalonians 3:13).

Key verses, 5:23-24
Now may the God of peace Himself sanctify you entirely;
and may your spirit and soul and body be preserved complete,
without blame at the coming of our Lord Jesus Christ.
Faithful is He who calls you, and He also will bring it to pass.

Message of 1 Thessalonians
Personal: Paul's Relationship to the Thessalonians (1:2-3:13)

Paul recalls his ministry among them and their response (chap. 1). First Thessalonians takes the reader behind the scenes to reveal life in the early church. The epistle also provides an intimate look into the heart and mind of Paul, the missionary. His methods and motives shine through this very personal letter. Paul begins by expressing his prayerful gratitude to God for the church at Thessalonica (1:2). Though young in the faith, they demonstrate faith, love, and diligent labor (1:3). Their response to the gospel proves the genuineness of both Paul's work and of their faith (1:4-6). These believers should be as encouraged as Paul is by the fact that their dramatic conversion to God from idols had been reported all across Macedonia and Achaia, thus opening the way for Paul to proclaim Christ (1:7-10). Their transformed lives demonstrate and proclaim the power of the gospel.

Paul defends the motives and methods of his ministry (2:1-16). Paul's primary desire is to encourage and exhort them, but first he is compelled to defend his own ministry. His defense is warmhearted and brief, but intense (2:1-12). They well know how much it cost Paul in personal suffering to bring the gospel to their city and how compassionate and selfless he was among them. He has been tender like a nursing mother and faithful like a father. Paul returns to the theme of thanksgiving when he considers their response to the gospel message. They embraced the gospel wholeheartedly as the word of God, and willingly endured suffering with him (2:13-16). They became imitators of the church in Judea as they shared a similar suffering.

Paul explains his absence and his efforts to return to them (2:17-20). Paul's departure from Thessalonica was abrupt but necessary. He had been *torn away* from them. He had an *intense longing* to see them and had *made every effort* (NIV) to return. Opposition to his return has been so intense that it can be explained only by Satan's personal involvement (2:17-18). However, not even Satan's opposition or Paul's suffering could diminish his joy over this church and his high expectation for the glory they will share at the return of Jesus Christ (2:19-20). They are Paul's *glory and joy.*

> Paul ends each of these five chapters with a reference to the Second Coming of Christ. That was the dominant thought behind this letter.

Paul's elation at their progress in the faith (3:1-13). Paul has been so anxious about them that he sent Timothy to *find out about* their faith. He has confidence that they will stand true under the pressure of persecution, yet he realizes the potential for them to be overwhelmed by the tempter (3:1-5). Paul is overjoyed at the report brought by Timothy (3:6-8). This is the only time in all his letters that he uses the words *good news* for anything other than the message of salvation in Christ! Paul's joy knows no bounds and neither does his prayer on their behalf (3:9-10). Having expressed his joyful prayer for their past and present devotion to Christ (and to Paul), he now prays for the future strengthening of their hearts. He again focuses on the Second Coming. *So that He may establish your hearts without blame in holiness before our God and Father at the coming of our Lord Jesus with all His saints* (3:13).

Practical: Paul's Instructions for the Thessalonians (4:1-5:22)
Instructions for completing what is lacking in their faith (4:1-12). Paul now turns his attention to some of the areas of need reported by Timothy. No criticism or condemnation is involved, only clarifying instructions and loving exhortation. As fishing nets are broken by use and need mending, so their faith has been sorely tested and needs "repair." Two areas that need attention are sexual purity and brotherly love. They are urged to *excel still more* in godly living, particularly regarding sexual purity (4:1-8). This is God's will and calling for them and sets them apart from the Gentiles around them. This is in keeping with the Holy Spirit who has been given to them. Paul has a second exhortation introduced with commendation. They have already gained a wide reputation for brotherly love, but there is room for growth. They are urged *to excel still more* in love

(4:9-10). The way to do that is by minding their own business and being diligent in their work so they will not be dependent on others (4:11-12).

The Rapture: comforting hope of Christ's return for believers (4:13-18). Paul is now ready to address the anxieties they had with reference to the return of Jesus Christ. They expected the imminent (any moment) return of Christ and hence were grieving for those Christian brethren who had died already. This reflected a fear on their part that these believers might somehow miss out on the full benefit of the return of Christ. One of the most valuable contributions of 1 Thessalonians is its clear teaching on the rapture of the church (4:13-18). Both the dead in Christ and the believers living at the time of Jesus' return will share fully in Christ's triumphant return. Paul makes it clear that they will be caught up to meet the Lord in the air and be reunited with him forever. That is truly a "comforting hope" and cause for encouragement (4:18).

The day of the Lord: the judgment that follows for those in darkness (5:1-11). Believers naturally have questions about the when as well as the how of Christ's return. The prophets of the Old Testament had much to say about the day of the Lord, and Paul had sufficient time during his ministry at Thessalonica to teach them about that aspect of Christ's return. The day of the Lord in prophecy focused especially on the restoration of the nation Israel and the accompanying judgment of the nations (the seventieth week of Daniel 9:24-27 and the subject of Revelation chaps. 4-19). The fact that Paul's discussion of the day of the Lord follows his discussion of the rapture suggests that the day of the Lord also follows the rapture of the church. The tribulation period will be marked by an outpouring of God's wrath on unbelievers who are children of darkness (5:1-7). However, Christians are *sons of light and sons of day* and appointed by God for salvation, not wrath (5:6-10). As "daytime people" they should be self-controlled and live in hope of Christ's coming for them. Far from causing complacency, their deliverance from the coming day of wrath should prompt believers to watchfulness and mutual edification (5:11). Paul now explains whom they should encourage and how they are to do it (5:12-15).

Paul's closing challenge to a young, growing church (5:12-22). Having dealt with his major purpose for writing, Paul provides some closing exhortations and encouragement. Three groups or types of people are to be the objects of this ministry of encouragement: helpful leaders, hurting believers, and hurtful people. Leaders had begun to arise in the church. Taking their cue from Paul, they worked hard on behalf of the church.

There was need for the church to be supportive of them and to hold them in high esteem (5:12-13). They were also to reach out to other believers who were hurting (5:14). Some were unruly, some were discouraged, and still others were too weak to hold on by themselves. The care the Thessalonians were to give was unique and appropriate to each and was always to be given patiently.

First Thessalonians closes with some of the shortest but most pregnant verses in the New Testament. Their walk with God is to be characterized by joyfulness, persistent prayer, thankfulness, and obedience to the direction of the Holy Spirit (5:16-22). They are to exercise discernment and hold firmly to what is good. Of particular importance is that they not *quench the Spirit.*

Paul's benediction and prayer for their full and final sanctification (5:23-28). Above and beyond their faithfulness, Paul is convinced of God's faithfulness on their behalf (5:23-28). God must and will sanctify them. Paul again prays for them in the light of the second coming of Jesus Christ. His prayer, like this letter, is marked by confidence. *Now may the God of peace Himself sanctify you entirely; and may your spirit and soul and body be preserved complete, without blame at the coming of our Lord Jesus Christ. Faithful is He who calls you, and He also will bring it to pass* (5:23-24). In this, one of Paul's first letters, we see a young church under attack but vibrantly in love with Jesus Christ and living on the growing edge. We also see the comfort and encouragement of their confident hope in the second coming of the Lord Jesus Christ.

Outline of 1 Thessalonians

I.	Salutation	1:1
	A. Author(s): Paul, Silas, and Timothy	1:1a
	B. Addressees: The church of the Thessalonians	1:1b
	C. Salutation: Grace and peace	1:1c
II.	Personal: Paul's Relationship to the Thessalonians	1:2-3:13
	A. Paul's thanksgiving for the Thessalonians	1:2-10
	1. The content of Paul's thanksgiving	1:2
	2. The cause for Paul's thanksgiving	1:3-10
	a. Their Christian virtues	1:3
	b. Their election by God	1:4-5
	c. Their acceptance of the gospel	1:5
	d. Their example to others	1:7-10

B. Paul's past ministry among them defended   2:1-12
   1. Paul's ministry among them was effective   2:1-2
   2. Paul's motives were approved by God   2:3-4
   3. Paul's methods were above approach   2:5-12
      a. Paul's ministry was not a masquerade   2:5, 6a
      b. Paul's ministry was like a mother's love   2:6b-8
      c. Paul's ministry was sacrificial   2:9
      d. Paul's ministry was with a father's firm love 2:10-12
C. Paul's thanksgiving renewed   2:13-16
   1. For how they embraced the gospel   2:13
   2. For how they exemplified the gospel   2:14a
   3. For how they endured persecution   2:14b-16
D. Paul's absence explained   2:17-3:13
   1. Paul's attempts to return were hindered   2:17-18a
   2. Paul's reason: Satan's opposition   2:18b
   3. Paul's rejoicing: their final triumph in Christ   2:19-20
   4. Timothy was sent to confirm their faith   3:1-5
   5. Paul's elation at Timothy's good report   3:6-10
   6. Paul's plan to return to them   3:11
   7. Paul's prayer for their progress in the faith   3:12-13

III. Practical: Paul's Instructions for the Thessalonians   4:1-5:22
  A. Exhortations to godly living   4:1-12
   1. By excelling in sexual purity   4:1-8
      a. The object: pleasing God   4:1
      b. The authority: the Lord Jesus Himself   4:2
      c. The exhortation: to maintain sexual purity   4:3-7
      d. The alternative: rejecting God   4:8
   2. By excelling in brotherly love   4:9-10
      a. Commendation for existing love   4:9-10a
      b. Call to excel in love   4:10b
   3. By engaging in productive work   4:11-12
      a. Aim: quiet self-reliance with insiders   4:11
      b. Outcome: positive testimony to outsiders   4:12
  B. Instructions concerning the rapture   4:13-18
   1. The question: what about the dead in Christ?   4:13
   2. The answer: they will be raised at the rapture   4:14-17
      a. Foundation: Jesus' death and resurrection   4:14
      b. Assurance: they will be raised   4:14-15
      c. Signal: the Lord's return from heaven   4:16a
      d. Sequence: resurrection then the rapture   4:16b-17a

		e. Culmination: reunited with the Lord forever	4:17b
	3.	Application: encourage each other	4:18
C.	Instructions concerning the day of the Lord		5:1-11
	1.	Uncertainty regarding the time	5:1-3
		a. They have already been informed	5:1
		b. That day will be unexpected	5:2
		c. The unprepared will not escape	5:3
	2.	Assurances regarding that day	5:4-9
		a. That day will not surprise them	5:4
		b. They belong to a different world	5:5
		c. They ought to lead a different life	5:6-8
		d. They are appointed to a different future	5:9
	3.	Application resulting from these truths	5:10-11
D.	Exhortations to build up the body of Christ		5:12-22
	1.	By upholding those in leadership	5:12-13
	2.	By building up other believers	5:14
	3.	By avoiding retaliation when wronged	5:15
	4.	By caring for the inner life	5:16-18
	5.	By caring for assembly life	5:19-20

IV. Conclusion		5:23-28
A.	Paul's prayer for their full sanctification	5:23
B.	Paul's confidence in God's faithfulness	5:24
C.	Paul's personal greetings	5:25-28

322

2 THESSALONIANS: The Day of the Lord has not come!

Key Verses: 2:1-3, *Let no one in any way deceive you, for it (the day of the Lord) will not come unless...*

Key Words:
Day of the Lord,
Coming of
Jesus Christ,
Lawless one,
Restrainer,
Revelation

1	2	3
Encouragement: To Persevere under Persecution	**Instruction:** Events Preceding the Day of the Lord	**Exhortation:** To Prayer and Discipline
Do not be disturbed!	*The Day of the Lord has not come yet!*	*Be steadfast! Work!*
Lord Jesus revealed- from heaven in blazing fire	Lawless one revealed- slayed by Christ at His coming	The Lord will strengthen, protect you from the evil one
Sharing in the suffering	Sharing in the glory	Sharing in the labor
Be persevering till Jesus comes	Be patient till Jesus comes	Be productive till Jesus comes
Prayer: Lord Jesus will be glorified in you	*Prayer: May God strengthen your hearts*	*Prayer: May the Lord grant you peace*

Paul,
A.D. 52
from
Corinth

323

Occasion and Purpose of 2 Thessalonians

Occasion for the letter. Reports reaching Paul indicated that the church at Thessalonica was growing stronger and persevering under intense persecution (1:3-4). However, there were also negative elements in the reports. The church at Thessalonica had been disturbed by forged letters and reports purporting to come from Paul (2:1-5). According to this false teaching, the day of the Lord had already come and the persecution the believers was experiencing was actually the end-time tribulation from which they had expected to be spared by the rapture (2:3-12). This was a very serious threat and had to be corrected. Anticipating the soon return of Christ, some believers were becoming idle and disruptive (3:6-15).

Paul's purpose for writing. Paul's primary reason for writing was to declare that the letters and messages in circulation were not from him but were forgeries and their teaching was false. This false teaching that the day of the Lord had already come contradicted Paul's teaching regarding the return of Christ. In Paul's first letter he felt assured that they had adequate knowledge about the time and signs relating to the day of the Lord (1 Thessalonians 5:1). But false teachers, who claimed Paul endorsed them, were infiltrating the church. Their teaching contradicted Paul's gospel (2 Thessalonians 2:2). To set the record straight Paul carefully documents the events that must precede the day of the Lord (2:3-12). Because of the forged letters being circulated, Paul felt compelled to authenticate this letter of correction by affixing his own signature (3:17).

The false teaching prompted some believers to abandon productive work in anticipation of Christ's soon return. Paul writes to counteract the idleness and disruptive behavior of this minority in the church. It was necessary for Paul to remind them of the importance of watchful living and productive employment while they waited for the return of Christ (3:6-12). It was also necessary to give instructions on how to discipline unruly members who might choose to disregard this letter from Paul (3:14-15).

In spite of these serious threats to the health of the congregation there was much for which to commend them. Paul opens this letter with heartfelt thanksgiving to God for their growing faith and love (1:3). He had good reason to *speak proudly* of them among the churches, and so he commends them for their perseverance and faith in the midst of intense persecution and reassures them that judgment awaits their tormentors (1:4-10).

Prayer and praise permeate the letter as Paul concludes every chapter with a prayer for them (1:11-12; 2:16-17; 3:16).

Theme of 2 Thessalonians

The second coming of Christ is the dominant theme of Paul's second letter to the Thessalonians. However, the emphasis differs from that of his first letter to them. False teachers were circulating forged letters and messages that supposedly came from Paul and were teaching that the day of the Lord had already come. Paul now explains the events that mark Christ's coming and that will precede the day of the Lord. Since these events have not yet occurred, they cannot be in the day of the Lord!

Key verses, 2:1-3

Now we request you, brethren, with regard to the coming of our Lord Jesus Christ and our gathering together to Him, that you not be quickly shaken from your composure or be disturbed either by a spirit or a message or a letter as if from us, to the effect that the day of the Lord has come.

Message of 2 Thessalonians

Paul's thanksgiving for the persecuted but persevering church (1:1-10). Paul's deep gratitude for the Thessalonian believers continues even though reports indicate conditions at Thessalonica are less than ideal. Paul's gratitude is appropriate in light of their growing faith and love (1:3). They have persevered under severe trials (1:4). The progress and perseverance of the church at Thessalonica is an indication of their worthiness for the kingdom of God (1:5). Paul offers encouragement by reminding them that God is just and will severely punish those who now persecute them (1:6-9). The return of Christ will bring judgment on their tormentors, but glorious triumph for those who have believed the gospel (1:10).

Paul's first prayer for their steadfastness in the face of persecution (1:11-12). Paul concluded each of the five chapters in his first letter with a reminder that Jesus Christ was coming again. In this second letter he closes each of the three chapters with a prayer for their steadfastness in light of Christ's return. His prayer for them in this first chapter is that God will enable them to accomplish the good they have purposed to do to the end that He will be glorified in them (1:11-12).

Paul's corrective teaching regarding the day of the Lord (2:1-12). This is the heart of Paul's letter. The serious matter that occasioned this letter is false teaching regarding the Day of the Lord (2:1-3). They have been disturbed by teaching that purported to be from Paul that was in reality false and contradictory. The point of this false teaching was that the day of the Lord had already come (2:3) and thus that the current persecution was actually the tribulation of the day of the Lord (1 Thessalonians 5:1-10). That teaching was false and did not come from Paul! Paul had taught them that they would be caught up to meet Christ before that day of wrath (1 Thessalonians 4:13-18).

Paul identifies the events that must precede the day of the Lord including:
1. The *apostasy* (2:3a), literally "***departure***," refers either to spiritual apostasy in the end times (1 Timothy 4:1-5), or to the rapture of believers before the tribulation (1 Thessalonians 4:13-18).
2. The "revelation" of the ***man of lawlessness*** (2:3b-5). Lawlessness is already present and working, but under restraint. In the day of the Lord it will be unleashed and embodied in a person elsewhere identified as the antichrist.
3. The "removal" of the ***restrainer***. The restrainer must first be removed (2:6-7). Only then will the man of lawlessness be revealed (2:8-10). Then the day of the Lord will come! The ***lawless one*** is destined for judgment at the return of Christ, but immediately before that he will be given supernatural power by Satan and will succeed in deceiving an unbelieving world during the day of the Lord (2:10-12). The restrainer is generally viewed as the Holy Spirit since only He, as God, has the power to restrain evil. Another possibility is that the restrainer is the archangel, Michael, who will be removed as Israel's protector (Daniel 12:1-2).

The call to stand firm in their hope under the present persecution (2:13-15). The believers are reminded that God has chosen them for salvation not judgment. Their calling was made effective through the preaching of the gospel. As a result they are called to stand firm against false teaching just as they have stood against persecution (2:13-15).

Paul's second prayer for their steadfastness against false teaching (2:16-17). Paul concludes this chapter of instruction with a prayer that God would comfort and strengthen their hearts in every good work (2:16-17). This call to steadfastness prepares the way for Paul's concluding exhortations.

Paul urges them to pray for him and for the progress of the gospel (3:1-5). Paul calls them to pray earnestly for his ministry. Like them he faces opposition from evil men. The message of the Lord has spread rapidly, but prayer, not complacency, is in order. It is still God's faithfulness that assures the outcome. He has confidence that they will be faithful to God even as He is faithful to them (3:1-5).

Paul's exhortation and instructions for dealing with the disorderly (3:6-15). False teaching about the Lord's return prompted some to be preoccupied with the future to the neglect of their present responsibilities. The result was idleness (living on the welfare of other believers) and disorderly conduct. In his first letter Paul urged them to warn those who were idle. That warning has not been heeded and now he calls for disciplinary action against brethren who are idle (3:6-15). Idle believers are not to be given support when they refuse to work for it. They are to be publicly rebuked when they persist in being disruptive. When rebuke fails, the church is to withdraw fellowship from the offender and thus shame them into action. While strong action is called for, they are to remember that they are brothers not enemies (3:15). The strength of Paul's appeal rests on his own example of self-support (3:7-10).

Paul's third prayer for their steadfastness (3:16). The concluding salutation contains a prayer for them to know peace in place of the alarm that has been occasioned by false teaching. This peace is possible because it comes from the Lord of peace Himself (3:16).

Paul's authenticating signature and benediction (3:17-18). In light of spurious letters purporting to be from Paul, the apostle is compelled to authenticate this letter by his own personal signature (2:17). This letter is from the pen of Paul and written *in my own hand.* Stand fast! The day of the Lord has not come!

Outline of 2 Thessalonians

I. Salutation		1:1-2
II. Encouragement: To Persevere under Persecution		1:3-12
A. Commendation for growth and steadfastness		1:3-4
1. Paul's gratitude for them		1:3a
2. Their growth in faith and love		1:3b
3. Their example for other churches		1:4
B. Comfort through Christ's return		1:5-10
1. God's justice guarantees it		1:5-6a
2. God will judge their persecutors		1:6b-9
3. God will be glorified in them		1:10
C. Paul's constant prayer for them		1:11-12
1. That God will fulfill their good intentions		1:11
2. That Christ will be glorified in them		1:12
III. Instruction: Events Preceding the Day of the Lord		2:1-17
A. Appeal for calmness		2:1-2a
1. Subject: return of Christ and the rapture		2:1
2. Source of the false alarm		2:2
3. False report: day of the Lord has already come		2:2c
B. Events that must precede the day of the Lord		2:3-12
1. The apostasy (departure) must come first		2:3a
2. The man of lawlessness must come		2:3b-5
3. The restrainer must first be removed		2:6-7
4. The man of lawlessness will then be revealed		2:8-12
a. He is destined for judgment		2:8
b. He will display supernatural power		2:9
c. He will deceive the unbelieving		2:10-12
C. The call to steadfastness		2:13-15
1. They were chosen by God for salvation		2:13
2. They were called through the gospel		2:14
3. They are challenged to stand firm		2:15
D. Paul's prayer for their encouragement		2:16-17
IV. Exhortation: To Prayer and Discipline		3:1-15
A. The call to prayer		3:1-5
1. The focus for their prayer		3:1-2
a. Spread of the message		3:1
b. Safety of the messengers		3:2
2. The foundation for their prayers		3:3-4

	a. God's faithfulness to them	3:3
	b. Their faithfulness to God	3:4
3.	The fruit of their prayers	3:5
B.	The command to discipline the disorderly	3:6-15
1.	The command to withdraw from the disorderly	3:6
2.	The challenge of Paul's example	3:7-9
3.	The constant rule: you must work to eat	3:10
4.	The command to the disorderly	3:11-12
5.	The challenge to the faithful brothers	3:13-15

V.	Conclusion	3:16-18
A.	Paul's prayer for them	3:16
B.	Paul's authenticating signature	3:17
C.	Paul's closing benediction	3:18

Bibliography for 1 and 2 Thessalonians

Beale, Gregory. *1 & 2 Thessalonians.* Pillar New Testament Commentary. Grand Rapids: Wm. B. Eerdmans Publishing Co., 2004.

Bruce, F. F. *1 and 2 Thessalonians.* Word Biblical Commentary. Waco, TX: Word Books, 1982.

Furnish, Victor. *1 and 2 Thessalonians.* Abington New Testament Commentary. Nashville: Abingdon Co., 2002.

Green, Gene. *1 and 2 Thessalonians.* Pillar New Testament Commentary. Grand Rapids: Wm. B. Eerdmans Publishing Co., 2002.

Hiebert D. Edmond. *The Thessalonian Epistles.* Chicago: Moody Press, 1971.

Kelly, William. *The Epistles of Paul the Apostle to the Thessalonians.* London: C. A. Hammond, 1953.

Marshall, I. Howard. *A Commentary on the Epistles to the Thessalonians.* New Century Bible Commentary. Grand Rapids: Wm. B. Eerdmans Publishing Co., 1982.

____. *1 and 2 Thessalonians.* New Century Bible Commentary. Grand Rapids: Wm. B. Eerdmans Publishing Co., 1993.

Morris, Leon. *The First and Second Epistles to the Thessalonians.* New International Commentary on the New Testament. Grand Rapids: Wm. B. Eerdmans Publishing Co., 1959.

Ryrie, Charles Caldwell. *First and Second Thessalonians.* Chicago: Moody Press, 1959.

Stott, John. *The Gospel & the End of Time.* Downers Grove, IL: InterVarsity Press, 1991.

Thomas, Robert. *1 and 2 Thessalonians.* Expositor's Bible Commentary. Vol. 11. Grand Rapids: Zondervan Publishing House, 1978.

Walvoord, John F. *The Thessalonian Epistles.* Findlay, OH: Dunham Publishing Co., 1955. Rev. ed. Mark Hitchcock and Philip Rowley, eds. Chicago: Moody Press, 2012.

Witherington, Ben. *1 and 2 Thessalonians.* Grand Rapids: Wm. B. Eerdmans Publishing Co., 2006.

PASTORAL EPISTLES

The Pastoral Epistles are the last will and testament of the apostle Paul. His passion for declaring the gospel of Jesus Christ is undiminished but he is now aged and standing on the threshold of martyrdom. He has poured out his life for Christ and for His church; soon his life's blood will be poured out on the stand of a Roman executioner. Throughout his ministry Paul has surrounded himself with young men who shared his passion for Christ and the church. Now it is time for him to turn the work over to these young co-workers. The Pastoral Epistles are private and personal letters; yet they are written for public use and benefit. Paul has fought the good fight, finished the course, and kept the faith. Now it is time for the torch of the gospel ministry to be passed on to others.

The three letters addressed to Timothy and Titus are personal in nature and are known as "the Pastoral Epistles." Hiebert notes that "although the term is convenient, it is not altogether appropriate" (*An Introduction to the New Testament*, 2:307). Timothy and Titus were apostolic representatives, not pastors. However, the type of care they provided for the churches at Ephesus and Crete has much in common with that of a pastor. They are the most personal of Paul's letters, but were intended for the benefit of the churches served by these two young associates of the apostle. Because they share a common nature and form the last group of letters credited to Paul, it is best to consider them as a unit in regard to authorship, authenticity, and historical setting. They will be treated separately with respect to their recipient, purpose, and arguments.

Authorship and Authenticity

Bible students who cherish the Pastoral Epistles are surprised and disappointed to discover that "these epistles have been more assailed than any of Paul's other letters" (Guthrie, *New Testament Introduction*, 607). The twin issues of authorship and authenticity are at the heart of the debate. "Since the beginning of the nineteenth century the Pastoral Epistles have been a fierce battleground, being more severely attacked than any other Pauline writings" (Hiebert, *An Introduction to the New Testament*, 2:308). Readers are referred to Donald Guthrie who devotes forty-five pages to a thorough examination of the charges against their authenticity and presents strong evidence in support of their Pauline authenticity (*New Testament Introduction*, 607-52).

Traditional view of authorship. The Pauline authorship of the Pastoral Epistles was unchallenged until the beginning of the nineteenth century. Homer A. Kent has translated and reproduced extensive quotations from early church fathers demonstrating their acquaintance with and acceptance of these epistles (*The Pastoral Epistles*, 24-40). Clement of Rome, Ignatius, Polycarp, Justin Martyr, Clement of Alexandria, Tertullian, and Irenaeus all support the Pauline authenticity of all three epistles. They were included as part of the Pauline collection of letters in the Muratorian Canon. The fact that Marcion excluded these epistles from his canon supports rather than contradicts Pauline authenticity. Marcion likewise rejected Matthew, Mark, and John and mutilated Luke (Guthrie, *New Testament Introduction*, 609). Marcion's views were rejected by the orthodox church of his day because he rewrote Scripture to accommodate his views. George G. Findlay says of the external evidence, "There is not a shred of historical evidence against the letters. The witness of the early Church to their place in the New Testament Canon and their Pauline authorship is as clear, full, and unhesitating as that given to the other epistles" (*The Epistles of Paul the Apostle*, 211).

The critical attack on the Pauline authenticity of these letters has been intense and must be addressed. However, the burden of proof rests on the critics who challenge the weight of history and the external evidence for Pauline authorship and authenticity. "If the external testimony is allowed to decide, there is no doubt that the balance is heavily in favor of authenticity. This means that the onus of proof must fall on the opponents of authenticity. Added to this is the fact that not until the nineteenth century were doubts cast on the Pauline authorship and it must be wondered why no-one before then raised any problems about them" (Guthrie, *New Testament Introduction*, 611-12).

Recent Challenges to Pauline Authenticity

Challenges to the Pauline authenticity of the Pastoral Epistles began in earnest with Friedrich Schleiermacher in 1807 when he denied the genuineness of 1 Timothy. Critics have attempted to find an acceptable alternative to the traditional view of Pauline authorship. These efforts have focused on the content of the Pastorals. Hiebert asserts, "All criticism of the traditional view is based entirely on objections derived from the internal evidence" (*An Introduction to the New Testament*, 2:311). Objections to Pauline authenticity are based on historical, ecclesiastical, doctrinal, and linguistic issues. The following is a summary of the

332

objections, some of the major supporting arguments, and the answers provided by conservative scholars.

The historical problem. The Pastoral Epistles contain references to travels and activities by the apostle Paul that are impossible to fit into the framework of the Acts history (Guthrie, *New Testament Introduction*, 612). Examples are Paul's joint ministry with Timothy in Ephesus (1 Timothy 1:3), with Titus in Crete (Titus 1:5), and his plan to spend the winter in Nicopolis (Titus 3:12).

The ecclesiastical problem. Critics of Pauline authenticity claim that the church organization reflected in these epistles is too advanced for the time of Paul, and is more uniform and important than in Paul's earlier letters. The view of church organization is said to be more in keeping with the second century, a date preferred by those who object to Pauline authenticity.

The doctrinal problem. Doctrines generally cited as absent are the fatherhood of God, the mystic union of the believer with Christ, and the indwelling work of the Holy Spirit. Some critics also suggest that doctrine, which appeared in an unstructured manner in Paul's earlier letters, has now been systematized under such terms as *the faith, the deposit,* and *the sound teaching.* Also critics assert that Paul viewed the return of Christ as imminent in his earlier letters to the Thessalonians and now as a more distant event in 2 Timothy. However, critics of authenticity recognize genuine Pauline elements in the Pastoral Epistles. This has led to the theory that these letters were written in the second century by an anonymous admirer of Paul who had access to fragments of several unpublished letters of Paul.

The linguistic problem. A large number of Greek words found in the Pastoral Epistles are unique to the New Testament and are absent from Paul's other letters (a phenomenon known as *hapax legomena,* "appearing only once"). Though answerable, Hiebert notes, "The linguistic peculiarities of these Epistles is admittedly one of the strongest arguments against Pauline authorship" (*An Introduction to the New Testament*, 2:315).

Critical theories regarding authorship. Attempts to solve these problems have led critics to hold that the Pastoral Epistles were written in the second century by a highly skilled author who was both an admirer of Paul and an articulate churchman and theologian. The Pauline elements in the Pastoral Epistles are so numerous and so genuine that the forgery is difficult for critics to detect. Hence there has been wide disparity regarding the amount and value of genuinely Pauline thought in these letters. Critical alternatives to Pauline authorship may be divided into two camps, those that see genuine Pauline material woven together by a later editor, the **fragment view**, and those that see the epistles as fictional, the **fiction view**.

Radical critics (the fiction view) see these epistles as entirely fictionalized but so masterfully done that the early church accepted them as authentic. However, most critics who reject the traditional view favor the fragment theory, and object to the fiction theory on two grounds. One, the amount of genuine Pauline material in these epistles cannot be attributed to a forger, no matter how masterful. These, it is maintained, reflect fragments of genuine, unpublished letters of Paul that were incorporated by a skillful editor of the second century who greatly admired Paul (thus the term fragment theory). Two, the improbability that the second-century church would accept such a forgery as being Pauline argues against their being completely fictional. The fragmentary view is the most widely held alternative to the traditional view. It attempts to explain the genuinely Pauline nature of the Pastoral Epistles while at the same time rejecting full Pauline authorship and authenticity.

Support for Pauline Authenticity

The external evidence for Pauline authorship is so uniform and overwhelming that it was essentially unchallenged until the modern era. Though debated, the internal evidence is so strong that critics must attribute at least parts of these epistles to Paul himself. Given the unanimous external support and the inescapable internal support, the burden of proof rests with those who would deny Pauline authenticity. The following is a summary of evidence supporting Pauline authorship of all three of the Pastoral Epistles.

Acts and chronology. The abrupt ending of Acts has often perplexed scholars. The circumstances of Paul's imprisonment in Rome do not indicate that Paul is soon to be executed. Rome seems indifferent to Christianity not opposed to it. A strong case can be made for Paul's release from imprisonment in Rome following Acts 28, a subsequent ministry in the East (including Ephesus, Crete, and Corinth), the fulfillment of his planned visit to Spain (Romans 15:24, 28), and a second Roman imprisonment which ended in his martyrdom (2 Timothy 4:6). A second imprisonment in Rome is at least a possibility if not a probability.

Pauline language and literary style. The language and style of these letters is so unmistakably Pauline that scholars have been forced to admit that they at least contain fragments of genuine Pauline writings. The occurrence of an estimated 175 *hapax legomena* in the Pastorals is explainable (Guthrie, *New Testament Introduction*, 633-36). Though the percentage is higher in the Pastorals than in other portions of Paul's writings, such one-time appearances occur throughout the other ten epistles of Paul. Further, these words are no more characteristic of the second century than they are of the first. We would expect Paul to use different words and phrases in letters that are written at the close of his life, to close personal associates, and for such a distinct purpose. If pressed, the linguistic peculiarities of these epistles could be used to raise doubts about the genuineness of all of Paul's epistles. Thayer sounds an appropriate warning. "The monumental misjudgments committed by some who have made questions of authorship turn on vocabulary alone will deter students, it is to be hoped, from misusing the list exhibiting the pecularities of the several books" (*A Greek-English Lexicon of the New Testament*, 689).

Theological perspective. The supposed absence of Pauline themes such as the fatherhood of God, the believer's union with Christ, and the work of the Holy Spirit is not sustained by a careful analysis of these letters. These doctrines do appear in general, if not in specific statements (1 Timothy 2:5, 6; 4:1; 2 Timothy 1:9-11, 14; 2:11-13; Titus 3:4-7). One is being contradictory if he argues that Pauline doctrines are absent from these epistles and at the same time maintains that the epistles evidence a systematized theology too advanced for the time of Paul. Reference to *the faith* (1 Timothy 1:2; 4:1, 6; 5:8) is to be expected in letters written at the close of Paul's life. The doctrine that Paul had been preaching was submitted to the church at Jerusalem for validation (Galatians 2:1-10), had been faithfully proclaimed for a lifetime (2 Timothy 3:10-17), and was now a matter of settled conviction (2 Timothy 4:1-5). Paul's frequent references to *the faith* and to *sound doctrine* reflect Paul's concern that the truth he proclaimed throughout his life be preserved just as it had been revealed to him (Titus 1:1-3). Of significance is the fact that no doctrinal disparity exists between the Pastoral Epistles and Paul's earlier letters.

Errors addressed. Early charges that the errors addressed in these letters resemble second-century Gnosticism has been abandoned by recent scholars. The heresies combated in these epistles were Jewish in nature (1 Timothy 1:7; Titus 1:10, 14). Rather than being a powerful attack on the Christian faith, these heresies were foolish and irrelevant (Titus 3:9). The doctrinal errors referred to in these letters favor rather than discredit Pauline authorship (Guthrie, *New Testament Introduction*, 630-32).

Church organization. The Pastoral letters stress the importance of elders, bishops and deacons in the church. It is often asserted that such emphasis on church organization is characteristic of the second century, not the first. However, the terms bishop and elder are used interchangeably (Titus 1:5-7) whereas they came to be viewed as two separate offices in the second century. Such attention to church organization was characteristic of Paul's missionary activity and appropriate in the closing days of his ministry (Acts 14:23). Guthrie argues, "If there is some ground for supposing that Paul was an ecclesiastical architect during the course of his missionary labors, it would be foolish to suppose that at the end of his life with the knowledge that he must soon hand over to younger men Paul had shown complete disinterestedness in the way in which his successors were to set about the task. With his vast experience of missionary statesmanship Paul of all men was best qualified to lay down stipulations for the appointment of officers and to give general instructions regarding Church order. He would have been the most shortsighted of men if he had not done so" (*New Testament Introduction*, 625).

Early acceptance by the church fathers. Early acceptance and use of these epistles by the church argues strongly for their Pauline authenticity. External evidence is early and extensive. "There is not one trace of suspicion in the early church. If this were a forgery (or even a 'pious fraud'), it is certainly strange that it gained immediate approval, even by those who could have been personally acquainted with Paul, and there are no dissenters (apart from the heretics previously discussed) until the nineteenth century, the uniform testimony of early history must carry more weight than the variety of the vocabulary" (Kent, *The Pastoral Epistles*, 71).

Facts and forgery. Highly unlikely is the idea that a forger could have so masterfully imitated Pauline thought and expression that he would escape detection by the church or that he would have risked exposure by undertaking such a massive forgery. The historical detail is too Pauline to be missed. At the same time people, places, and events mentioned only in the Pastoral letters would have been immediately discredited if the church had not viewed them as genuine. Forgers were at work very early in Paul's career (2 Thessalonians 2:2). The early church was alert to the problem of forgeries, and spurious writings that have survived are clearly inferior to these letters. However pious the imitator of Paul may have been, the moral issue of a forgery cannot be overlooked. In fact, the author himself condemns *speaking lies in hypocrisy* (1 Timothy 4:2, KJV). Guthrie is kind but firm in rejecting pseudonymous authorship. "We have refrained from calling the author a 'forger' because many scholars consider this term contains a moral stigma, which prejudices the issue. But does the term 'imitator' or 'devout Paulinist' really obviate the moral problem? Can we believe that the author was motivated by the highest intentions of modesty when he attributed these Epistles to Paul, as if it would have been almost an injustice to call his own what was in effect a reproduction of the thought of his master? ... to begin with, not a single comparable parallel from early Christian literary practice can be produced in support, which raises suspicions about its probability" (*New Testament Introduction*, 645).

Conclusion. The critical objections have been carefully examined and ably answered by many scholars, including Guthrie, Hiebert, and Kent. Kent underscores the importance of Pauline authenticity. "It certainly makes a great difference to a Christian whether these letters were actually written by the apostle Paul to his protégés Timothy and Titus, or whether they were the work of a forger (regardless of his motives) who fabricated them from Pauline fragments, liberally sprinkled with his own ideas. It means the difference between a properly attested portion of Scripture from the pen of Christ's apostle, and an intriguing piece of literature, not quite as trustworthy as the works of an Ignatius, Polycarp, Irenaeus, and other second-century writers" (*The Pastoral Epistles*, 11).

Background and Dates
Paul's itinerary between imprisonments in Rome
1. Paul had an effective but probably brief ministry in Crete (Titus 1:5). He did not have sufficient time to organize the churches that had been planted in cities across the island, and so he left Titus with that responsibility.
2. Paul visited Corinth once again either before or after his ministry in Crete (2 Timothy 4:20). Erastus remained in Corinth.

3. Paul continued his travels eastward ministering in Macedonia (1 Timothy 1:3). At that time he sent a message to Timothy, urging him to remain at Ephesus and later wrote his first epistle to Timothy.
4. Paul planned to send either Artemas or Tychicus to Crete, thereby enabling Titus to join him for the winter in Nicopolis (Titus 3:12). Confirmation of that visit does not exist, but Paul probably fulfilled his plan to winter at Nicopolis.
5. Paul made a second visit to Miletus, accompanied by Trophimus. Trophimus became ill and had to be left behind in Miletus (2 Timothy 4:20).
6. Paul made an abrupt departure from Troas (2 Timothy 4:13), perhaps because he was arrested and transported quickly to Rome. Paul left behind the scrolls and parchments he valued so highly, and the cloak he needed for protection against the winter cold of the Roman prison.
7. Paul was again imprisoned in Rome (2 Timothy 1:8). His close associates had been sent on other important ministries. Others who might have stood by him to give help and comfort deserted him (2 Timothy 1:15). Paul expected his first imprisonment to end with his release and further ministry in Philippi (Philippians 1:25-26), and he had earlier planned a ministry in Spain following a visit to Rome (Romans 15:24, 28). If that plan was fulfilled, it may have occurred before he traveled to the east or afterward. When Paul wrote 2 Timothy he anticipated martyrdom (2 Timothy 4:6-8). He longed for the company of Timothy, his closest companion and most trusted representative (4:9).
8. Paul was probably executed by Nero as part of Nero's attempt to destroy the growing movement of Christianity. The date was probably around AD 67.

Date of Paul's letters to Timothy and Titus. All three letters were written between Paul's release from his first Roman imprisonment in AD 62-63 and his martyrdom in Rome around AD 65-67. First Timothy was the first of the three pastoral letters and was probably written between AD 63 and 65. Titus was the second letter, which Paul probably wrote soon after he wrote his first letter to Timothy. The arrest and pending execution of Paul formed the background for Paul's last letter, 2 Timothy. A probable date for his martyrdom is AD 67.

Bibliography for the Pastoral Epistles

Fee, Gordon D. *The Pastoral Epistles.* Peabody, MA: Hendrickson Publishers, 1988.

Findlay, George G. *The Epistles of Paul the Apostle.* Cambridge Greek Testament for schools and colleges. Cambridge: University Press, 1904.

Guthrie, Donald. *New Testament Introduction.* Downers Grove, IL: InterVarsity Press, 1990.

____. *The Pastoral Epistles.* Grand Rapids: Wm. B. Eerdmans Publishing Co., 1957.

Hiebert, D. Edmond. *An Introduction to the New Testament.* Vol. 2. Chicago: Moody Press, 1975.

____. *First Timothy.* Chicago: Moody Press, 1957.

____. *Personalities Around Paul.* Chicago: Moody Press, 1973.

____. *Titus and Philemon.* Chicago: Moody Press, 1957.

____. *Second Timothy.* Chicago: Moody Press, 1958.

Kelly, J. N. D. *A Commentary on the Pastoral Epistles.* Black New Testament Commentary Series. Peabody, MA: Hendrickson Publishers, 1993.

Kent, Homer A. *The Pastoral Epistles.* Chicago: Moody Press, 1958.

Kostenberger, Andreas. "The Pastoral Epistles." In *The Expositor's Bible Commentary.* Rev. ed. Vol. 11. Grand Rapids: Zondervan Publishing House, 2006.

Knight, George W. III. *The Pastoral Epistles. A Commentary on the Greek Text. New International Greek Testament Commentary.* Grand Rapids: Wm. B. Eerdmans Publishing Co., 1992.

Marshall, I. Howard. *The Pastoral Epistles.* London: T. & T. Clark, 2000.

Mounce, William. *The Pastoral Epistles.* Nashville: Thomas Nelson Publishers, 2000.

Prior, Michael. *Paul the Letter-Writer and the Second Letter to Timothy.* Sheffield: Sheffield Academic Press, 1989.

Rutherford, John D. "The Pastoral Epistles." In *The International Bible Encyclopedia.* Ed. James Orr. Vol. 4. Grand Rapids: Wm. B. Eerdmans Publishing Co., 1939.

Seekings, Herbert S. *The Men of the Pauline Circle.* London: Charles H. Kelly, 1914.

Stott, John R.W. *Guard the Truth.* Downers Grove, IL: InterVarsity Press, 1997.

____. *The Message of 1 Timothy & Titus.* Downers Grove, IL: InterVarsity Press, 1996.

Thayer, Joseph Henry. *A Greek-English Lexicon of the New Testament.* Grand Rapids: Zondervan Publishing House, 1956.

Towner, Philip. *Letters to Timothy and Titus.* New International Commentary on the New Testament. Grand Rapids: Wm. B. Eerdmans Publishing Co., 2006.

____. *The Pastoral Epistles.* Downers Grove, IL: InterVarsity Press, 1994.

1 TIMOTHY: Pastoral Care and Conduct in the Church

Key verses 1:18; 6:20, *This command I entrust to you, Timothy, ... guard what has been entrusted to you.*

Key words:
Command,
Godliness,
Instruction,
Doctrine,
Grace,
Truth,
Faith,
Love

	Commission	Pastoral Care	and Conduct	Challenge
	1:1 — 1:20	2:1		6:10 — 6:11 — 6:21

Paul's Assignment for Timothy

Commission

Paul's commission: entrusted with the glorious gospel

Paul's commission for Timothy: entrusted with that glorious gospel

Fight the good fight!

Paul's Instructions for Timothy

Pastoral Care

Instructions regarding:

Church Worship 2:1-15

Church Officers   3:1-13

Purpose statement 3:14-16

and Conduct

Church Doctrine   4:1-16

Church Members 5:1-6:2

Church Finances   6:3-10

Paul's Charge to Timothy

Challenge

Paul's charge: flee, follow, fight, keep the commandment without reproach until the appearing of Jesus Christ

Guard what has been entrusted to you

Fight the good fight of faith!

Paul
A.D. 63-65
from
Macedonia

341

1 TIMOTHY

I write so that you will know how one ought to conduct himself in the household of God, which is the church of the living God, the pillar and support of the truth (3:15).

Profile of Timothy

The measure of the man. Paul's partnership with Timothy was the most intimate and enduring of all his personal relationships. The fact that Timothy is mentioned 24 times in the New Testament points up his importance to the apostle Paul. Timothy is associated with the apostle in the salutation of six of Paul's epistles. Paul always refers to Timothy with unqualified praise and appreciation. His name means, "honoring God." No doubt conferred by his godly grandmother and mother, the name reflected both their hope for him and the reality of his life in Christ. Timothy was unparalleled in his devotion to gospel ministry and in the sharing of Paul's heartbeat (Philippians 2:19-23). His somewhat frail health was exacerbated by his aversion to wine and the prevalence of contamination in drinking water (1 Timothy 5:23).

Timothy was by nature timid and retiring in spite of being placed often at the forefront of public ministry (1 Corinthians 16:10-11; 2 Timothy 1:7). This may have been due in part to his youth, but this was probably a matter of temperament as well (1 Timothy 4:12). He may have been timid, but he was a man of perseverance, remaining at Ephesus for some length of time. Both of Paul's letters found him engaged in ministry at Ephesus. Exhorted to share in Paul's suffering (2 Timothy 1:8), Timothy himself endured the hardship of prison (Hebrews 13:23). Above all, Timothy was deeply devoted to the apostle Paul (2 Timothy 1:4). This last letter from Paul must have been heart-wrenching for young Timothy. One can only imagine how much he longed to be with Paul in his final hours. Surely he lost no time in heeding Paul's plea; *Make every effort to come before winter* (2 Timothy 4:21). "This then, was Timothy—young in years, frail in physique, retiring in disposition—who nevertheless was called to exacting responsibilities in the church of God. Greatness was being thrust upon him" (John Stott, *The Message of 2 Timothy*, 20).

Background and calling of Timothy. Timothy was a native of Lystra (Acts 16:1; 2 Timothy 3:11). He was the child of a racially and religiously mixed marriage (Acts 16:1-3); his father was Greek and his mother and grandmother were Jewish. His father apparently did not become a proselyte to Judaism since Luke always refers to him as Greek without the qualifying adjective "devout." The fact that Timothy remained uncircumcised also suggests that his father remained a pagan. Timothy's mother Eunice and grandmother Lois were godly Jewish women (2 Timothy 1:5). Their influence is reflected in his name, "honoring God," and in their careful instruction of Timothy in the Scriptures (2 Timothy 3:15). As a young child he was steeped in the Scriptures (2 Timothy 3:14-15). Timothy's childhood absorption with Scripture prepared him for the reception of Jesus as the Messiah of the Old Testament. No doubt his mother and grandmother preceded him in the faith (2 Timothy 1:5).

The many references to Timothy as Paul's *son* or *child* in the faith (1 Corinthians 4:17; 1 Timothy 1:2, 18; 2 Timothy 1:2) argue for his being a convert under Paul's ministry. This would probably have occurred during the first mission of Paul and Barnabas to the Gentiles (Acts 14:8-21). In his home city of Lystra, Timothy saw Paul's compelling example of fervent devotion to the gospel ministry. He saw also the high cost of following Christ as he witnessed the stoning of Paul (Acts 14:19; 2 Timothy 3:10-12). He made a public profession of his faith in Jesus as the Messiah (1 Timothy 6:12). Timothy made rapid progress in the faith. In little more than a year he already enjoyed wide recognition in the Christian community (Acts 16:2).

Timothy was called to missionary service through public endorsement and the prophetic action of the Holy Spirit (Acts 16:2-3; 1 Timothy 1:18). The gift of God that formed the basis of Timothy's ministry was uniquely bestowed on him through the laying on of Paul's hands (2 Timothy 1:6). He was circumcised for the sake of the gospel ministry, not as an act of compromise (Acts 16:3). Perhaps Paul himself, acting in the place of the father in Jewish custom, administered the circumcision. Timothy must have been very young when he began his career as companion and apostolic representative to Paul. Approximately 15 years later he is referred to as a youth, a term used for one under 40 years of age (1 Timothy 4:12). His age at ordination is variously estimated between 18 and 25 years, probably when he was 21 or 22.

Timothy's travels and ministry. Timothy joined Paul and Silas on their second mission to the Gentiles (Acts 16:1-5). He is next mentioned with Paul at Berea (17:14). Since he is not referred to during their ministry at Thessalonica, Timothy may have remained at Philippi with Luke to consolidate the work among new believers (17:1-4, 10). Timothy remained with Silas at Berea when the Jews forced Paul to move on to Athens. Then Paul urged Timothy to join him in Athens as soon as possible (17:15). Timothy was sent back to Thessalonica on an urgent and potentially dangerous mission (1 Thessalonians 3:2-5). Timothy rejoined Paul in Corinth, where his positive report of the church at Thessalonica encouraged Paul (Acts 18:5) and prompted the writing of 1 Thessalonians (1 Thessalonians 3:6-8). Timothy was more than a messenger and became a valued partner in the extended ministry of Paul at Corinth (2 Corinthians 1:19). Timothy next appears on Paul's third mission to the Gentiles. He was sent into Macedonia along with Erastus (Acts 19:22). His primary assignment was probably to facilitate the offering that Paul was organizing for the Jerusalem church (1 Corinthians 16:1-4, 10-11).

The number and length of Timothy's visits to Corinth are difficult to determine as are Paul's own (1 Corinthians 4:16-17). Timothy is accompanying Paul in Macedonia when Paul's second letter to the Corinthians is written (2 Corinthians 1:1). He probably wintered with Paul in Corinth (Acts 20:2-4; 1 Corinthians 16:3-4; 2 Corinthians 8:19-21). He was present with Paul when the book of Romans was written from Corinth (Romans 16:21). Timothy is not mentioned in Luke's record of Paul's imprisonments at Caesarea or Rome. However, he must have rejoined Paul at some point during his first Roman imprisonment. Paul includes Timothy in the salutation of his prison epistles, Philippians, Colossians, and Philemon. Paul's intention to send Timothy to Philippi occasioned the apostle's highest praise of Timothy (Philippians 2:19-23). "Never did Paul allow himself such freedom in the praise of any of his co-workers as in this tender and generous outburst of feeling concerning one who had toiled with him in the holy work and whom he had come to esteem as a genuine son" (Seekings, *The Men of the Pauline Circle*, 60). Paul's first letter to Timothy reveals that this young co-laborer had an extended ministry in Ephesus (1 Timothy 1:3). This was a demanding and a large task in view of the problems of the church and the widespread influence of this congregation (Acts 19:10).

Purpose and Distinctives of 1 Timothy

Purpose. Paul clearly states his primary reason for writing this letter in 3:14-15. *I am writing these things to you, hoping to come to you before long; but in case I am delayed, I write so that you will know how one ought to conduct himself in the household of God, which is the church of the living God, the pillar and support of the truth.* A secondary purpose for this letter was to encourage young Timothy in a task that was growing more difficult and had extended beyond the expected time frame (1:18-20; 4:11-16; 6:11-16). Timothy had the difficult task of confronting false teaching (1:3: 4:6). To exercise this authority Timothy needed Paul's endorsement (1:3-7, 18; 4:11-14). The gospel was continuing to progress, and Paul felt it necessary to equip Timothy for changing, challenging times (4:1-5, 15-16).

Distinctives. First Timothy comes as near to providing a manual for the conduct of the church as is to be found in the New Testament (3:14-15). While the instructions are in harmony with other passages, their detail and concentration are unique to this letter. Guidelines for the officers of the church include the detail of their qualifications and selection process. They are not to be a *new convert* (3:6) and are to be subjected to careful and private examination before appointment (3:10). Even the remuneration of elders and its relation to their performance is discussed (5:17-20).

Surprisingly little is said about the order of service in the public meetings held by the New Testament church. However, some telling information can be gleaned from 1 Timothy. This information includes the place and the nature of prayer (2:1-10) and the importance of public Scripture reading (4:13). This last reference reveals that services in the early church appeared to follow the order of services in the synagogue: the reading of Scripture, followed by an exposition. Stress was placed on the teaching of doctrine.

Women made up a substantial portion of the New Testament church, and 1 Timothy gives some unique instructions regarding them. Though brief and comparable to 1 Corinthians, Paul is explicit about the role of women in public worship (3:11-15). Most distinctive is Paul's extended discussion regarding the care of widows (5:3-16). Depending on one's interpretation, Paul may also have included instruction regarding the character of deaconesses (3:11).

Timothy appears often in the book of Acts and in other epistles of Paul, but most of our insights into his personal characteristics are gleaned from 1 Timothy. Here we find indications regarding his age (4:12), his health (5:23), and his call to ministry (1:18; 4:14). Paul's guidelines regarding money are explicit and revealing. He discusses both the right and the wrong use of wealth (6:3-10, 17-19).

Key Verses

This command I entrust to you, Timothy, my son, in accordance with the prophecies previously made concerning you, that by them you fight the good fight, keeping faith and a good conscience (1:18).
I write so that you will know how one ought to conduct himself in the household of God, which is the church of the living God, the pillar and support of the truth (3:15).
O Timothy, guard what has been entrusted to you (6:20).

Message of 1 Timothy

First Timothy opens with Paul declaring his apostolic mandate (1:1, 11) and commissioning Timothy to carry on that work (1:18), and closes with his solemn charge for Timothy to keep that sacred stewardship faithfully until the return of Jesus Christ (6:11-21). The majority of the letter focuses on Paul's instructions on how Timothy is to carry out this commission (2:1-6:10). Paul's divine commission as apostle and Timothy's commission as an apostolic delegate appear several times throughout these instructions (2:7; 4:6, 11, 14; 5:21; 6:13-14, 20). In tracing the thought of 1 Timothy one must remember that this is a personal letter, not a doctrinal thesis. Paul provides a statement of purpose for the letter (3:14-15), but not until he is half way through the writing. This central passage provides the supporting pillar for Paul's instructions on how Timothy is to carry out this commission Paul is giving him. Retroactively it explains the instructions regarding worship in the local church (2:1-15) and the officers of the church (3:1-13). Proactively it introduces Paul's instructions to Timothy regarding the teaching of the church (4:1-16), the people of the church (5:1-6:2), and the financial integrity of the church (6:3-10).

Encouragement and authentication of Timothy's ministry are vital secondary purposes for this letter from Paul. Several personal sections are interwoven with the more public instructions given to Timothy. Most of the time these are closely related to the context, but in at least one case the appearance is abrupt and apparently unrelated (5:23). These capsules of personal encouragement include (1) the foundation of Timothy's ministry

(1:3, 18-20); (2) the importance of his teaching ministry and its exemplification in his life (4:6-16); (3) the need for Timothy to give attention to his own health (5:23); and (4) the concluding charge (6:11-16) and challenge (6:20-21).

Salutation (1:1-2)

In his opening sentence Paul introduces himself and reveals his purpose for writing. He is *an apostle of Christ Jesus according to the commandment of God our Savior, and of Christ Jesus.* In this letter he will entrust to Timothy that "commandment" or sacred trust (1:18). Paul is nearing the close of his life and ministry and is commissioning Timothy to carry on the work of the *glorious gospel* that has previously been entrusted to Paul (1:11). Timothy is Paul's *child in the faith* (1:2). In all his other epistles Paul combines the Christian and Jewish elements, *grace and peace*, in twin fashion. In his two letters to Timothy *mercy* is inserted between them. This triad of blessings originates in *God the Father and Christ Jesus our Lord* (1:2).

Paul's Assignment for Timothy (1:3-20)

Paul's original assignment to Timothy was to remain at Ephesus to counteract the false teaching that had arisen (1:3-7). At first glance 1:8-17 may seem parenthetical. However, on further examination one can see that it relates closely to the preceding statement regarding Timothy's assignment at Ephesus. The false teachers Timothy is to correct are *teaching strange doctrines* involving the misuse of the Mosaic Law (1:7). Therefore it is essential that Paul state the rightful use of the Law (1:8-11). As the mention of the Law (1:7) occasions Paul's explanation of its appropriate use (1:8-11), so the mention of the gospel entrusted to Paul (1:11) occasions Paul's explanation of his conversion and call to ministry (1:12-17). The right use of the Law contrasts with its wrong use by the false teachers. Paul's conversion and call contrast with the self-motivated ministry of these false teachers. Timothy is charged with the responsibility of teaching true doctrine that is in keeping with *the glorious gospel* that has been entrusted to Paul (1:18-20).

Paul's Instructions for Timothy (2:1-6:10)

Instructions regarding church worship (2:1-15). Prayer is to occupy first place in Timothy's ministry and in the life of the church (2:1-2). These prayers should be on behalf of all men but particularly for those in public office so that Christians may live in peace. The ultimate purpose of prayer is to spread the gospel message and fulfill God's desire for *all men to be* *saved and come to the knowledge of the truth* (2:3-4). The essence of that truth is the redemptive work of Jesus Christ (2:5-6) that Paul earlier called *the glorious gospel* (1:11). Again Paul declares his apostolic appointment on behalf of that gospel (2:7). Wherever and whenever men meet they need to pray in holy harmony (2:8). Men are to be characterized by prayer and are to provide the leadership in the church.

Paul has given instruction on the role of men, and now he gives Timothy instructions on the role of women in the worship of the church (2:9-15). This may be the most debated and least understood section of 1 Timothy. Paul wrote extensively to the church at Corinth about the role of women in public worship (1 Corinthians 11:3-16; 14:26-40), but here the instructions are directed toward women who are disrupting the public worship of the church either by their immodest behavior or by their speaking out during the teaching. The instructions seem to go beyond wives whose husbands have just been challenged to pray (1 Timothy 2:8). Ephesus was the home of the temple to the goddess Artemis, and the city was noted for the deification of female beauty and sexuality (Acts 19:26-27). Against that background Christian women are to dress modestly and lead godly lives (1 Timothy 2:9-15). Younger widows are later censured for wanton behavior, for gossip, and for talking about things that may be in keeping with the false teaching Timothy is to correct (5:11-13). Paul instructs women to be "quiet" (2:11), the same word he uses for all believers in 2:2. They are to leave the teaching and leadership role to the elders (3:2; 5:17)

Instructions regarding church officers (3:1-13). If a man is to lead the church he must be well qualified. Two leadership roles are described: (a) overseer, that is, elder (3:1-7) and (b) deacons (3:8-13). Paul does not give a job description for either office. He assumes that those properly qualified will know what to do and will be prepared for whatever responsibility is thrust on them. One who aspires to be an elder must be "unimpeachable" and must evidence an impressive list of qualifications. He must manage his own life well, have a genuine love for others, and be capable of teaching. At home he must be the husband of one wife (literally, a one-woman man), and a father who manages his own family well. The overseer (elder) must also have a good reputation outside the church. This position is definitely not a role for new believers. Leadership in the church is a high calling demanding high qualifications.

Qualifications for deacons are equally high (3:8-13). They must be good family men, self-controlled, honest and faithful in all they do, and be beyond reproach. While they are not required to teach, they must be knowledgeable in the faith. Deacons may be younger in the faith but must be tested before being appointed. Women are mentioned along with Paul's discussion of deacons (3:11). They are the wives of deacons or possibly deaconesses.

Paul's purpose statement for these instructions (3:14-16). Paul intends to join Timothy in Ephesus soon, but he anticipates that he may be delayed; hence this letter. He is writing these instructions so Timothy will know how to carry out his duties but also so that the church will have a "manual of operations." The church belongs to the living God and is to embody and express the truth. As is often the case with Paul, the mention of "truth" prompts him to include the church's confessional statement (3:16).

Instructions regarding church doctrine (4:1-16). Paul's confessional statement in 3:16 leads naturally to his warning about future apostasy and doctrinal perversion (4:1-5). False doctrine and moral deviation go hand in hand. As a good servant of Christ, Timothy is to privately adhere to and to publicly teach sound doctrine, and to exemplify godliness in his lifestyle (4:6-10). To do that he must be constantly *nourished on the words of the faith and of the sound doctrine (4:6)* and lead a disciplined life (4:7-8). Such a demanding lifestyle is prompted by the hope Timothy and Paul both share in the living God (4:10). These instructions have been personal for Timothy but are not his responsibility alone. He is to command and teach these things in the church (4:11). Timothy is to be an example of all that he teaches so that no one has cause to look down on him because of his relative youthfulness (4:12). The role of speaking naturally fell to Paul but now Timothy is to devote his full effort to the public reading and exposition of Scripture (4:13-16). This requires healthy self-awareness and persistent effort in his ministry, and promises great benefit for him and for the church.

Instructions regarding Timothy's relations with church members (5:1-6:2). The church is the "family of God" and Timothy should treat older men like fathers, younger men like brothers, older women like mothers, and younger women like sisters, but in all purity (5:1-2). The church is to provide care for widows but with clear guidelines (5:3-16). The family, particularly their own children, bear the responsibility of caring for widows. The church should not support widows unless they are at least 60 years of age and have demonstrated Christian virtues and service to the church. Younger widows must not be lazy and disruptive; they should marry and be productive homemakers.

The previous instructions relate to Timothy's relationships with members in the church. As an apostolic delegate he also has responsibility for the care of elders, those who "rule" in the church (5:17-22). The word for "elder" here is *presbuteros*, not *episkopos* as in chapter 3:1. However, the office is that of the teaching elder. Elders who fulfill their leadership role well in preaching and teaching merit the financial support of the congregation. Elders may be subjected to criticism and Timothy is not to act on an accusation against them unless it has the support of two or three witnesses. When rebuke of an elder is justified it must be done in public. This is not a welcome task and Timothy is to follow these directions without showing any bias or partiality. Paul may have envisioned that drunkenness could lead to an elder's failure, and this may have prompted Timothy to avoid alcohol entirely. So in a somewhat parenthetical note Paul calls on Timothy to use a little wine for his stomach and frequent health problems (5:23).

The sins of men are not always evident, but neither are good works (5:24-25). Sin will certainly be judged and good work cannot be concealed. This applies equally to the elders just mentioned and to Paul's instruction to Timothy regarding slaves. Slavery was common in the Roman world of the first century, but slaves were a welcome and important part of the church. They were considered equal with all believers in the church though not under Roman law. Believers under the yoke of slavery had a unique challenge: how to live as free in Christ while under bondage. Timothy is to instruct them to serve their masters faithfully as a witness to the grace of God (6:1-2).

Instructions regarding sound doctrine, godliness, and financial gain (6:3-10). Sound doctrine and godly living are inseparable. Those who think that the Christian faith leads to financial gain are deluded. Christians are to focus on their future hope in heaven, not on financial gain on earth. For the believer godliness itself is gain when it is accompanied by contentment (6:3-8). People obsessed with becoming rich face temptations that lead to their ruin. They depart from sound doctrine and abandon the truth (6:9-10).

Paul's Concluding Charge to Timothy (6:11-21)

Timothy is not exempt from the temptations for wealth that Paul has just decried. As he closes this letter Paul exhorts Timothy to "flee from these things." Instead he is to follow after "righteousness, godliness, faith, love, perseverance and gentleness" (6:11). Timothy is urged to "fight the good fight of faith" and to follow after his calling. Paul's charge to Timothy is a solemn one, witnessed by both God, who gives life to all things, and by Jesus Christ, who set the ultimate pattern of faithful witness (6:13). The charge is to keep the commandment, which is the sacred trust he has received from God and from Paul (1:1, 5, 11, 18), without stain or reproach until Jesus Christ returns (6:14). Mention of the appearing of Christ prompts Paul to include another doxology of praise to God the Father (6:15-16). Paul began this closing section with a warning about the lure of riches, and he again reminds Timothy that he must instruct them to fix their hope on God, and not on uncertain riches. They should focus their efforts on giving generously and invest in what is eternal (6:17-19). Paul closes this personal letter with an impassioned plea to his beloved young colleague Timothy. *O Timothy, guard what has been entrusted to you* (6:20). The conclusion of 1Timothy is unusually short and abrupt. Following his final challenge to Timothy, Paul simply declares, *Grace be with you* (6:21b).

Outline of 1 Timothy

I.	Salutation	1:1-2
II.	Paul's assignment for Timothy	1:3-20
	A. Remain at Ephesus	1:3
	B. Refute false teaching	1:4-7
	C. Reinforcement for Timothy	1:8-20
	1. Paul has been entrusted with the true teaching	1:8-11
	2. Christ has saved Paul as an example of grace	1:12-16
	3. Doxology to this King eternal, the only God	1:17
	4. Paul now entrusts this calling to Timothy	1:18-20
III.	Paul's Instructions for Timothy	2:1-6:10
	A. Regarding church worship	2:1-15
	1. The primacy of prayer	2:1-2
	2. God's undergirding purpose for prayer	2:3-7
	3. The prerequisites for effective prayer	2:8
	4. The role of women in prayer and worship	2:9-15

351

B.	Regarding church officers	3:1-13
	1. The qualifications for overseers	3:1-7
	2. The qualifications for deacons	3:8-13
C.	Purpose statement for Paul's letter	3:14-16
	1. Instruction for conduct within the church	3:14-15
	2. The confessional statement of the church	3:16
D.	Regarding church doctrine	4:1-16
	1. The threat of false teaching	4:1-5
	2. The antidote to false teaching	4:6-16
	a. Adhering to the doctrine of the faith	4:6-10
	b. Exemplifying the truth in one's personal life	4:11-16
E.	Regarding church members	5:1-6:2
	1. The guiding principles for ministering to people	5:1-2
	2. The proper care of widows	5:3-16
	3. The proper care of elders	5:17-22
	4. Timothy's care for his own health	5:23
	5. The proper conduct of slaves	5:24-6:2
F.	Regarding godliness and financial gain	6:3-10
	1. Sound doctrine leads to godliness	6:3-5
	2. Godliness with contentment is the real gain	6:6-10

IV.	Paul's concluding charge to Timothy	6:11-21
A.	The charge: keep the faith till Christ comes!	6:11-16
	1. Flee from the false doctrine that seeks wealth	6:11a
	2. Follow after righteousness and godliness	6:11b
	3. Fight the good fight of faith	6:12
	4. Keep this commandment until Christ returns	6:13-15a
	5. Doxology to Christ, the Sovereign, King of kings	6:15b-16
	6. Keep instructing those with their eye on wealth	6:17-19
B.	The concluding challenge: guard this sacred trust!	6:20-21

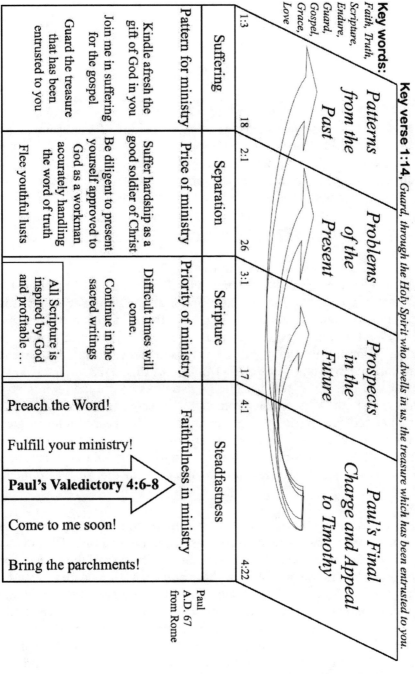

2 TIMOTHY

"Second Timothy has appropriately been called Paul's 'swan song.' In it we have the final, moving words of that mighty warrior of the cross as he faces death unafraid. It is the dying appeal of the Apostle to his young associate, exhorting him to steadfastness in the ministry in the face of appalling difficulties. It is the most personal of the Pastoral Epistles. It is rich in personal details and gives us a closing picture of the dauntless messenger of Christ, tender and sympathetic, heroic and grand to the very end" (Hiebert, *An Introduction to the New Testament*, 2:350).

Purpose and Distinctives of 2 Timothy

Purpose. Urgency and loneliness mark this, Paul's last known letter. He anticipates the arrival of a Roman executioner at any time. Yet even as his life hangs in the balance, he is still thinking of others, particularly Timothy, his most trusted and devoted co-worker. Paul writes this letter to encourage Timothy in the light of increased persecution and Paul's approaching martyrdom (1:6-8, 13-14; 2:1-3, 15, 22-23; 3:14; 4:1-5). "Down through centuries this priceless epistle has continued its ministry of giving strength and encouragement to discouraged and troubled workers, needed consolation to isolated missionaries yearning for human sympathy and Christian fellowship, and new inspiration to weary messengers of God confronted with seemingly insuperable obstacles and relentless antagonisms" (Hiebert, *An Introduction to the New Testament*, 2:356).

The apostle is also writing to summon Timothy to join him in Rome and to bring with him personal items Paul treasured and needed (4:9, 13, and 21). Hiebert captures the pathos of Paul's appeal. "At the end of life he has not lost interest in life; in the face of death he is still eager to read and to study. His busy life has not afforded much time for such activity, but in his present confinement he longs to improve the long hours, which hang heavily on his hands. He gives us a glimpse of the Apostle as a student and lover of books" (*An Introduction to the New Testament*, 2:358). This short letter alerts Timothy to the future threat of false teaching (3:1-9) and the long-term responsibilities that are about to descend on him following Paul's martyrdom (3:10-4:8).

Distinctives. Second Timothy has well been called Paul's "valedictory address." This epistle is our final portrait of the greatest servant of the Lord Jesus Christ and a man who shaped Christianity more than any other man apart from Christ Himself. This letter is the portrait of a lonely champion. Second Timothy takes us inside a Roman prison cell with Paul and takes us inside the prisoner himself. The apostle Paul faces death without fear and reflects triumphantly on a life well lived in faithful service for Christ (4:6-8). The prophetic element of this letter is unique. Paul warns Timothy and us about the threat of apostasy that hangs over the future of the Christian church. Though not a "doom—and— gloom" report or a sign of defeat, it does paint a realistic picture of the future (3:1-6; 4:3-4).

This second epistle is more personal than the first letter Paul wrote to Timothy. The first was more nearly pastoral, and this is overwhelmingly personal. Paul mentions twenty-three people in this epistle, twelve of whom are mentioned nowhere else. Both the good and the bad are mentioned. Most of all, it highlights the enduring relationship of Paul and his young co-laborer Timothy. At the end of a lifetime of ministry Paul sought the companionship of a young man who shared his heartbeat (Philippians 2:19-23; 2 Timothy 2:1-5; 3:10-16). The central passage regarding the inspiration of Scripture is 2 Timothy 3:16-17. Though not the sole proof for the doctrine, it stands alone in its clarity and value to the doctrine of inspiration. Paul's charge to Timothy, *Preach the word; be ready in season and out of season; reprove, rebuke, exhort, with great patience and instruction* (4:2); is a charge to all who would follow in the footsteps of Paul and Timothy. This call to expository preaching is the guiding beacon for Christian ministry.

Key verses, 1:14 and 4:2

Guard, through the Holy Spirit who dwells in us, the treasure which has been entrusted to you. ... Preach the word; be ready in season and out of season; reprove, rebuke, exhort, with great patience and instruction.

Message of 2 Timothy

At the heart of this last letter from Paul is his charge to Timothy. *Guard, through the Holy Spirit who dwells in us, the treasure which has been entrusted to you* (1:14). Like a great symphony, this theme appears over and over again with variations. Timothy is urged to *kindle afresh the gift of God which is in you through the laying on of my hands* (1:6). Timothy is exhorted to *join with me in suffering for the gospel* (1:8). Timothy is to *retain the standard of sound words which you have heard from me, in the faith and love which are in Christ Jesus* (1:13). To these three exhortations from the first chapter, at least nine are in the second chapter, one in the third chapter, and fourteen are in the final chapter. Paul clearly intended to stir the heart and strengthen the resolve of his young co-laborer.

Introduction, 1:1-2. Paul's greeting to Timothy is warm and personal. This is a letter from the aged apostle to his *beloved son* in the faith. As Paul faces the prospect of death he sees his life and legacy in the light of the *promise of life in Christ Jesus*.

Patterns from the past, 1:3-18. The skillful blending of past, present, and future dominates the structure of the book. Drawing on the past, both his own conversion and calling, and that of Timothy's training and gifting, Paul reminds Timothy of the pattern that will guide him in the days ahead (1:3-18). Paul has served God with a "clear conscience," and he reminds Timothy of the "sincere faith" of his mother and grandmother that Paul is convinced now resides in Timothy (1:5). The gift of God Timothy received when Paul laid his hands on him is Timothy's calling to the ministry of the gospel. Like a glowing ember Timothy is to fan this gift into flame (1:6). This ministry of the gospel is to be carried out with power, love, and discipline, not with timidity (1:7). The triumph of Christ over death gives Timothy the assurance of ultimate victory and the incentive he needs to endure suffering (1:8-10). The suffering of Christ that has brought salvation provides a pattern for Paul's suffering and for Timothy's suffering as well (1:11-12). Timothy has received *the standard of sound words* from Paul and now must, *guard the treasure* that was entrusted to him (1:13-14). Paul concludes by citing examples of faithlessness and also faithfulness among Paul's other co-workers (1:15-18).

Problems of the present (2:1-26). After drawing on the past (1:3-18), Paul now directs Timothy's attention to the present and to the problems he must address (2:1-26). Once again we see Paul's compelling logic at work. In a summary statement he outlines the twofold task confronting Timothy in the present (2:1-2). The first task is in the area of Timothy's personal life (2:3-13). To be strong in grace is to *endure hardship with me as a good soldier of Christ Jesus* (2:3) Paul leaves no doubt about his meaning. He explains it through a trio of illustrations: a soldier, an athlete, and a farmer (2:4-7). The soldier is "on active duty" and avoids anything that hinders him from pleasing his commanding officer (2:4). The athlete knows that to "win the prize" he must compete according to the rules (2:5).

356

The hardworking farmer looks forward to sharing in the harvest that his labor produces (2:7). Paul reinforces this call to endure hardship by appealing to the example of Christ and to his own suffering (2:8-13). Paul is bound in prison, but the Word of God is not imprisoned. Paul again quotes a Christian hymn or an established faith statement. It *is a trustworthy statement* (2:11-13). Paul uses this phrase five times in these three Pastoral Epistles. God will remain faithful, and Timothy must remain faithful as well.

Still on the subject of present problems, Paul moves from Timothy's personal life to his public ministry (2:14-26). Timothy has been reminded of the *standard of sound words* that he has received from Paul. Now he is to remind others of these same truths (2:14). In doing so, he must be a skilled craftsman in handling the Word of God (2:15). Some have already strayed from the truth and Timothy is to avoid their error (2:16-19). The Lord Himself is the owner and final arbiter of the believer's workmanship. Timothy must strive to be a vessel, an instrument, that is useful to the Master and prepared for any and every good work (2:20-21). The high calling and accountability of God's servants require that they practice what they preach (2:22-26). Timothy must be firm in opposition to error, patient when attacked, and gentle in how he confronts the false teachers. The goal is to bring them to repentance and to a proper understanding of the truth.

Prospects for the future (3:1-17). Paul now turns his attention from the past (1:3-18) and the present (2:1-26) to the future prospects for the church (3:1-17). He predicts a tragic and widespread apostasy (3:1-7). He lists nineteen sins that will manifest themselves among religious people in the future. The apostasy will be marked by religion without reality. The apostasy may be threatening, but it is not new. Moses himself faced opposition to the truth, and truth triumphed (3:8-9). Timothy witnessed the intense persecution Paul suffered on his first missionary journey and is reminded of how God rescued Paul (3:10-11). All who would live godly can expect the same treatment (3:12-13). But Timothy and the true church have a solid defense against apostasy, the inspired Scriptures (3:10-17). Timothy was nurtured in the sacred writings from infancy (3:15). Now he must rely on those same Scriptures to nurture him in adulthood and to fortify him against apostasy.

Paul's final charge to Timothy (4:1-8). Time is of the essence and Paul moves quickly to his final charge to Timothy (4:1-8) and to his concluding appeal for Timothy to join him in Rome (4:9-22). The essence of his charge to Timothy is to *preach the word* (4:2). It is a solemn charge, and Paul calls as witnesses God and Jesus Christ, who will judge the living and the dead. Timothy is to be ready at all times to proclaim the Word of God. Like a guiding beacon, expounding the Scriptures will keep Timothy on course in a time when multitudes turn away from sound doctrine (4:3-5).

Paul's valedictory address (4:6-8). No greater reinforcement could be found for Paul's charge to Timothy than his own example of unwavering faithfulness (4:6-8). No greater commendation could be given a servant of Christ than what Paul is honestly able to state as his own valedictory. Just as this letter has focused on the past, the present, and the future, so Paul's valedictory incorporates all three. Paul is presently being poured out just as the drink offering of the Old Testament was slowly poured out at the climax of the burnt offering and was a pleasing aroma to God (Numbers 15:1-10). As he reflects on the past he affirms, *I have fought the good fight, I have finished the course, I have kept the faith* (4:7). Looking to the future Paul anticipates receiving the crown of righteousness that the Lord has already prepared for him (4:8). Timothy can surely draw strength from Paul's assurance that the crown awaiting Paul himself awaits all who follow in his footsteps. Of Paul's valedictory, Hiebert says, "In these stirring words he reviews his whole life, present (6), past (7), and future (8). It will ever remain the classic expression concerning the triumphant death of the Christian. Although the Apostle is in very distressing circumstances, there is not a word of fear, complaint, or murmuring, but rather the confident shout of victory" (*An Introduction to the New Testament,* 2:357).

Paul's concluding appeal (4:9-22). Paul's concluding appeal reveals his loneliness and cold discomfort as he awaits execution (4:9-22). Only Luke is with him, and he longs for the companionship of Timothy. He once questioned John Mark's usefulness, but now he asks Timothy to pick him up on his way to Rome. He longs also for the scrolls and parchments that have nurtured his soul for so long. He needs the cloak to protect him against the dampness and cold of the Roman dungeon. Paul's first appearance before a Roman tribunal did not go well and "all deserted me." Paul was not alone, however, as "the Lord stood with me." The Lord has delivered him this time but Paul expects he will be executed soon. There is a compelling urgency in his request, *make every effort to come before winter* (4:21). Paul closes this final and poignant letter with the benediction, *the Lord be with you. Grace be with you.*

358

Outline

I. Introduction	1:1-2
II. Patterns from the Past	1:3-18
A. Remembering Timothy's sincere faith	1:3-7
1. Paul remembers Timothy with thankfulness	1:3-5
2. Paul reminds Timothy of his gift from God	1:6-7
B. Remembering Paul's suffering	1:8-12
1. Invitation to join in Paul's suffering	1:8
2. Explanation of Paul's suffering	1:9-12
C. Remembering Paul's sound teaching	1:13-14
1. Paul has given Timothy a pattern of truth	1:13
2. Now Timothy must guard the truth	1:14
D. Remembering the faithless and the faithful	1:15-18
1. Everyone in Asia has deserted Paul	1:15
2. Onesimus has devoted himself to Paul	1:16-18
III. Problems of the Present	2:1-26
A. Timothy's twofold task outlined	2:1-2
1. Personal: to be strong	2:1
2. Public: to disciple others	2:2
B. Timothy's personal responsibility explained	2:3-13
1. Reflect on the call to endure hardness	2:3-7
2. Remember the Christ who called you	2:8-13
C. Timothy's public ministry explained	2:14-26
1. To preach these things to others	2:14-21
2. To practice these things before others	2:22-26
IV. Prospects for the Future	3:1-17
A. The alert: a great apostasy is coming	3:1-9
B. The antidote: stay grounded in Scripture	3:10-17
1. Remember Paul's teaching and example	3:10-13
2. Remember the Scriptures you were taught	3:14-17
V. Paul's Final Charge to Timothy	4:1-8
A. Authority of the charge: the coming Christ	4:1
B. Statement of the charge: preach the Word	4:2
C. Reason for the charge: coming apostasy	4:3-4
D. Responsibility of the charge: discharge your duty	4:5
E. Pattern for the charge: Paul's own ministry	4:6-8

VI. Concluding Appeal	4:9-22
A. To come quickly	4:9-13
B. To guard against Alexander	4:14-15
C. The Lord's unfailing presence with Paul	4:16-18
D. Personal greetings for faithful friends	4:19-22

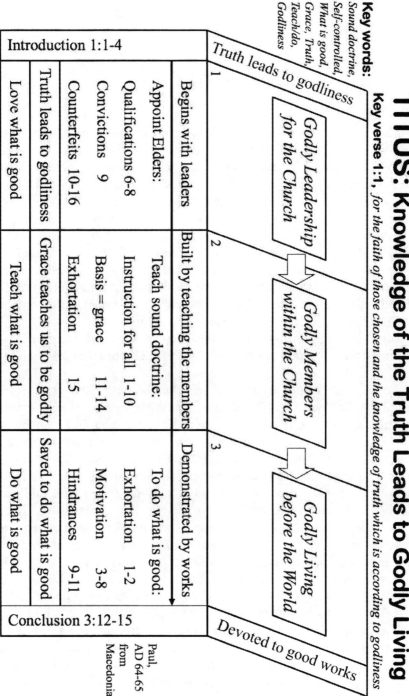

TITUS

Profile of Titus

The man himself. Like Timothy, Titus was a young co-laborer of Paul (1 Corinthians 8:23; Galatians 2:1-3). He was probably a native of Syrian Antioch (Galatians 2:1). His name does not appear in Acts and he is mentioned in only four of Paul's epistles (2 Corinthians, Galatians, 2 Timothy, and Titus). This has led some to conclude that Titus was a brother of Luke and hence not mentioned in the record of Acts. This view was strongly proposed by Eusebius in the early church but is supported by Ramsay and other recent scholars (Hiebert, *Personalities Around Paul*, 114-15). Titus was a Greek and not a proselyte to Judaism. He remained uncircumcised in spite of pressure from Judaizers at Jerusalem (Galatians 2:3-5). In distinction from Timothy, Titus had no Jewish roots and accepting circumcision would have compromised the gospel. He was probably converted under Paul's ministry in the early days of Paul's partnership with Barnabas at Antioch (Acts 11:25-26; Titus 1:4).

Titus progressed rapidly in the faith and showed both gifting and promise for ministry (Galatians 2:1-5). Judging from the assignments Paul gave him in Corinth and in Crete, he was a tactful troubleshooter (2 Corinthians 2:13; 12:18; Titus 1:5). Hiebert describes him in this way: "From the difficult tasks that Paul assigned to him, it is clear that Paul considered Titus a capable and trustworthy co-laborer, possessing a forceful personality. He was capable, energetic, tactful, resourceful, skillful in handling men and affairs, and effective in conciliating people" (*Personalities Around Paul*, 114). While young like Timothy, he was more aggressive and more oriented toward administration. Titus shared Paul's concern to avoid any financial impropriety and was given a large role in the offering being gathered for the church at Jerusalem. Like Paul, he avoided being manipulative or mercenary in the process (2 Corinthians 12:18). Titus was a true partner in Paul's motivation (2 Corinthians 8:16) as well as in his ministry (8:23). "He breathed the spirit of Paul, and in his conduct, manifested the same unmercenary attitude that characterized Paul. Titus has variously been characterized as 'the bridge-builder,' the 'conciliator, and 'a successful trouble-shooter'" (Hiebert, *Personalities Around Paul*, 114).

Travels and ministry of Titus. Titus appears first in Galatians (likely Paul's earliest letter) as one who accompanied Paul on a crucial visit to Jerusalem (Galatians 2:1-5). As noted in the introduction to Galatians, scholars differ on whether this was the "famine visit" of Acts 11 or the "Jerusalem Council visit" of Acts 15. Titus formed a test case for the salvation of the Gentiles by faith apart from the rite of circumcision (Galatians 2:1-5). He appears again approximately eight years later at Ephesus during Paul's third mission to the Gentiles (Acts 19:10; 20:31; 2 Corinthians 8:23). He served as Paul's representative on several trips to Corinth. Titus was charged with the vital but delicate task of arranging the collection for the saints at Jerusalem from a church with a stormy relationship with its founder, Paul (2 Corinthians 9:2; 12:13). One of Titus's trips to Corinth was especially sensitive and Paul was disturbed by the absence of Titus at their prearranged rendezvous in Troas (2 Corinthians 2:12-13).

Titus reunited with Paul in Macedonia with a positive report of change at Corinth (2 Corinthians 7:6-14). He loved the troubled believers at Corinth and shared Paul's joy at the progress they had made (2 Corinthians 7:13-15). The absence of Titus from Corinth during Paul's winter there (1 Corinthians 16:5-7) is suggested by the fact that he is not named with Timothy and others in Paul's letter to the Romans which was written from Corinth. Nor is Titus mentioned in the list of those who accompanied Paul when the offering was delivered to Jerusalem (Acts 20:4; 2 Corinthians 8:19-21). He resurfaces in the New Testament record five years later as the recipient of this letter bearing his name. During the interim he has been engaged in ministry along with Paul at Crete. He remained behind to complete the organization and establishment of the young church (Titus 1:5).

Titus was an apostolic representative with delegated but full authority to appoint elders and administer discipline (Titus 1:5; 2:15; 3:9-11). Paul planned to send a replacement for Titus and hoped to spend the winter with him in Nicopolis (3:12). The last reference to Titus is found in Paul's second letter to Timothy that was written on the eve of his martyrdom in Rome (2 Timothy 4:10). One should not infer that Titus was in the same class as Demas who "forsook Paul." Titus was likely about the business of the gospel in Dalmatia (modern Yugoslavia) as Paul's personal and trusted representative. No doubt Titus ended his ministry as he began, as a devoted co-laborer with Paul.

Purpose and Distinctives of Titus

Purpose. The primary reason for Paul writing to this epistle was to give Titus the necessary authorization and instructions he needed to complete the organization of the church at Crete (1:5). Though a church had been planted in this pagan center, it remained "a work in progress." Another reason for the letter was to summon Titus to join Paul for the winter at Nicopolis (3:12). The opportunity was provided by the planned visit of Zenas and Apollos (3:13).

Distinctive features. The epistle to Titus provides an excellent case study of how the gospel impacts a pagan society. The conditions in Crete were among the most difficult to be encountered by the gospel (1:10-16). Yet the calling and expectation set for the church were the most demanding (2:11-14; 3:4-8). This epistle provides an excellent overview of the church's ministry. Godliness in leadership (1:5-16) is linked with the development of godly members through teaching (2:1-15) and culminates in effective witness to a pagan world through godly living (3:1-14). The teaching ministry of the church by age, gender, and social grouping is clearly presented in the second chapter and provides a model for Christian education in the local church. The marks of godliness for the church in society stand out in this epistle (2:11-14). Christians are to be "do-gooders" in the best sense (1:16; 2:14; 3:8, 14). Though the reference to church discipline is brief, it makes a significant contribution to our knowledge of discipline in the early church (3:10).

Key Verse, 1:1

Paul, a bond-servant of God and an apostle of Jesus Christ, for the faith of those chosen of God and the knowledge of the truth which is according to godliness

---

Message of Titus

Paul's commission for Titus (1:1-4). Paul's statement of his apostolic calling embodies the theme of the letter to Titus, *for the faith of those chosen of God and the knowledge of the truth which is according to godliness*. That truth has as its source in God who eternally embodies truth and it has been made evident now in Jesus. Paul has been entrusted with the proclamation of that truth and is commissioning Titus to carry on that work. Titus is Paul's "true child in a common faith." Truth that leads to godliness is the essence of Paul's lifelong ministry and the urgent need of the young churches in Crete.

Knowledge of the truth issues in godly living and must begin with elders (chapter1), must characterize all believers (chapter 2), and must be evident to a pagan world (chapter 3). Following the opening salutation, Paul launches immediately into his purpose for writing this letter to Titus. *That you set in order what remains and appoint elders in every city, as I directed you* (1:5). The young church planted at Crete represented an "unfinished project." They have been saved out of a pagan society and are called on to know the truth and to live godly lives as a witness to their former world.

Appointing godly leadership for the church (1:5 -16). Building a godly church begins with leadership. Churches were springing up in cities across the island of Crete. These new congregations would not progress to maturity without godly leadership. Paul outlines three important issues regarding church leaders: their qualifications (1:6-8), their convictions (1:9), and the threat of counterfeits (1:10-16). The qualifications for elders are high because they are entrusted with God's work (1:6-8). As Paul directed Timothy, elders are to be above reproach, be good family men, hospitable, and must manage their own lives well. Above all, they must hold firm to the established doctrine and be capable of teaching it and also of refuting those who deny it (1:9). Their character and their conviction matter because both of these are lacking in the counterfeit leaders who oppose sound doctrine (1:10-16). The contrast between elders and those false teachers who oppose them is striking. Elders *love what is good* (1:8), while their Judaizing opponents are *worthless for any good deed* (1:16). As the leadership goes, so goes the congregation! Paul now moves to the needs of the congregations and Titus's teaching ministry among them.

Teaching truth to equip godly members within the church (2:1-15). Titus is also to teach that truth to the members of the various congregations. This task may later fall to the elders he is to appoint but for now it is his responsibility (2:1, 15). Godly leaders are charged with the task of developing a godly membership within the church (2:1-15). This they do by teaching sound doctrine to the various age, gender, and social groups in the church. Each group has unique needs and is to be taught accordingly. The system of sound doctrine that Titus himself has embraced also meets the needs of every age and situation, from old men and women to young wives and single men. Paul's instructions to Titus are a wise model for all pastors to follow. They must leave the teaching of young women to the older women and be careful to lead the young men, their peers, by personal example. Slaves have unique challenges and temptations, but they have the high calling to *adorn the doctrine of God our Savior in every respect* (2:10).

The teaching ministry of the church finds its ultimate source and its prime example in the grace of God (2:11). That grace has been personified in the redemptive work of Jesus Christ. Grace not only saves the sinner; it also teaches believers to say no to the appetites of the flesh and to say yes to the claims of Christ (2:12). It focuses on *the blessed hope and the appearing of the glory of our great God and Savior, Christ Jesus*. Sound doctrine and godly living flow from the wellspring of Christ's redemptive work. Jesus gave Himself for the express purpose of redeeming us from evil and creating us as His very own representatives eager to do what is right and good (2:14). Paul's mandate to Titus is to *speak and exhort and rebuke with all authority* (2:15).

Truth is evidenced by godly living before a pagan world (3:1-11). The mandate Paul gave Titus (2:15) is both a summation of chapter 2 and an introduction to chapter 3. Godly leaders (1:5-16) faithfully teaching the Word of God will produce a godly membership (2:1-15). This "finishing process" in the church culminates in believers who live godly lives before a pagan world (3:1-11). High standards are set for the conduct of believers (3:1-2) just as for the leadership of the church (1:6-9). Such godliness is in stark contrast with the depravity that marked their former lives (3:3). The saving grace of Jesus Christ transforms sinners into saints (3:4-7). Spiritual regeneration is the work of the Holy Spirit who has been lavishly poured out on us. This is all of grace and results in believers who are *careful to engage in good deeds*. Real truth produces real godliness that is beneficial to believer and unbeliever alike (3:8). All that hinders the church from growing in godliness, whether ideas or individuals must be avoided (3:9-11). The false teachers Paul warned Titus about are unprofitable and worthless. Titus is to warn them, and after a second warning he is to dismiss them as self-condemned.

Concluding requests and greetings (3:12-15). The conclusion of Paul's letter to Titus is practical and personal. Paul intends to send a replacement, thus enabling Titus to join him for the winter months in Nicopolis (3:12). In the meantime Paul requests that Titus do all in his power to aid Zenas and Apollos on their journey through Crete (3:13). Titus 1:1 and 3:14 form an inclusio. The gospel of Jesus Christ is truth and leads to godliness (1:1). Believers have been saved for the purpose of good works (2:14; 3:8) and Paul returns to that vital theme with his final exhortation. *Our people must* *also learn to engage in good deeds to meet pressing needs, so that they will not be unfruitful* (3:14).

Outline

I.	Introduction	1:1-4
	A. The author Paul and his commission	1:1-3
	B. The addressee and his common faith	1:4
II.	Appointing Godly Leadership for the Church	1:5-16
	A. Paul's commission for Titus to appoint elders	1:5
	B. The qualifications for elders	1:6-8
	1. Private qualifications in the home	1:6
	2. Public qualifications before others	1:7
	3. Personal qualifications of the inner life	1:8
	C. The convictions of elders	1:9
	D. The counterfeit of false teachers	1:10-16
	1. Characteristics of false teachers	1:10
	2. Conduct of false teachers	1:11-12
	3. Correction of false teachers	1:13-14
	4. Condemnation of false teachers	1:15-16
III.	Teaching Truth to Equip Godly Members in the Church	2:1-15
	A. Foundation: teaching sound doctrine	2:1
	B. Implementation: teaching by age and social groups	2:2-10
	1. Teaching older men to be sound in the faith	2:2
	2. Teaching older women to behave reverently	2:3
	3. Enlisting them to teach younger women	2:4-5
	4. Teaching young men	2:6
	5. Teaching by personal example	2:7-8
	6. Teaching slaves to exemplify the truth	2:9-10
	C. Motivation: grace, the master teacher	2:11-14
	1. Grace that saves	2:11
	2. Grace that teaches leaving and cleaving	2:12
	3. Grace that focuses on the return of Christ	2:13
	4. Grace that leads to doing good	2:14
	D. Exhortation: teach with authority	2:15
IV.	Truth Is Evidenced by Godly Living before the World	3:1-11
	A. Exhortation to godly living	3:1-2
	B. Motivation for godly living	3:3-8
	1. What we were before Christ	3:3

367

2.	What Christ did to transform us	3:4-6
3.	What we have become because of His grace	3:7
4.	What we ought to do because of His grace	3:8
C.	Confronting those who hinder godly living	3:9-11
1.	Avoid foolish controversies	3:9
2.	Warn quarrelsome people	3:10-11

V.	Conclusion	3:12-15
A.	Request for Titus to rejoin Paul	3:12
B.	Request for Titus to assist Paul's messengers	3:13
C.	Repeating Paul's purpose for writing	3:14
D.	Personal greetings	3:15

PHILEMON: Appeal to Forgive a Slave Who Became a Brother

Key verses: 9-10, *I appeal to you for my child Onesimus, whom I have begotten in my imprisonment,*

Key words:
Brother, slave,
Useless-useful,
Owes-repay,
Love, heart,
Prisoner,
Appeal

	Salutation (1)	Basis of the Appeal (4)	Object of the Appeal (8)	Source of the Appeal (17)	Conclusion (22, 25)
	A personal letter from prison to a beloved brother	*Philemon's* Love	*Onesimus's* Salvation — Service (12)	*Paul's* Love	Greetings from fellow prisoner, fellow workers
		Praise for Philemon	*Plea for Onesimus*	*Promise of Paul*	Paul, A.D. 62 from Rome
		Your faith	Was useless : Now useful	I will repay it	
		Your love	No longer a slave : Now a dear brother	I am confident	
		Your work	My chains : Your choice	I know you will…	
			If he owes : I will repay		
			You owe : Refresh my heart		
			I appeal : Your obedience		

PHILEMON

"Nowhere is the social influence of the Gospel more strikingly exerted; nowhere does the nobility of the Apostle's character receive a more vivid illustration than in this accidental pleading on behalf of a runaway slave" (Lightfoot, *Saint Paul's Epistles to the Colossians and to Philemon,* 303).

Authenticity and Authorship

External evidence. The Pauline authorship and authenticity of this book is strongly and consistently supported by early church fathers including Ignatius, Eusebius, Jerome, and Augustine. The book of Philemon is named as authentic in all of the early canons, most notably the Marcion and the Muratorian. "The letter's canonicity is beyond question" (Carson, Moo, and Morris, *An Introduction to the New Testament,* 389). The only early challenge to its authenticity was in the fourth century. Philemon was successfully defended against the charge that "it was unworthy of Paul because it contained no doctrinal teaching" (Hiebert, *An Introduction to the New Testament,* 2:242). A recent attack on the Pauline authenticity of the book has rejected it because the book of Philemon gives support for the authenticity of Colossians. That is merely guilt by association. "None but the most extreme negative critics have disputed the Pauline authorship of the epistle" (Guthrie, *New Testament Introduction,* 664).

Internal evidence. A wealth of Pauline material is in this epistle, both in the words used and in the style of writing. Eight Greek words occur nowhere else in Paul's epistles, and five of them are unique in the New Testament. The number of words unique to this epistle is in keeping with Paul's other letters. The personalities and biographical references point very strongly to Paul. He is aged and now also a prisoner of Christ Jesus (Philemon 9). "We may safely conclude that in this brief epistle we are listening to the authentic tones of Paul's own pleading" (Guthrie, *New Testament Introduction,* 664).

Occasion and Date

Conversion of Onesimus. Onesimus, a slave owned by Philemon, has wronged his master and fled. Onesimus has providentially come into contact with Paul who is in prison in Rome. Christ has changed Onesimus,

370

thereby making him useful to Philemon (vv. 15-16). The former slave of Philemon has endeared himself to the apostle Paul, and he rendered valuable service to the apostle Paul (vv. 12-13). Paul would benefit greatly from the continued ministry of Onesimus, but he recognizes the need for Onesimus to be reconciled with Philemon (v. 14). Under Roman law, Onesimus possessed no rights and was entirely at the mercy of his master, Philemon (Lightfoot, *Saint Paul's Epistles to the Colossians and to Philemon,* 321). In addition to the restoration of Onesimus, Paul establishes a model for the church in dealing with slaves. The fact that Paul addressed this issue in his epistles testifies to the prevalence of slavery in the early church (Ephesians 6:5-9; Colossians 3:22-4:1).

Visit of Tychicus to Colossae. Alerted by a report from Epaphras, Paul felt compelled to address the problem of false teachers at Colossae (Colossians 1:3-8). Tychicus was commissioned to carry Paul's letter to the Colossians and to represent Paul in dealing with the false teachers (4:7-8). Onesimus was commissioned, along with Tychicus, to represent Paul and to carry the letter to the Colossians (4:9). This represents a strong endorsement of Onesimus, but also reflects a practical necessity. A runaway slave would have a price on his head and be at grave risk of arrest and mistreatment. Placed under the care of Tychicus, Onesimus enjoyed much needed protection.

Paul's planned visit. Paul is currently a prisoner in Rome, but anticipates being released. Philemon is asked to prepare a guestroom because Paul hopes to visit Colossae on his release from prison (22).

Date and place of writing. Paul is writing from prison and the traditional and prevailing view is that this was Paul's first imprisonment in Rome (Hiebert, *An Introduction to the New Testament,* 2:244). The letter to Philemon was probably written in A.D. 62. "Its close connection with Colossians makes it virtually certain that the two epistles belong to the same period" (Guthrie, *New Testament Introduction,* 664). Philemon together with Colossians, Ephesians, and Philippians constitute the group known as "the prison epistles." Colossians, Ephesians and Philemon were most likely written near the same time and were sent with the same messengers (Colossians 4:7-9). Philippians was probably the last of the group to be written and may have been sent separately.

Distinctive Features

Christian grace. Though the briefest of all New Testament books, Philemon has a special grace and beauty. "As an expression of simple dignity, of refined courtesy, of large sympathy, and of warm personal affection, the Epistle to Philemon stands unrivaled" (Lightfoot, *Saint Paul's Epistles to the Colossians and to Philemon,* 319).

Personal correspondence. The New Testament raised the existing Greek custom of letter writing to an art form. Of the many letters contained in the New Testament, none is as personal and intimate as this letter to Philemon. Paul undoubtedly wrote many personal letters, but this is the only one preserved in the New Testament. Even the Pastoral Epistles are instructional in nature and written for the larger edification of the church.

Absence of doctrine. There is no doctrinal issue or problem addressed in the epistle. However, there is a rich foundation of truth implied by Paul's appeal. Salvation in Christ has transformed Onesimus from an unprofitable slave to a profitable brother. The request that Philemon charge the debt of Onesimus to Paul's account illustrates the doctrine of imputation. As our sin was charged to Christ when He died on the cross, so the righteousness of Christ is imputed to us when we believe, that is, "credited to our account."

Personalities around Paul. No fewer than eleven persons are mentioned in this short epistle. Most significantly, several of them apparently come from one household. Based on the proximity of names in the opening salutation, Apphia is likely the wife of Philemon and Archippus is their son (v. 2). The list of Paul's *fellow workers* includes Mark, Aristarchus, Demas, and Luke (v. 24). (Hiebert, *Personalities Around Paul,* 178-95).

Approach to slavery. This is the most substantial and enduring distinctive of the letter to Philemon. Paul does not launch a frontal attack on the matter of slavery, yet he effectively deals it a deathblow. Lightfoot has a helpful, extended treatment of this issue (*Saint Paul's Epistles to the Colossians and to Philemon,* 319-29). Hiebert notes that this letter has been "confidently appealed to both by those who sanctioned slavery as well as those who advocated its abolition" (*An Introduction to the New Testament,* 2:248). Slavery was part of the fabric of Roman life and a serious, but delicate issue for the New Testament church. Guthrie summarizes the contribution of Philemon to this social problem very well.

"This epistle brings into vivid focus the whole problem of slavery in the Christian church. There is no thought of denunciation even in principle. The apostle deals with the situation as it then exists. He takes it for granted that Philemon has a claim of ownership on Onesimus and leaves the position unchallenged. Yet in one significant phrase Paul transforms the character of the master-slave relationship. Onesimus is returning no longer as a slave but as a dear brother (16). It is clearly incongruous for a Christian master to 'own' a brother in Christ in the contemporary sense of the word, and although the existing order of society could not be immediately changed by Christianity without a political revolution (which was contrary to Christian principles), the Christian master-slave relationship was so transformed from within that it was bound to lead ultimately to the abolition of the system" (*New Testament Introduction*, 665-66).

Principal Characters

Philemon. Philemon was first and foremost a gracious Christian gentleman (3-7). He was likely a prominent and well-to-do businessman. This can be inferred from the fact that his home was large enough to accommodate meetings of the local church (2). Philemon was a slave owner. Though the number is not known, it is probable that he had numerous other slaves in addition to Onesimus. One may infer that the church saw nothing wrong in their culture with a believer owning slaves. The congregation at Colossae contained both slaves and masters (Colossians 3:22-4:1). Philemon was characterized by an outgoing love and generosity (Philemon 5, 7). It is likely that he was a mature individual and the father of Archippus. Paul had never visited Colossae, but he indicates that Philemon owes his conversion to Paul's ministry (v. 19). Probably Philemon came to faith in Christ through the ministry of Paul on one of Philemon's business trips to the city of Ephesus (Acts 19:9-10).

A warm friendship existed between Paul and Philemon (Philemon 7, 17, and 21). Philemon was an active leader in the church whether by position or simply by the service he rendered. The designation *fellow worker* may be interpreted as one who serves as pastor, but also it could suggest some other less official capacity. Philemon had a reputation of going beyond what was required and ordinary in loving service for Christ (v. 21). He exemplified Paul's exhortation to wholehearted service in the Colossian letter (3:17, 22-4:1). He was capable of forgiving and loving a renegade slave who was now a repentant brother in Christ. This too exemplified Paul's exhortation to forgiveness (Colossians 3:12-14). The response of

Philemon to this letter is not known. But the fact that Paul was so confident of the outcome and also the inclusion of the letter in the New Testament argue for a positive reaction on the part of Philemon (Hiebert, *Personalities Around Paul,* 190-95).

Onesimus. The name Onesimus means "profitable." Slaves were often given functional names and Onesimus was expected to be useful to his master. This is a significant play on words because Onesimus formerly proved to be *useless* but now has become *useful* (v. 11). By whatever means or cause, Onesimus was a slave owned by Philemon. It is possible that he was purchased as a captive in war, but more likely he was a second-generation slave born in bondage. In his letter to the Colossians Paul describes Onesimus as "one of you" (4:9). This would indicate that either by birth or by ownership Onesimus was a native of Colossae. Onesimus bore the added burden of being a Phrygian slave. Phrygian slaves were considered of the lowest order and noted for "rascality." "Onesimus represented the least respectable of the least respectable class in the social scale. He was regarded by philosophers as a 'live chattel,' a 'live implement'" (Lightfoot, *Saint Paul's Epistles to the Colossians and to Philemon,* 311).

Onesimus had wronged Philemon by theft of property or by some other means and had fled to Rome to escape the consequences of his actions (v. 18). The size and distance of Rome made detection less likely. "Rome was the natural cesspool for these offscourings of humanity" (Lightfoot, *Saint Paul's Epistles to the Colossians and to Philemon,* 312). The providence of God intervened and Onesimus was drawn into life- changing contact with the apostle Paul (v. 10). While technically still a slave, Onesimus is now both a child of God and a *child* of Paul by faith (vv. 10-11). The fact that Onesimus was free to return to Philemon indicates that he was not a prisoner and had not been identified as a runaway slave by Roman authorities.

Onesimus was transformed from a useless slave into a useful son and servant of God. The heart of Paul had wrapped itself around Onesimus. In sending him back Paul was sending *my very heart* (v. 12). Onesimus appears to have been very willing to seek reconciliation and to attempt to make restitution to Philemon, the master he had wronged. "Onesimus had received the forgiveness of his heavenly Master, but he still needed to be forgiven and restored by his earthly master" (Hiebert, *Personalities Around Paul*, 181). Runaway slaves were subject to arrest and even death.

Onesimus faced grave danger in trying to return to his master. Paul seized the opportunity to send Onesimus along with Tychicus on his mission to the church at Colossae. The safety of Onesimus was assured and his status elevated by Paul's linking him with Tychicus. *They will inform you about the whole situation here* (Colossians 4:9b). Accompanied with this letter, Onesimus returned to Philemon to accept the consequences of his action. Paul took on himself the responsibility for and the cost of restitution (Philemon 17-19). This was at once a genuine offer by Paul and also an act of great tact. "Paul was a master of sanctified psychology" (Hiebert, *Personalities Around Paul*, 182). Ignatius (A.D. 110) made an intriguing reference to one Onesimus as the bishop of the Ephesian church. According to Guthrie, "There seems to be no positive reason for rejecting the theory that Onesimus the slave later became bishop of the Ephesian church, but mere similarity of name cannot of itself confirm the identity" (*New Testament Introduction*, 665). The trio of Paul, Philemon, and Onesimus is as unique as it is intimate.

"An ex-Jewish rabbi, to whom all Gentiles were untouchables; a wealthy Gentile patrician, to whom an itinerant Jewish preacher in a Roman prison would normally be an object of contempt, and to whom a runaway thieving slave was a dangerous animal to be beaten or put to death; a ruthless slave without hope of human sympathy, or even human justice— in all conscience, humanly speaking, an impossible trio, yet all three are caught up through their common allegiance to Christ into an entirely new relationship, where each acknowledges the other as one of God's adopted sons, and a brother for whom Christ died" (Neil, *Harper's Bible Commentary*, 504).

Message of Philemon

Paul's letter of appeal to Philemon is compelling and yet casual in its structure. In his opening Paul identifies himself as *a prisoner of Christ Jesus* and Philemon as *our beloved brother and fellow worker* (v. 1). Apphia is likely the wife of Philemon and Archippus their son. The church at Colossae meets in their home (v. 2).

The gratitude that Paul expresses for Philemon in his opening thanksgiving (vv. 4-7) highlights the positive Christian character of Philemon. Philemon's love has brought joy to Paul and has refreshed the saints (v. 7). Based on that example of love and service Paul has confidence that the appeal he is about to make will be positively received (vv. 8-9a). Paul makes his appeal on the basis of Christian duty and love (vv. 8-9). The fact that Paul is now *the aged* and a prisoner makes his appeal all the more compelling. But the principal basis of the appeal is the spiritual transformation of Onesimus. Onesimus is no longer a useless slave, he is now Paul's child in the faith and a proven servant of God in Paul's ministry. The central thrust of this brief letter is Paul's request that Philemon forgive Onesimus and restore him to good standing as a brother in Christ not as the useless slave he was before (vv. 10-11). The rationale Paul gives for returning Onesimus with this letter is that he does not want to enjoy the benefit of Onesimus's service without the wholehearted consent of Philemon (vv. 12-14). Paul wished to keep Onesimus with him while he is in prison, but he is determined to do what is right. He is sending Onesimus back with his *very heart*, confident that Philemon will do what is right just as Paul has done. Philemon should now receive Onesimus back as a beloved brother in the flesh and in the Lord not as a slave (vv. 15-16).

Onesimus has filled a room in Paul's heart so Paul requests that Philemon would make room in his heart for this runaway slave (vv. 17-20). Aware that Onesimus owes Philemon a debt, Paul assumes that debt and requests that it be charged to his own account (v. 18). The appeal is made even more compelling by the fact that Paul is writing this letter with his very own hand and asks Philemon to refresh his heart by an affirmative response (vv. 19-20). As an added incentive he reminds Philemon that he owes his salvation to Paul's ministry. He is not presuming the outcome but is confident that Philemon will live up to his reputation of going beyond what is necessary (v. 21). He expects Philemon to fulfill the high expectation he holds. Paul adds additional weight to this appeal by saying he intends to visit and asks that Philemon prepare a guestroom for him. If the letter and the appeal are not compelling enough, the prospect of explaining his actions personally to Paul would surely influence Philemon to do what Paul considers right regarding Onesimus. The request that he prepare lodging for Paul leaves Philemon no room to ignore Paul's appeal (v. 22).

Outline

I.	Introduction	1-7
	A. Salutation	1-3
	1. Author	1a
	2. Addressee	1b-2
	3. Greeting	3
	B. Thanksgiving and prayer	4-7
	1. Thanksgiving for Philemon	4-5
	2. Prayer for Philemon	6
	3. Gratitude for Philemon	7
II.	The Appeal to Philemon	8-22
	A. The basis of the appeal	8-11
	1. Christian duty	8
	2. Christian love	9a
	3. Paul, the aged prisoner	9b
	4. Onesimus is a son of God and of Paul	10
	5. Onesimus is now a useful servant	11
	B. The rationale: Onesimus filled a room in Paul's heart	12-16
	1. Onesimus sent back with Paul's heart	12-13
	2. Paul's desire to do what is right	14
	3. Onesimus now a brother, not a slave	15-16
	C. The request: make room for Onesimus in your heart	17-22
	1. Welcome Onesimus on Paul's account	17
	2. Charge Onesimus's debts to Paul's account	18-19
	3. Refresh Paul's heart	20
	4. Fulfill Paul's high expectations	21
	5. Make room for Paul in your home	22
III.	Conclusion	23-25

HEBREWS: Hold Firmly to Faith in Jesus, the Great High Priest

Key verse- 4:14, *Therefore, since we have a great high priest.... Jesus the Son of God, let us hold fast our confession.*

Key Words:
Son, High Priest,
Better, Perfect,
Let us go on,
Once for all,
Faith, hope,
Heavenly

Introduction- statement of theme	1:1-3

In His Person — 1:4

Exposition

Danger!
- To Angels 1:4 - 2:18
- *Drifting* 2:1-4
- To Moses 3:1-6
- *Disobedience* 3:7-4:13

Warnings
- Personal qualifications 4:14-5:10 — 4:14
- *Declension* 5:11-6:20
- Perfect priesthood 7:1-28
- Better covenant 8:1-13
- Better sanctuary 9:1-10
- Better sacrifice 9:11- 10:18

In His Priesthood

Superiority of Jesus as God's Son, Great High Priest

Exhortation

Danger!
- Application: Enjoy fellowship 10:19-25 — 10:19
- *Defection* 10:26-31
- Endure affliction 10:32-39
- Live by faith 11:1-12:14
- *Despising* 12:15-29
- Live godly 13:1-19

In the Lives of His Saints

Conclusion- benediction	13:20-25

AD 64
To second generation Jewish Christians facing increased persecution and tempted to return to Judaism

379

HEBREWS

Therefore, since we have a great high priest who has passed through the heavens, Jesus the Son of God, let us hold fast our confession. (Hebrews 4:14).

The epistle to the Hebrews stands alone in the New Testament in both its message and its purpose. It offers a ringing endorsement of Christ as superior to all elements of the old order (written revelation, angels, Moses, Aaron, and the entire Levitical system of sacrifices, and earthly tabernacle). It is a rousing call for believers enamored with the old order to embrace the superiority of Christ and go on to maturity in their faith. It signals the fulfillment of what the Old Testament promised. Hebrews unites the old and the new. It calls believers to a triumphant faith in this life and to a rewarding hope in the next.

Hebrews is as abounding in introductory and interpretive problems as it is rich in content. Debate as to the authorship, readers, and place of writing continues unresolved. Notwithstanding these difficulties, Hebrews remains an unquestioned classic among the books of the New Testament. "It is unexcelled in its literary excellence and makes a unique theological contribution to the New Testament revelation. No other book of the New Testament breathes more deeply the Spirit of God nor more clearly authenticates its own inspiration than Hebrews, yet no other book leaves us with so many puzzling and enigmatical problems as does this book. Nearly all of the usual points of introduction have been the occasion of much controversy. And most of these matters are still keenly debated and the majority of them seem quite incapable of a decisive solution" (Hiebert, *An Introduction to the New Testament*, 3:68).

Authenticity

The inspiration and the canonicity of Hebrews were not seriously questioned in the early church in spite of uncertainty regarding its authorship. The content of the epistle bore such clear evidence of inspiration that it was accepted in both the Eastern and Western branches of the church. Pauline influence was recognized in the content, but opinions differed as to the matter of Pauline authorship. That is not surprising. Neither internal nor external evidence is definitive. Rather, both are suggestive of Pauline influence, but doubtful of Pauline authorship. Guthrie concludes, "There was no firm tradition on this matter in the earliest period" (*New Testament Introduction*, 668).

Support for the canonicity of the epistle comes from numerous sources. (1) Close parallels between Hebrews and the epistle written by Clement of Rome around AD 95 indicate that Clement accepted and used Hebrews. (2) Justin the Martyr (100-165) seemed to draw ideas from the epistle. (3) Clement of Alexandria (155-215) quotes directly from Hebrews in a way that shows he accepted its apostolic authority. (4) Origen (185-253) discussed both the epistle itself and the question of authorship. He recognized the Pauline influence, but expressed uncertainty about the authorship. His conclusion has been often quoted, "But who actually wrote the Epistle God only knows certainly" (Guthrie, *New Testament Introduction*, 669). (5) The Chester Beatty papyrus of the mid-third century places Hebrews among the Pauline Epistles. This association with Paul continued in the Eastern Church from that time on. (6) In the west, Tertullian (150-212) attributed it to Barnabas, but did not seem to place it on the same level as the epistles written directly by Paul. (7) Jerome (340-420) and Augustine (354-430) endorsed both the canonicity and the Pauline authorship. Augustine later revised his view, but both the authenticity and the Pauline influence became firmly established in the tradition of the church (Hiebert, *An Introduction to the New Testament*, 3:70-71).

Recent Acceptance

The Reformation revived and intensified the debate about the authorship of Hebrews. Luther raised some doubt about its canonicity. But Luther's reluctance to accept the canonicity of Hebrews may have been the result of his strong anti-Semitism. Luther placed the epistle toward the end of the Bible and attributed it to Apollos. Calvin endorsed Hebrews as canonical, but questioned the traditional view of Pauline authorship. Today, Paul, Barnabas, Apollos, Luke, and several others all have their advocates as authors of Hebrews. "The question of the authorship of Hebrews presents one of several apparently insoluble problems in connection with this epistle. The ancient Church was not united in its answer to the question and the modern Church presents even a greater diversity of answers" (Hiebert, *An Introduction to the New Testament*, 3:71).

Authorship

Support for Pauline authorship. Support for Pauline authorship is substantial but indirect. Timothy was the constant companion of Paul and the author's reference to Timothy's release from prison (13:23) suggests Paul is the author. The conclusion of the epistle (13:22-25) is characteristic of Paul's letters. Even those who attribute the letter to another author, suggest that Paul may well have written the last chapter himself. The author's reference to "compassion in my bonds" (10:34) points to Paul's imprisonment in Caesarea. (Westcott, *The Epistle to the Hebrews*, 334-35). J. Dwight Pentecost lists thirty-two similarities between Hebrews and Paul's epistles (*Faith That Endures*, 13-20). Some interpret Peter's reference to a letter written by Paul (2 Peter 3:13-16) as a reference to the book of Hebrews. Hebrews certainly does contain "many things hard to be understood." It is significant that the early church accepted Hebrews as Pauline in spite of its anonymity. It is argued that Paul was viewed as a traitor by the leaders of Judaism and thus would appropriately exclude his characteristic opening and other self-identification. The King James Version titles the book "The Epistle of Paul the Apostle to the Hebrews." But this designation rests on late manuscripts and is not supported by older manuscripts though it does bear some weight.

Objections to Pauline authorship. Several objections are raised against Pauline authorship. Its anonymity would not conform to Paul's style. "Nowhere in the epistle does the author lay claim to any apostolic authority, which would certainly be strange for Paul" (Guthrie, *New Testament Introduction*, 672). Difference of style is apparent and argues against Pauline authorship. The letter includes no reference to Paul's crisis on the road to Damascus or his other apostolic experiences. Several theological differences between Hebrews and the epistles of Paul may be noted, in spite of many similarities. These differences are not disagreements, but are substantial. The most telling objection is the indication that the author is a second-generation believer in Christ. In Hebrews 2:3 the author says he received his instruction directly from those who had heard the Lord, whereas Paul claims he received it by direct revelation from Christ (Galatians 1:11-12). Guthrie represents most current scholars when he concludes, "There seems little doubt from these considerations and from the uncertainty of early Christian attestation that Paul was not the author of this epistle" (*New Testament Introduction*, 674).

Conclusion. Guthrie, Bruce, and Hiebert join a majority of contemporary scholars in rejecting the Pauline authorship of Hebrews. Hiebert adds the author's extensive use of the Septuagint, the use of singular rather than compound titles for the Lord Jesus Christ, and the stylistic differences between Paul and Hebrews as further evidence against Pauline authorship (Hiebert, *An Introduction to the New Testament*, 3:76-78). Bruce is emphatic in challenging Pauline authorship. "What Paul and the author of Hebrews have in common is the basic apostolic teaching: but when we come to distinctive features we may say with certainty that the thought of the epistle is not Paul's, the language is not Paul's, and the technique of the Old Testament quotation is not Paul's. In brief, 'I can adduce no reason to show that Paul was its author.' So Calvin wisely sums up" (Bruce, *The Epistle to the Hebrews*, 19-20).

Support for Barnabas as author. Early church tradition placed Barnabas next to Paul as the probable author. Tertullian (150-212) reflected the thinking of his contemporaries in suggesting Barnabas as the author. Barnabas had a close association with Paul and Timothy. Paul and Barnabas had settled their earlier difference of opinion regarding John Mark, and Barnabas certainly absorbed the theological framework of Paul. Barnabas was a cultured Jew, a skillful communicator, and a thorough-going convert from Judaism to Christianity. A Levite from Cyprus, Barnabas was well suited to discuss the Levitical priesthood and to appreciate the superiority of the priesthood of Christ. Barnabas was given the name "son of consolation" (Acts 4:36; 11:22-25) and the author of Hebrews describes his work as "a word of consolation" (13:22).

Objections to authorship by Barnabus. The rise of the Pauline tradition would be difficult to explain if the readers of Hebrews and others in the early church perceived it to be a letter by Barnabas. However, in fairness, the same objection would pertain to all other associates of Paul with the possible exception of Luke acting as a translator. Barnabas enjoyed a more direct and close association with apostolic authority than that suggested in Hebrews 2:3. The elegance of language would suggest that the author was a Hellenistic Jew. This literary quality was not as common in Cyprus and Jerusalem where Barnabas had his roots, but there is nothing to prohibit Barnabas from possessing such a good command of the Greek language.

Conclusion. The evidence pointing to Barnabas is not strong, but neither are the objections against his being the author. The closeness of Barnabas to Paul and the early tradition of the church make Barnabas a likely candidate (if one rejects Pauline authorship).

Support for Luke as author or translator. Clement of Alexandria proposed that Paul wrote the original manuscript in Hebrew and Luke translated it into Greek. While Origen doubted that Hebrews was a translation, he did favor it being written by Luke or by Clement of Rome (Bruce, *The Epistle to the Hebrews*, 17). There are strong affinities of language and style between Hebrews and Luke's writing in Acts and Luke. Luke certainly knew the mind and heart of Paul and was capable of expressing Paul's thoughts.

Objections to Luke as author. Hebrews shows no traces of being a translation. In fact, the extensive use of the Septuagint makes it unlikely that the original was in the Hebrew language. The alliteration is not translatable. Luke was a Gentile but the author of Hebrews evidently was a Jew.

Conclusion. Aside from the suggestion by Clement of Alexandria, there is scant evidence to support authorship by Luke. Luke could be the author only if the epistle was no more than a translation from a Hebrew original by Paul, and that seems unlikely.

Support for Apollos as author. Apollos was thoroughly Jewish and closely associated with Paul and his ministry (1 Corinthians 16:12; Titus 3:13). He was noted for his eloquence (Acts 18:24) and possessed the kind of linguistic skill demonstrated by the author of Hebrews. Apollos possessed the knowledge of the Old Testament Scriptures that permeates the epistle to the Hebrews. "He was an eloquent man" and also "mighty in the Scriptures" (Acts 18:24). Apollos was a native of Alexandria where both Greek culture and Judaism were highly developed.

Objections to Apollos as author. Apollos was never suggested as the author by the early church. Luther was the first to suggest Apollos. We have no writings by Apollos to make a comparison with Hebrews. No other internal or external evidence points to Apollos. His association with Paul was meaningful, but not of the duration and intensity suggested by the Pauline influence in Hebrews.

Conclusion. A number of scholars are attracted to Luther's view, and on the surface it does seem plausible. However, the total absence of support throughout church history makes it very doubtful that Apollos was the author.

Silas. Hardly any evidence gives much weight to the view that Silas was the author of Hebrews, though he was a long and close associate with Paul. Silas may have had a substantial role in the writing of 1 Peter and there are significant commonalties between 1 Peter and Hebrews. But Silas was a Jerusalem Jew and even less likely than Barnabas to possess the linguistic skill evidenced by the author of Hebrews.

Conclusion. Recent opinion has shifted away from Pauline authorship, but it has found no unanimous or authoritative alternative. Numerous suggestions have been made in the last century including Clement of Rome, Phillip, Pricilla, Epaphras, and even Mary, the mother of Jesus. These suggestions find no support in antiquity and little evidence to justify taking them seriously. It must be remembered that doubt about the authorship does not necessitate doubt about the inspiration and hence the authenticity of Hebrews. The identity of the author remains a mystery, but his knowledge and literary skill are evident. Bruce concludes,

> "The author was a second-generation Christian, well versed in the study of the Septuagint, which he interpreted according to a creative exegetical principle. He had a copious vocabulary and was the master of a fine rhetorical style, completely different from Paul's; we might well describe him as 'a learned man, ... mighty in the Scriptures.' He was a Hellenist who inherited the outlook of those Hellenists described in Acts 6-8; 11:19ff, the associates of Stephen and Philip, pioneers in the Gentile mission" (*The Epistle to the Hebrews*, 20).

Hiebert feels that the anonymity is a blessing in disguise. "The more we contemplate this enigma concerning the authorship of this marvelous revelation of the supremacy of our Lord Jesus Christ, the more we feel that our ignorance is divinely intended to direct our attention rather to the message of the book. In this Spirit-breathed book the attention is centered upon Christ. He must ever remain preeminent. Throughout the epistle the unnamed author refrains from any mention of men, except to set them aside if they come at all, in the minds of the readers, in competition with Christ" (*An Introduction to the New Testament*, 3:81).

Original Audience

Jewish Christians. Internal evidence points strongly to a specific congregation of believers who had come out of Judaism to embrace Christ as the Messiah promised in the Old Testament and their Savior. Circumstances were causing them to waver and were tempting them to return to Judaism. Internal evidence includes the following points: (1) While it may not be original, the title "to the Hebrews" has been continuously attached to the epistle since late in the second century. (2) The strongest argument rests on internal evidence. The author writes from the Jewish point of view to people who were once in Judaism and were now being tempted to return to it (Bruce, *The Epistle to the Hebrews*, 3-5). (3) The book has 93 direct references to the Old Testament. These include 38 quotations and another 55 allusions. The NIV identifies 39 quotations with 18 of them coming from the Psalms. This extensive use of and dependence on the Old Testament would be most meaningful for Christians of Jewish extraction. While relevant to Gentiles, it would likely have required more explanation by the author but familiarity is assumed throughout the Epistle of Hebrews.

Situation. Personal references indicate that the recipients constitute a specific, local assembly of Jews (12:4; 13:19, 23-24). The fact that the author hopes to visit them soon indicates that the letter was not a general epistle written for universal circulation. They had received the gospel through apostolic representatives and had seen "signs and wonders" performed by the Spirit (2:3-4). They had been Christians long enough that the author expected them to have become mature in their faith and able to teach others (5:12). Good works and ministry to the saints characterized them both in the past and the present (6:10). They had suffered persecution, including imprisonment and confiscation of property (10:32-34), but they had not yet experienced martyrdom (12:4). Some of their former teachers had already passed away, (13:7) and they were called on to obey new leaders (13:17). Spiritual complacency had set in. They had become "slow to learn" (5:11). The author found it necessary to treat them as spiritual babies (5:12-14). They were in danger of drifting away from their firm commitment to Christ (2:1) and thus turning away from the living God (3:12). They had become quite worldly minded (13:5) and some had given up attending public meetings of the church (10:25). They were losing their sense of resolve (10:35-39). Some had last their focus on the person of Christ and their future hope (12:1-3, 12-13, 25-29). Some were taking a casual view of sin (10:26-31). Marriage relationships were being neglected or abused (13:4) and money was becoming much

386

too important (13:5, 16). For all their problems, they were clearly believers and not merely professors. They are called brothers (3:1, 12; 10:19; 13:1, 22). They are referred to as those "who have believed" (4:3), had personally shared in the benefits of salvation (6:4-5), and had anchored their hope in Christ (6:18-19) (Bruce, *The Epistle to the Hebrews*, 9).

Location. The location of both the author and the recipients is uncertain. Suggestions have included Rome, Jerusalem, Alexandria, Judea, and even Spain. "Certainty on the destination of the epistle is unattainable in the present state of our knowledge, and fortunately its exegesis is for the most part independent of this question" (Bruce, *The Epistle to the Hebrews*, 14). Hiebert, Bruce, and the majority of current scholars favor Rome. However, the statement, "those from Italy send you their greetings" (13:24) is not definitive. The use of *apo* indicates that they are native to, but now removed from Italy. That has also prompted many to identify the readers as a small Jewish house church located in Rome. The author would then be writing from a location outside Rome, where displaced Christians from Italy had settled. Guthrie lists seven evidences favoring Rome, but he has major reservations (*New Testament Introduction*, 698-700).

The traditional view has been that the readers were Jewish Christians living in Jerusalem or at least in Palestine. But the fact that their membership had not yet experienced martyrdom (12:4) would seem to exclude Jerusalem itself and perhaps Judea also. Stephen, James the son of Zebedee, and James the brother of our Lord had all been martyred in Jerusalem. The Jerusalem church was on the receiving end of support whereas the readers of Hebrews were generous givers (6:10). The Jewish nation was disintegrating at the time that this epistle was probably written and it seems unlikely that Jewish Christians would be tempted to revert to Judaism when it too was under siege from Rome (Hiebert, *An Introduction to the New Testament*, 3:85). The reference to those "from Italy" is hard to explain if both the readers and the greeters were away from Rome. Rome is the first place where the epistle appears to have been known in the early church. While there is not enough evidence to decide the matter, the most probable location of the readers is Rome, and the author was probably in some location away from Rome. There were congregations of believers in Rome at an early date, and Paul had a productive ministry there during his imprisonment (Acts 28:30-31; Romans 15:22-24).

Occasion and Date

Occasion. The traditional view has identified the readers as Jewish Christians who were in danger of forsaking Christianity and going back into Judaism. The evident Jewish background of the readers and the specific warnings within the book strongly support this contention. Recently, some scholars have argued that the "falling away" represents a return to paganism, or Gnosticism. However, the evidence seems overwhelming in support of the traditional view that these are Jewish Christians who have not understood the true nature of Christianity and thus are in danger of drifting back into Judaism (Bruce, *The Epistle to the Hebrews*, 5-9). The entire argument of Hebrews is designed to prove that Christ is the fulfillment of Old Testament promises and that the new order fulfills and supersedes the old. The situation of the readers as described above constitutes the background or occasion for the writing of Hebrews. Hiebert suggests this situation:

If we may think of the readers as members of the Jewish-Christian synagogues in Rome, the situation may be conceived as follows. With the outbreak of the Neronian persecution Christianity became an illegal religion. The fury of the persecution at first fell directly on the old, established Roman congregation consisting chiefly of Gentile Christians. These Jewish Christians still meeting in their synagogues were as yet officially regarded as Jews by the government. But their sympathy with their suffering brethren had expressed itself in definite efforts to help these unfortunate victims. This had aroused popular resentment against them also. They too were beginning to feel the weight of the persecution. Although martyrdom had not yet been extended to them, there was danger that it might. Because of this prospect their temptation was to minimize as much as possible their Christian distinctives and emphasize their Jewish background and beliefs. Their danger lay in the temptation to hide their Christian faith under the protective coloring of Judaism. Perhaps, as Manson thinks, they had no intention in giving up their Christian profession to return to open Judaism, but were hanging back and not accepting the full consequences of their Christian profession. Thus they were not pressing on to perfection and were in danger in falling short of the rest of God through unbelief (4:9). Such a compromising position resulted in spiritual dullness and foreshadowed a casting away of their confidence (10:35). They are therefore urged to 'go forth unto him without the camp, bearing his reproach'" (13:13) (*An Introduction to the New Testament*, 3:87-88).

Date. Hebrews must have been written before AD 95 since Clement of Rome used the epistle extensively in his own letter written in AD 96. It must also have been written before AD 70. The sacrificial system is spoken of in the present tense. The temple at Jerusalem was destroyed by the Romans in AD 70 and sacrifices ceased. The author makes no reference to this event and it would surely have been a most telling argument against going back to Judaism. A previous generation of Christian leaders had passed away (13:7), but the members themselves were still second-generation converts (2:3; 10:32). Timothy is still active in ministry. His release from prison favors a date around the time of Paul's imprisonment and the Neronian persecution (Bruce, *The Epistle to the Hebrews*, 21-22). If Paul was the author, then the epistle must have been written before his martyrdom around AD 64-66.

If Paul is not the author we do not have a clear explanation for the absence of reference to his martyrdom if the epistle was written after 64. Persecution poses an immediate threat, but which persecution? Many Jews were expelled from Rome under Claudias around AD 50. While the epistle could have been written that early, it seems much more likely that the persecution of Nero from AD 65 to 68 is in view. A date of AD 64 to 70 best fits the conditions described within the book and the external evidence available. This author favors a date of AD 64 shortly before the fierce persecution under Nero. Guthrie concludes, "In view of all the data available, it would seem reasonable to regard this epistle as having been sent just before the fall of Jerusalem, if Jerusalem was the destination, or just before the Neronian persecutions if it was sent to Rome" (*New Testament Introduction*, 705).

Purpose and Theme

Purpose. There are several interrelated reasons for the writing of Hebrews.

1. **Supremacy of Christ.** Treating lightly the person and work of Jesus Christ was a serious matter (10:26-31). Thus the writer set out to demonstrate the superiority of Christ over all that the old order represented. This essential truth forms both the primary purpose and the central theme for Hebrews.
2. **Maturity.** The major goal of the author is to see that the readers progress to maturity in Christ (5:11-14). They made a good start (6:10; 10:32-34), but they were in danger of drifting and going back rather than progressing on to maturity.

3. **Exhortations.** The author's primary intent was to encourage Christians whose faith was wavering to persist in their devotion to Jesus Christ. Hebrews is a book of exhortations (13:22). The author introduces these exhortations sixteen times with the expression *"let us"* (4:1,11,14,16; 6:1; 10:22, 23, 24, 25 (twice); 12:1 (twice), 2, 28; 13:13, 15).
4. **Persecution.** The author is conscious that persecution is breaking out and these believers are vulnerable. One important purpose of the letter is to encourage and fortify them for these persecutions (12:3-15).
5. **False Doctrine.** The exhortation comes near the end of the letter, but apparently there were "strange teachings" that threatened to undermine the faith of the readers (13:9-10).
6. **Commitment to Christ.** The summary challenge in 13:13 is a call to absolute commitment to Christ whatever the cost. *So, let us go out to Him outside the camp, bearing His reproach.*

> "The purpose of our author's exegesis of Old Testament Scripture, as of his general argument, is to establish the finality of the gospel by contrast with all that went before it (more particularly, by contrast with the Levitical cultus), as the way of perfection, the way which leads people to God without any barrier or interruption of access. He establishes the finality of Christianity by establishing the supremacy of Christ, in his person and work. As regards his person, Christ is greater than all the servants and spokesmen of God who have gone before—not only greater than other human servants and spokesmen (even Moses) but greater than angels. For he is the Son of God, his agent in creating and maintaining the universe, who yet became the Son of Man and submitted to humiliation and death. He now is exalted above all the heavens, enthroned at God's right hand, and he lives forever there as his people's representative" (F. F. Bruce, *The Epistle to the Hebrews*, 29).

Theme. The superiority of Christ is the unifying theme of the book of Hebrews. This is the basis on which the author exhorts his readers to progress to maturity in Christ (6:1). The practical purpose of Hebrews is exhortation (13:22), but the central thesis is that Christ is superior to all that characterizes the old order. This is evident by the author's use of 3 key words. (1) **Better** occurs thirteen times in Hebrews (1:4; 6:9; 7:7, 19, 22; 8:6 [twice]; 9:23; 10:34; 11:16, 35, 40; 12:24). (2) **Perfect** indicates completion or finality. Perfect or its equivalent occurs twelve times (2:10; 5:9, 7:11, 19, 28; 9:9, 11; 10:1, 14; 11:40; 12:23). (3) **Once** occurs eight times and the combination **once for all** three times (6:4; 7:27; 9:7, 12, 26,

390

27, 28; 10:2, 10; 12:26, 27), thus highlighting the uniqueness and finality of the work of the Lord Jesus Christ.

The finality and superiority of the once-for-all sacrifice of Christ is highlighted in contrast to the repeated and ineffectual Levitical sacrifices (1:1-10:18). Three of the author's five warnings occur in this section. The author then gives a series of exhortations that flow naturally from the truth of Christ's superiority (10:19-13:19).

Key Verse, 4:14
Therefore, since we have a great high priest who has passed through the heavens, Jesus the Son of God, let us hold fast our confession

---

The key that unlocks the book of Hebrews lies in a proper understanding of the readers and the occasion of the book. The epistle was written to second-generation Jewish Christians who had left Judaism and turned by faith to Christ. Now, however, persecution had arisen and was prompting them to return to the familiar life of the synagogue. The problem they face then is whether to go on to maturity in Christ (6:1), or to drift back into the apparent safety of Judaism (2:1-4). The author argues convincingly for the superiority of Christ and for the salvation provided under the New Covenant as the fulfillment of all that was promised and sought under the Old Covenant. He calls for them to press on to maturity in Christ. Bruce offers this description of the recipients and their situation.

"The addressees appear, then, to have been a group of Jewish Christians who had never seen or heard Jesus in person, but had learned of him (as the writer of the epistle also did) from some who had themselves listened to him. Since their conversion they had been exposed to persecution—particularly at one stage shortly after the beginning of their Christian career—but while they had had to endure public abuse, imprisonment, and the looting of their property, they had not yet been called upon to die for their faith. They had given practical evidence of their faith by serving their fellow-Christians and especially by caring for those of their number who had suffered most in the time of persecution. Yet their Christian development had been arrested; instead of pressing ahead they were inclined to come to a full stop in their spiritual progress, if not indeed to slip back to a stage which they had left." (*The Epistle to the Hebrews*, 9).

391

Literary Character of Hebrews

The Nature of Hebrews. Like everything else about this epistle, the literary nature of Hebrews has been the subject of debate. Hebrews has the well-reasoned quality of a theological treatise, the alliteration and passion of a sermon, and the warmth and conclusion of a letter. It is not surprising that some are convinced that it is an essay; others maintain that it is a series of sermons, and many hold that it is a personal letter. Hebrews fits all three descriptions. Rees is right when he says, "Hebrews begins like an essay, proceeds like a sermon, and ends like a letter" ("The Epistle to the Hebrews," in *The International Bible Encyclopedia,* 2:1355).

Probably the author had often given a series of messages on the subject of the superiority of Christ and of Christianity. The truth involved was urgently needed by the readers and the author proceeded to reduce the messages to a personal letter. The well-reasoned quality of a theological treatise is permeated with personal warmth and frequent appeals like a sermon. Hebrews deserves to be considered a letter, though it stands in a class by itself. The author himself describes it as *a word of exhortation* (13:22). He incorporates the logic of a treatise with the passion and appeal of a sermon but in a letter format.

Literary Features. Hebrews is filled with direct quotations or allusions to the Old Testament. Longenecker has identified 38 quotations and 55 allusions (*Biblical Exegesis in the Apostolic Period,* 164-66). The epistle has many *hapax legomena*: 157 words in Hebrews occur nowhere else in the New Testament. The author makes use of several inclusios. An *inclusio* is a paragraph or section that contains a complete thought and has a common beginning and ending. Often this is a repeated phrase or clause. Examples include 2:5-16; 3:1-4:14; 5:11-6:12; 7:1-10, and 12:14-13:20. (MacLeod, "The Literary Structure of the Book of Hebrews," in *Bibliotheca Sacra,* 146:187). The author of Hebrews frequently links sentences (verses) together by using "link words," that is, identical or similar words. Examples include "angels" (1:4-5), "children" (2:13-14), "enter" (4:5-6), and "promises" (6:12-13). Lightfoot cites these and several other examples of catch words in Hebrews (*Jesus Christ Today,* 49). Moffat has identified 20 examples of alliteration in the book of Hebrews. Though lost in English translations, this is a significant device and reflects the high quality of the Greek (*A Critical and Exegetical Commentary on the Epistle to the Hebrews,* lx).

Message of Hebrews

I. Introduction: Thesis Statement: The Son Is Superior to All Things (1:1-3). In the past God spoke to our ancestors in many and varied ways in the prophets, but His full and final revelation has been made to us in a person, His Son. The Son expresses God's glory, being of the very same nature as God. The Son is Creator, Sustainer, and Heir of all things. Having secured salvation for humanity, the Son has taken His rightful place of authority in heaven at the right hand of God.

II. Exposition: Evidence for and effect of the Son's Superiority (1:4-10:18).
The Son is superior to the angels (1:4-2:18). In the Scriptures God repeatedly declared that His Son is superior to the angels (1:4-14). They are servants, but Jesus is God's Son. The Son has been enthroned forever as God, has created all things, and will remain unchanged but all creation will perish. Now seated at the Father's right hand, the Son awaits the day when He will rule over all things while angels are occupied with serving those who will inherit the salvation purchased by the Son. What angel can make such a claim?

First warning: the danger of drifting/neglect (2:1-4). What lesson are we to draw from this? Just this: we must pay attention to this superior revelation by the Son and not drift away from it through neglect. If the message of the angels carried with it a severe penalty for those who disobeyed it (and we know that it did), surely we cannot escape the consequences if we neglect the salvation announced by the Son Himself. That salvation was confirmed to us by eyewitnesses and authenticated through many miraculous demonstrations by the Holy Spirit!

Lest there be any doubt as to the superiority of Jesus over angels, believers need to remember that God has given dominion over the world to come to Jesus, not to angels. The dominion that God intended to be exercised by humanity was lost but has been restored through Jesus, the perfect representative of humanity. To accomplish salvation and restore this dominion, it was necessary for Jesus to share fully in our humanity. His suffering and death was essential and effective in breaking the devil's grip on humanity, a grip he held through our fear of death. Because He fully shared our humanity, Jesus has become the kind of high priest we need to secure our full release from sin. Jesus' experience of suffering and temptation enables Him to help those who are now being tempted. The Son is sovereign (2:5-9), but as one with humanity He has suffered vicariously (2:10-16) and thus He is well able to come to the aid of those who are tempted (2:17-18).

The Son is superior to Moses (3:1-4:13). Jesus is also superior to Moses, the great lawgiver of Israel (3:1-6). Moses was faithful as a servant **in** God's house, but the Son is faithful **over** God's house. As the builder is superior to the house that he builds and the son ruling the house is superior to the servant in the house, so Christ, as both builder and Son, is superior to Moses. Since God appointed his Son and considers him worthy of greater glory than Moses, so should we! Remember that we are partakers of Christ and thus we are His house.

Second Warning: the danger of disobedience because of unbelief (3:7-4:13). Take care, brethren that you do not make the same mistake that our forefathers made. Because of their hard-hearted unbelief they disobeyed God's revelation and promise through Moses! As a consequence they incurred God's wrath and were denied entrance into the land and the rest that God had promised (3:7-19). Don't let that kind of unbelieving heart cause you to fall away from God. Rather, trust Jesus fully and experience the rest God still promises. After all, it is evident that not even Joshua gave our ancestors rest because God promised a future rest through David years later. God is still promising rest. Let us be diligent to enter God's rest and not fall victim to their disobedience and unbelief (4:1-11). God's word penetrates our inmost being and we cannot escape giving account to him. Therefore let us draw near to God's throne of grace where Jesus, our great and sympathetic High Priest, stands ready to help us. He knows our temptation firsthand and will give us the grace and mercy we need to go on to maturity (4:11-16).

The Son has a superior priesthood to the Levitical order (4:14-10:18). Since our ability to resist the temptation to unbelief and disobedience depends on Jesus as our High Priest, you need to understand how superior His priesthood is in every aspect to that of Aaron and the Levitical order that you find so attractive. Every priest must be appointed by God and represents humanity in offering sacrifices. He shares their weakness and must offer sacrifice for his own sins as well as for theirs. But Jesus was declared by God himself to be a priest forever. He suffered death and is now the source of eternal salvation to all who obey Him. Jesus belongs to the order of Melchizedek, not to that of Aaron. His priesthood is perfect and eternal like that of Melchizedek because He was not weakened by sin and because He was appointed by God Himself (5:1-10).

Third Warning: the danger of declension (falling away) (5:11-6:20). There are many intricate and important details involved in Jesus' perfect, Melchizedekian priesthood. But unfortunately you have not grown to maturity and are unable to digest such solid food (5:11-14). You are still in spiritual infancy and need to press on to maturity (6:1). Instead you have looked longingly at the old institutions of Judaism (6:1-3). If you do *fall away* in going back to those things, there is no possibility of removing that stigma of failure before the judgment seat of Christ (6:4-8). But beloved, we expect better things of you (6:9-12). Our confidence is bolstered by your past performance in the faith, but you must diligently follow the example of those who persisted in their faith. Above all, our confidence rests on the certainty of God's character and the sufficiency of Christ's priesthood (6:13-20). Just as God confirmed His promise to Abraham through an immutable oath, so also our hope is firmly anchored in Jesus who has entered into the very presence of God as our forerunner and our High Priest.

Christ is a perfect and indestructible priest who is able to save us forever (7:1-28). Consider Melchizedek. He was greater than Abraham and also than Abraham's descendant Levi (7:1-10), just as the one receiving tithes is greater than the one giving them. Jesus is a priest like Melchizedek. His priesthood is eternal and unchanging because of His indestructible life. Also, Jesus was made a priest by divine oath and has become God's guarantee of a better covenant. Here at last, after the failure of the Levitical system to perfect us (7:11-19), is a high priest who can bring us to maturity. Sin and death do not limit His priesthood, because He is absolutely holy and is now exalted above the heavens. He can save forever those who draw near to God as we have. He is everything we need in a priest. He did this through the once-for-all sacrifice of Himself (7:20-28).

Jesus is the mediator of a better covenant (8:1-13). From these facts it is obvious that Jesus is a superior high priest. It is thus to be expected that His priesthood is also based on a better covenant. As evidence, note that He is now seated in the heavenly tabernacle. The fact that God promised a New Covenant means that the old was not faultless. The New Covenant promised before and now fulfilled in Jesus is eternal and is based on superior promises. This covenant promises to transform the recipients from the inside out. The Old Covenant is now obsolete. And since the old covenant is obsolete, why would you want to go back to it?

Jesus ministered in a better sanctuary (9:1-10). Jesus has also entered into a better sanctuary, the heavenly and true tabernacle (9:1-10). The very design of the old sanctuary made it clear that the way of access to God was not yet open. Only the high priest could enter the most holy place and then only once a year and only with the blood of a sin offering. The Holy Spirit was thus giving an object lesson for us today that the old system of sacrifices could not make the worshiper perfect (9:1-10).

Jesus offered a better sacrifice (9:11-10:18). The blood of animals that was offered by the priest under the Old Covenant could never take away sin or remove the sense of guilt. It only effected an outward cleaning. What those sacrifices could not do, Jesus has done. Jesus' sacrifice was not that of bulls and goats, nor was it temporary and ineffective with regard to sin. Rather, He made one sacrifice for sin that was sufficient for all time. He sacrificed His very own blood and body. Therefore no other sacrifice is needed or possible. Real, inward, and eternal holiness is now possible. The proof is in the fact that He is now seated in heaven at the Father's right hand awaiting the day when every enemy will be brought under His sovereign rule. Sin, the great problem of the human heart, was vanquished, and there is now eternal forgiveness in the work and person of this High Priest (9:11-10:18).

III. Exhortation: Superiority of Jesus in a Believer's Life (10:19-13:19). The author has proved his point that Jesus is the completion of and is superior to the old order (1:1-10:18). He now proceeds to apply the truth of Jesus' supremacy to the life and fellowship of his readers. *Therefore* signals the application of truth now well established. Believers ought to use their position of privilege in Christ to draw near to God and hold fast to the hope they have professed (10:19-25). They ought to be encouraging one another to persevere.

Fourth Warning: the danger of defection (10:26-31). Armed with the truth that Christ is superior to the old order to go back to a dead, external ritual would be a willful sin. It is a serious matter to deliberately and willfully continue in sin. This is comparable to rejecting Christ and trampling Him underfoot. To go back to Judaism is to declare Christ *common and unclean.* If the past consequence of rejecting Moses' law was physical death, how much more severely do you think those should be punished who reject the Son who is greater than Moses? Those who do cannot expect to escape God's judgment. Remember, It *is a dreadful thing to fall into the hands of the living God* (10:26-31).

Exhortation to endure affliction (10:32-39). Persecution may be severe, but it does not justify turning away from Jesus Christ. The readers are now encouraged to endure affliction. Their past faithfulness is remembered and they are urged to hold firmly to that same confidence against the rising tide of opposition (10:32-39). Now is no time to abandon their confidence.

Exhortation to triumph through faith (11:1-12:14). Encouragement to press on even under severe persecution comes from the great host of heroes of the faith. Faith is able to triumph as demonstrated by men and women of God out of the past. Great men and women like Abel, Enoch, Noah, Abraham, Isaac, Jacob, Moses, and Rahab prove the value of persevering faith (11:1-31). So also do the nameless heroes of faith who accepted suffering and even death because of God's eternal promise (11:32-40). The readers themselves are now urged to join the throng of the faithful to *lay aside every encumbrance and the sin that so easily entangles us, and let us run with endurance the race that is set before us* (12:1). Jesus Himself is the prime example of overcoming faith and we must always keep our eyes fixed on Him. The hardships of life are part of God's loving discipline (12:4-14). God disciplines us for our good and so that we might share in His holiness.

Fifth Warning: the danger of despising our high privilege (12:15-29). It is a serious and irreversible error to reject the covenant blessings we have in Christ. To do so is to *come short of the grace of God.* Esau is a tragic reminder of the great loss suffered when covenant blessing is abandoned. No amount of tears can recover the lost opportunity. However, our hope already rests in the heavenly Jerusalem (12:22). We have already come to Jesus, the mediator of the New Covenant (12:24). We are already receiving a kingdom that cannot be shaken (12:28). Surely then we together should press on to maturity and not follow in Esau's tragic footsteps.

Exhortation to live honorably in every dimension of life (13:1-19). The exhortations to persevere in their allegiance to Christ must be translated into everyday experience. The author now gives a series of brief, practical exhortations (13:1-19). Hospitality, faithfulness to marriage vows, submission to leaders, and the rejection of false teaching are incumbent on all that would follow Jesus. The argument of the letter and its exhortations come down to one final appeal. *So let us, then, go out to Him outside the camp, bearing His reproach* (13:13).

397

Conclusion (13:20-25). The author concludes this essay as a personal letter with the request that they take his *word of exhortation* to heart (13:22). A personal visit is planned in the near future. In the meantime greetings are extended from all in Italy who share their common faith in Jesus Christ (13:23-25).

Outline

I. Introduction: The Son Is Superior to All Things	1:1-3
II. Exposition: Evidence of the Son's Superiority	1:4-10:18
A. The superiority of the person of Christ	1:4-4:13
1. Superior to the angels	1:4-2:18
a. As the Son of God he was made higher	1:4-14
First warning: the danger of drifting/neglect	2:1-4
b. As the Son of Man he was made lower	2:5-18
2. Superior to Moses	3:1-4:13
a. In His person as builder of the house	3:1-4
b. In His position as Son over the house	3:5-6
Second warning: the danger of disobedience	3:7-4:13
B. The superiority of the priesthood of Christ	4:14-10:18
1. In its nature and scope	4:14-7:28
a. Christ's personal qualifications	4:14-5:10
Third warning: the danger of falling away	5:11-6:20
b. Christ prefigured in Melchizedek	7:1-10
c. Christ's perfection as priest	7:11-28
2. In its ministry	8:1-10:18
a. Christ is mediator of a better covenant	8:1-13
b. Christ ministered in a better sanctuary	9:1-10
c. Christ offered a better sacrifice	9:11-10:18
III. Exhortation: Superiority of Jesus on Believer's Life	10:19-13:19
A. To avail ourselves of this new access to God	10:19-25
1. The present privilege	10:19-21
2. The present responsibility	10:22-25
Fourth warning: the danger of defection	10:26-31
B. To endure affliction	10:32-39
1. Encouragement from their past	10:32-34
2. Encouragement from their future	10:35-39
C. To triumph through faith	11:1-12:14
1. Evidence of the life of faith	11:1-40
2. Exhortation to the life of faith	12:1-14

Fifth warning: danger of despising our privilege　12:15-29
D.　To live honorably　13:1-19
　　1.　Social obligations　13:1-6
　　2.　Religious obligations　13:7-17
　　3.　Personal obligations　13:18-19

IV. Conclusion　13:20-25

Bibliography

Bruce, F. F. *The Epistle to the Hebrews.* Grand Rapids: Wm. B. Eerdmans Publishing Co., 1990.

Cockerill, Gareth Lee. *The Epistle to the Hebrews.* New International Commentary on the New Testament. Wm. B. Eerdmans Publishing Co., 2012.

Ellingworth, Paul. *The Epistle to the Hebrews.* New International Greek Testament Commentary. Grand Rapids: Wm. B. Eerdmans Publishing Co., 1993.

Guthrie, Donald. *New Testament Introduction.* Downers Grove, IL: InterVarsity Press, 1990.

____. *The Letter to the Hebrews.* Tyndale New Testament Commentaries. Grand Rapids: Wm. B. Eerdmans Publishing Co., 1983.

Hiebert, D. Edmond. An *Introduction to the New Testament.* Vol. 3. Chicago: Moody Press, 1975.

Johnson, Luke Timothy. *Hebrews.* Anchor Bible Series. New York: Doubleday, 2006.

O'Brien, Peter T. *The Letter to the Hebrews.* Pillar New Testament Commentary. Grand Rapids: Wm. B. Eerdmans Publishing Co., 2010.

Moffat, J. *A Critical and Exegetical Commentary on the Epistle to the Hebrews, lx).* International Critical Commentary. Edinburgh: T. & T. Clark, 1924.

Pentecost, J. Dwight. *Faith that Endures.* Grand Rapids: Kregel Publications, 2000.

Westcott, Brooke Foss. *The Epistle to the Hebrews.* Grand Rapids: Wm. B. Eerdmans Publishing Co., n.d.

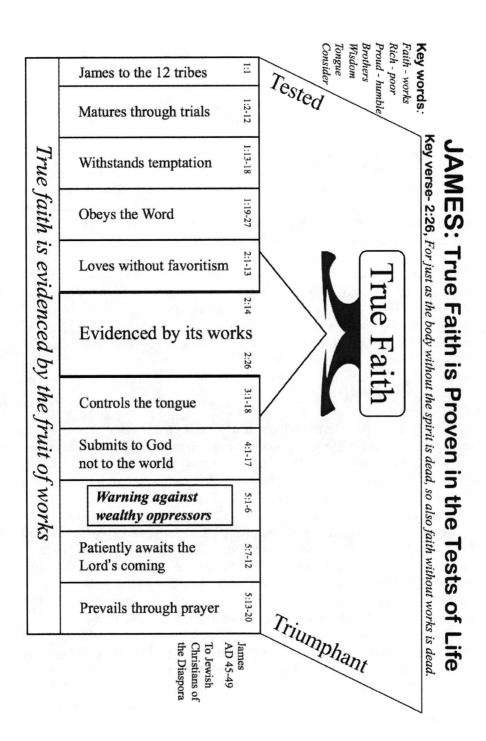

JAMES

The epistle of James is probably the earliest of all New Testament writings. It reflects the challenges faced by Christians before the church expanded across the Roman Empire. In it James provides a practical guide for believers who find themselves plagued by their old sin nature and persecuted by a hostile world. It explains how true religion works in the real world. James calls for radical faith that changes everything, inside and out. It is both pragmatic and positive. Some of the choicest gems of the New Testament are found in James. It is a timeless book because Christians still encounter trials. Temptation still wreaks havoc within. Our tongues still cause trouble. Rich and poor are still rivals. Prejudice continues to pervade our attempt at fellowship. Above all, God still gives grace to those who humbly draw near to him and Scripture still liberates the soul that takes its truth seriously. Though often misunderstood and much maligned, the epistle of James is an important part of Scripture and deserves our careful study.

Authenticity and Acceptance

External Authentication. The earliest and strongest endorsement comes from Origen (AD 185-254). Though some would argue the opposite, James likely influenced other Christian works including, *Shepherd of Hermas* and *1 Clement.* Eusebius and Jerome give guarded, but clear support. While calling attention to questions of authorship, both these early authorities quote the epistle of James as Scripture (D.A. Carson, Douglas J. Moo, and Leon Morris, *An Introduction to the New Testament,* 417). The Eastern Church was earlier and stronger in its endorsement of the epistle than was the Western Church. Uncertainty about the identity of the author and the absence of major doctrines are probable causes for this variation. The epistle of James relates to early Christianity following the dispersion from Jerusalem in Acts 8. Theological issues came later and were addressed by Paul rather than James. Leaders like Athanasius (298-373), Gregory of Nazianzus (330-390), and Chrysostom (347-407) accepted the epistle of James. "By the time of Jerome (340-420) and Augustine (354-430) it was all but universally accepted" Hiebert, *An Introduction to the New Testament,* 3:34).

Internal Authentication. The strongest support for the authenticity of James comes from within the epistle itself. The remarkable similarities between James and Jesus' Sermon on the Mount argue for first hand familiarity by the author. The absence of direct quotations points toward James as an authentic eyewitness and away from a later editor-author. Likewise, remarkable similarities exist between this epistle and the letter drafted by James at the Jerusalem conference (Acts 15). The idea that James constitutes an attack on Pauline theology does not stand up under careful scrutiny. Rather, it points to the traditional view of composition by James before the Jerusalem Conference. The theological controversy addressed by Paul occurred later. "Considered in a more balanced way, James can be seen to be making an important contribution to our understanding of Christian theology and practice. One that in no way conflicts with Paul or any other biblical author. On both historical and theological grounds, James fully deserves the canonical status that the church has accorded it" (Carson, Moo, and Morris, *An Introduction to the New Testament*, 418).

Recent Opinion and Acceptance. Martin Luther's description of James as "an epistle of straw" has been oft quoted and overworked. Though critical of James because of the perceived difference between James' view of faith and that of Paul, Luther did not exclude James from the canon of Scripture. In fact, he quoted James with approval many times and acknowledged that there were many good sayings in James. The epistle of James is not widely studied or frequently preached in evangelical circles though excerpts from the book are occasionally quoted. James' scathing denunciation of the rich and of social injustice has made this epistle a favorite in liberation theology.

Author

Identity. The author refers to himself simply as *"James, a servant of God and of the Lord Jesus Christ"* (1:1a). English translations have obscured the actual Greek word *Iakobos*. Jacob was a common and revered name in Israel because of its association with the patriarch, Jacob. There are four men identified as "James" in the New Testament, hence the debate over the author's identity. The simplicity with which the author introduces himself indicates that he was well known and occupied a position of authority in the early church. Tradition has identified the author of this epistle as James, the Lord's brother (Matthew 13:55; Mark 6:3; Galatians 1:19). It is highly unlikely that the author could have been James, the son of Zebedee and brother of John, one of the twelve disciples (Matthew 4:21;

10:2; Mark 10:35; Acts 1:13). The beheading of this James by Herod Agrippa in AD 44 (Acts 12:2) makes it unlikely that he was the author. Neither James the son of Alphaeus (Matthew 10:3; Mark 3:18; Acts 1:13), nor James, the father of Judas "not Iscariot" (Luke 6:16; Acts 1:13) held a position of leadership in the early church. Frequent allusions to the teaching of Jesus, the Jewishness of the book, textual similarities with James' letter of Acts 15 and the prominence of James in the early church (Acts 15:13; Galatians 1:19; 2:9), support the traditional view. Guthrie provides a detailed explanation of six strong arguments for identifying James, the brother of our Lord, as the author (*New Testament Introduction*, 726-33).

1. The author's self-identification
2. The author's Jewish background
3. Similarities between James and Acts
4. Similarities with the teaching of Jesus
5. Agreements with the New Testament account of James
6. The conditions within the community

Several alternative theories have been proposed for the authorship of the epistle of James. Some suggest that it was an unknown James. Others propose that the letter is pseudonymous, written by a later author assuming the name of James. Still others argue for the work of a second century editor using original material from James himself. The high quality of the Greek language and perceived differences between James and Paul are most often cited as evidence against the traditional view. Some also charge that James is dependent on 1 Peter. After examining these alternative views and their supporting evidence, Guthrie concludes, "None of these views has any better claim to credibility than the tradition. In these circumstances the authorship of James, the Lord's brother, must still be considered more probable than any rival" (*New Testament Introduction*, 746).

Character of James. The author says little about himself but reveals much within the letter itself. "There are yet few writings which in the same space reveal more of the individual character of their author" (Hiebert, *An Introduction to the New Testament*, 3:37). Like our Lord, James was a keen observer of nature. He used vivid, natural images to teach spiritual truth. Intensity and integrity are evident qualities. He had a no nonsense approach to the Christian faith. He clearly grasped the role of the flesh, the world and Satan in the spiritual warfare of believers. His language was direct and authoritative. As reflected in Acts 15, James was discerning and decisive. He was a thorough going Christian yet remained a devout Jew.

History. James was probably the oldest of the brothers of Jesus since he is always mentioned first (Matthew 13:55; Mark 6:3). His early doubts about the messianic mission of Jesus dissolved following the resurrection. Jesus appeared personally to James after the resurrection (1 Corinthians 15:7). James was already among the other followers of Jesus gathered in the upper room (Acts 1:14). He rose quickly to prominence in the church and was sought out by Paul for confirmation of his understanding of the gospel (Galatians 1:18-19). He was the leader of the church and the first to be informed of Peter's release from prison (Acts. 12:17). At the Jerusalem conference (Acts 15) and at Paul's last visit to Jerusalem (Acts 21:18-25) James was the leader of the church at Jerusalem. James was not in conflict with Paul. He supported Paul's position against the Judaizers and reaffirmed his support toward the end of Paul's ministry (Acts 15, 21). It is probable that the legalists confronted by Paul at Galatia overstated their authority when they represented themselves as coming "from James" (Galatians 2:12).

Tradition indicates that James continued as an orthodox Jew in respect for the Law and lived as a Nazarite. It was reported that he spent so much time in prayer on his knees that they became callused and earned him the nickname, "camel's knees." His integrity and respect for the law earned him the title "James the Just." He was well accepted in the Jewish community though he served as leader in the Christian congregation of Jerusalem. James continued his ministry in the city of Jerusalem until martyred in AD 62. His death by stoning at the hands of Jewish leaders was condemned by most Jews (Hiebert, *The Epistle of James*, 34-36).

Relationship to Jesus. The earliest and prevailing view has identified James as a younger brother of Jesus and the child of Mary and Joseph. That Mary and Joseph had additional children following Jesus is indicated by the term "first born son" found in Luke 2:7. Numerous references to Jesus' brothers and sisters add support (Matthew 13:55; Mark 6:3; Acts 1:14). Later emphasis by the Roman church on the perpetual virginity of Mary led to the development of other views. Some held that the brothers were actually children of Joseph by a previous marriage. That would appear impossible since they would have been older brothers to Jesus and hence the legitimate claimants to David's throne. Jerome rejected that view and proposed that they were actually cousins, not brothers. The traditional view that James and the others were brothers of Jesus, born to Mary and Joseph after Jesus' birth, best fits the biblical text and the historical evidence (Hiebert, *An Introduction to the New Testament*, 3:46-49).

Recipients

Jewish Christians. The letter of James is addressed to "*the twelve tribes dispersed abroad*" (1:1). That was a common designation for the Jewish people and is best understood in the literal sense. That does not preclude them being Christians. It points to their Jewish heritage as believers in Christ. James is not given to figurative language and it is unlikely he would use a common Jewish term to describe Christians with no Jewish roots. References to the Lord Jesus Christ (1:1; 2:1, 7), to the coming of the Lord (5:7) and to the new birth (1:19) identify them as Christians. Their Jewishness is evident from the fact that they still meet in the synagogue (2:2) and from the frequent appeals to the Old Testament (2:21, 25; 5:11, 17-18). Hiebert concludes, "The common, and doubtless the correct, view is that it was addressed to Jewish Christians outside Palestine" (*An Introduction to the New Testament*, 3:49).

Diaspora: Outside Palestine. The Greek term, *diaspora* was in use even before the destruction of Jerusalem in AD 70. It was used to describe Jews who were scattered (whether by choice or force) outside Palestine (John 7:35). Peter uses the word also in reference to believers (1 Peter 2:11). The book of Acts indicates that believing Jews were forced out of Jerusalem by persecution (8:1-4). The gospel thus spread to the Jews of surrounding regions and later to Greeks as well (Acts 11:19-21). This letter from James was probably sent as a general, pastoral letter to believing Jews living outside, but comparatively near Palestine. "Identifying James' readers with these early Jewish Christians would fit the date of the letter and would furnish an explanation of the circumstances that called it forth: James, the leader of the Jerusalem church, must minister to his scattered flock by mail. While tentative, this suggestion is better than most in explaining the circumstances of the letter" (Carson, Moo, and Morris, *An Introduction to the New Testament*, 415).

Occasion and Date

Circumstances. The Epistle provides numerous indicators of the conditions existing among these Jewish Christians. The following can be gleaned from James: 1) The believers were enduring persecution for their faith (1:2). 2) They were largely poor and were victims of social injustice (1:9; 2:6; 5:1-6). 3) Though harassed by the rich, they still showed favoritism to their tormentors (2:1-7). 4) They were often succumbing to the old sin nature and being defeated by temptation (1:13-15; 4:1-3). 5) Worldliness often replaced God's heavenly wisdom and produced quarrels within the church (3:13-4:6). 6) Patience was lacking and so was effective prayer (1:2-8; 4:2-3; 5:7, 13-18). 7) Above all else, they were flirting with the notion that faith was sufficient in and of itself without the evidence of a holy life (2:14-26).

Date. James, the brother of our Lord, was martyred in Jerusalem in AD 62. The dispersion of Jewish Christians from Jerusalem began at least by AD 35. The gospel had spread widely among the Gentiles when the Jerusalem conference was held in AD 49. The most probable date for the epistle of James is either AD 45-49 (before the Jerusalem council) or AD 60-61 (shortly before the martyrdom of James). Guthrie prefers the earlier date and gives eight supporting arguments (*New Testament Introduction*, 750-52).
1. The absence of reference to the fall of Jerusalem.
2. The absence of reference to the Jewish-Gentile controversy.
3. The primitive character of church order.
4. The Jewish tone of the letter.
5. The state of the Christians.
6. Exposure of Christians to persecution.
7. The relation to other New Testament letters.
8. The relation to the apostolic fathers.

Hiebert cites similar evidence and states his conclusion firmly. "We conclude that the preponderance of the evidence points to an early date for the epistle, sometime before the Jerusalem Conference. The epistle may thus be dated at about AD 46, at least not later than AD 49. This view makes James the earliest book in the New Testament" (*The Epistle of James*, 41).

Purpose
The epistle of James is clearly ethical and practical but it is also doctrinal. His readers were in danger of straying from the true faith. In response, James provides a series of tests to determine the genuineness of their Christian faith. The situation is unique to the early church, but the tests are timeless. Orthopraxy, not just orthodoxy, is the issue. Paul will combat legalism. James combats laxness and license. He aims to restore the vital Christian faith and a genuine fellowship that characterized the church immediately after Pentecost.

Distinctive Features and Contributions

Emphasis on Works as a Necessary Evidence of Faith. James is noted primarily for his stress on holy living as a necessary outcome of the Christian faith. *Even so faith, if it has no works, is dead, being by itself* (2:17). Faith that does not manifest itself in a transformed life and active obedience is useless and dead (2:20, 26). Many have concluded from this emphasis that James is opposed to Paul's teaching of justification by faith. Galatians and Acts indicate otherwise. James joined Peter in confirming the conversion and call of Paul (Galatians 1:19). James is listed first among the apostles who gave Paul "the right hand of fellowship" (Galatians 2:9). At the Jerusalem Conference, it was James who supported Paul's ministry among the Gentiles, while at the same time conciliating the Jews (Acts 15:13-21). He was also the one Paul reported to with the collection sent by Gentile Christians for their impoverished brethren at Jerusalem (Acts 21:7-26). However, James' emphasis on faith that works is so strong that some have taken exception. Hiebert notes, "James believes that faith justifies, but not a 'faith' that remains alone and produces no works. James rejects it as not being true faith. He demands a working faith" (*The Epistle of James*, 197).

Correspondence with Jesus' Teaching. There are more parallels between this epistle and the teaching of the Lord Jesus in the Gospels than in any other New Testament book. Both the frequency and the nature of these occurrences are significant. James never directly quotes the Lord. Rather, James reproduces the Lord's teaching in an authentic, original manner. "The degree to which James is permeated by parallels to Jesus' teaching can be accounted for only if James so thoroughly knew that teaching-probably in oral form-that it had molded his own views and attitudes" (Carson, Moo, and Morris, *An Introduction to the New Testament*, 416).

Hiebert lists the following parallels between the epistle of James and Jesus' Sermon on the Mount (*The Epistle of James*, 17).

James	Matthew
1:2	5:10-12
1:4	5:48
1:5; 5:15	7:7-12
1:9	5:3
1:20	5:22
2:13	5:7; 6:14-15
2:14-16	7:21-23

3:17-18	5:9
4:4	6:24
4:10	5:3-4
4:11	7:1-2
5:2	6:19
5:10	5:12
5:12	5:33-37

Old Testament Roots and Jewishness. James has been called "the Amos of the New Testament." Like Amos, James uses word pictures that are drawn from nature. James attacks social injustice and also appeals to the Jewish heritage he shares with his readers. He writes as a devout Jew who has found completion in Christ, the Messiah. James contains allusions to over twenty Old Testament books (Bailey and Constable, *Nelson's New Testament Survey*, 538). Some claim it is the most Jewish writing in the New Testament.

Omission of major doctrinal teaching. James is noted for what he does not say. He makes no reference to the incarnation, crucifixion, or resurrection of Jesus. Paul began his epistles with a major doctrinal section. By contrast, James makes brief allusions to essential doctrines, but only as support for his ethical teaching (Guthrie, *New Testament Introduction*, 737). Hiebert offers this explanation, "But these omissions do not mean that the writer was devoid of doctrinal convictions. The practical purpose of James did not call for an exposition of his doctrinal views, but there is a good deal of what has been called 'compressed theology' in the epistle" (*An Introduction to the New Testament*, 55).

Imperatives. No other New Testament book contains such a concentration of commands. James addresses the problems directly and with compelling authority. Imperatives abound! Fully one half of the verses contain a call to action. "He assumes the position of an official teacher, sure of his ground, with no questions about his authority. In the 108 verses of the epistle, he uses 54 imperatives" (Hiebert, *An Introduction to the New Testament*, 55).

Literary Style. James defies easy characterization. Some have classified it as a "diatribe," a collection of individual discourses lacking a central theme. Others see James as a carefully constructed work with several recurring themes (Davids, *The Epistle of James*, 23-25). Parallelism, prominent in Hebrew poetry, appears in the structure of James. The themes of testing, wisdom and wealth are introduced (1:2-11) and then repeated with new elements added (1:12-25) (Blomberg, *From Pentecost to Patmos*, 393-404). Contrasts are drawn between rich and poor, heavenly and earthly wisdom, and obedience and disobedience. James also makes use of a feature that Hiebert calls *duadipelosis,* "the linking together of clauses and sentences by the repetition of the leading word or some of its cognates" (*An Introduction to the New Testament*, 3:55). He identifies patience, lacking, asking, and doubting as examples found in 1:2-6.

Quality of Greek. One of the arguments used against the traditional view of authorship is that the author uses excellent Greek, but Robertson and others contend that the quality issue is overstated. The language is exceptionally good, but not of the caliber exhibited by Luke and Paul. Galilee was a bilingual region and James would have had opportunity to master the language. His leadership of the church and dealings with Hellenistic Jews would have further improved his Greek. Still, it is worth noting that James, the brother of our Lord used Greek with compelling force. He was clearly a man of uncommon intellectual ability as well as moral integrity.

> "The distinctness of the book of James from other New Testament books is a witness to the manysidedness of Christianity. Its contribution is needed to convey the full revelation of the truth in Christ" (Hiebert, *The Epistle of James*, 47).

Theme and Structure

Theme. The primary emphasis of James is on the genuineness of faith as evidenced in its outworking before men (2:14-26). "Paul and James, then, are talking about different things: Paul of the declaration of our righteousness and James about the demonstration of our righteousness" (Carson, Moo, and Morris, *An Introduction to the New Testament*, 419). True religion is known by the fruit it bears (1:26-27). James proposes a series of tests to distinguish the living faith from dead faith. These include controlling the tongue as the supreme example of self-mastery (3:1-18), love that extends fellowship without showing favoritism (2:1-13), and submission to God that shows itself in humble service to others (4:1-12).

Key verse, 2:26
For just as the body without the spirit is dead, so also faith without works is dead

---

Structure. The epistle of James is difficult to outline. The number of proposed divisions within the book range from 2 to 25. Some have despaired of finding any cohesive design, treating it rather as a series of disjointed exhortations. Ironically, those who practice form criticism or redaction criticism have been the strongest proponents of structure (Davids, *The Epistle of James*, 22-27). The epistle contains a series of exhortations centered on the thesis that true faith is proven in the tests of life and is authenticated by works. The recurring themes of wisdom, testing, riches and the tongue are interwoven as unifying cords that bind these exhortations together.

Outline
True faith is proven in the tests of life and authenticated by works.

Salutation   1:1

I.   True faith matures through trials   1:2-12
    A. Exhortation: Consider trials with joy   1:2
    B. Explanation: Trials develop perseverance   1:3
    C. Outcome: Perseverance produces maturity   1:4
    D. Enablement: Prayer secures God's wisdom   1:5-8
    E. Application: Life's true value is eternal   1:9-11
    F. Conclusion: Crown of life awaits the tested 1:12

II. True faith withstands temptation   1:13-18
    A. Exhortation: Don't blame God for temptation 1:13
    B. Explanation: Temptation comes from within   1:14
    C. Outcome: Yielding leads to sin and death   1:15
    D. Explanation: God gives only/all good gifts   1:16-17
    E. Conclusion: God has created us to overcome   1:18

III. True faith obeys the Word   1:19-27
    A. Exhortation: follow a new standard of life   1:19-20
    B. Enablement: allow the Word to do its work   1:21
    C. Explanation: Obedience to the Word is essential 1:22-25
    D. Application: Obedience is evidenced by actions 1:26-27

IV. True faith loves without favoritism   2:1-13
    A. Exhortation: Don't show favoritism   2:1
    B. Example: Favoring the rich over the poor   2:2-4

C.	Explanation:	2:5-11
	1. God has chosen the poor	2:5
	2. The rich oppress you	2:6-7
	3. Scripture condemns favoritism	2:8-11
D.	Application: Prepare to be judged by Scripture	2:12-13

V.	True faith is authenticated by works	2:14-26
A.	Question: Can inoperative faith save?	2:14
B.	Illustration: Words without works can't meet needs	2:15-16
C.	Conclusion: Faith without works is dead	2:17
D.	Application: True faith shows itself in works	2:18-19
E.	Evidence: From Abraham	2:20-23
F.	Application: Works authenticate faith	2:24
G.	Evidence: From Rahab	2:25
H.	Application: Faith without works is dead	2:26

VI.	True faith controls the tongue	3:1-18
A.	Principle: Mature faith controls the tongue	3:1-2
B.	Explanation:	3:3-8
	1. The tongue has great power	3:3-4
	2. The tongue is destructive	3:5-6
	3. The tongue is untamable	3:7-8
C.	Application: True faith must control the tongue	3:9-12
D.	Enablement: Wisdom from above	3:13-18

VII.	True faith submits to God not the world	4:1-17
A.	Question: What causes fights and quarrels?	4:1-2
B.	Answer: It is the fruit of submitting to the world	4:3-4
C.	Explanation: Indwelling Spirit is offended	4:5-6
D.	Exhortation: Submit to God	4:7
E.	Explanation: Humble yourselves before God	4:8-10
F.	Application:	4:11-16
	1. Don't slander or judge others	4:11-12
	2. Life is uncertain, but God is sovereign	4:13-16
G.	Conclusion: Knowing without doing is sin!	4:17

VIII.	Warning against wealthy oppressors	5:1-6
A.	Announcement: Judgment is coming	5:1
B.	Explanation: Wealth will be destroyed	5:2-3
C.	Cause of judgment: Oppression of the poor	5:4-6

IX. True faith patiently awaits the Lord's coming	5:7-12
A. Exhortation: Be patient until the Lord's coming	5:7
B. Explanation: Stand fast, He is coming soon	5:8-9
C. Illustration: Prophets and Job persevered	5:10-11
D. Application: Don't lose control of your tongue	5:12
X. True faith prevails through prayer	5:13-20
A. Exhortation: To prayer and praise	5:13
B. Application:	5:14-16
1. In sickness-prayer and faith	5:14-15
2. In sin-confession and forgiveness	5:16
C. Illustration: Elijah prevailed by prayer	5:17-18
D. Summation: Restoring brethren brings blessing	5:19-20

Bibliography

Adamson, James B. *The Epistle of James*. The New International Commentary on the New Testament. Grand Rapids: Wm. B. Eerdmans Publishing Co., 1976.

Davids, Peter H. *The Epistle of James*. New International Greek Testament Commentary. Grand Rapids: Wm. B. Eerdmans Publishing Co., 1982.

Guthrie, George H. "James." In *The Expositor's Bible Commentary*. Vol.13, rev. ed. Grand Rapids: Zondervan Publishing House, 2006.

Hiebert, D. Edmond. *The Epistle of James*. Chicago: Moody Press, rev. ed. 1992.

Martin, Ralph P. *James*. Word Biblical Commentaries. Waco, TX: Word Books, 1989.

McKnight Scot. *The Letter of James*. The New International Commentary on the New Testament. Grand Rapids: Wm. B. Eerdmans Publishing Co., 2011.

Moo, Douglas J. *The Letter of James*. Pillar New Testament Commentary. Grand Rapids: Wm. B. Eerdmans Publishing Co., 2000.

Motyer, J. A. *The Message of James*. The Bible Speaks Today. Downers Gove, IL: InterVarsity Press, 1985.

Nystrom, David P. *James.* NIV Application Commentary. Grand Rapids: Zondervan Publishing House, 1997.

Osborne, Grant R. *James, 1-2 Peter, Jude.* Cornerstone Biblical Commentary. Carol Stream, IL: Tyndale House Publishers, 2011.

Varner, William. *The Book of James: A New Perspective.* Kress Biblical Resources. The Woodlands, TX: 2010.

1 PETER: True Grace for Fiery Trials

Key verse: 5:12, *I have written to you briefly, exhorting and testifying that this is the true grace of God. Stand firm in it!*

Key words: Jesus Christ, God, Holy, Suffering, Grace, Glory, Love, Faith, Hope

Standing Firm In The Midst of Suffering

Strangers- scattered — *Stand firm!*

1:1-2 Peter, an apostle, to God's elect			
Salvation:	**Sanctification:**	**Submission:**	**Suffering:**
1:3-12 **Our Destiny**	1:13-2:12 **Our Duty**	2:13-3:12 **Our Duty**	3:13-5:11 **Our Discipline**
Living hope	Be holy like our Father	To the state	For the right reason
Secure inheritance	Love from the heart	To masters/employers	With the right attitude
Glorious joy	Grow in the Word	To wives and husbands	With praise not shame
Future glory	Restrain the flesh	To the body of Christ	Will result in eternal glory
Gave us new birth and a living hope	Redeemed us with His precious blood	**Jesus Christ:** Bore our sins, set the example of suffering	Rose from the dead and now is exalted in heaven
Grief in all kinds of trials prove our faith	Holy living leads to false accusations	**Suffering:** Unjust/for doing good Called to it for Christ	Painful for a little while, but God will make you strong
5:12-14 Purpose: to exhort and testify			AD 64 Peter to Jewish and Gentile Christians of the Diaspora, from "Babylon"

1 PETER

First Peter has been one of the most warmly received and widely used books in the New Testament. It breathes a spirit of confidence and hope in the midst of suffering. It is a loving call to action and a source of strength for those enduring suffering. Saints through the ages have drawn strength from Peter's instruction on how to face "fiery trials" (4:12). Jesus had warned the disciples, especially Peter, that intense persecution awaited them as His followers (John 15:18-16:4, 33; 21:18-19). Jesus' promise was being fulfilled when Peter penned this letter. Christians were coming under attack from local Roman governments as well as from the Jewish religious establishment. The believers were citizens of heaven, but suffered as strangers on earth (1:1; 2:11). Like the Jews of the diaspora, Christians were aliens in a hostile environment. "The first epistle of Peter has appropriately been called 'the epistle of the living hope.' It sets forth the hope of the believer in the midst of a hostile world. Addressed to those who stood as strangers in the midst of an antagonistic and oppressive world, it is a ringing appeal to steadfast endurance and unswerving loyalty to Christ" (D. Edmond Hiebert, *An Introduction to the New Testament*, 1:105).

Authenticity and Acceptance

Early acceptance. The church recognized the authenticity and apostolic authority of 1 Peter early and universally. It stands in stark contrast to the second letter attributed to the pen of the apostle Peter. First Peter was widely and warmly embraced as apostolic while 2 Peter was slowly and cautiously affirmed as authentic. "The early Church had no doubts concerning the authenticity of 1 Peter. The evidence for the epistle is early and clear, and it is as strong as for any other book in the New Testament. It was universally received as an acknowledged part of the Christian Scriptures. ... Only since the 19th century have radical critics sought to discredit the epistle" (Hiebert, *An Introduction to the New Testament*, 3:105-6).

Recent criticism. Recently some scholars have questioned the genuineness of the salutation, *Peter, an apostle of Jesus Christ* (1:1). Critical objections focus on (1) the language and style of the epistle, (2) historical questions, and (3) doctrinal issues (Donald Guthrie, *New Testament*

416

Introduction, 763-67). To these might be added the challenge regarding the unity of the letter. Much is made of the contrast between the general suffering that characterizes the first portion of the letter and the "fiery trials" introduced in 4:12-5:11. These objections are examined fairly and answered very well by Guthrie. The early and universal acceptance of 1 Peter is so strong that Guthrie asserts, "Our conclusion must be that this epistle not only exerted a wide influence on early Christian writings, but that it also possessed for them apostolic authority. This makes clear that the primitive church, as far back as any evidence exists, regarded it as a genuine epistle of Peter, and thus any discussion of objections to Petrine authorship must sufficiently take account of this fact" (*New Testament Introduction,* 762).

Author

Internal evidence for Petrine authorship. Personal references by the author point unmistakably to Peter. The humility and reticence with which Peter speaks of himself argues against a forger using Peter's name. A pseudo-author would make much more of this apostolic authority than does Peter himself. Critics question 1 Peter because the author mentions himself somewhat obliquely, but they use the frequent personal references of 2 Peter as an argument against Petrine authorship. One cannot have it both ways! Several lines of evidence support Petrine authorship. (1) The author makes a direct claim to be *Peter, an apostle of Jesus Christ* (1:1). (2) The author claims to have been *a witness of Christ's sufferings!* (5:1). He writes as one who was deeply and personally impacted by the Lord's death on the cross (1:18-20; 3:18; 4:1). (3) The Gospels and the book of Acts paint a clear portrait of the apostle Peter and the content, style, and convictions of 1 Peter breathe that same spirit. (4) The author shows familiarity with Jesus' teaching. Thirty-two passages directly parallel the words of Jesus in the Gospels. (5) This epistle is appropriate to Jesus' commission to Peter. In his post-resurrection interchange with Peter, Jesus repeatedly called Peter to be a shepherd to the church (John 21:15-19). The shepherd motif and the author's claim to be a *fellow elder* ring true (5:1-4).

External evidence for Petrine authorship. The church never seemed to entertain doubts about authorship by Peter. Polycarp (AD 69-155) and Clement of Rome (AD 30-100) both quote the letter. Irenaeus (AD 140-203) is the first to formally mention Peter as the author. Eusebius placed it among the *homologoumena,* the books universally accepted by the church. In exploring the evidence Guthrie claims, "The very great weight of patristic evidence in favor of Petrine authorship and the absence of any dissentient voice raises so strong a presupposition in favor of the correctness of the claims of the epistle to be Peter's own work that it is surprising that this has been questioned" (*New Testament Introduction,* 762).

Objections to Petrine authorship. The most credible objection to authorship by Peter is on historical grounds. It is charged that the persecution described by Peter is systematic and has been initiated by the Roman emperor. The expression "fiery trials" (4:12) is taken as a reference to second century persecution under Trajan. Peter was martyred under Nero around AD 64, making it impossible for him to be the author of this 2nd century letter. But the language of 1 Peter does not require such an understanding. The persecution seen in the epistle is local not universal. Christians from the earliest times suffered at the hands of local governments. "Suffering 'for the Name' was known to Christians even before the time of the Neronian persecutions. ... They may be explained as the result of the spasmodic outbursts of pagan fanaticism against Christians (4:4). At any rate, it is now generally admitted that there is nothing in the epistle which *compels* us to date it later than the Neronian persecutions" (Hiebert, *An Introduction to the New Testament*, 3:108).

The stylistic and linguistic objections are answered by the social conditions of Galilee during Peter's lifetime. The excellence of the Greek language and familiarity with the Septuagint are consistent with the culture found in Peter's home territory, Galilee. Similarities between 1 Peter and the epistles of Paul are explainable. Frequent interaction between Peter and Paul, widespread circulation and use of Paul's letters (particularly Romans and Ephesians), and their common source in the Lord Jesus Christ all help to explain the similarities. Recent scholarship has added support by highlighting the originality and value of 1 Peter (Guthrie, *New Testament Introduction,* 774-76).

Silas hypothesis. Similarities of thought and language between 1 Peter and the letters of Paul have caused some scholars to credit Silas with the actual writing of the letter while incorporating the ideas of Peter. Silas may have helped in the writing of the letter (5:12). However, the similarities are usually overemphasized in this approach and the distinctives diminished. Guthrie counters that argument with evidence that "suggests that Silas played a far less important part than the amanuensis hypothesis implies. Not only so, 5:12 would stand as a rather obnoxious piece of self-commendation, unless in fact Peter himself added this conclusion. It is further difficult to imagine that the direct appeal of 5:1 and ff. could have been the indirect work of a secretary. The personal authority is so real that it would be necessary to maintain that for this part of the letter the apostle had dictated. ... If Peter had the help of Silas it would seem improbable, by reason of the whole tone of the letter, that the author allowed too much freedom to his secretary. At least the finished article was given out very definitely as Peter's personal message, invested with his own special authority" (*New Testament Introduction,* 770).

Audience

Jewish and Gentile Christians. Peter's use of the term *diaspora* (1:1) and the frequent quotations from the Old Testament are cited as evidence that Peter is writing to Jewish Christians. However, Peter also refers to them as formerly *not a people* (2:9). They also share a past with the Gentiles (4:3). Such references point strongly toward Gentile Christians as the intended recipients. "The correct interpretation of the facts requires a combination of both views. As in the case of most churches outside of Palestine, their membership was of mixed racial origin. They were composed of both Jewish and Gentile Christians, with perhaps the Gentiles in the majority in most churches. Peter thinks of them not as Jews or Gentiles but as all members of one Body in Christ" (Hiebert, *An Introduction to the New Testament,* 3:113-14).

Location. The letter is addressed to *God's elect, strangers in the world, scattered throughout Pontius, Galatia, Capadocia, Asia, and Bithynia* (1:1). That may refer to Roman provinces at the time or designate old geographical areas. The Roman provinces would include all of Asia Minor, whereas the designation of old geographic locations would restrict the area. The area is now part of Northern Turkey. Peter does not claim responsibility for planting the churches (1:12). They were probably an extension of Paul's ministry in Ephesus (Acts 19:10). Co-workers of Paul probably did the actual evangelization as Epaphras did at Colosse (Colossians 1:3-8). Both Paul and Peter had contact with these churches. First Peter is a general letter addressed to Christians across the region as a part of Peter's shepherding ministry.

Occasion

Growing persecution. Peter sensed a gathering storm that would bring intensified persecution to the Christian community. The church had known opposition ever since Pentecost, but it was increasing in severity as

Peter wrote. Some appeared surprised by the escalation (4:12). Thus the two strands of suffering and hope are intertwined throughout the letter.

Slander because of separation. A high tide of evil was washing over the Roman Empire. Peter describes conditions as a *flood of dissipation* (4:3-4). Those believers who separated from pagan indulgence found themselves misunderstood and slandered as a result of their disciplined and pure lifestyle (2:12, 15; 3:16).

Charges of disloyalty to the state. Corruption and abuse permeated the Roman government. Peter found it necessary to exhort the Christians to submit to Roman authorities in spite of the corruption and to persist in doing what was right (2:13-17).

Tendency to compromise with the world. The old sin principle still carried on its internal war against their souls (2:11). The world around them solicited that old tendency toward sin (4:1-6). The devil was orchestrating the campaign and was alert for stragglers (5:8-9). Along with equipping the saints for suffering, Peter was exhorting them to holy living (1:13-17; 2:1, 12; 4:1-2).

Leadership challenges. Greed, pride, and authoritarianism were insidious enemies (5:2-3). There was considerable room for improvement in the area of brotherly love (3:8-9; 4:8-9). Spiritual gifts were not always faithfully or enthusiastically used to benefit others (4:9-11; 5:1-6).

Immaturity. Not all believers were making satisfactory progress toward maturity (2:1-3). They were destined to be severely tested by persecution and needed to become *strong, firm, and steadfast* (5:10).

Place and Date of Writing

Identity of Babylon. Controversy has surrounded Peter's reference to Babylon (5:13). Three different locations have been suggested. One location, a city by that name in Egypt, is highly unlikely. Most of the debate alternates between the actual city named Babylon on the Euphrates and a veiled reference to Rome as "Babylon." If Peter is using the term literally then it would indicate he had a ministry in Babylon and was writing from that location prior to his arrest and martyrdom in Rome. However, church history is silent regarding such a ministry and the existence of a Christian church in Babylon. It is more likely that Peter is using Babylon as a metaphor for Rome. Like Babylon, Rome had become the world center of wealth and power. Seeds of decay were already sown through emperor worship, overindulgence, and rampant immorality. Rome was powerful but morally bankrupt. The great Roman Empire would later collapse under the weight of its own indulgences and excesses. Both Peter and John sensed that Rome was the "Babylon" of their day.

Date. Authorship by Peter suggests a date of AD 64 or earlier. That was the year Nero unleashed his blood bath. Nero himself died in AD 68. Most conservative scholars favor a date immediately before or at the beginning of the Neronian persecution. Conditions described in 1 Peter support that conclusion. "We conclude that the epistle was written on the eve of the outbreak of the Neronian persecution. The date then assigned to it must be in the summer of AD 64" (Hiebert, *An Introduction to the New Testament*, 3:121).

Distinctive Features and Contribution

Theology. If theology was "absent" in James, it abounds in 1 Peter. The letter opens with a doxology rich in theological truths (1:3-12). The divine plan of redemption is outlined from eternity past to eternity future. Peter explains the distinct roles of the Father, Son, and Holy Spirit in salvation. The regenerating power of Scripture (1:23-25), the unique nature of the church (2:9-10), and the substitutionary atonement of Christ (1:18-21; 2:24; 3:18) are briefly but clearly explained. Most notable of all is the frequency with which Peter refers to God. God is mentioned thirty-nine times (an average of once in every forty-three words). Peter describes God as *Father* (1:2), *judge* (1:17), *living* (1:23), and *faithful Creator* (4:19). He is also the *God of all grace,* another favorite word of Peter that appears ten times in this letter (5:10). "There is more, but this is sufficient to make it clear that Peter is giving us a full and satisfying understanding of who God is and what he is doing" (D. A. Carson, Douglas J. Moo, and Leon Morris, *Introduction to the New Testament*, 428).

Suffering of Christ and the saints. Peter leaves no doubt that salvation is possible only through the suffering of Christ. The verb *paschō,* "suffering," appears twelve times in 1 Peter and only eleven times in all the rest of the New Testament epistles. Redemption through the shed blood of Christ was planned even before creation (1:18-21). The sin- bearing work of Christ on the cross is treated uniquely in 1 Peter 2:24 and Hebrews 9:28. Peter mentions the sufferings of Christ during His life repeatedly as an example for saints to follow (2:21-23; 4:1). The disciple who so strenuously resisted the cross and suffering of Christ (Matthew 16:21-23) now clings to that saving reality. Christians are called to share in Christ's suffering (2:21). The trials they are enduring are *painful* (NIV) and *fiery* (KJV). Though severe, their suffering is only for *a little while* and will result in glory (1:7; 5:10). In this brief letter Peter tells the saints how to handle suffering by following the pattern set by their Lord.

Christ's decent into Hades. Peter's statement that Christ preached "to the spirits in prison" (3:19) is one of the most difficult passages to be found in Scripture. The nature of this preaching, the identity of the "spirits," and the relation with baptism challenge the interpreter.

Focus on the future. There is good reason for calling 1 Peter "the epistle of the living hope." Believers have a secure hope (1:3-4) and a glorious future (1:13, 21; 5:4, 10).

Practical content. The language of Peter is direct and forceful, much like the author himself. Peter uses thirty-four imperatives. Unlike James, these are frequently rooted in theology. Peter speaks directly to husbands and wives (3:1-7), to slaves (2:18-21), and to elders (5:1-4). Peter covers a wide range of subjects with deep theological insight and practical application. This letter bears evidence of how well Peter took to heart Jesus' call to be a shepherd to His sheep (John 21:15-19).

Purpose and Plan

Purpose. Peter left no doubt about the primary purpose of this letter. He stated it in a closing paragraph. *Through Silas, our faithful brother, (for so I regard him), I have written to you briefly, exhorting and testifying that this is the true grace of God. Stand firm in it!* (5:12). Peter's purpose is twofold: first, to exhort (call to action), and second, to testify (confirm the truth of the gospel they had trusted for their salvation). "The hortatory character of the epistle is its prominent feature. It is always entirely hortatory. It is not a doctrinal treatise but a powerful appeal to courage, purity, and faithfulness to Christ amid the sufferings which they are experiencing. It is full of that 'comfort which only a true Christian, rich in faith and rich in love, can give to the suffering'" (Hiebert, *An Introduction to the New Testament*, 3:122). "Exhortation" is a strategic word for Peter to use. It comes from *parakaleō* and conveys the idea of one called alongside of another person to help, admonish, comfort, or exhort. It is the verbal form of the word Jesus used to describe the promised Holy Spirit (John 14:26; 16:7, 14). Peter was acting as an agent of the Holy Spirit in this call to action. Peter ends with a summation of all these exhortations, "stand firm!"

Peter's second purpose, *testify*, is equally significant. "Testify," is an intensified form of *martureō*, "to testify emphatically, appear as a witness decidedly for something" (Spiros Zodiates, *The Complete Word Dictionary: New Testament*, 631). Peter is writing about suffering and is giving a personal witness to the truth of the gospel. The term has been transliterated into English as *martyr*. The intense form used by Peter appears only here in the New Testament. "Peter bore witness to the reality that the message of salvation that the readers had received was indeed the true grace of God. *Grace* points to the objective message of salvation in Christ, and *true* confirms that message to be genuine and trustworthy. *This (tauten)*, the demonstrative pronoun, looked back to the message of salvation presented in the epistle. The message of God's grace that the readers received at conversion and were experiencing in their Christian growth was no delusion; they were to allow their sufferings to cast no shadow of uncertainty of that reality" (D. Edmond Hiebert, *First Peter: An Expositional Commentary*, 308-09).

Key Verse, 5:12
I have written to you briefly, exhorting and testifying that this is the true grace of God. Stand firm in it!

Message of 1 Peter

First Peter offers the Christian "true grace for fiery trials." Peter lays a solid theological foundation and gives a strong personal witness authenticating the gospel these believers have trusted. From his opening declaration of salvation (1:3-12) to his closing promise of eternal glory (5:10) Peter validates the faith of these suffering saints.

Introduction (1:1-2). Peter identifies himself simply as *an apostle of Jesus Christ* without mentioning his leading role as a follower of Jesus Christ, thus exemplifying the humility and servant spirit that he urges on other leaders (5:1-7). His readers are *aliens,* indicating that they live in a foreign and often hostile environment, and are *scattered,* διέσπειρα indicating that they are dispersed (*diaspora*) like seeds sown throughout the territory with the expectation that they will take root and produce fruit where they have been planted. Whatever their status on earth they are special because they have been *chosen* by God. God's choice of them was planned in eternity past, made effective through the Holy Spirit and purchased by the blood of Jesus Christ. Peter's prayer for them is that the grace and peace of the God who has chosen them would be theirs *in the fullest measure* (1:2).

> "Christians are not distinguished from the rest of mankind by either country, speech or customs. ... They reside in their respective countries, but only as aliens. They take part in everything as citizens and put up with everything as foreigners. Every foreign land is their home, and every home a foreign land. ... They find themselves in the flesh, but do not live according to the flesh. They spend their days on earth, but hold citizenship in heaven" (*The Epistle to Diognetus*, anonymous, quoted in David Otis Fuller, *Valiant for the Truth: A Treasury of Evangelical Writings*, 9-10).

The Believer's Destiny: Salvation (1:3-12). Their destiny: they have a living hope that is secure in heaven (1:3-12). The Christian's life is as secure in heaven as it is tenuous on earth. Their future hope is certain and their present faith is shielded by God's power until that triumphant day (1:3-5). A note of expectancy pervades the entire epistle in light of the Lord's return. It is a living hope (1:3) that triumphs over as well as through suffering (1:5-8). Christians rejoice because of their position in Christ though it may lead to suffering (1:1-12). The prophets told of this coming salvation and understood by revelation that it was not for them but for a yet future time. Angels marvel at the salvation that believers in Christ enjoy.

The Believer's Duty: Sanctification (1:13-2:12). Believers are to grow in their relationship with God (1:13-21), in their relationship with other believers ((1:21-25), and in their inner life (2:1-12). Holiness is essential not optional in light of, (1) the Holy One who called them, (2) the One before whom they must give account (1:13-17), and (3) the high cost of their redemption. They have been purchased by the blood of Christ, the precious blood of a perfect lamb unblemished and untainted by sin (1:18-21). Obedience to that saving truth ought to result in fervent love for one another, and the believer has been given the Scriptures as food to nurture growth (1:22-25). Salvation is secure in heaven but calls for spiritual growth here on earth (2:1-12). Growth is not automatic but is the result of intentional effort (2:1-3). Believers have come to Christ, the living stone, and the divine plan is that they should be *a chosen race, a royal priesthood, a holy nation, a people for God's own possession, so that you may proclaim the excellencies of Him who has called you out of darkness into His marvelous light* (2:1-10). Peter makes a closing appeal by reverting to his opening description of the readers as *aliens and strangers* and reminds them that the world may misunderstand and malign them just as it did Christ (2:11-12).

The Believer's Duty: Submission (2:13-3:12). Believers are to live godly lives in the midst of a hostile world. A high and holy position in Christ carries with it the responsibility to submit to those in government (2:13-17), to their masters in the marketplace (2:18-25), and to others within the family (3:1-7). Submission is in every dimension of life and may include false accusations and unjust suffering (2:13-20). If submission seems unappealing they are reminded that Christ himself set the example of submission and did not retaliate when He was reviled (2:21-25). Peter will soon remind them that Christ did not submit in vain since He is now in heaven and seated at the Father's right hand (3:22). Wives are to be in submission to their husbands, husbands are to thoughtfully respect their wives, and both are to be in submission to God (3:1-6). Submission is primarily that of the heart to God (3:7-12) and its effect is seen in all facets of earthly life.

The Believer's Discipline: Suffering (3:13-5:11). A holy life infuriates those under Satan's control and causes them to persecute the Christian (3:13-4:6). If believers suffer for righteousness' sake at the hands of pagans, this is normal and to be endured without shame. Christ established a pattern in His suffering for them. Being armed with the same mind, they ought to continue to live holy lives even though it occasions unjust suffering for Christ's sake. Suffering is temporary (4:7-11). Though a "fiery trial" it is a means of partaking in Christ's sufferings (4:12-19). God's remarkable plan for His children and the pattern set by Christ enable Christians to praise God and persist under suffering (4:19). An additional responsibility is placed on the elders who, as undershepherds, are to be examples to the flock (5:1-4). The young are to submit to their elders (5:5). Humble submission to God and alertness toward the devil are the norm for all suffering saints (5:6-9). Believers who humble themselves now *under the mighty hand of God*, will be *exalted at the proper time*. They are reminded that the devil is the ultimate source of their suffering, that they are not suffering alone, and that God's sovereign purpose is being surely worked out in them.

Peter's benediction is a synopsis of the entire book and the believer's sure hope in suffering. *After you have suffered for a little while, the God of all grace, who called you to His eternal glory in Christ, will Himself perfect, confirm, strengthen and establish you. To Him be dominion forever and ever. Amen* (5:10-11).

Conclusion (5:11-14). A clear statement of purpose and personal greetings closes out Peter's letter of encouragement, confirmation, and hope (5:12-14). Peter has had a twofold purpose in writing: (1) to confirm that the faith they have embraced is beyond doubt *the true grace of God* and (2) to encourage them to *stand fast* in that grace.

Outline

I. Introduction	1:1-2
A. The writer	1:1a
B. The readers	1:1b-2a
1. Special to God	
2. Strangers in the world	
3. Scattered for a purpose	
4. Saved by the triune God	
C. The greeting	1:2b
II. The Destiny of the Christian: Salvation	1:3-12
A. Its source	1:3a
1. The God of great mercy	
2. The death and resurrection of Christ	
B. Its substance	1:3b-4a
1. A new birth	
2. A living hope	
3. A heavenly inheritance	
C. Its certainty	1:4b-9
1. The inheritance is safeguarded in heaven	1:4b
2. The heirs are shielded on earth	1:5
3. The faith triumphs through testing	1:6-7
4. The future hope brings present joy	1:8-9
D. Its significance	1:l0-12
1. Predicted by the Spirit	
2. Pondered by the prophets	
3. Admired by the angels.	
III. The Duty of the Christian: Sanctification	1:13-2:12
A. Toward God: holiness	1:13-21
1. Conforming to our hope	1:13
2. Conforming to our Father	1:14-16
3. Conforming to our salvation	1:17-21

B. Toward fellow believers: love — 1:22-25
    1. Exhortation: to love from the heart — 1:22
    2. Explanation: through the power of the Word — 1:23-25
C. Toward ourselves: grow — 2:1-12
    1. Get rid of sin — 2:1
    2. Grow to maturity in salvation — 2:2-3
    3. Grow together with fellow believers — 2:4-8
    4. Glow as God's people in a dark world — 2:9-10
    5. Say no to the old sinful appetites — 2:11
    6. Show your salvation by actions — 2:12

IV. The Duty of the Christian: Submission — 2:13-3:12
A. Submission in the state — 2:13-17
    1. The exhortation: submit to authority — 2:13a
    2. The explanation: it is God's will — 2:13b-15
    3. The application: live as servants of God — 3:16-17
B. Submission to owners/employers — 2:18-25
    1. Exhortation: submit to your masters — 2:18
    2. Explanation: it is commendable to God — 2:19-20
    3. Example: Christ did not retaliate, He trusted — 2:21-23
    4. Application: trust the Shepherd of your soul — 2:24-25
C. Submission in the family — 3:1-7
    1. Exhortation to wives: submit to your husbands — 3:1-6
    2. Exhortation to husbands: honor your wives — 3:7
D. Submission in the church — 3:8-12
    1. Exhortation: love as brothers — 3:8-9a
    2. Explanation: blessing rests on those who do — 3:9b-12

V. The Discipline of the Christian: Suffering — 3:13-5:11
A. Anticipating unjust suffering — 3:13-22
    1. Issue: unjust suffering — 3:13-14
    2. Exhortation: set Christ as Lord in your hearts — 3:15-16a
    3. Explanation: suffer unjustly don't do evil — 3:16b-17
    4. Example: Christ died, was raised, is now exalted — 3:18-22
B. Arming ourselves with the right attitude — 4:1-11
    1. Example of Christ: He suffered in the body — 4:1a
    2. Exhortation: adopt the same attitude — 4:1b
    3. Explanation: live for God not for the flesh — 4:2-6
    4. Incentive: the end is near — 4:7a
    5. Application: serve in God's strength — 4:7b-11a
    6. Outcome: that God may be praised — 4:11b

C. Understanding and accepting suffering	4:12-19
1. Reason: participating in Christ's suffering	4:12-15
2. Response expected: commit yourself to God	4:16-19
D. Concluding appeal	5:1-9
1. To elders: serve willingly, by example	5:1-4
2. To young men: submit to elders in authority	5:5a
3. To all: humble yourselves before God	5:5b-7
4. To all: resist the devil	5:8-9
E. Benediction	5:10-11
VI. Conclusion	5:12-14
A. Purpose for writing: to encourage and testify	5:12a
B. Final appeal: this is the true grace, stand fast in it!	5:12b
C. Personal greetings: from Babylon	5:13-14

Bibliography

Blomberg, Craig L. *From Pentecost to Patmos.* Nashville: Broadman & Holman Publishers, 2006,

Blum, Edwin A., and Glenn W. Barker. "1, 2 Peter; 1, 2, 3 John; Jude." In *The Expositor's Bible Commentary*. Grand Rapids: Zondervan Publishing House, 1996.

Carson, D. A., Douglas J. Moo, and Leon Morris, *Introduction to the New Testament.* Grand Rapids: Zondervan Publishing House, 1992.

Charles, J. Daryl. "1, 2 Peter, Jude." In *The Expositor's Bible Commentary*. Vol.13, rev. ed. Grand Rapids: Zondervan Publishing House, 2006.

Davids, Peter H. *The First Epistle of Peter.* New International Commentary on the New Testament Series. Grand Rapids: Wm. B. Eerdmans Publishing Co., 1990.

Fuller, David Otis, compiler and editor. *Valiant for the Truth: A Treasury of Evangelical Writings.* New York: McGraw-Hill, 1961.

Grudem, Wayne A. *The First Epistle of Peter: Introduction and Commentary.* Tyndale New Testament Commentaries. Grand Rapids: Wm. B. Eerdmans Publishing Co., 1988.

Guthrie, Donald. *New Testament Introduction.* Downers Grove, IL: InterVarsity Press, 1990.

Hiebert, D. Edmond. An *Introduction to the New Testament.* Vol. 3. Chicago: Moody Press, 1975.

____. *First Peter.* Chicago: Moody Press, 1984.

Jobes, Karen H. *1 Peter.* Baker Evangelical Commentary on the New Testament. Grand Rapids: Baker Academic, 2005.

Kelly, J. N. D. *First Peter.* Peabody, MA: Hendrickson, 1993.

Kistemaker, Simon J. *James, Epistles of John, Peter, and Jude.* New Testament Commentary. Grand Rapids: Baker Book House, 1996.

Michaels, J. Ramsey. *1 Peter.* Word Biblical Commentary. Nashville: Thomas Nelson Publishers, 1988.

Schreiner, Thomas. *The First Epistle of Peter.* New American Commentary. Nashville: Broadman and Holman Publishers, 2003.

Walls, David, and Max Anders. *1, 2 Peter, 1, 2, 3 John, Jude.* Holman New Testament Commentary. Nashville: Broadman and Holman, 1999.

Wuest, Kenneth S. *First Peter in the Greek New Testament.* Grand Rapids: Wm. B. Eerdmans Publishing Co., 1954.

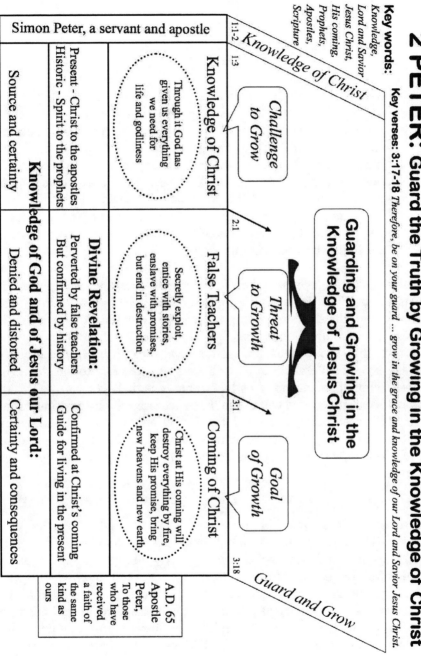

2 PETER

Second Peter is the last testament of Simon Peter (1:12-15). Peter is conscious that his martyrdom is rapidly approaching, 2 Peter is reminiscent of Paul's second letter to Timothy. The church is facing assault from a hostile world, but it is also being infiltrated by false teachers (2:1-22). The church is at risk of being infected by the growing indifference to Christ's return and the judgment to follow (3:1-16). Second Peter might well have been written today at the dawning of a third millennium. Like a mirror, it reflects the pagan culture of our times and the prevailing condition of the church. Second Peter is greatly needed, yet it is little known and is lightly regarded in our time.

Each of the Petrine epistles presents a timely message. In 1 Peter the emphasis is on Christian suffering inflicted by a hostile world; in 2 Peter the stress is on the dangers arising from apostasy within the church. The first is an exhortation to endurance and loyalty to Christ amid undeserved opposition; the second is an appeal for loyalty to Christ in the midst of subtle heresy. First Peter instructs believers how to react to their external enemies, while the second epistle strengthens believers to resist the internal adversaries of the truth. The first encourages hope amid suffering; the second accentuates the need for full knowledge as the safeguard against vicious error. Thus, the pertinent message of 1 Peter to persecuted believers is supplemented by the equally apt warning against prevalent apostasy in 2 Peter.

Authenticity

Readers of 2 Peter may be surprised that this letter is the most controversial of all New Testament epistles. Acceptance by the early church was slow and guarded. However, "early doubts nowhere took the form of definite rejection" (Guthrie, *New Testament Introduction*, 806). The same cannot be said for modern scholarship. Recent critics have all but abandoned the authenticity of 2 Peter as a genuine letter from Peter. The issues of authenticity and authorship are inseparably linked. While important in our assessment and use of 2 Peter, it is impossible to explore the issue here in an exhaustive fashion. Guthrie and Hiebert treat both the epistle itself and the critical objections thoroughly and fairly.

External support for the authenticity of 2 Peter. Several lines of evidence support the authentic nature of this epistle. (1) The earliest and strongest support for 2 Peter is the epistle by Jude. This of course depends on accepting the view that 2 Peter was written before Jude. (2) The Apocalypse of Peter, a second-century writing, contains coincidences with 2 Peter that are more than accidental. This again assumes the priority of 2 Peter. Support comes from the fact that the church did not recognize the Apocalypse of Peter as authentic and was cautious in accepting any book. (3) Writing early in the third century, Origen cited 2 Peter six times. He showed little hesitation in accepting 2 Peter as canonical, probably reflecting the thinking of his day. (4) Almost a century later Eusebius placed 2 Peter among the disputed books, but implied that it was regarded as authentic. (5) At the close of the fourth century Jerome placed 2 Peter in the canon of Scripture, but proposed a new solution to the question of authorship. He suggested that Peter used two different amanuenses, hence the difference in literary style. Doubt about its authenticity seemed to vanish from the fourth century until recent years. "The external evidence for 2 Peter, compared to the first epistle is meager and late. The second epistle had a much narrower circulation than the first and came much more slowly to general recognition. It was not expressly quoted during the first two centuries, and when it did come into general circulation, questions concerning its authenticity were naturally raised. But, as Guthrie observes, those 'early doubts nowhere took the form of definite rejection.' No other name than that of Peter was ever connected with it" (Hiebert, *Second Peter and Jude*, 5).

Critical Objections. There are five arguments raised against Petrine authorship. These include (1) the personal allusions, (2) historical problems, (3) literary problems, (4) stylistic problems, and (5) doctrinal problems. After careful analysis Guthrie concludes that the evidence supports and adequately explains the authenticity of 2 Peter (Donald Guthrie, *New Testament Introduction*, 812-42).

Internal Evidence. The author claims to be Peter and identifies himself as an apostle. The writer calls himself Simon Peter (1:1). He claims to be a personal eyewitness of the transfiguration of Christ (1:16-18) and recalls the Lord's prediction of His death (1:14; John 21:18-19). The author places himself on a par with the apostle Paul (3:15). He also claims to have written a previous letter (3:1). While critics reject these personal claims as excessive, a forger would hardly have made such a blatant attempt to imitate Peter, nor would the church have accepted such a forgery.

433

A comparison of other pseudonymous writings of the time truly sets 2 Peter above the rest. Inspiration of the epistle is validated by its doctrinal integrity and its moral value. Second Peter is unquestioned on both counts (Hiebert, *An Introduction to the New Testament*, 3:147). Peter boldly claims inspiration for the writing of Paul (3:15). While less direct, he appears also to be associating himself and all apostles alongside the Old Testament prophets as recipients of divine revelation (1:16-21). Rejection of the doctrine of inspiration is not an acceptable ground for rejecting the authenticity of 2 Peter. "The conservative position is that the Petrine authorship is not without rational explanation, and that it furnishes the best and least confusing solution to the difficult problem. This view receives at face value the claims of the epistle and eliminates all implications of deception in the personal references in the epistle. We accept this as the best working solution" (Hiebert, *An Introduction to the New Testament*, 3:149).

Authorship

Peter. The early church cautiously embraced the epistle as a genuine work of the apostle Peter. The marked difference in literary style and the prevalence of pseudo-epistles help explain the slow acceptance of the epistle. Based on strong internal evidence, the test of time and integrity, the church accepted Peter as the author of the epistle.

Testament of Peter. Jerome suggested that Peter was not the direct author, but that the material was genuinely Petrine, that is, it was written by an associate utilizing Peter's teaching. Calvin and a number of recent scholars have adopted this position. While this preserves the authenticity of the material, it does not satisfactorily explain the epistle's claim to be written by Peter.

Pseudonymous. The majority of critical scholars today assign the writing of 2 Peter to an unknown author in the second century. They do not doubt that the author claims to be Peter, but they consider those claims to be "a harmless literary device" or a "pious fraud." Given the poor quality of such psuedepigraphal writings of the second century and their rejection by the early church, it is unlikely that 2 Peter would have been confirmed as an authentic work of Peter by the early church (Michael Green, *Second Peter and Jude*, 33-39).

Audience

The readers of this letter are not specifically identified. The author indicates that this is his "second letter" to the same readers (3:1). Based on this statement, it is likely that the intended audience was the same as the audience addressed in 1 Peter. Both are general letters intended for a wide audience. The conditions described are specific to the readers, but are symptomatic of conditions in the church at large. Second Peter was apparently intended for Jewish and Gentile Christians in Asia Minor (1 Peter 1:1).

Occasion and Date

Peter's approaching martyrdom. A sense of personal urgency pervades this letter. Peter is now "old," but that is not the underlying reason for urgency. The Lord Jesus Christ has made clear to him that his death is just over the horizon (1:13-14). An interesting interpretive issue is raised by Peter's use of the term "soon" in describing his departure. "This adverb, placed prominently forward, may indicate the time of his death as approaching speedily, or it may describe the manner of his death as swift, that is, violent. If Peter means that he is to die soon, there is good reason to admonish them [his readers] earnestly now. If he means that he will die quickly, giving no opportunity for any deathbed exhortations, the sense of urgency is even stronger. ... In light of the confirmatory statement it seems more natural to hold that Peter is thinking of a sudden death by crucifixion. But it may well be that both elements were in Peter's mind; Christ's prophecy to him that he would die a violent death related to the time of his old age (John 21:18). His advanced years assured him the time was near" (Hiebert, *Second Peter and Jude*, 67).

Infiltration of False Teachers. Peter was concerned by an outbreak of heresy that was threatening the church. In the first epistle Christians faced an external threat from persecution. In this second epistle they face an internal threat from an infectious heresy (2:1). As the false prophets of the Old Testament destroyed the faith of Israel, so these false teachers threatened the faith of the church. Peter's use of the future tense through most of chapter 2 suggests that the problem was likely to be a continuing threat to the church. Second Peter is reminiscent of Paul's second letter to Timothy. Peter gives a graphic detailed description of the false teachers (2:1-22). Some take this as a description of second-century Gnosticism. However, it is more likely that the heresy is simple antinomianism (against law or regulations). Paul had to battle this at Corinth as well. Christian liberty has always faced the dual threat of legalism on the one hand and license on the other. At most, the heresy addressed by Peter is an incipient form of Gnosticism that would later blossom into a philosophical movement. "This false teaching was characterized by antinomianism with its resultant immoral tendencies. It was marked by immorality, irreverence, and insubordination" (Hiebert, *An Introduction to the New Testament*, 3:152).

Date. The date of 2 Peter hinges on our view of its authorship. Those who see it as pseudepigraphal place it in the middle of the second century. Authorship by Peter requires a date no later than AD 68, the year of Nero's death. Nero unleashed his campaign of terror against Christians in the later part of AD 64. If Peter was martyred by Nero, and before Paul, then a probable date is AD 65.

Purpose

Guarding the faith. The primary intent of this letter is to warn Christians about the infiltration of false teachers (3:17; 2:1-22). These Christians have already been well established in the truth (1:12). However, there is a risk that they will "fall from their secure position" as a result of these false teachers (1:10; 3:17). Christians are capable of being enticed and exploited by clever manipulators of truth (2:1-3). Second Peter is a warning against false teachers (2:1-22) and an appeal to the Christian readers to think correctly (1:12-13) by acquiring true knowledge (1:16-21; 3:18).

Growing in Grace and Knowledge. Guarding and growing are Siamese twins in Peter's thought. Growth in grace and knowledge represents both the cause and the cure for their problems. Immaturity, the lack of growth, makes them highly susceptible to false teachers. In turn, error will keep them from maturing in Christ. Thus the cure for infectious false teaching and the best defense against it is growing to maturity in Christ (1:2-11; 3:18).

Theme. The twin themes of guarding the faith and growing are woven together throughout the epistle and highlighted at its conclusion (3:17-18).

Distinctive Features

Inspiration. Peter makes a major contribution to our understanding of the doctrine of inspiration. He attributes the recording of divine revelation to the work of the Holy Spirit (1:21). He also describes the unique process by which the Spirit of God works in and through human authors (1:20-21). By ranking Paul's writings with "the other Scriptures" Peter is equating Paul's letters (and for that matter, other New Testament writings) with the inspired writings of the Old Testament (3:15-16). These are key passages on the doctrine of inspiration. Along with 2 Timothy 3:16 they explain the nature and origin of the Scriptures.

Knowledge. This brief epistle begins and ends with an emphasis on knowledge (1:2; 3:18). Knowing Christ is the most important issue in life and eternity. Knowing Christ is the key to guarding the faith and to growing to maturity. Hiebert explains, "The keynote of 2 Peter is knowledge. A prominent place is given to it. The words *know or knowledge*, in their varied forms, occur sixteen times in the epistle. Six times the intensive form, signifying *full knowledge*, is used (*An Introduction to the New Testament*, 3:153).

License. This epistle provides the most comprehensive description of license to be found in the New Testament. References to this perversion of grace are also found in James, Jude, and the writings of Paul. Second Peter provides an excellent analysis of the false beliefs and deceptive practices of those who turn Christian liberty into license (2:1-22).

Epochs of Time. Much was made of Peter's statement, "With the Lord a day is like a thousand years" (3:8) when we approached the new millennium in 2000. Peter's emphasis on the second coming of Christ is not unique, but it is valuable. What is unique to Peter is his division of human history into three distinct epochs (3:4-13).

"Here Peter divides history into three vast cosmic epochs and indicates something of the characteristics of each. There was the antediluvian world, the world destroyed by the Flood (vv. 5-6); there is the present cosmic system, 'the heavens that now are, and the earth' (v. 7), which will come to a fiery apocalyptic consummation; then there is the future order, the 'new heavens and a new earth' (v. 13) wherein righteousness shall be at home. In the light of our own atomic era this prophetic message in 2 Peter has suddenly taken on striking relevance. Until well within the 20th century the skeptics continued to say, 'all things continue as they were from the beginning of the creation' (3:4). But with the bursting of the atomic age it is becoming frightfully evident that Peter's picture of the destruction of this present world's system by means of a universal conflagration is not just an impossible fantasy but offers evidence that gives a sober picture of prophetic revelation" (Hiebert, *An Introduction to the New Testament*, 3:154-55).

Vocabulary. For a man who was unschooled, Peter exhibited a flare for unusual words when he penned this letter. One of the arguments critics use against the authenticity of 2 Peter is the large number of words unique to both of these two letters by Peter. There are 361 Greek words in 1 Peter that do not occur in 2 Peter. Similarly there are 231 words found in 2 Peter that do not appear in 1 Peter. The difference is striking. Less often noticed, but even more significant is the comparison of these two letters to the rest of the New Testament. Proportionately, there are seven times as many rare words in 1 Peter as in the New Testament as a whole and ten times as many in 2 Peter. Similarities between the two epistles are often overlooked, as are their differences from the rest of the New Testament. The Greek language of 2 Peter lacks the smoothness of 1 Peter, but is equally rich in unique words and ideas (Homer Kingsley Ebright, *The Petrine Epistles: A Critical Study of Authorship,* 121).

Key Verses

You therefore, beloved, knowing this beforehand, be on your guard so that you are not carried away by the error of unprincipled men and fall from your own steadfastness, but grow in the grace and knowledge of our Lord and Savior Jesus Christ. To Him be the glory, both now and to the day of eternity. Amen (3:17-18).

"Know," (*gnosis*) is one of Peter's favorite words. He uses it or a variation of it sixteen times in this short letter. Six of those occurrences involve an intensified form of knowing, *epignosis,* "full knowledge" (1:2, 3, 8; 2:20, 21 [twice]). Grace and truth come through the knowledge of God and the Lord Jesus (1:2). Everything the Christian needs for life and godliness comes through the knowledge of Christ (1:3). Their knowledge rests on God's revelation in the Old Testament Scriptures and through Christ Himself (1:12-21). That is also the source of their knowledge about the future day of the Lord (3:1-13). Right thinking precedes right living. The best way to guard against error is to grow to maturity in our knowledge of Christ. Peter may have been "unschooled" and "ignorant" (Acts 4:13), but he had discovered the overwhelming power of knowing Christ.

Peter's thesis:

Guard the truth and yourselves against error by growing in the grace and knowledge of our Lord and Savior Jesus Christ (3:17-18).

Message of 2 Peter

Challenge to grow to maturity in Christ (1:1-21). Grace and peace are centered not in ourselves, but in the knowledge of God and of Jesus our Lord (1:2). Through this knowledge Jesus supplies all we need for life and godliness (1:3). Claiming God's precious promises enables us to become more like Christ and less like our fallen world (1:4). Our present fruitfulness and future reward depend on the extent to which we develop these spiritual qualities (1:5-11). The certainty of this knowledge is that of inspiration. Our faith rests on established truth that has been divinely revealed and recorded (1:12-21).

False teachers: the threat to growing in the knowledge of Christ (2:1-22). False prophets have existed in the past, and in our day false teachers will seek to undermine this knowledge (2:1-19). Their heresies are shameful and blasphemous. These false teachers infiltrate the body of Christ and spread their corruption like a virus. They solicit the old sin nature and bring our past enslavement to sin back to life. God is able to deliver his own, but these false teachers are destined for judgment. Their repudiation of Christ indicates their true character and calls for greater guilt and judgment (2:20-22).

Christ's coming: the goal of our growing in knowledge (3:1-18). Our knowledge of Christ awaits the Second Coming for its full and glorious completion. Scoffers oppose all thoughts of future judgment and blessing. They do not recognize the signs and deliberately reject the promises of Christ's coming (3:1-7). However, Christ will certainly come and the day of the Lord will be accompanied with an outpouring of divine wrath (3:8-13). Such a judgment calls for holy living and patient endurance on the part of believers (3:14-16).

Peter concludes with a call to guard this precious faith and to grow in the grace and knowledge of our Lord and Savior Jesus Christ (3:17-18). Knowing Christ is our best defense against the subtle error that would cause us to fall. Knowing Christ is also the source of a productive life now and a guarantee of our glorious future. Guarding that faith and growing in that knowledge is our high calling.

Outline

I.	Introduction	1:1-2
	A. The writer	1:1a
	B. The readers	1:1b
	C. The greeting	1:2
II.	Challenge to Grow in the Knowledge of Christ	1:3-21
	A. The provision for growth	1:3-4
	1. God has given us everything we need for growth	1:3a
	2. Knowing Christ is the basis of growth	1:3b
	3. Christlikeness is the fruit of growth	1:4
	B. The process of growth	1:5-7
	1. Growth requires nurturing	1:5a, 10a
	2. Seven qualities to nurture	1:5b-7
	C. The results and incentives for growth	1:8-11
	The characteristics of spiritual growth:	
	1. When abounding; we are effective and fruitful	1:8
	2. When absent; we are blind and unproductive	1:9
	3. When present; they are evidence of our election	1:10a
	4. When present; they safeguard us against failure	1:10b
	5. When complete; we receive a rich welcome	1:11
	D. The grounds for growing in knowledge	1:12-21
	1. Contemporary revelation	1:12-18
	a. Peter's timely reminder of known truth	1:12
	b. Peter's reason for the reminder	1:13-14
	c. Peter's commitment to their future	1:15
	d. Peter's source is revelation from Christ	1:16-18
	2. Historic revelation	1:19-21
	a. Its authority and importance	1:19
	b. Its divine origin	1:20-21
III.	False Teachers: Threaten Growth in Knowledge	2:1-22
	A. Description of false teachers	2:1-3
	1. Their evil intent	2:1
	2. Their effect and effectiveness	2:2
	3. Their motives and methods	2:3
	B. Destruction of false teachers	2:4-9
	1. Example of angels	2:4
	2. Example of the pre-Flood world	2:5
	3. Example of Sodom and Gomorrah	2:6

4.	Deliverance of Lot	2:7-8
5.	Conclusion: certainty of divine justice	2:9
C.	Denunciation of false teachers	2:10-22
1.	Lawless arrogance	2:10-11
2.	Brutish ignorance	2:10
3.	Sexual perversion	2:13-14a
4.	Obsessive greed	2:14b-16
5.	Spiritual bankruptcy	2:17
6.	Depraved sensuality	2:18-19
7.	Apostate character confirmed	2:20-22

IV. Christ's Coming: The Goal of Our Growing in Knowledge 3:1-18
   A. Peter's timely reminder of known truth — 3:1-2
      1. Goal of the reminder: wholesome thinking — 3:1
      2. Grounds of the reminder: divine revelation — 3:2
   B. The issue: scoffers who deny Christ's coming — 3:3-7
      1. Their accusation: "Where is this coming?" — 3:3-4
      2. Their error: they deliberately forget: — 3:5-7
         a. Past destruction by the Flood — 3:5-6
         b. Future destruction by fire — 3:7
   C. The answer to scoffers: Christ's coming is certain — 3:8-10
      1. The Lord is patient — 3:8-9
         a. The Lord's perspective on time — 3:8
         b. The Lord's purpose for delay — 3:9
      2. The judgment is certain — 3:10
   D. Application to the saints: in light of Christ's coming — 3:11-16
      1. Issue: what kind of people ought you to be? — 3:11a
      2. Answer: — 3:11b-16
         a. Live holy and godly lives — 3:11b
         b. Live expectantly — 3:12-13
         c. Live purposefully — 3:14
         d. Live thoughtfully — 3:15-16
   E. Appeal: guard the truth and grow in knowledge — 3:17-18
      1. The appeal to guard the truth from error — 3:17
      2. The appeal to grow in the knowledge of Christ — 3:18a
   F. Doxology — 3:18b

Bibliography

Charles, J. Daryl. "1, 2 Peter, Jude." In *The Expositor's Bible Commentary*. Vol. 13, rev. ed. Grand Rapids: Zondervan Publishing House, 2006.

Ebright, Homer Kingsley. *The Petrine Epistles: A Critical Study of Authorship*. Cincinnati: Methodist Book Concern, 1917.

Green, Michael. *The Second Epistle General of Peter and the General Epistle of Jude*. Grand Rapids: Wm. B. Eerdmans Co., Revised, 1998.

Guthrie, Donald. *New Testament Introduction.* Downers Grove, IL: InterVarsity Press, 1990.

Hiebert, D. Edmond. *Second Peter and Jude: An Expositional Commentary*. Greenville, SC: Unusual Publications, 1989.

____. *An Introduction to the New Testament.* Vol. 3. Chicago: Moody Press, 1975.

Kistemaker, Simon J. *James, Epistles of John, Peter and Jude*. New Testament Commentary. Grand Rapids: Baker Book House, 1996.

Moo, Douglas J. *2 Peter and Jude*. The NIV Application Commentary Series. Grand Rapids: Zondervan Publishing House, 1996.

Osborne, Grant R. *James, 1-2 Peter, Jude.* Cornerstone Biblical Commentary, Carol Stream, IL: Tyndale House Publishers, 2011.

Walls, David and Max Anders. *1, 2, Peter, 1, 2, 3 John, Jude*. Holman New Testament Commentary. Nashville: Broadman and Holman Publishers, 1999.

Wuest, Kenneth S. *In The Last Days: II Peter, I, II, III, John and Jude.* Grand Rapids: Wm. B. Eerdmans Publishing Co., 1954.

1 JOHN: Fellowship in Eternal Life

Key verses: 1:3 & 5:13: *That you may have fellowship... that you may know that you have eternal life.*

Key words:
Jesus Christ,
Son, Truth,
Know, Abide,
Light, Love,
Life, Sin,
World

Fellowship

		In Light	In Righteousness	In Love	
Introduction		*Certainty of the Incarnation*			
1:1-4	1:5		2:29	4:7	5:13-21

First Cycle of Tests:
- Obedience: Moral Test 1:5-2:6
- Brotherly Love: Social Test 2:7-17
- Truth about Christ: Doctrinal Test 2:18-28

Second Cycle of Tests:
- Doing Right: Moral Test 2:29-3:10
- Brotherly Love: Social Test 3:11-24
- Truth about Christ: Doctrinal Test 4:1-6

Third Cycle of Tests:
- Brotherly Love: Social Test 4:7-21
- Obedience: Moral Test 5:1-5
- Truth about Christ: Doctrinal Test 5:6-12

God is Light — *We are children of God!* — *God is Love*

Conclusion

The Certainties of Life

AD 95-100
Apostle John to the church in Asia Minor invaded by false teachers and inclined to worldliness

1 JOHN

What we have seen and heard we proclaim to you also, so that you too may have fellowship with us; and indeed our fellowship is with the Father, and with His Son Jesus Christ. These things we write, so that our joy may be made complete (1 John 1:3-4). *These things I have written to you who believe in the name of the Son of God, so that you may know that you have eternal life* (1 John 5:13).

The first epistle of John is one of the most widely read and best-loved books of the New Testament. It succeeds in being personal without a single person being named. It breathes a spirit of intimacy without openly identifying either the writer or the readers. The assembly addressed is local, specific and well known, yet the letter is universal in appeal and application. The style of the author is authoritative, but not abrasive. It is stern yet tender. It treats profoundly important truths such as the deity and humanity of Christ, yet it includes practical truths for everyday life. It reflects the spirit of its author who is at once a "son of thunder" and the "apostle of love." "The forcible simplicity of its sentences, the note of finality behind its utterances, the marvelous blending of gentle love and deep-cutting sternness of its contents, and the majesty of its ungarnished thoughts, have made 1 John a favorite of Christians everywhere. The simplicity of its language makes it intelligible to the simplest saint, while the profundity of its truths challenges the most accomplished scholar. Its grand theological revelations and its unwavering ethical demands have left their enduring impact upon the thought and life of the Christian church" (D. Edmond Hiebert, *An Introduction to the New Testament*, 3:181).

Authenticity and Acceptance

The first epistle of John was accepted and used early and widely by the church. Polycarp (AD 69-115), Papias, (80-155), Irenaeus (140-203), Tertullian (155-222), and Origen (185-253) endorse the epistle as apostolic and authoritative. "The evidence shows that this epistle, undoubtedly one of the latest of the New Testament books to be written, took an immediate and permanent position as an authoritative writing of inspiration" (Hiebert, *An Introduction to the New Testament*, 3:184). Some recent scholars have questioned the Johannine authorship and thus the authenticity of this epistle primarily due to their doubts about the authorship of the Gospel of John. Moffatt, Bultmamn, Brown and Dodd are representatives of those who argue against the authorship by the apostle John. But none have succeeded in countering the definitive work of Westcott in defending apostolic authorship by John. Regarding the theory that an unknown John is the author, Donald Guthrie concludes, "It is extremely difficult on this hypothesis to account for the unchallenged tradition of the church in favor of apostolic authorship. It is admitted by most students of the New Testament Canon that this epistle gained acceptance on the grounds of its supposed apostolic origin, but were the Church Fathers likely to become confused about two Johns? In spite of all assertions to the contrary, it must be admitted that these alternative theories do not provide as adequate an explanation of the high regard in which the epistle was held as the traditional testimony" (*New Testament Introduction*, 863-64).

Authorship by John the Apostle

External evidence. Earliest writings of the church are clear and unanimous in identifying the apostle John as the author of this epistle. Polycarp claimed to know John personally, as did Papias. Irenaeus refers to this familiarity and expressly identifies John as the author in his quotations of 1 John. The Muratorian Canon (AD 170) includes the epistle and ascribes it to John. John did not identify himself in the book, but the church immediately recognized his voice and attributed it to him. Eusebius (AD 260-340) wrote, "But of the writings of John, not only his Gospel, but also the former of his epistles, has been accepted without dispute both now and in ancient times." Burdick adds, "It was, therefore, the universal opinion of the church throughout the second and third centuries that John the apostle was the author of the first epistle. No voice was raised in opposition to that view; no other person was suggested as author. It was furthermore commonly assumed that the same John wrote both the fourth gospel and the first epistle" (*The Letters of John the Apostle*, 26).

Internal evidence. Internal evidence confirms the opinion of the early church that this epistle was written by the apostle John himself. Internal evidence includes the following:
1. The author claims to be an eyewitness of the life and ministry of Christ (1:1-4; 4:14).
2. The author demonstrates a familiarity with his readers that suggests a long personal ministry among them (2:1, 12, 28; 3:7, 18; 4:4; 5:21). Early church writings indicate John had an extensive ministry to the

Christians of Asia. The addressees of the book of Revelation add further support.

3. The authoritative manner of the writer flows from his apostolic authority (1:6-8, 10; 2:4-5, 15; 4:1; 5:21). "Whereas others might, and did, possess such authority and exercise it in their writings, there was no one to whom it was more becoming than to an apostle. Hence, in the authoritative tone of the epistle we find another corroboration of the church Father's witness to John as the author" (Burdick, *The Letters of John the Apostle*, 30).

4. John's character as a "son of thunder" (Mark 3:17) is evident in the epistle. It was John who sought to prevent an exorcist from casting out demons in Jesus' name (Mark 9:38). It was John who suggested calling down bolts of lightning to destroy an inhospitable village in Samaria (Luke 9:54). The love and tenderness of this epistle do not obscure the decisive call for purity so characteristic of John (1:6; 2:4, 18, 22; 4:1). "A forceful personality cannot readily be concealed. It is inevitably reflected in a person's style of speaking and writing. To this rule 1 John is no exception. Whoever wrote the epistle was obviously a blunt and vigorous individual—a son of thunder. Again the internal evidence is in harmony with the external. Both point to John the apostle as author" (Burdick, *The Letters of John the Apostle*, 31).

5. Similarities between 1 John and the Gospel of John point to a common authorship. In fact, similarities in style and terminology abound. Brooke lists 51 references in the Epistle of 1 John that parallel statements in the Gospel (A. E. Brooke, *A Critical and Exegetical Commentary of the Johannine Epistles*, li-iv). Both make frequent use of contrasting parallels such as light and darkness, life and death, love and hate, truth and falsehood, the children of God and the children of the devil, etc. William M. Ramsey concludes, "There can be no doubt that the same hand can be traced in the First Epistle and the Fourth Gospel. No two works in the whole range of literature show clearer signs of the genius of one writer, and no other pair of works are so completely in a class by themselves, apart from their work of their own and of every other time" (William M. Ramsey, *The Church in the Roman Empire Before AD 170*, 302-3).

Alternative Views. Two popular opinions circulated during the last century. One identified the author as John "the elder." The existence of this second John and his ministry at Ephesus rests on a disputed reference attributed to Papias. The existence of a second John actually came about because Eusebius was opposed to the Jewishness and millennialism of

Revelation and used Papias for support. Recent scholars who doubt the existence of John "the elder" propose a third, anonymous John as the author. But the early and unbroken tradition of the church, along with the compelling internal evidence, argues for the apostolic authorship of 1 John.

Readers, Location and Date

Readers. The destination of the letter is not stated. From comments within the epistle we are able to draw the following conclusions or at least inferences: (1) they were believers in the Lord Jesus Christ. John calls them brothers (3:13, 14, and 16). Many statements are made about them that are only true of born-again believers (2:12-14, 20-28; 3:1, 3, 13-14; 4:4, 6, 13, 16; 5:4, 13-15). (2) They had a long, personal association with the author. He is not actually writing something "new" to them (2:7, 18, 20, 21, 24, 27; 3:11). They had probably been Christians for some length of time (2:7, 24). (3) They were probably Gentile converts. This is inferred from the fact that there are no quotations from the Old Testament. The warning against idolatry (5:21) would be true of former pagans as well as converts from Judaism. (4) They are under attack from false teachers (2:18-27; 4:1-6). The epistle contains many tests to be applied to those claiming to be imparting new truth. (5) The believers are tempted to worldliness (2:15-17). Either because of the false teachers' misuse of Christian freedom, or the readers growing complacency, John had to emphasize the seriousness of sin and the necessity for righteousness (1:6-2:6). (6) The readers were occasionally lacking in love for another (3:11-15; 4:7-12).

Location. The epistle contains no geographical clues. Strong and well-documented evidence from early church history indicates that John had an extended ministry in Asia, particularly at Ephesus. The letters to the seven churches found in Revelation corroborates this. The content of the epistle points to the readers as being members of a particular local church or at least churches sharing a common area and relationship with John. Though not a "general" or "circular" letter, 1 John is appropriate to what is known of the churches in Asia at the close of the first century. "In view of the tradition about John's ministry in Asia and the fact that the earliest testimonies to the epistle come from that province, it seems most natural to locate the readers there. The scope of John's Asian ministry, as well as the absence of all that which is merely local in the epistle, leads to the conclusion that it was addressed to a group of congregations under the supervision of the writer" (Hiebert, *An Introduction to the New Testament*, 3:198).

Date. Suggested dates for the writing of 1 John extend all the way from AD 60 to 100. The absence of any reference to the destruction of Jerusalem suggests a date before AD 70 or a considerable time later. Hodges is among those who place the epistle early. He suggests a date of "somewhere between AD 60 and 65." He says a date even earlier than that is possible (Zane C. Hodges, "1 John," in *The Bible Knowledge Commentary*, 882). Such an early date is not widely held. It rests, at least in part, on the idea that the epistle was written before the Gospel of John. Hodges also suggests that the writing was based in Jerusalem and the false teachers who "went out from us" (2:19) originated in the Jerusalem church. While possible, these arguments and the early date are not widely accepted. Most place the writing of 1 John sometime between AD 80 and the close of the first century. The status of the readers does suggest that they have been Christians for a long time. The false teaching is more characteristic of the region of Ephesus than Jerusalem. Indications from early church history point to an extended ministry by John in Ephesus, Corinth, and surrounding areas. Hiebert favors a date around AD 80 but most scholars favor a date of AD 95 to 100 (Guthrie, *New Testament Introduction*, 879).

Occasion: False Teaching

The immediate occasion for writing this letter was the infiltration of the church by false teachers (2:26; 4:1). The error being taught centered on two cardinal doctrines: the incarnation of the Lord Jesus Christ, and the nature of sin and the believer's responsibility. Several heresies were being propagated among the churches even before the close of the first century. Burdick offers this summary; "The heresy combated in John's first epistle was, as previously seen, perverted in its Christology and woefully deficient in its morality. It denied that Jesus was the Christ, the pre-existent Son of God. It was not necessarily a denial of the historicity of Jesus, nor of the existence of the Christ, but it was a denial that the two were to be identified as one and the same Person. Such a disavowal was a repudiation of the incarnate Jesus of whom the apostles had intimate knowledge. In the area of morality the heresy was decidedly antinomian, not a careless kind of antinomianism, but a reasoned, purposeful kind. Even though those heretics walked in darkness, they insisted that they neither committed sin nor possessed a sinful nature" (Burdick, *The Letters of John the Apostle*, 61). The heresy combated by John was an early, incipient form of Gnosticism. Gnosticism took many shapes, but always exhibited two primary characteristics: intellectualism and dualism.

Intellectualism. Gnosticism is derived from the Greek word *ginoskō*, "to know." Gnostics considered themselves the "knowing ones." They were the "elite" of Christendom and they viewed the "unenlightened" of the church with contempt. According to Hiebert, "For them spiritual excellence consisted not in a holy life but in a superior knowledge which enabled a man to rise above the earthbound chains of matter into the heavenly apprehension of truth. This not infrequently led to a disregard of the ethical demands of Christianity. ... In opposition to this dangerous teaching John insisted on the intimate relation between doctrine and conduct. He points out that Christian knowledge, possessed as the result of the anointing from the Holy One (2:20), is a knowledge which involves holiness of life and conduct as well as intellectual enlightenment (1:5-2:5)" (*An Introduction to the New Testament*, 3:202).

Dualism. Gnostics held that matter is evil and spirit is good. These two were in constant conflict. They were most often represented as light (spirit) and darkness (matter). This had many implications, but the most crucial was in the area of the incarnation. Gnosticism could not accept the union of deity and humanity in the person of the Lord Jesus Christ. If matter is absolutely evil, then the Son of God could not be united with humanity. To them the incarnation was impossible. John wrote to defend and explain the incarnation (1:1-3; 2:22-23; 4:1-3, 15; 2 John 9). The denial of the incarnation took two forms, Docetism and Cerinthianism.

Docetism taught that Christ only seemed to have a human body. Docetism is derived from the Greek term *dokeo*, "to seem, to appear." "The idea of an incarnate deity was unintelligible and, therefore, rejected. Docetism evolved a means of getting over the intellectual difficulty by making a distinction between the human Jesus and the heavenly Christ, the latter only appearing to take a human form. The incarnation was not, therefore, a reality. This solution, which made a wide appeal, had the added advantage, so it was thought, of avoiding the anomaly of Christ sharing in such an inherently evil thing as matter" (Guthrie, *New Testament Introduction*, 864-65).

Cerinthianism, also known as adoptionism, derived its name from the founder, Cerinthus. He and his followers taught that Christ, the divine spirit, came upon the human Jesus at his baptism and left him before the crucifixion. "Cerinthus separated Jesus from Christ. He denied the virgin birth of Jesus, but recognized that He was preeminent for righteousness, prudence and wisdom. He taught that the Christ spirit came upon Him following His baptism, empowered His ministry, but left Him before the crucifixion. The man Jesus suffered and rose again but the Christ, a pure spirit, remained impassable. In thus splitting the person of Jesus Christ, Cerinthus destroyed the reality of the incarnation and the atonement. Apparently both of these forms of error come into view in the epistle" (Hiebert, *An Introduction to the New Testament*, 3:202-03).

John's Answer

Regarding the incarnation: Jesus is the Christ (2:22; 4:15; 5:6). John refers to Jesus Christ seven times. Jesus has come in the flesh. John speaks of His: being sent (4:9-10, 14), His coming (5:20), His appearing (1:2; 3:5, 8; 4:9), His coming in the flesh (4:2; 2 John 7), and by water and blood (5:6).

Regarding sin: John charges that sin is real and contrary to God's nature (1:8-10; 2:1; 3:8). "Sin" is mentioned thirteen times, "sins" eight times, and "sinned" one time. Sin disrupts fellowship with God (1:6). It cannot continue to be practiced by believers (3:6-10) because Christ appeared to put away sin (3:5).

Regarding knowledge: John counters false intellectualism with the claim that believers have an "annointing" of the Holy Spirit (2:20; 3:24: 4:13). They "know" because they are taught by the Spirit (2:27; 3:24; 4:13; 5:6-10).

Regarding love for the brethren: John says love is intrinsic with God, and hence must be reflected in and by believers (3:16-21). Love for Christian brothers is a necessary outcome and evidence of knowing God (2:9-10; 3:10-20; 4:7-12, 17-21). The word "love" is used thirty-five times, "loves" five times, "loved" four times and "loving" once. Love is validated by actions not just expressed in words (3:17-18).

Regarding salvation: Salvation is by the new birth alone and not by intellectual enlightenment. "Born of God" is used eight times (3:9; 4:7; 5:1). It is from God and by faith. The Incarnation was essential to the atoning sacrifice (2:2; 4:9-10). "Life" or "eternal life" is used thirteen times and it is only "in the Son" (5:10-11). The Incarnation is essential to eternal life (5:20).

Purpose

John is very helpful in including a purpose statement in the epistle. The problem stems from the fact that he includes not one, but two purpose statements (1:4; 5:13). Both involve or are expressed through a series of "tests." The first occurrence (1:3-4) is a "test of fellowship," a series of tests by which a believer can determine if he or another believer is walking in fellowship with God. The second purpose statement involves the "test of life," by which a person can determine if he or others are believers. The tests of fellowship focus on communion with God, while the tests of life focus on union with God. The actual tests are the same in both cases. The three recurring tests in 1 John are obedience, or the moral test (2:3-6; 2:28-3:10); love, or the social test (2:7-11; 3:11-18; 4:7-12); and belief, or the doctrinal test (2:18-27; 4:1-6, 13-15). The instructor's preference is for the fellowship view, but both are true. Fellowship with one another is possible only because believers share a common life (1:2-3). The life they share is eternal because it is the life of the Son of God who appeared in the flesh for them (4:9-12; 5:13, 20).

Theme and Structure

Theme. The central theme of 1 John is **fellowship in eternal life.** John's purpose is to encourage believers to be assured of eternal life (5:13) and to grow in fellowship with God and with one another (1:3-4). Eternal life and fellowship are secured by the atoning work of the incarnate Son of God (1:1-2; 3:5; 4:2, 9-12; 5:10-13).

Key verses:

What we have seen and heard we proclaim to you also, so that you too may have fellowship with us; and indeed our fellowship is with the Father, and with His Son Jesus Christ. These things we write, so that our joy may be made complete (1:3-4).

I write these things to you who believe in the name of the Son of God so that you may know that you have eternal life (5:13).

John is writing to combat the false teaching concerning the Incarnation that has led not only to confusion regarding the true nature of Christ, but also to a lack of morality and brotherly love. "In as much as the specific occasion for writing was the presence of one or more forms of earlier Gnosticism, the primary purpose of John was to counteract the pressures that the false teachers were bringing to bear upon the Asian Christians" (Burdick, *The Letters of John the Apostle*, 64).

The method by which John counteracts the false teaching is twofold. He does this by repeatedly stressing the truth of the Incarnation (2:22; 4:2, 15; 5:6, 10). He also presents a clear and compelling view of the life of the believer in Christ. It is this emphasis on life in Christ that pervades the epistle and provides an answer to the false teachers that is both positive and practical.

"It was a critical period for the church, and the apostle recognizes this. He will write a letter, somewhat in the form of a tract to warn and instruct the believers in his own district about the seriousness of the peril. But his approach is to be wholly positive. He will present a wholesome picture of the true Christian life, and only incidentally denounce the error. He believes that truth is the best answer to false teaching, although he makes perfectly plain what his own estimation of that teaching is. ...

"Quite apart from the false teachers, therefore, the author has an edificatory purpose. Christians need to be challenged about the distinctive features about their faith, especially the need for the exercise of love. Nowhere else in the New Testament is the combination of faith and love so clearly brought out, and it seems probable that this is emphasized because the behavior of the readers leaves much to be desired" (Guthrie, *New Testament Introduction*, 866-67).

Structure. Students will readily agree with the assessment of Zane C. Hodges, "The First Epistle of John is notoriously difficult to outline" (Zane C. Hodges, "1 John," in *The Bible Knowledge Commentary, New Testament*, 882). Burdick explains the problem. "It is commonly agreed that the organization of 1 John is most difficult. This is true because of the intricate interrelation of its major concepts resulting in a closely-knit fabric that is not easily unraveled. For example, notice the theme of love as it reappears repeatedly in ever new and varying associations. ... A second reason for the difficulty involved in the structure of the book lies in the kind of transitions John employs. Rather than be clearly marked, they are subtle and unobtrusive, often occurring in the middle of a statement. ... The difficulty incurred in discovering the epistle's organization is also due in part to the aphoristic nature of its many statements. ... John's writing may be characterized as intuitive rather than analytical and deductive. And, whereas the structure of analytical composition is most easily discernible, the organization of intuitive writing is by no means as obvious" (Burdick, *The Letters of John the Apostle*, 85).

452

Most recent commentaries draw on the analysis of Robert Law who published, *The Tests of Life,* in 1909. He viewed the book as consisting of a prologue (1:1-4) and three cycles of tests: the first cycle (1:5-2:28) focuses on walking in the light; the second cycle (2:29-4:6) focuses on divine sonship; and the third cycle (4:7-5:21) focuses on the correlation between righteousness, love, and belief (Burdick, *The Letters of John the Apostle*, 87).

Two elements are essential to discern the outline. First, John's use of purposeful repetition, there are three cycles of tests (1:5-2:28; 2:29-4:6; 4:7-5:12). Second, three tests are repeated in each of the three cycles. Law called them, "the three cardinal tests" by which we may judge whether we possess eternal life or not. Stott explains them as follows.

> "The first is theological, whether we believe that Jesus is 'the Son of God' (3:23; 5:5, 10:13). The Christ "come in the flesh" (4:2; 2 John 7). ...The second test is moral, whether we are practicing righteousness and keeping the commands of God. Sin is shown to be wholly incompatible with the nature of God as light (1:5), the mission of the Son to take away sins (3:5) and the new birth of the believer (3:9). Now, as then, any claim to mystical experience without moral conduct is to be rejected (1:6). The third test is social, whether we love one another. Since God is love and all love comes from God, it is clear that a loveless person does not know him (4:7-8)" (John R. W. Stott, *The Letters of John*, 58-59).

Similarities with the Gospel of John

The similarities between 1 John and the Gospel of John are many and striking. They treat essentially the same subject matter. They have a similar love of opposites, light and darkness, life and death, love and hate, etc. They have the simple construction and use of parallelism evident in Hebrew literature. Christ is presented as *Logos,* "the Word." Both begin with the same emphasis on the incarnation and conclude with the emphasis on possessing eternal life through the Son of God. Similarities between 1 John and the Gospel of John are evident in the use of identical phrases. Brooke lists 51 direct parallels. Stott organizes them under 46 phrases, but an equal number of parallel occurrences (Stott, *The Letters of John,* 21-23). Stephen S. Smalley provides the following thematic list of the parallels between 1 John and John 14-17 (Smalley, *1, 2, 3 John,* xxx).

1. *The Godhead and the Christian*

The love of the Father	1 John 4:16	John 14:21
The abiding of the Son	3:24	15:4
The gift of the Spirit	4:13	14:16-17

2. *The Christian and the Godhead*
Mutual indwelling	3:24	14:20
Forgiveness	1:9	15:3 (13:8)
Eternal life	2:25	17:2
Righteousness	2:29	16:10
3. *Conditions for Christian Discipleship*
Renounce sin	1:8; 3:4	16:8
Be obedient	2:3; 3:10	14:15
Reject worldliness	2:12; 4:1	15:19
Keep the faith	2:18; 5:5	17:8

Distinctive Features

Sin unto death. John's reference to the "sin unto death" (5:16) has been intensely debated. While believers are instructed to pray for a "brother" committing a sin, they are discouraged from praying for those whose sin "leads to death." Interpretations differ substantially. Variations in interpretation center on four questions or issues.

1. What is the sin unto death (grave sin like murder or adultery, unpardonable sin of blasphemy against the Holy Spirit, persistent willful sin, or denial of the deity and incarnation of Jesus Christ)?
2. Who is the person committing the sin (unbeliever, false teacher, or Christian)?
3. What kind of death is involved (is it physical or is it spiritual, eternal death)?
4. What kind of prayer or limitation is involved (is prayer prohibited, is prayer permitted but not recommended, is it public or private prayer)?

Christology. John is writing to address a serious challenge to the truth about Jesus Christ. Christology is both the occasion and the central idea in 1 John. According to Burdick, "The Christology of 1 John revolves around two poles of equal importance: the Savior's humanity and His deity" (*The Letters of John the Apostle*, 71-73). John argues for the deity of Christ by designating him as "Son," a term he uses twenty-one times. The deity of Christ is supported by His preexistence (1:1; 2:13-14), His equality with the Father (1:2-3), and as the Messiah of Old Testament (2:22; 5:1). John ends the epistle with a ringing endorsement of the deity of Jesus Christ. *We know also that the Son of God has come and has given us understanding, so that we may know him who is true. And we are in him who is true - even in his Son Jesus Christ. He is the true God and eternal life* (5:20).

John argues with equal force for the genuine humanity of Jesus Christ. The preexistent Son has come "in the flesh" (4:2). His incarnation is as real as "water and blood" (5:6). The bodily reality of Jesus Christ is the foundation on which both the Epistle and the Christian life are based (1:1-3). "By the use of repetition and the Greek perfect tense, the apostle emphatically insists he has witnessed the reality of Christ's humanity and that the memory of that reality is still clearly with him when he writes some sixty years later. ... In contrast to the false teachers, John insists on the incarnation of the Son of God, the mystery of the divine Christ coming in human flesh—not coming *upon* human flesh, but coming in such an integral union with humanity that the result was one indivisible person, Jesus Christ (4:2)-not coming in the phantasmal semblance of human flesh, but in flesh that was real to sight, hearing, and touch (1:1)" (Burdick, *The Letters of John the Apostle*, 73).

Theology. John presents two important truths about the nature of God: *God is light* (1:5), and *God is love* (4:8). God is holy and righteous. His essence is that of absolute moral rightness. Consequently all who have fellowship with God must *walk in light* (1:6-7). This truth counteracts the false teaching that sin and physical matter are synonymous and hence not necessary or important issues in the Christian life. John insists that God takes sin seriously and so must believers. John's emphasis on *God is love* is also unique.

> "More than an assertion that God is loving or that He loves, this is an affirmation concerning the essential nature of God, what He is in His essence. All that He is, and thus all that He does, is conditioned by *agapē*, 'love,' that intelligent, self-determined, self-communicating disposition toward others that actively seeks their highest good. And because God is *agapē* essentially, He is the source of *agapē* on the human plain as well. Consequently, all who are related to Him by spiritual birth likewise possess and manifest *agapē*)" (Burdick, *The Letters of John the Apostle*, 71).

Love. The verb *agapaō* occurs twenty-eight times in 1 John. The noun, *agapē*, appears nineteen times. John has appropriately been called "the apostle of love." God's initiating love is expressed in the Incarnation (4:9) and in the atoning sacrifice of Christ for us (3:16; 4:10). The believer's love is reflective. It is the outcome of God's love (4:11-12, 19), and the necessary evidence of life in relationship to God (3:14; 4:16, 20-21). Love is to be expressed by obedience to God (5:3) and by practical, sacrificial love toward other believers (3:16-18).

Convictions based on evidence. John reaches conclusions based on the evidence. Truth is tested and confirmed by facts. The verb *ginoskō* occurs twenty-four times and the verb *oida* fifteen times. What we *know* is derived from solid evidence (2:3, 5-6, 18; 3:10, 14, 16, 18-19, 24; 4:2, 13; 5:2).

Outline of 1 John

I. Introduction: The Message Authenticated	1:1-4
A. Eyewitness proof of the incarnation	1:1-2
B. Result is fellowship with the Father and Son	1:3-4
II. First Cycle of Tests re: Fellowship in Light	1:5-2:28
A. Obedience: the moral test	1:5-2:6
1. Basis for fellowship: God is light	1:5-7
2. Conditions for maintaining fellowship	1:8-2:2
a. Confession of sin on our part	1:8-10
b. Continuous atoning advocacy by Christ	2:1-2
3. Obedience is the necessary evidence	2:3-6
B. Brotherly love: the social test	2:7-17
1. Basis for fellowship: command to love	2:7-8
2. Condition of love: no stumbling block	2:9-11
3. Call to action	2:12-14
4. Alternative condemned: loving the world	2:15-17
C. Truth about Christ: the doctrinal test	2:18-28
1. The crisis: antichrists have come	2:18-19
2. The solution	2:20-28
a. Anointing of the Spirit	2:20
b. Knowledge of the truth	2:21
c. Knowledge of the error	2:22-23
d. Abiding in the truth	2:24-28
III. Second Cycle of Tests: Fellowship in Righteousness	2:29-4:6
A. Doing Right: the moral test	2:29-3:10
1. Basis of righteousness: God is righteous	2:29-3:1
2. Consequence	3:2-6
a. Future: perfect likeness to him	3:2-3
b. Present: decisive break with sin	3:4-6

3. Call to action	3:7-10
B. Brotherly love: the social test	3:11-24
1. Basis of love: God's command	3:11
2. Wrong way to love: like Cain	3:12-15
3. Right way to love: like Christ	3:16-18
4. Consequence: confidence before God	3:19-24
C. Truth about Christ: the doctrinal test	4:1-6
1. The crisis: many false teachers	4:1
2. The criteria for testing error	4:2-3
3. The conquest through Christ	4:4-6
IV. Third Cycle of Tests: Fellowship in Love	4:7-5:12
A. Brotherly Love: the social test	4:7-21
1. Basis of love: God is love	4:7-10
2. Call to love one another	4:11-12
3. Consequence of loving one another	4:13-20
a. Confidence before God	4:13-18
b. Credibility before people	4:19-20
4. Call to love repeated	4:21
B. Obedience: the moral test	5:1-5
1. Basis: unity of belief, love, and obedience	5:1-2
2. Consequence	5:3-5
a. Love is expressed by obedience	5:3
b. Victory is assured by faith	5:4-5
C. Truth about Christ: the doctrinal test	5:6-12
1. Basis: the incarnation of Jesus Christ	5:6a
2. Confirmation: threefold witness	5:6b-12
a. External, historic witness	5:6b-8
b. Objective witness of the Father	5:9
c. Internal witness of the Spirit	5:10-12
V. Conclusion: Certainties of the Christian Life	5:13-21
A. Certainty of eternal life	5:13
B. Certainty of answered prayer	5:14-17
1. Basis: according to His will	5:14
2. Outcome: answered prayer	5:15
3. Qualification: prayer for sin unto death	5:16-17
C. Certainty of victory over the evil one	5:18-19
D. Certainty of the Incarnation	5:20
E. Call to cling to Christ not idols	5:21

2 and 3 JOHN

These two epistles are better known for their brevity than for their content. That is unfortunate. Both are a part of inspired Scripture and are valuable. They reflect the kind of correspondence that occurred frequently in the first-century church. These two letters along with Philemon help us appreciate the *koinonia* (fellowship) that existed among early believers. They also reveal the practice of Christian hospitality and the substantial role of women in congregational life. Second and 3 John are considered together because of their similarity in content and style. They have been described as "twin sisters."

Authenticity and Authorship

Authorship. Both epistles share a remarkable likeness to each other and to 1 John. The author identifies himself as "the elder" in the opening of both 2 and 3 John. Both focus on the twin themes of truth and love. "Truth" appears four times in 2 John (1, 2, 3, and 4) and six times in 3 John (1, 3 [twice], 4, 8, and 12). "Love" occurs five times in 2 John (1, 3, 5, and 6 [twice]) and twice in 3 John (1, 6). Both epistles deal with Christian hospitality. The numerous identical phrases found in both these shorter epistles and in 1 John are best explained by common authorship. More than half of the contents of 2 John are also found in 1 John.

> "It is not necessary to marshal arguments for the common authorship of 2 and 3 John; it is almost self-evident. ... There is a striking similarity of address, the same background situation of itinerant missionaries, the length, pattern, style, language and conclusion. They are 'like twin-sisters' (Alford). 'The similarity between them is too close to admit of any explanation except common authorship or conscious imitation' (Brooke); and the latter is hardly credible in view of the brevity and comparatively unimportant content of the letters" (Stott, *The Letters of John*, 30).

Authenticity. Second and 3 John were not as widely circulated as the first epistle. They were also slower to gain universal acceptance by the church. This is due to at least three factors: (1) their brevity, (2) their personal nature, and (3) the absence of major doctrine in the content. Irenaeus (AD 140-203) quotes 2 John in a manner to show he accepted it as inspired. References by Clement of Alexandria (155-215), Origen (185-253), and Cyprian (200-258) provide indirect proof of canonicity. Eusebius (AD 265-340) placed 1 and 2 John among the *antilegomena*. However, the

459

Council of Carthage (AD 397) recognized both as canonical. The church accepted the apostolic authorship by John and thus conferred canonical status on these two epistles. "The preponderance of the external evidence is definitely in favor of the apostolic authorship. The internal evidence is overwhelmingly in favor of the traditional view. The historical situation reflected in these brief letters harmonizes with our information concerning the closing years of John's life. The contents of the epistles point to the Johannine authorship" (D. Edmond Hiebert, *An Introduction to the New Testament*, 3:221).

Readers

The identity of the "elect lady" who is addressed in 2 John is debated. While some attempt to make it a proper name, it appears to be either a literal designation of an individual woman or a metaphorical reference to a local congregation. Burdick, Guthrie, and Hiebert are among those who favor identifying the "elect lady" literally with a woman who provided her home as a meeting place for the local assembly. Hodges and Stott are representative of those who favor the metaphorical understanding that the "elect lady" was actually a local congregation. Guthrie gives a fair treatment of the evidence on both sides (*New Testament Introduction*, 887-89).

The recipient of 3 John is clearly named, "my dear Gaius." This was a very common name and the actual identity of the recipient is not known. He was probably a leading believer in the local congregation. He may have been an official in the same church as that of 2 John or a church on the same circuit. Whatever the case, he distinguished himself by Christian hospitality and did so at some risk. Diotrephes was an autocratic leader and a negative example of Christian hospitality (vv. 9-10).

Occasion

The false teaching John had countered in his first epistle was apparently impacting the congregation involved in 2 John. Whether the letter was addressed to an individual woman or to the entire church, "antichrists" were at work (7-8). They were the deceivers John previously warned about who rejected the Incarnation. Christian hospitality was commendable, but not to be extended to such deceivers (vv. 10-11). Two additional reasons occasioned this letter. First, John was expressing his joy at finding "my children walking in the truth," (v. 4). Second, Demetrius was travelling to the region and probably carried all three epistles written by John.

The primary reason for 3 John seems to be the planned visit by Demetrius (3 John, 12). John wanted to ensure that this Christian friend would be shown hospitality by Gaius. This was important because Diotrephes had refused to extend Christian hospitality previously and had attempted to excommunicate those who did (vv. 9-10). John hopes to visit the area personally and will confront that situation when he arrives. In the meantime Gaius needs encouragement and Demetrius needs hospitality. This letter achieves both objectives.

Date

These two letters were probably written at the same time as 1 John. That conclusion is based on the similarities between these letters and the historical context in which they appear to have been written. As in the case of 1 John, the assigned date may vary from AD 60 to 100. Most scholars place the writing of 2 and 3 John around AD 95-100 based on the traditional understanding of John's ministry to the churches of that region.

Distinctive Features

Christian correspondence. Letter writing became an art and a major characteristic of the early church. These epistles provide a unique example of the kind of personal correspondence that strengthened the bonds between individual members and local congregations of the body of Christ. "They are valuable illustrations of a free and intimate correspondence between Christians such as have must have been very common in the early Church. They are not of any great doctrinal importance, but they do give us a vivid glimpse into the closing years of the apostolic era with its troubles and its triumphs" (Hiebert, *An Introduction to the New Testament*, 3:226).

Christian hospitality. Travelers of the first century found accommodations limited and often undesirable. Christian hospitality became a trademark of the early church. Travelers would sometimes carry letters of introduction from one congregation to another. Hospitality often included financial and other practical support as well as food and shelter. Hiebert notes, "The message of the two epistles is complimentary. They show the place and importance of Christian hospitality in the early Church. The second warns against false hospitality which would aid and further false teaching. The third commends Christian hospitality to missionary brethren as the inviolable duty of individuals and the churches. It is distinctly the epistle of missionary obligation" (*An Introduction to the New Testament*, 3:226).

Theme and Structure

Theme. Similarities between 2 and 3 John extend even to the central theme. Both concern "walking in the truth" (2 John 4; 3 John 3). A slight, but significant variation occurs in the expression of this common theme. In 2 John "love" and "obedience" are combined with "truth" in the Christian walk (vv. 3, 6). In 3 John "walking in the truth" results in "working together for the truth" (v. 8).

Structure. These epistles have an almost identical format. They begin with the common identification of the author, "the elder." They next identify the recipient, "elect lady" and "Gaius." Both epistles offer commendation to the recipient for their adherence to truth and for their love. The author makes a similar statement in both epistles about the length of the letter and about an intended visit (2 John 12; 3 John 13-14).

Key verse of 2 John

And this is love, that we walk according to His commandments. This is the commandment, just as you have heard from the beginning, that you should walk in it (2 John 6).

Outline of 2 John

I.	Introduction	1-3
	A. The writer	1a
	B. The reader(s)	1b-2
	C. The greeting	3
II.	Commendation	4-6
	A. Present example of walking in the truth	4
	B. Personal challenge to walk in love	5-6
III.	Caution regarding deceivers	7-11
	A. Warning about false teachers	7-9
	B. Warning against offering them hospitality	10-11
IV.	Conclusion	12-13
	A. The letter explained	12
	B. Greetings from children of your sister	13

Key verse of 3 John

I have no greater joy than this, to hear of my children walking in the truth (3 John 4).

Outline of 3 John

I.	Introduction	1-4
	A. The writer	1a
	B. The reader	1b
	C. The greeting	2-4
II.	Commendation of Gaius	5-8
	A. His personal example of hospitality	5
	B. Challenge to work together for the truth	6-8
III.	Criticism of Diotrephes	9-11
	A. His evil ambition	9
	B. John's intention to confront	10
	C. The appeal to imitate good not evil	11
IV.	Commendation of Demetrius	12
V.	Conclusion	13-14
	A. The letter explained	13-14a
	B. Greetings from friends	14b

Bibliography for the Epistles of John

Brooke, A. E. *A Critical and Exegetical Commentary of the Johannine Epistles.* The International Critical Commentary. Edinburgh: T. & T. Clark, 1912.

Burdick, Donald W. *The Letters of John the Apostle.* Chicago: Moody Press, 1985

Guthrie, Donald. *New Testament Introduction.* Downers Grove, IL: InterVarsity Press, 1990.

Hiebert, D. Edmond. An *Introduction to the New Testament.* Vol. 3. Chicago: Moody Press, 1975.

____. *The Epistles of John.* Greenville, SC: Bob Jones University, 1991.

Hodges, Zane C. *The Epistles of John*. Irving, TX: Grace Evangelical Society, 1999.

____. "The Epistles of John," in *The Bible Knowledge Commentary, New Testament*. Edited by John F. Walvoord and Roy B. Zuck. Wheaton, IL: Victor, 1983; reprint, Colorado Springs, CO: Cook, 1996.

Kruse, Collin. *1-3 John*. Grand Rapids: Wm. B. Eerdmans Publishing Co., 2000.

Lightner, Robert. *First, Second, & Third John & Jude*. Chattanooga, TN: AMG Publishers, 2003.

Marshall, I. Howard. *The Epistles of John*. Grand Rapids: Wm. B. Eerdmans Publishing Co., 1978.

Ramsey, William M. *The Church in the Roman Empire Before AD 170*. New York: G. P. Putnam's Sons, 1919.

Smalley, Stephen S. *1, 2. 3 John*. Word Biblical Commentary. Nashville: Word Books, 1984.

Stott, John R. W. *The Letters of John*. Grand Rapids: Wm. B. Eerdmans Publishing Co., 1998.

Thatcher, Tom. "Epistles of John." In *The Expositor's Bible Commentary*. Vol. 13. rev. ed. Grand Rapids: Zondervan Publishing House, 2006.

Westcott, B. F. *Commentary on the Epistles of St. John*. Grand Rapids: Reprint, Wm. B. Eerdmans Publishing Co., 1966.

JUDE: Contending for The Faith

Key verse: 3, *I felt the necessity to write to you appealing that you contend earnestly for the faith.*

Key words:
Keep/Kept,
The faith,
Judgment,
Ungodly,
Mercy,
Glory,
Lord

Kept by Jesus Christ

Kept from stumbling

Contend for the Faith

Apostates

Build yourselves up in the Faith

	Past	Present	Future
Introduction			**Doxology**
	Examples from the Past	Warning about the Present	Promise for the Future
	Ungodly, deny Jesus Christ, turn grace into license	**Apostates** *Polluting, profiteering, rejecting authority*	*Mockers, divisive, worldly, devoid of the Spirit*
	Unbelievers, angels, Sodom and Gomorrah	**Judgment** *The Lord is coming with His holy ones to judge ungodly*	*Spoken before by apostles, will be in the last times*
	Common salvation, remember that the Lord delivers His people	**Believers** *These men are hidden reefs in your love feasts,*	*Build yourselves up in the faith, Pray in the Holy Spirit, Keep yourselves in the love of God*

1-2 | 3 | 7 / 8 | 16 / 17 | 23 / 24-25

A.D. 67-70

Jude, bond-servant of Jesus Christ brother of James, to believers infiltrated by apostates.

JUDE

Beloved, while I was making every effort to write you about our common salvation, I felt the necessity to write to you appealing that you contend earnestly for the faith which was once for all handed down to the saints. For certain persons have crept in unnoticed, those who were long beforehand marked out for this condemnation, ungodly persons who turn the grace of our God into licentiousness and deny our only Master and Lord, Jesus Christ (Jude 3-4).

The epistle of Jude is one of the least known and least appreciated books of the New Testament. Its brevity, subject matter, and location have contributed to its obscurity. However, it is Scripture and deserves careful attention. It is particularly relevant for our generation and its neglect is our loss.

"The brief epistle of Jude is without a parallel in the New Testament for its vehement denunciation of libertines and apostates. While displaying affectionate concern for true believers, it burns with fiery indignation and vivid pronouncements of judgment upon religious sensualists. It heaps denunciation upon errorists who pollute the purity of the faith and insists that the revelation of God in Christ cannot be compromised. In our day when an increasing number regard truth as relative and are growing more willing to consider all religious systems as having some validity, many suppose that this epistle has lost its relevance for today. But as long as it is true that belief influences and motivates conduct, and as long as God's holiness continues to stand in opposition to all sin and evil, so long will this epistle retain its relevance by declaring God's unchanging message to men" (D. Edmond Hiebert, *Second Peter and Jude,* 185).

Authenticity

Early Acceptance. The canonicity of Jude was established early but not without caution and even some debate. Jude enjoyed wide acceptance and use in the second century. "The Epistle of Jude has stronger attestation than 2 Peter. In view of its brevity and the polemical character of its contents, the impression that this epistle made on the early church is indeed remarkable" (Hiebert, *Second Peter and Jude,* 185). Endorsements for the epistle come in the form of allusions, direct quotations, and comments on its canonicity. It was included in the Muratorian Canon (c.

466

170). Tertullian (AD 150-222) identified Jude as the author and designated it as Scripture. Clement of Alexandria (AD 155-215) wrote a commentary on Jude. Origen indicated that there were doubts regarding the epistle but he did not share them personally. He wrote, "And Jude wrote an Epistle, tiny in the extreme, but yet full of powerful words and heavenly grace" (Quoted by Green, *The Second Epistle General of Peter and the General Epistle of Jude,* 48). "The available evidence shows that there was little, if any, question concerning the authorship of the epistle. The doubts were rather concerning its canonicity. Did the author have the required authority for a canonical status? The epistle won a recognized place in the canon in the face of these questions. ... There was an awareness of the difficulties concerning it, yet the evidence for its canonicity, after full and ample testing, was considered to be adequate" (Hiebert, *An Introduction to the New Testament,* 3:161).

Critical Objections. Early objections to the epistle were based on Jude's quotations from apocryphal books. Evidence indicates that the epistle was accepted in the Western Church immediately and by the Alexandrian churches during the second century. However, the Syrian Churches delayed acceptance until the fourth century. Jerome (AD 340-420) verified the acceptance of Jude as canonical and attributed its slow acceptance to the author's use of the apocryphal Book of Enoch. Modern criticism has departed markedly from the cautious debate of the early church. Jude, along with 2 Peter, has been subjected to careful scrutiny and frequent criticism in the modern era. Some critics question the scriptural value of the book, but most critical debate centers on its authorship and is based largely on internal rather than external matters. Donald Guthrie concludes, "Enough has been said to show that the epistle had considerable use at an early period. And the later doubts, which occurred, must not be allowed to obscure this fact. The attestation for it is particularly strong and questionings appear to have arisen mainly because of the author's use of apocryphal books" (*Introduction to the New Testament,* 902).

Authorship

Internal Evidence. The author of the epistle identifies himself clearly at the outset. *Jude, a servant of Jesus Christ and a brother of James* (v. 1). "Jude" is adapted from "Judas," a common name in New Testament times. Judas the Maccabee had won independence for Israel much earlier and his name remained popular. Six men in the New Testament bear this name, including two of the original disciples. However, the designation "brother

467

of James" narrows the list to two men. The author's purpose in calling attention to that relationship indicates that James was a leading figure in the church. Only James, author of the Epistle of James and brother of the Lord Jesus fits that category. The early Church did not question the identity of the author, attributing it to Jude, the brother of Jesus and of James (Matthew 13:55; Mark 6:3)

The integrity and humility of the author is evident when he distinguishes himself from the apostles. *But, dear friends, remember what the apostles of our Lord Jesus Christ foretold* (v. 17). Like James, Jude did not believe the messianic claims of the Lord Jesus Christ until after the resurrection. He then appears among the believers gathered in the upper room (Acts 1:14). Like James, Jude recognized the deity of the Lord Jesus Christ and saw his own rightful place as that of a "bond servant." Later stories preserved by Hegesippius, combined with Paul's comment in 1 Corinthians 9:5, indicate that Jude was married and served as an itinerant evangelist.

Recent Objections. Critical objections to the traditional view of authorship have resulted from a rethinking of the date and occasion for the epistle. Critics charge that the epistle must have been written in the second century and hence could not have been written by the brother of our Lord and of James. Objections to the occasion and date and hence authorship are: (1) Jude's reference to "the faith that was once for all entrusted to the saints" (v. 3) is said to point to a well-developed body of doctrine. This, it is charged, would require a substantial passage of time. (2) Jude's reference to "the apostles" (v. 17) is taken to mean that they are no longer present. That too would indicate a date in the second century. (3) The error attacked by Jude is equated with second-century Gnosticism. (4) Jude's quotations from apocryphal books and the excellence of his Greek language are viewed as requiring an author other than a humble Galilean.

Conclusion. The above objections have been carefully examined and well answered. A forger would hardly have chosen an obscure name like Jude if he wished his letter to be accepted as genuine. Neither would he have risked quoting an apocryphal book. If 2 Peter were written first, a forger would not likely have used that letter so extensively. Guthrie concludes, "There seems, therefore, no reason to suppose that this Jude was other than the Lord's brother. In fact, although kinship with Christ was not stressed as a qualification of importance in the New Testament era, Christians would undoubtedly treat the Lord's brethren with respect, and this would account, not only for the authority with which Jude writes, but also for the wide regard which the epistle gained in the Christian Church" (*Introduction to the New Testament*, 904-05).

Jude, the Man. What we know of Jude must be gleaned from this brief epistle. He was a passionate defender of the faith. He was a man of strong convictions and forthright speech. His Jewish background shows through, but he has a firm command of the Greek language. He writes in a fluid style, with vivid imagination and a rich vocabulary. The sternness of the letter and the vigorous denunciation of error create a first impression of Jude that is harsh and unbending. Careful examination of the letter itself along with recognition of the importance of the issue being addressed, lead to a second and different opinion. "His love for the truth of God and the souls of men compelled him to speak forth in fiery denunciation against the destructive influences of the false teachers. But when addressing the brethren, there are glimpses of affectionate nature and a tender spirit. Thrice he addresses the readers as "beloved" (vv. 3, 17, 20). He has a heart concern for those who have been ensnared in the evils being combated and councils a compassionate and saving attitude towards them (vv. 22-23)" (Hiebert, *An Introduction to the New Testament,* 3:168).

The Relation of Jude to 2 Peter

Unmistakable Similarities. The similarities between Jude and chapter two of 2 Peter are so clear and substantial that some literary connection between the two seems necessary. "The similarities in thought and structure are so striking that they cannot be merely accidental. For points of resemblance between the two, compare Jude 7 with 2 Peter 2:6; Jude 8 with 2 Peter 2:10; Jude 9 with 2 Peter 2:11; Jude 10 with 2 Peter 2:12; Jude 16 with 2 Peter 2:18; and Jude 17-18 with 2 Peter 3:2-3. The common material relates almost entirely to the Libertines in the Church and only incidentally touches on other matters" (Hiebert, *Second Peter and Jude,* 195). Scholars have labored hard to provide a satisfactory explanation for the similarities between Jude and 2 Peter. Green says, "This problem is one of the most enigmatic in New Testament studies" (*The Second Epistle General of Peter and the General Epistle of Jude,* 58). There are four proposed solutions.

Independent revelation. A few scholars have maintained that both Peter and Jude received their revelation from God directly and wrote independently of each other. They argue that inspiration requires independence. However, that does not seem to explain the similarities between Old Testament prophets like Isaiah and Micah. Neither does it explain the familiarity of Peter with Paul's writings and Luke's use of sources in preparing his gospel. This approach has few adherents.

Common source. Green is among those who argue that both Peter and Jude used an existing document in composing their letters. According to this view Peter and Jude wrote independently of each other but both used a common source and this accounts for the similarities. After extended discussion, Green concludes, "This appears to me to be the simplest explanation of the perplexing literary phenomena linking 2 Peter with Jude" (*The Second Epistle General of Peter and the General Epistle of Jude*, 61-64).

Jude preceded 2 Peter. Kelly is representative of most recent scholars who believe that 2 Peter draws on Jude. He cites the expansion of the material in 2 Peter as supporting evidence. He claims the tendency in the early church was toward enlargement rather than curtailment. After a fairly brief discussion of the evidence, Kelly concludes, "For reasons like these the priority of Jude is all but unanimously accepted today; and a closer inspection of the text serves to confirm 2 Peter's secondary character" (J. N. D. Kelly, *The Epistles of Peter and Jude*, 226-27). Guthrie is not decisive on the issue, but does seem to favor the priority of Jude. He lists nine arguments that point to 2 Peter as a later work drawing on Jude. After presenting the case in support of Jude as preceding Peter, Guthrie ends the discussion with a suggestion that actually favors the priority of 2 Peter over Jude. Thus, it is not fair to equate Guthrie with either position. He concludes with the statement, "The problem, like so many other purely literary problems of New Testament criticism, must be left unresolved. It does not affect the authenticity problem of either letter. ... Yet the epistles are too short to lead to certainty. The verdict must remain open" (*Introduction to the New Testament*, 924).

Second Peter preceded Jude. Hiebert prefers the view that Jude was written shortly after and incorporated material from 2 Peter. He lists nine arguments in support of the view that Jude used 2 Peter. These may be summarized as follows. (1) Jude is writing under a sense of urgency and is more likely to utilize known material. (2) Jude did quote other sources whereas 2 Peter is more original. (3) It is more likely that Jude abbreviated Peter's remarks than that Peter expanded Jude's. (4) The error is present and more sinister in Jude than in 2 Peter, suggesting a later date. (5) The relative obscurity of Jude makes it more likely that he would borrow from the better-known apostle, (6) Jude's use of triplets indicates a sermonic treatment of existing material. (7) Second Peter warns against false teachers while Jude speaks to their victims. (8) Second Peter is essentially predictive, while Jude speaks of a present crisis. (9) Jude appears to be quoting from 2 Peter 3:3-4 when he writes, "Remember what the apostles of our Lord Jesus Christ foretold" (v. 17). The word for "scoffers" occurs only twice in the New Testament, here in Jude 18 and in 2 Peter 3:3 (Hiebert, (*Second Peter and Jude*, 198-99).

Further support for the priority of 2 Peter and its use by Jude is the matter of date and authorship. Nero martyred Peter before A.D. 68. If Jude was written first, then it must have been written sometime before 68. Many scholars consider this to be too early a date for Jude. Thus they propose that someone other than Peter wrote 2 Peter. The Petrine authorship of 2 Peter is sufficiently clear and important to make this unacceptable. If the evidence is of equal weight on both sides, it seems preferable to balance the scale toward the priority of 2 Peter and preserve its early date and Petrine authorship.

Conclusion. This instructor prefers the fourth view. It seems more likely that Jude was written after 2 Peter and that it incorporates ideas from the earlier epistle. Both men may have had opportunity to discuss the error threatening the church and thus have a common view. The error that was on the horizon in 2 Peter has already arrived with devastating results when Jude was compelled to write. Hiebert offers a conjecture as to how Jude may have been written.

> "The scholars will doubtless continue to debate the problem of priority, and each will decide according to the factors which impress him most. We conclude that the preponderance of the evidence is in favor of the priority of 2 Peter. That some kind of literary dependence exists between them seems obvious. ... It would seem that Jude did not actually have 2 Peter lying before him when he wrote, but rather that he drew on his own memory of Peter's picture of these false teachers; he wrote his epistle with the stirring words of Peter again and again running through his mind. This would account for the similarities between the two epistles and yet explain the independence of Jude" (*Second Peter and Jude*, 200).

Jude's Use of Apocryphal Books

The apocryphal books were quite widely known and used in the Jewish community of the first century, but they were not accorded canonical status. Jude is the only New Testament author quoting directly from this Jewish literature. Verse 14 is a nearly *verbatim* quotation of *1 Enoch* 1:9. Verse 9 appears to be a quotation from the *Assumption of Moses*, but this manuscript has not been preserved (Guthrie, *Introduction to the New Testament*, 914). Jude's use of *1 Enoch* prompted some in the church to attach canonical authority to Enoch. However, the excesses so evident within this apocryphal book dispelled that idea and prompted some to doubt the canonicity of Jude as a result. Jude does not appear to be citing *1 Enoch* as Scripture, only as a forecast of the future that has proven true. Jude is highly selective in his quotes and uses them only to prove a point about the current error. Jude's use of the apocryphal books does pose a problem, but it does not require the rejection of the authenticity of this epistle. "Whatever the answer to this problem, it is clear that Jude regards the words he cites as invested with some authority, although this need give no indication of what he thought of the rest of the book. ... He is clearly concerned to reinterpret the apostolic message in terms of a Christian understanding. But it should be noted that the mere citation of non-canonical books cannot be construed as a point unfavorable to the canonicity of the epistle" (Guthrie, *Introduction to the New Testament*, 916).

Occasion and Date

Date. Among those who accept the authorship and authenticity of Jude suggested dates range from AD 61 to 80. It does seem likely that Jude would have referred to the destruction of Jerusalem in AD 70 if he was writing after that event. The primary criteria for determining the date is whether Jude wrote before or after Peter wrote his second letter. Peter must have written 2 Peter shortly before his martyrdom around AD 64-65. If Jude was written after 2 Peter that would suggest a date of at least AD 67. Though younger than his brother James and our Lord Jesus, Jude would not likely have written this epistle much later. A date of AD 67-70 seems probable, but a date as late as AD 80 is possible.

Occasion. Jude had in mind writing a letter of exhortation to these friends, but found himself compelled to write this urgent letter of warning. He states the circumstance and his purpose for writing at the outset. The false teachers Peter warned about in 2 Peter have already infiltrated the church and done grave damage. They escaped detection when they entered the church (v. 4a). These apostates wore a cloak of Christianity, but their conduct was more evil than the pagans. Farrar captures their true nature. "They were doing the deeds of darkness while they stood in the noonday. They claimed higher prerogatives than the Jews, yet they lived in viler practices than the Gentiles. The fullness of their knowledge aggravated the perversity of their ignorance; the depth of the abyss into which they had sunk was only measurable by the glory of the height from which they had fallen" (F. W. Farrar, *The Early Days of Christianity,* 127). These were false teachers who perverted the grace of God into a license for sin. They were libertines who misrepresented and misused Christian liberty. While anticipated by the apostles, they are now at work and must be rooted out. True believers must *contend earnestly for the faith* (v. 3).

Location and Audience

The Epistle of Jude is written to believers, *to those who are the called, beloved in God the Father, and kept for Jesus Christ* (v. 2). Beyond their spiritual status, it is difficult to be very precise about the location of the readers. The use of the Old Testament and the reference to the Jewish apocryphal books suggest they were of Jewish extraction. However, the ability of the libertines to infiltrate the church suggests that it was located in a largely heathen environment. The false teachers would not likely have been able to exert such strong influence in Jerusalem itself. We cannot be definitive, but it is probable that the church was well known to Jude and was located in the region of Palestine. The reference to the apostles lends some support to Antioch as a possible destination.

Distinctive Features

Severity. The writing of Jude is much like that of his brother James. The language is poetic and picturesque. The denunciation of the libertines is passionate and the descriptions of their judgment graphic. "The severity of the tone of the epistle is without parallel in the New Testament. It is the outflashing of righteous indignation against blatant evil" (Hiebert, *An Introduction to the New Testament,* 3:175).

Similarity to 2 Peter. No two writings in the Scripture have as much in common as Jude and 2 Peter. Some scholars question the value of Jude because there is so little "original" material. "There are only three verses in the beginning and seven verses at the end of Jude which do not have extensive parallels in 2 Peter (Jude 1-3, 19-25), though verbal agreement is rare" (Green, *The Second Epistle General of Peter and the General Epistle of Jude,* 59).

The similarities are frequently discussed, but the differences overlooked. Both authors display independence in vocabulary and style regardless of which one wrote first. Hiebert notes several key differences between Jude and 2 Peter (*An Introduction to the New Testament*, 3:168). Guthrie has gone even further to count the number of words in each epistle and demonstrates that less than 30 percent of the vocabulary is common to both letters. "Out of the parallel passages comprising 2 Peter 1:2, 12; 2:1-4, 6, 10-12, 15-18; 3:2-3 and Jude 2, 4-13, 17-18, the former contain 297 words and the latter 256 words, but they share only 78 in common. This means that if 2 Peter is the borrower he has changed 70% of Jude's language and added more of his own, whereas if Jude borrowed from 2 Peter, the percentage of alteration is slightly higher, combined with a reduction in quantity. Clearly there can be no question of direct copying or of editorial adaptation" (*Introduction to the New Testament*, 925).

Angels bound in chains. Jude's description of angels who abandoned their former position and now are confined in chains is even more precise than the reference in 2 Peter. Jude does not link them to the days of Noah, but he does draw a parallel between their sin and the sexual immorality of Sodom and Gomorrah (vv. 6-7). Similarly, only Jude relates the dispute between Michael and the devil regarding the body of Moses (v. 9). Though brief, these references are as significant as they are problematic.

Triads. Jude has a fondness for triplets in arranging his material. Perhaps this is a reflection of his ministry as an itinerant evangelist! There are ten or twelve such triads in this brief epistle. Mercy, peace, and love appear together in verse 2. Israelites, angels, and cities of the plain are objects of divine judgment in verses 5-8. Cain, Baalam, and Korah are three notorious rebels against God in verse 11. The false teachers pollute, reject, and slander in verse 8. The concluding doxology of verse 25 links past, present, and future. Though writing with a sense of urgency, Jude is systematic and orderly in writing.

Doxology. The doxology is the most often quoted passage from Jude. In fact, it is usually the only reference made to this epistle. It is outstanding in its combination of comfort with warning as well as future triumph with present risk. *Now to Him who is able to keep you from stumbling, and to make you stand in the presence of His glory blameless with great joy, to the only God our Savior, through Jesus Christ our Lord, be glory, majesty, dominion and authority, before all time and now and forever. Amen* (vs. 24-25).

Key verse:

Contend earnestly for the faith which was once for all handed down to the saints (v. 3b).

Outline

I.	Introduction	1-2
	A. Writer	1a
	B. Readers	1b
	C. Greeting	2
II.	Reason for Writing	3-4
	A. Original purpose	3a
	B. Revised purpose	3b
	C. Reason: Apostates have infiltrated the church	4
III.	Examples of Past Apostates	5-7
	A. Unbelieving Israel	5
	B. Rebellious angels	6
	C. Immoral Sodom and Gomorrah	7
IV.	Denunciation of Present Apostates	8-16
	A. Description of apostates	8-10
	1. Their actions are defiling	8
	2. Their attitudes are defiant	9-10a
	3. Their ignorance is deliberate	10b
	B. Destruction of apostates	11-16
	1. Parallels with past judgments	11
	2. Their perversion exposed	12-13
	3. Their destruction predicted	14-15
	4. Their character summarized	16
V.	Duty of Believers amidst Apostasy	17-23
	A. Remember the warnings of Christ's apostles	17-19
	B. Keep yourselves in the love of God	20-21
	C. Reach out to those in doubt	22-23
VI.	Doxology	24-25

Bibliography

Blum, Edwin A., and Glenn W. Barker. "1, 2 Peter, 1, 2, 3 John, Jude." In *Zondervan NIV Bible Commentary*. Vol. 2, New Testament. Grand Rapids: Zondervan Publishing House, 1994.

Charles, J. Daryl. "1, 2 Peter, Jude." In *The Expositor's Bible Commentary*. Vol. 13, rev. ed. Grand Rapids: Zondervan Publishing House, 2006.

Davids, Peter. *2 Peter and Jude*. Pillar New Testament Commentary. Grand Rapids: Wm. B. Eerdmans Publishing Co., 2006.

Farrar, F. W. *The Early Days of Christianity*. New York: Cassell & Company, 1882.

Green, Michael, *The Second Epistle General of Peter and the General Epistle of Jude*. Grand Rapids: Wm. B. Eerdmans Co., Rev. 1998.

Guthrie, Donald. *New Testament Introduction*. Downers Grove, IL: InterVarsity Press, 1990.

Hiebert, D. Edmond. *Second Peter and Jude: An Expositional Commentary*. Greenville, SC: Unusual Publications, 1989.

_____. *An Introduction to the New Testament*. Vol. 3. Chicago: Moody Press, 1975.

Kelly, J. N. D. *A Commentary on the Epistles of Peter and Jude*. Thornapple Commentary Series. Reprint, Grand Rapids: Baker Book House, 1981.

Kistemaker, Simon J. *James, Epistles of John, Peter and Jude*. New Testament Commentary. Grand Rapids: Baker Book House, 1996.

Moo, Douglas J. *2 Peter and Jude*. The NIV Application Commentary Series. Grand Rapids: Zondervan Publishing House, 1996.

Osborne, Grant R. *James, 1-2 Peter, Jude*. Cornerstone Biblical Commentary. Carol Stream, IL: Tyndale House Publishers, 2011.

476

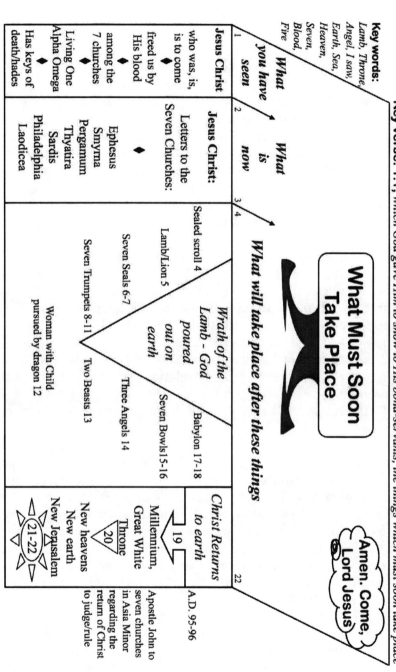

REVELATION

The Revelation of Jesus Christ, which God gave Him to show to His bond-servants, the things which must soon take place; and He sent and communicated it by His angel to His bond-servant John, who testified to the word of God and to the testimony of Jesus Christ, even to all that he saw (Revelation 1:1-2).

Therefore write the things which you have seen, and the things which are, and the things which will take place after these things (1:19).

The book of Revelation poses a major challenge to the interpreter. Its enigmatic language, elaborate use of symbols, and orientation toward the future make it difficult to understand. It is no surprise that Revelation has suffered at the hands of friend and foe alike. On the one extreme are those who regard the book as so enigmatic that it has little relevance or value to the modern student. Hiebert quotes Scott as saying, "This is a book which either finds a man mad or leaves him so." Similarly, Smith writes, "Calvin refused to write a commentary on Revelation, and gave it very little consideration in his massive writings. Luther for years avoided its teachings" (D. Edmond Hiebert, *An Introduction to the New Testament,* 3:232).

Calvin may not have written a commentary on Revelation, but others have not been so reluctant. Library shelves contain more volumes on Revelation than on most other New Testament books. While some have avoided the book, many have become obsessed with its end-times emphasis. Peter was referring to the apostle Paul's prophetic writings, but had he written later, he would no doubt have included Revelation in his assessment. *His letters contain some things that are hard to understand, which ignorant and unstable people distort, as they do the other Scriptures, to their own destruction* (2 Peter 3:16b).

The book of Revelation is God's final word to man. It completes and concludes the divine revelation begun in Genesis. While difficult to interpret, it is essential that we understand Revelation. It is the final chapter in God's redemptive story. Edmond Hiebert provides an excellent summary of its value.

"The book of Revelation is the true capstone of the Bible. It is the only distinctively prophetic book in the New Testament. Other New Testament books contain various prophetic portions, but none of them provides such a sustained prophetic picture of the future as is given in this concluding book of the biblical canon. Without it our Bible would be quite incomplete—like a stirring story without an ending or a drama without its climax. It brings the eschatological expectations of the Church to their fitting conclusion. It "supplies the finishing touch to the whole panorama of the biblical story." It is truly the book of consummation. That which is begun in the book of Genesis is brought to its conclusion in the book of Revelation. It is irreplaceable. For those who have spiritually illuminated eyes, the Apocalypse is one of the most precious and extraordinary writings in the world" (*An Introduction to the New Testament* 3:231).

Authenticity

Early acceptance. The book of Revelation was widely circulated and frequently quoted early in the second century. That was remarkable, given that it was probably written around A.D. 95-96. The usual explanation for this rapid circulation and acceptance is threefold. (1) It was addressed to a specific list of seven churches. These churches would have read it carefully and circulated it in their communities. (2) It addressed the rising tide of persecution and thus was eagerly received by Christians seeking information and encouragement. (3) The church recognized John as the author and thus circulated the book of Revelation. John was a well-known figure, an established leader in the church, and the last remaining apostle. Henry Barclay Swete has provided one of the most complete examinations of the early acceptance and use of Revelation. While examining the objections thoroughly, Swete notes that it received early and strong endorsement. "Thus it is not incredible that Ignatius (110-117) may show some knowledge of the Apocalypse of John in more than one of his letters to the Asian Churches. ... There is however abundant evidence that the Apocalypse was in circulation during the second half of the 2nd century, not only in Asia, but in the West. ... In Asia Minor and in Western Syria the book had already become a court of appeal to which Christians of opposite schools could submit their differences' (Swete, *The Apocalypse of St. John*, cvii-cxix).

Elmer E. Flack claimed, "Evidence of wide recognition at an early period is more abundant for Revelation than for any other book of the New Testament" ("The Revelation of St. John," in *New Testament Commentary*, 678). Quotations and endorsements include an illustrious list of early church leaders. Papias made use of the book early in the second century. Justin Martyr (100-165) confirmed Revelation as apostolic and canonical. Clement of Alexandria (155-215) accepted it as Scripture written by John, the apostle. Melito, Bishop of Sardis, wrote a commentary on Revelation around AD 175. One of the strongest witnesses for the authenticity of Revelation is Irenaeus (130-200). Irenaeus was a student of Polycarp, who heard the teaching of John directly. Irenaeus quotes from every chapter of Revelation. Tertullian (150-212) quotes from almost every chapter.

Critical objections. Marcion excluded Revelation from his list of canonical books because of its Jewish character. Dionysius was the first and most influential person to reject the apostolic authorship of Revelation. He did so on three grounds. (1) The author identifies himself in Revelation, but not in the fourth gospel or epistles. (2) The subject matter and terminology of the apocalypse differ from that of the gospel and epistles of John. (3) The difference in style between the Apocalypse and the other writings by John "is so striking as to preclude common authorship" (Hiebert, *An Introduction to the New Testament,* (3:244). It is significant that the writings of Dionysius vanished, and we are dependent on quotations of his work found in Eusebius (265-340). Modern critics have added little to the objections of Dionysius.

Conclusions. Early acceptance of Revelation was strong, clear, and widespread. "So strong is this evidence that it is difficult to believe that they all made a mistake in confusing the John of the Apocalypse with John the Apostle. ... If all this evidence is due to a mistake it would be an extraordinary case of mistaken identity" (Donald Guthrie, *New Testament Introduction,* 933). The objections of Dionysius are known only through the writings of Eusebius. Though Eusebius was opposed to Revelation on doctrinal grounds, he still felt compelled to list it among the accepted books of the canon because it was so clearly endorsed by the church at large. B. W. Bacon does not accept the apostle John as author of Revelation, but considers its authenticity undeniable. "There is no book of the entire New Testament whose external attestation can compare with that of Revelation, in nearness, clearness, definiteness, and positiveness of statement" (B. W. Bacon, *The Making of the New Testament,* 190).

Author

Internal evidence. Objections to the authenticity of Revelation seem to be motivated by theological issues. Opposition to the premillennial and Jewish emphases grew as the church became more popular in the Roman

Empire. Origen endorsed Revelation, but gave birth to the allegorical method of interpretation. With the adoption of Christianity by Constantine, the issue of emperor worship and the persecution of the church diminished. It is not surprising that the value of Revelation was then questioned and its message reinterpreted. It is against that background that the issue of apostolic authorship was raised. Dionysius suggested John Mark as the author. This met with little acceptance by the church. A debated reference by Papias that there were two John's at Ephesus has led some to attribute the Revelation to John, the elder, rather than to John, the apostle. The issue of authorship is thoroughly examined by Donald Guthrie and others and is only summarized here (*New Testament Introduction*, 935-38).

Internal support for John, the apostle. Internal support for apostolic authorship is strong and includes the following arguments.

1. The author identifies himself four times as John (1:1, 4, 9; 22:8). While he does not call himself an apostle, he was obviously well known to the churches and had no reason to doubt that they would recognize him without adding his title, apostle. It is all the more remarkable considering that apocalyptic literature of the day always excluded the author's name in favor of some notable personage from the past.
2. The personality of the author is evident in the book and appropriate to what we know of John the apostle.
3. There are marked similarities to the Gospel in spite of the often-cited differences. Both speak of Christ as the *logos* and as the *lamb*. Both employ contrasts between light and darkness, truth and falsehood, and the power of God versus the power of this world. Hiebert notes that the adjective *true* occurs ten times in Revelation, eight times in the Gospel of John, four times in 1 John, but only five times in the rest of the New Testament. Similarly, the words *witness* and *overcome* appear frequently in these writings, but rarely in the rest of the New Testament (Hiebert, *An Introduction to the New Testament*, 3:242-43).
4. The author claims divine revelation for the writing of the book (1:1, 11, 19; 22:6-8, 18-20). The boldness of such a claim and its immediate acceptance by the church argue convincingly for apostolic authorship. John Walvoord concludes, "There is really no solid evidence against accepting John the Apostle as the author, and there is much that confirms it" (*The Revelation of Jesus Christ*, 13).
5. The author's personal knowledge of the churches to which he is writing and his identification with them in suffering are appropriate to what is known of the apostle. There is strong evidence to support the

traditional view that John was exiled on the island of Patmos during the reign of Domitian (Robert H. Mounce, *The Book of Revelation*, 32-33).

External support for apostolic authorship. This matter has already been discussed under authenticity. External support for apostolic authenticity is so strong as to be overwhelming. Mounce claims, "Early tradition is unanimous in its opinion that Apocalypse was written by John the Apostle" (*The Book of Revelation*, 27). Morris reaches a similar conclusion. "There does not appear to be evidence of any early or well-grounded tradition which regards anyone other than the Apostle as the author" (Leon Morris, *The Book of Revelation*, 28).

Critical objections. Conservative scholars like Guthrie, Hiebert, Thiessen, Morris, Walvoord, and Mounce argue in favor of apostolic authorship. However, many current scholars reject apostolic authorship in favor of a lesser-known author named John. According to Hiebert, "The majority of modern critics agree that in the light of the differences between them, the John who wrote the Revelation cannot also be accepted as the author of the fourth gospel and the Johannine Epistles" (*An Introduction to the New Testament*, 3:248).

Conclusion. Differences in style between the Gospel of John and the book of Revelation do not require separate authors. In fact, there are many similarities between the two books and logical explanations for the differences. For a listing and discussion of the similarities see Edmond Hiebert, *An Introduction to the New Testament*, 3:246-49. Henry Barclay Swete concludes that the evidence "creates a strong presumption of affinity between the Fourth Gospel and the Apocalypse, notwithstanding their great diversity both in language and in thought" (*The Apocalypse of St. John*, cxxx).

Occasion for Writing

Revelation. The character and purpose of the book is made clear in the opening sentence. *Apokalypsis* declares that what follows is a "revelation, disclosure, or unveiling" (1:1). Jesus Christ himself is both the source and the subject of the revelation. John is writing in obedience to a divine order transmitted through an angel (1:1-4, 11, and 19). The natural understanding is that John was suffering as an exile on the Island of Patmos (1:9). Whatever other conditions may have influenced the content of the book of Revelation; the occasion was a direct command from God.

The Father, the risen Christ and the Holy Spirit all shared in the disclosure and the command to write (1:1, 8, and 10). The revelation was initiated *on the Lord's Day* (1:10). Many have understood that as referring to the first day of the week, but Walvoord is among those who see it as a prophetic term referring to the future day of the Lord (*The Revelation of Jesus Christ*, 42). Regardless of the time factor, the occasion was clearly a divinely initiated revelation that John was commanded to record.

Conflict between Christianity and the emperor cult of Rome. The Roman Empire is personified as a beast that demands universal worship (13:4, 15-17; 14:9; 16:2; 19:20). Most conservative interpreters see the writing of Revelation as a sign of the growing conflict between Christianity and the emperor cult (Mounce, *The Book of Revelation*, 32-33). While Revelation 13 is predictive of end-time conditions, it also reflects the official assault on Christianity under Domitian. Christians had experienced persecution ever since Pentecost, but now it took the form of government policy.

The danger had become acute because of the unprecedented demand of Domitian asking divine worship. Domitian's demand and the zeal of the leaders of the imperial cult in Asia had brought the churches to a terrible crisis. The prospect had terrifying possibilities for believers, who were well aware of the extermination power of imperial Rome. Needed was a message from God which would strengthen and encourage them to persevere under the impending ordeal and give them assurance that their faith would be vindicated with the return of Christ and His certain victory over all the forces of Satanic evil (Hiebert, *An Introduction to the New Testament*, 3:257-58).

Persecution. "Within the book itself are indications that the storm of persecution is about to break" (Mounce, *The Book of Revelation*, 33). John himself has been banished to the prison Island of Patmos *because of the word of God and the testimony of Jesus* (1:9). At Pergamum, Antipas has been martyred (2:13). Believers at Smyrna are warned to expect suffering and imprisonment, perhaps even death (2:10). Though probably referring to the future tribulation (about which John will write extensively in chapters 4-16) an "hour of trial" was going to come upon the whole world (3:10). "We may take it, then, that there had been some persecution of Christians, and that the indications were that much worse was in store" (Leon Morris, *The Book of Revelation*, 37).

483

Decline and compromise within the churches. Not all the dangers were coming from outside the church. False teaching, spiritual coldness, and immorality were sapping the strength of the church from within. The Nicolaitans were inviting the Christians to join the trade guilds and compromise with their hostile pagan environment (2:15). False apostles were testing the discernment of the church (2:2). Varying degrees of spiritual coldness were evident (2:4; 3:1, 14-16). Even the vilest forms of sexual immorality could be found inside the church (2:14, 20-24). Whether because they had drifted from their first love for Christ or because they had consciously embraced the world to avoid suffering, the churches needed a wake-up call. "The graphic portrayal of the fierce conflict and its glorious outcome was a message of hope suited to counteract their spiritual deterioration, induce repentance and purify their lives, encourage perseverance, fortify them against discouragement and despair, and encourage them with the knowledge of assured ultimate victory. ...This prophetic unveiling of the future has a practical ethical purpose. The purpose of prophecy is not simply to satisfy curiosity about the future, it is intended to have a sanctifying affect on the daily life of the saints" (1 John 3:3) (Hiebert, *An Introduction to the New Testament*, 3:259).

Date

Solid evidence supports the traditional date of AD 95-96 for the writing of Revelation. This coincides with the persecution under Domitian. Domitian had erected a Caesar-temple in Ephesus. Irenaeus (130-200) places the writing of Revelation near the end of Domitian's reign. Domitian committed suicide in A.D. 96, and external evidence favors a date shortly before his death. Internal evidence is in harmony with the external evidence for a date of 95-96. The marked spiritual deterioration within the churches would suggest that time had passed since their founding. Laodicea was destroyed by an earthquake in AD 62 but has once again become a prosperous city (3:14-22). The church at Smyrna did not likely begin until after AD 63. Only two dates are really feasible, the persecution under Nero (64-68) or the close of Domitian's reign (95-96).

Place

The place of writing and the destination are quite well established in the book. John is on the island of Patmos when he receives the revelation (1:9). Some have suggested that he did not write the book until later, but it is probable that the writing and the revelation occurred at the same time. That partially explains the abruptness of the style and the so-called "bad grammar."

The revelation was addressed "to the seven churches in the province of Asia" (1:4). There were other churches in the region, but these seven are identified by name and described in detail. John was obviously familiar with the churches and seems to have had some responsibility for their oversight. The question is sometimes asked why these seven churches were identified and others in the region were excluded. William M. Ramsey suggests that these churches were located in strategic centers of influence and constituted a circuit that the messenger would follow in carrying the letter. "All the Seven Cities stand on the great circular road that bound together the most populous, most wealthy and influential part of the province, the west-central region" (Ramsey, *The Letters to the Seven Churches of Asia*, 80). Though addressed to the seven churches, the book of Revelation was intended for a larger audience and for future generations of the church. *Blessed is he who reads and those who hear the words of the prophecy, and heed the things which are written in it; for the time is near* (1:3). *He who has an ear, let him hear what the Spirit says to the churches* (2:7, 11, 17, 29; 3:6, 13, 22).

Apocalyptic Character of Revelation

Apocalyptic literature. A literary genre known as "apocalyptic" flourished in the biblical world from 200 BC to AD 100. It originated in the Jewish and Christian communities. It was rooted particularly in the work of the Hebrew prophets, but did not possess their quality and inspiration. Mounce describes apocalyptic literature as follows.

"It is generally true that an apocalypse normally purports to be a divine disclosure, usually through a celestial intermediary to some prominent figure in the past, in which God promises to intervene in human history to bring times of trouble to an end and destroy all wickedness. The writers were normally pessimistic about man's ability to cope with the evil world. The great cosmic forces which lie behind the turmoil of history are portrayed by vivid and often bizarre symbols. Visions abound. The apocalyptists followed a common practice of rewriting history as prophecy so as to lend credence to their predictions about that which still lay in the future" (Mounce, *The Book of Revelation*, 18).

Writers of apocalyptic literature never used their own names. They chose to write under the pseudonym of a notable person from history, but the lack of authenticity was quite evident in the writing. When the book of Revelation identifies itself in the opening word as an "apocalypse" it automatically raises the question of the relationship between this book and the body of apocalyptic literature that the church rejected as noncanonical. The book of Revelation shares many characteristics with apocalyptic literature, but departs from it radically in its divine origin and quality. The characteristics of apocalyptic literature include the following.

1. **It is always eschatological**. It treats a period of time yet future when God will break into this world of time and space to bring the entire system to a final reckoning.
2. **Apocalyptic is dualistic**. There exist two opposing supernatural powers, God and Satan. There are also two distinct ages: the present one which is temporal and evil, and the one to come, which is timeless and perfectly righteous.
3. Apocalyptic is also **characterized by a rigid determinism** in which everything moves forward as divinely preordained according to a definite time schedule and toward a predetermined end. While this led to a complete pessimism about man's ability to combat the evils he encountered, it nevertheless bred confidence that God would emerge victorious even in the apocalyptist's own life-time.
4. The content of apocalyptic normally **comes to the author by means of a dream or vision** in which he is translated into heavenly realms where he is privileged to see revealed the eternal secrets of God's purpose. Apocalyptic visions were supposedly given to ancient seers and handed down for generations by means of a secret tradition, which now in the last days was being revealed to the people of God.
5. **Symbolism plays a major role in apocalyptic**. In giving free reign to the imagination, symbols of the most bizarre sort become the norm. The origin of a specific image is difficult if not impossible to determine with any degree of certainty, while much of it stems from the Old Testament, some of it extends back into ancient mythology.
6. **The apocalypses are normally pseudonymous**. The apocalyptist did not write in his own name but projected his work back into the past by assigning its authorship to some outstanding person of antiquity. As a result, past history is rewritten as prophecy. Although symbolically portrayed, this march of events is usually quite clear up until the time of the actual writer (who understood himself to be standing at or near the end of time). From this point on "prediction" loses its clarity (Mounce, *The Book of Revelation*, 19-22).

Revelation as apocalyptic. The book of Revelation bears some, but not complete resemblance to standard apocalyptic literature. The cities named are real, the twelve tribes of Israel are literal, and John is a real person.

The differences are so striking that the book of Revelation cannot be placed in the same class as the pseudepigrapha (spurious, false writings).

A sharp distinction should be observed between apocalyptic works outside the Bible and apocalyptic works which are Scripture, whose writing was guided by the inspiration of the Holy Spirit. Apocalyptic literature outside the Bible can be classified as pseudepigrapha. They were works pretending to emanate from characters of the Bible who are cast in the role of predicting the future. The actual authors, however, often lived long after the character to whom the work is ascribed. ... It is characteristic of apocalyptic literature outside the Bible to have a pessimistic view of the contemporary situation and to paint the future in glowing terms of blessing for the saints and doom for the wicked. The real author's name is never divulged in apocalyptic works outside the Bible. Apocalyptic portions of the Scriptures are in sharp contrast to these pseudepigrapha. The more important apocalyptic works of the Old Testament are Isaiah, Ezekiel, Daniel, Joel, and Zechariah (Walvoord, *The Revelation of Jesus Christ*, 23-24).

The eschatology of Revelation differs substantially from general apocalyptic literature. Revelation predicts the future from the vantage point of the present. Apocalyptic literature predicts the present and near future from the standpoint of the past. The prophetic element is evident and reliable in Revelation, but it is distorted in apocalyptic literature. Revelation presents the conflict between good and evil and the ultimate triumph of Christ, but not as a strict dualism or determinism. The willfulness of man and Satan is evident. God's justice is always appropriate, never arbitrary. Redemptive love undergirds and permeates the triumph of Christ.

Symbolic language is used extensively in Revelation, but it is drawn from the Old Testament and appropriate to the real world. Students of Isaiah, Ezekiel, Daniel and Zechariah see a familiarity in the symbolism of Revelation. Like those prophets, Revelation draws heavily on nature to portray the supernatural. In Revelation John clearly identifies himself as the author and claims to be a firsthand witness of what he records. The pseudonymity of apocryphal literature is absent in Revelation. The obscurity of dates and places that characterizes apocalyptic literature is missing from Revelation. The author identifies his location, the place and circumstance of his readers, and the places and personages involved in future events.

487

> "Whatever view may be taken of his indebtedness to Jewish sources, there can be no doubt that he has produced a book which, taken as a whole, is profoundly Christian, and widely removed from the field in which apocalyptic occupied itself. ... The faith and the hope of the Church had diverted apocalyptic thought into new channels and provided it with ends worthy of its pursuit. The tone of St. John's book presents a contrast to the Jewish apocalypses, which is not less marked. ... In the apocalypse of John the presence of the Spirit of Revelation is unmistakably felt" (Swete, *The Apocalypse of St. John*, xxx).

Interpretation of Revelation

Interpretive approaches. The message and meaning of Revelation is dependent on the system of interpretation used by the student. Many who normally follow the literal (grammatical-historical) method of interpretation feel compelled to abandon it when approaching Revelation. Different methods of interpretation lead to different meanings of the biblical text. Nowhere is this more evident than in Revelation. Variations are many, but there are four major interpretive approaches.

Preterist. The Latin *praeter* means "past." Preterist Kenneth L. Gentry says, "Preterism refers to that understanding of certain eschatological passages which holds that *they have already come to fulfillment* ... In Revelation, most of the prophecies before Revelation 20 find fulfillment in the fall of Jerusalem (AD 70)" (*He Shall Have Dominion: A Post Millennial Eschatology*, 159). Leon Morris (an idealist not a preterist) explains the preterist interpretation of Revelation thus, "This starts with the situation of the church in the 1st century and ends there. It sees the book as arising out of the situation of the first Christians and that is its outstanding merit. The Roman Empire dominates the scene. The Seer was wholly preoccupied with the church of his day. He wrote out of its situation and indeed has nothing more in mind than its situation' (Morris, *The Book of Revelation*, 18).

Preterists see all but the final three chapters of Revelation as fulfilled in the fall of Jerusalem (AD 70), or for "mild or partial" Preterists, the fall of Rome (AD 476). This view tends to diminish the current or abiding value of Revelation and its treatment of the ultimate triumph of Christ over Satan. R. C. Sproul is one of the best-known "mild Preterists" (*The Last Days According to Jesus*).

Historicist. Historicists see the book of Revelation as being fulfilled throughout church history. The tribulation (Revelation 6-19) is being fulfilled in the current age. Historicists use the allegorical or "spiritual" method of interpreting the language and symbols of Revelation. Thus the tribulation and the millennial kingdom can co-exist. Historicism owes much to the allegorical method initiated by Origen and championed by Augustine. The Reformers adopted and popularized this view. Historicism is synonymous with amillennialism. Under this view there is no literal seven-year tribulation or one-thousand- year millennial reign of Christ on earth. Walvoord points to the following deficiencies in historicism. "Its major difficulty is that its adherents have succumbed to the tendency to interpret the book as in some sense climaxing in their generation. As many as fifty different interpretations of the book of Revelation therefore evolve, depending on the time and circumstances of the expositor. The very multiplicity of such interpretations and identifications of the personnel of Revelation with a variety of historical characters is its own repudiation. If the historical method is the correct one, it is clear until now that no one has found the key" (*The Revelation of Jesus Christ*, 19).

Futurist. Futurists follow a more literal interpretation of Revelation. They see a future for Israel and literal significance to the time elements of Revelation. They also correlate the Old Testament prophecies, particularly those of Daniel, with Revelation 4-22. Futurists are usually premillennial.

Adherents to this view generally hold that beginning with chapter 4, the book sets forth end-time events which will be fulfilled in the period immediately preceding and culminating in the return of Christ and the establishment of His millennial kingdom. They hold that chapters 6-19 relate to the end-time period known as "the great tribulation" (7:14) which is generally regarded as a period of seven years (cf. Daniel 9:24-27). ... The futurist view gives due recognition to the prophetic character of the book. It points to the second advent as the central, unifying theme of the book and holds that its interpretation must be understood in the light of that dominating event. ... This view does not resort to wholesale allegorizing. While recognizing the use of symbolic language, futurists generally tend to interpret as literally as possible (Hiebert, *An Introduction to the New Testament*, 3:266).

Idealist. This view understands the book of Revelation to be a book of principles, not predictions. It views the book as timeless and symbolic. The idealist relies on the allegorical method of interpretation and interprets

Revelation as a description of the ageless struggle between the kingdom of light and the kingdom of darkness. It sees the hand of God in human history and maintains that Christ will ultimately triumph. The second coming of Christ and the eternal state are the only prophetic and are more or less literal events of Revelation. The idealist approach is explained and adopted by Leon Morris (*The Book of Revelation*, 20-24).

Millennial Views

Interpreters of Revelation also differ widely on their understanding of the one thousand year reign of Christ described in chapter 20. At issue is whether the millennium should be interpreted literally or figuratively and whether it is for the church or for Israel. If it is interpreted literally, then a future millennial kingdom on earth must follow the second coming of Christ. This is known as Premillennialism. If interpreted figuratively (allegorically, spiritually) then the millennium may be a general time (indefinite length) culminating in the second coming of Christ. This position is identified as either postmillennialism or as amillennialism. One primary issue, the method of interpretation, determines these different millennial systems, as well as views regarding the rapture of the church.

> "No question facing the student of Eschatology is more important than the question of the method to be employed in the interpretation of the prophetic Scriptures. The adoption of different methods of interpretation has produced the variant eschatological positions and accounts for the divergent views within a system that confront the student of prophecy. The basic differences between the premillennial and amillennial schools and between pretribulation and posttribulation rapturists are hermeneutical, arising from the adoption of divergent and irreconcilable methods of interpretation" (J. Dwight Pentecost, *Things to Come*, 1).

Millennialism in the early church. The apostolic fathers (the generation of church leaders immediately following the New Testament apostles) were apparently literal in their method of interpretation and hence were premillennial. The early church fathers saw the book of Revelation as "being fulfilled contemporaneously in the trials and difficulties of the church" (Walvoord, *The Revelation of Jesus Christ*, 22). Premillennialism in the early church actually took the form of septamillennialism. They viewed past history as encompassing six thousand years and expected the second coming of Christ would be soon and would usher in the millennial kingdom. "Although the early church's staunch adherence to premillennialism is generally acknowledged, the origin of the doctrine and the reason for its prevalence are disputed. In truth, the early fathers considered premillennialism to be the settled, orthodox belief of the church because they believed Scripture taught it, the apostle John validated it, and a literal hermenutics required it" (Mal Couch, ed., *A Dictionary of Premillennial Theology*, 256).

Amillennialism. The rise of the allegorical school of interpretation (AD 200-400) and the adoption of Christianity as the religion of Rome changed the prevailing view regarding the millennium. Augustine (354-430) saw the triumph of Christ as already having occurred. The church on earth was fulfilling the tribulation and the millennium simultaneously. This approach dominated the study of Revelation until the modern era. Amillennialist L. Berkhoff defines it in this way: "The Amillennial view is, as the name indicates, purely negative. It holds that there is no sufficient Scriptural ground for the expectation of a millennium, and is firmly convinced that the Bible favors the idea that the present dispensation of the Kingdom of God will be followed *immediately* by the Kingdom of God in its consummate and eternal form" (Berkhoff, *Systematic Theology*, 708).

Postmillennialism. Postmillennialism treats the one thousand years more realistically, but rearranges and spiritualizes the events involved. Christianity is seen as progressively triumphing over evil and unbelief. This optimistic view of history sees the second coming of Christ as concluding, not introducing the millennium. Though currently experiencing revival, postmillennialism actually began in the twelfth century, flourished in the eighteenth and nineteenth centuries, and declined in the first half of the twentieth century. Postmillennialist Lorraine Boettener explains it this way: "Postmillennialism is that view of the last things which holds that the kingdom of God is now being extended in the world through the gospel and the saving work of the Holy Spirit in the hearts of individuals, that the world eventually is to be Christianized and the return of Christ is to occur at the close of a long period of righteousness and peace commonly called the millennium. It should be added that on postmillennial principles the Second Coming of Christ will be followed immediately by the general resurrection, the general judgment, and introduction of heaven and hell in their fullness' (*The Meaning of the Millennium*, 117).

Premillennialism. Premillennialism is distinguished by three characteristics. One, there will be a literal kingdom on earth (either involving Israel or the church). Two, there will be a literal return of Christ to the earth prior to the establishing of the millennial kingdom. Three, a more literal method of interpretation is applied to Revelation. Historic or covenant Premillennialism maintains that the church has replaced Israel and therefore the millennium will be for the church, not for national Israel. Dispensational Premillennialism holds that Israel will be restored as the Old Testament prophets maintained and that the millennium applies to Israel and is in fulfillment of those restoration promises. Premillennialism is prevalent among churches and schools associated with conservative or fundamental Christianity.

"The *premillennial* view accepts the thousand years as a definite chronological period and holds that Christ will return to earth personally in glory to initiate His millennial kingdom. The righteous dead will be raised and rule with Him during the Millennium. This view generally assumes that the Old Testament eschatological teaching must be taken at face value and demands belief in a literal, glorious kingdom on earth in the end time. ... A regular feature of Premillennialism is the view that the Second Advent will be in two phases, the *Rapture*, when the Church will be caught up to meet her Lord and be eternally united with Him, and the *Revelation*, when Christ will return to earth in open glory with His Church to establish His millennial reign" (Hiebert, *An Introduction to the New Testament*, 3:269).

Premillennialists differ on the timing of the rapture of the church in the book of Revelation. Some place the rapture at chapter 4 (pretribulation view), some place it in chapter 19 (posttribulation), and still others place it somewhere between chapters 6 and 13 (mid-tribulation view). This study of the book of Revelation is based on the literal method of interpretation. The frame of reference is that of pretribulational Premillennialism.

Distinctive Features

Symbolism. The symbolic nature of the book is clear from the very method by which the Revelation was communicated to John. *Semianō* (1:1) has the root meaning "sign or token." The King James term "signified" is actually more appropriate than the NASB "communicated" and the NIV "made it known." Merrill Tenney explains, "This term evidently meant a kind of communication that is neither plain statement nor an attempt at concealment. It is figurative, symbolic, or imaginative, and is intended to convey truth by picture rather than by definition" (*Interpreting Revelation*, 186).

The symbols of Revelation fall into three categories: (1) those explained within the book; (2) those explained in the Old Testament; and (3) those that are unexplained or are explained by apocalyptic literature of John's day. Symbolism in Revelation includes color, people, objects, and events. Tenney provides a good overview of the symbols and their parallels (*Interpreting Revelation*, 186-93). According to Hiebert, "Its symbolism is the most distinctive feature of the book of Revelation" (*An Introduction to the New Testament*, 3:259).

Christocentric. Jewish apocalyptic writings generally focused on a person from the past who served as God's agent in revelation. The book of Revelation leaves no doubt that the Lord Jesus Christ is both the agent and the object of the book of Revelation. He is both its source and its subject. *The Revelation of Jesus Christ, which God gave Him to show to His bond-servants, the things which must soon take place; and He sent and communicated it by His angel to His bond-servant John, who testified to the word of God and to the testimony of Jesus Christ, even to all that he saw* (Revelation 1:1-2).

In chapters 1-3 Jesus is in the center of the churches as the Savior, Sustainer, and Judge. In chapters 4-5 Christ is the Lamb who has purchased redemption by His blood and the Lion who is worthy to rule over all. Throughout the tribulation on earth (chaps. 6-18) the wrath of Christ is being poured out on His adversaries on earth (6:15-17). In chapter 19 Christ is the conqueror returning to earth in triumph to judge the antichrist and the nations. In the great white throne judgment, the new heavens and the new earth, Christ is the Lamb on the throne, the Light of the kingdom, and the center of attention (20-22; 21:22-26) (Tenney, *Interpreting Revelation*, 117-34).

Numerology. Numbers occur often throughout the book and are important to its message. While an element of symbolism is involved (7 is the number of perfection, 666 is the number of man) they convey a literal meaning. The number 7 occurs 54 times and provides one of the keys to the interpretation of Revelation. Twelve, 10, and 4 are other frequently used numbers. "These numbers may be understood literally, but even when understood in this way, they often carry with them also a symbolic meaning. ... From these indications it is clear that the use of these numbers is not accidental. Though the symbolism is not always obvious, the general rule should be followed to interpret numbers literally unless there is clear evidence to the contrary." (Walvoord, *The Revelation of Jesus Christ*, 28).

Theology. Preoccupation with the prophecies of Revelation frequently obstructs one's awareness of the extensive theology contained in the book. "Few books of the Bible provide a more complete theology than that afforded by the book of Revelation" (Walvoord, *The Revelation of Jesus Christ*, 30). Walvoord gives an excellent survey of the theology and theological value of Revelation. Doctrines treated in Revelation include bibliology, theology proper, anthropology, hamartiology, angelology, soteriology, ecclesiology, and eschatology.

Use of the Old Testament. It is impossible to fully understand and appreciate Revelation apart from the Old Testament. Swete says that out of 404 verses of Revelation, 278 refer to the Old Testament. Tenney identifies 348 allusions to the Old Testament. Yet in spite of these allusions, there is no direct quotation from the Old Testament. Revelation comes from God, the author of the Old Testament, and it is not surprising that allusions abound and quotations are absent. Revelation draws on all parts of the Old Testament, but most frequently on Exodus, Psalms, and the prophets.

Judgment. God does not delight in judgment, but His justice ultimately demands it. The rebellion of Satan and the subsequent rebellion of mankind lead inescapably to divine judgment. Judgment pervades the book of Revelation. In the first three chapters Christ stands as judge in the midst of the churches. Throughout the tribulation period (chaps. 6-18) God's judgment is poured out on the antichrist and the rebellious on earth. The judgment of the nations at Christ's Second Coming (chap. 19) and the judgment of unbelieving individuals at the great white throne (chap. 20) form the climax. While wrath is poured out on the unbelieving (6:15-17; 20:11-15), God's redeeming love undergirds and overshadows this judgment (1:5; 21:3-8).

Worship and song. The judgments described in Revelation are so striking that they easily overshadow the songs of praise and worship contained in the book. There are twenty songs of praise and worship identified in Revelation. Saints, angels, and all of nature join in the worship of God (5:8-14; 19:10; 22:9) (Hiebert, *An Introduction to the New Testament*, 3:262).

Purpose and Theme

Purpose. The purpose of this prophetic unveiling is identified in the opening statement, "*to show to His bond-servants the things which must shortly take place;*" (1:1). Blessing is promised to those who read and heed the message that follows (1:3). The book concludes with a stern warning to any that would alter or ignore the content of this revelation. *I testify to everyone who hears the words of the prophecy of this book: if anyone adds to them, God will add to him the plagues which are written in this book; and if anyone takes away from the words of the book of this prophecy, God will take away his part from the tree of life and from the holy city, which are written in this book* (22:18-19). The message of Revelation is both urgent and important. The term "shortly" (*en tachei*) indicates that the events will be sudden, not necessarily soon. "The idea is not that the event may occur soon, but that when it does, it will be sudden (cf. Luke 18:8; Acts 12:7; 22:18; 25:4; Rom. 16:20). A similar word, *tachys,* is translated "quickly" seven times in Revelation (2:5, 16; 3:11; 11:14; 22:7, 12, 20)" (Walvoord, *The Revelation of Jesus Christ,* 35).

Theme. The prophetic events that will occur in the last days form the central idea of Revelation. However, at the center of these prophetic events is a person, the Lord Jesus Christ. The theme is like two concentric circles. The events of Revelation emanate from Christ, the focal point. Even when one approaches Revelation from the linear point of view, the Lord Jesus Christ is central. *"I am the Alpha and the Omega," says the Lord God, "who is and who was and who is to come, the Almighty"* (1:8).

Key Verse:
The Revelation of Jesus Christ, which God gave Him to show to His bond-servants, the things which must soon take place (Revelation 1:1a).

Structure
The literary structure of Revelation is simple and yet complex. The overall structure or outline is given in 1:19: *Therefore write the things which you have seen, and the things which are, and the things which will take place after these things.* Using this as an outline, the book of Revelation may be divided into three major sections: (1) things which were past at the time of writing (chapter 1), (2) things which were addressed as immediately present (chaps. 2-3), and (3) things which were yet future (chaps. 4-22). The complexity of the structure comes from the use of repeated phrases. The expression "in the Spirit" occurs in 1:10, 4:2, 17:3, and 21:10. In each instance John is transported to another place and given a new perspective. Other significant phrases include "and I saw" and "lightnings, voices, thunders, and an earthquake." For a full discussion of the structure of Revelation see Tenney, *Interpreting Revelation,* 32-41, and Hiebert, *An Introduction to the New* Testament, 3:270-72.

495

The literary structure within chapters 6-18 is frequently debated. These chapters describe three series of judgments, each in seven parts. There are seven seals, seven trumpets, and seven bowls. Those who hold to "concurrent fulfillment," that is, occurring at the same time, maintain that the three series are actually parallel, and terminate with the return of Christ. Some hold that they are not completely parallel, but are at least overlapping, the "partially concurrent fulfillment" view. A third view is "consecutive fulfillment" that sees the three series as following one another. The seventh seal marks the beginning of the seven trumpets (8:1-7). The seven bowls appear to follow and flow from the seventh trumpet (11:15-19).

Another feature of the literary structure of Revelation is the use of "insets" or "interludes." These do not represent a break in the action, but are explanatory notes regarding what has just proceeded. Dwight Pentecost refers to these as "parentheses" and identifies two (7:1-17; 10:1-11:14). Hiebert identifies three additional insets that he calls "episodes" (12:1-14-20; 16:13-16; 17:1-18:24). Most commentators agree "that the book of Revelation was composed according to a carefully devised plan," but they do not agree on that structural plan.

Outline

I. What You Have Seen: The Divine Vision	1:1-20
A. The Introduction	1:1-3
1. Revelation of Jesus Christ to John	1:1-2
2. Blessing promised to readers	1:3
B. The Greeting	1:4-8
1. Grace to the seven churches	1:4-5a
2. Glory to the Son	1:5b-6
3. Guarantee of His coming	1:7
4. Sovereignty of the Father	1:8
C. The Vision	1:9-20
1. The setting of the vision	1:9-11
2. The vision of Christ	1:12-16
3. The result of the vision	1:17-20
II. What Is Now: Letters to the Seven Churches	2:1-3:22
A. The message to Ephesus	2:1-7
1. The command	2:1
2. The commendation	2:2-3
3. The condemnation	2:4

4. The correction	2:5-6
5. The challenge	2:7

A similar pattern is followed for each of the seven churches except that condemnation is absent from the second (Smyrna) and the sixth (Philadelphia), and commendation is omitted from the seventh church (Laodicea).

B. The message to Smyrna	2:8-11
C. The message to Pergamum	2:12-17
D. The message to Thyatira	2:18-29
E. The message to Sardis	3:1-6
F. The message to Philadelphia	3:7-13
G. The message to Laodicea	3:14-22

III. What Will Take Place Later: End Time Events	4:1-22:21
A. The heavenly throne and the sealed scroll	4:1-5:14
1. The open door to heaven	4:1
2. The sovereign God on His throne	4:2-11
3. The scroll no one could open	5:1-5
4. The Lamb who opens the scroll	5:6-8
5. The song of worship to the Lamb	5:9-14
B. The events of the tribulation period	6:1-18:24
1. The judgment of the seven seals	6:1-8:1
a. First seal: rider on white horse	6:1-2
b. Second seal: rider on red horse	6:3-4
c. Third seal: rider on black horse	6:5-6
d. Fourth seal: rider on pale horse	6:7-8
e. Fifth seal: martyrs under the altar	6:9-11
f. Sixth seal: global upheaval	6:12-17

First Parenthesis: Redeemed of the Tribulation	7:1-17
(1) Sealing of 144,000 in Israel	7:1-8
(2) Saved multitude of Gentiles	7:9-17

g. Seventh seal: silence in heaven	8:1
2. The judgment of the seven trumpets	8:2-11:19
a. Preparation: prayers of the saints	8:2-6
b. First trumpet: third of earth is destroyed	8:7
c. Second trumpet: third of sea is destroyed	8:8-9
d. Third trumpet: third of fresh water polluted	8:10-11

	e.	Fourth trumpet: third of stars destroyed	8:12-14
	f.	Fifth trumpet: locusts from the pit	9:1-12
	g.	Sixth trumpet: third of humanity destroyed	9:13-21

Second Parenthesis: Turning Point of the Tribulation	10:1-11:14
(1) The little scroll	10:1-11
(2) The two witnesses	11:1-14

h.	Seventh trumpet: temple in heaven opened	11:15-19

Third Parenthesis: Key Personages of the Tribulation	12:1-14:20
(1) The woman, the child, and the dragon	12:1-17
(2) The two beasts, from sea and earth	13:1-18
(3) The Lamb and the 144,000	14:1-5
(4) The three announcing angels	14:6-12
(5) The blessed dead	14:13
(6) The harvesting angels	14:14-20

3.		The judgment of the seven bowls	15:1-16:21
	a.	Preparation in heaven	15:1-16:1
	b.	First bowl: painful sores	16:2
	c.	Second bowl: sea turned to blood	16:3
	d.	Third bowl: fresh water turned to blood	16:4-7
	e.	Fourth bowl: scorching heat	16:8-9
	f.	Fifth bowl: darkness and pain	16:10-11
	g.	Sixth bowl: Euphrates dried up	16:12

Fourth Parenthesis: Satanic Assembly for Armageddon	16:13-16

h.	Seventh bowl: cosmic upheaval	16:17-21

Fifth Parenthesis: Overthrow of Babylon	17:1-18:24
(1) Harlot: religious Babylon destroyed	17:1-18
(2) City: political Babylon destroyed	18:1-24

C.		The second coming and the eternal state	19:1-22:5
	1.	Return of Christ in glory	19:1-21
		a. Rejoicing in heaven	19:1-10
		b. Return of Christ to earth	19:11-21

2.	The millennial kingdom	20:1-10
	a. Satan bound one thousand years	20:1-3
	b. Saints rule with Christ	20:4-6
	c. Satan released—final rebellion	20:7-10
3.	Great White Throne Judgment	20:11-15
4.	New heaven, new earth, New Jerusalem	21:1-22:5
D. The conclusion		22:6-21
1.	Authentication of the Revelation	22:6-16
2.	Invitation to respond	22:17
3.	Warning against altering the Revelation	22:18-19
4.	Concluding promise	22:20
5.	Benediction	22:21

Bibliography

Berkhoff, L. *Systematic Theology.* Grand Rapids: Wm. B. Eerdmans Publishing Co., 1941

Bock, Darrell, ed. *Three Views on the Millennium and Beyond.* Grand Rapids: Zondervan Publishing House, 1999.

Couch, Mal, ed. *Dictionary of Premillennial Theology.* Grand Rapids: Kregel Publications, 1996. (Dispensational)

Gregg, Steve, ed. *Revelation, Four Views: A Parallel Commentary.* Nashville: Thomas Nelson Publishers, 1997.

Guthrie, Donald. *New Testament Introduction.* Downers Grove, IL: InterVarsity Press, 1990.

Hemer, Colin J. *The Letters to the Seven Churches of Asia in Their Local Setting.* Grand Rapids: Wm. B. Eerdmans Publishing Co., 2001.

Hiebert, D. Edmond. An *Introduction to the New Testament.* Vol. 3. Chicago: Moody Press, 1975.

Keener, Craig. *Revelation.* Grand Rapids: Zondervan Publishing House, 2000. (Premillennial)

Ladd, George A. *A Commentary on the Revelation of John.* Grand Rapids: Wm. B. Eerdmans Publishing Co., 1972. (Historic, Covenant Premillennial)

Mounce, Robert H. *The Book of Revelation.* Grand Rapids: Wm. B. Eerdmans Publishing Co., 1977. (Amillennial)

Morris, Leon. *The Book of Revelation.* Tyndale New Testament Commentaries. Rev. ed. Grand Rapids: Wm. B. Eerdmans Publishing Co., 1999. (Amillennial).

Pate, C. Marvin, Ed. *Four Views on the Book of Revelation.* Grand Rapids: Zondervan Publishing House, 1998.

Pentecost, J. Dwight. *Things to Come.* Grand Rapids: Zondervan Publishing House, 1958. (Dispensational, Premillennial)

Ramsey, W. M. *The Letters to the Seen Churches of Asia.* New York: A. C. Armstrong, 1904.

Sproul, R, C. *The Last Days According to Jesus.* Grand Rapids: Baker Books, 1998. (Amillennial, Preterist).

Swete, Henry Barclay. *The Apocalypse of St. John.* Grand Rapids: Wm. B. Eerdmans Publishing Co., n. d.

Tenney, Merrill C. *Interpreting Revelation.* Reprint. Peabody, MA: Hendrickson Publishers, 2001. (Premillennial)

Thomas, Robert. *Revelation: An Exegetical Commentary.* 2 vols. Chicago: Moody Press, 1992, 1995. (Dispensational, Premillennial)

Walvoord, John F. *The Revelation of Jesus Christ.* Chicago: Moody Press, 1966. (Dispensational, Premillennial)

____. "Revelation," in *The Bible Knowledge Commentary, New Testament.* Edited by John F. Walvoord and Roy B. Zuck. Wheaton, IL: Victor, 1983, reprint, Colorado Springs, CO: Cook, 1996. (Dispensational, Premillennial).

CPSIA information can be obtained at www.ICGtesting.com
Printed in the USA
LVOW06s1238240214

374946LV00001B/2/P